D0999630

# The Legal Profession in England and Wales

# The Legal Profession in England and Wales

*Richard L. Abel*

Basil Blackwell

First published 1988

Basil Blackwell Ltd
108 Cowley Road, Oxford, OX4 1JF, UK

Basil Blackwell Inc.
432 Park Avenue South, Suite 1503
New York, NY 10016, USA



**British Library Cataloguing in Publication Data**
Abel, Richard L.
The legal profession in England and Wales.
1. Lawyers —— England
I. Title
340'.023'42 KD460

ISBN 0-631-14111-1

**Library of Congress Cataloging in Publication Data applied for**

ISBN 0-631-14111-1

Typeset in 10 on 12 pt Plantin
by Photo·Graphics, Honiton, Devon
Printed in Great Britain by TJ Press, Padstow

To my parents, Reuben and Marion,
my wife, Emily,
and my daughters, Laura, Sarah and Heather

# Contents

# List of tables and figures

## Appendix 1 Barristers

### Tables

*Discipline*



## Figures

Appendix 2 Solicitors

## Tables

*Entry*



*Composition*

### Figures



## Appendix 3 Legal education

### Tables

## Appendix 4 Demographics

### Tables

Appendix 5 Work

## Tables

# Preface

The author of every book depends on the help of many people and institutions. Because I have been writing about a legal profession not my own, from across an ocean and a continent, I have had to ask for more assistance than usual and have been fortunate in receiving a very generous response. Geoffrey Bindman and his family offered me repeated hospitality, and he patiently answered my endless questions. David Sugarman, head of the Law Department at Middlesex Polytechnic, has gone to great lengths to keep me informed of ongoing developments. Simon Roberts arranged for a lengthy stay at the London School of Economics and several subsequent visits to its library. Stuart Anderson, of Hertford College, Oxford, gave detailed comments on an earlier draft. Michael Zander, now head of the Law Department of the London School of Economics, provided guidance not only through his extensive writings about lawyers but also during many discussions. Robert Stevens, Chancellor of the University of California, Santa Cruz, laid the foundation for all later studies of the legal profession in his book with Brian Abel-Smith, and he also commented on an earlier draft. Aubrey Diamond, Director of the Institute of Advanced Legal Studies, kindly organized a day-long seminar, whose participants offered me a great deal of useful criticism. Robert Hazell allowed me to see unpubished chapters of *The Bar on Trial*. Mr H. S. K. Peppiatt of Freshfields provided me with a copy of Judy Slinn's history of the firm. Kim Economides of the Law Department of the University of Exeter sent me the valuable research produced by the Access to Justice in Rural Britain Project. Charles Morrison and Mary Phillips, successive Deans of the Council of Legal Education, furnished me with statistical data on entry to the Bar. Walter Merricks, first as a contributor to the *New Law Journal* and now as Secretary to the Professional and Public Relations Committee of the Law

Society, has been generous with his archives and knowledge. Mr J. A. Tomlin, Assistant Secretary to the General Council of the Bar, provided many Senate publications. Mr A. J. Viner, Assistant Secretary of the Education and Training Department of the Law Society, helped me obtain statistics on the admission of solicitors. Mr D. B. Read, Senior Careers Adviser at the University of Sheffield, sent me the useful studies of entrants to the legal profession conducted by the Association of Graduate Careers Advisory Services. Mr David Lehman, a history graduate student at UCLA, was my research assistant at the beginning of this project, and Ms Nicola Shaldon, a law student at LSE, helped me fill in gaps at the end. And Ms Dorothe Brehove, my secretary at UCLA Law School, displayed her usual skill and patience in typing the first draft of this manuscript and formatting, typing and retyping the growing accumulation of tables.

I am also indebted to a number of institutions. The Law Department of the London School of Economics offered me hospitality during a research leave in the summer and autumn of 1982. I was also fortunate in being asked by the *Modern Law Review* to deliver the Chorley Lecture in June 1985, when I was able to try out some of the ideas in this book. I am grateful for the use of the British Library, the Institute of Advanced Legal Studies, the Institute of Education, the LSE library, the libraries of the Law Society and of Gray's Inn and Lincoln's Inn and the records of the Treasurer's Office of Inner Temple and the Treasury Office of Lincoln's Inn. The UCLA Law Library repeatedly obtained books for me. Two placement services, Chambers and Partners and Reuter Simkin, gave me statistical studies of their work in placing lawyers.

Finally, this book would not have been possible without research support from the Law and Social Science Program of the National Science Foundation and three sources within UCLA: the Academic Senate Research Committee, the Committee on International and Comparative Studies and the Law School Dean's Fund.

Readers reasonably may wonder how an American law teacher in Los Angeles came to write a book about lawyers in England and Wales. As I write this preface sitting in the warm February sun less than a mile from the Pacific – so far from England not just geographically but also in terms of social and cultural environment – it seems incongruous to me as well. When I first visited England in the summer of 1961 – a 19-year-old seeing Europe on $5 a day – I determined to return to live there some day. That became possible through the hospitality of the British government, which gave me a Marshall Scholarship for two years of postgraduate work at the School of Oriental and African Studies in 1965–7. The experience made a permanent impression on my wife and me: she also began her PhD at the University of London during that time; we made friendships, with Michael and Jane de Swiet for instance, that have lasted more than 20 years; and our eldest daughter was born at the end of the period, a citizen of both Britain and the United States. We have returned often since then, including a six-month stay as a family in 1982, when we were the beneficiaries of lavish hospitality from many friends.

I began teaching and studying the sociology of American lawyers in 1974. My interest in the profession in England and Wales was stimulated by an invitation from Phil Thomas to comment on the Final Report of the Royal Commission on Legal Services at a conference organized by University College Cardiff in the spring of 1980. At about the same time, I joined the Working Group for Comparative Study of Legal Professions initiated by Philip Lewis of All Souls College, Oxford. That latter project has now produced accounts of some 20 legal professions, which, together with comparative and theoretical essays, are being published in three volumes by the University of California Press. I agreed to write the national reports on the United States and on England and Wales. Each grew into a monograph in its own right, with the results you see here (the American book will be published by Oxford University Press, New York, in 1989).

I am painfully aware that I am twice removed from the subject of this book. I am a law professor writing about lawyers and an American writing about England and Wales. Such a distanced perspective has inescapable drawbacks. I know I have missed details, made factual errors and overlooked nuances. And a book on a moving target like the contemporary legal profession cannot help but be dated even before it is published (I have tried to include information available up to November 1986). Yet as an outsider I have no obvious axe to grind. And the eye of the stranger sometimes perceives features, connections and patterns hidden from those inside the system. I hope such insights may excuse the inevitable flaws.

Richard L. Abel
Santa Monica, California

# I

# Introduction

# 1

# Theories of the professions

This book seeks to describe and analyse barristers and solicitors in England and Wales. My framework for this task is the sociology of professions, a subdivision of the sociology of occupations. I have adopted this framework out of the conviction that the social organization of a profession helps to illuminate its role in society. Certainly little justification is needed for seeking to understand the social role of lawyers: both official spokespersons for the profession and external critics agree that lawyers significantly influence political, economic, social and cultural life. But if there is consensus about the importance of the subject, choices still must be made about how to approach it. This book is a sociology of the legal *profession*, not of lawyers' *work*. The reason for my focus is not the logic of explanation: the nature of legal work affects the social organization of the profession just as much as the reverse is true. Rather, it is a concession to what we know. Historical and sociological primary and secondary sources offer rich accounts of who lawyers are, how they are trained and certified, the structures within which and the rules by which they practise, how much they earn, how they organize themselves into professional associations and what those associations do. Except for a handful of very recent ethnographic studies of lawyer–client interaction (e.g. Cain, 1979; Griffiths, 1986; Sarat and Felstiner, 1986), we know little more about what lawyers do than how they allocate their time among different subject matters. One reason for writing this book is my hope that its description of the social organization of the legal profession will enable and stimulate others to undertake the more difficult task of studying the content and form of their daily work activities.

It is customary to begin any work of social science with a definition of the phenomenon under scrutiny – here the legal profession – both because the definition necessarily is stipulative and because the choice implicitly introduces theoretical assumptions. By the adjective 'legal' I include all those formally qualified and practising as barristers or solicitors, either independently or in the public or private sectors, as well as students preparing for either branch and law teachers training them. I also discuss the subordinates of private practitioners: legal executives and barristers' clerks. I exclude the myriad of other individuals without formal qualifications who perform equivalent functions, such as workers at citizens' advice bureaux, trade union shop stewards or accountants. I also exclude those who have qualified but are not practising law, such as politicians or company officials. And I do not deal with magistrates or judges. I have drawn the boundaries of my subject in this fashion because of my interest in exploring the relationship between the social organization of the occupational category and the way in which its members perform a set of overlapping tasks.

If this categorization of 'legal' occupations is a plausible starting point for analysis (though by no means the only possibility), the notion of a 'profession' is more controversial. There are three principal theoretical traditions in the study of professions: Weberian, Marxist and a structural functional approach with roots in Durkheim. Because each poses fundamentally different questions about society, it sees the professions from radically divergent perspectives. Consequently, although there is some overlap of interest, proponents of different traditions often fail to communicate with each other. I will outline the three perspectives below and explain why I have emphasized the Weberian approach, before offering a more detailed exposition of how each of the three theoretical frameworks informs my description and analysis of the legal profession.

For Weber (1978) and other theoreticians in his tradition, most notably Eliot Freidson (1970), Terence Johnson (1972), Magali Sarfatti Larson (1977) and Frank Parkin (1979), analysis begins with the sphere of distribution. The central question is how actors seek and attain competitive advantage within a relatively free market – one structured by the state but dominated by private producers. The goals are economic rewards and the social status that is partly a consequence and partly a legitimation of those rewards. Market competition constructs categories of adversaries who oppose each other *within* classes (Weber, 1978: 341–42; Parkin, 1979: 44). The functional division of labour among occupations is one by-product of this process. But unrestrained competition is certainly unpleasant and perhaps intolerable (Polanyi, 1957). Consequently, all economic actors seek protection from market forces. Professions are distinguished by the strategies of social closure through which they enhance their market chances. This Weberian tradition finds parallels in the positive and normative writings of neoclassical economists, although there is little communication between the two approaches (but see Begun, 1986). In recent decades, economists have studied and criticized the ways in which occupations that are recognized as, or aspire to become, professions seek to regulate the market for their services, to the detriment of both competitors and consumers. Thus, the neoclassical economists, like the Weberians, see the arena of struggle as the marketplace and the adversaries as members of the same class.

Marx and his followers make production, not distribution, the starting point. Although the mode of production has changed, relations of production have always defined a vertical division between two opposed classes. Under capitalism these are the bourgeoisie and the proletariat. I present this oversimplified Marxist conceptualization in order to highlight the marginality of professionals, who often appear to be little more than a historic residue of petty bourgeois artisans. At times, indeed, Marx seemed to argue that the petty bourgeoisie were destined to vanish in the progressive polarization between capital and labour. Yet Marx also recognized that the cumulative concentration of capital required more and more functionaries to mediate between the two opposed classes (Abercrombie and Urry, 1983: 49–51). The continuing focus of bourgeois, especially American, sociology upon this 'middle class' and the explosive increase in its numbers since World War II have compelled Marxists to reconsider its categorization and future. For Marxists, then, the fundamental question is whether the category of which professionals are a part – defined variously as the service class, the professional-managerial class, the 'new class', or black-coated or educated workers – is destined to ally itself with either labour or capital or to constitute an independent force within the ongoing class struggle, and what characteristics of its members will influence that affiliation.

For Durkheim (1933; 1957) and the structural functionalists who followed him, the critical question was social order (see Dingwall, 1983). In a society composed of egoistic individuals lacking common values and unconstrained by such traditional institutions as the family, religion and locality, what would prevent pursuit of self-interest from degenerating into Hobbesian anarchy? The professions appeared to offer one antidote to the insidious poison of selfish materialism. Indeed, it was particularly important that they remain disinterested because of the grave dangers were they to misuse their privileged knowledge (Rueschemeyer, 1983). The older professions, particularly law and medicine, actually did retain significant traces of a precapitalist tradition (Duman, 1979). And all professions and professionalizing occupations energetically promoted an image of themselves as a community within the anomic mass society, altruistic where other economic actors were egoistic, a self-regulating counterweight to an increasingly monolithic state.

This highly flattering portrayal may be part of the reason why study of the professions long dominated the sociology of occupations (Smigel, 1954; Smigel et al., 1963; Hall, 1983). Although many sociologists and other observers uncritically accepted this self-portrait (e.g. Carr-Saunders and Wilson, 1933: 497; Marshall, 1963), the best-known and most influential proponent of this position was Talcott Parsons (1951; 1964a; 1964b; 1968). It is worth quoting Parsons at length, if only to indicate the target at which much subsequent sociology of the professions was directing its fire:

> The professional complex, though obviously still incomplete in its development, has already become the most important single component in the structure of modern societies. It has displaced first the 'state', in the relatively early modern sense of that term, and, more recently, the 'capitalistic' organization of the economy. The massive emergence of the professional complex, not the special status of capitalistic or socialistic modes of organization, is the crucial structural development in twentieth-century society.
>
> (1968: 545)

Parsons's own tendency toward static categorization was paralleled by the dominant 'trait' approach to professions, which sought to demarcate them from other occupations by elaborating their allegedly socially integrative functions into a series of distinguishing characteristics (e.g. Lewis and Maude, 1952: ch. 4; Cogan, 1953; Goode, 1957; Greenwood, 1957; Barber, 1963; Vollmer and Mills, 1966; Hickson and Thomas, 1969; Moore, 1970: 5–6; Elliott, 1972; Cullen, 1978; 1985). The rhetorical power of this approach is evident in its influence on the Royal Commission on Legal Services, which defined 'the five main features of a profession' as:

> A governing body (or bodies) [that] represents a profession and … has powers of control and discipline over its members.
>
> [mastery of] a specialised field of knowledge. This requires not only the period of education and training … but also practical experience and continuing study of developments in theory and practice.
>
> Admission … is dependent upon a period of theoretical and practical training in the course of which it is necessary to pass examinations and tests of competence.
>
> [A] measure of self-regulation so that it may require its members to observe

higher standards than could be successfully imposed from without.

> A professional person's first and particular responsibility is to his client. ... The client's case should receive from the adviser the same level of care and attention as the client would himself exert if he had the knowledge and the means.
>
> (1979, vol. 1: 28, 30)

This reduction of sociological analysis to little more than professional apologetics eventually stimulated a critical reaction (e.g. Roth et al., 1973; Halmos, 1973a; 1973b; Roth, 1974; Boreham et al., 1976; Pemberton and Boreham, 1976; Krause, 1977; Spangler and Lehman, 1982). But except to the extent that critics were inspired by either the Weberian or the Marxist frameworks described above, they remained confined to the attempt to refute the traits claimed by the professions and attributed by the structural functionalists. Thus, critical sociologists sought to demonstrate that governing bodies were unrepresentative and ineffective regulators; professions lacked the expertise they claimed; admission criteria had little relevance to the actual work of the profession; ethical rules were motivated by economic self-interest and failed to ensure competence; and professionals repeatedly betrayed clients.

Although I will draw on all three theoretical traditions to present and analyse the data about the legal profession, I find the Weberian approach the most illuminating. Because professions are primarily a category in the horizontal division of labour, they are marginal to Marxism, which focuses on class conflicts (cf. Barbalet, 1982: 491). Because professions are primarily an economic activity, structural functionalism is marginal to them, since it is concerned with community, altruism and self-governance – the core of social movements and fraternal organizations, perhaps, but not of occupations. Because most lawyers in the common law world are private practitioners, the market for their services is, and must be, their central concern. The Weberian framework (and its parallel within neoclassical economics) offers the greatest insights into the dilemmas of professionals within such a market. Yet because legal professionals increasingly are becoming employers in the private sector and employees in both the private and the public sectors, Marxist class analysis poses questions that cannot be ignored. And the construction of community, the encouragement of altruism, self-governance and the regulation of ethicality and competence are not insignificant, even if they must be secondary concerns of professions. Structural functional theory and the critical response it has stimulated properly direct our attention to these activities.

## Weberian theories of professions in the marketplace

### *Constructing the professional commodity*

Professions produce services rather than goods. Unlike the farmer or herder before the industrial revolution or the manufacturer of goods today, the producer of services cannot rely on consumer demand for physical objects to constitute the market. Instead, such producers confront two distinct problems in particularly acute form. First, the consumer must acknowledge the value of the producer's services. If we address this issue by thinking of contemporary medicine or even law, the perception of value does not seem problematic. But if we think of the sorcerer in tribal societies (Freidson, 1970: ch. 1) or the rabbinate, ministry or priesthood in most contemporary Western societies, the difficulties are immediately apparent. Second, consumers must be convinced that they cannot produce the services themselves. Once again, if we reflect on neurosurgeons or corporate lawyers, consumer incompetence may be obvious. But, in fact, we doctor and lawyer ourselves much of the time, often resisting the urgings of others that we consult an 'expert'.

The success of producers in constructing a market for their services turns on several variables. What consumers 'need' is a function of cultural beliefs over which producers have only limited control. The most they can do is amplify or dampen demand by seeking to connect their services to fundamental values: mediation between man and God with transcendental beliefs, medicine with the desire for physical wellbeing, and law with justice or the protection of political and economic stability. Structural functional theory tends to treat the demand for professional services as unproblematic – merely a rational acknowledgement by the consumer of the objective 'utility' of those services. But professions emerge and thrive with little or no evidence that their services actually benefit consumers: religion, medicine before about 1900 and psychotherapy today are vivid examples (Goode, 1960: 912; Pemberton and Boreham, 1976: 24; Boreham, 1983: 695). Even established professions constantly must construct consumer confidence in the value of what they are selling (Grimm and Kronus, 1973). Freidson (1986: 225; see also 1984) frames the question starkly: 'Is professional power the special power of knowledge or merely the ordinary power of vested economic, political and bureaucratic interests?'

Once consumers believe in the value of the services, how are they persuaded to purchase them from others rather than produce the services themselves? Part of the answer is that the division of labour compels this: as producers become specialized, consumers necessarily become generalized and thus dependent on others (Friedman, 1962; Johnson, 1972: 41). But a number of other factors also shape that dependence. Perhaps the best-known formulation proposes that professional services contain an irreducible element of uncertainty or discretion, a balance between indetermination and technicality, art and science (Fox, 1957; Wilensky, 1964: 148; Jamous and Peloille, 1970). Too much art and consumers lose confidence (as in quack medicine); too much science and consumers (or lower status producers) can provide the service themselves (do-it-yourself home repairs or conveyancing) (Child and Faulk, 1982: 160).

We can identify other ingredients in the successful construction of a professional commodity. The producer's expertise should appear to be objective, not merely the arbitrary creation of the expert. For religious believers, the warrant often is traditional – a sacred text or church hierarchy – though religion also fosters the rise of charismatic leaders. But for most contemporary professions, the strongest warrant of objectivity is connection with natural science. Despite the efforts by lawyers to make law appear to be a logico-deductive system, it is clearly manmade and thus ultimately a reflection of political power. Professional knowledge must be esoteric, but legal language is just ordinary language used in strange and arbitrary ways, except for the cherished residues of Latin, French and English archaisms. Professional knowledge must reconcile stasis and change, traditional warrants of legitimacy and the novelty that ensures continuing uncertainty. But whereas scientific traditions can invoke the validation of repeated experience, ancient laws may be seen as the heavy hand of history. And whereas scientific novelty is progress and therefore good by definition, law 'reform' may be seen as a concession to some special interest. Professional knowledge is standardized; and heterodoxy threatens its very foundation – hence the difficulties that medicine encountered until the end of the nineteenth century. At least since the triumph of the nation-state, law has been the voice of a single sovereign and thus clearly unitary; but in pluralistic societies, unity may be seen as tyranny.

The construction of a marketable professional commodity also depends on variables other than the nature of professional expertise. The relation between producers and consumers clearly is critical; it can hardly be an accident that the two most successful contemporary professions, medicine and law, emerged by selling their services to individual consumers. And the failure of many latecomers to the market for services to become more than semi-professions certainly is connected to the fact that they sell their services either to existing professions (nurses, legal executives) or to large bureaucratic employers (social workers, teachers) (Etzioni, 1969; Larson, 1977). The commodity must be packaged in units that consumers can afford, which may be one reason why physicians have been relatively more successful than lawyers. And it is very helpful to have exclusive access to a vital arena: the hospital for physicians, the courtroom for lawyers, the document registry for European notaries.

The task of constructing the professional commodity never ends, for it is constantly being undermined (Bucher and Strauss, 1961). Other bodies of knowledge may challenge the hegemony of professional expertise, as natural science has been eroding the authority of religion at least since the Enlightenment, and as economics may be displacing law as the foundation of government today. Expert authority also may be unmasked as political domination (Pemberton and Boreham, 1976: 28–33): the feminist critique of medicine is a contemporary example, but law is far more vulnerable to political critique. And the ratio of indetermination to technicality may become unbalanced. Art may be revealed as fakery: apricot stones as a cancer cure, for instance, or a recent finding that the intake of cholesterol is not correlated with its presence in the blood, so that dietary prescriptions for avoiding heart attacks – long a staple of modern medicine – appear to be worthless. Or, more dramatically, politicians and the public may lose faith in the ability of economists to forecast or manipulate macroeconomic trends. At the other extreme, technicality opens the professions to competition from paraprofessionals – dental hygienists setting up independent practices, for instance – a threat that is amplified by the rise of information technology (Jamous and Peloille, 1970: 138; Toren, 1975).

### *Pursuing social closure*

Producers of a service who succeed in constructing a marketable commodity only become an occupation. In order to become a profession they must seek social closure. This project has two dimensions: market control and collective social mobility (Larson, 1977). Although these are inextricably linked, it is analytically useful to distinguish them, dealing with market control here and collective mobility below (see 'Closure as collective mobility', p. 17). All occupations are compelled by the market to compete. This may be advantageous to consumers – that is the market's fundamental justification after all – but competition is hardly pleasant for producers since it is the classic zero-sum game. Notwithstanding their ideological attachment to free markets, therefore, it is not surprising that producers energetically try to escape from that freedom (Polanyi, 1957; cf. Fromm, 1941).

Producers of goods can seek protection from market forces in a variety of ways: through horizontal monopolies or cartels, vertical control over raw materials and control over technology and other intellectual inputs (patent, trade mark and copyright). Because services are not embodied in a physical form, their producers have only one option: control over the production *of* producers (Larson, 1977). Indeed, state regulation of the markets for goods and services is roughly contemporaneous (ibid. 135). There is nothing new about control over the production of producers, and it certainly is not limited to capitalism. Tribal societies in precolonial Africa often limited specialized occupations, such as blacksmith, to a particular kinship group or clan; and of course Indian castes are one of the most elaborate forms of market control. Other non-professional forms of closure include guilds, trade unions, civil service employment, academic tenure and employment within large private bureaucracies. Weber suggests some of the permutations of closure:

> Both the extent and the methods of regulation and exclusion in relation to outsiders may vary widely, so that the transition from a state of openness to one of regulation and closure is gradual. Various conditions of participation may be laid down: qualifying tests, a period of probation, requirement of possession of a share which can be purchased under certain conditions, election of new members by ballot, membership or eligibility by birth or by virtue of achievements open to anyone.
>
> (1947: 142; see also 1978: 342; Saks, 1983: 5)

In recent years, a number of writers have elaborated this notion of closure (e.g. Freidson, 1970; Westergaard and Resler, 1975: 92, 346; Larson, 1977; Abbott, 1986). Johnson (1972: 45–6) has contrasted collegiate control through guilds or professions with control by the client (whether an oligarchic, corporate or individual consumer) and mediation of the producer – consumer relationship (by the state, a corporation or an insurer). Parkin (1979; see also Abercrombie and Urry, 1983: 90–1) makes closure his central analytic concept, analogizing it to the earlier capitalist asymmetry of ownership of the means of production, and Bourdieu and Passeron (1977) also view expertise based on credentials as a form of 'cultural capital'; indeed, Murphy (1984) suggests that capital is merely another form of closure, like credentials. Others have adopted the framework of political economy, examining the ways in which professions have sought to mobilize political power to structure their market (e.g., Tuohy and Wolfson, 1977; Bankowski and Mungham, 1978; Luckham, 1981).

Structural functionalists address this issue from a very different perspective. For them, closure is not a response to the market and certainly not a conscious, self-interested strategy by producers. It is simply the means by which society ensures that consumers receive quality services (cf. Young, 1958). Because it is so difficult to evaluate either the process of rendering services or the outcome, quality is maintained through input controls (Jamous and Peloille, 1970: 113). Weber rejected this interpretation in the strongest terms:

> When we hear from all sides the demand for an introduction of regular curricula and special examinations, the reason behind it is, of course, not a suddenly awakened 'thirst for education' but the desire for restricting the supply of these positions and their monopolization by the owners of educational certificates. Today the 'examination' is the universal means of this monopolization, and therefore examinations irresistibly advance.
>
> (1964: 241–2)

Parkin is equally emphatic: 'Once a professional monopoly has been established, the way then becomes clear for the elaboration of those purely ceremonial conventions by which access to specialised knowledge is carefully monitored and restricted' (1979: 104).

Adherents of the Weberian position can point to the lack of fit – and certainly the lack of any evidence of fit – between credentials and actual work (Collins, 1977; 1979), whether the credential is technical and the work manual (Blackburn and Mann, 1979) or the credential is a liberal education and the work white collar (Rawlins and Ulman, 1974). Even if there is some plausibility to the notion that education correlates with technical skill, the credentials required often far exceed the skill demanded (Berg, 1970; Kumar, 1977; Boreham, 1983: 707). A telling illustration of this disjunction is the fact that the very institution responsible for producing most professionals – the university – chooses its faculty on the basis of credentials that say *nothing* about competence to teach. And it would be hard to make the argument that the credentials required of lawyers are necessary to the practice of law when legal education varies so greatly. Lawyers in England and the United States perform many of the same tasks, but there are substantial differences in the degree to which their education is academic or apprenticeship, through lectures or socratic dialogue, based on treatises or casebooks, located in classrooms or clinics, and undergraduate or graduate.

Indeed, the little we know about what lawyers do suggests they make scant use of their formal legal education:

> Scottish solicitors explained that on average they would deal with the law, in the sense of technical knowledge, for something around one hour a week. The rest of their time – taken up with handling personal relationships and business negotiations, and with consultations and meetings – involved little legal skills; either they used totally routinised legal knowledge or else they moved out of, or beyond, specifically legal work. Solicitors further confirmed that in their practice, the most important factor in terms of giving clients satisfaction was *not* careful research, technical skills, or even (when a dispute was involved) winning a case, but rather maintaining relationships with clients on proper grounds.
>
> (Campbell, 1976: 34)

And Jerome Carlin's study of solo practitioners in Chicago in the late 1950s came to similar conclusions:

> Time devoted to writing legal briefs and memoranda is at a minimum for all but a very few respondents. Reading legal material either for 'keeping up' or on research in connection with some matter at hand accounts for only a small fraction of the individual practitioner's working day – less than a half hour a day, on the average. And only 6 respondents specifically mentioned engaging in any legal research.
>
> *Interviewer:* Do you spend any time reading legal material?
> *Respondent:* I'm ashamed to tell you, not even an hour a week. You can say I get by on cursory knowledge of the law. But it's mostly the same thing, not just bluffing.
> *Interviewer:* Do you spend any time preparing legal documents?
> *Respondent:* Zero. Well, pleadings, yes, but most are in subrogation cases, and I use a form, filling in the date, and so on, so it doesn't take too much time.
>
> (1962: 41 n. 2, 77)

To the extent that mandatory education serves a purpose other than market control, it helps to confer status through association with high culture (Parkin, 1979: 55; Klegon, 1978: 279), socializes entrants to their roles as professionals (Merton et al., 1957; Becker et al., 1961; Bucher and Stelling, 1977) and provides warrants of loyalty and discipline (Berg, 1970).

Strategies of closure can be exclusionary – directed against equals or inferiors – or usurpationary – attempts to seize the markets of superiors (Parkin, 1979). They may vary in their emphasis on training and testing (Johnson, 1982: 198, 205). Credentials may be demanded of individual producers or of the institutions through which producers are qualified or services delivered (Freidson, 1986: 64). Closure may be achieved through exclusive rights to use a title, registration or licensing, and the degree of closure sought may vary with the market conditions for the professional commodity (ibid.: 77). Associations of producers obviously play a critical role in imposing entry requirements (Millerson, 1964). Yet, paradoxically, the elite who typically organize and dominate the professional association and direct the professional 'project' stand to gain little economically by controlling the production of producers; they are more concerned with collective status (Larson, 1977: 133). Closure is negotiated among the profession, the university and the state. But despite the lip service paid to the shibboleth of professional autonomy, closure ultimately depends on state authority (Barbalet, 1982: 488), which has expanded as the state has become a major source of financing for training and reimbursing professionals (Freidson, 1986: 76; cf. Kronus, 1976).

One of the central questions for a Weberian approach – but also the most difficult to answer – is why some occupations successfully professionalize and others do not. A number of factors may be relevant. The strength of the value that the professional service ostensibly promotes is crucial: health and justice obviously rank high (Macdonald, 1985: 544). Collegial control of the market is easier to attain if the clientele consists of isolated individuals. Furthermore, the homogeneity of the clientele will influence the homogeneity of producers, which in turn can determine whether a single profession emerges or several occupations continue to compete (Parry and Parry, 1977; Macdonald, 1984; 1985). Elite sponsorship can advance the professional project (Johnson, 1972: 52; Macdonald, 1984); conversely, the presence of socially disadvantaged groups, such as women, can hinder it (Parkin, 1979). Elite universities can play an instrumental role, as in continental Europe; but England and such former colonies as the United States, Canada, Australia and New Zealand clearly demonstrate that professions can emerge that train largely or exclusively through apprenticeship. Many of these themes are explored in the histories of the emergence of the medical profession in the United States and England (Freidson, 1970; Stevens, 1971; Markowitz and Rosner, 1973; Berlant, 1975; Parry and Parry, 1976; Starr, 1982).

Social closure is an elusive goal, even for the most successful professions (Child and Faulk, 1982; Rothman, 1984). It constantly must be defended against threats from consumers and potential competitors and the consequences of adventitious events. Success itself intensifies pressure for entry by aspiring professionals, jurisdictional challenges and consumer complaints about excessive costs. Changes in ideology and social movements can render the continued exclusion of disadvantaged groups intolerable. Demographic shifts caused by wars or changing birth rates can alter both supply and demand. Changes elsewhere in the labour market can affect the relative attractiveness of a professional career (Ben-David, 1963: 275; Fuchs, 1968; Abercrombie and Urry, 1983: 2–6). And the expansion of education – secondary schooling at the end of the nineteenth century, the tertiary sector after World War II – can lead to the inflation of credentials (Berg, 1970; Dore, 1976).

### *Economic analyses of the professions*

Sociological theories of professions as closure find their parallel in economic analyses of professions as restraints on an otherwise free market. Although Adam Smith justified exempting professions from market forces as a means of guaranteeing quality (1937: 118–19; see Dingwall and Fenn, 1987: 1), many of his twentieth-century followers have been considerably more severe. A strong and growing tradition sees the limitations on entry to the profession and on competition among professionals as unfair to potential competitors (both outside the profession and within) and detrimental to consumers (e.g. Friedman and Kuznets, 1945; Gellhorn, 1956; 1976; Friedman, 1962; Rottenberg, 1962; 1980; Lees, 1966; Maurizi, 1974; Slayton and Trebilcock, 1978; Blair and Rubin, 1980; Foley et al., 1982; Nieuwenhuysen and Williams-Wynn, 1982; Hogan, 1983). Some economists subsume this within the broader critique that regulation inevitably is captured by and benefits the industry at the expense of the consumer (e.g. Moore, 1961; Stigler, 1971; Posner, 1974; Peltzman, 1976; White, 1979c). Although economists concede that licensing can increase the quality of services *delivered*, they emphasize that the quality of services *received* necessarily declines because higher prices drive down demand (Carroll and Gaston, 1979a; 1979b; 1983). These theoretical arguments have been tested and generally confirmed by numerous empirical studies on the effects of licensing and other restrictive practices. Most researchers have looked at medicine because of the high value placed on health, the magnitude of overall expenditures on medical care and their rapid rate of increase, and the expanding role of public and private third-party payers (e.g., Kessel, 1958; 1970; Holen, 1965; Scitovsky, 1966; Feldstein, 1970; Egelston, 1972; Frech, 1974; Masson and Wu, 1974; Pfeffer, 1974; Siebert, 1977; Lipscomb, 1978; Shepard, 1978; Pashigian, 1979; White, 1979a; 1979b; 1983; Muzondo and Pazerka, 1980; Begun, 1981; Lazarus et al., 1981; Maurizi et al., 1981; Conrad and Sheldon, 1982; DeVany et al., 1982; Monheit, 1982; Larkin, 1983); a few also deal with lawyers (Arnould, 1972; Freeman, 1975; Evans and Trebilcock, 1982).

Just as there are parallels within economics to Weberian theories of social closure, so there are analogies to structural functional theories of the professions. One approach simply argues that the allegedly adverse consequences of licensing do not occur: physicians do not enjoy monopoly rents when their lengthy working hours are considered (Lindsay, 1973; Leffler, 1978; Mennemeyer, 1978), nor do they engage in price discrimination (Ruffin and Leigh, 1973). Economists approach structural functionalism more closely, however, when they concede that professions reduce competition but justify such reduction on the ground that informational asymmetry between producer and consumer requires producer control in order to ensure quality (e.g. Arrow, 1963; Akerlof, 1970; Leland, 1979; Carroll and Gaston, 1983; Dingwall and Fenn, 1987). Yet such justifications are open to the objection that the professions themselves create the very market failure they purport to rectify (Begun, 1986: 122).

Human capital theory also seeks to justify the price of professional services as including a reasonable return on the investment in education (e.g. Schultz, 1961; Becker, 1964; Kiker, 1966). In another formulation, professional credentials signal to prospective employers the value of the employee's services (Spence, 1973). Yet there is no evidence that training correlates with either productivity or quality. And empirical studies find that the rate of return varies with the height of entry barriers, even when the length of educational preparation is controlled (e.g. Dodge, 1972; Psacharapoulos, 1975; Larson, 1977: 212; Riera et al., 1977: ch. 2). Finally, labour economists have noted the analogy between professions and segmented labour markets (Kreckel, 1980). Professions thus become simply a special instance of the more general phenomenon of the dual labour market (e.g. Kerr, 1954: 93; Doeringer and Piore, 1971; Gordon, 1972), although professionals have advantages by reason of the generalized skills that allow them mobility between employers (Kreckel, 1980: 541). But though economists attempt to justify this, too, on the basis of informational inequality (Creedy, 1982), it remains subject to the general critique of segmented labour markets.

Although much of the economic literature is strongly normative, positive analyses describe not only how professions distort the market for services but also the ways in which those markets are self-correcting. Barriers to entry may create monopoly rents in the short run, but these inevitably attract additional entrants who drive down the price of the professional commodity (Posner, 1975; Tullock, 1975). More generally, the use of credentials as a means of securing economic advantage and status leads to the overproduction of those credentials and their progressive devaluation (Freeman, 1976; Larson, 1980: 151–3).

*Closure as collective mobility*

The professional project is directed not only toward controlling the market but also toward enhancing professional status, an issue sociologists treat far more extensively than economists. Indeed, some sociologists define professions as a status – a quality and degree of respect enjoyed by virtue of occupational role (e.g. Dingwall, 1976; Saks, 1983: 4–5). This emphasis is consistent with the fact that professional elites whose economic privileges are secure energetically pursue (and often initiate) the project of raising the status of the occupational category; and occupations with no hope of achieving market control persist in seeking professional status.

The relationship between economic privilege and social respect is very complex. Although inequality always requires justification, entrepreneurs seem to feel that success within the 'free market' is self-legitimating, whereas professionals feel compelled to offer additional explanations, since they visibly control their markets. The lengthy training professionals must complete perhaps may better be understood not as the acquisition of technical skills but as a sacrifice necessary to justify future privilege; only this can make sense of the relative poverty endured by students, their prolonged celibacy, the tedium of study, the indignities of apprenticeship, the anxiety inflicted by examinations and the lengthy postponement of adulthood.

The status of a profession is affected by two principal factors (aside from its economic standing): membership and clientele. Limitations on entry, which are the foundation of market control, inevitably influence the profession's composition as well as its numbers, whether or not this is a conscious goal. When American physicians excluded 'persons of inferior ability, questionable character and coarse and common fiber' by implementing the reforms ultimately embodied in the Flexner Report, the proportion of women medical graduates declined from 4.3 per cent between 1880 and 1904 to 3.2 per cent in 1912 (Markowitz and Rosner, 1973: 95, 97; Frech, 1974: 124–5). Sociologists analyse entry barriers in terms of whether professional status is ascribed or achieved, the warrant is aristocratic or modern, entry is based on qualities that are particularistic or universalistic and mobility is sponsored or contested (Turner, 1960). Both the classic elite professions, such as the Bar, and those occupations that successfully professionalized during the nineteenth century, such as Scottish accountants, appear to have benefited from the fact that their members enjoyed high status by birth (Macdonald, 1984). Professions exhibit a movement from ascribed to achieved status during the nineteenth and twentieth centuries, as contact with higher education and the university came to confer status (Bledstein, 1976; Klegon, 1978: 275). But some professions resisted this transformation precisely because they feared that barriers based on achievement would admit entrants from lower social backgrounds (Johnson, 1982: 203). And many observers have noted the loss of status (and pay) within previously male occupations that were feminized during this period, such as schoolteaching and clerical work (e.g. Fox and Hess-Biber, 1984). But it is important not to allow the ideology of meritocracy to conceal the fact that all 'achieved' requirements disproportionately exclude those disadvantaged by class, race or gender (e.g., Dorsey, 1980; Freeman, 1980). Whatever mobility does occur tends to be found within the middle class rather than between classes (Larson, 1977: 5).

Professions also gain, and lose, status from their clients. The classic professions of law and medicine clearly benefited from their historical association with aristocratic patrons (Portwood and Fielding, 1981: 765). On the other hand, the failure of other occupations to professionalize during the twentieth century may be due, in part, to their services to low-status clients (ibid.: 759). Abbott (1981) has argued, paradoxically, that professions gain public status by conferring order on disorder, though they lose intraprofessional status through their connection with disorder.

Although one of the defining characteristics of a profession is the fact that the status of its members is collective – conferred by entry to the profession and enhanced by mobility of the professional category – status differences inevitably persist within the profession. These, too, may be a function of the characteristics of the particular member (ascribed or achieved) or of the member's clients. But whereas collective mobility tends to solidify the professional category, intraprofessional mobility can impair it, as lower strata challenge higher or higher seek to immunize themselves from taint by lower.

### *Controlling production by producers*

Controlling entry – the production *of* producers – is only the first step in the professional project. An occupation that seeks to professionalize must also control production *by* producers, both for economic reasons and to enhance its status. Weber, again, surveys the range of possibilities:

> Closure within the group as between the members themselves and in their relations with each other may also assume the most varied forms. Thus a caste, a guild, or a group of stock exchange brokers, which is closed to

> outsiders, may allow to its members a perfectly free competition for all the advantages which the group as a whole monopolizes for itself. Or it may assign every member strictly to the enjoyment of certain advantages, such as claims over customers or particular business opportunities, for life or even on a hereditary basis.
>
> (1947: 143)

Restrictions may be formal or informal, visible or invisible. If a principal reason for adopting such restraints is to protect members from competition with each other as well as with outsiders, they also may enhance the status of the profession by conferring an aura of disinterest (Larson, 1977: 62–3). The image of professionals as *honoratiores* is reinforced by such devices as the academic hood (into which students put the fees paid to professors at medieval universities), Pooh-Bah's references to bribes as 'insults' in *The Mikado* and the widespread convention that lawyers and physicians do not discuss fees in advance.

Neoclassical economics has discussed and criticized these forms of market control, as well as the restrictions on entry described above. Economists have found empirical confirmation for the theoretical prediction that limitations on advertising, fee schedules, prohibitions on interprofessional partnerships and other anticompetitive rules increase consumer prices (e.g. Newhouse, 1970; Newhouse and Sloan, 1972; Frech and Ginsberg, 1972; Benham, 1972; Benham and Benham, 1975; Cady, 1975; Feldman and Begun, 1978; 1980; Muzondo and Pazerka, 1979; Bond et al., 1983). Yet if the professional monopoly itself is difficult to construct and maintain against external attack, cartels also are very fragile. Anticompetitive rules protect some who would do worse within a free market only by disadvantaging others who would do better (Hall, 1948). And it is difficult to justify restrictive practices, although the profession may try to stigmatize violators as charlatans or encroachers (Goode, 1960) or argue that the rules are necessary to ensure quality (e.g. Leffler, 1983). The two forms of market control – overproduction *of* and *by* producers – appear to rise and fall together.

### *Demand for professional services*

The theories of professionalism as closure discussed above focus on the nature and extent of occupational control over the supply of services. This is particularly true of economic analyses, which view demand as an exogenous variable, independent of supply. Explanations of demand must be specific to the service, although demographic changes in the size of the population and its age distribution affect most services. A number of factors seem likely to influence the demand for legal services. Because law everywhere is intimately associated with the definition and transfer of property, the demand for lawyers will vary with the distribution of wealth and income (cf. Sugarman and Rubin, 1984: 86–88). Thus, the rise of the bourgeoisie, the spread of home ownership, the growth of pension funds, the concentration of capital and the proliferation of state welfare benefits all affect that demand. Within the private sector, the mix of economic activities – between the production of goods and services, for instance – may influence the level of demand. As portions of the economy are nationalized, administration may displace law, and economists or other technocrats may be substituted for lawyers (Luckham, 1981: 325). Indeed, where the growth of the state anticipates that of private capital, lawyers become civil servants rather than private practitioners (Johnson, 1973; Rueschemeyer, 1973; Larson, 1977: 144; Luckham, 1981: 298). Because law is state social control, it varies with the level of other forms of institutional control (Black, 1976); thus, the increase in geographic mobility, the contraction of kinship bonds, the decline of ethnic communities, secularization and other related trends may increase the demand for legal control. Whenever the state subjects new areas of social life to legal regulation the demand for lawyers will increase – the most notable contemporary example being laws that address the dissolution of marriage. Finally, there are differences between societies and across time in the extent to which recourse to law is culturally approved or discouraged (Galanter, 1983: 51–61).

But demand is not a given, which professions simply accept. Economists have argued theoretically and sought to demonstrate empirically that physicians create demand for their own services (e.g. Evans et al., 1973; Evans, 1974; Feldman, 1980). One way professionals do this is by developing new capabilities: thus, physicians increase their ability to preserve or restore health or prolong life by expanding their scientific knowledge or technological armoury; and lawyers multiply the benefits they can confer through every legal innovation – or complication. Professions also seek to rationalize and expand their markets by using intermediaries in both the private and the public sectors. Private insurance, frequently as an adjunct of employment or union membership, has dramatically affected the markets for medical services in the United States and legal services in Germany. State subsidies have been even more important to the professions, particularly where they allow clients to obtain services from private practitioners rather than from state employees (Bankowski and Mungham, 1978). These forms of 'demand creation' have important consequences beyond the economic benefits they confer on professionals. They introduce 'mediative' control over the production and distribution of professional services, increasing the heterogeneity of consumers, stratifying the profession and altering the relationship between producers and consumers (Johnson, 1972: 77–81). And they may also affect the collective status of the profession – perhaps enhancing it as a larger proportion of the population benefits from the services, but also possibly lowering it if demand creation is seen as motivated by economic self-interest.

## Marxist theories of professions in the class structure

If the problem for Weberian theories of the professions is the horizontal relations between occupational categories competing for market shares and social status, the problem for Marxist theories is the location of professions within the vertical system of classes defined by relations of production. Marxism makes class relations central because it views class conflict as the principal engine of change and, ultimately, the mechanism through which socialism will displace capitalism. Yet as I mentioned at the beginning of this chapter, professions are something of an anomaly for Marxist class analysis. There are only three solutions to the question of their class location. They could be categorized with capitalists – but they clearly do not own the means of production. They could be called workers – but both the work they do and the rewards they receive are vastly different from those of most workers. Or they could constitute a third category – but that would require a fundamental reworking of Marxist theory.

Marx did not devote much attention to the professions, since they were numerically insignificant and apparently marginal to relations of production. As members of the petty bourgeoisie – neither exploited labour nor exploiters of labour – they were a historical residue from an earlier stage of capitalism. Marx seems to have expected the professions either to disappear or to be assimilated to one of the two great class adversaries. At times, however, both he and later Marxists recognized that the increasing concentration of capital would require the expansion of a category of functionaries acting as agents for the owners of capital in their interactions with other capitalists and financiers or as managers of labour (Abercrombie and Urry, 1983: 31, 49). Because history did not follow the path initially predicted by Marx, later Marxist writers have had to rethink class analysis, especially as the number of educated workers and professionals has grown so rapidly during the last two decades. A wide variety of theoretical perspectives has been advanced to locate professionals within the class system.

*Orthodox Marxism: professionals and relations of production*

Marx defined classes in terms of their relations to the means of production. He argued that all societies have exhibited the opposition of two major classes, one of which exploits the other by extracting surplus value from its labour. Although Marxists have sought to apply this analysis to professions, they have encountered considerable difficulty in deciding whether the latter produce surplus value so that they can be considered exploited labour (Johnson, 1977a; 1977b; Larson, 1977: 213; Szymanski, 1979; Derber, 1982d: 200; Abercrombie and Urry, 1983: 77; Boreham, 1983). Certainly this criterion does not unambiguously define the class identity of lawyers. Much of their work relates to the sphere of reproduction rather than production (e.g., family law, inheritance or the transfer of unproductive property such as homes). And even within the capitalist enterprise, lawyers have considerably more influence on how surplus value is distributed among capitalists than on how it is extracted from workers.

Some authors have sought to construe Marxism in functional terms, distinguishing the global functions of capital and labour and assigning members of society to one category or the other on the basis of the function they perform (Carchedi, 1975; Abercrombie and Urry, 1983: 62–3). These analysts define the global functions of capital to include ideological inculcation, political repression and the management and supervision of the working class (Poulantzas, 1975; Esland, 1980). In these terms, physicians can be seen as members of the dominant class (Navarro, 1976; 1978) and so can engineers (Noble, 1979: 135–6). Lawyers are even more intimately associated with such 'global' functions as social control (criminal law), structuring the relations of production (labour law), exchange among capitalists (commercial law) and ownership of capital (company law). Yet such an expansive definition of capital subsumes a very large proportion of the population, leaving the working class a minority, class conflict a foregone conclusion and history static.

Erik Olin Wright (1979: 201) has argued that the Marxist concept of class is structural and therefore cannot be understood in such functionalist terms. Consequently, he and his associates have refined the basic categories to acknowledge that a number of crucial actors occupy contradictory class locations: semi-autonomous wage earners (such as assistant solicitors in firms and the lower ranks of employed lawyers in commerce and industry) between the proletariat and the petty bourgeoisie, small employers (such as law firm principals) between the petty bourgeoisie and the bourgeoisie, and managers (perhaps including senior house counsel) between the bourgeoisie and capitalists (Wright et al., 1982). This more discriminating picture highlights the ambiguity of professions in the class system, but in rejecting functionalism it becomes unable to distinguish between professionals.

### *Professional expertise as power*

At least ever since Berle and Means (1933) noted the increasing separation between ownership and control within the capitalist enterprise, analysts have had to assess whether the technical expertise acquired by managers (on the job) and professionals (in the academy) renders them servants of power or enhances their autonomy. A large and diverse group of observers has opted for the latter conclusion, although they differ about whether technocrats will use their power for selfish or unselfish ends (e.g., Galbraith, 1967; Bell, 1974; 1976; Bruce-Biggs, 1979; Steinfels, 1979; Crozier, 1982; Wuthnow and Shrum, 1983; Larson, 1984). Gouldner (1979) portrays the potential role of Western intellectuals in the most favourable light, as a 'flawed' universal class; Konrad and Szelenyi (1979; see also Szelenyi, 1982) offer a very bleak picture of the actual role of intellectuals in Eastern Europe. Frank Parkin equates the acquisition of formal credentials to the ownership of capital as an index of ruling class membership: 'The dominant class under modern capitalism can be thought of as comprising those who possess or control productive capital and those who possess a legal monopoly of professional services' (1979: 58). Yet as Gouldner has objected (1979: 19–20), credentials may produce monopoly rents, but they differ from capital in two essential respects: credentials do not valorize themselves, producing more credentials the way capital produces more capital; and there is no market for credentials comparable to the capital markets. Ehrenreich and Ehrenreich (1979) are equally emphatic that the 'professional-managerial class' – defined by its possession of specialized skills and its function of reproducing capitalist culture and class relations – is independent of and opposed to both capital and labour. But while I am persuaded that professionals are at least somewhat autonomous, such a conclusion suggests that class analysis can tell us relatively little about their behaviour.

### *Working conditions and the proletarianization of professionals*

The third possibility within Marxist class analysis is that professionals will become members of the proletariat as a result of changes in their working conditions (e.g. Haug, 1973; Oppenheimer, 1973). Just as proletarianization progressively extended from unskilled workers to skilled craftsmen during the early stages of the rise of capitalism, so now it will embrace educated workers. Derber (1982a: 5) notes the parallel between the nineteenth-century shift from putting out to factory work and the contemporary displacement of the independent professional by the employee. Indices of proletarianization include ever more detailed specialization and specification of tasks, increased working speed, subordination to external authority and the entry of disadvantaged categories into the profession (Larson, 1980: 162–71; see generally Wood, 1982). In the private sector, proletarianization is attributable to the investment of capital in service production in order to organize a dispersed clientele, reap the rewards of higher profitability and take advantage of technological development (Derber, 1982a: 6–7). In the public sector, proletarianization is an expression of the fiscal crisis of the state, which increasingly pays for or subsidizes the production of services (O'Connor, 1973).

Not all observers perceive these changes, and even those who acknowledge them disagree about their significance. Eliot Freidson is most vehement in rejecting the proletarianization thesis, noting that professions have not suffered any decline in their knowledge base or in the respect they elicit – indeed, quite the reverse has happened (1986: ch. 6; see also 1983; 1985). Derber concurs that it is essential to distinguish the deskilling and routinization of manual work that occurred under the banner of Taylorism from the situation of contemporary professionals, whose increased specialization actually may lead to greater autonomy (1982a: 7, 30–1). But Freidson concedes that professionals have lost control over the organization of their work (1986: ch. 6; see also Larson, 1980: 139). And Derber makes a useful distinction between ideological and technical proletarianization (1982c: 169; see also Salaman, 1979: 139). Technical proletarianization is a function of the progressive separation of mental and manual tasks, the substitution of computers for workers and the growth of a reserve labour force; it accurately characterizes the plight of the lower service class, which therefore also suffers an erosion of income (Derber, 1982d: 196–99; Abercrombie and Urry, 1983: 57, 114–18). Professionals avoid this fate only by embracing ideological proletarianisation. They retain autonomy in the selection of means, but the price they pay is allowing others to determine the goals. Extrinsic rewards (pay, career advancement, working conditions) displace intrinsic satisfaction, which is limited to the exercise of technical skill. I find this account thoroughly persuasive; indeed, the strongest evidence that professionals have relinquished control over the ends of their work may be their inability to perceive the loss. On the other hand, even a theory of ideological proletarianization may be guilty of romanticizing the situation of 'independent' professionals, who always embraced the ends of whichever clients they were able to find in the marketplace.

### *What does class analysis tell us?*

Although Marxist class analysis sometimes degenerates into mere taxonomy, its avowed purpose is to identify a category of actors who share a common outlook, engage in similar (even collective) political, economic and social behaviour, and thus can be agents of transformation. Several commentators argue that denominating professionals as capitalists, workers or some intermediate class also predicts their behaviour. Thus, Frank Parkin maintains that 'those who monopolize productive property and credentials share for the most part a broadly similar political and ideological stance' (1979: 58). At the other extreme, analysts who conclude that educated workers have been proletarianized predict that they will exhibit a working class consciousness (e.g. Gorz, 1964; 1976; Tourraine, 1971; Mallet, 1975); and there is evidence that educated workers are increasingly discontent with their conditions and rewards (Derber, 1982b: 22–7). They have joined unions in greater numbers and displayed more militant opposition to private and public employers (e.g. Kleingartner, 1967; Haug and Sussman, 1973). On the other hand, professionalism fosters individualism, status consciousness and concern for technical autonomy, all of which discourage union membership and collective action (Derber, 1982b: 27–9; 1982d: 204). If traditional class analysis assimilates professionals to capital or labour, 'new class' theories emphasize the autonomy of professional ideology. The few empirical data concerning the political attitudes of lawyers are consistent with this view (e.g., Heinz and Laumann, 1982: 143; Nelson, 1985); but again this suggests that class analysis is not a particularly powerful tool for understanding the legal profession.

## Structural functional theories of professions and social order

If the problem for Weberians and neoclassical economists is the market and the problem for Marxists is class, the problem for structural functionalists is social order: what holds together an aggregation of egoistic individuals? At least since Durkheim, professions have been an important part of the answer. Professions play a significant role within the system of stratification, which unites the extremes of society. Professions ensure that expertise is deployed in the general interest.

Professions exemplify a form of community that was undermined by the industrial revolution. And professions regulate themselves, thereby offering a counterweight to an increasingly imperial state.

### *Professions in the system of stratification*

Whereas Marxists conceptualize inequality as dividing society into two discrete opposed classes based on a single criterion (relations of production), structural functionalists see continuous differences along a multiplicity of variables, including wealth, income, occupation, education, religion, ethnicity, race, gender and parental background – none of which is theoretically pre-eminent (Abercrombie and Urry, 1983: ch. 2). They particularly reject the notion that professions can be identified with either capital or labour or that they constitute a coherent 'new class' (e.g. Freidson, 1986: ch. 3). In doing so, they stress the heterogeneity of the professions in terms of background, training, function, clientele, rewards and politics. Certainly it would be difficult to conceptualize class in such a way as to include within a single category judges, law teachers, lawyers in the civil service or employed by industry and commerce, and private practitioners. Even if lawyers take on the coloration of their clients (Luckham, 1981: 304–6; Heinz and Laumann, 1982), their affiliations are extremely diverse given the heterogeneity of the clientele.

The task of social analysis then becomes placing lawyers within the system of stratification according to some of the many criteria (e.g. Hodge et al., 1964; Blau and Duncan, 1967; Treiman, 1977; Coxon and Jones, 1978). The hierarchy as a whole, and the location of professions at or near the top, constitute an invitation to compete for rewards within the system rather than to challenge it. Studies of social mobility, especially through entry to the professions, are essential to ascertaining how the relative starting points of competitors affect their chances of retaining or improving their positions (Larson, 1977: 156–7).

### *Threats to professional autonomy*

A principal foundation of structural functional theories of the professions is the belief that, protected from outside interference, they will use their knowledge for the social good (Haskell, 1984). Talcott Parsons exemplified this approach in writing about lawyers:

> His [the lawyer's] function in relation to clients is by no means only to "give them what they want" but often to resist their pressures and get them to realize some of the hard facts of their situations, not only with

> reference to what they can, even with clever legal help, expect to "get away with" but with reference to what the law will permit them to do.
>
> (1964a: 384)

The first question raised by such a theory – to what extent does the 'independent' professional actually pursue client rather than personal interest and elevate the social good above both – is rarely investigated (but see Nelson, 1985). Instead, structural functionalism assumes that 'independent' professionals exhibit such desirable traits and then explores the threats to professional autonomy. The principal threat generally is seen to be employment and, to a lesser extent, third-party reimbursement. This is the functionalist equivalent of the Marxist inquiry into the proletarianization of professionals. There can be no doubt that employment is increasing – more rapidly outside the older professions originally organized around independent practice (primarily medicine and law) but also within them (Derber, 1982c: 167).

The problem typically is framed as a tension or conflict between professionalism and bureaucracy (e.g. Harries-Jenkins, 1970; Benson, 1973; Fielding and Portwood, 1980; Rueschemeyer, 1983: 52). Social scientists have made this a principal theme in studies of psychiatrists in the military (Daniels, 1969), scientists in industry and government (e.g., Glaser, 1964; Kornhauser, 1965; Marcson, 1966; Perucci and Gerstl, 1969) and physicians (e.g., Ben-David, 1958; Rothstein, 1973; Starr, 1982). Whether as employers or paymasters, private and public bureaucracies control professionals through hiring, promotion and retention policies and the allocation of resources, especially technology (Blau and Schoenherr, 1971; Freidson, 1986: 169). Indeed, a recent manual on managing professionals advised companies to permit internal mobility to allay boredom, create a promotional ladder within technical departments for the unusually gifted, ensure personal attention to avoid alienation and use part-time technicians to cushion full-time employees against fluctuations in demand (Raelin, 1986).

This literature has stimulated a revisionist reply, which questions the tension between professionalism and bureaucracy (e.g. Hall, 1968; Ritzer, 1975; Derber, 1982b: 16). Such authors note that the 'autonomy' of private practitioners is not only empirically undemonstrated but also theoretically dubious: the need to find and retain clients in the marketplace remains a powerful constraint, even when the profession has imposed limitations on entry and internal competition. Second, professionalism is not 'autonomy' but simply another form of control, different from but no less constraining than bureaucracy and a form that is particularly appropriate when tasks require high technical discretion and work is discontinuous and less predictable (Stinchcombe, 1969; Larson, 1977: 193, 199). Professionalism controls work through its lengthy socialization process and the selection of those predisposed to comply with authority (Derber, 1982d: 202). Third, external authorities, whether bureaucratic superiors or third-party payers, may be concerned with the organization of work and its cost, but they leave the technical details to the professional (Freidson, 1986: 161). These disagreements are to some extent questions of emphasis – whether independence of goal or technique is more important – and to some extent empirical questions about the behaviour of professionals in different environments.

### *Professions as communities*

Community remains an attractive but elusive goal in a mass society where ideologies of universalism and efficiency constantly tend to disrupt strong, multiplex, enduring interpersonal bonds. Structural functionalism sees professions as a powerful and valuable source of community (e.g. Durkheim, 1957; Goode, 1957). It is true that members of a profession do share some common role definitions, an esoteric language and social boundaries. Membership is attained through a long and painful socialization process (Rueschemeyer, 1964: 17 n. 2), and for most it is a terminal status (Heinz and Laumann, 1982: 206–10). And professions do engage in self-governance.

But there are serious problems with the notion of profession as community. Certainly other communities – such as those based on kinship, race, ethnicity, class, religion, gender or locality – are far more salient to most people most of the time. To the extent that professions do become communities for their members, they often achieve that quality by excluding others on the basis of class, gender or race – forms of discrimination that are no longer acceptable in the workplace. All professions are riven by major internal divisions between practitioners, administrators and teachers or researchers (Freidson, 1986: 213). And as an increasing proportion of professionals become employees, especially of large private or public bureaucracies, their community tends to become their employer rather than the profession as a whole.

The legal profession has even fewer communal characteristics than other professions. In an inegalitarian society, professionals necessarily reflect the stratification of their clients (Larson, 1977: 3). An extreme example within medicine is the social distance between the psychiatrist employed by a public mental hospital and the psychiatrist treating private outpatients, although they share common credentials and possess similar expertise (Johnson, 1972: 59). But even within private practice, the clienteles of lawyers vary more dramatically than those of physicians, from the poor individual to the largest company (Rueschemeyer, 1964: 23–4). The divisions within the legal profession – among employed, employing and independent private practitioners and between them and judges, prosecutors, civil servants, house counsel and law teachers – are more numerous and deeper than those within medicine, even disregarding subject-matter specialization. Partly for this reason and partly because lawyers practise within a specific polity, legal knowledge is more localized and particular than knowledge in other professions, such as medicine (Schudson, 1974: 358). And certainly there is a much lower degree of consensus about ultimate values among lawyers than among physicians; justice is more contentious than health (Rueschemeyer, 1964: 19). Thus, though lawyers may find community within their work, the legal profession as a whole is a weak community.

### *Self-regulation*

If functionalism had to identify professions by a single characteristic, self-regulation would be near the top of the list. Because professions are a manifestatation of the division of labour between producers and consumers, mechanisms are needed to ensure that producers are technically qualified and do not abuse the power they derive from their specialized knowledge. When consumers are powerful – aristocratic patrons in the past, large public or private entities today – they themselves may be able to ensure the loyalty and competence of producers (Johnson, 1972: 69). But most consumers must rely on other sources of control. Professions are adamant in insisting that they, not the state, must possess regulatory authority. They rest their claim on two grounds. First, they argue that only fellow professionals possess the necessary expertise; but since the profession painfully constructed the monopoly of expertise in the first place, that argument is self-serving. Second, they assert that the profession is independent of the state; but this assumes that the profession is more solicitous of client (and other public) interests than is the state and that the profession will oppose the state in defence of those interests – empirical propositions for which there is little if any support. Furthermore, despite its protestations of autonomy, the profession necessarily derives its regulatory power from the state.

Professions do not appear to perform their regulatory functions very effectively. Although they claim constantly to be refining their technical skills in the service of society, Weber notes that self-interest frequently dampens their ardour for reform:

> Whenever legal education has been in the hands of practitioners, especially attorneys, who have made admission to practice a guild monopoly, an economic factor, namely their pecuniary interest, brings to bear a strong influence upon the process not only of stabilizing the official law and of adapting it to changing needs in an exclusively empirical way but also of preventing its rationalization through legislation or legal science.
>
> (1954: 202–3)

Lawyers, like all professionals, also display their altruism in providing gratuitous or low-cost services; but the magnitude of such charity seems to vary inversely with how extensively it is publicized – conspicuous production being the necessary complement of conspicuous consumption (Veblen, 1915). Although professions portray self-regulation as a means of reducing client uncertainty, they deliberately draft ethical rules in vague and ambiguous language in order to preserve the indeterminacy that is an essential foundation of professional power (Jamous and Peloille, 1970: 141). Many ostensibly 'ethical' rules serve the Weberian objective of market control rather than the Parsonian goal of protecting clients and society. Rules focus on professional technique but ignore the ends to which that technique is directed. Enforcement is weak. Client confidentiality is invoked to forestall external surveillance of professional conduct (Johnson, 1972: 70; cf. Wilensky, 1964: 152). Larger productive units resist professional control over their members or employees. And the object of 'self-regulation' often appears to be protecting the inept within the profession rather than the society they ostensibly serve (Goode, 1967; Noble and Pym, 1970; Trebilcock et al., 1979; Haug, 1980), as has been documented with respect to physicians (e.g., Derbyshire, 1983; Dolan and Urban, 1983). One reason for systematic non-enforcement is that control of misconduct and incompetence readily becomes an arena for intraprofessional conflict, which threatens the very community self-regulation purports to express. Consequently, self-regulation may be more comprehensible as an assertion of status rather than a form of social control (Abbott, 1983; cf. Edelman, 1964). There is a danger, however, that the visible failure of self-regulation may lead to attempts to assert control by clients (Haug and Sussman, 1969) and external agents such as courts (Child and Faulk, 1982; Freidson, 1984; 1986: ch. 5).

## The plan of this book

In the chapters that follow, I will present a historical sociology of lawyers in England and Wales, using the theoretical framework developed above to organize the data and using the data to test and refine that framework. I will be concerned with the Weberian issues of how lawyers constructed their professional commodity (legal services) and sought to assert control over their market and to enhance their collective status by regulating the production *of* and *by* producers and stimulating demand. I will explore the Marxist questions of where lawyers fit within relations of production. And I will look at the structural functional questions of lawyers in the system of stratification, professional autonomy, self-governance and self-regulation.

In seeking to present a historical sociology of the legal professions, I have emphasized quantitative data over qualitative accounts. This is not because I believe one is superior to the other but simply because I could not do justice to both within a single book. In order to trace change over time, generalize about the national legal professions and make comparisons between and within the branches, it is extremely useful – often essential – to reduce complex features to something that can be counted. But I would be the first to admit that quantification frequently sacrifices depth for breadth and complexity for the memorable but incomplete summary. Furthermore, the selection of a numerical index assumes that we know the meaning of a social practice, although we have not asked the actors themselves how they understand their behaviour. I know I have drawn upon interpretative accounts, discussions with lawyers and my own experience in choosing the questions I have tried to answer quantitatively. I hope others will interrogate my generalizations through interpretative methods.

Because barristers and solicitors effectively constitute distinct (often rival) professions with different histories and structures (if also overlapping functions), I will address them separately in parts II and III, noting contrasts and tensions. I begin my story in the early nineteenth century; this is a natural divide for solicitors, who effectively lacked the hallmarks of a profession before then. Although the history of barristers is more continuous, the efforts of solicitors to professionalize ultimately affected the Bar as well (but see Prest, 1984). In part IV I examine the rise of academic legal education, which remained marginal to barristers and solicitors until its rapid growth in the 1960s transformed both branches. I conclude with some thoughts about the future of the English legal professions.

# II

# Barristers

# 2

# Controlling supply

## Defining the category

Barristers are defined formally by call to the Bar; those in private practice are also defined functionally by the conjunction of a privilege and a disability. The privilege is their monopoly of rights of audience in the higher courts (Crown courts, High Court, Court of Appeal and House of Lords). The disability is the prohibition on dealing directly with clients; barristers can take instructions only from solicitors.

The contemporary Bar is a nineteenth-century amalgam of several distinct occupational categories. The first group to achieve the monopoly of advocacy was serjeants-at-law, who were appointed by the Crown; beginning in the thirteenth century, only they could appear in the Court of Common Pleas. As the Crown gradually ceased to appoint Church officials to the bench, serjeants also became common law judges. Serjeants had their own Inns (and remained members even after elevation to the bench) and a collegiate life, but by the eighteenth century they had lost much of their prestige. Although they retained a nominal monopoly of appointments to the Court of Common Pleas until 1846, this had become a mere formality by the nineteenth century, for the Crown simply made serjeants of those it wished to appoint to the bench (Duman, 1982: 12–13).

Barristers originally were the apprentices of serjeants and thus aspired to similar appointments, but they soon formed the present four Inns – Lincoln's, Gray's and Inner and Middle Temple – and secured a monopoly of advocacy at King's (or Queen's) Bench by travelling on circuit with the Sovereign. A third category of advocates – King's (or Queen's) Counsel (also known as silks, by virtue of their gown, or seniors, to distinguish them from junior barristers) – consisted of barristers appointed by the Crown and originally paid an annual retainer to advise and represent it in litigation. They became an honorific category in the early nineteenth century and remain one today. The historical multiplicity of jurisdictions gave rise to additional divisions. Chancery had its own distinct Bar (even after the merger of law and equity Chancery remains a specialist practice, with its own sets based in Lincoln's Inn). Similarly, rights of audience in the ecclesiastical courts (with jurisdiction over marriage, divorce and succession) and in the Court of Admiralty were limited to Doctors of Law, who obtained a DCL at Oxford or Cambridge and apprenticed for a year before joining the College of Advocates housed in Doctors' Commons.

Finally, there were two groups on the fringes of the Bar, whose existence was not a by-product of judicial specialization. The increasing complexity of pleading during the seventeenth and eighteenth centuries generated the categories of special pleader in common law and equity draughtsman in Chancery, who had mastered the arcane formulae necessary to initiate litigation. They were attached to the Inns, though not themselves barristers. And similarly, ever more esoteric devices for encumbering and transferring land led to the emergence of conveyancers (a function that barristers originally shared with solicitors), located first in the Inns and then attached to the Chancery Bar (Abel-Smith and Stevens, 1967: 14–17).

Although these distinct categories flourished well into the nineteenth century, by its end all but the silks had disappeared or were about to do so. The number of serjeants actually grew during the the first half of the century (see table 4.2), but none was appointed after 1866; in 1873 all serjeants (including those who had been appointed to the bench) returned to the Inns in which they originally had been called, and the one remaining Serjeants' Inn was abolished. Doctors of Law, who had grown from 12 in 1779 and 9 in 1785 to 28 in 1815, gradually declined to 25 in 1835 and 22 in 1842. They also joined the Bar when the separate ecclesiastical and Admiralty jurisdictions were eliminated in 1857. The number of conveyancers fluctuated during the first half of the century but declined sharply by the end (see table 4.2). Special pleaders and equity draughtsmen (who, together with conveyancers, totalled 172 in 1800) also virtually had vanished by 1900 (Holdsworth, 1938: 4; Cocks, 1983: 122–3; Whishaw, 1835: 251–5, 282–3; Shaw's Calendar, 1877–8: 22–26; Commissioners of Inland Revenue, Annual Reports; Odgers, 1901: 30; S. Warren, 1845: 2; 1863, vol. 1: 2–3; Foster, 1885; Duman, 1982: 8). Thus, halfway through the period with which I am concerned (the nineteenth and twentieth centuries), barristers had succeeded in absorbing or eliminating most other occupational categories performing similar functions. Struggles over the market for legal services have continued, but they have been internal – between barristers and solicitors and, among barristers, between juniors and seniors, circuit members and outsiders and (more recently) across divisions of age, gender, race and specialization.

## Limiting entry

Entry barriers perform two tasks essential to the construction of any profession: they limit the number who can offer the service, thereby lessening competition, and they simultaneously shape the demographic characteristics of practitioners by making entry easier for some than for others. Members of an occupation need not conspire to pursue these ends; efforts to maintain standards of ethics and competence inevitably also affect the number and background of entrants. But the Bar has often been quite open about its actual objectives. In the 1840s, barristers complained repeatedly that the profession was overcrowded (Cocks, 1983: 122; Duman, 1983a: 1–2). Twenty years later, they expressed the fear that the standing of the Bar might be diminished by lower-class entrants who could surmount the minimal hurdles (Cocks, 1983: 122; Duman, 1979; 1983a: 20–2). And in recent years the Bar Council has publicized the unattractive financial prospects of young barristers in order to discourage aspirants (Senate, 1978d: 5). Yet the Bar entered the nineteenth century with a structure of professional qualifications that many other professions (including solicitors) would envy, even if eventually it felt the need to superimpose meritocratic criteria of technical knowledge upon the intensely personalistic criteria of wealth and social standing.

### Admission to an Inn

In order to become a barrister, an applicant first must be admitted as a student by one of the four Inns of Court. At least since the sixteenth century, control over admission has been lodged with the benchers of each Inn, an oligarchy of older barristers who select their own successors (see chapter 9, p. 128). Although Lord Mansfield announced in 1780 that judges could hear appeals from rejections, the first such appeal was not filed until 1837, and they have been extremely infrequent since then (Holdsworth, 1938: 28–33; Duman, 1981: 86; Abel-Smith and Stevens, 1967: 64; Cocks, 1983: 23).

Applicants in the 1830s had to state their age, residence and condition in life and provide references from two barristers or one bencher; furthermore, applicants could not be engaged in trade (S. Warren, 1835: 498–9, 501). Clearly, these conditions limited how many applied and who did so. In the light of this self-selection, it is not surprising that few applicants were rejected: Lincoln's Inn refused only four out of the nearly 2000 who applied between 1814 and 1834 (Manchester, 1980: 53). One reason for this hospitality is that the Inns depended for a large part of their income on student fees, as we will see below.

## Keeping terms

Although the Inns had ceased to be educational institutions long before the nineteenth century, they still preserved the rituals associated with collegiate life. Pre-eminent among these was the requirement that a student 'keep terms' by dining in hall a specified number of times: three in each of the four terms (associated with the judicial calendar) for graduates of English universities, six in each term for others (until 1968). Students had to keep terms for seven years until the end of the eighteenth century; this was reduced to five years in 1762 (three for university graduates) and to three in 1835 (Holdsworth, 1938: 23–4; N. Warren, 1978: 50). Today, all students must dine at least 32 times spread over at least eight terms (Royal Commission, 1979, Vol. 1: 620). Meeting this requirement represents a significant cost, both for the dinners themselves and for transportation if the student lives outside London (though these items are small in comparison with the other costs discussed below). It also inconveniences those living outside London and places a much more substantial burden on overseas students, who must remain in or return to England after completing their studies and examinations in order to attend any remaining dinners. And the custom was criticized before the Royal Commission as not only anachronistic but also an occasion for harassment of women students. Yet it persists, if only as another argument barristers can invoke when resisting fusion with solicitors.

## The cost of qualifying

At least until recently, the greatest obstacle to becoming a barrister has been simple cost. Some of the charges are imposed directly by the Bar, such as fees for admission to an Inn, for examinations and for call. Other costs are a residue of tradition: the price of a wig and gown (whose use the Royal Commission fervently defended) (1979, vol. 1: 471–2) or the customary fee for pupillage. And some, like stamp duties on admission and call, are imposed by the state. But the largest item has always been maintenance during the lengthy period of qualification and the early, unremunerative years of practice. Nor can students readily defray these expenses by part-time work: the Inns have prohibited students from undertaking work incompatible with the dignity of the profession (Zander, 1968: 230 n. 113); and though this rule may be honoured more in the breach, the demands of studying now render employment more difficult. Making entry to a profession contingent upon ability to pay is an extremely effective means of controlling both numbers and background, if one whose legitimacy increasingly is questioned.

In the first half of the nineteenth century, all aspiring barristers (except those tutored privately) would have attended a public school at a cost of £300–500 spread over four years; the majority also would have attended university for several years, representing at least another £150–200 (Duman, 1982: 47). In 1835, the Inns charged £30–40 for admission (of which £25 was stamp duty), £5–10 a year to dine in hall (for a minimum of three years) and £70–80 at call (of which £50 was stamp duty) (S. Warren, 1835: 504). Furthermore, the student had to deposit £100 on admission, which was refunded without interest only if the student ultimately was called (Abel-Smith and Stevens, 1967: 66). During the Georgian era, only 20–30 per cent of students ever were called (Duman, 1981: 87 n. 6). In 1845 Samuel Warren, a contemporary author, estimated the additional costs as: £6–8 a year for books; £150 a year maintenance as student, pupil and beginning barrister; 200 guineas premium for a pupillage; £100–200 initial investment in practice plus £15–20 a year expenses; 8 guineas for a wig and gown; and £90–100 a year for riding circuit. All told, Warren advised aspiring barristers to be prepared to invest £300 capital and possess a steady (unearned) income of £250 a year (1845: 74–5). In 1859, one Thomas Blofeld went to London to study for the Bar with an allowance of £250 a year, which was not overgenerous (Cocks, 1978a: 38). A modern historian of the Bar has estimated the total cost at £1200–2600, spread over 10 years (Duman, 1982: 48).

These costs continued to rise. In 1879, Walter Rouse Ball published an extremely successful *Students' Guide to the Bar*, in which he described in some detail the steps necessary to succeed as a barrister (quoted in Cocks, 1983: 181–83). These were: admission to Oxford or Cambridge to read classics or history at the age of 19; admission to an Inn at 20½; the Bar examination in Roman law at 21½; a university degree at 22; the Bar examination in English law at 22½; pupillage with a conveyancer or equity draughtsman until 23½; pupillage with a common law barrister until 24; half a year with a solicitor; call to the Bar at 24½, followed by another half year in the chambers of an established barrister. Even when the fully qualified barrister opened his own chambers, he could not expect to support himself for several years (see 'Surviving the early years of practice', p. 60). Ball deemed it too obvious to be worth mentioning that matriculation at Oxford or Cambridge presupposed several years at public school. The decade of preparation for a career as a barrister would cost a minimum of £300 a year, an income that could be produced only by capital of at least £2400 (see also Shaw's Calendar, 1877–8: 56; Napier and Stephenson, 1888: 11, 66). To put these figures into perspective, the average wage of the English worker during the nineteenth century ranged between £40 and £60 a year (Bowley, 1900: 64–70).

These costs remained a substantial barrier for 150 years, until after World War II. They greatly constricted the class backgrounds of those who became barristers (see chapter 4, p. 74). But since the war their significance has changed and diminished. Certain fixed costs have been eliminated – the £50 stamp duty on call was abolished in 1947, for instance (Abel-Smith and Stevens, 1967: 358). Others have remained relatively constant but have been overtaken by inflation: some Inns still charge a deposit of £75–150, but only to the minority of mature and overseas students (Senate, 1977a: XI.16–17). Michael Zander (1968: 44–5) estimated that it cost £550 out-of-pocket to qualify as a barrister in 1968 – less than it cost to become a solicitor (Abel-Smith and Stevens, 1967: 358). By 1980, this figure had almost doubled, but the increase was much slower than the pace of inflation. All aspiring barristers had to pay for admission to an Inn (£82–5), tuition for the vocational course at the Inns of Court School of Law (£550), the part 2 examination fee (£30), the call fee (£75), books (£150), the wig and gown (£135) and dining fees (£25–45 plus travel) – a total of more than £1000. Graduates in subjects other than law also had to pay for a year's tuition in law (£265) and the examination fee for part 1 (£30) (Zander, 1980: 76–7). But, as Zander emphasized, these items were insignificant compared with the cost of maintenance – a minimum of £1500 a year for the three years of undergraduate education, the additional year of legal education for non-law graduates, the year of vocational training, the year of pupillage and the early years of practice. Although means-tested grants are available to all UK undergraduates studying for their first degree, state support for the later years is partial at best.

## Bar examinations

Until the last quarter of the nineteenth century, *any* student who had been admitted to an Inn and kept terms for three years could ask to be called to the Bar. The benchers, who exercised unlimited discretion in this matter, made no inquiry into the legal knowledge of the applicant (S. Warren, 1835: 504). The first examination, introduced by Inner Temple in 1854 in response to the promptings of a parliamentary commission, did not test law but instead examined the general knowledge – Latin or Greek and history – of those students who had not matriculated at university (ibid.: 501; S. Warren, 1845: 938; Lucas, 1962: 479). This innovation seems to have been intended to control the class background of students, since matriculation at university constituted no guarantee of competence in the classics or in history. In any case, Inner Temple abandoned the examination after 35 years, perhaps because barristers were preferring the other Inns (Duman, 1983a: 20–1). Then, in 1888, all four Inns adopted an examination in English language, Latin and English history for non-matriculates (the Law Society had erected a similar hurdle for solicitors 27 years earlier). The examination was held every Saturday during term; 40–50 per cent were 'postponed' each time and could not try again until the next term (Napier and Stephenson, 1888: 22, 70–1). But this was not a significant barrier, especially since most students were matriculates even at this early date (see 'Formal Education', p. 46).

Pressure to institute an examination in law, engendered by unflattering comparisons with physicians, undoubtedly was intensified when solicitors – whom barristers condescendingly treated as the 'junior' branch of the legal profession – introduced such a requirement in 1836. Even in the rough colonies of Australia, a Bar examination was mandatory from the 1850s (Duman, 1983a: 121–2). Nevertheless, the Inns were very reluctant to take this step, and an early proposal was vetoed by the benchers of Lincoln's Inn in 1859 (Manchester, 1980: 58). Although the Council of Legal Education instituted an examination shortly after it was founded by the Inns in 1852, this was merely an *alternative* to attending lectures for a year (Cocks, 1983: 93). The Bar seemed to fear that an examination would render entry to the profession easier rather than harder, thereby admitting the wrong sort of people and endangering the status of the profession (ibid.: 179–80; Duman, 1983: 80–1; Lucas, 1962: 480). (Similar concerns were voiced in the early twentieth century by elite American lawyers, who warned – accurately – that Bar examinations represented no barrier to eager immigrants, especially Eastern European

Jews.) Nevertheless, faced with mounting external criticism and calls for fusion, the Inns agreed to institute a compulsory Bar examination in 1872 (Abel-Smith and Stevens, 1967: 74).

From the outset, it was perceived by contemporary commentators as easy, perhaps even laughable (Duman, 1983a: 81). At the end of the 1870s, three and a half months were regarded as ample preparation for university graduates, even though they had never previously studied English law (which was not taught at university). Questions were published semi-annually, together with sample answers (*Bar Examination Journal*, 1871–92). Crammers had already begun to assist the insecure student, though they were hardly necessary (Cocks, 1983: 181–2). A decade later, two contemporary advisers thought that students could pass the Roman law examination with three months of work, starting from scratch, though they would need six to seven months for the English law examination, and some might require as long as two years (Napier and Stephenson, 1888: 73–4). From 1891, graduates who had passed Roman law at university were exempt from that subject on the Bar examination (though they were a small minority of examinees) (Hazeltine, 1909: 918; Lawson, 1968: 134–5). Sometime between 1892 and 1910 the Council of Legal Education added examinations in criminal law and real property and a separate part 2 of the final examination (the only requirement for law graduates). Contracts and torts was substituted for criminal law in 1931, but the latter was restored in 1947. Since the 1960s, the examinations have been redesigned several times.

Incomplete statistics for the Bar examinations allow us to draw some tentative conclusions about their significance in controlling entry. During the first 20 years, pass rates gradually increased to 90 per cent on the Roman law exam and 80 per cent on the English law examination (see table 1.1); cumulative pass rates for those who resat the examination must have been even higher. Thereafter, two major trends are apparent. The first, and most dramatic, is the long-term secular decline in pass rates during the twentieth century (see table 1.1 and Figure 1.1). This trend is hard to interpret: it may represent either increasing stringency on the part of the examiners or decreasing preparation on the part of the examinees, or some combination. We do know that the proportion of overseas students, which was insignificant before World War I, increased steadily during the twentieth century, particularly after World War II. Before World War I, less than a fifth of the students admitted by Inner Temple were from overseas (see table 1.14d). In the interwar period, 53 per cent of those called in Middle Temple and Lincoln's Inn were from overseas, though only 35 per cent of those called in Gray's Inn (see table 1.14a-c). By 1959, 75 per cent of the students registering at the Council of Legal Education for the first time were from overseas (Denning Committee, 1961: para. 43). The following year 77 per cent of students at the Inns of Court School of Law were from overseas (Abel-Smith and Stevens, 1967: 363). The vast majority of these overseas students were from newly independent or soon-to-be independent African or Asian countries. The proportion of new Bar students from overseas domiciles then declined steadily to a low of 22 per cent in 1976, before rising somewhat during the last ten years (largely attributable to an influx of students from Singapore, Malaysia and Hong Kong) (see table 1.16).

Overseas students have posed a dilemma. On the one hand, the Bar has sought to attract them for reasons that are both economic and political. The Inns earned substantial income from the admission and call fees and the interest on deposits paid by overseas students – money that helped to subsidize the submarket chambers rents paid by English practitioners. The English Bar and bench, and the nation as a whole, greatly strengthened the bonds that tied the colonies and former colonies to the mother country by training colonial barristers. Furthermore, English barristers genuinely believed they were contributing to political stability and justice by inculcating British ideals. But in order to encourage overseas applicants, it was necessary to make call to the Bar a realistic possibility for students who often had difficulty with English as well as inadequate general education. In fact, the persistent seem to have been fairly successful: a very high proportion of those retaking part of their examinations passed (see table 1.2); and three fifths to three-quarters of overseas students admitted to Middle Temple in 1950 and 1960 ultimately were called (see table 1.18). At least until recently, virtually no overseas barristers remained in England to compete with the domestic Bar.

But if the pass rate were raised too high, was there not a danger that the Bar would be flooded with domestic entrants? The answer is no because, as we will see below, the significant constraints on the size of the practising Bar have been the stages following the final examination – pupillage, finding a tenancy and surviving the early years of practice – rather than the examination itself. Indeed, the pass rates for intending practitioners on part 2 of the final (the only examination for the increasing proportion who read law as undergraduates) reached a high of 87 per cent for first-takers in 1980 and 70 per cent for repeaters in 1977 and 1978 – confirming that the examination was not a real obstacle (see table 1.3). Barristers who took the examination in recent years tell the same story. A 1967 sample of a third of all London barristers called between 1963 and 1966 (95 per cent response rate) revealed that 9 per cent had studied less than two months for the part 2 examination, 25 per cent less than three months, 64 per cent less than four months and 85 per cent less than nine months; 80 per cent had passed the first time, another 18 per cent the second, and only 2 per cent had required a third try (Bolton Report, 1967). University law graduates undertook and passed the examination without difficulty five months after completing their degrees, and some even sat it in September, a mere two months after coming down from university (Senate, 1976c: 3). A survey of 276 Bar final students in the late 1970s revealed that most found the examination quite easy (AGCAS, 1981b: 7).

That the difference in preparation of domestic and overseas students explains a good deal of the postwar decline in pass rates is confirmed by the fact that, when the Council of Legal Education began differentiating in 1973 between the performance of intending and non-intending practitioners (a division largely paralleling that between domestic and overseas students), the disparity in pass rates consistently was 10 to 30 per cent (see table 1.3; this is more marked among the first-takers at Trinity Term than among repeaters at Michaelmas). Other evidence is consistent with the view that pass rates reflect differences in preparation. Repeaters were a growing proportion of those passing the examination after 1949, especially during the 1960s (see table 1.4). As the proportion of overseas students declined in the 1970s, the aggregate pass rate of all examinees (first-takers and repeaters) rose on both part 1 and part 2 (see table 1.2). Furthermore, the rising pass rates of both domestic and overseas students between 1973 and 1980 (see table 1.3 and Figure 1.2) are probably related to the fact that an increasing proportion had read law and that entry to law faculties was ever more competitive (see part IV). It is also noteworthy that those sitting the Michaelmas Term examination as a proportion of those sitting the previous Trinity Term examination – a crude index of the proportion resitting – declined by about two-thirds between 1973 and 1984 (see table 1.3).

But if part of the fluctuation in pass rates is attributable to changes in the composition and competence of the applicant pool, another part can be understood only as professional manipulation of supply. Pass rates rose dramatically during and after both wars (see table 1.1 and Figure 1.1). Since these applicants are likely to have been less well prepared rather than more, the most plausible explanation is the examiners' desire to recognize the sacrifice of those who had served in the armed forces and the need to make up for the deaths suffered by the Bar and the low rate of production during the wars. The pass rate on part 2 dropped just as dramatically at the beginning of the depression. I can think of nothing other than deliberate supply control to explain the fact that more than 80 per cent passed during the 1920s but less than 50 per cent during the 1930s. (Additional support for this interpretation can be found in the fact that bar examination pass rates in most American states also fell dramatically after 1929.) Changes in the structure of the examinations also suggest an intent to constrict entry: the reduction in the number of times the examinations were administered each year, from four to three in 1928 and from three to two in 1968; the limitation of resits to four in 1965 (Senate, 1976c: 4–5); and the 1967 requirement that examinees take three papers at a time (the three of Group A and/or the three of Group B) rather than singly. Finally, it is hard to imagine why the pass rate for first-takers on part 2, which climbed fairly steadily from the mid 1960s to 1980 (reflecting the higher quality of university graduates and the higher proportion of law graduates), suddenly reversed itself and fell precipitously to 1984 (see tables 1.1–1.3) – unless the examiners were responding to the enormous expansion of the Bar during the 1970s.

The ultimate measure of the profession's control over the supply of barristers is the relationship between admissions and calls. Not all the attrition can be attributed to the difficulty of the professional examinations. Some students drop out because they cannot afford to continue, others because they choose different careers. Nevertheless, calls as a proportion of earlier admissions is a crude index of supply control. I assumed three years between admission and call (following Layton et al., 1978a). In fact, my calculation of the actual period for the 47 barristers called in Lincoln's Inn in 1939 disclosed a median of four years and a mean of 3.5–4.4, with little variation between graduates and non-graduates, domestic and overseas students. My assumption therefore may render my calculations underestimates (Middle Temple records specifying which students were called indicate somewhat higher proportions; see table 1.13). Calls remained a fairly constant two-thirds to three-quarters of admissions from 1850 to World War I (see table 1.12). There was a dramatic drop during the War but an equally dramatic rise afterwards, with the result that calls in the 11 years 1914–24 were 72 per cent of admissions in the 11 years 1911–21. During the 1920s and 1930s the proportion remained about two-thirds (despite the decline in part 2 pass rates following the crash of 1929). But the decline of production during World War II was not made up afterwards: calls during the 11 years 1940–50 were only 56 per cent of admissions during the 11 years 1937–47. During the 1950s the proportion remained a steady 60 per cent but then dropped precipitously after 1962 to a low of 36 per cent in 1968 – only partly reflecting the admission of large numbers of overseas students. The disparity between the ratios for domestic and overseas students widened during the 1970s (see tables 1.17, 1.18). Although I readily grant the enormous difficulty of interpreting these figures, they seem to confirm my earlier conclusion that the Bar examination posed no real obstacle for domestic students.

## Formal education

Professions justify entry requirements on the ground that they ensure the competence of practitioners, thereby protecting clients. A profession can itself educate those who seek entry, it can examine applicants educated by other institutions, and it can adopt the credentials conferred by other educational institutions. The Bar pursued all three alternatives, though often with what seemed only lukewarm enthusiasm.

### *Secondary education*

The kind, quality and length of secondary schooling has little direct relationship to the technical competence of lawyers. Rather, it tends to confer a body of general knowledge and, perhaps more important, the repertoire of social skills associated with the status to which barristers aspire. Even before the Bar made any attempt to ensure mastery of the law it exercised control over entry to admit only the right sort of men. By encouraging university graduates (as we will see below), it ensured that they had completed a minimum of secondary schooling. Non-graduates had to pass a preliminary examination in the liberal arts. When uniform examinations were adopted by secondary schools, the Inns of Court School of Law required a minimum grade of 50 on two A-level examinations or 40 on three; after 1969, this was raised to a grade of C on two A-levels (Ormrod Committee, 1971: 233). And in 1975, school leavers were denied admission altogether (with rare exceptions for mature students) (Royal Commission, 1979, vol. 1: 619). Thus, as secondary education has become more widespread and uniform, the Bar progressively has raised its requirements in order to maintain its exclusivity.

### *University education*

Long before the Bar required a university degree it encouraged entrants to obtain one. In 1762, it allowed graduates of Oxford or Cambridge to keep only three years of terms instead of five; it extended this privilege to graduates of Trinity College, Dublin, in 1793 and subsequently to those of other universities (Abel-Smith and Stevens, 1967: 25). This gave an advantage to members of the Established Church, for dissenters and

Catholics were not granted degrees until the 1850s (Oxford University Act, 17 and 18 Vict. c.81, s.44; Cambridge University Act, 19 and 20 Vict. c. 88, s. 45; Winstanley, 1947: 37–8; Slinn, 1984: 62). Like secondary schooling, neither of these requirements had anything to do with legal knowledge: dining in hall was a social, not an educational, experience; and universities did not begin teaching English law until the end of the nineteenth century. Even when university legal education was available, aspiring barristers typically preferred to read other subjects, generally classics (Cocks, 1978a: 38; 1983: 185–94; Lawson, 1968: 33).

Whether they were motivated by the reduction in terms or whether a university education simply was part of the upbringing of the class who sought to be called to the Bar (the more likely hypothesis), a very substantial proportion of barristers always have been graduates. Forty-one per cent of a sample of barristers practising in 1785 had attended university, 58 per cent of a sample practising in 1835 and 70 per cent of a sample practising in 1885 (Duman, 1983a: 24). Among those barristers who ascended to the bench between 1727 and 1875, about 70 per cent had attended university (Duman, 1982: 43). Records of admissions and calls confirm this picture. In the first half of the nineteenth century, half or more of the students called in Lincoln's Inn were university graduates (see table 1.13). In the second half of the century, the proportion ranged from half in Middle Temple to three-quarters in Lincoln's Inn and four-fifths in Inner Temple (see tables 1.13, 1.14d). The dominance of university graduates is even more striking when we realize that there were fewer than 10,000 university students in Britain until 1870 and that they constituted only 0.2 per cent of the population (Edwards, 1982: 29, 33).

The representation of graduates continued to rise during the first half of the twentieth century, with the result that more than three-quarters of all those called to the Bar in the 1950s were university graduates (see table 1.14), and many of the non-graduates were former members of the military or civil service or solicitors. Furthermore, the vast majority of graduates had attended one of the elite universities. This was not so surprising in the nineteenth century, before the rise of the provincial universities: among graduates of British universities admitted to Middle Temple in 1877, 47 per cent had attended Cambridge, 36 per cent Oxford and 17 percent London (Shaw's Calendar, 1877–8: 146–78); the proportions at Inner Temple were similar, although Oxford was even more dominant (see table 1.14d). But it is noteworthy that these three universities continued to produce at least three-quarters of all graduate barristers through the 1950s, dwarfing the more than a dozen redbrick universities (see table 1.14).

This pattern has changed significantly in the last 20 years. The proportion of barristers who are university graduates rose steadily (see table 1.5), and in 1975 the Bar made graduation a prerequisite, except for a small number of mature students (only 10 of those doing the academic stage in 1982–3 and in 1983–4 and 15 in 1984–5) (Senate, Annual Statement, 1983–4: 42–3; 1984–5: 39). The proportion of entrants who read law also increased. In 1937, the Bar had exempted law graduates with a first or second class honours degree from the contract and tort, land law and criminal law papers of the part 1 final (Lawson, 1968: 135). This seems to have had little immediate effect, for the numbers sitting the part 1 examination remained comparable with the numbers sitting the part 2 through the 1950s (taking into account the fact that the lower pass rate on part 2 produced more repeaters) (see table 1.1). Nevertheless, the proportion who are law graduates rose to two-thirds of those called in the 1970s and is four-fifths today (see table 1.5a). In 1982–3, the Senate issued 439 certificates to students admitted to an Inn but not exempted from all of the part 1 examination, approximately a third of those admitted; of these, 308 were non-law graduates (another 10 were mature school leavers), and the rest were law graduates or magistrate's clerk's assistants who were not exempted from all the law subjects; the total number admitted with certificates of eligibility rose to 467 in 1983–4 and 476 in 1984–5; of course, not all were called (Senate, Annual Statement, 1983–4: 42–3; 1984–5: 39). Non-law graduates preparing for part 1 as a proportion of all those preparing for part 2 declined from more than half in the mid 1970s to less than a fifth in the mid 1980s (see table 1.5b).

A third change is the declining dominance of Oxbridge and London. In 1962, 91 per cent of the graduates admitted by one of the Inns were from Oxbridge (Zander, 1968: 41 n. 28). In a 1967 sample of London barristers called between 1963 and 1966, 76 per cent of university graduates were from Oxbridge (Bolton Report, 1967). Nevertheless, the proportion from Oxbridge and London among UK graduates called in Middle Temple in 1970 had dropped to 57 per cent (see table 1.14a). And only 38 per cent of those called in Gray's Inn in 1984 had attended Oxbridge or London (see table 1.14b). Indeed, the diversity of undergraduate institutions attended by Gray's Inn students is quite striking: 79 per cent had graduated from 36 different universities (including 5 outside the UK), and the remaining 21 per cent had attended 17 polytechnics and colleges of further education (see table 1.15).

If the Bar now draws from a broader cross-section of undergraduate institutions, it no longer seems to attract their best students. Declining proportions of Oxford and Cambridge law graduates with first class or upper second class degrees have been choosing the Bar since the early 1950s (and increasing proportions have become solicitors) (see table 1.6; Senate, 1985a: 6). Much of this shift seems attributable to the fact that a career as a solicitor offers far greater security and immediate financial rewards than are available to the new barrister. On the other hand, in 1984 the Bar unilaterally excluded anyone with less than a second class honours degree. Since a 1967 sample of London barristers called between 1963 and 1966 found that two-thirds had a lower degree (Bolton Report, 1967), this requirement is likely to have a significant effect, even though barristers with poorer degrees already had been experiencing great difficulties in obtaining pupillages and tenancies (79 *LSG* 105, 1982). In fact, the Dean of the Council of Legal Education, who retains discretion to admit those with lower degrees, receives more than 100 such applications each year and grants a significant proportion (Senate, Annual Statement, 1983–4: 40–1; 1984–5: 38).

Thus the role of undergraduate education in controlling entry to the Bar has changed significantly in the last 100 years. Originally, attendance at Oxford or Cambridge was a concomitant of class background, encouraged by social pressures rather than formal rules. It had nothing to do with technical competence: students did not read law and were not expected to excel academically. In the last few decades, formal requirements have been established to mandate a university degree and a (high) minimum level of performance. Almost all entrants now read law, strongly influenced by the desire to avoid an additional year of study and another examination. Undergraduate education thus has become a vehicle for imparting technical skills. At the same time, the Bar has become both more exclusive and less elite. It is more exclusive because of the difficulty of entering a law faculty (see chapter 17) and acquiring a second class degree. It is less elite because more than 50 institutions confer law degrees, and fewer of the best graduates now go to the Bar.

### *Professional education*

We have seen that the Bar early embraced two means of controlling supply: it adopted the credentials of other institutions (secondary schools, universities and law faculties), and it administered its own examinations. But until very recently it has been quite half-hearted about ensuring competence by taking direct responsibility for training. The Inns of Court ceased educating students in the seventeenth century. Thereafter, they represented little more than a finishing school, a convenient gentleman's club, most of whose members had no intention of practising at the Bar. In 1846, the Inns began teaching law again, appointing three (part-time) readers for this purpose. Six years later the Inns united to establish the Council of Legal Education (CLE), which appointed two more readers and offered instruction to students as an alternative to the newly instituted Bar examination. But when the Bar examination was made compulsory in 1872, students quickly turned to private crammers, the largest and best-known of which was Gibson and Weldon. In 1908, the CLE staff consisted of six readers, four assistant readers and two lecturers, but most students preferred commercial tutors (Hazeltine, 1909: 888). This situation continued virtually unchanged until the 1960s. As late as 1945, CLE had *no* full-time teachers, relying instead on moonlighting university lecturers and practising barristers (Senate, 1976c: 2). Even after CLE opened the Inns of Court School of Law (ICSL) in 1964, Gibson and Weldon continued to dominate professional education. A 1967 sample of London barristers called between 1963 and 1966 concurred that Gibson and Weldon was invaluable in preparing for the Bar examination and CLE virtually useless; 63 per cent of them had studied with the former, 8 per cent privately and only 28 per cent with CLE (Bolton Reports, 1967).

In the last two decades, however, there have been major changes. The Law Society's College of Law absorbed Gibson and Weldon in 1962 (Abel-Smith and Stevens, 1967: 353). But though the expanded institution continued to prepare Bar students for their examinations, the increasing number of prospective solicitors, as well as tensions between the two branches, led the College of Law to exclude Bar students for several years. As the proportion of prospective barristers reading law increased, the number preparing for the part 1 final diminished, and the academic year required of non-law graduates was transferred to the polytechnics in 1978 (Senate, 1976c: 8; Annual Statement, 1975–6: 29; see table 1.5b). (It is noteworthy that the Bar still assumes that the three years of an undergraduate law degree course readily can be compressed into a year of cramming.)

Under pressure from the rapidly rising numbers seeking to become barristers – which doubled at the beginning of the 1970s (see table 1.16) – the ICSL greatly expanded its staff to 19 full-time teachers, assisted by 14 part-time university and polytechnic instructors teaching two hours a week and 130 practising barristers teaching one or two hours a week (Senate, Annual Statement, 1983–4: 43). Even so, the approximately 1000 students enjoyed a far worse student:teacher ratio than the 10:1 at most universities and polytechnics. It is not surprising that 276 Bar Final students questioned in the late 1970s were quite critical of the quality of instruction (AGCAS, 1981b: 6–7). Indeed, because the Bar required all those sitting the part 2 final to complete a year of vocational training (though this could be taken elsewhere), and all intending practitioners had to take a practical course (which was offered *only* at the ICSL), that institution became a major bottleneck in the production of lawyers.

There is considerable evidence that this was not mere accident. The Bar, whose numbers have increased even more rapidly than those of solicitors during the last two decades (compare table 1.16 with tables 2.11–2.12), has been quite open about its desire to reduce entry. We saw above that the Bar (unlike solicitors) moved to all-graduate entry and then to the requirement of a second class honours degree. In the spring of 1983, the Senate held a special meeting 'to consider entry numbers to the Bar' (80 *LSG* 744, 1983). Mr Justice Bingham, Chairman of the CLE, deplored admitting three times the numbers who could be absorbed by the profession, a view that was seconded by Sir Rawden Temple QC, Treasurer of Inner Temple. Charles Morrison, Dean of the ICSL, said the School could not expand and opposed the creation of another institution. Lord Justice Ackner said the Bar final should be made more difficult. Professor Ronald Graveson QC, Treasurer of Gray's Inn, favoured greater selectivity at the earlier stages of the entry process. Richard Scott QC, Chairman of the Bar, said that the Bar could not train every qualified applicant who wished to practise. And Peter Atherton, speaking for the northern circuit, said there was not enough work. The meeting concluded by opposing any further consideration of the idea that the ICSL might open a second school in the provinces and confirming the authority of the CLE to limit enrolment at the ICSL to 1000 and give preference to intending practitioners. As a result, applications to the ICSL have been running about 20 per cent above registrations since at least 1978 (see table 1.19). In 1983, the school made 1239 offers to the 1404 applicants; the following year it made 1202 offers to the 1375 applicants (Senate, Annual Statement, 1983–4: 40–1; 1984–5: 38). Recently, the number of applications has declined, because non-intending practitioners anticipate rejection and go to Holborn Law Tutors and because Malaysia, which accounted for many non-intending practitioners, has initiated its own vocational course. As a result, the school accepted all 1230 applicants in 1985, ending up with 916 students (Senate, Annual Statement, 1985–6: 60–1; see table 1.19).

The requirement of professional education restricts entry not only by limiting the number of places but also by increasing the cost of preparation. Until 1967, an educational fee of 25 guineas entitled the student to attend unlimited lectures at the ICSL (Senate, 1976c: 7); in 1985, tuition for intending practitioners for the vocational year exceeded £1000, to which must be added the cost of maintenance (see table 1.19).

Financial support is very limited after the student has completed a first degree. The Inns have offered a small number of scholarships, but many are earmarked for graduates of particular universities or for men; between 1971 and 1975 they totalled little more than £100,000 a year – certainly less than 5 per cent of the cost to students of the vocational year (Senate, 1978d: 18–23). Furthermore, they tend to go to those least likely to need them: between 1957 and 1962, graduates of Oxbridge received 94 per cent of all scholarships awarded by Middle Temple, and the proportion at Inner Temple was similar (Zander, 1968: 44 n. 34). The principal source of student support is grants from local education authorities. In 1967, only 250 students received such grants – less than half of the number called and a much smaller proportion of those preparing for the part 2 final (Abel-Smith and Stevens, 1968: 100). Ten years later, only 21 per cent of Bar students at the Law Society's College of Law received local authority grants to prepare for part 1 (because they already had been supported for a first degree in a subject other than law), although 68 per cent received some support for the part 2 course (Royal Commission, 1979, vol. 1: 655; Zander, 1980: 78). In the late 1970s, 70 per cent of a sample of 276 Bar Final students received local authority grants, and 9 per cent obtained grants or loans from their Inns; by the early 1980s, the proportions were 85 per cent and 9 per cent (AGCAS, 1981b: 3; 1984b: 3). Since 1980, four-fifths of UK intending practitioners have received some support; but more than half the local authorities provide only partial support; and only two-fifths of intending practitioners from overseas obtain any support (see table 1.19). Thus, the limited number of places at the ICSL and the inadequate level of financial support for the vocational year both present additional hurdles to the aspiring barrister.

## Continuing education

The medical profession in Britain and elsewhere and the legal profession in other countries have developed programmes of continuing education that not only seek to preserve or enhance competence but also may control supply by eliminating practitioners who fail examinations or decline to take compulsory courses. The Law Society recently adopted such a requirement for new entrants. Nevertheless, the Senate has asserted: 'Little or no post-qualification education or training is undertaken on a formal basis. It is not generally appropriate to the circumstances of practice at the Bar' (Senate, 1976c: XI.23).

## Pupillage

It has long been customary for students and young barristers to spend some time under the tutelage of a more senior practitioner – sometimes a barrister but also attorneys, special pleaders and conveyancers (Duman, 1983a: 82). In 1845, most barristers did two years of pupillage (S. Warren, 1845: 74). In 1879, a contemporary commentator urged students to do a year of pupillage with a conveyancer or equity draughtsman, then six months each with a special pleader or common law barrister and with a solicitor and then, after call, another half year with a barrister (Ball quoted in Cocks, 1983: 182–3). Yet Gower and Price (1957: 322 n. 19) estimated that only a fifth of young barristers served any pupillage in the 1950s; and subsequent authors thought the proportion was only a third to two-fifths (Abel-Smith and Stevens, 1967: 359; Hazell, 1978a: 83). In 1959, however, the Bar Council ruled that barristers would be required to complete 12 months of pupillage (Hazell, 1978a: 83).

This requirement affects the production of barristers in several ways. First, it imposes additional costs. In 1845, Samuel Warren advised students that the premium for a pupillage would be 200 guineas (presumably for two years) (1845: 74–5). It seems to have remained at this level for a century; following World War II it was 100 guineas for a year and 50 for six months (Abel-Smith and Stevens, 1967: 358; 1968: 101; Hazell, 1978a: 83; Gower and Price, 1957: 322). With post-war inflation, the premium soon became a trivial element in the cost of pupillage and of qualifying in general; and in 1975 the Bar Council resolved that no pupillage fee should be required, a decision that eventually was accepted by all barristers, if reluctantly (Hazell, 1978a: 92).

But the real cost of pupillage has always been maintenance; and unlike the fixed costs described above, this has increased with inflation, especially for the majority of barristers who do their pupillage in London chambers. In 1978, the minimum needs of a pupil were estimated to be £2000 (Id. 91). The pupil cannot expect any professional income during this period: in 1965 the Bar Council ruled that pupils could not accept briefs during the first six months (ibid.: 83), and even thereafter briefs tend to be rare. Scholarships offered by the Inns are thoroughly inadequate to the needs of pupils: the number granted is small, the value of each (£300) is only a fraction of the total cost, and many are restricted to Oxbridge graduates, who are least likely to require them (ibid.: 92). A survey of 276 Bar final students in the late 1970s found that they had obtained 67 grants and 19 loans (with some duplication); but only 2 of the 38 polytechnic graduates received either, though they were least able to draw on parental support (AGCAS, 1981b: 3). A subsequent survey of 274 pupils in the early 1980s found that they obtained a total of 58 grants and 40 loans (with duplications), but that the 46 polytechnic graduates obtained only four grants and eight loans (again with duplications) (AGCAS, 1984b: App. D). Although the Royal Commission on Legal Services recommended that mandatory grants for the vocational stage be extended to the first six months of pupillage (1979, vol. 1: 658), the Lord Chancellor's Department has opposed this on the ground that it is not the government's policy to give mandatory grants to those who have attended higher education (1983: 29).

Nevertheless, there has been some easing of the financial plight of pupils. Chambers are beginning to offer pupillage awards, typically at the rate of £1000 a year; in 1984, 84 of the more than 200 London chambers (but no provincial chambers) offered a total of £175,000 in awards (Senate, 1985a: 27). A few chambers are guaranteeing a minimum income for the second six months of pupillage (Senate, Chambers pupillage arrangements and awards, 1983–5). And there are signs of an even more radical change: some 20 private employers, under the direction of the Bar Association for Commerce, Finance and Industry, have obtained the Senate's approval to offer pupillages for the second six months and are paying pupils at an annual rate of £4000–6000 (132 *NLJ* 353, 1982; Senate, Annual Statement, 1985–6: 48). The Bar has felt the need to make these changes in order to compete with solicitors for the better qualified graduates; but it would be ironic if employed barristers were the ultimate beneficiaries. Still, this may be a step towards accepting employment within the Bar, at least for young barristers.

Pupillage began to pose an additional obstacle in the early 1970s, when the rapid increase in the number of barristers called was not matched by any comparable increase in the number of juniors of more than five years call willing to accept pupils (Senate, 1976d: 4). As early as 1971, 100 newly called barristers were unable to find pupillages (Coldstream Committee, 1973). The following year, there were 305 pupils but only 177 pupilmasters, an unsatisfactory ratio of 1.7 pupils per master (Chambers Report, 1973). Very few chambers took on pupils for the first time, and the number of pupillages said to be available in response to a Senate questionnaire was little more than a third of the number of barristers called (half the British domiciliaries) (ibid.). Furthermore, from 1974 to 1983 the number of pupils remained relatively constant although the number called (including the number of British domiciliaries) continued to rise (compare table 1.7 with table 1.16). Indeed, the proportion of chambers answering the questionnaire and indicating that they took no pupils actually increased sharply in 1983 and 1984 (see table 1.7).

Despite these figures, several studies in the mid-1970s claimed that pupillages were available to all who wanted them: every intending practitioner called in 1973 had a place within six months (Wilmers Committee, 1974); 38 per cent of the 472 students who wanted pupillages for the autumn of 1976 had found them by December 1975 (Council of Legal Education, 1976); 83 per cent of those who took the part 2 final in Trinity term 1976 had arranged pupillages for the following autumn by mid year (Bar Students' Working Party, 1976). In 1983, the Senate reiterated: 'Until recently all practitioners requiring a pupillage are enabled to obtain one except in the most exceptional cases' (1983: 5). And the Senate's own estimates of pupillages available, based on answers to Accommodation Committee questionnaires, actually have exceeded the number of intending practitioners completing the Bar final each year since 1976 (see table 1.7); a survey of chambers confirmed that there were more pupillages available in both London and the provinces than were taken between 1982 and 1984 (Senate, Annual Statement, 1983–4: 21). Bar students themselves concurred: it was easy to obtain a pupillage in London (where it did not lead to a tenancy), though not in the provinces (where it did) (AGCAS, 1981b: app. D at iii).

It is hard to know whether the scarcity of pupillages (if there ever was one) discouraged any barristers from seeking to enter private practice (or affected earlier career choices). But it may have had other consequences. The process of obtaining a pupillage traditionally has been intensely particularistic, focusing on personal qualities other than technical competence. A 1976 study revealed that the largest proportion of students (37 per cent) obtained places through personal acquaintance or introduction by an intermediary, and another 7 per cent did so through their universities, whereas only 29 per cent succeeded through the Inn pupillage or sponsorship schemes, which were intended to be more universalistic (Bar Students' Working Party, 1976). Only 2 per cent obtained a pupillage by contacting chambers directly, which was thought to be bad form (Hazell, 1978a: 84). Furthermore, the different procedures differed greatly in success rates: all who were personally acquainted with a barrister obtained a pupillage, as did 78 per cent of those introduced by an intermediary and 46 per cent of those who used their university placement office; but only 41 per cent of those who used the Inn schemes and a mere 14 per cent of those who approached chambers directly were successful (Bar Students' Working Party, 1976; see also Senate, 1976d: 30). Because students were desperate to obtain a pupillage they took whatever was available – a choice that could determine their specialities for the rest of their careers (Hazell, 1978b: 23).

Here, again, the Bar has sought to rationalize the allocation process and equalize the chances of all applicants. In 1983 the Senate published the first edition of 'Chambers pupillage arrangements and awards', containing listings by 111 chambers (a third of the total); the next year 161 chambers appeared (half the total). In 1983 it also announced the joint pupillage awards scheme, intended to set a common deadline for applications and decisions and to facilitate multiple applications by circulating letters of reference. Yet the persistence of particularistic selection may be seen in the fact that two years after its inception, only 28 London sets participated in the scheme. It is not just those seeking pupillages who are dissatisfied with the situation. The Griffith Committee enquiry in 1984 found that 17 of the 29 heads contacted were unhappy with the quality of applicants. And a survey of some 180 sets found that 40 percent had encountered difficulty finding pupils of the right calibre between 1980 and 1984 (Senate, 1985a: 9).

Pupillage continues to be criticized on other grounds. The Inns exercise virtually no supervision over the selection of pupilmasters (Hazell, 1978a: 88). The experience tends to be very narrow because the pupil is apprenticed to a single master (ibid.: 87). And masters sometimes exploit pupils, using pleadings and papers drafted by them without making any changes (Hazell, 1978b: 21) and taking on as many as four pupils at a time (Hazell, 1978a: 93). Young barristers still complain that pupilmasters are too busy to offer meaningful guidance (AGCAS, 1984b: 8). Despite all the criticism of articles, the clerk apprenticed to a firm of solicitors generally enjoys greater opportunity for interaction with experienced practitioners. Yet pupillage also may be changing. There is a tendency for the pupillage to be with an entire chambers rather than a single pupilmaster (Senate, 1983: 5). And many pupils are spending a third or even a fourth six months, each with a different chambers, in order to gain more varied experience.

## Tenancies

The barrister who has completed a pupillage and wishes to practise privately must find a tenancy. Barristers can practise only in chambers, which must be staffed by a clerk and, until recently, had to be located within the Inns of Court (if in London). During the early nineteenth century, when most of the Bar practised individually, a newly qualified barrister would simply open his own chambers (Cocks, 1983: 9; Duman, 1983a: 83; Lewis, 1982). Today, however, the novice would encounter numerous obstacles: capital outlay for new chambers is prohibitive; overhead is very high (even with rent relief), especially as computers become prevalent; space within the Inns is unavailable; and the new barrister would be unable to attract briefs from solicitors, who favour established chambers (Royal Commission, 1979, vol. 1: 451, 462). Therefore, the barrister must find a set of chambers willing to provide a seat.

The rapid growth of the Bar, starting about 1970, has led to an acute shortage of physical space, aggravated by the fact that much of the Inns were let to non-barristers (60 per cent in 1975, 52 per cent in 1981). Even after the Senate relaxed the rule that London chambers had to be located within the Inns, only five sets moved outside because the Inns offer sub-market rents and a real or imagined advantage in obtaining business (Senate, Annual Statement, 1981–2: 34–5). As early as 1967, London sets had crammed 14 barristers into six rooms, 12 into five, 15 into seven and 14 into eight (Zander, 1968: 70–1). The situation undoubtedly has worsened. In 1985, 228 pupils, 309 tenants and 73 squatters each shared a *desk* with another barrister (Senate, 1985b). Indeed, 10 per cent of the London Bar shared a desk, and one out of every ten London sets lacked a waiting room (2(1) *Counsel* 39, 1986).

The Bar did little to alleviate this situation. Although the 'accommodation crisis' was discussed in the mid 1960s, little new space for chambers was created. Between 1975 and 1981, only 71,770 additional square feet were found for barristers in the Inns of Court, an increase of 9 per cent during a period in which the Bar grew 28 per cent (Senate, Annual Statement, 1981–2: 34–5; see table 1.16). Between 1979 and 1985, only 25,797 additional square feet were obtained within the Inns, an increase of 6.7 per cent despite the fact that the Bar grew 17.9 per cent from 1979 to 1984 (Senate, 1985b; see table 1.16). As a result, the average of 1.74 tenants per room in London in 1979 had worsened slightly to 1.77 in 1985 (ibid.). Indeed, a 1985 survey of London chambers (with an 83 per cent response rate) found that there was an average of 2.5 people per room (including pupils and floaters) (1 *Counsel* 17–18, 1985). Of the chambers responding, 60 per cent wanted additional space and would take on another 187 pupils and 284 tenants if they had it. But their eagerness to expand was contingent upon more subsidized accommodation within the Inns. They wanted 409 such rooms but only 259 if Inn rents increased 25 per cent; they would have 209 rooms if the rooms were located outside the Inns and 141 if rents for these rooms increased 25 per cent (ibid.). Even in the provinces the situation was not much better. As early as 1963 there were no seats in the larger assize towns of Birmingham and Bristol and the major cities of Wales (Zander,

1968: 70–1). Nevertheless, the Senate imposed on the provinces the very rigidity from which London suffered, requiring all new chambers to secure approval from their circuits (33 *NLJ* 671, 1983).

Consequently, many pupils encountered severe difficulties in finding tenancies. As early as 1969, the number of barristers seeking to enter practice greatly exceeded the number of vacant seats, often by a factor of two to one (compare table 1.7 with table 1.16). Even in May 1965, 47 pupils were unable to find tenancies (see table 1.7). In 1973–4 a questionnaire (60 per cent response rate) revealed that 239 pupils and floaters in Lincoln's Inn were competing for 177 seats in common law chambers, and 43 were competing for 21 seats in Chancery sets, while in the provinces 74 were competing for 13 seats. In the mid 1970s, 50 pupils a year were unable to find tenancies (Senate, 1978d: 9–11). And of the 361 UK domiciliaries called to the Bar in July 1974, only 176 had secured tenancies by 1976 (Senate, 1976d: 8).

The difficulties of finding seats are vividly illustrated by the plight of 'floaters' – qualified barristers who practise out of temporary accommodation. Their numbers – about a sixth of the British domiciliaries called each year – have remained relatively constant since these data first were collected in 1974, although there were significant increases in 1981, 1982 and 1984 (see table 1.7). Between 1974 and 1976, there were an average of 550 pupils each year but an average of only 348 starts in practice (63 per cent) (Senate, 1977a: XI.2); between 1974 and 1977, there were an average of 407.5 pupils but only 342 starts (84 per cent) (Senate, 1978c: D.16). Although most persistent floaters eventually find a seat, some have been stuck in this status for a considerable time. In November 1976, 24 per cent of all floaters had just begun looking for a tenancy, another 63 per cent had been looking for a year, 8 per cent for two years, 4 per cent for three and 1 per cent for four (Senate, 1976a: 9–10). A year later the situation appeared worse (Senate, 1978c: D.19): 3 percent had been looking for less than a year, 58 per cent for one to two years, 27 per cent for two to three years, 8 per cent for three to four years, 2 per cent for four to five years, one barrister for six to seven years, and one poor soul had been called in 1947! And though the Senate offered new barristers accommodation in the Middle Temple library and the use of clerks in existing chambers, only ten barristers took up the offer, the rest recognizing that this arrangement could not lead to a secure practice (Senate, 1978c: D.20).

Recent studies suggest that the situation has deteriorated further. A 1981 survey of 276 graduates of universities and polytechnics between 1976 and 1978 (excluding Oxford) found that of those who started the vocational course with an intent to practise privately (84 per cent of the total), fewer than half obtained tenancies (39 per cent of the total). A 1980 survey of Oxford law graduates in the same cohort found that only 33 per cent had obtained tenancies, though another 27 per cent were still looking (AGCAS, 1981b: 2 and app. E). A follow-up of 104 in the first category found that 60 were in private practice (AGCAS, 1984a: 1–2). A subsequent survey of 366 graduates of the classes of 1979–81 who took the Bar final revealed that 79 per cent intended to enter private practice, and 75 per cent found pupillages, but only 47 per cent obtained tenancies. Furthermore, it was the inclusion of Oxford graduates in the later sample (71 per cent of whom obtained tenancies) that accounted for the higher percentage (AGCAS, 1984b: 1–2).

Clearly, the lack of accommodation has become a major bottleneck, discouraging many undergraduates from ever aspiring to practise at the Bar and persuading others taking the vocational course, in pupillages, or working as floaters to abandon the idea. Furthermore, the shortage of space has made sets very selective about whom they choose for the rare tenancy. Particularistic factors such as class background, schooling and personal contacts play a major role; pupils have a considerable advantage, but even they are unable to penetrate the secrecy surrounding the selection process or ascertain when the decision is made, by whom and according to what criteria (Hazell, 1978a: 97). Nevertheless, although the Royal Commission recommended the creation of a register of available tenancies (1979, vol. 1: 459–60), the Senate rejected the idea on the ground that 'in private practice there is always room for the right person' (1983: 8). That is just the problem. Among a sample of graduates in the years 1979–81, 71 per cent of those from Oxford obtained tenancies, 54 per cent of those from Cambridge, 45 per cent of those from other universities and only 32 per cent of those from polytechnics (AGCAS, 1984b: 3). Twice as many tenants had completed pupillages in the set where they ultimately found their seats as had not (AGCAS, 1984a: 1–2; 1984b: 3). Given the intense competition for places, a graduate with a lower second class degree and no distinguishing qualities was unlikely to find a seat; only those with first class degrees could expect to join a specialist set (AGCAS, 1984a: 5). Nevertheless, a 1985 survey of 180 sets found that 33 per cent claimed to have had difficulty filling tenancies because of the poor quality of applicants (Senate, 1985a: 9).

The Bar finally seems to be doing something about one aspect of the problem – the shortage of physical accommodation. The Senate and the Bar Council have appointed an estate agent to advise and represent sets of barristers seeking accommodation outside the Inns. Gray's Inn is completing an extension of Raymond Court Buildings to house the Council of Legal Education and provide 30,000 square feet for chambers.

And Middle Temple has acquired Devereux Court, with another 9000 square feet capable of housing 60 barristers (1(4) *Counsel* 15–16 1986).

## Surviving the early years of practice

The barrister who has found a seat in chambers must still earn a living. Because the Bar claims to be a collection of wholly autonomous individuals, beginning barristers must subsist very largely on the briefs they receive in their own right. Unlike assistant solicitors, they cannot spend several years in salaried employment while they find their feet. In the eighteenth century, those with family connections could obtain government sinecures (Duman, 1981: 95). During the nineteenth century, social networks played a pivotal role in generating business, especially on circuit (Cocks, 1978a: 41; Duman, 1983a: 89–94). Even the barrister without family ties might pick up briefs on circuit that no other barrister wanted (Duman, 1983a: 84–5). And for the barrister who did not set his sights on attaining the pinnacle of professional success, emigration to the colonies offered yet another, perhaps less competitive, arena, although most colonial barristers of the period had been born and bred in the colonies, to which they returned after qualifying (Duman, 1983a: ch 4).

For those determined to remain in England (which then meant London), the cost of practising was substantial. In 1804, chambers for a single barrister and clerk rented for £32 a year; by 1820 this had risen to £50–70. The barrister had to invest £100–200 in a library and spend £15–20 annually to keep it up. Maintenance required a minimum of £100–200 a year. And travel on circuit (which was mandatory, since the London courts were closed for part of the year) cost another £180–200 a year. All told, the beginning barrister required an income of about £400 a year (Duman, 1982: 55–7). No one could earn these sums in the early years of practice. In 1862, a barrister on the Norfolk circuit who was earning more than £1000 a year after 13 years (and thus had succeeded handsomely) recalled that he had earned only £5 in his first year and £12, £49, £67, £116 and £129 annually during the next five (Cocks, 1978a: 42). Even barristers who ultimately were very successful rarely earned more than £100 in their early years (Duman, 1982: 58). Unless the young barrister had a very substantial independent income, he had to rely on other work: law reporting, until this was taken over by commercial firms at the end of the nineteenth century (ibid.: 41; cf. Dickens, 1850: ch. 27); devilling, i.e. piecework on the brief of a more senior barrister in the set (in 1961 the Bar Council allowed the devil to work for a quarterly salary or a 50:50 split of the fee) (Zander, 1968: 254); marking examination papers; lecturing in the evenings; writing articles for legal periodicals; or editing for law publishers (Gower and Price, 1957: 329–30). The difficulty of making ends meet must help to explain the fact that, in 1885, only 38 per cent of those called actually started in practice even though call had already become somewhat more onerous by reason of the Bar examination (Duman, 1983a: 5).

Matters had not improved much as late as the 1950s. It was estimated that a barrister starting practice in 1952 would lose £10 his first year and earn a net income of £100, £280, £370 and £590 in the succeeding four years (Gower and Price, 1957: 329). A national survey conducted in 1955–6 found that barristers called in 1955 had an average income of £181, and those called during the preceding three years had incomes of £250, £536 and £490 (Doctors and Dentists, 1960: 283). One measure of the financial difficulty of the early years is the fact that, of 172 barristers who started practice in 1950–1, 49 (28 per cent) had abandoned it by October 1956 (Gower and Price, 1957: 329 n. 42). Despite the Bar's pretence of individualism, success depended heavily on the amount of business attracted by the more experienced barristers in the chambers and the willingness of the clerk to entrust the newcomer with briefs that other tenants were unable or unwilling to handle. This, again, suggests that particularistic factors influencing the selection of pupils and tenants and the new barrister's relationship with the head of chambers and the clerk were, and remain, critically important to success.

Legal aid, which was just beginning when the cohort of barristers described above started practice, has significantly changed the financial situation of the novice. Young barristers depend heavily on legal aid: juniors with less than nine years experience at the family, common law and criminal bars in London earned 59–62 per cent of their gross fees from legal aid in the late 1970s; their counterparts on circuit earned 68–72 per cent (Senate, 1977c: addendum 9; see also Royal Commission, 1979, vol. 2: 596). As a result, income levels have risen. Juniors with three years of experience or less earned a median of £2753 in 1974–5 and £5361 by 1981–2 (see table 1.41). A survey in March 1981 found that barristers in practice for less than three years enjoyed a median gross income of £5250, those practising three to four years earned £7100, and those practising four to five years earned £9000 (AGCAS, 1981b: 4). A similar survey two years later found that London practitioners with two to three years experience grossed £7080, and those with four years grossed £9420 (AGCAS, 1984b: 4–5).

At the same time, legal aid provides a very low level of remuneration for most. In 1974–5, the median income of juniors with less than three years of experience practising in the London family, common law or criminal bars was only £1,572, while the lower quartile earned £545 and the lowest decile £229 (see table 1.42). And from 1967 to 1979, between 12 and 20 per cent of barristers earned less than £500 a year (see table 1.43). As recently as 1977, 51 out of 1026 juniors with three years of experience or less reported net losses (Royal Commission, 1979, vol. 2: 590). Furthermore, expenses consume a far higher proportion of the gross income of juniors with three years experience or less (about 50 per cent) than they do for more senior practitioners (about 30 per cent), even though the contribution to chambers overhead increases with seniority (Royal Commission, 1979, vol. 2: 590). Although the Senate has placed £500,000 in a loan scheme for new practitioners, both the number of loans (about 40 a year) and the amounts (£1000–2750) are grossly inadequate to the need (Senate, 1983: 14; Annual Statement, 1984–5: 32).

The difficulty of surviving the early years can be seen in the numbers abandoning practice (see table 1.16). These began to decline in the late 1950s, most significantly among those in practice less than ten years. Furthermore, although the absolute numbers began to rise in the 1960s, this trend was very gradual and seems to have peaked by 1980. The proportion leaving practice continued to decline until the mid-1970s, and even afterwards it barely attained half the level that had characterized the late 1950s (see table 1.8). Nevertheless, it is not insignificant that over a ten-year period about a fifth of those who began practice appear to have abandoned it.

## Solicitors seeking to become barristers

As we have seen, the route to practice at the Bar is extremely onerous. The only alternative was to become a solicitor (surmounting a different, but no less difficult, series of hurdles) and then transfer to the Bar. Whether solicitors should have to repeat all the qualifications has been a point of considerable contention between the two branches for the last 150 years. At the end of the eighteenth and beginning of the nineteenth centuries the Inns required that an attorney or solicitor cease practising and have his name removed from the Roll for two years before being called (Kirk, 1976: 179). In 1844, the benchers insisted that the solicitor also keep terms for three years and thus abstain from practice for a total of five years (ibid.; Christian, 1896: 227 gives the date as 1825). Although the justification for the hiatus was to prevent a solicitor from securing briefs from his former colleagues, the effect of having to forgo all professional income for five years clearly was to prevent transfer. In 1877, solicitors sought to lower the barriers to transfer by offering barristers with five years of experience the right to become solicitors immediately after passing the Law Society's final examination, without any waiting period (Kirk, 1976: 180). In 1881, under threat of legislative action, the Inns allowed solicitors of five years' standing to be called, though only after a waiting period of one year (Abel-Smith and Stevens, 1967: 227). Two years later, even this requirement was dropped, and solicitors could take the Bar final without keeping any terms, though the solicitor still had to give 12 months notice before taking the examination (ibid.: 230, 236). In 1926, the notice period was reduced to six months and solicitors were categorically exempted from the part 1 examination (instead of having to apply individually), though pupillage was still required (ibid.: 236). Finally, in October 1969, solicitors with three years standing were excused from six months of their year's pupillage (Kirk, 1976: 180; Senate, 1977a: IV.10).

The controversy appears to have concerned status competition between the two branches more than supply control by the Bar. Each branch wanted to ensure that it gained reciprocal privileges for every concession. The number of solicitors seeking to transfer was always insignificant (see table 1.9). Even fewer completed the process. Between 1919 and 1923, 50 solicitors became barristers, and this figure may have been inflated by the end of the war (Abel-Smith and Stevens, 1967: 236). In the early 1970s, the number of transfers was less than 1 per cent of calls (Senate, Annual Statements). In the years 1981–2 to 1985–6, the number of solicitors who even applied to transfer varied between 14 and 32, an average of 26 a year or less than 3 per cent of calls (Senate, 1986: 10 n. 19).

## The changing configuration of supply control

The process of becoming a practising barrister vividly illustrates the alternatives and tensions within the project of supply control. The central question has been whether barristers should be men of good breeding or people of the highest technical competence. Until the end of the nineteenth century, the answer was clear. The Inns enjoyed total discretion to admit and call whomever they wished. They asked for character references and lineage instead of testing legal knowledge. They made concessions to university graduates at a time when only upper-class men who belonged to the Established Church attended university, and none of them read English law. They insisted that students keep terms for the social graces and contacts they acquired, not because the dinners had any educational content. And the very substantial cost of the lengthy process of qualifying and developing a practice ensured that only the sons of the wealthy would complete the course. The focus on who the entrant was rather than on what he knew may reflect the security of the Bar's monopoly over its rights of audience and the fact that advocacy skills were more akin to art than to science.

The barriers to entry have changed greatly since the mid-nineteenth century. Quasi-public institutions like the Inns no longer can make decisions based explicitly on personal qualities. The cost of the early stages of qualification has declined, both because fixed charges have failed to keep pace with inflation or been abolished and because the state supports secondary schooling, universities and polytechnics and even defrays some of the cost of vocational training. The Bar was shamed into adopting an examination, although it consistently has been easier than the Law Society examinations. The expansion of undergraduate education has made a degree less of a barrier, although academic institutions still play an important role in ranking students through the admissions and grading processes. Technical competence has become far more central, since most entrants read law as undergraduates (and the rest must do an academic year), and all complete a year of vocational training. Yet the Bar retains the hurdles of pupillage, tenancy and the early years of practice – the second of which became significant only in recent decades. Although these barriers do not affect overseas students returning home (whose numbers are diminishing in any case), they do continue to control *who* enters private practice. First, they are low visibility decisions made by private individuals – pupilmasters, heads of chambers and clerks – who make no secret that they are greatly influenced by personality and background as well as the candidate's technical competence. Second, barristers must defray some of the cost of the academic and vocational years and all of the year of pupillage and survive the early years of practice – financial demands that strongly favour those whose families can continue to support them well into their twenties.

# 3

# Numbers

## 1800–1950

Statistics on the size and growth of the Bar are very unreliable until the Bar Council, and later the Senate, began keeping records in the 1950s (see table 1.16). Earlier data are not only incomplete and unreliable but also very difficult to interpret. Admissions to the Inns and calls to the Bar do not differentiate between domestic and overseas students, although we know that the latter increased both absolutely and proportionally through the 1970s and that until very recently few remained in England to practise. The number of barristers called cannot tell us the number who started to practise, since the fraction varies considerably over time. We know that during the early nineteenth century, many men found it worth while to claim the status of barrister although they never intended to practise (Duman, 1980: 619 n. 21). And even starts in practice do not tell us the strength of the practising Bar, since many barristers leave practice before retirement age. A 10 per cent sample of all men living in 1885 who had ever been called to the Bar (80 per cent traceable) found that only 38 per cent were still practising (Duman, 1983b: 142).

The cumulative effect of these uncertainties undoubtedly explains the wildly varying estimates of 'the Bar' offered by different sources. Thus, at the turn of the century several authors give the number of barristers as 1000–1500, but the Law List for 1900 contained the names of 9457 barristers (Odgers, 1901: 30). The latter figure presumably included all those ever called, regardless of whether they started to practise or remained in practice. And the census of 1951 lists 3235 barristers, although the Bar Council stated that only 1907 were in practice in 1953 (compare table 1.16 with table 4.1); the former figure may include those called to the Bar but employed in the public or private sectors.

With these cautions, what can we learn from the historical statistics? Admissions to the Inns seem to have increased significantly during the first half of the nineteenth century (see table 1.10). They nearly doubled in the decade following 1853 and then remained at that level for the rest of the century (see table 1.12; see also Council of Legal Education, 1982–3: 4). Duman (1983a: 2–4, 25) suggests significant fluctuations in admission rates, rising steadily from about 130 a year in 1800 to 330 in 1835, then dropping back almost as far by 1850, rising to about 260 in 1870 and finally exhibiting a slight decline until 1885. He attributes these variations to external factors: the economic expansion associated with the Napoleonic wars, the crash of 1835 and depression of the 1840s, the prosperity of the 1850s and the great depression of the 1870s.

Nineteenth-century admission figures tell us least of all about the Bar, because many men viewed the Inns as a club, providing convenient and inexpensive accommodation and a good social life. Even though call had no significant prerequisites until the last quarter of the century, the number called does tell us a little more about the attractions of the Bar. Calls, too, seem to rise during the first half of the century, from fewer than 100 in the 1820s to about 150 in the 1840s, before dropping in the 1850s. They rose quite steadily from 113 in 1857 to 280 in 1873, an increase of almost 150 per cent (see table 1.12 and figure 1.3). Part of this was a function of the increase in admissions, and part reflected the fact that a higher proportion of students admitted were being called. Duman estimated that this proportion increased from 21 per cent in 1784 to 68 per cent in 1864, although it declined slightly thereafter (1983a: 28; see also 1981: 89). Clearly, it was and remained easy to qualify as a barrister. Given this trend, it is striking that the number called dropped sharply from 1873 to 1878 and that it remained within 72 of the average of 259 between 1873 and 1904 – indeed, within 32 of that average (a fluctuation of only 12 per cent) in all but five of the 32 years (see figure 1.3). It seems plausible to attribute this, at least in part, to the introduction of the Bar examination in 1872, which, if it remained easy, at least discouraged those students not intending to practise from seeking call.

But it is almost as difficult to extrapolate the practising strength of the Bar from calls as from admissions. Duman (1981: 88–9) estimated that, of the 4800 students admitted to the Inns between 1745 and 1780, about 1200 were called and between 120 and 300 practised. Thus, though the Law List of 1785 contained 385 barristers, the number of practitioners actually ranged from 121 to 295. If we make the (dubious) assumption that the ratio of practitioners to calls remained constant, then the Law List reveals a growth from just over 200 in 1779 to about 2000 in 1840 (see table 4.1). This is consistent with bitter complaints about overcrowding among barristers in the 1850s (Duman, 1980: 621). Thereafter, the Bar appears to have done no more than double during the rest of the nineteenth century, most growth occurring by 1870 (see table 4.1); this is about the same rate of growth as that of the age cohort from which beginning barristers were drawn (see table 4.2). Cocks (1983: 123) argued that the practising Bar experienced a net increase of 80 in 1866: 200 calls, 100 starts and 20 deaths or retirements. This is consistent with the notion that the Bar examination did retard growth. Furthermore, the ratio of starts to calls seems to have fallen significantly during the century, 1:2.5–5 in 1835 to 1:4–9 in 1885 (Duman, 1983b: 148). Duman, who has made the most careful studies, estimates that the Bar grew 250 per cent between 1800 and 1850 but only 50 per cent in the second half of the century (1983a: 8). The number of living barristers ever called increased almost threefold between 1835 and 1885 (Duman, 1980: 619–20). Circuit lists, which may be a more accurate index of practising strength, grew from a total of 132 in 1785 to 319 in 1820, 449 in 1830 and 626 in 1860 (Duman, 1980: 620; but the number of barristers belonging to a circuit more than tripled between 1860 and 1900). Other historians present pictures that are similar in outline if different in detail (Birks, 1960: 214; Reader, 1966: 208).

The Bar experienced enormous ups and downs during the first half of the twentieth century. Admissions rose dramatically until 1910 (twice the level of 1900) and calls even more dramatically until 1913 (2.4 times the level of 1900) (see table 1.12 and figure 1.3). The reasons are unclear, although it may be significant that half the barristers called in Gray's Inn in 1913 were from overseas (see table 1.14b), and overseas students increased from 35 per cent of admissions to Middle Temple in 1900 to 62 per cent in 1910 and from 39 per cent of 1900 admissions ever called to 64 per cent in 1910 (see table 1.13). The hypothesis that overseas students account for much of the increase in admissions and calls is consistent with the fact that the size of the practising Bar remained constant during this decade (see table 4.1).

World War I caused substantial losses to the Bar, through both deaths and injuries among practising barristers and the production of few new barristers. The number called fell from a high of 503 in 1913 to a low of 136 in 1917, a decrease of 73 per cent. Although postwar production made up some of the losses, 805 fewer barristers were called in the ten years 1914–23 than in the 11 years 1904–13, a shortfall of 23 per cent (see table 1.12). This undoubtedly explains the decrease of 28 per cent between the 1911 and 1921 censuses in the figures for the number of barristers (see table 4.1). After the postwar recovery, there was a sharp decline in calls following 1924, when the pass rates on part 1 of the Bar examination also fell (compare figure 1.1 with figure 1.3). Following a slight increase in the late 1920s, both admissions and calls fell during the depression, a period when the number of solicitors continued to rise (compare figure 1.3 with figure 2.6).

World War II also inflicted great losses on the Bar. Half the barristers with professional addresses before the war served full time in the war services (General Council of the Bar, Annual Statement, 1945: 6). The number of calls fell from 319 in 1939 to 92 in 1944, a drop of 71 per cent to a level lower than it had been in 100 years. Although some of this loss was made up after the war, 663 fewer barristers were called in the 1940s than in the 1930s, a difference of 21 per cent (see table 1.12). This undoubtedly explains why the census of 1951 showed almost exactly the same number of barristers as those of 1931 and 1921 (see table 4.1). It also must be relevant that the number of men in the age cohorts of beginning barristers (20–24 and 25–34 years old) remained relatively constant between 1911 and 1951 (see table 4.3). Furthermore, during the 1920s and 1930s, overseas barristers represented half or more of the calls at Middle Temple and Lincoln's Inn and a similar proportion of the admissions at Inner Temple; though overseas barristers were a lower proportion of calls at Gray's Inn, it was smaller than either Middle or Inner Temple (see tables 1.12–1.14).

Thus the Bar seems to have grown rapidly during the first half of the nineteenth century but more slowly during the second half and to have remained static or actually to have declined during the first half of the twentieth century. If census counts are to be believed, the number of barristers in 1951 was identical to the number in 1861 (see table 4.1).

## 1950–1985

We have a much better picture of the growth of the practising Bar since 1950, because the Senate has compiled statistics distinguishing overseas and domestic admissions and calls and tabulated the numbers starting and leaving practice and in practice (see table 1.16). There are two distinct periods within the postwar era. First, following the postwar recovery of the Bar (which ended in the early 1950s), it entered a period of stasis and even decline, lasting until almost 1970. This is particularly striking because it coincided with the postwar economic boom, which should have stimulated demand for barristers' services (see 'supply and demand', p. 70). The number of UK admissions was the same in 1970 as it had been in 1963 (although it fluctuated in between). The number of UK calls fell 45 per cent from 1952 to 1960 and did not exceed the 1952 level until 1969. Calls as a proportion of admissions three years earlier declined in the 1960s (see table 1.12). Some of this may have been caused by the drop in the Bar examination pass rates after the war (see figure 1.1), although part of the drop is attributable to the growing proportion of overseas students. Most dramatically, the number of barristers entering practice fell 57 per cent from 1947 to 1960. During this period, fewer than half of the UK barristers called started practice (see table 1.17). As a result, the practising strength of the Bar actually declined every year from 1954 to 1961 and grew only slowly through 1969. It seems reasonably clear that the barriers of a university education, the cost of professional training and the Bar examination, the importance of personal connections in obtaining a pupillage and tenancy and the inability of beginners to earn a living drastically limited the size of the Bar in the quarter century following the end of World War II.

The years since 1970 exhibit a dramatic change. The number of UK admissions doubled between 1970 and 1976; the mean number of UK students admitted rose from 671 in 1963–71 to 797 in 1972–84. The number of UK calls more than doubled between 1968 and 1971 and increased almost fourfold between 1963 and 1983. UK calls as a proportion of admissions rose dramatically from the late 1960s to the early 1970s and thereafter have remained high – virtually 100 per cent (see table 1.17). Some of this must be explained by the increase in the pass rate on Part 2 of the Bar final (see figure 1.2) and the decline in the number taking part 1, both of which probably are related to the higher proportion of Bar students who have read law as undergraduates. The number starting practice increased fourfold between 1964 and 1973. An average of 104 started practice annually in the period 1955–64, 150 in 1965–9, 246 in 1970–4 and 317 in 1975–84. Nevertheless, starts as a proportion of UK calls actually declined during the 1970s and 1980s (see table 1.17) – in 1982–3 it had fallen to the level of 1966 (Senate, Annual Statement, 1982–3: 49) – although an increasing proportion of those called may have become employed barristers.

All of this suggests that the expansion of undergraduate law teaching and the provision of government grants reduced and even eliminated any obstacle posed by the Bar examination (although entry to law faculties became a new bottleneck). At the same time, however, the cost of pupillage, the scarcity of tenancies, the importance of personal contacts in obtaining both and the difficulty of making a living during the early years of practice remained significant hurdles and may even have grown in magnitude. Nevertheless, the practising Bar expanded at an annualized rate of 8.2 per cent between 1969 and 1978 and at an annualized rate of 3.7 per cent beween 1978 and 1984; there were 2.7 times as many practising barristers in 1984 as in 1961. It is interesting, none the less, that growth has declined in the 1980s as the pass rate on part 2 of the Bar final has dropped and the scarcity of tenancies has become more acute.

## Supply and demand

I argued above that fluctuations in the number of practising barristers are at least partly a function of restraints on entry imposed by the Bar. Both the restraints and the fluctuations typically are justified in other terms–ensuring the character or technical competence of entrants or responding to market demand (cf. Royal Commission, 1979, vol. 1: 336, 517). There is virtually no evidence concerning the relationship between entry barriers and character or competence, and it seems extremely far fetched that dining in hall, for instance, advances either goal. Although it would be even more difficult to test the proposition that the size of the practising Bar reflects the demand for barristers' services, such a relationship seems inherently implausible. Entrants cannot possibly know, when they are seeking to qualify, what the demand for their services will be for the next 40 years, yet having made a major investment in attaining the status of barrister, most remain in practice for at least that long.

I have developed some crude indices of barristers' work, which suggest there is considerable independence between supply and demand. During the interwar period, the number of calls was declining, the number of UK calls may have been declining even more rapidly than the aggregate, and the practising strength of the Bar was constant at best. Yet the number of High Court original proceedings, trials in assizes and quarter sessions and divorce proceedings actually were increasing, if slowly (see tables 5.1–5.3). We saw that about 20 per cent fewer barristers were called during the 1940s than during the 1930s and that growth was stagnant or actually negative until the 1970s. Yet this period displayed dramatic increases in barristers' work. High Court original proceedings nearly doubled between 1958 and 1968 (see table 5.1). Full trials of indictable offences more than doubled between 1950 and 1970 (see table 5.2). And the number of divorce proceedings increased nearly threefold between 1959 and 1970 (see table 5.3). An index of all cases (1953 = 100) rose from 98 in 1958 to 207 in 1973 (Williams Report, 1985: 4–6).

But if supply remained resistant to rising demand during the half century between 1920 and 1970, the rapid increase in supply since then seems to have outstripped demand. High Court original proceedings remained nearly constant between 1973 and 1983; full committals for crimes increased only 64 per cent between 1970 and 1983, and summary trials rose only 75 per cent; and though divorce proceedings increased 153 per cent between 1970 and 1983, these no longer are the exclusive province of the Bar (see tables 5.1–5.3). The index of all cases increased from 207 in 1973 to 305 in 1983, or only 47 per cent (Williams Report, 1985: 4–6). The single demand variable that has paralleled or exceeded the growth in supply is legal aid (which, I suggested above, has helped beginning barristers survive the early years of practice). The civil legal aid budget increased 14 times between 1966 and 1983, while the criminal legal aid budget rose from £550,000 to £62,318,000 (see table 5.10), though a significant part of this demand has been satisfied by the much larger solicitors' branch.

Even after we acknowledge all the uncertainties about the indices of both supply and demand, it seems clear that the variation in the latter does not explain the variation in the former. Demand was expanding between 1910 and 1970 – slowly until 1950 and rapidly thereafter. But supply contracted during both world wars and the intervening depression and continued to contract from the end of World War II until 1970. A more plausible interpretation of the relationship between these two variables is that the Bar successfully prevented supply from rising in response to demand until the 1970s, when the combined effect of the long-term imbalance between the two variables and the expansion of state-supported tertiary education led to an explosion of supply.

It seems equally clear that the Bar has become increasingly concerned over its diminished ability to control supply, fearing that the growing numbers of young barristers will intensify competition, depress prices and impair the profession's prestige. In response to an enquiry by a Senate committee, the Family Bar Association saw no prospect of further growth; the revenue Bar was losing work because of judicial attacks on tax avoidance schemes and competition from solicitors; the chancery Bar was encountering competition from 'hyperbodies' providing comprehensive services; the criminal Bar expected to suffer as a result of the new Crown Prosecution Service, which planned to hire 425 lawyers, and there was fear that, even if solicitors were unable to obtain greater rights of audience, the loss of the conveyancing monopoly would stimulate their interest in advocacy in industrial tribunals and county courts (Whitfield and Walker Report, 1985). I will return below to the efforts of the Bar to create demand for their services. Here I simply want to reiterate that the Bar has not been content to allow demand to influence supply. Its concern to control supply is visible not only in the continuing shortage of seats in chambers but also in recent suggestions that the Bar examination be made more difficult and that character tests be adopted (80 *LSG* 744, 1983; 33 *NLJ* 671, 1983).

# 4

# The composition of the Bar

## Age

Although the Bar never consciously sought to shape the age profile of barristers, and most barristers would have no views on the subject if asked, fluctuations in the entry rate inevitably affect the age distribution. There are few historical data against which to compare the contemporary situation, although I calculated that 22 percent of all barristers in 1835 were within 5 years of call, 19 percent were 6–10 years, and 12 percent were 11–14 years (based on Whishaw, 1835: 162–233). In October 1954, the profile looked roughly similar, with 49 percent within 8 years of call and another 5 percent within 9–14 years (General Council of the Bar, Annual Statement, 1954: 34). But the impact of World War II (in which some younger barristers died and very few new barristers were called) and especially the small number of calls in the late 1950s made the Bar top-heavy. In 1966, only 34 percent were within 10 years of call (General Council of the Bar, Annual Statement, 1968: 61; Senate, 1977a: I.4; Royal Commission, 1979, vol. 1: 585). The next 15 years reversed this situation, as the small cohort of barristers called during the 1950s became the senior members of the profession and were overwhelmed by the numbers entering in the 1970s. By 1976, 57 per cent were within 10 years of call; two years later the proportion was 59 per cent (Royal Commission, 1979, vol. 1: 585; Senate, Annual Statement, 1978–79: 19). As expansion has slowed, the Bar has begun to age again. In the Spring of 1984, 21 per cent of juniors were within 5 years of call, 32 per cent were 6–10 years, 26 per cent were 11–15, and 21 per cent were more than 15 years (10.5 per cent of the Bar were silks and thus at the upper end of this spectrum) (Senate, Annual Statement, 1983–84: 19). Most barristers are young when called: in 1900, 25 per cent of the barristers called at Middle Temple were under 21, and another 37 per cent were under 26 (Sturges, 1949); in 1970, 90 per cent of those called were between 21 and 27 years old (see table 1.20). Consequently, the age profile follows that of experience. In 1976, 38 per cent of all barristers were under 30, and 71 per cent were under 40 (Royal Commission, 1979, vol. 2: 56 and table 1.15 in that report).

These realignments in the age distribution can be extremely significant for the internal politics of the Bar. As we will see below, there are many tensions between younger and older barristers, which intensify during periods of rapid change, such as the last two decades. These tensions are aggravated when the gerontocratic structure of Bar governance allows the small number of older barristers to resist the challenge to tradition posed by the large number of younger barristers. Both the intense conservatism, which characterized the Bar through the 1970s, and the present rumblings of reform may be attributed, at least in part, to shifts in the influence of different age cohorts.

## Class

In analysing the process by which barristers are recruited, I stressed the way in which family wealth and connections and elite education all tended to produce a strong class bias within the Bar, admitting only those who could afford to qualify and allocating pupillages, tenancies and business on the basis of personal contacts. The Bar frequently has been quite open about its desire to preserve its upper class character (Lucas, 1962: 467, 470–73). Even today the Inns require students to state their father's occupation (but not their mother's!) when seeking admission and call. During the eighteenth century, the proportion of barristers drawn from the gentry gradually fell from 40 per cent between 1715 and 1744 to 28 per cent between 1745 and 1756 and 22 per cent between 1765 and 1774 (Duman, 1981: 91–92). This decline continued into the nineteenth century partly because, even with connections, success at the Bar was more problematic than it was in the Church, the army or navy or the civil service (Duman, 1981: 94; 1983a: 16–22; 1973). Thus, 45 per cent of judges between 1727 and 1760 were from landowning families compared to only 8 per cent between 1850 and 1875 (Duman, 1982: 51 and table 4).

The place of the gentry was taken by the professional and merchant classes. Between 1850 and 1875, 54 per cent of the judges were from professional families and 29 per cent from those of merchants or proprietors (ibid.). In a 10 per cent sample of all men living in 1885 who ever had been called to the Bar, about three-quarters came from the urban middle and upper-middle classes (Duman, 1983b: 144). But privilege did not significantly diminish. Throughout the nineteenth century, about a third of all barristers were educated at public schools (Duman, 1983a: 23; 1983b: 151). In the late nineteenth century, 60 per cent of the practising Bar was educated at Oxford or Cambridge (Duman 1983a: 108–9). I found that more than 90 per cent of UK graduates admitted to Inner Temple in the late nineteenth and early twentieth centuries were from Oxbridge (see table 1.14d). Furthermore, most of them described their fathers as gentlemen or professionals, although the former category shrank and the latter expanded after the turn of the century (see table 1.21d).

During the interwar period the category of gentleman declined (perhaps as much because it ceased to be a culturally acceptable description as because barristers' families enjoyed less unearned income) while that of professional continued to expand. There were more entrepreneurs, and company officials began to appear as businesses grew in size. But there still were virtually no workers' sons (see table 1.21). In the 1950s, approximately equal numbers of barristers were the children of business executives, entrepreneurs and white-collar employees, and these categories together equalled the children of professionals (ibid.). I indicated earlier that the dominance of Oxbridge and London continued after World War II (see table 1.14). There was little change in the 1970s (see table 1.21b).

Other studies confirm the class homogeneity of the Bar. Among those who took the final examination in Trinity Term 1976, 55 per cent were graduates of private secondary schools, 32 per cent had graduated from Oxford or Cambridge, 55 per cent received family support while preparing for the examination, and 24 per cent had family connections with the law (Senate, 1976d: 31). Among the fathers of students called to the Bar at Middle Temple in 1977, 76 per cent were professionals or managers, compared with only 21 per cent of the fathers of all those between 16 and 19 in 1975 (Royal Commission, 1979, vol. 2: 59). Since most of these figures pertain to calls, and class affects pupillage, tenancy and ultimate success in practice more strongly, if anything, it is not surprising that 77 per cent of a sample of 105 QCs practising in 1973 were Oxbridge graduates (Cain, 1976: 237 cf. Paterson, 1974; Griffith, 1977).

Yet this apparently monolithic image must be qualified in two important ways. First, it is *class* position that is being reproduced more than membership in the profession. In the nineteenth century, clergymen greatly outnumbered barristers or solicitors among the fathers of entrants; in the twentieth century, engineers and physicians often outnumbered lawyers (see table 1.21). Among university graduates in 1976 and 1977, only 5 per cent of law entrants and 8.4 per cent of those taking the Bar examination had lawyer fathers (Royal Commission, 1979, vol. 2: 60–1). Second, a small number of workers' children do manage to be called to the Bar, thereby vindicating the myth of social mobility. Among those called at Middle Temple in 1977, 14 per cent had working class fathers; among those called at Gray's Inn in 1984, 12 per cent had working class fathers; yet these token figures must be viewed in the light of the fact that 66 per cent of those aged 16–19 had working class fathers in 1975 (ibid.: 59; see table 1.21a). Thus, though the middle classes have gained entry to the Bar, it hardly represents a cross-section of the population.

## Race

Unlike the solicitors' branch, which excluded non-citizens until 1974, the Inns always welcomed overseas students, although until recently they expected those called to return to practise in their home countries. As we have seen, the number of overseas Bar students was small throughout the nineteenth century: less than 2 per cent in 1835, only 12 per cent in 1885 (Duman, 1983a: 10). They were 5 per cent of students admitted to Inner Temple in 1867 and about 20 per cent in 1886 and 1907 (see table 1.14d), though they were 30–40 per cent of both admissions and calls at Middle Temple in the latter half of the nineteenth century (see table 1.13). Until the end of the century, most came from Ireland; thereafter, increasing proportions travelled from India, Mauritius, the West Indies, Africa and Australia.

Their numbers increased steadily during the twentieth century – most dramatically after World War II, as the prospect of independence promised attractive careers in the former colonies for those qualified as barristers (see table 1.14). Because this growth coincided with a decline in the number of British domiciliaries called, the relative proportions of the two categories changed even more. Whereas overseas students had been only a third of calls from 1947 to 1951, they rapidly grew to three-quarters by 1963 (see table 1.16). In 1949, 40 per cent of students registering at the Council of Legal Education for the first time were from overseas; ten years later the proportion was 75 per cent (Denning Committee, 1961: para. 43). In 1960, the Inns had 3600 students, of whom more than three-quarters were overseas: 1100 from Nigeria, 300 from Malaysia, 300 from Pakistan, 150 from the West Indies, 100 from Ceylon, 100 from Cyprus, 100 from India and 50 each from Tanganyika, British Guyana and Uganda (Abel-Smith and Stevens, 1967: 363).

By the mid 1960s, however, the numbers declined rapidly (both absolutely and proportionally) as the newly independent nations (especially those in Africa) opened their own law faculties, and the number of UK students began to rise. By 1971, overseas students were only a third of those admitted to the Inns, and the proportion fell to less than a quarter in 1977, where it has remained ever since (see table 1.16). The majority of these students come from countries that lack legal training institutions at home: 290 of the 484 overseas students admitted to the Inns in 1982 were from Malaysia and Singapore, as were 231 of the 380 admitted in 1983; in the latter year, no other country accounted for more than 16 students (Senate, Annual Statements, 1982–3; 1983–4: 42).

One reason for the drop is that the Bar did little to accommodate the massive influx of overseas students, who came from radically different cultures and educational backgrounds and would return to practise in very different societies, polities and legal systems (beyond allowing them to take an optional paper on African, Hindu or Moslem law as part of their final examination). Not surprisingly, overseas students performed much less well on the Bar examination than domestic students: their pass rate (for first-takers) on part 2 of the Bar final was about 20 per cent lower between 1973 and 1982 (see table 1.3), and the ratio of calls to admissions consistently was 10–20 per cent lower between 1966 and 1979 (see table 1.17; see also Layton et al., 1978a: 73–4 and nn. 10–11). Overseas students repeated the examination far more often than domestic students. A crude measure is the ratio of those sitting the part 2 final at Michaelmas term (typically a resit) to those sitting it the previous Trinity term; this index consistently is two to three times higher among overseas students than among domestic students (see table 1.3). Several commentators have suggested that the Inns were insensitive at best and possibly even mercenary in their treatment of overseas students. During the 1960s, when the numbers were greatest, the Inns earned £1 million in admission and call fees and interest on deposits (N. Warren, 1978: 49); in the late 1960s, £450,000 was on deposit, earning interest for the Inns, not the students (Zander, 1968: 41 n. 29). Given that those never called forfeited their deposits, the Inns' 1964 decision to limit resits to three seems somewhat self-serving. And most of those who were called never used the facilities of the Inns again.

Throughout this period it was assumed that overseas students would return home to practise. Although no law prevented non-citizens from setting up practice in the UK, Zander (1968: 31) stated that it was virtually impossible for a black student to obtain a pupillage. Even if the barrister overcame this barrier and also secured a tenancy, he was very unlikely to receive briefs from a solicitor (all of whom were white) on behalf of a client, who almost certainly also would be white. In the last ten years, however, a small but significant racial minority has emerged in the Bar as the black population of Britain has grown, and legal aid has helped them secure representation. The Royal Commission (1979, vol. 1: 501) estimated that there were about 200 black barristers in 1978, less than 5 per cent of the Bar but perhaps somewhat more in London. In 1983, the Senate identified 210 black barristers, 4.3 per cent of the practising Bar (Annual Statement, 1983–4: 32–6).

Although the Senate (1983: 13) has acknowledged the existence of racial discrimination, it rejected affirmative action as a solution. It did amend the Code of Conduct in 1984 to prohibit discrimination against pupils, tenants or applicants on the grounds of race or sex (para. 76; *Legal Action* 5, August 1985). And in autumn 1986 it issued guidelines on applications for pupillages and tenancies and on distribution of work in chambers, prohibiting racial discrimination; but it may be equally noteworthy that barristers' clerks objected to these limitations on their discretion and the Senate chose not to make them practice rules in order that they might remain hortatory but unenforceable (82 *LSG* 2482–3 and 2493, 1986). Although the 1985 Senate AGM voted overwhelmingly to support the activities of the Minority Access to the Legal Profession Project, the 'know-nothing' attitudes that survive within the Bar were indicated by those who spoke without embarrassment in opposition to the resolution:

> Charles Beattie QC said he had never heard of the project. ...He was troubled by the frequent references to race. He had never himself noticed anything different about coloured people and had never come across racial discrimination.
>
> Mrs Purie Harwell thought resolutions 2 and 3 were absurd. The Bar was not the social services department of a local council with a responsibility to give help to minority groups. This was a free country. For people to think others should support them was nonsense. The sooner the Race Relations Committee was abolished the better.
>
> (Senate, Annual Statement, 1985–6: 25)

There is evidence that greater efforts will be needed. Black students still have considerably more difficulty obtaining pupillages: a 1976 sample of Bar students found that only 26 per cent of the blacks had secured pupillages at a time when 51 per cent of the whites had done so (Senate, 1976d: 28). Black pupils have even greater problems obtaining tenancies, especially outside predominantly black chambers. The Race Relations Committee of the Senate noted that none of four black pupils got tenancies in white chambers, although two had lower second class law degrees from Cambridge, one an upper second from another university and one a lower second from a polytechnic; one of them was rejected in favour of a white pupil who had *no* degree and only a third class pass on the Bar final (Senate, Annual Statement, 1983–4: 32–6; see also Senate, 1985c). And there is evidence that barristers' clerks (all of whom are white except in 'ghetto' chambers) remain prejudiced against black tenants (Flood, 1983: 50).

It is not surprising, then, that black barristers are concentrated in so-called 'ghetto' chambers, which are relatively isolated from the rest of the Bar. In 1983, 164 black barristers (78 per cent of the total) practised in just 14 sets, all of which had at least 5 black tenants; the remaining 46 practised in only 34 other sets, leaving 238 sets (83 per cent of the total) without a black barrister. Only 5 black barristers were in chambers outside London. The 'ghetto' sets are unequally distributed: they are only 4 out of the 152 in the Temple and 1 out of the 22 in Gray's Inn but 6 out of the 43 in Lincoln's Inn and 2 of the 5 outside the Inns. Almost all black barristers are involved in predominantly criminal practices. In October 1983, only 1 black barrister was in a specialist chambers. Two years later, however, the number had grown to 17, and 10 of the 40 new tenants joining specialist practices in 1984–5 were black (83 *LSG* 2482–3 and 2393, 1986). Even those who find a tenancy have difficulty obtaining work. Several black barristers have complained that white solicitors' firms refuse to brief them, overruling the explicit wishes of the clients (Cohen, 1982c: 8); in one instance, a firm appointed by the Law Society to handle the affairs of a suspended solicitor withdrew 14 briefs from a black barrister. Despite complaints to the Industrial Tribunal, the courts have ruled that relations between solicitors and barristers are not covered by the Race Relations Act. However, the Law Society has instituted a pilot scheme to monitor the instruction of black counsel (*Legal Action* 3, June 1985; 5, August 1985). It seems likely that unless white sets actively seek to integrate (a course for which they show no enthusiasm), the Bar will become increasingly segregated, with black barristers in black chambers serving a black clientele with a distinct configuration of legal problems.

## Gender

Both branches of the legal profession excluded women until compelled to admit them by the Sex Disqualification (Removal) Act of 1919. In 1920, 32 women were admitted to Middle Temple, and 23 were called

(Sturges, 1949). Twenty were practising when the 1921 census was taken, a mere 0.7 per cent of the Bar; by 1931, their numbers had tripled to 79 (2.7 per cent), and they doubled again in the next two decades to reach 151 in 1951 (4.9 per cent) (see table 4.1; Sachs and Wilson, 1978: 174). The number of women called fluctuated between 2 and 6 per cent of calls during the 1920s and 1930s; surprisingly, the proportion declined drastically during World War II (see table 1.12). Those women who sought to enter the Bar were very isolated: through the 1950s there rarely were more than half a dozen women called at any Inn in a given year (see table 1.14). Because few women went to university at that time, the non-graduate women barristers started at a disadvantage. The fact that a higher proportion of women than men had barrister fathers suggests that their families had an even stronger influence on both their choice of career and their likelihood of success. Furthermore, both the census and the call give an exaggerated picture of the number of women practitioners; Gower and Price (1957: 337 n. 79) estimated that only 68 women were even nominally in practice in 1957, and no more than 45 actually were practising.

Little changed until 1965, when the entry of women barristers, like that of men, increased dramatically. Since the base of women practitioners was so small, their rate of increase in the ensuing 17 years (more than 500 per cent) far outstripped that of men (just over 200 per cent), with the result that women slightly more than doubled their representation in the Bar, to over 10 per cent (see table 1.16). There is reason to expect this trend to continue, since women were 39 per cent of entering university law students in 1978 and 37 per cent of all polytechnic law students (see tables 3.7, 3.8). Although there is evidence that women prefer the solicitors' branch (for reasons discussed below), it is striking that they were 38–9 per cent of those called in Lincoln's and Gray's Inns in 1984 (see table 1.14).

The Bar has a better record than some other professions. In 1972, women were smaller proportions of town planners (5.4 per cent), architects (4.2), chemists (3.8) and insurance salespersons (3.7), only half the proportion of solicitors (3.2) and far fewer in the hard and applied sciences. But the proportion of barristers who were women did not begin to compare with that of physicians (17.8) or dentists (13.1) (Special Committee, 1972, citing a 1972 survey by the Royal Institute of British Architects). For women must still overcome very substantial barriers in order to succeed at the Bar. Undergraduate and professional education is not one of these; indeed, it is largely the increase in the proportion of women undergraduates that explains what success they have had at the Bar. A survey of all practising women barristers in the winter of 1977–8 (50 per cent response rate) found that only 8 per cent felt they were disadvantaged in obtaining a place at university or elsewhere in preparing for part 1 of the Bar final, and none felt disadvantaged in preparing for part 2 (Senate, 1978c: K, Annex 2). Indeed, women do better than men as undergraduates (see Chapter 18).

Sexism re-emerges at the later stages of the barrister's career (Podmore and Spencer, 1982: 343–4) – when selection processes are less centralized and visible, and decision makers can indulge in particularistic biases without fear of public criticism. Women have greater difficulty than men in obtaining pupillages. A 1972 survey of all women barristers (50 per cent response rate) revealed that 15 per cent experienced difficulty in obtaining a pupillage, though only 8 per cent suffered any delay (Senate, 1978d: 9, quoting Special Committee, 1972). Five years later, however, the proportion reporting disadvantage in securing a pupillage had increased to 25 per cent, and 70–5 per cent said that other women had told them of encountering problems at this stage (Senate, 1978c: K, annex). The difference between the two surveys may be explained by the psychological difficulty all victims of discrimination experience in acknowledging their humiliation to any but intimates. It also may be attributable to the fact that the number of women barristers had doubled in the interim (while pupillages had increased less rapidly), possibly engendering greater resistance among men.

For women, as for blacks, obtaining a tenancy is an even greater hurdle. Among the respondents to the 1972 survey, 39 per cent had problems finding a tenancy, and 23 per cent experienced delay – 9 per cent for longer than nine months; in the 1977–8 survey, 56 per cent felt at a disadvantage in seeking a tenancy, and 92 per cent said other women had reported this. Although 60–70 per cent of men seeking tenancies obtained them, only 40–45 per cent of women did so (Kennedy, 1978: 150–1). Nor did problems cease with a seat in chambers. Half the respondents in the 1977–8 survey said they were disadvantaged in obtaining work once in practice, and 82 per cent said other women complained of this.

The manifestations of discrimination are numerous. Many of the scholarships that the Inns grant to pupils are closed to women (Kennedy, 1978: 151). The circuits long discriminated against women. As late as 1964, the Midland circuit excluded them from both meetings and the mess, and the Northern circuit admitted them only to certain occasions (Zander, 1968: 73). This may help to explain why, even in 1980, they were only 5–10 per cent of the members of each circuit (see table 1.25). Banks refused to grant overdrafts to beginning women barristers (Kennedy, 1978: 151). But the most important source of sexism is the heads of chambers and clerks. As late as 1984, there were only nine women heads (one of whom practised by herself) and 15 women clerks in the 219 London chambers, though the proportion of the latter was higher in the provinces (see table 1.23). Heads appear to express simple prejudice; clerks are also motivated by economic self-interest, fearing (correctly, as we will see) that women tenants will earn lower incomes than men, which in turn reduces clerk incomes (Kennedy, 1978: 151–2; see also Senate, 1976d: 27; Flood, 1983: 50). In the 1972 survey, although only seven women practitioners felt they were treated differently by other barristers in their chambers, 24 per cent experienced different treatment from their clerks, and 44 per cent did so from solicitors. This had not improved significantly five years later: 20 per cent still felt at a disadvantage in getting along with the clerk.

The results of this discrimination are visible in the distribution of women in chambers (see tables 1.23, 1.29). In 1967, two-thirds of London chambers and nearly 60 per cent of those in the provinces had *no* women members. In 1984, the proportion without women remained virtually the same, and another 29 per cent of London chambers and 34 per cent of provincial chambers still had only one woman. Indeed, the dispersion of women in provincial cities seems to have created even greater isolation. Women were only 4 per cent of the provincial practising Bar, compared with 16 percent of the London Bar; there were *no* women in eight provincial Bars, only one in each of nine, and two in each of two more. The law does nothing to remedy this, since the Sex Discrimination Act 1975 (like the Race Relations Act) does not apply to the Bar because private practitioners are not employees. It remains to be seen whether the 1984 amendment to the Code of Conduct condemning sex discrimination will have any effect.

A final obstacle for women is less the explicit sexism of male barristers, solicitors and clerks than their unconscious acceptance of the traditional division of labour in childrearing. For a long time, women had to sacrifice marriage in order to be barristers: in 1921, only 20 per cent of women barristers were married, compared with 67 per cent of men; 30 years later the proportions were still 32.5 per cent and 72 per cent (census). In the 1972 survey, half the respondents were unmarried, a sixth had no children, and another sixth had gone to the Bar only after their children were grown (Kennedy, 1978: 161). The one out of six who tried to raise young children while practising had a difficult time: respondents to the 1977–8 survey took an average of less than three months maternity leave and spent an average of £30–40 pounds a week on childcare. And one out of three found it difficult to reconcile practice with family responsibilities (only three of the 33 women found it easy, and the husband of one of them had given up work). Women who had taken the Bar final in the late 1970s continued to reflect these tensions:

> I only left the Bar because I wanted a family. I was advised by my pupil master to leave, have a family, and return with grey hair.
>
> (AGCAS, 1981b: app. D at iv)

> I feel a woman's chances prior to marriage and children are slender. Doing Finals once your children are of school age is more likely to lead to success.
>
> (AGCAS, 1984a: 3)

These obstacles explain why the number of women at the Bar and their positions within it are not what the number and quality of aspirants would have led us to expect. Women Bar students declare an intention to enter private practice more frequently than do men: 75 versus 58 per cent in 1976 (Kennedy, 1978: 151), nearly 100 per cent of women in 1978 (Royal Commission, 1979, vol. 2: 438). Nevertheless, the proportion of women actually starting practice is far lower. Of the 255 men called in 1965, 56 per cent started practice, compared with only 37 per cent of the 46 women (Id. 440). Of the 306 men called 10 years later, 50 percent had started practice by 1979, compared to only 33 percent of the 41 women (ibid.: 439). This is consistent with statistics showing that women were 24 per cent of those studying for the Bar examination in 1977, 21 per cent of those taking it in 1976 and 24 per cent of those called to the Bar in 1977–8, but they were only 12 per cent of those starting practice between 1975 and 1978 (ibid.: 446; Rule, 1980: 33). It is instructive to compare these figures with the situation in Scotland, where advocates practise individually rather than in chambers and are served by a common clerical staff; there women and men now are equal proportions of beginners (Paterson, 1988).

Furthermore, the wastage of women who enter practice in England is also higher. In 1971, only 4 of the 101 women called between 1922 and 1929 were still practising, 5 of the 122 women called in the 1930s, 9 of those called in the 1940s, 43 of those called in the 1950s and 69 of those called in the 1960s (Knightly and Colton Report, 1971); only some of this can be attributed to normal retirements and deaths. Among those who entered practice after being called to the Bar in 1965, 47 per cent of the women had left within ten years compared with 13 per cent of the men; as a result, only 20 per cent of the women were still practising ten years later, compared with 40 per cent of the men (Royal Commission, 1979, vol. 2: 440).

Individual and institutional sexism affect not only whether women enter and remain in practice but also the kind and profitability of the work they secure. Women are concentrated in certain fields: in 1972, half practised mainly in criminal, general civil or family law; only 5 per cent had a Chancery practice, and none practised tax or commercial law (Kennedy, 1978: 154, quoting Special Committee, 1972, multiple responses permitted; Senate, 1976d: K.2). This distribution was not always a matter of choice: 53 per cent of the respondents in the 1977–8 survey said they felt disadvantaged in getting the sort of work they wanted to do (Senate, 1978d: K, annex). Women appear to be overrepresented within central government offices: in 1984 they were only 12 per cent of the Bar but 21 per cent of lawyers employed by the central government (not all of whom were barristers) – particularly in the Office of Fair Trading (45 per cent women, 55 per cent barristers) and the Official Solicitor's Department (42 per cent women, 17 per cent barristers) (see table 4.4). Furthermore, women earned considerably less than men, even when we control for other variables. Those less than 30 years old earned about three-quarters the incomes of their male counterparts, but this proportion declined drastically among older age cohorts, reaching a mere third among those over 50 (Royal Commission, 1979, vol. 2: 443). Women with 3 years of experience or less earned 86 per cent as much as their male counterparts, but those in practice 9–15 years earned less than half (ibid.: 444). And though women who practised on the circuits earned 60 percent as much as their male counterparts, those in London family and common law practices earned only half (ibid.). Overall, women earned just over half as much as male barristers (ibid.; AGCAS, 1984c: 12).

Women are even more disadvantaged with respect to other measures of status and power within the Bar. They were heads of chambers in only 5 out of 181 London sets in 1975 (2.8 per cent) (see table 1.23); in 1984, they were heads in 9 out of 222 London sets (4.1 per cent; one was a barrister sole) and 4 out of 115 provincial sets (3.5 per cent). They constituted 0.5 per cent of all benchers in 1976 and only 1.7 per cent in 1980 (see Podmore and Spencer, 1982: 342; table 1.22). In 1977–8, women were only 2 out of 109 benchers in Lincoln's Inn, 1 out of 140 in Inner Temple, 2 out of 142 in Middle Temple and 1 out of 89 in Gray's Inn. There were no women officers or Inn representatives in the Senate, just one woman Bar Council representative and one additional woman member (Royal Commission, 1979, vol. 1: 497). Despite the rapid influx of women since the late 1970s, there has been little change. In 1985, women were only 1 out of 119 benchers in Inner Temple, 2 out of 151 in Middle Temple, 0 out of 118 in Lincoln's Inn and 0 out of 93 in Gray's Inn (excluding honorary and supernumerary benchers). Of the more than 100 members of the Senate, there were only 5 women:

4 Bar Council representatives and 1 additional member (Solicitors' and Barristers' Directory and Diary, 1985). Women still are only 2 per cent of QCs; between 1960 and 1985, no women were granted silk in 15 of those years, and only one received an appointment in each of seven years (see table 1.22). Some of these differences can be explained by the age profile of the Bar, since honours are conferred on older, more experienced barristers. In 1976–7, 56 per cent of women barristers but only 37 per cent of men were under 30, and 49 per cent of women but only 29 per cent of men had practised less than three years (Royal Commission, 1979, vol. 1: 497). Women therefore were 10.3 percent of barristers under 30 but only 3.9 per cent of those over 50, and 11 per cent of barristers with less than four years experience but only 4 per cent of those with 15 years (ibid.: vol. 2: 442; Rule, 1980: 36). Even so they are underrepresented. Half of the men but less than a quarter of the women who have practised more than ten years have been appointed to the bench (Sachs and Wilson, 1978: 175).

Thus there seems to be little basis for the extraordinary complacency about sexism recently expressed by the Bar:

> In regard to discrimination against women, the Senate believes that this is a thing of the past. That is not to say that sex discrimination is nowhere to be found, only that it has ceased to be a serious problem.
>
> (Senate,1983: 13)

> Some years ago it was claimed that women were discriminated against in seeking to become and remain barristers. Whatever the truth of this accusation, it is clearly now the case that women at the Bar are competing on merit with their male colleagues – and rightly so.
>
> (Michael Wright, Attorney-General and Chairman of the Bar, in Senate, Annual Statement, 1983–4: 7)

# 5

# Controlling production by producers

In order to control the market for their services, producers must seek to regulate not only the production *of* producers – how many barristers there are and who becomes one – but also production *by* qualified producers. This second task, the promulgation and enforcement of rules of professional conduct, can be undertaken only after significant progress has been made on the first. For if anyone can hold himself out as a barrister, it would be economic suicide for a subset of 'barristers' voluntarily to adopt practices that limit their ability to compete with others who claim the same title but refuse to be bound by similar rules. The Bar had acquired a significant degree of control over the production of producers well before the nineteenth century, although, as we have seen, some of these controls were becoming anachronistic and had to be replaced by others framed in terms of technical competence rather than personal qualities. Therefore, we should expect to find a well-elaborated set of rules governing the production of services *by* barristers. I will begin with the most important: the boundary that demarcates the Bar's monopoly from the claims of its most immediate challengers – solicitors. Then I will discuss limitations that derive from the structures of practice, anticompetitive rules governing who will do the work, what fees will be charged and how they will be collected, and two domains within the Bar that further limit the production of and by producers – the circuit and the silk systems.

## The Bar's monopoly – rights of audience

Barristers do some non-contentious work, such as providing legal opinions, but they define themselves, and are perceived by others, as advocates. Consequently, the most important restriction on production by producers is their exclusive rights of audience in the higher courts (they share rights of audience with solicitors in the magistrates' and county courts). This monopoly is even more important because it tends to define who can become a judge, with the concomitant rewards of income, status and power. Barristers have enjoyed these privileges without serious challenges, until very recently.

Although solicitor interest in High Court advocacy waxed periodically during the last 100 years, whenever conveyancing income declined, the Law Society rarely pressed the issue. A motion favouring fusion passed at a meeting of the Law Society in 1919 was reversed by a two-thirds vote in a subsequent postal ballot, and a 1922 bill to the same effect died after its first reading (Reeves, 1986: 7–8). Solicitors made a claim to Quarter Sessions in the interwar period, but it came to nothing (Abel-Smith and Stevens, 1967: 236). In 1967, 64 out of 111 local law societies presented evidence to the Royal Commission on Assizes and Quarter Sessions. Although almost three-fifths (37) strongly sought a right of audience at Quarter Sessions, nearly a fifth were opposed to any change, four sought only a slight increase, and another fifth had no opinion (Zander, 1968: 159–60). The British Legal Association, formed to pursue the economic interests of solicitors more vigorously, found that responses from 27 per cent of its 2400 members indicated that 70 per cent sought rights of audience in Quarter Sessions, 43 per cent in Assizes and 35 per cent in all courts (ibid.: 162). But its campaign to secure a right of audience at Quarter Sessions failed (Reeves, 1986: 9).

When 108 out of the 121 local law societies responded to the Royal Commission on Legal Services in the late 1970s, only 33 (31 per cent) sought greatly extended rights of audience, 15 (14 per cent) sought a more limited extension, and 60 (56 per cent) preferred the status quo (Royal Commission, 1979, vol. 1: 211). Only the Prosecuting Solicitors' Society made a strong case for extension (Glasser, 1980: 31). Not surprisingly, the Bar was adamantly opposed (Senate, 1978c: annex, 1). And its views prevailed (Royal Commission, 1979, vol. 1: 220). What little erosion the Bar did suffer occurred through expansions of the jurisdiction of magistrates' and county courts – for instance, the extension of some divorce jurisdiction to the latter in 1967 – or the grant to defence solicitors of the right to continue in the Crown Court proceedings begun in magistrates' courts. Yet even today, solicitors encounter discourtesy and prejudice from both opposing counsel and judges when they seek to exercise these limited rights (ibid.: 88–90).

Though solicitors gained formal rights of appointment to some lower judicial positions, few actually were appointed (Lord Chancellor's

Department, 1976). Solicitors became eligible to chair Quarter Sessions in 1938, but 30 years later they held only 1 out of the 64 chairs and 4 out of 204 deputy chairs (Kirk, 1976: 183). Solicitors could become stipendiary magistrates in 1949, but the first was appointed in 1956 and the third in 1969. And solicitors with ten years experience could become Crown Court recorders in 1971; five years later there were 36 (ibid.: 184–5). In the North-eastern Circuit in 1986, only 13 out of some 3000 practising solicitors had been appointed recorders, assistant recorders or deputy circuit judges (5 in the preceding five years), compared with 116 out of some 300 practising barristers (60 of whom had been appointed in the preceding five years) (Letter to 'Postbox' by J.J. Pearlman, President, Leeds Law Society, 83 *LSG* 744–5, 1986). At the beginning of 1987, solicitors were 41 of 388 circuit judges and 31 of 540 recorders, although they outnumbered barristers five to one.

There the matter might well have rested but for challenges from an unlikely source – the Conservative government. Prime Minister Thatcher is herself a barrister, and the Tories consistently have been solicitous of the interests of the Bar. Nevertheless, their strong attachment to free market ideology and their desire to cut government expenditures tended to undermine the monopoly of the Bar in two ways. First, the government initiated the Crown Prosecution Service, which became operative in London on 1 April 1986 and in the rest of the country on 1 October. The Bar was suspicious from the outset, and the 1984 annual general meeting condemned any erosion of barristers' exclusive rights of audience, especially from the proposed service (134 *NLJ* 593, 1984). The Bar had reason to be afraid: it derived about £40 million from Crown Court criminal work, a significant part of which would be threatened by a service that planned to hire more than 400 lawyers (134 *NLJ* 668, 1984). Although the Attorney-General sought to reassure the Bar that the employed lawyers would be allowed to appear only in situations where solicitors had existing rights of audience (82 *LSG* 920–21, 1985), the Law Society made a cogent case for the monetary savings to be gained from substituting employed lawyers for independent barristers (81 *LSG* 3004, 1984). The effects of the new service on the Bar are still to be evaluated. More recently, the Legal Aid Scrutiny Report by the Lord Chancellor's Department recommended granting solicitors a right of audience in all Crown Court cases not involving jury trials in order to save the government £1 million a year in legally aided matters (136 *NLJ* 622, 1986).

The second challenge to the Bar is a by-product of the erosion of the solicitors' conveyancing monopoly (see chapter 12, p. 178), which reinvigoratied solicitor interest in higher court advocacy. Following the government's 1984 accord with Austin Mitchell to seek legislation allowing non-solicitors to do conveyancing, the Law Society promptly asked for equal rights of audience with barristers. The Bar Council vehemently opposed the demand, and the Prime Minister rejected it (81 *LSG* 858, 1218 and 1330, 1984). But it was clear that solicitors were not going to allow the issue to die. In October 1985, a solicitor sought to read in High Court an agreed statement disposing of a libel action. The High Court judge refused, stating that he lacked discretion to allow a solicitor a right of audience in the absence of exceptional circumstances, and the Court of Appeal affirmed (*Abse* v. *Smith, The Times* 6, 12 December 1985). Nevertheless, the Master of the Rolls did indicate that judges had inherent power to regulate rights of audience. The Law Society immediately sought a hearing from the panel of 105 High Court and Court of Appeal judges, requesting rights of audience not only to read agreed statements in personal injury actions but also to appear in unopposed *ex parte* hearings and whenever the barrister briefed is absent. On 13 January 1986 the panel granted only the first of these requests (*Abse* v. *Smith* [1986] 1 All ER 350), but the Bar still saw that as the thin end of the wedge. Its anxiety was intensified in June 1985, when Austin Mitchell tabled a private member's bill that would grant solicitors full rights of audience in all courts (although it had no chance of passage). And tension between the branches mounted in January 1986 when the Law Society published 'Lawyers and the courts', a discussion paper by its Contentious Business Committee, recommending something approaching fusion, with all lawyers entitled to practise in all courts and to be appointed to their benches (Law Society, 1986). In May, the Young Solicitors' Group seconded this with a paper 'The reorganisation of the legal profession', endorsing virtually all the recommendations (83 *LSG* 1682–3, 1986). The First National Conference of Litigation Solicitors also sought expansion of their rights of audience, although they voted 2:1 against the removal of all restrictions (83 *LSG* 1438, 1986). To no one's surprise, the Senate (1986) flatly and vehemently rejected all these claims. Austin Mitchell intends to reintroduce in 1987 his private member's bill to grant solicitors full rights of audience (136 *NLJ* 837, 1986). But though fusion is very unlikely to occur in the immediate future, the barristers' monopoly is more tenuous at present than it has been in over a century.

## Structures of practice

The Bar strictly controls the location and structure of the chambers within which barristers may practise. One of the influences was economic:

the Inns long have leased chambers to barristers at submarket rents, and indeed, until the end of the eighteenth century (1870 in Middle Temple), barristers obtained a tenancy for life on payment of a lump sum (Holdsworth, 1938: 37). Until recently, chambers in London had to be located within an Inn – a rule that limited both the opening of new sets and the fission of old ones. Although that rule has been relaxed, sets seeking to locate outside the Inns must obtain the approval of the Bar Committee, and very few have done so, perhaps fearing the loss of competitive advantage (as well as subsidized rents). Circuits must approve chambers and annexes in provincial cities. These rules recently were reaffirmed at the 1983 annual general meeting of the Bar Council (which can hear appeals in such matters) because, in the words of David Savill QC, 'There are obvious dangers in a free-for-all' (Senate, Annual Statement, 1983–4: 10–12). Barristers (unlike solicitors) cannot practise in their homes, an arrangement that would reduce expenses (and perhaps costs to consumers) and facilitate part-time practice, especially by women. This rule was reaffirmed by the Royal Commission (1979, vol. 1: 456) and the Senate's response (1983: 8).

We have seen that these restrictions strengthen the profession's control over the production *of* producers by limiting the availability of pupillages and especially tenancies. They also reinforce control of production *by* producers by increasing the average size of sets (see chapter 6, p. 103), thereby subjecting the more than 5000 private practitioners to the strong influence of the little more than 300 heads of chambers, almost all of whom, as we have seen, are elderly men. The Legal Profession Reform Bill tabled by Austin Mitchell in June 1985 and likely to be reintroduced in 1987 would curtail these restrictive practices by allowing barristers to practise anywhere and by regulating recruitment to pupillages and tenancies (*Legal Action* 4, June 1985; 136 *NLJ* 837, 1986).

Chambers also must have a clerk. The Senate (1983: 8) rejected the Royal Commission's recommendation (1979, vol. 1: 493) to dispense with this requirement, on the ground that barristers would be encouraged to tout, although it has relaxed the prohibition on spouses acting as clerks. As we will see in chapter 6 (p. 107), the clerk plays a central role in securing business for the chambers, allocating it among the tenants and negotiating their fees. Barristers also must practise as independent professionals: they cannot form partnerships, nor can one barrister employ another (although the practice of devilling, in which a novice works on the briefs of a more senior member of chambers, comes very close) (Royal Commission, 1979, vol. 1: 463; Zander, 1968: 229, 254). The Planning Committee of the Senate began an investigation in 1985 into a 'purse-sharing' arrangement within the Wellington Street chambers, whereby all fees are paid into a common pool and shared equally among those with at least two years' call (Senate, Annual Statement, 1985–6: 54). These rules limit the division of labour within chambers and may create inefficiencies. Finally, barristers cannot combine another occupation with the practice of law (Zander, 1968: 229; but see Mortimer, 1982), which both aggravates the difficulty of the early years of practice (by eliminating additional sources of income) and may prevent barristers from obtaining a competitive advantage by developing additional forms of expertise. It is interesting to contrast the solicitors' profession, which provides a salary to assistant solicitors, permits and indeed encourages partnerships among solicitors and is considering (though still unlikely to allow) partnerships with other professions.

## The allocation of work

In a capitalist economy, the free market is supposed to be the principal mechanism for allocating resources. But professions define themselves as exceptions to this rule, and they *are* exceptional in fact. Barristers are prohibited from seeking work and do not advertise or solicit business. Dicey said that the rules of etiquette on circuit 'may be summed up under one law – thou shalt not hug attorneys' (quoted in Duman, 1983a: 46). And during the nineteenth century, restrictions on transfer from the solicitors' branch to the Bar and even on socializing between barristers and solicitors were justified in these terms. In March 1986, the Northern circuit unanimously and vehemently reiterated its opposition to any advertising by barristers (1(3) *Counsel* 8, Easter term 1986).

But in a classical illustration of the ethical division of labour (Hughes, 1971: 345–6), barristers' clerks devote much of their effort to maintaining good relations with solicitors' firms, promoting the members of their own chambers and knocking those in others (Flood, 1981a). Although a formal market in information about barristers may have been less important in the nineteenth century, when little more than 1000 practised in London, today the professional ban on self-promotion favours those with established (but perhaps undeserved) reputations and disadvantages newcomers.

The Bar has taken some very tentative steps toward freeing the market for information by allowing barristers to announce their starts in practice or changes in chambers in a 'suitable publication' and to list in a directory the areas in which they hold themselves out to practise (Senate, 1983: 4); it is considering further liberalization (Senate, Annual Statement, 1985–6: 54–5). One reason why barristers, apparently even younger ones, have not been overly eager to enlarge the means of self-promotion is that their immediate consumers are solicitors' firms, which are relatively knowledgeable about the market and typically linked to barristers' chambers by an ongoing relationship. However, there is some indication that if the Law Society continues to press for expanded rights of audience, the Bar may respond by seeking to bypass solicitors and deal directly with clients. Austin Mitchell's Legal Profession Reform Bill would authorize this (*Legal Action* 4, June 1985), and, surprisingly, so would the Discussion Draft by the Law Society's Contentious Business Committee (1986). If individuals and companies become the market for barristers' services, I would expect increased enthusiasm within the Bar for advertising and other promotional devices.

Rules of etiquette restrict competition in other ways. A barrister must refuse a brief if another has already been briefed in the matter, unless the solicitor offers a satisfactory explanation for withdrawing the first brief (Zander, 1968: 121). The rule adopted in 1965 prohibiting pupils from accepting briefs during their first six months (Abel-Smith and Stevens, 1967: 428), when combined with the requirement of a year of pupillage (introduced six years earlier), could be seen as restricting competition by the rapidly increasing number of new barristers. But in fact the rule was enacted before the period of rapid growth, and new barristers have considerable difficulty obtaining briefs even after their first six months. The best-known rule governing the allocation of work – the cab-rank principle – appears to enhance the freedom of clients to choose among barristers rather than to further the interests of the Bar. Yet it may also dampen competition by limiting the capacity of a barrister to shape his or her career. However it, too, like the rule against self-promotion, readily can be evaded. For the cab-rank rule offers the client a uniquely capitalist right – to buy what you can afford. This, in turn, allows the barrister to avoid unpopular cases, which might prejudice the chance for a judgeship, by having the clerk mark up the brief fee or find some conflicting obligation (Caplan, 1978: 134; Zander, 1968: 83).

Perhaps the greatest competitive threat to the private Bar comes from employed barristers (see 'The Bar's monopoly', p. 86; and chapter 6, p. 111). But even in the absence of employment, barristers form long-term relationships with consumers, which exclude other producers. This is true not only in the private sector, where it is mediated by solicitors' firms, but also in the public. All the government's important civil work goes to the first junior Treasury counsel, who are chosen by the Attorney General and typically are appointed to the High Court after serving in this role. Central government departments and the directorates of legal services (of the military) also brief private practitioners in civil matters.

The heaviest cases at the Central Criminal Court are handled by Treasury counsel, also chosen by the Attorney General. Major prosecutions in other courts go to barristers on a secret Director of Public Prosecutions list prepared by the Attorney General's clerk and divided into three categories according to the seriousness of the matter; barristers' clerks are significant intermediaries in getting their principals on the list (Flood, 1983: 67–8). In 1984 Sir Michael Havers, the Attorney General, indicated his intention of pruning the list and distributing prosecution work more broadly – perhaps another reflection of the government's ideological commitment to a free market (134 *NLJ* 776 and 799, 1984). Finally, less important criminal prosecutions are distributed by local police departments, the largest of which, by far, is the Solicitor of the Metropolitan Police. Competition to get on that list is fierce: in the late 1970s, 200 were waiting to be added, and the number had been as high as 1000 (Flood, 1983: 68–9).

## Setting and collecting fees

Just as barristers do not compete by seeking business, so they do not engage in price competition. Fees are set exclusively by barristers' clerks; only in cases of special difficulty are QCs (since 1951) and juniors (since 1966) allowed to discuss fees with solicitors (Hazell, 1978c: 105), which is a continuous source of grievance to the latter (ibid.: 113). Clients are never directly involved in these negotiations. Whether this is viewed as protecting the Bar from the stigma of commercialism or as a form of market control, the result is that barristers are twice removed from those paying their bills. The small number of senior clerks (just over 200 in London, half as many in the provinces and only a handful in any one provincial city) also makes it easier for them to reach 'understandings' about the going rate. Sometimes this price fixing is explicit. In 1888, the newly formed Bar Council established a minimum fee of 1 guinea, raised to 2 guineas in 1951 (Abel-Smith and Stevens, 1967: 410); a barrister who charged less would be reported to his Inn (Abel-Smith and Stevens, 1968: 280). The Bar Council has also negotiated informal agreements with the Law Society (ibid.). On occasion, leading sets of London chambers have sought collectively to increase the level of fees: in 1957–8, 15 common law sets doubled the fee for interlocutory work, and though solicitors for insurance companies resisted, the clerks held firm (Abel-Smith and Stevens, 1967: 418–19; Zander, 1968: 187 n. 10). As a result, most set fees doubled between 1957 and 1962, and some increased threefold; even brief fees rose 25 per cent during this period

(Abel-Smith and Stevens, 1967: 425 and n. 25). As recently as 1985 the Professional Conduct Committee of the Bar Council ruled that there was no objection to one clerk consulting other clerks as to the 'going rate' in a particular type of case (Senate, Annual Statement, 1985–6: 68). It cannot be coincidence that the Bar exercised this leverage during the period when it enjoyed the greatest control over the production *of* producers. But even when the Bar does not act collectively, barristers' clerks can reach less formal agreements. The Bar Council acknowledges that it is common practice for a clerk to consult the clerk of opposing counsel on a matter in order to set a comparable fee, and the Council sees nothing wrong with this as long as the solicitor agrees (82 *LSG* 1215, 1985; Flood, 1983: 107–8).

The Bar has used its cartel power to enforce other uniform practices that clearly promote its self-interest. The full brief fee is due once the brief is delivered, even if the case is settled without a hearing; during the 1962 autumn assizes, half the cases (457 out of 908) were settled after the brief was delivered (Abel-Smith and Stevens, 1967: 274). Although the client is not protected against overcharging, the barrister *is* protected against undercharging by the practice of refreshers, which require additional payments after the first five hours of court time (ibid.: 213). A barrister must be briefed separately for every client, even if their cases are virtually identical (Zander, 1968: 125).

Yet counterbalancing these forms of market power derived from the Bar's control over the production *of* producers are two sources of weakness. The first, and less serious, is the difficulty barristers experience in collecting fees. The genesis of this problem reveals some of the inherent contradictions in the professional project. The barrister cannot sue a solicitor (or client) for non-payment of fees because this would undermine the profession's pretence that economic gain is of little or no importance – a hypocritical claim that is believed to enhance the status of the Bar. This is one of several conflicts between the two facets of the professional project – market control and collective mobility.

But perhaps more problematic is the Bar's symbiotic yet strained relationship with solicitors. As in many marriages, neither can live without the other, yet they have considerable difficulty living together. Solicitors have their own grievances – such as late return of briefs and inadequate preparation (see chapter 12, p. 188). Barristers' grievances include late or inadequate instructions and court attendance by a less experienced solicitor or legal executive from the firm. But in recent years, these have been dwarfed by anger at solicitors who delay in paying barristers' fees or never do so. In the late 1970s, it was said that many barristers were owed up to £10,000 by solicitors (Hazell, 1978c: 118).

The Bar Council Working Party on Fee Collection (1982) obtained 379 responses to a survey of fees received during the first six months of 1982. It found that two-thirds had been outstanding for more than three months, 45 per cent for more than six and 22 per cent for more than 12. This apparently was not due to dilatoriness among barristers: two-thirds of the fee notes had been submitted within a month of completing the work and only 19 per cent later than four months. The average amount outstanding was £14,396, which varied little by experience. The existing system for fee collection clearly was inadequate: only 32 of the 379 barristers had referred matters to the Law Society or threatened to do so, although 23 of those obtained satisfactory results; 186 of those who did not mobilize the complaint process stated that they feared retaliation by solicitors' firms in the form of a boycott.

In response, the July 1982 annual general meeting of the Bar resolved that solicitors who failed to pay within three months of a fee note should be blacklisted. The Bar Council objected and obtained a legal opinion that it was an unlawful restraint of trade (*The Guardian* 4, 13 December 1982). An extraordinary general meeting of the Bar was convened in December 1982 to choose between compulsory reporting of delinquent solicitors together with a modified blacklisting scheme and a more discretionary obligation to report followed by institutional responses from the Bar Council and the Law Society. A substantial majority chose the latter. The immediate result was a doubling in the number of complaints by barristers to the Senate, from 174 in 1980, 157 in 1981 and 187 in 1982 to 326 between May 1983 and April 1984 and 368 between April 1984 and March 1985. In the first 12 months under the new rules, 253 complaints (78 per cent) contained sufficient information for the Bar Council to take action (in the rest, the fee notes were insufficient or late). The chairman's letter elicited 195 full and 10 partial payments (80 per cent). The chairman also wrote 112 letters to the Law Society, producing 51 full and 12 partial payments and leading to 14 disciplinary proceedings. In the second year of the scheme's operation, 309 complaints contained adequate information (84 per cent), and the chairman's letter led to 212 full and 18 partial payments (74 per cent); he also wrote 155 letters to the Law Society. Despite the better results, some barristers remained seriously dissatisfied, feeling that many barristers' clerks refrained from using the system, especially against the larger firms, for fear of retaliation. Consequently Robin de Wilde again sought a compulsory obligation to report in a second extraordinary general meeting in December 1984, though this too was defeated. In the six months October 1985 to March 1986, 554 barristers filed a total of 900 complaints against 242 solicitors (80 *LSG* 2995, 1983; 81 *LSG* 915 and 3567–8,

1984; 82 *LSG* 1554, 1985; 132 *NLJ* 1136, 1982; 133 *NLJ* 610, 625 and 922, 1983; 134 *NLJ* 593 and 1075, 1984; Bar Council, 1984a; 1984b; Senate, Annual Statement, 1983–4: 54; 1984–5: 16, 54; 1985–6: 79–80).

Although the anger expressed by barristers has cooled, this episode remains highly instructive. At times, professions truly are the enclaves within capitalism they purport to be, immune from competitive pressures and capable of restraining greed even if they cannot eliminate it. But such insulation from the market is a precarious achievement. The erosion of control over the production *of* producers appears to have widened divisions between the two branches and opened fissures within the Bar. Barristers, especially the less experienced, can no longer pretend to be unconcerned with money. As both branches grow, informal understandings between them tend to be replaced by formal procedures and relationships, with the inevitable deviance that this engenders. Indeed, Austin Mitchell's Legal Profession Reform Bill would give barristers contract remedies for unpaid fees (*Legal Action* 4, June 1985). The rapid expansion of the Bar has also led to a growing divergence of interests between younger barristers and those they contemptuously refer to as the 'fat cats'. Here, as elsewhere, barristers are having to choose between the honorific status of professionals and the open pursuit of economic interests.

The second – and more fundamental – source of the Bar's diminished control over production *by* producers is its increasing reliance on the public purse. The public sector – both criminal prosecutions and criminal and civil legal aid – has expanded rapidly as a source of barrister income (see chapters 7 and 8). Fees for these services are set by the taxing authorities (Senate, 1977b: VI.1) and tend to be based on estimates of the amount of time reasonably necessary to do the work (ibid.: XVI.15). It is possible that the introduction of the Crown Prosecution Service will lead to greater government control over the fees paid for the diminished number of prosecution briefs sent to private practitioners (82 *LSG* 920–1, 1985). And given the prominence of legal aid, especially in the work of younger barristers, the government fee structure tends to be followed even when the client is private (Royal Commission, 1979, vol. 1: 563, 566). That barristers are growing restive under the constraints of government fee-setting is seen in the threat by the chairman of the Criminal Bar Association in 1985 to refuse prosecution briefs unless the Treasury increased the level of legal aid payments (Helm, 1985a). It seems plausible to expect the evolution of two distinct markets for legal services: the larger one dominated by the public sector, where the state determines fees, and a smaller market for private clients, in which barristers' clerks continue to set fees.

## Circuits

The rules and practices described above primarily regulate the ways in which legal services may be produced by those formally qualified. The circuit system does this too, but it also controls the production *of* producers by dividing England and Wales into circuits, to one of which a barrister must belong. The circuits arose as barristers followed the King, and later the King's judges, during their periodic travels throughout the realm. In the early nineteenth century the number of barristers practising on each circuit was small (see table 1.25), and their behaviour was governed by implicit understandings reinforced by informal sanctions. Circuit life was intensely social and arguably, at this time, a more important locus of self-regulation than the Inns (Cocks, 1976a; 1983). As the century progressed, however, the circuits underwent substantial change. The number of barristers increased dramatically – the membership of the circuits grew threefold between 1800 and 1860, more than fourfold on the Home, Northern and Western circuits (Duman, 1983a: 51; see table 1.25). Improved transportation allowed barristers to appear before the assize courts by making daytrips out from London without travelling on circuit with the other barristers and judges. The circuits were reorganized, undermining their organic solidarity. Permanent provincial Bars emerged in the major cities (see table 1.26). And the Bar Council, founded in 1883, increasingly spoke for barristers as a whole.

Consequently, circuits began to formalize regulations prescribing practices that probably had been in effect for decades. Electoral rules were strengthened so that a minority of members could block the entry of an applicant (Cocks, 1976a: 40). A barrister who wished to appear outside his circuit was required to demand of his client a special fee of 100 guineas if he was a QC, 50 if he was a junior (in addition to his ordinary brief fee); earlier in the century the special fee for a QC had been 300 guineas (ibid.: 44–5). At these prohibitive levels, the purpose clearly was to exclude non-members of the circuit rather than to enhance the income of the Bar. At Quarter Sessions the fee customarily was 5–30 guineas, and the Bar Council fixed a minimum of 10 guineas in 1898 (Abel-Smith and Stevens, 1967: 220–21). The client who briefed a non-member of the circuit also had to pay an additional 'kite' brief to a circuit member (Cocks, 1976a: 40). A barrister was required to make an irrevocable choice of circuit (ibid.: 45).

These rules effectively created a number of submonopolies, whose members were protected against competition from outside their circuit. But, like the other restrictive practices of the Bar, these came under increasing attack in the 1960s, both from within the Bar and from outside. In 1965, as a result, the Bar abolished both special fees and kite briefs. But it retained several less extreme anticompetitive practices: a barrister was required to join one circuit (and only one) in order to appear on any; he could not attend court outside his own circuit unless he already had been briefed; and he had to pay 5 guineas a day place money when visiting a circuit other than his own (Abel-Smith and Stevens, 1967: 431–2). But place money was a pale shadow of the earlier restrictive practices, and it appears to have fallen into disuse (it is not mentioned in the discussion of circuits by the Royal Commission, 1979, vol. 1: 434–5).

## Silks

Queen's Counsel and King's Counsel (generically called silks, by reference to their gowns, or seniors, by contrast with juniors) originally were named by the monarch to assist the law officers of the Crown. These obligations ended in the eighteenth century, however, and the annual emolument of £40 ceased in 1831 (Duman, 1983a: 35). Since then silks have been simply an elite within the Bar – a profession within the profession, enjoying the benefits of both limited numbers and restricted competition from juniors. Silks are appointed by the Lord Chancellor, who nominally advises the Crown and takes counsel from senior judges and practitioners. According to Abel-Smith and Stevens (1968: 118), appointment was virtually automatic for any barrister who applied, until the chancellorship of Jowitt (1945–51). A barrister elected to Parliament was entitled to take silk as of right until 1959 and retains a special claim to the privilege even today (Podmore, 1980: 76 n. 16).

These observations seem to be substantiated by the numbers appointed. Although these consistently were small – 2–3 a year before William IV, 9 a year during his reign, 11–12 a year at the end of the Victorian era and 20 a year during the early 1960s (Megarry, 1962: 89–90) – there was enormous annual variation (see table 1.24). Furthermore, silks do not seem to have been a constant proportion of the Bar prior to 1920 but rather to have grown from about 3–4 per cent throughout much of the nineteenth century to 10 per cent following World War I (ibid.). Since then, the number of silks has paralleled the size of the Bar, shrinking with it in the 1950s and expanding rapidly in the 1970s (ibid.).

Until 1961, an applicant had to notify all juniors on his circuit with greater seniority so that they could apply before he did (Zander, 1968: 137 n. 7). And until 1983 the junior had to furnish two references, preferably from judges (Monopolies and Mergers Commission, 1976a: 5; Lord Chancellor's Department, 1983: 25). In addition, the Lord

Chancellor asks the leaders of the circuits and of the specialized bars not only about the qualifications of the applicant but also whether there is sufficient business to justify the appointment of another silk in that region and substantive area (Monopolies and Mergers Commission, 1976a: 5). Indeed, the anticompetitive nature of the institution was made even more explicit by a Lord Chancellor who indicated that there should not be more than four silks, or two active silks, in any set (Zander, 1968: 134 n. 6).

The ratio of applicants to appointments has been high since at least the 1960s: in 1964, 180 applied and only 18 patents were granted (Abel-Smith and Stevens, 1968: 119); in the late 1960s, about 120 applied a year and 25–30 were appointed (Zander, 1968: 131); and since the 1970s the proportion of applicants appointed has varied between 10 and 25 per cent (*Economist*, 1983: 47; 134 *NLJ* 503–4, 1984; 135 *NLJ* 1048, 1985; see table 1.24). Although Lord Chancellors repeatedly have maintained that the relationship between the number of silks and the size of the Bar is mere fortuity, and though the Royal Commission recommended that silks henceforth be appointed exclusively on merit (Royal Commission, 1979, vol. 1: 470; Lord Chancellor's Department, 1983: 25), the figures tell their own story (see table 1.24).

By itself, the limitation on numbers would create an honorific category, whose members might expect to enjoy higher prestige and income. But the institution of silk is surrounded by additional restrictions on the production of legal services by both seniors and juniors, which further serve to dampen competition between the two categories. Queen's Counsel are disqualified from accepting preliminary work, which thereby has become the monopoly of juniors. In the early nineteenth century, when the circuit messes still were the primary mechanism of self-regulation, QCs consistently refused to appear without the assistance of juniors (Cocks, 1976b; 1978b; cf. Abel-Smith and Stevens, 1967: 56; Monopolies and Mergers Commission, 1976a: 9). The Bar Council formulated an explicit rule to this effect in 1890, in both jury and bench trials, reaffirming it in 1935 and extending it to tribunals in 1951 (Monopolies and Mergers Commission, 1976a: 10). The third rule in this constellation of restrictive practices required the junior to be paid a fixed proportion of the leader's fee. Although there was some uncertainty in the nineteenth century whether this was two-thirds or three-fifths, the former fraction was adopted by the Bar Council in 1900 (Abel-Smith and Stevens, 1967: 223–4). If juniors thus receive significant advantages from the silk system, seniors benefit even more. They are required to charge substantially higher fees; and though this may subject many to a temporary drought, it generally is followed by higher, sometimes extraordinary, incomes (see chapter 8). And silks are the exclusive source of appointments to the higher courts.

Like the rules governing the circuit system, these also were attacked in the postwar years. The Bar abrogated the two-thirds rule under strong external pressure in 1971. But a study conducted three years later indicated that the practice persisted: in 22 per cent of a sample of High Court personal injury cases in which a QC appeared, the junior's fee was two-thirds the senior's; in another 50 per cent it was one-half; and the overall average was 55 per cent. Juniors briefed with QCs earned an average fee of £107, whereas they only charged an average of £80 when performing the same functions on their own (Zander, 1976: table 10). The barristers' clerks of the leader and junior still consult with each other in setting fees in order to preserve a proportion of roughly two-thirds (Flood, 1983: 107–8). In 1977, at the insistence of the Director of Fair Trading following an enquiry by the Monopolies and Mergers Commission, the Bar abolished the two-counsel rule. But because it preserved the right of a QC to refuse to act unless a junior was briefed, this change also had little effect. A more significant challenge to the tradition of two counsel is refusal by legal aid committees to pay for both (Monopolies and Mergers Commission, 1976a: 16). This is not surprising, given that the maximum legal aid fee in a jury trial was ten times higher for a QC than for a junior! The recent Legal Aid Scrutiny Report by the Lord Chancellor's Department recommended greater caution in using more than one counsel in legally aided matters – a measure it hoped would save the government £1 million a year (136 *NLJ* 622, 1986). But even without the financial incentive, some clients may prefer a junior who has abandoned the hope of being appointed a silk or a judge and thus may be a more vigorous advocate. Consequently, some of the more senior juniors have been poaching the heavier briefs and acting as leaders with a second junior, a practice naturally resented by silks (and some judges). In 1975, the Bar Council recommended that any leader have at least seven years experience; in 1983, the Criminal Bar Association suggested a minimum of ten years (133 *NLJ* 587–8, 1983).

The continuation, and indeed intensification, of these struggles for competitive advantage between more and less experienced practitioners is attributable, in part, to the erosion of control over the production of barristers. As a result, control over the production of *silks* becomes that much more important and control over production *by* both juniors and seniors that much more difficult to enforce. The logical next step would be the elimination of the category altogether, as proposed in Austin Mitchell's Legal Profession Reform Bill (*Legal Action* 4, June 1985; 136 *NLJ* 837, 1986; see also Samuel, 1987; Gifford, 1986).

# 6

# The structures of production

The relations of production are influenced by the rules and practices described above. But they are also shaped, perhaps even more profoundly, by the structures within which barristers and related occupations practise, even when these are not imposed upon them. This chapter examines changes in the geographic distribution of barristers, the size of the unit of production, the relationship between barristers and subordinated occupations and the growth of employed barristers.

## Geographic distribution

Until the end of the nineteenth century the Bar, like the bench, was centralized in London. Both judges and barristers left the capital twice a year to travel on circuit to the assize towns, but at least two-thirds of the year would be spent in London (Cocks, 1978a: 41). Towards the end of the century, however, this began to change. The fact that courts were open in both London and the provinces throughout the judicial year meant that barristers had to choose between them. Many ceased to travel on circuit, which experienced a substantial decline in attendance (Cocks, 1976a). By 1971, although most London barristers (1311 out of 1981) nominally belonged to a circuit (for this was a prerequisite if they wished to practise on *any* circuit), many rarely appeared: for each nominal member, the contribution to active barrister strength on circuit ranged from 0.21 on the Northern to 0.37 on the Midland and Oxford (Bar and Quarter Sessions, 1971).

Paralleling this decline in circuit activity (and explaining much of it) was the emergence of a provincial Bar permanently based in the larger commercial cities. There was none to speak of until about the middle of the nineteenth century. The 1785 Law List included no barristers with provincial addresses, the 1798 Law List included 3, the 1815 Law List 34 (perhaps 5 per cent of the practising Bar) and the 1830 Law List 81 (perhaps 7 per cent) (Duman, 1981: 97). Most cities had only one or two barristers, although the larger ones contained more: Manchester had 5 in 1830, 13 in 1850 and 56 in 1880; Liverpool had 13 in 1830, 17 in 1850 and 59 in 1880 (ibid.; Duman, 1980: 620). Yet no more than 60 of the 3268 barristers in the 1850 Law List had addresses outside London, and some of those practised part time; no cities except Liverpool and Manchester had more than 7 barristers (Duman, 1980: 620; 1982: 8 n. 2).

The establishment of the county courts in 1847 and subsequent expansions in their jurisdiction, together with the changes in the assize system effected by the Judicature Act of 1875, contributed to the gradual expansion of the provincial Bar (Duman, 1980: 620). In 1874, 24 per cent of the 213 members of the Northern circuit had chambers in a provincial city; 21 years later, 37 per cent did so, and another 5 per cent had chambers in both London and the provinces. Between 1880 and 1900 the local Bar grew from 13 to 22 in Birmingham, 14 to 20 in Leeds, 59 to 95 in Liverpool and 56 to 99 in Manchester (Duman, 1983a: 86–8). At the turn of the century there were about 300 provincial barristers, some 7 per cent of the practising Bar. Since then, the number has grown steadily, both absolutely and proportionally: 373 (9 per cent) in 1910–11, 340 (11.5 per cent ) in 1920–1, 346 (11.7 per cent) in 1930–1, and 444 (14.4 per cent in 1950–1 (see table 1.26). Even these percentages may be understated if the denominator is more likely than the numerator to include barristers not in private practice. The more accurate figures available since 1953 show an increase from 24 to 29 per cent of the Bar (see table 1.27). The provincial cities themselves have become important centres of Bar life and activity. The very largest (Birmingham, Bristol, Cardiff, Leeds, Liverpool and Manchester) consistently have contained two-thirds to three-quarters of all provincial barristers (see table 1.26). Others, like Newcastle-upon-Tyne and Nottingham, emerged into prominence only after World War II. Today there are another half dozen provincial cities with significant Bars (Chester, Leicester, Nottingham, Preston, Sheffield, Southampton and Swansea).

The coherence, colleagueship, ease of communication and sense of common interest that characterized the nineteenth-century Bar inevitably diminished as nearly a third of its members dispersed to live and work in some 30 cities outside London. The conditions of provincial practice appear to differ significantly from those in London (see 'Size of sets',

p. 103; and chapter 7). At the same time, this geographic dispersion has not resolved the problem of access to the Bar by clients and their solicitors. The location of barristers mirrors the placement of courts and the level of commercial activity, not the distribution of people. The ratio of population to provincial barristers varied from 22,323:1 on the Northern circuit to 123,408:1 on the Western; the ratio of population to active barrister strength (including London barristers practising on circuit) varied from 17,989:1 on the Northern circuit to 44,351:1 on the North-eastern. And many cities with substantial populations still have no local Bar (Zander, 1968: 71 n. 15). Even those with small Bars do not offer clients and solicitors a wide range of choice, especially given the degree of specialization in practice today. And all silks still must have chambers in London, although they may belong to a provincial set as well (Duman, 1983a: 87). Several solicitors in Devon and Cornwall in 1985 (albeit a minority) had little respect for the local Bar and sent their briefs to London (Blacksell et al., 1986: 17 and table 52).

## Size of sets

Although the Bar has been housed in chambers in the Inns of Court for centuries and in provincial chambers for more than 100 years, the structure of the productive unit recently has experienced dramatic changes. In the early nineteenth century, barristers practised individually, each assisted by his own clerk and perhaps also by pupils and by recently admitted barristers without tenancies, who were devilling (Cocks, 1983: 9; Duman, 1983a: 83). As late as World War II, the average set of chambers contained only four to six barristers (Senate, 1976b: 4); in 1959, provincial chambers still had only five to six (see table 1.27). But the extraordinary growth of the Bar in the last 20 years, combined with the restriction of London chambers to the Inns (and provincial chambers to comparable boundaries), has transformed the productive unit. Between 1959 and 1984, the average size of chambers more than doubled in both London (7.5 barristers to 16.7) and the provinces (5.6 to 12.6) (ibid.). Whereas a quarter of all London sets had contained 5 barristers or fewer in 1960, and four-fifths contained 10 or fewer, by 1984 only 3 per cent contained fewer than 5, and just 13 per cent contained fewer than 10; in the Temple, only 9 per cent contained fewer than 10. By contrast, the proportion of sets with at least 16 tenants grew from 2 per cent in 1960 to 51 per cent in 1979; by 1984, 65 per cent of London sets had at least 15 tenants. Indeed, nearly half of all the sets in the Temple and a third of those in Gray's Inn contained at least 20 barristers. In the provinces, the proportion of sets with 5 barristers or fewer declined from half in 1960 to a fifth in 1979; by 1984, only 8 per cent contained fewer than 5 barristers. The proportion with 10 barristers or fewer declined from nine-tenths of all sets in 1960 to four-tenths in 1979; by 1984 they were only a quarter. And whereas no set had contained more than 15 barristers in 1960, a third did so in 1979, and half contained 15 or more by 1984; indeed, 27 per cent contained more than 20 (see tables 1.28, 1.29). The change is even more extreme if expressed in terms of the number of barristers rather than sets. A tenth of all London barristers practised with fewer than 5 colleagues in 1960, and two-thirds practised with fewer than 10; by 1979, these proportions had shrunk to less than a hundredth and a tenth, respectively, whereas the proportion practising with at least 15 others had grown from 3 per cent to two-thirds. In the provinces, the proportion of barristers practising with fewer than 5 colleagues had declined from a quarter to a sixteenth, those practising with fewer than 10 had declined from four-fifths to a fifth, and two-fifths were practising with at least 15 other barristers, whereas none had done so previously (see table 1.28).

The growth of the Bar and the physical limitations of the Inns undoubtedly magnified this tendency toward concentration, but they do not explain all of it. For one thing, the Bar itself is responsible for much of the pressure to practise within the Inns in London and within similar confines in the provinces. And external forces cannot account for the fact that the number of sets actually declined in both London and the provinces between 1959 and 1970. Several other factors may be significant. As barristers and their clerks have (very slowly) adopted computer technology for word processing, scheduling, accounting and billing, the capital investment of practitioners has become substantial. This means both that efficiencies of scale encourage the growth of chambers and that it is increasingly difficult for a group of barristers – especially the younger ones who might be so inclined – to obtain the capital needed to launch a new set. Although the Inns offer loans for this purpose, they are few and small (an average of eight loans and grants of rent relief a year at £11,759 per loan between 1971 and 1978); and they find even fewer takers (Royal Commission, 1979, vol. 1: 451). Rising labour costs also would foster concentration; but barristers employ relatively little subordinate labour, and what they use they pay on a commission basis (see 'Barristers' clerks', p. 105). Although such an arrangement may reduce the barristers' interest in concentration, it strongly reinforces the senior clerk's interest, because the clerk's income increases directly with the number of tenants. Finally, size may enhance the prominence and internal diversity of a set, allowing it to attract more business as well as demonstrating to others its continuing ability to do so. (In most market economies, as in Alice's Wonderland, you have to run as fast as possible just to stay in place.) Among the 188 London sets who responded to a 1985 accommodation questionnaire, 60 per cent said they would take on an additional 284 tenants if they could obtain further space (1 *Counsel* 17–18, 1985).

Since all these forces seem likely to persist, and indeed to intensify, barristers' chambers should continue to expand (within space limitations). This, in turn, is likely to have several noteworthy consequences. It tends to enhance the authority of the head, who legally is the sole tenant of the set and can admit or dismiss the others at will. But as chambers grow there may be pressure to subject this autocratic power (and the governance of chambers generally) to bureaucratic structures, if not yet democratic control. The sets themselves are likely to become ever more important units in relation to such larger professional associations as the circuits, the Inns and the Senate. Chambers will also become more differentiated from each other in terms of specialization, composition, income and prestige. The prominence of these intermediate units of production will make it more difficult to contend that the Bar is merely a collection of independent professionals.

## Barristers' clerks

The paradoxical position of the barristers' clerk is central to an understanding of the production of services by the Bar. For though clerks come from a much lower social class than barristers, possess little formal education and have failed in their efforts to professionalize, they wield extraordinary authority within chambers and reap equally surprising financial rewards. It is said that barristers first began using clerks in the eighteenth century in order to distance themselves from solicitors, who were just beginnning to brief them. Payments to clerks originally were voluntary and nominal; but as clerks demanded more, the recently organized Law Society successfully sought a formal scale of charges in 1834 (Abel-Smith and Stevens, 1967: 56 and n. 4). The number of senior clerkships is fixed by the number of chambers (although two or even three people may share a position, and several smaller chambers may share a clerk). Consequently the number of senior clerks, like the number of sets, has grown far less rapidly than the Bar as a whole, increasing from 277 in 1959 to 341 in 1982, or 23 per cent (only 15 per cent in London) (see table 1.27). This slow rate of growth clearly benefits the senior clerks, whose income varies directly with the number of barristers they serve. I presume they have done what they can to discourage both attrition or fission within their own chambers and the creation of new sets. In this respect, the two branches exhibit inverse relationships between staff within the productive unit: whereas the income of barristers' clerks increases with the number of tenants in chambers, the income of principals in solicitors' firms increases with the number of fee-earning subordinated personnel (see chapter 13, p. 205).

Senior clerks are assisted by junior clerks, whose numbers are more flexible. In 1964–5 it was estimated that there were three juniors for every two seniors, or a total of approximately 400 juniors (Johnstone and Hopson, 1967: 426). In 1977, the Royal Commission obtained 172 replies from 53 per cent of all chambers, which would extrapolate to 325 junior clerks (1979, vol. 2: 412). However, the survey also showed that the typical set of chambers has one or two junior clerks and perhaps a typist, which suggests double the number. Flood (1981a: 396; 1983: 5) believes the figure is between 600 and 900, which seems plausible since the number of junior staff should increase with the size of chambers. On the other hand, estimates of the ratio of barristers to all other staff have grown from 3:1 in the early 1960s to 4:1 in the late 1970s (compare Johnstone and Hopson, 1967: 428 with Royal Commission, 1979, vol. 1: 485).

Barristers' clerks, both senior and junior, come from working or lower-middle class backgrounds, an identity London clerks tend to accentuate by the display of cockney accents (Flood, 1981a: 391; Johnstone and Hopson, 1967: 437). A survey of all senior clerks at the end of 1976 (59 per cent response rate) revealed that just 1 out of the 156 was a university graduate, only 14 per cent had A-levels, and less than half had even O-levels (Royal Commission, 1979, vol. 2: 402). Two-thirds of a similar sample of junior clerks had left school at 16, i.e. before their A-levels and often without any O-levels (ibid.: 429). Half the senior clerks were under 40, and four-fifths of the juniors were under 30 (ibid.: 401, 413). Senior clerks were surprisingly inexperienced (perhaps because they attain their positions relatively late or retire early): a third had served less than 2 years, two-thirds less than 11 (ibid.: 402), though all had spent substantial periods as juniors.

Career advancement tends to occur laterally, between sets (Johnstone and Hopson, 1967: 437; Flood, 1983: 21). Recruitment as a junior clerk is usually mediated by contacts, often a relative who is a clerk; nearly two-thirds obtained their positions this way (Royal Commission, 1979, vol. 2: 433). It is not surprising, then, that the proportion of women is small: less than 2 per cent of seniors and 5 per cent of juniors in 1963–4 (Johnstone and Hopson, 1967: 426); 14 per cent according to a 1971 study (Knightly and Colton Report, 1971); 10 per cent of seniors and 19 per cent of juniors in 1976 (Royal Commission, 1979, vol. 2: 401, 412). In 1981, women were 4 per cent of London clerks and 22.5 per cent of those in provincial chambers (Flood, 1983: 45); in 1984, there were 15 senior women clerks in the 222 London chambers and 24 in the 115 provincial chambers. As always, women are less well represented in senior positions and in the more prestigious (and remunerative) London chambers, which may be attributable to the prejudices of both senior clerks and heads of chambers (Flood, 1981a: 387, 396).

The role of the senior clerk is defined by his relationship to the head of chambers, who employs and can dismiss him. In 1977, a prominent head dismissed a senior clerk who refused to accept a reduction in his commission from 10 to 8 per cent unless he were relieved from paying his juniors; the industrial tribunal ruled that he was an independent contractor and thus not protected by law (Hazell, 1978c: 115; Flood, 1983: 7). This relationship tends to be long and close; in the past, a head of chambers who went to the bench often took his clerk with him, although today clerks tend to decline such offers because of the income they must sacrifice, unless they are close to retirement and interested in the government pension (Flood, 1983: 26). That the relationship still retains some of these personal qualities is suggested by the fact that only a quarter of all senior clerks had written contracts in 1976 (Royal Commission, 1979, vol. 2: 403). Nevertheless, this may be changing as chambers grow larger and more bureaucratic; in 1982, the Senate published a proposed form contract for barristers' clerks (Annual Statement, 1982–3: 69).

The senior clerk performs a large number of indispensable functions. He accepts briefs from solicitors on behalf of the barristers in his chambers. This is anything but a passive activity. Clerks carefully cultivate ongoing relationships with solicitors' firms, which come to be viewed as chambers' firms (Flood, 1983: 69). Indeed, clerks aggressively promote the barristers in their set and deprecate the abilities of competitors. Although the Barristers' Clerks' Association (BCA) has rules against touting, and especially against poaching from firms that have established a relationship with another set, there is no enforcement mechanism beyond informal sanctions (Flood, 1978: 12; 1983: 106). The obverse of attracting business is declining less remunerative or prestigious work on behalf of successful barristers, circumventing the obligations of the cab-rank rule (Flood, 1983: 70–1).

Getting business is intimately associated with negotiating fees, which is the exclusive province of the clerk in most cases. Although payment by commission motivates the clerk to set the fee as high as possible, short-term gains must be balanced against the danger of damaging ongoing relationships with solicitors' firms and driving business elsewhere (Flood, 1981a: 403–4). Indeed, clerks will cut fees to initiate or preserve relationships with firms (Flood, 1983: 72). The clerk's role in negotiating fees has diminished in importance with the growth of legal aid work, where fees are set by taxing masters. Finally, the clerk must collect these fees from solicitors, a process that often can take years and where vigorous demands again are constrained by fear of losing future business (Flood, 1981a: 403–4).

These primary tasks carry with them several collateral responsibilities. Each court appearance must be scheduled so that the barrister can do the most work with the fewest conflicts (Flood, 1983: ch. 5). This can be an extremely demanding and tense operation, requiring excellent working relationships with court clerks (some of whom may be former barristers' clerks) constructed through long acquaintance, much convivial drinking and even presents (ibid.; Hazell, 1978c: 107–8). When conflicts do arise, the clerk must try to persuade the solicitor to accept another barrister from the same chambers or risk losing the brief to a competitor, which not only will deprive the clerk of his fee but also may lead the solicitor to send future business to the competitor (Hazell, 1978c: 107–8; Flood, 1981a: 385). One solution is to establish reciprocal relationships (return circuits) with other sets, which refer business back and forth but do not poach chambers' solicitors (Flood, 1983: 102). According to evidence submitted by the United Lawyers' Association to the Royal Commission, barristers are replaced in 58 per cent of all briefs (quoted in Reeves, 1986: 57).

In order to achieve these objectives, the clerk must work to develop a set of chambers that attracts business and keeps returned briefs. Therefore, he has a vital interest in shaping the composition of the set. He consults with the head and with the other tenants in deciding which pupils will be offered tenancies and helps those rejected to find tenancies elsewhere through his contacts with other clerks (Flood, 1983: 57–8). Perhaps even more important, he can make or break a young barrister by channelling business to or away from him when solicitors send a brief to chambers rather than to a particular barrister or when the clerk needs a substitute barrister for a returned brief (Zander, 1968: 85). He may even try to convince an unsuccessful tenant to find another chambers, enter employment or change careers (Flood, 1983: 58–9).

The performance of these functions confers significant power. It is also rewarded financially. And the two are often connected symbolically. At least since World War I, clerks received the extra shilling in every guinea the barrister earned and also charged the client a further percentage of the barrister's fee (Royal Commission, 1979, vol. 1: 487; Flood, 1983: 6). In 1967, the clerk's commission was 10 per cent of the first £50 and 2.5 per cent thereafter (Abel-Smith and Stevens, 1968: 111; Hazell, 1978c: 114). With the conversion to decimal currency in 1971, the clerk ceased billing the client directly and instead was paid an agreed percentage of the fee by the barrister (Royal Commission, 1979, vol. 1: 488; Flood, 1983: 6–7). The BCA and the Bar Council agreed that this should be a minimum of 5 per cent, though a head and clerk could negotiate higher amounts (General Council of the Bar, Annual Statement, 1969–70; Senate, 1977a: III.7–8). In 1976, about 10 per cent of senior clerks received a salary from their heads (often with some additional commission), 15 per cent received 5 per cent of gross fees, 17 per cent received 6–7 per cent, 16 per cent received 8–9 per cent and 42 per cent received 10 per cent (Royal Commission, 1979, vol. 1: 486, 488). The senior clerk usually must pay the salaries of the junior clerks (although some of these may also get commissions of 1–2 per cent) as well as those of other office staff (Senate, 1977a: III.7–8). However, these are fairly low; in 1975–6, the average junior clerk earned £2527 a year (Royal Commission, 1979, vol. 1: 487).

Senior clerks do very well financially. In 1975–6, salaried clerks averaged £7604 a year, those earning commissions of 5–7 per cent and making no contribution to junior staff salaries earned £8968, and those receiving commissions of 8–10 per cent and making such a contribution earned £11,378 (Royal Commission, 1979, vol. 1: 486). The average income of all senior clerks was nearly 50 per cent higher than the average earnings of all junior counsel and significantly higher than even the upper quartile of juniors (ibid.: 487). Clerks reach an income plateau fairly early: between 31 and 40 years old and after six to ten years' experience (Royal Commission, 1979, vol. 2: 407–8). The major factor influencing earnings is the size of the set: clerks in sets with more than 20 barristers earned nearly four times as much as those who clerked for 6–10 barristers; in sets with 16–20 the ratio was 3:1; and in sets with 11–15 it was 2:1 (ibid.: 408). Thus the growth in the size of chambers has had a direct and very strong effect on clerk income: in 1960, when there were an average of seven barristers per senior clerk, the latter earned two-thirds the average of his principals; in 1976, when the size of chambers had doubled, the clerk earned 1.4 times the average of his principals (Hazell, 1978c: 114–15). The Senate noted (1983: 11) that a clerk receiving the minimum 5 per cent commission in a larger set that grossed £750,000 would earn £37,500, which it characterized as 'a ridiculously excessive figure to pay to any clerk in any circumstances'. Yet some clerks make more than £100,000 (*Economist*, 1983: 47).

Despite the enviable amounts of power and income enjoyed by senior clerks, they have been singularly unsuccessful in attaining professional status. Or perhaps material success is the reason for professional failure: status alone may be an insufficient motivation to pursue the professional project. Barristers' clerks formed an associaton in 1922, but it was just a friendly society intended to pay for burials, provide pensions and perhaps assist the families of deceased members (Flood, 1978: 6–7). In 1956, the BCA attempted to control the supply of clerks by requiring membership, but it was rebuffed by the Bar Council (ibid.: 13). Yet formal supply control may be superfluous. The number of senior clerkships is fixed by the number of sets, and numerous forces restrain the growth of the latter. The category is so small – just 200 in London and another 100 in the provinces – that informal controls can be quite effective. And most senior clerks belong to the BCA anyway – 78 per cent in London and 51 per cent in the provinces (Johnstone and Hopson, 1967: 438; Senate, 1977a: III.14; Solicitors' and Barristers' Diary and Directory, 1985).

The BCA performs some of the functions of a professional association but only half-heartedly. It defended the commission system in 1949 when it was under attack and even challenged the Bar Council (if unsuccessfully) when the latter sought to impose a 2 guinea minimum fee, which clerks feared would reduce their leeway in negotiations (Flood, 1978: 8, 11). It lost the struggle to retain a separate clerk's fee in 1971. Although the BCA claims disciplinary powers, it does not exercise them, perhaps because the ultimate sanction of expulsion has no real bite (Johnstone and Hopson, 1967: 438; Flood, 1983: 122–3). Instead, clerks are disciplined by the Bar – a visible symbol of their subordinate status (Flood, 1978: 17). Although the BCA began lectures for junior clerks in 1972 and introduced an examination in 1972, open to those who had three O-levels, only about 15 clerks a year seek to qualify (out of some 600) (Flood, 1978: 17; 1983: 22). And only recently have senior clerks begun to adopt modern accounting practices in response to external criticism (Flood, 1978: 18). Senior clerks retain their privileges because the only categories that have reason to challenge them – younger barristers and junior clerks – are too weak to do so. Yet even without such challenges, barristers' clerks are being transformed from entrepreneurs into administrators as the flow of work depends increasingly on ongoing relationships with ever-larger solicitors' firms, as taxing authorities determine fees in the expanding public sector and as court calendars are computerized.

## Employed barristers

Although there are no registries of employed barristers, their numbers appear to be at least as large as those in private practice. Between 1947 and 1984, 15,634 UK domiciliaries were called to the Bar, but only 7607 started practice; many of the others – more than half the total – entered employment as barristers (though some undoubtedly abandoned law altogether). Furthermore, only two-thirds of those who started practice during this period were still practising at the end of it; since few of the missing third would have died or retired, some of those who left practice undoubtedly went into employment as barristers (see table 1.16). Until recently, barristers were disadvantaged in seeking employment: unlike private practitioners, they could not appear in the higher courts; and unlike solicitors, they could not brief barristers, do conveyancing or even appear in the lower courts (except as agents of their employers) (Zander, 1968: 163–4; 81 *LSG* 2639, 1984). The Royal Commission (1979, vol. 1: 242) recommended that the first two disabilities be removed; the Senate agreed (1977b: XIV.2; 1978c: B.3; 1983: 3) and set up a procedure, which approved most applications. In 1985–6, 20 employed barristers were certified to perform conveyancing and have direct access to private practitioners; another 270 had only direct access (Senate, Annual Statement, 1983–4: 48; 1984–5: 47; 1985–6: 75). The Bar Association for Commerce, Finance and Industry (BACFI) also persuaded the Senate to allow employed barristers the same rights of audience that solicitors enjoy in the lower courts (135 *NLJ* 138, 1985).

### *Industry and commerce*

In 1962 it was estimated that there were 800–900 employed barristers in the private sector (Megarry, 1962: 6; Wheatcroft, 1962; Zander, 1968: 163); by 1978 the number was said to have grown to 3000 (Royal Commission, 1979: vol. 1: 232). Most work for the larger companies – in 1967, those with assets over £100 million (Zander, 1968: 179; see also Cohen, 1984). Although salaries are high, they do not equal the incomes enjoyed by the most successful private practitioners, perhaps because employment offers much greater security at the early stages of a career. Nevertheless, salaries have been rising: £5000–6000 in 1972, £7000–8000 in 1974 and £9000–10,000 in 1976 (*Solicitors' Journal*, 1972; Senate, 1977c: 17). Salary increases with age, peaking in the early fifties (Royal Commission, 1979, vol. 2: 623). The 1976 median of £9750 compared favourably with the average for private practitioners of £8715; but employed barristers retained their advantage only in the early years. Those under 30 made half again as much as private practitioners (£6089 versus £3970); those in their thirties made about as much as private practitioners 30–34 years old (£8303 versus £8081) but less than those 35–39 years old (£10,534); and employed barristers remained behind in the later years (ibid.: 602, 626). The professional association of employed barristers enrolled 576 members in 1977, 800 in 1985; it is seeking to expand by involving barristers employed in government and academia (ibid.: 622; 135 *NLJ* 138, 1985).

### *Government*

There are very few barristers in local government (compared with the number of solicitors) because barristers, until recently, could not perform an essential function – conveyancing. In 1962 they were only 2.9 per cent of town clerks (the chief executive officer) (Zander, 1968: 179; Wheatcroft, 1962: 15); in 1978, there were only 60 barristers in local government, compared with 1700 solicitors (Royal Commission, 1979, vol. 1: 232; Local Government Group, 1977; see generally Hamm, 1986).

On the other hand, barristers are overrepresented in central government, where they hold nearly half the positions, even though there are about five times as many qualified solicitors (Drewry, 1981: 30; see table 4.4). Central government did not begin to employ lawyers in significant numbers until well into the twentieth century. In 1877, only eight departments besides the Treasury had legal divisions. The Director of Public Prosecutions was formed only in 1879, the Lord Chancellor's Department in 1885, the Legal Adviser to the Foreign Office in 1876 and the Home Office Legal Adviser in 1933 (Drewry, 1981: 18–19). A Law Officers' Department was created only in 1893; before then, the officers of the Crown (the Attorney-General and Solicitor-General) practised from their chambers in the Inns and were allowed to retain their private clients (Edwards, 1964: 141; Duman, 1982: 13). Even after that date, the government minimized the number of barristers it employed by briefing juniors in private practice (known, confusingly, as 'devils') (ibid.: 143). One reason for this arrangement was that barristers employed by the government (aside from the Attorney General and the Solicitor General) could not appear in court. A legal secretary was appointed head of the Law Officers' Department in 1931, and two legal assistants were added in 1964, but that was the entire staff (ibid.: 151). There were 332 barristers in central government in 1961 (Wheatcroft, 1962: 15; see also Griffith, 1961). In 1964, there were 15 in the Legal Adviser's Department of the Foreign Office, 16 in the Parliamentary Counsel's Office and 13 in the Lord Chancellor's Office (Abel-Smith and Stevens, 1967: 444–5). In addition, barristers dominated the Charity Commissioner, the Colonial Office and the Director of Public Prosecutions (Johnstone and Hopson, 1967: 376 n. 55). Yet with the exception of a few elite departments, central government has never been very attractive to barristers, for it offers neither the high starting salaries found in private employment nor the long-term prospects of wealth and status offered by private practice. In 1965, there were only 3 applications for some 50 vacancies (Abel-Smith and Stevens, 1968: 121).

Today there are between 400 and 450 barristers in central government offices (Drewry, 1981: 30; Zander, 1980: 5; see table 4.4). This suggests a growth of about a third in the last 20 years, whereas the number of barristers employed in the private sector and the number practising privately each has grown more than 200 per cent. The largest concentrations are in Customs and Excise (see MacFarlane, 1986), Employment, Environment and Transport, the Foreign and Commonwealth Office, Health and Social Services, the Home Office, Inland Revenue (see Easton, 1986), the Law Officers' Department, the Office of Fair Trading, the Parliamentary Counsel and the Director of Public Prosecutions. Furthermore, barristers head 23 of the 31 law offices even though they outnumber solicitors in only 13 (Drewry, 1981: 29–30; see table 4.4). In 1919, lawyers employed in central government formed their own association, the Civil Service Legal Society, which enrolled 250 members in 24 departments at the end of the first year; it now is the Legal Section of the First Division Association and claims 1000 members (solicitors as well as barristers) (Drewry, 1981: 21).

# 7

# The work of the Bar

The last 100 years have seen significant changes in the amount and range of work performed by barristers and in its distribution – the relative importance of different kinds of work and the type and degree of specialization. Barristers always have been specialized. Indeed, the amalgamation of several professional categories during the nineteenth century actually reduced specialization by court (see chapter 2, p. 36). Throughout the century, many barristers held minor judicial and administrative offices (which may have provided a secure, if small, income necessary to survive the early years of practice, which barristers today derive from legal aid); they were commissioners in bankruptcy (abolished in London in 1831 and in the provinces in the 1860s), revising barristers and recorders or part-time borough Quarter Sessions judges (Duman, 1983a: 96–7). Even the Judicature Acts, which eliminated many specialized courts, did not obliterate the differences between the common law Bar (which practised in Queen's Bench Division and at assizes), the Chancery Bar, barristers who appeared before the Privy Council, those who practised in the courts of Admiralty, Probate and Divorce, parliamentary counsel and specialists in conveyancing and patent law (Abel-Smith and Stevens, 1967: 211).

These specializations still exist, and others have been added: revenue law, town and country planning law, pensions, transport tribunals, rating, building arbitration, national insurance, banking, company law and criminal law (Senate, 1976a: 18; Abel-Smith and Stevens, 1968: 104). Almost all provincial barristers are common law practitioners (Hazell, 1978b: 17–18). But in London, a substantial number of sets are known for their specialities: in 1967, there were six in tax, six in patents, two in Admiralty, two in shipping, about six in heavy commercial matters, two in defamation and others in criminal law, local government and conveyancing (Abel-Smith and Stevens, 1968: 104). Thus about one out of seven London sets specialized in 1967, and the proportion almost certainly has grown. This is another indication that chambers are becoming the significant unit of production despite the fact that barristers cannot form partnerships.

As specialization has increased there have been major reallocations in the time barristers devote to different subjects. The most important shift has been from civil matters to criminal. In the early nineteenth century (1843), criminal work was thought to be disreputable as well as unprofitable; not surprisingly, it represented only 10 per cent of barrister income (Abel-Smith and Stevens, 1967: 32). This has changed dramatically. In 1975, 63 per cent of judicial time was devoted to criminal matters in the Crown Court, whereas civil matters occupied only 9 per cent of the High Court's time and 23 per cent in the county courts (Munby, 1978: 185). In the quarter century 1958–83, the number of county court proceedings increased 63 per cent, and the number of original High Court proceedings doubled, while full trials of indictable offences increased 161 per cent, and summary trials grew more than fourfold (see tables 5.1, 5.2). In 1974–5, more than half the income of juniors was derived from criminal matters and just under half that of all barristers (see table 1.30).

Because criminal work pays relatively poorly (see chapter 8), barristers have had to specialize in order to generate the volume necessary to achieve profitability. Thus, there is a category of criminal law practitioners in both London and the provinces who spend virtually all their time (85–97 per cent) in the Crown Courts (Coopers & Lybrand, 1985a: 11). Furthermore, although English criminal procedure long has boasted that the barrister who prosecutes one day may defend the next, this rarely happens in practice (and will become even less frequent with the establishment of the Crown Prosecution Service). A 1976–7 study of London barristers who derived 90 per cent of their income from criminal work found that a third worked exclusively for either prosecution or defence, and 55 per cent devoted at least 70 per cent of their time to one side (Bar Council, n.d.b). A contemporaneous study agreed that only 30–40 per cent of barristers practising in Crown courts worked for both sides (Zander, 1976). Civil work is also strongly specialized. Personal injury is the largest single category – three-quarters of all cases in the Queen's Bench Division (Munby, 1978: 181). Since the number of deaths and serious injuries on the roads and railways and in industry has actually declined since World War II (see tables 5.5, 5.6), this predominance may have been even greater in the past. On the other hand, divorce, which accounts for most of the rest of the High Court caseload, increased

570 per cent in the quarter century 1958–83, although the number stabilized after 1977 (see table 5.3).

Many factors influence the mix of work that barristers perform. One is the rate of profit. Interlocutory work is notoriously underpaid: barristers earned less than £10 in 77 per cent of a sample of personal injury matters heard between 1970 and 1974 and more than £15 in only 2 per cent of the sample (Zander, 1975: 679). In personal injury cases, barristers earned only £32 for the average pretrial settlement but £271 for cases settled at the door of the court and £284 for cases that went to trial (ibid.: 682). But though these differences generate a strong incentive to litigate, it is important to remember that: barristers are entitled to their brief fees even if the cases are settled before trial; 46 per cent of cases are settled after the brief fee is paid and before trial; and the brief fee is rarely waived, although the barrister is entitled to do so (Zander, 1974; Hazell, 1978c: 112). At the other end of the reward hierarchy, commercial and Chancery QCs spend 15–20 per cent of their time abroad – in Hong Kong, Singapore, Bermuda, Barbados and other former colonies – because the fees for such work are substantially higher than those they can charge at home (Hughes, 1985).

A second factor affecting the mix of work is court jurisdiction, for barristers enjoy a monopoly only in the higher courts and must compete with solicitors in magistrates' and county courts. In the late 1940s, the Bar successfully fought to preserve exclusive High Court jurisdiction in divorce (even though the cases actually were heard by county court judges sitting as special divorce commissioners). But in 1967, jurisdiction was transferred to the county courts, with the result that solicitors quickly obtained about half the work (Munby, 1978: 180; Elston et al., 1975: 613).

But in recent years, by far the greatest influence on barristers' work, has been legal aid. Indeed, it hardly overstates the case to say that legal aid paid for the doubling of the Bar since the late 1960s: 40 per cent of barrister income came from public funds in 1983 (33 *NLJ* 1052, 1983). The civil legal aid budget grew tenfold from 1970 to 1983, the criminal legal aid budget more than twentyfold (see table 5.10). The total legal aid budget, which was £94.7 million in 1980, grew to £259 million in 1984 and was expected to reach £360 million in 1986–7 (Lord Chancellor's Department, Legal Aid Annual Report, 1980–1: 49). Legal aid payments to counsel increased from just under £3 million in 1975–6 to £17.5 million in 1983–4 – almost sixfold in eight years (Lord Chancellor's Department, Legal Aid Annual Reports). It is legal aid (and to a lesser extent state payment of 'private' practitioners for prosecution) that explains the incredible growth in criminal law work. Barristers earn 90 per cent of their income from the state in criminal matters but only 15 per cent in civil matters (see table 1.31). In the Crown Court in 1977, legal aid paid for 97 per cent of the representation of accused tried on indictment and 99 per cent of proceedings relating to sentence (Royal Commission, 1979, vol. 1: 156). The growth of legal aid also paralleled (and partly caused) the rise in matrimonial work: in 1975–6, 87 per cent of the 208,000 civil legal aid certificates concerned matrimonial and family matters; two years later, after the government withdrew legal aid for undefended divorces, family matters still accounted for 74 per cent of the 149,000 legal aid certificates issued (ibid.: 107). The increase in divorces from 1951 to 1981 (38,489 to 176,162) closely tracks the rise in civil legal aid certificates granted (37,772 to 270,451) (see tables 5.3, 5.10). Nevertheless, the Bar derives a much smaller proportion of its income from civil legal aid than from criminal (see table 1.34). Eighty per cent of the public funds paid to barristers in 1983 went to criminal practitioners (33 *NLJ* 1052, 1983).

Barristers depend on public payments to very different degrees. Many earn little or nothing: in 1975–6, three-quarters earned less than £1000; in 1983–4, half earned less than £2000. At the other extreme, a small number earn most of their income from legal aid: in 1975–6, 10 per cent earned more than £2000 and 3 per cent more than £4000; in 1983–4, 28 per cent earned more than £4000, 16 per cent more than £6000 and 9 per cent more than £8000 (see table 1.32). Although some of the change is attributable to inflation, the shift does suggest that an increasing proportion of the Bar is deriving much of its income from legal aid. The degree of dependence varies strongly with status, specialization and experience. In 1974–5, Queen's Counsel earned only a quarter of their income from the state, but juniors obtained half of theirs (see table 1.31). In 1981–2, the proportion of QC income derived from public funds had fallen to 18 per cent (Bar Council, n.d.a: table A). The disparities are even greater if status is combined with specialization: QCs with a specialized or Chancery practice in London received only 2 per cent of their income from legal aid in 1974–5 (1.5 per cent in 1976–7); juniors practising on circuit received 65 per cent from that source in 1974–5, and juniors with a London criminal practice received 91.7 per cent in 1976–7 (see table 1.33). Dependence on legal aid tends to decline as the junior barrister gains more than eight years of experience, though this is less true of civil than of criminal legal aid; on the other hand, the amount of prosecution work (which pays better) increases with experience (see table 1.34; Zander, 1976). One consequence is that more experienced prosecutors consistently confront less experienced defence counsel. Finally, the effect of the three variables is additive: specialist

QCs who had taken silk at least two years earlier earned 1 per cent of their income from public funds in 1974–5; juniors with four to eight years experience practising on circuit earned 72 per cent (see table 1.35).

The increasing dependence of the Bar on public funds has very important consequences. It creates a division between barristers who earn little and those who earn most of their income from public funds – a division that largely parallels age differences (and therefore also gender) and is deepening. Animosities between the two categories are visible in struggles over governance (see chapter 9). The experience of being a barrister has changed radically for those who are paid by the public purse. The Bar traditionally has operated in a market in which it has wielded considerable economic power by virtue of its control over production and the fact that most consumers are relatively unorganized. Now barristers must deal with the state. Where barristers' clerks used to mark brief fees before the work was done, taxing masters (who are state employees) now set those fees after the fact. The state often is even worse than private clients about paying promptly for services rendered. In 1982–3, the Bar negotiated payment on account for civil legal aid; 2564 barristers made claims concerning 23,615 certificates and received £3,935,924; in 1984, another £2 million was paid for 15,551 claims (Senate, Annual Statement, 1983–84: 54).

Most important, it is the state that establishes the fee schedule; all the Bar can do is seek to influence the decision. To this end, it has commissioned research on the earnings of barristers, particularly those specializing in criminal defence (134 *NLJ* 593, 1984). The most comprehensive was the Coopers & Lybrand study submitted to the Lord Chancellor in September 1985, on the basis of which the Bar urged an increase of 30–40 per cent in legal aid fees. The Lord Chancellor summarily rejected this request and, without further negotiation, raised fees only 5 per cent. The following day more than 1000 members attended a previously scheduled extraordinary general meeting of the Bar and unanimously deplored the Lord Chancellor's actions, narrowly refraining from a boycott of prosecution briefs by voting to challenge the decision in court (Senate, Annual Statement, 1985–6: 32–41). The divisional court agreed to review the matter (83 *LSG* 666, 1986). In the end, the Lord Chancellor and the Bar settled the case by conducting further negotiations (1(3) *Counsel* 25, 1986). Much of the dispute has come to turn on the interpretation of statistics: where Coopers & Lybrand assumed that a guilty plea took 2 hours, the Lord Chancellor's Department (LCD) found that it took only 0.7 hours; where Coopers & Lybrand assumed that an appeal against sentence required 5 hours of preparation, the LCD thought this excessive for a proceeding that consumed only half an hour of court time. The Bar sought to bolster its claim by invoking the salaries of barristers in the civil service, though this seems somewhat inconsistent with the Bar's perennial boast that the independence of private practitioners renders them unique. But the LCD rejected the comparison (83 *LSG* 577, 611 and 618–19, 1986; *Financial Times* 4, 10 February 1986). In July 1986, the Lord Chancellor finally awarded the Bar an additional 3 per cent increase (on top of the 5 per cent initially offered) plus another 2 per cent if the Bar would change its working practices (83 *LSG* 2282–7, 1986). It seems clear who won this battle. At about the same time, the Lord Chancellor's Department published its Legal Aid Scrutiny Report, which recommended (among other things) that special authority be required before counsel was instructed in the county courts – a measure it expected to save the government £2 million a year (136 *NLJ* 622, 1986).

These controversies, which are certain to be renewed, indicate the extraordinary transformation wrought by legal aid. The Bar as a collectivity is negotiating with the state; these negotiations are couched in the language of statistics and comparability; and though the state has ultimate authority, some barristers are prepared to take industrial action. Two public organizations contesting within the political arena have displaced private individuals negotiating within the market.

# 8

# Barrister income

It is extremely difficult to make meaningful statements about barrister income: statistics are unavailable, unreliable and uncomparable; and there is greater variation within the profession than between it and many other professions. In this chapter I will present the limited data in order to trace changes over time, compare the Bar with other professions and explore the dimensions of internal variation.

Time series data are subject to sharp, significant jumps because the total income of the Bar is small enough that annual fluctuations can deviate greatly from long-term trends; in 1976–7, the total income of barristers was only £30 million (Glasser, 1980: 31). Median barrister income appears to have been fairly stable during the first half of the twentieth century, probably because it was contained by the depression; the retail price index in 1934 was also at almost the same level as in 1907 (see table 4.7). Immmediately after World War II, barrister income rose steeply and continued to do so through the early 1970s (see table 1.36). In the years between 1939 and 1954–5 it increased 210 per cent, while the retail price index increased 284 per cent (ibid.). The sharpest rise appears to have occurred at the end of this period: between 1969–70 and 1975–6, income increased 75–100 per cent (see table 1.37). In the first half of the century the gain was both absolute and relative: 596 per cent between 1913–14 and 1955–6, compared with an increase in the cost of living of only 425 per cent between 1913–14 and 1960 (Routh, 1980: 60, 63). Since the early 1970s, however, the substantial absolute increases actually have signified a decline relative to the cost of living. Between 1974–5 and 1976–7, the net profits of barristers rose 15 per cent, but retail prices increased 44 per cent and weekly earnings 51 per cent (Royal Commission, 1979, vol. 1: 517). Between 1976–7 and 1981–2, on the other hand, barrister earnings substantially outstripped inflation, with the result that for the entire period between 1974–5 and 1981–2, barristers basically held their own (see table 1.38).

This pattern is consistent with the interpretation offered earlier. The control over supply, which the Bar exercised through the 1960s, combined with the postwar economic boom to produce a substantial rise in earnings. This rendered the Bar more attractive to undergraduates at the same time that state-supported legal education reduced the cost of qualifying and legal aid payments cushioned the early years of practice. The resulting growth in the production of barristers from the late 1960s created a large cohort of beginners with very low earnings, thereby depressing the median income of the Bar, although senior juniors and QCs may well have continued to enjoy rising living standards (see the figures for 1974–6 in table 1.36, which exclude low earners; compare the increases in the incomes of juniors and QCs between 1976–7 and 1981–2 in table 1.38). Indeed, the proportion of barristers earning less than £500 remained fairly constant (12.6–18.8 per cent) between 1967 and 1979 *despite* inflation, whereas the proportion earning high incomes increased dramatically: from 7.1 per cent to 24.7 per cent for those earning £6000–12,000, from 1.0 to 18.1 per cent for those earning more (see table 1.42).

The median income of barristers consistently has been lower than that of solicitors, although the gap has narrowed somewhat with time (see tables 1.36, 1.40). Both barristers and solicitors fell way behind doctors and dentists in the immediate postwar era and then rapidly gained parity as the medical professions lost ground following the introduction of the National Health Service. In the 1970s, most professions enjoyed roughly comparable median incomes (if lowest earners are excluded). However, the 1976–7 medians again show barristers significantly behind the other professions, presumably as a result of the large cohort of novices – for the only category earning less than barristers is assistant solicitors and salaried partners, almost all of whom are relatively inexperienced. This interpretation is strengthened by looking at the highest deciles of each profession, where barristers earn almost as much as hospital doctors, significantly more than general medical practitioners and only slightly less than solicitors. And the fact that salaried barristers in industry have higher median incomes than private practitioners can only be because the former have higher starting salaries, since later in their careers they earn less (see table 1.40).

As I indicated at the outset, however, medians conceal more than they illuminate because of differences within each profession. This is particularly true of barristers. Throughout the present century, the Bar has displayed greater internal variation than any comparable occupation

(Routh, 1980: 61). Median barrister income was only 11 per cent of the highest decile in 1913–14, 17 per cent in 1922–3 and 25 per cent in 1955–6; among doctors, dentists and solicitors the ratio was 30 per cent at the first date, 30–40 percent at the second and 40–65 per cent at the third (ibid.). This remains true even when we control for age; in 1955–6, the coefficient of variation for barrister income was 57 per cent, compared with 30 per cent for solicitors, 22 per cent for accountants and less for other occupations (Lees, 1966: 38 n. 1). Between 1974–5 and 1981–2 the ratio of the highest decile of barristers to the lowest remained roughly 10:1 (see table 1.44). This spread between top and bottom is a product of two factors – the depressed earnings of beginners and the extraordinary incomes of high-flyers – both of which are attributable to the fact that barristers produce services as individual entrepreneurs rather than in larger productive units.

As the figures just cited indicate, these disparities were even greater in the past than they are today. In 1850, it was estimated that 5 barristers earned £11,000 a year, 8 earned £8000 and 24 earned £5000, but most juniors made only £500–1200 (Reader, 1966: 200–1). Among a sample of 208 barristers who became judges between 1727 and 1875, 20 had earned about £10,000 when they ascended to the bench, and towards the end of this period a few had earned more than £20,000 (Duman, 1982: 106–7 table 8). The incomes of the highest earners increased during the succeeding 50 years and consistently exceeded those of any other profession (Duman, 1983a: 144–5, 148). In 1928, Lord Maugham earned £25,000 at the Chancery Bar and Lord Birkett £30,000 at the common law Bar (Abel-Smith and Stevens, 1967: 243 n. 1), although median barrister income could not have been much more than £600 – a ratio of 50:1. Even in 1983, *The Economist* estimated that some QCs grossed more than £200,000, though this is probably only about ten times the median income of all barristers (*Economist*, 1983: 47; Bar Council, n.d.a). And the Bar's own survey of remuneration during 1981–2 (26 per cent response rate) found that the highest decile of QCs grossed £163,000 (33 *NLJ* 1052, 1983). The gradual convergence of the extremes (although they still are further apart at the Bar than in any other profession) presumably reflects the emergence of legal aid as a source of income for beginners and the increasing significance of chambers as a unit of production.

Barrister income varies with status, age, experience and speciality – all of which are also indices of the degree of dependence on public funds (see chapter 7). The great divide is between QCs and juniors – that is, after all, the purpose of the distinction, which has grown in salience as the Bar's control over the production of barristers has eroded. In 1971, it was estimated that the median income for all QCs was twice that for all juniors of more than 12 years call – groups with roughly equivalent seniority (Office of Manpower Economics, 1974: 154–5). In 1974–5, 1975–6, 1976–7 and 1981–82, the median income of all QCs consistently was more than three times that of all juniors – an indication that the median income of juniors has been depressed by the flood of entrants while that of QCs has been sustained by the perpetuation of supply control (see table 1.41). In 1974–5, QCs appointed at least two years earlier earned seven times as much as juniors with less than four years of experience (Review Body, 1978: 108). The highest decile of QCs earned £29,600, the lowest decile of juniors £800; the median QC earned £16,300, the median junior £4800 (Zander, 1980: 30). In 1976–7, the highest quartile of QCs earned nearly three times as much as the highest quartile of juniors and more than seven times as much as the lowest quartile (see table 1.41). Forty-six per cent of QCs earned more than £20,000, compared with 3 per cent of juniors; two-thirds of QCs earned more than £15,000, compared with 7 per cent of juniors (Royal Commission, 1979, vol. 2: 601). In 1981–2, the highest quartile of QCs earned three and a half times as much as the highest quartile of juniors and nearly nine times as much as the lowest quartile (see table 1.41). Nor are overheads proportional to earnings: QCs paid 27 per cent of their gross income in 1974–5, while juniors paid 33 per cent; the following year the percentages were 31 and 36 (INBUCON, 1977: table 27).

Some of these differences can be attributed to age and experience. Indeed, the age spread in incomes is greater at the Bar than in other professions (see table 1.40). Even in 1955–6, before the influx of the large cohort of younger barristers (but also before the expansion of legal aid), barristers under 35 earned only a quarter as much as barristers 45–54 (Doctors and Dentists, 1960: 282). Age has an impact within the two major status categories as well. The income of juniors triples during the first 15 years, after which it declines for those who do not take silk (see table 1.41). Furthermore, the incomes of younger juniors increased more rapidly between 1976–7 and 1981–2 than those of more senior juniors (see table 1.39). For QCs, the increase with experience is more gradual (Doctors and Dentists, 1960: 282; Zander, 1980: 31–3; see tables 1.41, 1.43).

Specialization also affects income. One survey found that the upper half of the London Chancery and specialist Bars earned one and a half to two times as much as general practitioners in London, although this relationship was reversed in the lower half (INBUCON, 1977: tables 14, 15). Another survey found that London Chancery and specialist QCs made one and a third to one and a half times as much as other QCs, and juniors with a London Chancery and specialist practice made one and a third to one and three-quarters as much as other juniors (see table 1.41). At the other extreme, London criminal practitioners earned less than the Bar median (ibid.). Their incomes rise little with experience, unlike those of practitioners in other categories (see table 1.44). Between 1976–7 and 1981–2, the incomes of criminal practitioners (both QCs and juniors) increased more slowly than those of family and common law or Chancery and specialist barristers (see table 1.39). Between 1982–3 and 1983–4, the earnings of criminal practitioners remained relatively static, and those of London specialists devoting more than 90 per cent of their time to criminal law actually declined (see table 1.45). This, of course, reflects the low level of legal aid fees and was the reason for the Bar's (unsuccessful) demand for a major increase. Differences among specialities persist when we control for age (see table 1.42).

Barristers increasingly have been attracted to employment outside private practice (see chapter 6, p. 111; Grand Metropolitan Ltd, 1976; Bar Association for Commerce, Finance and Industry, 1977). The salaries of lawyers employed in industry (both barristers and solicitors) have risen steadily since the mid 1970s at rates that generally exceeded inflation (1974–5: 24.3 per cent; 1975–6, 9.3 per cent; 1976–7, 3.8 per cent; 1977–8, 12.9 per cent; 1978–9, 17.0 per cent; 1979–80, 24.5 per cent; 1980–1, 18.4 per cent; 1981–2, 11.8 per cent; 1982–3, 12.4 per cent; 1983–4, 8.8 per cent; 1984–5, 9.8 per cent) (Chambers & Partners, 1985: table 2). Surveys by BACFI found a 17 per cent increase in salary between 1982 and 1984, during a period in which the retail price index rose only 10 per cent (82 *LSG* 919, 1985). For the years in which comparable figures are available for private practitioners, employed lawyers appear to have done better (see table 1.38). Between 1974–5 and 1981–2, the average income of private practitioners rose 157 per cent while the minimum income of senior legal assistants increased 189 per cent and the maximum income 206 per cent (Bar Council, n.d.a). The Bar Association for Commerce, Finance and Industry has estimated that employed barristers earned a median salary of £18,000–19,900 in 1982, compared with a median of £10,000–15,000 for private practitioners (ibid.). The differences are most marked for beginners. Among barristers who took their undergraduate degrees in 1978, private practitioners were earning £5250 by March 1981, whereas employed barristers were earning £7280. Among barristers who took their degrees in 1981, London practitioners were making £7080 in 1983 and provincial practitioners £6500, whereas employed barristers were making £8110. Similarly, a survey by the Bar Association for Commerce, Finance and Industry found that only 2 per cent of employed barristers were making less than

£8000 in 1982, compared with 25 per cent of private practitioners (Bar Council, n.d.a). I mentioned above the Bar Council's claim that legal aid fees would have to be increased 30–40 per cent in order for the specialist criminal practitioner to earn an income comparable with that of a barrister in the civil service with equivalent experience (Coopers & Lybrand, 1985a). But though the career structure of employment does offer considerable scope for advancement, each survey also found that the gap between the two categories diminished with experience (AGCAS, 1984a: 11; 1984b: 4–5). In 1985, legal assistants averaged £21,755, legal advisers £29,992 and senior legal advisers £44,408 (Chambers & Partners, 1985: table 2). And most employed lawyers have the use of a company car, a pension scheme and other benefits (ibid.). Nevertheless, there are fewer high-flyers. In 1982, 4.7 per cent of employed barristers earned more than £40,000, compared with 7.7 per cent of the private Bar (Bar Council, n.d.a). Even so, employment seems likely to attract an increasing proportion of barristers: it offers a paid pupillage; it avoids the scramble for tenancies at the end of the pupillage; it guarantees an income; and the income is likely to be higher than that attainable in private practice for many years. Of course, the greater supply of barristers will affect the employment market as well; but employers may choose to seek better credentials rather than reduce labour costs.

Finally, income varies with geography. In 1955–6 (before the erosion of supply control), the median income of barristers with chambers in London was twice that of provincial barristers (Doctors and Dentists, 1960: 282). The lower pace of work outside London is suggested by the fact that the number of court days per month per active barrister ranged from 9.2 on the Northern circuit to 22.6 on the Western (Bar and Quarter Sessions, 1971). Nevertheless, though the regional disparity still prevailed in 1970 among QCs, whose supply remained tightly controlled, by 1976–7 juniors on circuit made more than London juniors practising family and common law or criminal law, particularly during the earlier years of practice (see tables 1.41, 1.42). And there is evidence of the same reversal in the 1980s (AGCAS, 1984a: 11; 1984b: 4–5; see table 1.45). This suggests that the enormous increase in beginners has affected practice in London more than in the provinces.

# 9

# Governance and discipline

Given the early date at which barristers acquired the trappings of a profession, it is not surprising that they are governed by a multiplicity of institutions with overlapping jurisdictions and very different structures. The circuits and the Inns embody traditional modes of organization. The Bar Council reflects nineteenth-century pressures to professionalize, especially competition with solicitors; in recent years it has taken on a new role as the forum in which younger dissidents express their dissatisfactions. Finally, the Senate represents postwar attempts to rationalize administration.

## The circuits

Throughout most of the nineteenth century, the circuits rivalled the Inns as centres of social and professional life (Cocks, 1983: ch. 2 and p. 214). For the first half of the century they remained sufficiently small to exercise considerable control over their members by means of informal sanctions (see table 1.25; even these figures overstate actual attendance). The circuits influenced entry and conduct through relatively unstructured patterns of authority that emerged gradually and depended on seniority and tradition (Cocks, 1976a).

These informal mechanisms broke down in the last quarter of the century. The circuits grew with the Bar (Cocks, 1976a: 37; see table 1.25). Some were reorganized to accommodate this expansion, creating larger units and disrupting accepted conventions. Barristers seeking admission, and even those who seconded them, were unknown to the regular members of the circuit mess (Cocks, 1983: 165–6). In any case, once informal barriers collapsed, the circuits lacked formal power to exclude anyone (ibid.: 148; Cocks, 1976a: 39). Attendance at circuit declined because the courts sat simultaneously in London and the provinces, and a provincial Bar emerged to represent litigants in the latter (Cocks, 1976a: 41; 1983: 125, 148, 152; see chapter 6, p. 102). Coincidentally, civil litigation on circuit declined between 1886 and 1906 (Abel-Smith and Stevens, 1967: 88, 94). Those circuits close to London lost their social functions as the railways allowed barristers to return home after a day in court rather than dine with the circuit mess (Cocks, 1983: 126, 156). Implicit rules of etiquette that generally had been observed (and that reflected geographic limitations before the railways) – such as the custom that a barrister could practise only on a single circuit – were not enforced by the new county courts (ibid.: 125). Circuit messes tried to deal with these problems by formalizing their rules and organizations, but the attempt failed (Cocks, 1976a). The creation of the Bar Council promised a more centralized institution to address the problems of barristers at the end of the nineteenth century. Yet the circuits still exercise both authority (over the opening of provincial chambers, for instance) and influence (over the appointment of silks and judges). And they remain a vehicle through which provincial barristers can voice their opinions within the newer governing bodies.

## The Inns

Although these are by far the oldest continuous professional associations of barristers (perhaps of any English occupation), they were in decline throughout the eighteenth and nineteenth centuries. They performed no significant educational functions. Although they offered a convenient gathering place for young men ostensibly preparing for the Bar, the circuits were at least as important foci for the social life of practising barristers (but see Duman, 1983a: 194–5). And until the end of the nineteenth century the Inns exercised little formal control over either entry into the profession or practice by barristers. Although they had exclusive jurisdiction over discipline until 1966, they used it sparingly (see 'Discipline', p. 133).

One reason for their relative inactivity and intense conservatism may have been the structures of governance. Each Inn was autonomous and refused to surrender any independence until the creation of the Senate in 1966. Although the Inns co-operated in creating the Council of Legal Education in 1852, they gave it few resources and little authority. Because the Inns differed significantly in size, wealth, income, prestige and tenants, their interests diverged as well. Furthermore, the internal governance of each Inn was archaic, gerontocratic and oligarchic. Although junior barristers once had played an important part, they were supplanted by silks during the nineteenth century (Duman, 1983a: 35–6). With the elimination of the rank of serjeant and the closure of Serjeants' Inn in 1875, judges returned to the Inns in which they had been called and also assumed a prominent role in governance.

In 1966, the 394 benchers who governed the four Inns consisted of: 71 honorary appointments (such as members of the royal family and aristocrats), 140 judges, 130 QCs, 10 academics and only 30 juniors. Thus, more than 90 per cent of the Bar was represented by less than 8 per cent of the governors. The benchers were unrepresentative in other ways as well. Of those whose appointments were not honorary, three-quarters were graduates of Oxbridge colleges, two-thirds were over 60 and 50 of the 323 were more than 76 years old (Abel-Smith and Stevens, 1968: 96). In the mid 1970s, judges constituted 45 per cent of the benchers, retired barristers another 25 per cent and juniors only 5 per cent, although they were 90 per cent of the practising Bar (N. Warren, 1978: 61). As we have seen above, women are grossly underrepresented, and there are no black barristers to represent the 5 per cent of the Bar who are black.

Because the benchers are a self-perpetuating oligarchy who choose their own successors, this is unlikely to change quickly (Royal Commission, 1979, vol. 1: 418). Some indication of the level of enthusiasm for reform may be seen in the Senate's response (1983: 8) to the Royal Commission's recommendation (1979, vol. 1: 444) that benchers retire at 70 – it referred the matter to the Inns! Although the Inns no longer control entry or discipline (except through their influence within the Council of Legal Education and the Senate), they still exercise extraordinary control over the profession in their role as landlords, determining who shall have space within the Inns and how much it will cost. And despite repeated challenges, only the benchers are privy to the accounts of the Inns – which are essential for evaluating rental policies (Senate, 1983: 7).

## The Bar council

In the last two decades of the nineteenth century, a number of factors converged to stimulate interest in new structures of governance. The circuits were declining in importance. The great majority of barristers had lost control over the Inns to silks and judges. In any case, neither institution met the growing need for centralized action. At the same time, critics inside and out saw barristers losing status to solicitors, now led by the Law Society. And junior barristers were fearful that the changes introduced by the Judiciary Acts and the new rules of court would mean a loss of business; they were also alarmed by talk of fusion (Cocks, 1983: 154, 215; Hazell, n.d.: 1). A meeting called to discuss these matters drew over 2000 barristers – certainly more than half the practising Bar. Although barristers lost the fight against the rules of court, they did form the Bar Committee in 1883. But though the new organization cut across membership in the Inns for the first time, it experienced all the problems inherent in voluntary associations. The 257 barristers who launched the Bar Committee quickly secured a total of 566 subscriptions; but the number of people voting declined from 800 to 367 in 1892, and the number paying the half guinea subscription fell to 200. The moribund organization was revived under the name of the Bar Council in 1893 at a meeting attended by 800, and 1700–1800 voted in its first elections in 1895 (General Council of the Bar, Annual Statements; Abel-Smith and Stevens, 1967: 215; Duman, 1980: 623 and nn. 40–2). Thereafter membership grew steadily, reaching a very respectable 90 per cent of all private practitioners in 1968 (though much smaller proportions of employed barristers) (Zander, 1968: 2). By a narrow margin, the Bar Council rejected compulsory membership (Hazell, n.d.: 35).

Apart from the proceeds of its very small subscription fee, the Bar Council has been dependent on the Inns for finance, and the latter have been singularly ungenerous. In 1895, each Inn agreed to donate £150 per year on condition that the Bar Council not interfere in Inn affairs; this was increased to £250 a year in 1909 (Abel-Smith and Stevens, 1967: 216, 219 n. 3). As late as 1968 the contribution was only £900 per Inn and actually fell to £810 between 1969 and 1972 before growing to £1,400 for the years 1973 and 1974 (Hazell, n.d.: 8 n. 12). The Bar Council has never had jurisdiction over discipline, which remained with the Inns until 1966. Its primary concern, consistent with its origins, has been to promote the interests of barristers. In 1892 it agreed that barristers could take instructions only through solicitors; in 1902 it insisted that silks be accompanied by juniors (Hazell, n.d.: 2–3). It was relatively dormant between the wars, perhaps because barristers were content with the control they exercised over their market (Carr-Saunders and Wilson, 1933: 17–18). After World War II it became increasingly concerned with fees and effectively tripled barrister income in a few years (Abel-Smith and Stevens, 1967: 409; Hazell, n.d.: 10–11).

In recent years, the Bar Council has taken on new life. First, it has become the primary vehicle through which barristers negotiate with the state over the scope of legal aid and the level of fees – negotiations that have become increasingly acerbic (see chapter 7). Second, the critical importance of public funds for the economic wellbeing of most juniors has focused renewed attention on the composition of the Bar Council. It has always been a more representative institution than either the Inns (see 'The Inns', p. 128) or the Senate (see 'The Senate', p. 131). In the 1930s, a majority of the Council was elected; half of the elected members had to be juniors, and an eighth within ten years of call (Carr-Saunders and Wilson, 1933: 17). Today, the Bar Council consists of: the chairman and vice-chairman of the Senate (the latter is also chairman elect), selected by the Bar Committee, the Council's executive body; 9 members *ex officio* (the treasurer of the Senate, the Attorney-General and Solicitor-General and the 6 circuit leaders); 33 elected representatives, 18 of whom must be juniors, 6 under seven years of call; 2 members each nominated by the Bar Association for Commerce, Finance and Industry, the Legal Section of the Association of First Division Civil Servants and the Bar Association for Local Government and the Public Service; and up to 12 co-opted members. This reserves only 30 per cent of the places to the 90 per cent of the practising Bar who are juniors; it guarantees only 10 per cent to employed barristers, about half of all those called who are performing legal functions; and it ensures only 10 per cent of the places for those under seven years of call – more than a quarter of the practising Bar and perhaps a higher proportion of employed barristers (Senate, Annual Statement, 1983–4: 19). In actuality, the Bar Council is both slightly more and considerably less representative than these figures suggest. In 1984–5, there were 25 juniors, though only the minimum of 6 under seven years of call; on the other hand, there were only 4 women – 7 per cent of the Council – in a Bar that is more than 12 per cent women. Furthermore, the Bar Committee (the executive of the Council) contained only 2 juniors in 1983–4 (82 *LSG* 1245, 1985).

The anger of younger barristers at what they saw as the failure of an unrepresentative Bar Council to press their case with the government led to the formation of the Campaign for the Bar in the spring and summer of 1985. It ran a slate of ten on a broad platform: opposing any expansion of solicitors' rights of audience, raising the level of funding for legal aid and criminal prosecutions, pressing solicitors to pay fee notes promptly, direct election of the chairman of the Bar, greater representation for younger barristers and provincial barristers, and a public relations campaign to improve the image of the Bar. The circumstances and demands closely parallel those that characterized the founding of the Bar Council by younger barristers almost exactly 100 years earlier. All members of the slate won with at least 62 per cent of the vote. It immediately urged that henceforth the chairman of the Bar be elected by a postal ballot of all practising barristers (excluding those employed). It also asked that all ten members of the slate be placed on the 25-person Bar Committee. The 1985 Senate AGM voted to put both resolutions to a postal ballot (Senate, Annual Statement, 1985–6: 16–22). And it promised to run a second slate in the 1986–7 elections (1(4) *Counsel* 15, 1986). Clearly, there will be further reorganization of the structure of the Bar Council to reflect the changing composition of the Bar and the very divergent interests of the different categories.

## The Senate

In 1966, the four Inns of Court created a Senate to co-ordinate their activities. Eight years later it incorporated the Bar Council. As the creature of the Inns, it assumed their disciplinary functions. They have also supported it far more generously than they ever did the Bar Council: in 1975–6 they contributed £80,000; ten years later the contribution had doubled (Hazell, n.d.: 8; Royal Commission, 1979, vol. 1: 432; Senate, Annual Statement, 1984–5). Its total income exceeds £500,000. But in return for this devolution of authority and financial support, the Inns retained considerable power. The Senate is composed of 6 representatives of the benchers of each of the four Inns; 3 representatives of each Inn who are not benchers; the 39 Bar Council representatives (described above); the president, chairman, vice-chairman and treasurer; and, *ex officio*, the Attorney-General, Solicitor-General, chairman of the Council of Legal Education and chairman of the Disciplinary Tribunal; and it can co-opt up to 16 additional members (Royal Commission, 1979: vol. 1: 430). In 1985, 32 of its 104 members were junior barristers (31 per cent), 6 were employed barristers (6 per cent); the rest were judges or silks; and women were less than 4 per cent (Senate, Annual Statement, 1984–5: 63–5). QCs are even more dominant in the Senate committees, in which much of the work is done (Hazell, n.d.: 33).

The unrepresentative quality of the Senate may explain why a fairly constant 10 per cent of the private Bar has not belonged during the decade 1974–5 to 1985–6 (another 5–10 per cent has failed to increase their payment levels as they have become more senior or taken silk); and only about half the estimated number of employed barristers subscribed. Furthermore, the proportion of non-subscribers was higher among younger barristers (who may feel unrepresented by it) and the most senior juniors (who may feel it can do nothing for them (see table 1.50). Nevertheless, the Senate (1983: 6) rejected the recommendations

(Royal Commission, 1979, vol. 1: 443) that its structure should be changed and laypersons co-opted on to committees. It argued that 'the great majority' of its members are elected and noted that laypersons do serve on the Professional Conduct Committee, the Disciplinary Tribunals and the Oral English Panels. Yet if the movement to democratize the Bar Council progresses, it seems inevitable that the Senate will have to accommodate, or it will be bypassed.

In 1986 the Rawlinson Committee on the Constitution of the Senate of the Inns of Court and the Bar submitted its report, recommending substantial changes in the governance of both bodies. The present Senate would be replaced by a bicameral body. Real power would reside with the General Council of the Bar and the Inns of Court, consisting of 93 barristers (not judges) representing the circuits, speciality bar associations, Inns and the Bar generally. A Treasurers' Council of the Inns would appoint and regulate disciplinary tribunals but otherwise could only refer matters back to the General Council, which could overrule the Treasurers' Council by a two-thirds vote. These proposals were supported by the Bar Council, the Bar Committee, the Inns (with reservations), the circuits, the Chancery Bar Association, the London Common Law Bar Association, the Bar Association for Commerce, Finance and Industry, the Family Law Bar Association and the Campaign for the Bar. Extraordinary general meetings of both the Senate and the Bar on 21 June also endorsed the recommendations by a vote of 1896 to 85. At the same time, the issue of compulsory membership in the new General Council was considered and approved by a postal ballot vote of 1831 to 150, although a motion to allow opting out was defeated by a smaller margin: 1270 to 499 (83 *LSG* 2493, 1986). Even so, membership fees will have to be doubled in order to pay the increased costs of discipline and of the staffing changes recommended by the Coopers & Lybrand report (83 *LSG* 1278 and 2321–4, 1986; Senate of the Inns of Court and the Bar, notice of a ballot of the practising Bar, 1 August 1986).

## Speciality and regional associations

Real power within the profession lies with the Inns and the Senate, although these are being challenged by the Bar Council. Nevertheless (or perhaps because these institutions are so resistant to change), barristers have formed a number of associations to represent more specialized interests and to exchange information, including the Criminal Bar Association, the London Common Law and Commercial Bar Association, the Administrative Law Bar Association, the Bar Association for

Commerce, Finance and Industry, the Legal Section of the Assocation of First Division Civil Servants (for barristers employed in central government), the Bar Association for Local Government and the Public Service, the Local Government and Planning Bar Association, the Chancery Bar Association, and the Probate and Divorce Bar Association. And each of the major provincial centres has a local Bar association (2(1) *Counsel* 9 and 11, 1986; Caplan, 1978: 146; Johnstone and Hopson, 1967: 364–5).

## Discipline

Professional associations, like those described above, engage in a wide variety of activities: exchanging information, providing benefits and services, lobbying and negotiating with the government, promoting the economic interests of their members, overseeing the education of entrants and practitioners, engaging in public relations and seeking to reform the law and legal institutions. But two functions are essential for any occupation that claims to be a profession: control over the market and control over the behaviour of its members. I have described the forms of market control that the Bar enjoyed at the beginning of the nineteenth century and the ways in which these have been transformed and eroded (see chapters 2–5). Structures of self-regulation have undergone a similar evolution. Although the Inns long have claimed authority to discipline their members (and so did the circuit messes until the end of the nineteenth century), the first published account of barrister etiquette appeared only in 1875 (Duman, 1983a: 38; Cocks, 1983: 157). During the nineteenth century it was the Attorney General who formulated professional rules, not the Bar (Abel-Smith and Stevens, 1967: 217). Only with the creation of the Bar Council did the latter assume that role, although it had no authority to make binding rules (Carr-Saunders and Wilson, 1933: 19). The Royal Commission (1979, vol. 1: 310) recommended that the Bar promulgate written professional standards, and in 1980 the Senate published the Code of Conduct for the Bar of England and Wales (Senate, 1983: 3).

Efforts to centralize and institutionalize the disciplinary process failed in the 1860s, and only in 1896 were the judges of the Supreme Court allowed to hear appeals from benchers in disciplinary matters (Cocks, 1983: 170–2; Abel-Smith and Stevens, 1967: 217). Although the Bar Council never acquired the power to discipline, it did hear complaints and referred a few of them to the Inns (Carr-Saunders and Wilson, 1933: 18). Shortly after the Senate was established it assumed jurisdiction in disciplinary matters. Today complaints are reviewed by the Professional Conduct Committee of the Bar Council, which consists of 15 practising and non-practising barristers (including one employed barrister) and two laypersons. Unlike the governing bodies of the Bar Council and Senate, this committee is not dominated by QCs. It can recommend no action, admonish the barrister, report the matter to the treasurer of the barrister's Inn or transmit a charge to the Disciplinary Tribunal. The latter consists of four to six practising members of the Senate and a layperson. The lay members of both committees are selected from a panel named by the Lord Chancellor (Royal Commission, 1979, vol.1: 354–7). The Disciplinary Tribunal can dismiss the charges, reprimand, suspend or disbar. Recently it was empowered to exclude barristers from legal aid payments (Administration of Justice Act 1985 s. 42). A barrister who is punished by the Disciplinary Tribunal has a right of appeal to the judges who sit as visitors to the barrister's Inn (Royal Commission, 1979, vol. 1: 358).

All these institutions deal exclusively with misconduct, not incompetence, which constitutes misconduct only if blameworthy. Although complaints occasionally have alleged blameworthy incompetence, the Disciplinary Tribunal has never punished a barrister on this ground (Senate, 1977a: VII.3–4). Thus, the profession exercises no control over post-admission competence, despite the Royal Commission's recommendation that it take action on complaints of bad professional work (1979, vol. 1: 359). In an important decision in 1969, the Court of Appeal held that barristers were immune from civil liability for malpractice with respect to their conduct in the course of litigation but suggested, by way of dictum, that they might be liable for conduct outside litigation (*Rondel* v. *Worlsey* [1969] 1 AC 191). Between 1971 and 1978, four malpractice claims were settled by insurers for a total of £35,000 (Royal Commission, 1979, vol. 1: 333). In 1976, barristers could purchase £50,000 of insurance for an annual premium of only £5–20 (Senate, 1977a: IX.3–4). Finally, in October 1983, barristers were required to take out a minimum of £250,000 in indemnity insurance (Senate, Annual Statement, 1982–3: 75). Although I have no data about claims experience, it is noteworthy that the number of insurers in the field has declined in recent years from seven to two, while premiums in 1985 increased 50–80 per cent for criminal chambers, 100–150 per cent for civil, 500 per cent for the glossier commercial chambers and a staggering 1800 per cent for a set with a record of claims against tenants (135 *NLJ* 1132, 1985). The Senate anticipates further substantial increases (Annual Statement, 1985–6: 70).

How well does the disciplinary system function? First, it is entirely reactive, relying on complaints to initiate the process of investigation and hearing. The number of complaints is extremely small: fewer than 100 a year until the mid 1970s and only about 150 a year since then (see table 1.46). Furthermore, there are less than a fifth as many complaints per practising barrister as there are complaints per practising solicitor (compare tables 1.49 and 2.41). There are several reasons for these low numbers. Lay clients have the greatest stake in redressing misconduct and indeed file the majority of complaints: 58 per cent between 1972 and 1978 (see table 1.47). Yet the lay client – who has little direct contact with the barrister (since this is mediated by the solicitor) and is ignorant of the law, the rules of etiquette and performance standards – is in a poor position to perceive misconduct. The fact that nearly a quarter of complaints are filed by prisoners suggests that complaining is an act of desperation by those with low opportunity costs. Legal professionals, who are in the best position to witness and identify misconduct, seem singularly indisposed to report it: judges and court clerks filed only 14 per cent of complaints, solicitors 13 per cent and barristers a mere 8 per cent (ibid.). Another explanation for the low numbers may lie in the content of the grievances (see table 1.48). The single largest category – inadequate representation (nearly a quarter) – obviously originates with lay clients. If we include other matters that pertain to the barrister–client relationship – such as bad advice, acting without or contrary to instructions, lack of courtesy, withholding information, refusing to act, undue influence, conduct of proceedings and delay – then this category grows to nearly three-quarters of all complaints. Yet the Senate declines to act with respect to incomptence that is not 'blameworthy'. All this suggests that only a fraction of actual misconduct is reported. It is interesting, in this regard, that the ratio of complaints to barristers increased by more than half since the early 1970s (see table 1.49) – the period in which entry to the Bar accelerated – but it is impossible to know whether this signifies more frequent misconduct or a change in the perceptions and actions of complainants.

The ultimate test of a system of social control is the extent to which it punishes those who have committed offences. By this criterion, barrister discipline is highly suspect. The Bar Council dismissed three-quarters of all complaints between 1957 and 1974, finding no evidence of misconduct (see table 1.46.a). Its reconstituted Professional Conduct Committee dismissed 57 per cent of complaints between 1968 and 1985 for lack of evidence of any misconduct, and another 28 per cent were either withdrawn or handled informally or by summary procedures; thus, less than a quarter still went to formal hearing (see table 1.46.b). The Royal Commission recognized that lay clients often find it difficult to frame a complaint and to collect the relevant evidence, and it recommended that the Senate interview all lay complainants (1979, vol. 1: 354–5); but the latter rejected this suggestion (1983: 4). Yet the Professional Conduct Committee can be quite energetic on occasion, as when it investigated the conduct of barristers involved in the miners' strike and the defence of the Greenham Common protesters (Helm, 1985b).

Few barristers are punished in the very small number of cases that receive a formal hearing. Between 1968 and 1985, the Disciplinary Tribunal disbarred only 48 barristers, suspended 21, reprimanded 27 and dismissed the charges against 21 (in two other cases it either disbarred, suspended or reprimanded) (see table 1.46.b). To put the matter more strongly, less than 3 per cent of complaints during this period led to disbarment, and only 1 per cent resulted in suspension. This may be another reason for the low level of complaining: those aggrieved have little faith in the process. The Senate (1983: 4) rejected the Royal Commission recommendation (1979, vol. 1: 359) that it adopt less severe sanctions – such as fines or orders of further training – which it might be willing to use more often. Yet even with the low level of complaining, there is evidence that the Senate's disciplinary processes are being strained by the caseload. The budget for discipline increased more than sixfold in the seven years between 1977–8 and 1984–5, from £6948 to £39,350 (Senate, Annual Statements). Nevertheless, the backlog of cases pending before the Disciplinary Tribunal has been high since 1977 – several times the number of cases forwarded each year (see table 1.46.b).

# III

# Solicitors

# 10

# Controlling supply

## Origins

Unlike the Bar, the occupational category of attorneys and solicitors did not acquire real coherence until well into the nineteenth century. They lacked a collegiate institution like the Inns of Court to define boundaries and instil solidarity. Indeed, they had been expelled from the Inns in the sixteenth century (Kirk, 1976: 15). They enjoyed no monopoly comparable with the barristers' exclusive rights of audience in the higher courts. Attorneys and solicitors gradually accreted around two functions within the division of labour: acting as general agents for the gentry and other landowners and handling the necessary preliminaries to litigation. The first function led to the conveyancing monopoly, which has been the financial base of solicitors for at least two centuries; the second evolved into the role of essential intermediary between barristers and lay clients, as well as full responsibility for litigation in the local lower courts. In both capacities, the very characteristic that made it difficult for attorneys and solicitors to organize also gave them a market advantage: they were dispersed throughout the country and thus accessible to clients and near local courts, whereas the Bar was concentrated in London. But it is important to recognize that attorneys and solicitors acquired these functions only gradually and against considerable opposition, especially from barristers. Until the end of the nineteenth century, barristers maintained their right to perform conveyances and to deal directly with lay clients, if they rarely exercised these powers; and litigation only became a significant function for provincial solicitors with the creation of county courts and the decline of the circuits.

Similarly, there was little effective control over either who became an attorney or solicitor or their numbers. Each court established individual criteria and maintained its own Roll of authorized practitioners (attorneys were admitted by common law courts, solicitors by Chancery). These were not combined into a single Roll until 1843. Some courts insisted on a period of apprenticeship as early as the seventeenth century (Carr-Saunders and Wilson, 1933: 43–4). But the facts that an attorney or solicitor admitted in one court could gain admission to any other and that apprenticeship was policed loosely, if at all, made a mockery of these requirements. Throughout the seventeenth and eighteenth centuries there were constant complaints about the number and incompetence of solicitors and attorneys. The Act of 1729 was intended to remedy this: it instructed judges to examine candidates before admitting them to the Roll, required five years of articles, prohibited attorneys and solicitors from supervising more than two articled clerks at a time and specifically provided that the Act should not be construed to require or authorize the admission of more attorneys 'than by the ancient usage and custom of such court hath been heretofore allowed' (Holdsworth, 1938: 54–5). But these measures had little effect. In 1730–1, the first comprehensive review of the Rolls disclosed 2236 attorneys in Common Pleas and 893 in King's Bench and 1700 solicitors in Chancery (Birks, 1960: 139). Despite some duplication, the occupational category certainly was many times larger than the Bar, which was estimated to contain only 208 practising barristers in 1779 (see table 4.1). The number of solicitors and attorneys admitted to the Rolls increased fairly steadily from 262 in 1750 to 428 in 1790, an increase of nearly two-thirds (Birks, 1960: 142).

Attorneys and solicitors originally shared the first of their central functions, handling lucrative land transactions, with members of the Scriveners' Company, who had acquired a monopoly of that privilege within the City of London in 1712. Attorneys successfully attacked the monopoly in 1760, but they still had no means of preventing others (including laypersons) from performing conveyances (Abel-Smith and Stevens, 1967: 15–16; Birks, 1960: 148, 195). The second provincial law society was founded in Yorkshire in 1786, partly to seek limitations on licensed conveyancers (Lawton, 1986). Solicitors finally acquired their monopoly almost by chance. In 1785, the government imposed a stamp duty on the annual practising certificates held by attorneys and solicitors: £5 in London and £3 in the provinces. It also imposed a further duty on each conveyance they performed (Robson, 1959: 14; Kirk, 1976: 129–34; Christian, 1896: 131). In 1794, the government added a tax on articles – £100 in London and £50 in the provinces – and three years later it placed a duty of £8 on the certificate admitting the attorney or solicitor to the Roll (Kirk, 1976: 129–34).

As these actions show, the government had discovered at the end of the eighteenth century that attorneys and solicitors were an excellent source of revenue. Faced with the rising cost of the Napoleonic Wars, Pitt sought in 1804 to increase these charges, raising the stamp duty on annual practising certificates held by those who had practised for more than three years to £10 and £6 in London and the provinces and the duty on articles to £110 and £55, respectively. Attorneys and solicitors vigorously resisted and demanded recognition of their monopoly over conveyancing as a quid pro quo. The government readily granted this, enforcing it by a £50 fine for unauthorized conveyancing (Abel-Smith and Stevens, 1967: 23 nn. 1–2). Yet the Bar Council did not unequivocally relinquish the right of barristers to do conveyancing until 1903 (Zander, 1968: 178–9). In 1815, the government raised these duties again: £12 and £8 for annual practising certificates, £120 and £80 to register articles and £25 for admission to the Roll (Birks, 1960: 141, 212; Christian, 1896: 134, 218). The Yorkshire Law Society responded by renewing the attack on licensed conveyancers, who were not required to keep terms at the Inns of Court while attorneys and solicitors had to serve five years of articles, and who paid fees of only £28 compared with the £130 paid by attorneys and solicitors (Lawton, 1986). Attorneys and solicitors objected to the increased fees and, indeed, sought the repeal of all stamp duties, successfully reducing the duty on London articles to £80 and the fee for the annual practising certificate to £8 and £6 in London and the provinces (ibid.). But these charges do seem to have had the effect of slowing the rapid proliferation of attorneys and solicitors that had occurred during the latter half of the eighteenth century (Birks, 1960: 141–2). The Attorney and Solicitor Act gave the recently formed Incorporated Law Society responsibility for issuing annual certificates; it quickly established a central Roll of attorneys and solicitors (in place of those previously maintained by individual courts) and subjected the renewal of certificates to stricter regulation (Law Society, Annual Report, 1844).

The role of attorneys and solicitors as intermediaries between lay clients and barristers in the conduct of litigation in the higher courts was confirmed by statute in 1729 (Abel-Smith and Stevens, 1967: 19–20). It was not until the end of the nineteenth century, however, that the Bar clearly conceded that it could not offer advice directly to lay clients outside litigation (Kirk, 1976: 174 n. 35; Forbes, 1979: 15, 17). Until the mid-nineteenth century attorneys and solicitors shared the role of intermediary with proctors in Doctors' Commons, who briefed advocates appearing before the ecclesiastical and Admiralty courts. There were 44 proctors in 1775, 111 in 1842 (Kirk, 1976: 20). But the ecclesiastical courts were abolished in 1857 and Admiralty in 1859. Although solicitors and attorneys obtained reciprocal privileges in 1751, the dual categories persisted into the nineteenth century. By the mid 1800s, attorneys were abandoning their title for that of solicitor, which had attained higher social status. Finally, the distinction was obliterated with the merger of law and equity by the Judicature Act of 1873, and the title of attorney dropped from use.

At the beginning of the nineteenth century, the procedures for entering the Bar had been well established for several hundred years. But solicitors had to construct their entry requirements almost from scratch. In the absence of strong traditions, they embraced contemporary nineteenth-century ideas about technical knowledge and meritocracy, producing a series of hurdles that seem more familiar to modern eyes than those of the Bar. Aspiring solicitors had to complete a period of formal education. Then they had to serve several years of apprenticeship. During this time they had to pass one or more examinations. Those who succeeded were hired as salaried employees by solicitors' firms, government and occasionally private industry. Only after several years in this status were they entitled to practise on their own or in partnership.

## Formal education

### *Secondary schooling*

Solicitors apparently did not demand any secondary education until the 1860s, more than 30 years after Inner Temple first required Bar students to demonstrate competence in Latin or Greek. The Law Society introduced a preliminary examination in 1861 but exempted those who had completed the prerequisites for matriculating at university (and, *a fortiori*, those who had attended or graduated from university). A crude index of the proportion seeking entry without sufficient secondary schooling to be exempted from the preliminary examination is the ratio of those passing the exam to those taking the intermediate examination the following year (I have aggregated several years in order to dampen annual fluctuations). The ratio declined steadily from 90 per cent in the 1860s to less than 1 per cent in the 1960s (see table 2.1). Other evidence is consistent with this general picture. The proportion of articled clerks who had taken and passed the preliminary examination fell from two-thirds in 1881 to less than half in the first decade of the twentieth century (see table 2.2). After World War II, the number seeking to become solicitors without completing secondary school dwindled into insignificance. In 1956, one commentator stated that few grammar school boys were willing to enter a solicitor's office without articles, and few secondary modern students who did so ever would be granted articles (Jones, 1956). In 1962, only 4 per cent of the 1304 clerks entering articles had failed to complete secondary school (Ormrod Committee, 1971: 112). In 1963, five O-levels exempted a candidate from the preliminary examination; four years later the requirement was increased to two A-levels with a grade of C or three passes at A-level and one at O-level (Royal Commission, 1979, vol. 1: 613). The only exceptions were made for mature students over 28 years old (mostly managing clerks), who could continue to sit the preliminary examination. But the numbers have become trivial, and the pass rate has declined (see table 2.10).

### *Undergraduate education*

An undergraduate degree never has been a prerequisite for becoming a solicitor and still is not. Although the data are incomplete, they consistently indicate that the university graduate was very much the exception during the nineteenth century. In the 1870s, only 5 per cent of those admitted to the Roll were graduates (Kirk, 1976: 57–8). In the 1880s, the proportion of articled clerks with degrees varied between 11 and 15 per cent; in the first decade of the twentieth century it remained between 15 and 17 per cent (see table 2.2). Until World War II, less than a third of beginning solicitors had university degrees (see table 2.3). Even as late as 1969, the proportion was less than half (ibid.). A 1965 survey of about 5 per cent of practising solicitors revealed that 48 per cent of those in practice more than 30 years were university graduates, 53–4 per cent of those in practice 10–30 years and 64–5 per cent of those in practice less than 10 years (Wilson, 1966: 5, 7). The prevalence of non-graduate entry can still be seen today: in Devon and Cornwall in 1985, only 60 per cent of solicitors were graduates (Blacksell et al., 1986: table 2).

But as undergraduate enrolment in universities and polytechnics rose in the 1970s, so did the proportion of new solicitors who were graduates, which now exceeds 90 per cent (see table 2.3). Whereas the Bar sought the status attached to an all-graduate profession, solicitors stressed the opposite symbolism – access for all, even those without a degree (Royal Commission, 1979, vol. 1: 630–1). Nevertheless, the incentives to obtain a first degree are substantial. Graduates serve two years less in articles; because state support is available for undergraduate education but not for apprenticeship, three years in a university or polytechnic may be preferable to another two in poorly paid articles. As we will see below, solicitors prefer graduates in choosing articled clerks, hiring assistant solicitors and offering partnerships. On the other hand, there is no evidence that graduates perform better than non-graduates on the Law Society's examinations (AGCAS, 1984c: 7). In August 1986, 88.9 per cent of Institute of Legal Executives fellows passed the final examination in whole or in part, 50 per cent of justices' clerks' assistants and 64.8 per cent of those with 'other qualifications', compared with 72.5 per cent of all examinees (83 *LSG* 3499–3500, 1986). Today, the proportion of non-graduates is minimal. Of the 845 students who obtained certificates of eligibility to take the common professional examination (CPE) in 1982, there were only 20 mature students without any university training (most of the rest had read a subject other than law as undergraduates) (Law Society Standing Committee, 1983: 3). Among those admitted to the Roll between 1980 and 1985, the proportion of mature students remained a constant 2–3 per cent but the proportion of school leavers declined from 11 to 3 per cent (see table 2.4). In 1984, only 8 per cent of those admitted to the Roll were mature students, legal executives or school leavers without a baccalaureate; the following year the proportion fell to 3 per cent (Marks, 1986).

Another contrast between the two branches of the profession is that, whereas most barristers used to read subjects other than law, most solicitors who obtained a first degree did so in law. While the Bar claimed to seek entrants with a liberal education, solicitors did not hide their interest in ensuring that entrants had acquired technical legal knowledge. In 1895, the Law Society began excusing law graduates from the intermediate examination in law (later the part I final and now the CPE). Furthermore, given the greater difficulty of the Law Society's examinations (see 'Examinations', p. 156), a first degree in law may have helped examinees to pass (although it does not help today – law graduates actually do slightly worse on the Law Society's final examination than graduates in other subjects) (AGCAS, 1984c: 7; 82 *LSG* 3430–3, 1985); 83 *LSG* 3499–3500, 1986). Once again I calculated the ratio of those passing the intermediate examination in law to those taking the final examination as a crude index of the proportion of those seeking to become solicitors who had a law degree (see table 2.5). Although the curve is not as smooth as before, the proportion of those with a law degree did rise steadily and approximated the proportion with an undergraduate degree. Law graduates as a proportion of those admitted, only 40 per cent in 1969, increased to almost two-thirds in 1980 and nearly three-quarters in 1984 (see table 2.4; Marks, 1986).

Now that most of those seeking to become solicitors obtain a first degree, and most graduates read law, other characteristics of undergraduate education influence subsequent career. As we will see below, the quality of the degree and the school attended affect where the clerk finds articles and the assistant solicitor secures employment. They also relate to success on the final examination. In 1980, 95 per cent of those with a first class honours degree passed, but the proportion declined with the quality of the degree, falling to only 23 per cent of those with a third; in 1983, the proportion varied from 100 to 31 per cent (AGCAS, 1982: 4; 1984c: 5; 1980a: 2–3). Almost without exception, university graduates do better than those from polytechnics. In 1979, 52 per cent of university graduates passed six papers compared with 24 per cent of polytechnic graduates, and only 18 per cent passed fewer than three, compared with 41 per cent; in 1980, 82 per cent of university graduates passed all seven papers, compared with 42 per cent of polytechnic graduates and 37 per cent of those from institutes of higher education (AGCAS, 1980a: 2–3; 1981a: 4). These two correlations overlap considerably: university law graduates obtain a much higher class of degree than polytechnic graduates (AGCAS, 1980a: 2–3; 1982: 4). But there are also substantial differences among undergraduate institutions within each category: the pass rates on the Law Society final between 1980 and 1985 ranged from 84 per cent for Cambridge to 44 per cent for Kent, and from 52 per cent for Trent Polytechnic to 30 per cent for Chelmer Institute of Higher Education (105 *Law Notes* 80–2, 1986). It is disturbing that students who obtain mixed degrees or pursue innovative curricula appear to do less well.

### *Professional education*

Whereas the Bar did not take professional education seriously until after World War II, the Law Society initiated lectures for articled clerks in 1833, during its first decade and even before it required entrants to pass an examination. For the following 60 years it employed three lecturers, each of whom gave 9–12 lectures annually at the Society's headquarters on Chancery Lane (Law Society, Annual Report, 1901: 12–13). After 1863, classes were also offered to smaller groups of students, and in 1879 a fourth lecturer was hired to prepare students for the intermediate examination (ibid.). In 1893, the Society hired two tutors for small group instruction. It finally opened the Law Society's College of Law in 1903, which five years later had a staff of ten (Hazeltine, 1909: 889). But attendance at lectures and classes remained low, actually declining in proportion to the number of students taking the Law Society's examinations once Gibson and Weldon opened their private coaching school in 1876 (Kirk, 1976: 60; compare tables 2.6 and 2.10). Indeed, seven-eighths of the examination candidates attended *no* Law Society lectures, and only 3 per cent attended all of them (ibid.).

Another reason for the low attendance, of course, was that the Law Society offered its lectures only in London, whereas two-thirds of those who took the examination in 1871 were articled in the provinces, where two-thirds of solicitors practised (Proceedings of a Special General Meeting of the Law Society, 14 April 1871: 12). Provincial law societies sometimes filled this gap: Manchester instituted lectures in 1844, Liverpool in 1871 and Yorkshire in 1898 (Kirk, 1976: 60; Williams, 1980: 317–18). Nevertheless, a questionnaire asking 50 provincial law societies in 1888 about their educational activities elicited no response from 19; 18 thought the idea would fail; and only 11 thought it desirable. At that time, only Manchester, Liverpool, Birmingham and Newcastle-upon-Tyne offered lectures (Law Society, Annual Report, 1888: 4–5). The Law Society sought to encourage provincial education by grants to local law societies: £800 each to Birmingham, Leeds, Manchester, Sheffield and Yorkshire in 1900, increased to £2,400 in 1909 and extended to Newcastle, Bristol, Nottingham, Sussex and Swansea (Abel-Smith and Stevens, 1967: 171).

In 1922 the Law Society made two major changes in professional education: it introduced a compulsory year of lectures prior to the intermediate examination, and it increased its subsidy of provincial law faculties in order to allow clerks articled outside London to attend. Attendance at the latter grew rapidly, both because provincial universities welcomed the income and because most provincial clerks did not have the alternative of a private crammer (see table 2.6). But the Law Society's trump card was to merge with its principal competitor – Gibson and Weldon – in 1962, creating the present College of Law. Simultaneously it withdrew subsidies from the provincial law faculties and authorized commercial and technical colleges in Birmingham, Bristol, Leeds, Liverpool, Manchester, Newcastle and Nottingham to offer instruction for the Society's examinations (Abel-Smith and Stevens, 1967: 353–5; Ormrod Committee, 1971: 18). This, basically, is the present position. Everyone without a law degree must take a one-year course at the Law Society's College of Law in London, Guildford or Chester or at a provincial polytechnic. Those without an undergraduate degree also take additional correspondence courses (if they have completed secondary school) or a two-year course (if they are mature entrants, i.e. over 25) (Royal Commission, 1979, vol. 1: 615). Finally, all potential solicitors must take a one-year vocational course.

Professional education has restricted entry in two ways: by virtue of its cost and, more recently, through limitations on the number of places.

Even in 1914, some students might spend as much as £500 on private crammers (Offer, 1981: 14). In 1979, tuition alone at the Law Society's College of Law was £914 for the one-year course and £1614 for two years, to which must be added substantially greater amounts for maintenance (Royal Commission, 1979, vol. 1: 668; Zander, 1980: 78). The state only recently has begun supporting students during their professional training, and the grants are far less generous than those for undergraduates. In 1956, the Law Society offered a small number of studentships, but each was worth only £40 and was awarded only after the intermediate examination (Jones, 1956). The situation gradually improved with the expansion of local authority support. In 1968, half the students at the Law Society's College of Law had such grants (Abel-Smith and Stevens, 1968: 130). The College's own survey in 1976–7 showed that 69 per cent of students at the vocational stage had grants, and 17 per cent had been rejected; among non-law graduates taking the academic year, 48 per cent had grants, and 33 per cent had been rejected (Royal Commission, 1979, vol. 1: 655; vol. 2: 702–3). In 1980, the proportion receiving grants at the two stages had increased to 71 and 52 per cent (Zander, 1980: 78). In a 1979 survey of the 104 local education authorities (LEAs), 79 of the 83 replying said they provided grants for professional legal education.

But the actual situation of those preparing for the Law Society's examinations is more complicated than these numbers suggest (AGCAS, 1981a: 4–5). First, LEAs distinguish between the academic and the vocational years: in 1980, 45 out of 83 LEAs gave no grants for the CPE, and 30 out of 83 gave grants for either the CPE or the final but not both; in 1985, 85 out of 89 gave grants for the final, but only 59 supported study for the CPE, and only 34 did so if the student had received support as an undergraduate (AGCAS, 1981a: 4; 82 *LSG* 859–60, 1985). In a 1983 survey, only 24 per cent of LEAs said they offered grants to graduates for the academic year, whereas 96 per cent said they offered such grants for the vocational year (Law Society Standing Committee, 1983: app. 6). Furthermore, few grants cover the full cost of professional education. A 1979 survey found that only 19 per cent received full awards, 60 per cent received need-based awards, and 11 per cent got partial awards (AGCAS, 1981a: 4–5). Consequently, 62 per cent of CPE students relied on their families, 46 per cent for more than half of their expenses; 48 per cent drew on savings and earnings, 28 per cent for more than half of their expenses (AGCAS, 1980b: 4). And of those studying for the final, only 10 per cent lived on their grant: 54 per cent received money from their families, 27 per cent more than half their costs; and 29 per cent drew upon savings and earnings; the previous year two-thirds had relied on their families and a third on savings or earnings (AGCAS, 1980b: 4; 1981a: 5).

Thus far I have not distinguished between the College of Law and the polytechnics as forms of professional education. But in fact they differ significantly. Although the Law Society refuses to disclose the exact figures, surveys of students consistently show that those at the College of Law do better on their professional examinations. The relative rates for full passes among students at the two categories of institution were: 1978, 46 and 15 per cent; 1979, 50 and 27 per cent; 1980, 65 and 41 per cent (AGCAS, 1981a: 3–4; 82 *LSG* 3430–3, 1985). This is not attributable to differences in the quality of instruction. Virtually all the disparity is explained by the characteristics of the two student bodies: undergraduate institution attended, quality of degree and gender ratios (ibid.; AGCAS, 1984c: 6). But these, in turn, have their own causes. First, fees at the College of Law are about twice as high as those at the polytechnic, and maintenance – in London and away from home – is also much higher (135 *NLJ* 72–3, 1985). Second, the better credentials of College of Law students are explained by the fact that competition for places is more acute – partly because the Law Society has directed the polytechnics to admit students according to some random selection process rather than on the basis of prior performance (135 *NLJ* 72–3, 1985).

Indeed, the number of places in the mandatory courses is itself becoming a limitation on entry to the profession. In 1982–3, there were approximately 1300 applications for 590 places in the CPE course, though some of these were multiple applications. The College of Law accepted only 455 of the 733 applicants (Law Society Standing Committee, 1983: 7–8). In 1984 and 1985 there were about 3300 places for the vocational course. The City of London Polytechnic received 700 applications for 90 places (135 *NLJ* 72–3, 1985; Marks, 1984: 2608).

### *Continuing education*

Just as the Law Society showed an earlier, more serious concern for professional education than did the Bar, so it has taken more interest in continuing education. Courses have been offered for many years. In 1985, the Law Society required all new entrants to take approximately four half-day courses in each of their first three years of practice. A quarter of these will be compulsory courses in professional conduct and office management, offered by the Law Society and local law societies; the other three-quarters will be a wide variety of options offered by the

College of Law and other approved educational institutions (80 *LSG* 2987–8, 1983; 81 *LSG* 3251–3, 1984).

## Apprenticeship

Apprenticeship was the traditional mode of qualifying as a solicitor. It preceded formal education by several centuries and survives even today, when four years of academic and vocational education have become mandatory. A 1729 statute required five years of apprenticeship, though it was enforced only loosely during the eighteenth century (Christian, 1896: 112, 131). At the turn of the century, taxes were imposed on articles, as well as on admission to the Roll and the annual practising certificate (see 'Origins', p. 140). The stamp duty on articles was £100 in London and £50 in the provinces in 1794, £110 and £55 ten years later, and a uniform £120 in 1845 (S. Warren, 1845: 913). It was reduced to £80 in 1853 and remained at that level until its elimination in 1947 (Kirk, 1976: 113). The length of the apprenticeship was shortened to three years for university graduates in 1821 and for managing clerks with ten years' experience in 1860 (Abel-Smith and Stevens, 1967: 26–7). In 1963, the period was reduced from five years to four for school leavers and from three to two for graduates and mature students (Royal Commission, 1979, vol. 1: 614–15).

In addition to the stamp duty, clerks had to pay substantial premiums In the eighteenth century, this was about £100 in London, at a time when the average annual income in England was about £75 (Slinn, 1984: 16; Lane, 1977: 172). In 1835, the average was £200, and it could be as high as £500 (Kirk, 1976: 51; Birks, 1960: 163–4). In 1845 the normal premium was still 200 guineas but again might range from £300 to £500 for the best attorneys (S. Warren, 1845: 913). In 1914, it varied between £100 and £500 and remained at this level through the 1950s (Offer, 1981: 13–14; Williams, 1980: 241; Abel-Smith and Stevens, 1967: 349; 1968: 131; Gilbert, 1977: 30; Jones, 1956; Gower and Price, 1957: 323). But both the stamp duty and the premium were dwarfed by the cost of maintenance during articles, which, until recently, lasted five years for most apprentices. In 1914, the total cost of articles was £700–1000 (Offer, 1981: 13–14); in the 1920s, it was £1200–1300 (Abel-Smith and Stevens, 1967: 181). In 1956, one commentator estimated that the total cost of becoming a solicitor was £5500, including private secondary school, professional education and articles (Jones, 1956).

Just as stamp duties and premiums were eliminated for barristers after World War II, so they disappeared for solicitors – as for other professions

(Gower, 1950: 156 n. 49). A 1963 survey of 333 graduates of Durham and Manchester Universities who entered articles (71 per cent response rate) found that the proportions paying premiums sharply declined by year of graduation, from 74 per cent of the class of 1955 to 19 per cent of the class of 1962 (Elliott, 1963). Other sources confirm this picture: half of all clerks were paying premiums in 1958 (Birks, 1960: 286); just 12 per cent of a sample of 359 clerks in 1962 (Council of the Law Society, 1962: 266); and only 10–15 per cent in 1963 (Johnstone and Hopson, 1967: 414). Among the 321 clerks admitted to the Roll in the first five months of 1964, 23 per cent had paid premiums; and 90 per cent of those articled in London and 50 per cent of those articled in Kent, Surrey and Sussex paid no more than a nominal £10 (Abel-Smith and Stevens, 1967: 365; 117 *NLJ* 365, 1967). By 1968, only 5 per cent of solicitors' firms acknowledged charging premiums (National Board for Prices and Incomes, 1968: 5).

Even more important than the elimination of fixed fees was the introduction of salaries to defray at least part of the cost of maintenance. The survey of Durham and Manchester graduates found that third-year clerks were paid a pound or two a week in 1957–8, £5 by 1960; second-year clerks were paid £2–4 a week starting in 1959 and first-year clerks £3–4 in 1960 (Elliott, 1963). Again, other sources confirm these findings: in 1956, the clerk's salary repaid the £300 premium in 18 months, and thus was about £2 a week (Jones, 1956). In London, the larger City firms were paying a couple of pounds to £7–8 a week (Abel-Smith and Stevens, 1967: 350; Gower and Price, 1957: 323; Birks, 1960: 286); by the mid 1960s, those firms were paying £8–16 a week to graduates, though only £2 to non-graduates (Abel-Smith and Stevens, 1967: 355). Just as premiums persisted longer outside London, so pay was much lower – just under £5 a week in Sheffield – with the result that the national average was about £8 a week (Abel-Smith and Stevens, 1968: 131; National Board for Prices and Incomes, 1968: 5).

In 1962, the Law Society recommended an annual salary between £100 and £400–500 (Council of the Law Society, 1962). By 1976, a two-thirds sample of students in an accounts class at the College of Law reported that the average weekly wage was £38–43 in the City and £31.25 outside London (Winyard, 1976). Some large City firms were paying as much as £75 a week (Hazell, 1978a: 92 n. 25, 94 n. 30). A 1976 survey of 70 per cent of all articled clerks found a median salary of £1635 (50 per cent higher in firms with ten or more partners), beginning at £1498 in the first year and reaching £1755 in the third (Royal Commission, 1979, vol. 2: 466–7). Law graduates who had passed their final examinations before taking articles (first allowed in 1962) commanded the highest salaries; and today three-quarters of new solicitors are law graduates (see 'Undergraduate education', p. 143). And whereas in the 1960s firms had released clerks without pay to study for their Law Society examinations, by 1976 they were paying them for this released time (Elliott, 1963; Winyard, 1976). Yet despite these rises, few articled clerks could live on their salaries. The 1976 survey of College of Law students found that 60 per cent of clerks had other sources of income: 45 per cent relied on their parents, 31 per cent on their spouses and 16 per cent on personal income or savings (Winyard, 1976). And increasing numbers were taking out bank loans to defray educational expenses: 51 in 1979, 513 in 1981 (Law Society Standing Committee on Entry and Training, 1983: app. 7).

The economic situation of articled clerks has continued to improve during the last decade. Toward the end of the 1970s they organized the Articled Clerks' Action Group within the Transport and General Workers' Union and the London Trainee Solicitors' Group (a symbolically significant change of name) within the Law Society (Podmore, 1980: 31 n. 11; London Trainee, 1977). Their advocacy persuaded the Law Society to prescribe a minimum salary scale in 1980 and to increase it annually since then at least as fast as the rate of inflation (see table 2.7). Local law societies can, and do, recommend even higher levels (80 *LSG* 152 and 1358, 1983). At first, actual salaries fell well below the minima. A 1980 survey of 1978 law graduates found that the median income of clerks was £1750, but 14 per cent earned less than £1250 and only a third more than £2250 (AGCAS, 1980a: 6–8). Among clerks starting in 1980, a third earned less than the minimum and only 17 per cent more than £3750 (AGCAS, 1981a). In 1981, half earned less than £2750 and a quarter less than £2250 (AGCAS, 1981a: 8–10). Yet within a few years most firms met or exceeded the minima (AGCAS, 1984d: 8). In 1985, the median was £6050 in Inner London and £4860 in outer London (Law Society Committee on Education and Training, 1985). Outside London, only a third of articled clerks received the bare minimum of £3375, although 70 per cent received less than £4000 (81 *LSG* 211–12, 1985).

The small minority who clerked for government or private industry did much better. Among the tenth of a sample of 1978 law graduates who fell into this category, 88 per cent earned between £2750 and £3749, compared with only 13 per cent of those in private practice (AGCAS, 1980a: 6–8). Among the approximately 5 per cent of a sample of 1979 graduates who fell in this category, the median salary was £4250, compared with £2750 for those in private practice (AGCAS, 1981a: 8–10). Among a survey of 1980 law graduates, ten of those clerking in private firms earned less than £2750, but the minimum was £4150 in local government and £4650 in private industry (AGCAS, 1984d: 8).

Even so, apprenticeship still imposes an opportunity cost upon clerks. In 1979, when clerks were earning a median of £1750, trainee chartered accountants earned £2750, and even undergraduates were given grants equivalent to £3016 for twelve months (AGCAS, 1981a). And in 1985, when the minimum for articled clerks in the provinces was £3375, other university graduates were starting at £6300 (82 *LSG* 211–12, 1985; Law Society Committee on Education and Training, 1985). Nevertheless, articles no longer present an economic barrier, though some graduates may find other careers more attractive.

Instead, apprenticeship is acquiring a new significance: limitations on the number of places and differences in the rewards they offer have intensified competition for articles, which have become the principal mechanism for allocating entrants to roles within the professional hierarchy. Obtaining articles has not been a problem until very recently. During most of the nineteenth and twentieth centuries the number of solicitors was growing very slowly: between 1800 and 1835 it appears to have doubled (although this may signify a consolidation of the Rolls of different courts); then it remained constant until the 1870s, when it began another period of growth, increasing by half in the 1890s. Thereafter it remained virtually constant for 60 years, with minor fluctuations. Only in the 1950s did it begin to grow, doubling by 1980 (see tables 2.14, 2.15). Since the eighteenth century, solicitors had been limited to two clerks; the Law Society rejected a 1908 proposal to reduce this to one (Christian, 1896: vii; Offer, 1981: 62–3).

Given the slow rates of growth prior to the 1960s, there was no shortage of articles. During the period for which statistics are available, the number of clerks admitted each year rarely exceeded about 5 per cent of solicitors in private practice (see table 2.14). Even assuming that all clerks were articled for five years (though as many as half were articled for only three by the end of this period) and that there was no attrition (though as many as a third may have dropped out) (Johnstone and Hopson, 1967: 414), there still would have been only one clerk to every four solicitors. In the late 1940s and early 1950s, the market remained favourable to those seeking articles. A study of advertisements in the pages of the Law Society's register reveals that the number of replies to each listing of articles vacant increased from about one and a half in the late 1940s to about three in the late 1950s, and the number of replies to each advertisement of articles wanted declined from between four and five to between three and four (see table 2.8).

The situation began to change in the 1960s. There were 5100 articled clerks in 1966 and 5800 three years later, still only about a quarter of the solicitors holding practising certificates (National Board for Prices and Incomes, 1969: 7). Nevertheless, the number was already twice what it had been ten years earlier (Johnstone and Hopson, 1967: 413; Ormrod Committee, 1971: 16). And the proportion of firms who took on no clerks in 1977 was high: 79 per cent of sole practitioners, 67 per cent of firms with two partners, 45 per cent of those with 3–4 partners, 17 per cent of those with 5–9 and 3 per cent of those with 10–14 (Law Society, 1978: 7). Furthermore, newly qualified solicitors cannot accept apprentices for five years, creating an additional lag between the expansion of the number wishing to clerk and the number of solicitors capable of supervising them. Indeed, the rapid production of assistant solicitors during the last two decades has tended to displace articled clerks within the workforce of firms (see chapter 13, p. 204). And while the number of solicitors has grown more rapidly outside private practice than within (see chapter 13, p. 212), the former generally do not take on clerks. Among a sample of 1977 law graduates, 91 per cent served their articles with private practitioners, 6 per cent in local government, 2 per cent in magistrates' courts and 1 per cent in industry and commerce (Royal Commission, 1979, vol. 2: 47). Among a sample of 1979 law graduates, 31 per cent sought articles in local government, 29 per cent in magistrates' courts, 24 per cent in industry and commerce and 17 per cent in civil service (many applied to more than one category); but only 4 per cent ultimately articled in local government and 1 per cent in industry and commerce (AGCAS, 1981a). A survey of 1982 law graduates found that only 18 out of 730 clerked in local government, 4 in industry and commerce and 1 in the central government (AGCAS, 1984d: table 29). Clerks also express a strong regional preference: although London had 25 per cent of firms and 30 per cent of principals, it attracted 43 per cent of new articles in 1985–6 (Marks, 1986). A recent Law Society rule that the supervising solicitor be able to offer training in at least four specified areas of work may reduce opportunities outside private practice.

Heightened competition for increasingly varied clerkship opportunities has affected both how clerkships are allocated and who gets which ones. There are several indices of this competition. A sample of 1977 law graduates wrote an average of 29 letters in order to obtain three interviews and a single offer (Royal Commission, 1979, vol. 2: 48). That year there were 800 applications for the 30–40 articles offered in the Law Society register, a ratio of 25:1; this may be compared with the ratios of 1.5:1 in the 1940s and 3:1 in the 1950s (London Trainee, 1977). One medium-sized central London firm (by no means the most prestigious) received 247 applications for 4 places, a ratio of 61:1 (Wallace, 1977). Those seeking articles were increasingly energetic – even frantic. Among a sample of 1979 law graduates, 27 per cent had made fewer than 6 applications, 30 percent more than 25 and 15 per cent more than 40 (AGCAS, 1981a: 8–10; cf. AGCAS, 1980b). Among a sample of 1982 law graduates, 21 per cent made fewer than 6 applications, 19 per cent more than 40 and some more than 100 (AGCAS, 1984d: 3). Applicants were beginning their search earlier. Among the 247 applications received by a London firm in 1977, 17 per cent wanted to begin that year, 38 per cent the following year and 45 per cent two years later (Wallace, 1977). Although a third of non-law graduates did not begin to look until they had passed the CPE (AGCAS, 1980b), 18 percent of law graduates applied more than two years before they intended to begin their articles, despite the fact that this violated a Law Society rule (AGCAS, 1984d: 2). The concern revealed by these data was not fear of failing to obtain articles. By the summer of 1979, the proportion of law graduates who had found articles was 78 per cent of the class of 1978, 79 per cent of the class of 1977, 77 per cent of the class of 1976 and 75 per cent of the class of 1975 (AGCAS, 1981a: 6; see also Royal Commission, 1979, vol. 2: 47). In the autumn of 1983, 80 per cent of 1982 law graduates had accepted offers, and another 3 per cent had offers outstanding (AGCAS, 1984d: 6).

Rather, the concern was to obtain the best articles possible. For the search had come to depend less on contacts and more on achievement. Although the Law Society long had provided a register to connect together those seeking and offering clerkships, few used it. Between 1948 and 1956, those seeking articles through the register remained a mere 5 per cent of new articles, although the proportion had increased to 14 per cent by 1962 (Johnstone and Hopson, 1967: 491; see table 2.8). The situation had changed only gradually by the mid-1970s: a third of a sample of 1977 law graduates, a third of a sample of London clerks and more than half of a sample of West Midlands practitioners obtained their articles through personal contacts (Winyard, 1976; Royal Commission, 1979, vol. 2: 48; Podmore, 1977a: 611). Indeed, in the West Midlands, 14 per cent had articled with a father or close relative (Podmore, 1977a: 611). Still, change was evident. The proportion relying on relatives or friends to find articles had declined from 41 to 27 per cent between 1976 and 1982, while the proportion using careers services rose from 24 to 47 per cent (AGCAS, 1984d: 7; see also AGCAS, 1981a: 8–10). In order to rationalize the application process further, the Association of Graduate Careers Advisory Services (AGCAS) created the Register of Solicitors Employing Trainees (ROSET), which it subsequently handed over to the Law Society (*LAG Bulletin* 126–7, June

1981; 81 *LSG* 481 and 1890, 1984). But applicants remained dissatisfied with the amount of information available. And a third of 1979 graduates still found their articles through family and friends (AGCAS, 1981a: 8–10).

Because academic credentials significantly influenced success within the more universalistic processes, graduates with better degrees from more prestigious institutions preferred those mechanisms, while others preferred personal contacts: nearly two-thirds of non-law graduates obtained their articles through relatives and friends, compared with slightly more than a third of law graduates (AGCAS, 1980b: 4–8; 1984d: 7). A higher proportion of university law graduates than polytechnic law graduates obtained articles (1978 graduates, 82 versus 66 per cent; 1979: 82 versus 65 per cent) (AGCAS, 1980a: 5–6; 1981a: 6–7; cf. AGCAS, 1984d: 6). A degree from Oxford or Cambridge still conferred substantial advantages on those seeking clerkships in large City firms (see table 2.9). A higher proportion of 1979 law graduates than 1979 non-law graduates obtained articles (80 per cent versus 66 per cent) (AGCAS, 1981a: 6; 1980b: 5; see also Johnstone and Hopson, 1967: 355; Zander, 1968: 32; table 2.9). Those with better degrees were more successful: among 1978 law graduates, all firsts, 87 per cent of upper seconds, 76 per cent of lower seconds and 59 per cent of thirds had obtained articles by the summer of 1979 (AGCAS, 1980a: 5–6; cf. AGCAS, 1984d: 6). Those who took the vocational year at the College of Law were more successful than those who studied at polytechnics, though this may reflect the other differences already mentioned (1978 law graduates, 81 versus 63 per cent) (AGCAS, 1980a: 6; but see AGCAS, 1984d: 6). Undergraduate institution, class of degree and success on the Law Society final also correlated with the clerk's salary (AGCAS, 1980a: 7–8). Interestingly, although women reported discrimination by solicitors who interviewed them for articles at firms, they were at least as successful as men, if not more so (AGCAS, 1980a: 5–6; 1981a: 6–7; 1984d: 6).

The cost of apprenticeship to the clerk and the problems inherent in allocating articles perhaps could be justified if their educational value were clear. But there has been a constant current of criticism during the last 150 years, if not longer. The 1846 Select Committee on Legal Education heard evidence that solicitors did nothing to supervise their clerks, merely setting them to copying documents (Select Committee, 1846). These criticisms were echoed more than a century later by the Ormrod Committee (1971: 60) and the Royal Commission on Legal Services (1979, vol. 1: 650). Indeed, the latter recommended that articles should be abolished if they were not reformed. Clerks today tend to agree. The 1963 survey of Durham and Manchester graduates revealed that 39 per cent were only partially satisfied and 24 per cent dissatisfied with their articles; 85 per cent received no guidance concerning the Law Society examinations; 39 per cent never discussed cases with their principals; half received no guidance concerning studies and training; and 65 per cent received training in only three out of the five categories the Law Society deemed essential. One reason for the pedagogic inadequacy is that solicitors are using clerks to produce income: 69 per cent of the 1963 sample spent more than half their time during the first year in fee-generating work; in subsequent years, 90 per cent spent more than half their time and 54 per cent spent *all* their time on such work (Elliott, 1963). A decade later, another study found 80 per cent of clerks 'satisfied' but unhappy that their training was too narrow (Winyard, 1976). A more recent survey found that only 26–30 per cent of clerks spent more than 10 per cent of their time receiving 'positive legal instruction' (quoted in Sherr, 1982). Thus far the only step the Law Society has taken to remedy these deficiencies is to institute a monitoring scheme, beginning 1 August 1986, in which one clerk will be interviewed in every firm during the last three months of the first year of articles (82 *LSG* 15, 1985; 83 *LSG* 163, 259 and 2460, 1986). Since the monitoring will be conducted by the local law society, it seems unlikely that the standards of supervision will change dramatically.

## Examinations

The third hurdle an aspiring solicitor must surmount is the professional examinations. In this respect, as well, solicitors differ from barristers: they introduced compulsory examinations 36 years earlier, and those examinations have always been more difficult. But though examinations have long been a major obstacle to entry, their significance has changed greatly over time.

When the notion of an examination first was floated in 1794 or 1795, the Society of Gentlemen Practisers (the predecessor of the Law Society) actually opposed it, successfully, on the ground that it would surrender control over entry to the judges (who of course were barristers, not solicitors) (Abel-Smith and Stevens, 1967: 26–7 and n. 5). Nevertheless, within a decade after the Incorporated Law Society was founded in 1826 it introduced examinations for attorneys and solicitors. The common law judges appointed 16 attorney members of the Council of the Law Society to examine attorneys; the Master of the Rolls appointed 12 solicitor members to examine solicitors; and these boards were combined to administer a single examination in 1853. The written examination lasted a day, but the standard was said to be very low (Select Committee, 1846; Abel-Smith and Stevens, 1967: 54; Law Society, Annual Report, 1837: 4; 1850: 6; 1855: 26–31). At its first administration, several candidates handed in their papers within two hours, although five hours were allowed; ten papers (10 per cent) were failed, but the examiners reconsidered them the next day, passing six; several days later the remaining four failures were re-examined and passed (Birks, 1960: 179).

Yet even this minimal requirement may have had an immediate impact on the rate of entry, which dropped from 500 a year in 1836 to 391 a year between 1837 and 1852 (Reader, 1966: 48–9). It is worth noting that the number of barristers called showed no such decline during this period (see tables 1.11, 1.12). When the first attorneys' examination was administered, the number of clerks declaring their intention to apply for admission fell by half, but the number seeking admission as solicitors (who were not examined for another six months) increased tenfold (Birks, 1960: 179). Aspiring lawyers energetically sought to evade the requirement. In the 1840s there was an increase in the number admitted to practice without examination by the judges of the County Palatinate Court of Lancaster and Durham; they then claimed admission to the court at Westminster, although this was denied (Law Society, Annual Report, 1848: 25). In 1858, the Law Society required solicitors admitted in the colonies to pass the examination before practising in the UK (ibid., 1858: 4). And in 1873 the Society brought proceedings against a solicitor who sought to impersonate a candidate and take the examination on his behalf; the solicitor was struck from the Roll and the candidate prevented from taking the examination the following year (ibid., 1873: 17). Furthermore, commercial tutors and crammers quickly responded to an eager market of anxious articled clerks, publishing a 'Key to examination questions' in the 1830s and 1840s, Barnham's 'Series of questions' in 1840 and Halliday's 'Examination questions' in 1856; and student societies met to prepare together. Yet it is not clear why candidates were so apprehensive. As I will discuss below, the pass rate on the first two sittings of the examination was 100 per cent; and a total of 94 per cent of the candidates passed during the first 15 years of examinations (Law Society, Annual Report, 1851: 16; see table 2.10). The cumulative pass rate for those who resat the examination was even higher – 99 per cent in 1870–1 (see table 2.10 and accompanying notes).

Perhaps in recognition of the failure of this examination to regulate supply, the Law Society introduced two further tests in 1861. A preliminary examination of general (i.e., non-legal) knowledge was discussed in the mid 1850s; it was to contain Latin, French, English, history, geography and arithmetic (Law Society, Annual Report, 1857: 14; Birks, 1960: 237). The Law Society appears to have chosen this method for influencing the number and quality of entrants, rather than specifying a minimum level of secondary education, because it exercised less control over the latter, which offered too many soft options. Furthermore, just as American lawyers defended the part-time night law schools from which so many of them graduated in the 1920s and 1930s, so solicitors may have felt reluctant to demand from entrants educational standards that they themselves had not attained.

Nevertheless, demands immediately arose for exemptions from the preliminary examination on the basis of educational credentials, especially since 28 per cent failed the first time the examination was given, to the great embarrassment of the Society (Birks, 1960: 238; see table 2.10). Initially, authority to grant exemptions was lodged in the Lord Chief Justice, the Chief Baron and the Master of the Rolls. Chief Baron Kelly alone exempted 141 applicants in the two years 1877–8 (nearly 10 per cent as many as passed the exam during that period), while the other two officials only granted 29 exemptions between them; and his generosity was ended only by his death in 1881. (When Kelly had been Treasurer of Lincoln's Inn 25 years earlier, he testified against a qualifying examination for barristers: 'I do not see the mischief of men being called to the Bar, who are after all incompetent, whether it is from want of means, or from idleness, or from incapacity, or anything else' (quoted in Duman, 1983a: 80).) In 1878, 80 out of 100 applicants who sought exemptions were granted them. That year, however, the Law Society persuaded the responsible officials to refer applications for exemption to the Council. As a result, only 14 out of 30 applications were allowed in 1888, and the number granted averaged 20 a year in the 1880s, dropping to 4–12 a year between 1900 and 1907 (Law Society, Annual Report, 1877: 6–7; 1881: 11–12; 1888: 7; Offer, 1981, 14; Kirk, 1976: 56–7). The fact that more aspirants had to take the examination may help to explain the sharp decline in the pass rate after 1885 (see table 2.10). Thereafter, efforts to avoid the preliminary examination shifted from individual applications to securing Law Society approval of institutional credentials that would exempt all who held them (university graduates had been exempt since 1877) (Law Society, Annual Report, 1908: 65–84). In 1908, for instance, at least half a dozen examinations excused those who passed from taking the preliminary examination, although the pass rates on the former were lower than those on the Law Society's examination (see table 2.11). The preliminary examination remained a significant obstacle (or at least irritant) until the 1950s, when the expansion of university education exempted almost all those aspiring to become solicitors.

The intermediate examination, also introduced in 1861, was a law examination originally taken by clerks during the period of their articles (Law Society, Annual Report, 1863: 11). Questions on bookkeeping and trust accounts were included until 1871 and then reintroduced as a separate examination in 1906. In 1921, the Law Society required candidates to take a year of professional training prior to sitting the examination and commencing their articles. Law graduates were exempted from the law part, though they still had to take the accounts part (Hazeltine, 1909: 918). The intermediate examination was replaced by part I of the final in 1963 and by the common professional examination in 1980. (Although the latter was intended to serve both branches of the profession, the Bar has refused to recognize it.) In addition, the Law Society offered an optional honours examination in 1880, although honours had been granted on the basis of final examination performance as early as 1859 (Law Society, Annual Report, 1880: 4; Kirk, 1976: 5). The separate honours examination was suspended during World War I (1916–22) and World War II (1940–6) and again after 1962, but honours continued to be awarded on the basis of the final examination grade (Kirk, 1976: 65).

Did these examinations control the production of producers of legal services? The Law Society certainly thought so. In 1875 it urged that the final examination be made more difficult, and that year the pass rate did drop 15 per cent (Annual Report, 1875: 22–3; see table 2.10). Three years later, it succeeded in assuming direct control over the entire examination process, displacing the judges who previously had appointed the examiners (Law Society, Annual Report, 1878: 5; Abel-Smith and Stevens, 1967: 169). In 1886, a resolution was introduced to raise the standard of the preliminary examination in order to remedy 'overcrowding'; although it was defeated, the pass rate did decline steadily thereafter (Proceedings and Resolutions of the Special General Meeting of the Law Society, 30 April 1886; see table 2.10). And in 1887 there was a drop of 17 per cent in the pass rate on the final examination (Kirk, 1976: 65; see table 2.10). In 1908, the Law Society raised the standard of the intermediate examination, and it considered doing so again in 1911; but noting the decline in the number of new articles registered (from an average of 580 between 1902 and 1911 to 428 in 1913) it decided to leave matters alone for the time being. In any case, the pass rate did drop from 74 per cent in 1907 to 62 per cent in 1913 (Law Society, Annual Report, 1911: app. p. 53; see tables 2.10, 2.14). Finally, in response to the loss of business during the depression, the

Society again increased the difficulty of the examination: the pass rate on the final fell from an average of 83 per cent between 1923 and 1932 to an average of 66 between 1933 and 1940, halving the number of new articles between 1934 and 1939 (Abel-Smith and Stevens, 1967: 183; see tables 2.10, 2.14).

But the Law Society's intentions are just one measure of the significance of its examinations. The difficulty of those examinations and their impact is another matter. Later I will relate the total configuration of supply control to fluctuations in the number of solicitors (see 'The efficacy of supply control', p. 164; cf. Offer, 1981: 63). Here I will examine only the pass rates on the five examinations (see table 2.10). The preliminary examination served to control *who* became a solicitor (as defined by their secondary education and general knowledge) more than it affected the number of entrants. In order to enhance the status of solicitors, the examination became progressively more difficult. The pass rate shows a linear decline from a high of 86 per cent in the third year the examination was administered (1863–4) to a low of 22 per cent in 1977 (see figure 2.1). This trend must be attributable, in part, to the fact that an increasing proportion of candidates were exempt from the examination, so that those who took it were less qualified (see 'Secondary schooling', p. 142). Yet even then the examination served its purpose by encouraging entrants to complete the secondary schooling necessary for exemption, thereby raising the collective status of solicitors.

The pass rate on the intermediate examination in law, introduced at the same time as the preliminary examination, also displays a steady decline from a high of 97 per cent in its second year (1863) to a low of 35 per cent in its last two years (1981 and 1982) (see table 2.10). Within this general trend there are several significant peaks and troughs. During World War I there was a sudden increase in the pass rate, as the number taking the examination plummetted, and this higher level was sustained through the 1920s. This may have been a conscious effort to compensate for the deaths of solicitors and reduced number of solicitors who qualified during the war. The pass rate dropped again after 1930, most markedly in 1933, at the bottom of the depression, and then climbed during World War II even more dramatically than it had during World War I. But after 1949 it resumed its long-term decline through to the 1980s. As before, one reason for the decline was the increasing proportion of candidates who were exempted from the examination by virtue of their law degrees (see 'Undergraduate education', p. 143). But at least until the 1970s, the examination served to control supply either by requiring students to prepare for and pass it or by encouraging them to choose the even more onerous alternative of a three-year law degree.

The pass rate on the intermediate examination in accounts, introduced in 1906, rapidly declined from a high of 84 per cent in its first three years to an average of 61 per cent during the next six (see figure 2.3). Thereafter, the pattern came to resemble that of the intermediate examination in law, even though the populations were different (law graduates were exempt from the latter but not the former): both rose dramatically during and after World War I, dropped during the depression, recovered following World War II and then declined steadily after 1950. This examination probably served less to control numbers than to respond to the recurrent scandals caused by solicitor misapplication of client funds.

The final examination has the longest history and is, of course, the ultimate entry barrier, which every candidate must surmount. It showed the same steady decline we have seen above, from a pass rate of 100 per cent when it was initiated in 1836 to a low of 48 per cent in 1952 and 1953 (see figure 2.4). It also rose dramatically during and after World War I and fell even more dramatically during the depression. Although it fluctuated erratically during World War II (partly because of the small number of candidates), it did not exhibit anything like the increase found during and after World War I, and it remained low throughout the 1950s and early 1960s. Then the pattern deviates markedly from other examinations, for the pass rate began a steady increase and has remained at a higher level ever since. I would attribute this to the increasing proportion of law graduates in the 1960s and 1970s (we will see below that the pass rates for university law graduates in the 1980s are very high indeed).

The honours examination does not serve to define the size or even the characteristics of the solicitors' branch. At most, it allocates entrants to places within the professional hierarchy, and even this influence may be weak. Therefore, we should not be surprised to find that it displays no obvious pattern – and certainly not the pattern repeatedly found above (see figure 2.5). It is difficult to interpret these figures because honours were awarded during the two world wars on the basis of final examination performance; since the denominator (those taking the examination) in that period is much larger, the percentages are artificially deflated. What is clear, nevertheless, is that the proportion of candidates granted honours rose abruptly in the 1950s, when performance on all other examinations was declining or had stabilized at a low level, and it ended at a level far above that at which it began.

Study of fluctuations in the pass rates on all five Law Society examinations seems to support the following conclusions. First, though the change in pass rates was gradual, the direction was quite constant.

Even had it wanted to do so, the Law Society could not have raised standards abruptly: those who had invested years in preparation would have been outraged; and the Law Society also contained many solicitors who wanted their sons to join them in practice. Second, the examinations that control entry show significant similarities in overall pattern even though different populations took them. There was a long-term secular decline in pass rates, broken by sudden increases during and after the two world wars (to make up for losses of practising and future solicitors) but accelerating downwards during the depression (because of falling demand). Third, examinations are not the same as quotas: they can be surmounted. Thus we find a pattern of troughs, when the examination was made more difficult, followed by increases, as students (and crammers) responded to the challenge.

These patterns cannot be attributed to changes in the ability or preparation of candidates. True, some of the decline in performance on the preliminary examination and the intermediate examination in law may have occurred because an increasing proportion of the better-qualified entrants were exempt. But that was not the case for the final: while that pass rate was declining, the ability and preparation of candidates was increasing as the proportion of the population seeking to become solicitors expanded and formal education became more accessible and widespread. Nor could quality and preparation have varied sufficiently from year to year to account for the occasional sudden changes in pass rates. Furthermore, it is highly implausible that quality would have increased dramatically during the wars and decreased just as dramatically during the depression. Indeed, the reverse is more likely – that quality declined during the wars and increased during the depression as the number of candidates fell and rose. Perhaps the strongest evidence against the hypothesis that pass rates varied with quality is the results of the Law Society's own honours examination, for the award of honours bore no relationship to the pass rates on other examinations. The pattern that emerges, therefore, is the progressive intensification of Law Society control over supply through the multiplication and increased stringency of professional examinations. This was relaxed briefly during and after the two world wars. It peaked during the 1950s. Thereafter it was eroded by the limited equalization of secondary education and the expansion of state-supported tertiary education, which excused candidates from the preliminary examination and the intermediate examination in law and helped them pass the CPE and the final. Since the early 1960s the pass rate (full and partial) on the final has remained between two-thirds and three-quarters of all candidates, with surprisingly little fluctuation. Although the Law Society instituted a rule in 1979 limiting candidates to three attempts (81 *LSG* 778, 1984), there is evidence that the pass rate for repeaters is almost as high as that for first takers (*Law Notes*; AGCAS, 1982: 6–7; see table 2.10), with the result that the cumulative pass rate is even higher. Thus, professional examinations, introduced by the Law Society in 1836 to control numbers, no longer perform that role very effectively 150 years later.

Even if examinations have little effect on the number of entrants they still may influence *who* enters. This was the explicit motive behind the preliminary examination: to allow solicitors as a category to claim greater respect by demonstrating that they possessed the rudiments of a liberal education. We also saw that prior education enhanced success in obtaining articles and influenced where the clerk was apprenticed. Not surprisingly, prior education is also related to performance on the Law Society's examinations. A 1970 generational analysis of clerks entering articles in 1961 showed that 82 per cent of university graduates (in *any* subject) had passed all their professional examinations, compared with 19–65 per cent of other clerks; larger proportions of the other clerks had also given up trying to pass (Ormrod Committee, 1971: 112). Performance on the final examination in the 1980s shows the same pattern: pass rates vary strongly with the class of the undergraduate degree, and there is a smaller difference between university and polytechnic graduates (see table 2.12). Those who studied at the College of Law did better on both the CPE and the final than those who prepared at polytechnics, but much of this variation is explained by prior educational credentials (AGCAS, 1980b: 2–3; 1982: 6–7; 1984c: 4; 83 *LSG* 3499–500, 1986; see table 2.13). It is interesting that there is virtually no difference between law graduates and all first-takers, suggesting that it is the examination skills undergraduates obtain, rather than substantive knowledge, that influence performance on professional examinations (see table 2.12).

## Barristers becoming solicitors

The onerous route just described could be abbreviated by barristers who wished to become solicitors. Of course, this did not significantly ease entry into the profession because it was, if anything, more difficult to qualify at the Bar. Furthermore, until recently the barrister would have to relinquish the status of a member of the 'senior' branch, presumably in the expectation of higher income. Indeed, there was so little demand for transfers in this direction prior to 1860 that there were no rules governing the process. Thereafter, barristers were required to serve three years in articles and pass both the intermediate and final examinations

(Forbes, 1979: 8). In 1877, the Law Society sought to elicit reciprocal rights for solicitors wishing to become barristers by admitting those with five years' call on completion of the final examination (Abel-Smith and Stevens, 1967: 226). Nevertheless, there was no rush to take advantage of this privilege: between 1919 and 1923, only 29 barristers did so, less than 1 per cent of the new solicitors admitted during that period (ibid.: 236; see table 2.14). Today, a barrister must be disbarred and pass the final examination papers in accounts, revenue law and conveyancing; those with less than three years' experience must pass the rest of the final and serve two years in articles (Senate, 1977a: IV.11). Given the greater security of a solicitor's practice and the fact that partners in large firms enjoy exceptionally high incomes, it is not surprising that a 1984 survey elicited the following response from a recent transfer: 'Of the 65 lawyers I work with in a firm of solicitors, 18 are ex-barristers, all of whom have left the Bar in the past five years' (AGCAS, 1984b: 18).

## The efficacy of supply control

How effective was supply control? The boundary that initially defined the solicitors' profession, the stamp duty on annual practising certificates, is no longer a significant barrier. Although it was £60 in 1979, plus a contribution to the compensation fund for those who had practised more than six years, it serves only to raise revenue, not to discourage entry (Royal Commission, 1979, vol. 1: 383). But the combination of liberal and professional education, articles and examinations undoubtedly continues to have some effect. We can begin to understand it by looking at the number of new articles registered, solicitors admitted and solicitor deaths and the change in the number of practising certificates (see tables 4.1, 2.14 and 2.15, and figure 2.6).

During the first third of the nineteenth century the annualized rate of growth in the number of practising solicitors was very high (3 per cent) – an expansion not attained again until the 1970s, with the result that the number of practising certificates nearly doubled during this period. The number of new articles registered annually fluctuated irregularly between 300 and 600, another indication that there was little control over entry. Such rapid growth may have been one stimulus for the revival of a national professional association. In 1835, this growth abruptly ended, and both the rate of entry and the size of the profession remained constant for the second third of the century (despite population growth and economic expansion). It may not be entirely coincidental that the final examination was instituted in 1836, although it is always dangerous to impute causality to a single factor, especially since the pass rates were so high in the early years. The profession began to grow again in the 1870s, and this growth accelerated in the early 1880s. Although the preliminary and intermediate examinations had been introduced a decade earlier, pass rates on both were still very high. This period of expansion may have been a reaction to 35 years of stasis, as well as to the passage of the Judicature Act in 1875, which significantly increased the business available to solicitors (at the expense of barristers). But in the two decades prior to World War I the number of new articles registered and solicitors admitted declined, and growth fell to a negligible level (an annualized rate of 0.5 per cent), which may reflect the combined effect of the three examinations (four after 1906), whose pass rates were dropping during the period.

Soon, however, events beyond the control of the Law Society constricted supply. World War I had a catastrophic effect. Nearly a quarter of the profession (3324 solicitors) served in the war; 588 were killed and 669 seriously wounded. The next generation of solicitors was affected even more drastically: 1485 articled clerks served, probably more than half the total; 358 were killed and 458 seriously wounded (Law Society, Annual Report, 1919: 8; Kirk, 1976: 198). Furthermore, the rate of production during the six postwar years 1920–5 (2789 new solicitors) actually fell below that of the comparable six prewar years 1908–13 (3042 new solicitors), thus failing to compensate for the very low rate of production during the six war years 1914–19 (1131 new solicitors). Thus, the apparent relaxation in examination standards following the war was an insufficient corrective. The result was a net loss of several thousand solicitors through deaths and underproduction – perhaps 10–20 per cent of the profession. Between 1928 and 1938 the salaries requested by those seeking jobs through the Law Society Employment Register dropped from £250 to £200, and the number of applicants doubled while the number of jobs advertised fell by half (Birks, 1960: 285). Although the rate of production increased again after the early years of the depression, annualized growth between 1920 and 1939 was an insignificant 0.8 per cent. One reason was that the large cohort admitted during the 1870s and 1880s was retiring and dying. But the low growth rate also represented successful supply control in the face of greater numbers seeking entry, as shown by the decline in the pass rates on the Law Society's examinations.

World War II also had a catastrophic effect on the profession. Solicitor deaths (excluding retirements) exceeded admissions by several hundred for each of five years. More than a third of the profession (6124 solicitors) served in the war, and 314 were killed; 2490 clerks served (perhaps two-thirds of the total), and 223 were killed (Kirk, 1976: 198). The rate of production during the eight postwar years 1947–54 (6159 new solicitors) barely exceeded that during the comparable eight prewar years 1931–8 (5704 new solicitors) and certainly failed to compensate for the low rate of production during the eight war years 1939–46 (2048 new solicitors), so that once again the profession lost several thousand actual or potential members, or 20–30 per cent of its strength.

As a result, the profession entered the postwar economic boom almost exactly the same size it had been in 1890, with just 447 more solicitors than had held practising certificates 58 years earlier – a net increase of 3 per cent in six decades or an annualized growth of 0.05 per cent. The combined effect of the cost and length of articles and the four professional examinations kept the growth of the profession at an annualized rate of 1.2 per cent a year for the decade 1952–62. Although the Law Society occasionally bemoaned this fact, it did nothing to encourage entry. Instead, it was the combination of market forces and changes in the educational system that ultimately broke down the barriers. Solicitors ceased charging premiums and began paying salaries to clerks. Higher education expanded (including law faculties), and state grants supported students. As a result, the profession grew at an annualized rate of almost 3 per cent between 1962 and 1970 and nearly 6 per cent between 1970 and 1982. A profession that had grown only 31 per cent in 72 years (an annualized 0.4 per cent) grew 117 per cent in 22 years (an annualized 5.3 per cent).

Before concluding that the Law Society exercised increasingly effective control over supply from the early nineteenth through the mid-twentieth centuries and has lost significant control in the last two decades, it is necessary to consider at least two other explanations for the fluctuations in the number of solicitors. The first is demographics. The rate of entry into the profession might simply vary with the size of the appropriate age cohort. Yet if we construct a ratio of male lawyers (most of whom would be solicitors) 25–34 years old to the total male population in that cohort, we find that it also fluctuated (see table 4.3). Furthermore, it tended to decline from 1881 to 1931 and then increased, gradually to 1971 and rapidly to 1981. These changes are not the explanation for the size of the profession but another variation to be explained.

I referred above to the pressure of market forces. No occupational group can disregard these entirely, particularly in a relatively free economy. It seems plausible that the increasing imbalance during the 1960s between the relatively rigid supply of solicitors and the growing demand for their services generated by rapid economic expansion explains some of the growth of the profession during the last two decades. Do market forces also explain the size and growth of the profession in earlier periods? If it is difficult to devise indices of demand for barristers, it is even more difficult to do so for solicitors, because the latter perform more varied tasks. Some of the fluctuation in entry rates in the nineteenth century may be attributable to the depressions of 1836–7, 1847–8, 1857–8 and 1866 (Slinn, 1984: 80). But the evidence is quite clear that the nearly constant number of solicitors between 1890 and 1948 and the slow growth from then until 1962 cannot be attributed to stagnant demand. Indictable offences in magistrates' courts – a staple of solicitors' criminal practice – grew only slightly between the wars but then doubled by the end of the 1950s (see table 5.2). Although deaths and personal injuries at work and on the railways declined during the first half of this century (except for bulges during the two wars), they were quickly eclipsed by road accidents, in which deaths rose from 1000 in 1910 to between 4000 and 8000 after 1926, serious injuries grew from 50,000 in 1937 to nearly twice that by the end of the 1950s, and all injuries multiplied from 26,000 in 1910 to well over ten times that number by the end of the 1950s (see tables 5.5, 5.6). Civil litigation as measured by county court original proceedings did not increase greatly until the 1960s (see table 5.1). On the other hand, divorce proceedings, which always involve a solicitor (and also required a barrister, until recently) tripled in the 1910s, doubled in the 1920s, doubled in the 1930s and increased fivefold in the 1940s (see table 5.3).

The facilitative work that solicitors do is even harder to measure, but if bankruptcies, other insolvency proceedings and company dissolutions remained constant or declined during this period, there were 683 companies registered in 1863 alone as a result of the liberalization of company law (Slinn, 1984: 113–14), and the number of registrations doubled between 1875 and 1885, doubled again before World War I and doubled yet again by the 1930s (see table 5.4). But the most important measure of demand is conveyances, from which solicitors consistently have earned half their income (see chapter 14, p. 223). Gross advances on building society mortgages are a crude index of solicitor income from conveyancing, since fees vary with the value of the property conveyed. This measure doubled between 1910 and 1920, increased fourfold during the 1920s, tripled again immediately after World War II and doubled once more by the end of the 1950s (see table 5.7). Although each index requires refinement and qualification, there can be no doubt that increases in demand greatly exceeded increases in supply until 1960 and that the Law Society magnified this imbalance.

In the 1960s and 1970s, these measures of demand rose even more rapidly, continuing to outstrip supply. The number of solicitors holding practising certificates increased 135 per cent between 1960 and 1986 (see table 2.14). The number of crimes tried summarily increased 265 per cent (see table 5.2). Industrial and railway deaths and injuries continued to decline, and now so did road deaths and injuries (see tables 5.5, 5.6). Yet county court proceedings increased (see table 5.1). And divorce proceedings multiplied 515 per cent, at a time when solicitors began to handle them without barristers (see table 5.3). The growth of both criminal and civil litigation was greatly accelerated by the introduction and expansion of legal aid. As I mentioned earlier, the civil legal aid budget increased 1287 per cent between 1966 and 1983, while the criminal legal aid budget grew from £550,000 to £62,318,000, although of course this was shared with barristers (see table 5.10). Legal aid payments to solicitors rose from £40,046,927 in 1975–6 to £183,020,571 in 1983–4 (see table 2.33). Bankruptcies and company acquisitions also increased (see table 5.4). And again, most important, conveyancing boomed. Gross advances on building society mortgages increased 3277 per cent between 1960 and 1983, and other indices showed similar increases (see tables 5.7–5.9). (At the same time, net building society mortgage commitments dipped during the 1973–4 recession, and the real value of property sales remained depressed to at least 1978, even though this was the period when the production of solicitors grew most rapidly) (Bowles, 1981). It seems clear that, though state-subsidized tertiary education has lowered the barriers posed by professional examinations, education itself has become a new rationing device (see chapter 18).

# 11

# The sociography of solicitors

The efforts of the Law Society to control the number of solicitors also affected the characteristics of those who entered the profession. In some instances this was intentional and explicit – such as the exclusion of women until 1919 and of non-citizens until 1974. In other instances it was intentional but implicit – such as the class bias introduced by the preliminary examination and extended by the preference given to graduates. And sometimes it was inadvertent – as in the impact of supply control on the age composition of the profession.

## Age

The age profile of any group is a product of the age and rates of entry and exit. The last has been virtually constant for solicitors. Nearly all attrition occurs through death and retirement by reason of age; very few leave the profession during their working lives (by contrast with the high rate of attrition during the early careers of barristers). Despite the large proportion of solicitors who served in both world wars, deaths did not increase greatly during those periods (see table 2.14 and figure 2.6). There is no evidence of any dramatic change in the age at which solicitors were admitted: although there has been a shift toward graduate entry, apprenticeship for graduates has been shortened from five years to two. In 1984, 83 per cent of the men law graduates and 87 percent of the women law graduates admitted were 23–6 years old, although the much smaller number of non-law graduates were several years older (Marks, 1985: 2914).

Changes in the age profile of solicitors, therefore, have been a consequence of variation in the rate of entry. Given the fact that solicitors have always been at least three times, and often five times, as numerous as barristers, census data describing all male lawyers can be used as a rough surrogate for male solicitors. The profession consistently grew older between 1871 and 1921: solicitors under 35 declined from 30.5 per cent of the profession to 15.6 per cent; those over 54 increased from 25.2 per cent to 35.2 per cent (see table 4.5b). This suggests the progressive refinement of supply control as well as the effect of World War I.

The number of younger male lawyers increased somewhat in 1931 and 1951, in the aftermath of the two world wars. But the dramatic change in the profession occurred after 1961. The proportion of male lawyers under 35 increased to 39.5 per cent in 1966 and 48.9 per cent in 1981 – nearly half the male profession and three times what the proportion had been 60 years earlier. The proportion of solicitors on the Roll who were under 40, which was a constant 47 per cent in 1939 and 1969, increased to 55 per cent in 1984 (National Board for Prices and Incomes, 1969: 6; Marks, 1984; cf. Royal Commission, 1979, vol. 2: 52). Rural lawyers tend to be older than urban (Blacksell et al., 1986: table 3). Women solicitors were even younger than men: not only did they tend to enter the profession at younger ages (Marks, 1984), but few had entered the profession before the 1970s. As a result, a staggering 80 per cent of women solicitors were under 35 in 1981, compared with 48.9 per cent of men (see table 4.5a). Therefore, 54 per cent of all lawyers recorded by the 1981 census were under 35 (ibid.). Thus, both branches are youthful – a situation that aggravates the tensions generated by the gerontocratic structure of self-governance (see chapter 16).

## Class

The class background of solicitors has always been considerably less exalted than that of barristers – one basis for the latter's claim to be the 'senior' branch of the profession. There are numerous symbolic representations of this inequality, which the Bar has fought doggedly to preserve. In the mid-nineteenth century, the distinguished attorney Sir George Stephen complained that, though he was related to more barristers than perhaps any other member of his profession, he had been invited to dine with a barrister only once during his 32-year career and had been told explicitly that this was because of his calling (Parliamentary Papers, 1846, vol. 10, p. 366, quoted in Holdsworth, 1965: 229). During World War II, barristers automatically received commissions as officers, whereas solicitors generally entered as enlisted men. It still is the case that solicitors call on barristers, even though the offices of the former almost always are far more commodious than the chambers of the latter. And solicitors generally must discuss fees with barristers' clerks, so that barristers are not tainted by contact with pecuniary matters. The greater class-consciousness of the Bar is also shown in the fact that father's occupation is recorded at admission to an Inn or at call but not at admission to the Roll of Solicitors.

But these distinctions should not suggest that solicitors constitute a cross-section of the population. The cost of articles and formal education and the class bias inherent in admission to and success within tertiary education, the selection of articled clerks and the content of professional examinations ensure that background variables will continue to affect the likelihood of entry. A 1965 survey of 81 articled clerks in firms located in a middle class section of Manchester revealed that their fathers included 21 professionals, 22 managers, 14 businessmen, 5 white collar workers and only 4 manual workers (Hilton and Lerner, 1965). This is strikingly similar to the class composition of those called to the Bar in the postwar period (see table 1.20). A survey of solicitors in the West Midlands in the late 1970s confirmed this pattern, although it also indicated that the class backgrounds of private practitioners were superior to those of solicitors employed in business, whether measured by the proportion who had attended an independent secondary school (44 versus 24 per cent) or a grammar school (53 versus 72 per cent), the proportions from the Registrar-General's classes I, II and III (38 versus 32 per cent, 37 versus 40 per cent and 16 versus 12 per cent) or the proportion whose fathers were solicitors or managing clerks (18 versus 8 per cent) or professionals (29 versus 16 per cent) (Podmore, 1977a: 611; 1980: 92–3). Among solicitors practising in Devon and Cornwall in 1985, 54 percent had attended an independent secondary school (Blacksell et al., 1986: table 2).

The dramatic changes in entry barriers between the 1950s and the 1970s (see chapter 10) inevitably will affect the class composition of solicitors. Elimination of stamp duties and premiums and the payment of a salary during articles facilitate entry by those without private means. And aspiring solicitors who lack connections and upper class backgrounds can obtain articles and employment as assistant solicitors more easily than Bar students can secure pupillages and tenancies. On the other hand, the virtual necessity of an undergraduate degree (preferably in law), strenuous competition for entry to law departments and the high cost of professional education create new barriers that may accentuate class advantage.

Surveys of recent entrants do not suggest any significant diversification in class background. A 1976 sample of 207 of the 331 London articled clerks in a class preparing for the accounts paper revealed that 28 per cent belonged to the Registrar-General's class I and 54 per cent to class II (Winyard, 1976: 2). And a survey of 1448 solicitor students at the College of Law in 1977 found that the fathers of 61 per cent were professionals or managers (compared with 21 per cent of all youths aged 16–19), 15 per cent were executives or administrators, 10 per cent were self-employed entrepreneurs, 5 per cent were clerical workers, and only 3 per cent were manual workers (compared with 66 per cent of all youths aged 16–19) (Zander, 1980: 23; Royal Commission, 1979, vol. 2: 59). The class profile of Bar students did not differ significantly (ibid.). If anything, entry to the profession appears to have narrowed during the last two decades.

## Race

Until 1974, the Law Society prohibited non-citizens from qualifying as solicitors (Royal Commission, 1979, vol. 1: 496). Because racial minorities constituted a small proportion of citizens until the 1960s, few became solicitors. In the last decade, as the minority population has grown and a second generation has matured, the number of black solicitors and articled clerks has increased, to an estimated 200 in 1982 – a mere 0.25 per cent of solicitors, compared with approximately 5 per cent of the Bar (Cohen, 1982b: 11). The Law Society effectively ignored problems of discrimination until recently. Indeed, Ashe Karim, a black solicitor whom the Law Society had struck off the Roll, won reinstatement (on payment of a £750 fine) from the division court on the grounds that he had been treated more harshly than a white solicitor would have been (ibid.: 14). Following the First National Conference on Minority Entry to the Legal Profession in June 1985, the Law Society finally established a Race Relations Committee and agreed to monitor access to clerkships, positions as assistant solicitor and partnerships and to investigate complaints of discrimination (83 *LSG* 163, 1986). Applications for the 1986 annual practising certificate asked about race for the first time, in order to establish the statistical information necessary to do something about discrimination (83 *LSG* 2802, 1986).

## Gender

The single most effective device for limiting the number of solicitors, of course, was the exclusion of women. Although mores and informal social pressures were partly to blame, the Law Society bears considerable responsibility. In 1879, it rejected a woman's request to take the professional examinations. In 1914, it again denied such an application, this time from a woman with a university law degree, and the Court of Appeal upheld its refusal. Only the passage of the Sex Disqualification Act of 1919 compelled the Society to admit women (Kirk, 1976: 110–11). The first woman was admitted in 1922, and two others passed their final examinations that year (ibid.; cf. Sachs and Wilson, 1978: 174). There was an average annual intake of 8–9 women solicitors during the 1920s, 16 during the 1930s, 12 during the 1940s and 30 in the 1950s (Kirk, 1976: 112). But not all of these entered or remained in practice, for the census indicated that women were only 0.7 per cent of the profession in 1931 and 2.7 per cent in 1951; indeed, the proportion dropped to 1.8 per cent in 1957 (see table 2.16).

The situation changed significantly in the 1970s with the expansion of higher education, and especially legal education, partly in response to the increasing number of applications by women (see part IV). Women were less than 10 per cent of new admissions in 1971; they were 40 per cent in 1985 (see table 2.16). Whereas admissions of men peaked in 1980 and had declined 39 percent by 1985, admissions of women continued to increase 14 per cent during these five years (Marks, 1986). Indeed, the erosion of supply control in the 1970s was very largely attributable to the determination of women to qualify through the relatively meritocratic route of the academy. Women undergraduates perform better than men: 38.4 per cent of those taking the 1983 final examination had an upper second class degree or better, compared with 30.0 per cent of men (AGCAS, 1984c: 5; cf. 82 *LSG* 3430, 1985; see chapter 18). They also perform better on the Law Society's examinations: in 1980, 63 per cent of women passed completely, compared with 58 per cent of men; in 1983, the proportions of women and men with full or partial passes were 75.1 and 65.6 per cent; and in August 1985 they were 61.4 and 54.6 per cent (AGCAS, 1980a: 2, 4; 1981a: 4; 1984c: 4; 82 *LSG* 3430, 1985). And, in sharp contrast to the situation at the Bar, women are approaching half of all those seeking to become solicitors. They were 41 per cent of all students enrolled at the Law Society's College of Law in 1982, 44.2 per cent of those applying for admission to the College in 1983 and 45.4 per cent in 1984 (Law Society, Annual Report, 1982–3; 1983–4; 1984–5). They were 29 per cent of new articles registered in 1982, 49.6 per cent in 1983 and 46.5 per cent in 1985–86 (ibid.; Marks, 1986).

Yet the fact that women now are 40 per cent of new solicitors admitted to the Roll is no assurance that they are the same proportion of practitioners or that they are attaining the same positions as men. First, there is evidence of considerable attrition following admission. In 1957, only 337 out of the 560 women on the Roll took out practising certificates (60 per cent); in 1974, only 1299 of the 2296 women on the Roll did so (57 per cent); in 1975 the proportion was 68 per cent; and in 1976–77 it was 83 per cent (Birks, 1960: 278; Sachs and Wilson, 1978: 231; Kirk, 1976: 112; Royal Commission, 1979, vol. 2: 442). A 1985 survey of the members of the Association of Women Solicitors found that the proportion temporarily retired from practice in order to raise children ranged from 8.6 per cent of those 36–40 years old to 17.4 per cent of those 31–35. Furthermore, those in private practice took short maternity leaves (an average of 5.2 months, but only 2.4 months for partners), and though 87.2 per cent returned to the same job, only 53.7 per cent kept the same hours; 22.7 per cent of those in private practice were working part time, and 34 per cent of those with children thought their career prospects were changed by motherhood (Molyneux, 1986). Until recently, women had to sacrifice marriage as well as motherhood to become solicitors: in 1921, 18 per cent of women solicitors were married compared with 74 per cent of men; in 1951, the proportions were 24 and 70 per cent; and as late as 1966, only a third of all women lawyers were married (census). Although it is encouraging that an increasing proportion of enrolled women take out practising certificates, the fact that the proportion remains smaller than that of men suggests that women either are not practising or are not practising privately (Marks, 1985: 2914). (It also may reflect the fact that a higher proportion of women are assistant solicitors, who often do not take out certificates.) A smaller proportion of women than men seek articles in private practice, and a higher proportion seek articles in local government (AGCAS, 1984d: table 28). The disparity between the proportions of enrolled men and women solicitors in private practice grew from 81 versus 74 per cent in the cohort under 30 to 73 versus 47 per cent among those 35–39 years old, before converging again (see table 2.17). An analysis of solicitors holding practising certificates in 1984 also reveals gender differences. Women are proportionally represented in public and private sector employment; but since many employed solicitors do not take out practising certificates, and a smaller proportion of enrolled women solicitors take out practising certificates, they almost certainly are overrepresented in those areas (see table 2.18). They are overrepresented among assistant solicitors – though in proportion to their share of the relevant age cohort they almost certainly are underrepresented (see table 4.5a) – and underrepresented among partners, even controlling for age. And they are underrepresented among solo practitioners. The 1985 survey of the members of the

Association of Women Solicitors found that only a fourth of those in private practice and 31–35 years old were equity partners, and more than a third of those 36–45 years old were assistant solicitors. Furthermore, it took women an average of 4.8 years to be admitted to partnership, compared with 3.5 years for all solicitors in firms with two to four partners (some of the difference may be due to the overrepresentation of women in larger firms) (Molyneux, 1986; 83 *LSG* 170, 1986). Although a surprisingly large proportion of women private practitioners specialize in litigation (15.3 per cent, 19.2 per cent of those under 36), the next most common categories are areas to which women traditionally have been relegated: probate and trust (12 per cent), family (10.7 per cent) and domestic conveyancing (8.3 per cent) (Molyneux, 1986; see also Podmore and Spencer, 1982: 349).

These differences are a product of both overt discrimination and passive acceptance of the traditional sexual division of labour. The City firm of Freshfields hired their first woman articled clerk in 1926, but she left the firm soon after she was admitted, in the 1930s; they admitted the first woman partner only in 1979 (Slinn, 1984: 147, 169–70). A survey of solicitors in Devon and Cornwall found that a third thought there were disadvantages to having women in their firms, and nearly half could see no advantages. Those who did see advantages felt that women would be good at family law and with women clients (Blacksell et al., 1986: table 50). Another survey of potential clients in that area found that a quarter preferred to deal with a male solicitor (Watkins et al., 1986d: 12). Women also have difficulty obtaining positions with the more prestigious firms: in the mid-1970s, women were only 5 per cent of the solicitors at the 15 leading City firms and only 3.5 per cent at the 6 leading London trade union firms (Equal Opportunities Commission, 1978: 20–1). Among most of the firms with 20 or more principals in 1984, women were only slightly smaller proportions of assistant solicitors than of the relevant age cohort. But two City firms (with 75 and 62 lawyers respectively) had *no* women; and at ten other firms, women were 20 per cent or less of assistant solicitors (see table 2.25). Large firms clearly were much less ready to make women partners; in 1980, they were only 5 of the 555 principals in the 15 leading City firms (Podmore and Spencer, 1982: 342). They were less than 20 per cent of principals in all but 1 of the 47 firms with at least 20 principals and less than 10 per cent in all but 8; half of the firms had fewer than 2 women principals, and a quarter had none. This cannot be explained entirely by age, for women were 11 per cent of private practitioners 35–39 years old, 7 per cent of those 40–44 and 4 per cent of those 45–64 (see table 2.17). Undoubtedly some of the reason is the reluctance of firms to allow maternity leave (AGCAS, 1981a), so that women who want to have families must sacrifice the seniority and continuity necessary to become partners.

Women fare no better in the governance of the profession than they do in attaining the most remunerative and prestigious positions in practice. The first woman joined the Council of the Law Society in 1977–8; until that date none had even been proposed (Kirk, 1976: 112; Royal Commission, 1979, vol. 1: 497; vol. 2: 442). In 1984–5, there still was only one woman on the Council – and she had been admitted to practice 27 years earlier! Such patriarchy may have been one of the stimuli for forming a rival association, the British Legal Association, which had a woman chair in 1975 (Kirk, 1976: 112). But if women are not found at the pinnacle of the profession, we should not be surprised to find them at its base: women clerical staff constitute 50,000 of the 98,000 people working in solicitors' offices (Sachs and Wilson, 1978: 178). This is a twentieth-century development: women were not welcome in solicitors' offices in the nineteenth century; in 1891, there were only 165 women law clerks compared with 22,009 men; but by 1901 women were 39 per cent of the 32,168 non-managing clerks (census; Kirk, 1976: 121). Even among the unadmitted staff, women suffer discrimination: they constitute less than a third of legal executives and consistently earn only about two-thirds as much as their male counterparts at each level of seniority (Royal Commission, 1979, vol. 2: 445).

# 12

# The control of production by producers

The initial attraction of the professional form is that it allows producers to exercise some control over the size and characteristics of their occupational group. A further advantage is that professionals can influence not just who produces the services but also how they are produced, distributed and consumed. This latter project necessarily depends on the success of the first, for if an occupation without control over the production *of* producers seeks to impose self-restraints on its members, new producers will enter the market and ignore those restraints, thereby achieving a competitive advantage. This chapter will begin by exploring the ongoing efforts of solicitors to define and defend the jurisdictional boundaries of their monopoly. Then I will analyse the ways in which solicitors have sought to suppress intraprofessional competition by limiting self promotion and by price fixing.

## The conveyancing monopoly

Although the Law Society always refers to conveyancing as 'a so-called monopoly', the inverted commas cannot disguise the fact that for nearly two centuries solicitors have been able to earn half their income from transferring property because virtually no one else may perform that function. Solicitors gained their monopoly at the beginning of the nineteenth century almost by accident, as a by-product of the government's need for increased revenue, some 40 years after they successfully challenged the exclusive right of scriveners to convey property within the City of London (Manchester, 1980: 20–30; see chapter 10, p. 140). During the nineteenth century, enforcement of this monopoly was in the hands of HM Commissioners of Inland Revenue (which collected the stamp duty on conveyances), and the procedure was cumbersome and ineffective. Unauthorized conveyancing became summarily punishable at the instance of the Law Society only in 1921 (Kirk, 1976: 130, 134). Solicitors shared the market with notaries public, barristers (who are still entitled to convey property but rarely exercise that right) and certified conveyancers (non-barrister members of the Inns of Court). The latter category remained significant throughout the first three-quarters of the nineteenth century and were a constant irritant to solicitors, but their numbers declined after 1860, and they virtually disappeared by the end of the century (see table 4.2).

During the first half of the present century, the principal threat to the income solicitors derive from conveyancing was the movement for land registration, which the Law Society successfully opposed for many years (Abel-Smith and Stevens, 1967: 196–206; Offer, 1981: 47). As a result, only 7 million out of 19 million homes were registered as late as 1984, and the increasing complexity of land use controls has allowed solicitors to continue earning similar profits conveying registered land (National Board for Prices and Incomes, 1971; Taylor, 1984). Ironically, the Society has responded to the recent threats to its monopoly by embracing land registration and urging that it be made compulsory (Annual Report, 1984–5: 10). When the Bar Council asserted in 1949 that employed barristers could execute conveyances, the Law Society protested vigorously, and the Bar Council was forced to back down in 1955 (Zander, 1968: 178–9). In the 1960s, lay competitors such as Sidney Carter and the National House Owners' Service asserted the right of laypersons to execute their own conveyances and to advise others for a fee, but the Law Society successfully contained such threats (Zander, 1968: 172–3; Abel-Smith and Stevens, 1968: 156; Kirk, 1976: 147–8). In 1976, a solicitor actually published a scathing attack on conveyancing practices in a book whose popularity can be judged by the fact that eight years later it had reached a seventh printing and sold 44,000 copies (Joseph, 1976). Although discontent with the conveyancing monopoly was a major stimulus for the Royal Commission on Legal Services, it concluded with a blanket endorsement for preserving the solicitors' monopoly. Indeed, it urged that the power to convey be withdrawn from newly appointed provincial notaries and that the penalties for unauthorized practice be increased (1979, vol. 1: 265–6, 281–2).

The Law Society appeared to have won not just the battle but also the war. It therefore surprised almost everyone when a private member's bill, introduced in June 1983, reopened the debate, leading to a period of intense controversy among potential competitors and great uncertainty concerning the future of the solicitors' monopoly. I cannot tell the story in full here, both because it deserves (and undoubtedly will get) a book of its own and because it is unfinished and continues to unfold too rapidly to permit sufficient historical distance. But since few recent events are likely to have greater impact on the legal profession, I must outline what has happened thus far.

Austin Mitchell, the Labour MP for Great Grimsby, introduced the House Buyers' Bill, drafted and supported by the Consumers' Association. Because of his luck in the lottery, it received a first reading on 20 July 1983. On 14 November, Sir Gordon Borrie, the Director-General of Fair Trading, gave a speech in which he urged that house buying costs be lowered by combining the functions performed by several occupations. Two weeks later, the government ended the opticians' monopoly on the supply of spectacles (*LAG Bulletin* 4, December 1983). The Law Society was not backward in stating its vehement opposition to deregulation, participating in 4 national and 25 local radio broadcasts and 8 national and 8 local television programmes (81 *LSG* 162, 1984). Although Conservative governments typically have been sympathetic to the professions, and especially to lawyers, this government had a strong ideological commitment to free markets. Consequently, it persuaded Austin Mitchell to withdraw his bill (which could not hope to pass without Government support, although the vote on the second reading had been 96 to 76) in exchange for the Government's promise to introduce its own (134 *NLJ* 161, 1984). For nearly two years after he did so on 17 February 1984, solicitors and their potential competitors sought to influence both the government and public opinion in order to shape the pending legislation, and each tentatively launched new commercial ventures for conveyancing.

Both sides commissioned public opinion polls to support their respective cases. Market Opinion and Research International conducted a survey for the Law Society in October 1983 (MORI, 1984; 81 *LSG* 1817–18, 1984). Among those who had purchased a home in the previous 12 months, 74 per cent had a generally favourable opinion of solicitors, 61 per cent could say nothing bad about the services rendered (though 10 per cent could say nothing good), and 28 per cent praised the solicitor's speed (though 9 per cent were critical). However, 40 per cent of first buyers and 51 per cent of second buyers thought the completion took too long, 40 per cent of recent buyers thought the solicitor's fees were too high, and 50 per cent did not agree that 'solicitors are worth every penny you pay them.' Although a third of recent buyers knew about alternatives to solicitors, a quarter were thinking of do-it-yourself conveyancing, and many of the others mistakenly thought that building societies and estate agents could convey property. MORI concluded that

87 per cent of recent buyers were satisfied (59 per cent very satisfied) and only 11 per cent dissatisfied. A later MORI poll found that 65 percent of respondents preferred their own solicitor for conveyancing, and 20 per cent preferred a building society or bank solicitor; one third also thought the private solicitor would be cheapest (81 *LSG* 2258, 1984). A January 1986 study by Research Surveys of GB Ltd found that two-thirds of respondents associated solicitors with conveyancing, and a quarter of these knew of *no* other resource. Half of the sample were aware of alternatives, but 57 per cent of these still preferred their own solicitor, a preference that varied directly with age, socioeconomic status and prior use (83 *LSG* 1113, 1986).

The Halifax Building Society, one of the largest such institutions, commissioned surveys that, not surprisingly, came to different conclusions. First, it found that there was a market for its services: 13 per cent of buyers would use a national conveyancing service, 33 per cent a regional one and 86 per cent a local one (82 *LSG* 998–1002, 1985). Second, it surveyed 1200 of its own most recent borrowers (41 percent response rate). A third had used a solicitor previously, a quarter of whom found the service more expensive than they had expected. Among the borrowers who responded, 94 per cent thought that building societies should be able to convey property, 51 per cent thought banks should do so, and 44 per cent endorsed licensed conveyancers. If Halifax had offered conveyancing, 94 per cent of borrowers would have used the service, though 37 per cent would have done so only if it were cheaper than a private solicitor (134 *NLJ* 492, 1984; Halifax Building Society, n.d.).

Like most opinion polls, these resolved nothing. The Law Society pointed to the fact that 87 per cent of those who used solicitors for conveyancing were satisfied with their services. Halifax responded that 94 per cent of its borrowers would have chosen it to convey the property had they been allowed to do so.

Therefore the interested parties were forced to begin competing for the conveyancing market, indicating the services they would like to offer and launching pilot projects, to the extent this was permitted. The principal actors in this confrontation were the building societies (and to a much lesser degree the banks), estate agents, chartered surveyors and, of course, solicitors themselves. Even before Austin Mitchell introduced his bill, the Building Societies Association proposed that its members be able to perform conveyances for borrowers (133 *NLJ* 95, 1983; 82 *LSG* 998–1002, 1985). They were already able to contract with independent solicitors to perform conveyances for their borrowers at fixed rates (134 *NLJ* 1081, 1984). Building societies were the greatest threat to solicitors for several reasons. First, potential buyers frequently contacted them to secure financing before seeking a solicitor to perform the conveyance. And second, they were large and and wealthy. As the Law Society hastened to point out, mortgage lending was a highly concentrated industry: the 5 largest societies owned 55 per cent of the total assets; the 16 largest owned 83.5 per cent (81 *LSG* 1259 and 1265, 1984). Furthermore, proposed reforms in the law regulating financial services would allow the building societies complete vertical integration: they could build houses, operate estate agencies, lend money to purchasers and perform conveyances (*Financial Times*, 7 November 1985). In addition, banks were entering the mortgage market and would pose another threat to solicitors (82 *LSG* 998–1002, 1985).

The second category of players, estate agents, seem to have been drawn into the fray reluctantly. Although they did not really want to engage in conveyancing, they had to threaten to do so in order to resist the efforts by solicitors to set up estate agencies (discussed below). However, a few estate agents took the initiative. Morleys Estate Agents in Manchester began offering free conveyancing to vendors selling property through them and also offered purchasers conveyances through Morleys Legal Services at prices lower than those charged by solicitors. This naturally raised the ire of the local profession, and Alain Cohen, a Manchester solicitor, sought an injunction against Morleys. Although the Law Society initially kept its distance, it eventually agreed to finance and prosecute an appeal against the denial of the injunction and also considered disciplining the solicitor who was performing conveyances for Morleys Legal Services. In the end, Morleys was taken over by Oystons of Blackpool and abandoned its conveyancing services, though not before it took £260,000 in conveyancing fees away from local solicitors. At the same time, Shipways launched Central Conveyancing Ltd in Birmingham, using legal executives when local solicitors refused to co-operate (134 *NLJ* 930–2, 1984; 81 *LSG* 2195, 2502 and 3404–6, 1984; 82 *LSG* 2 and 998–1002, 1985).

Others were also interested in the conveyancing market. Chartered surveyors, like estate agents, saw no reason why they should remain the inferiors of solicitors, and they asserted their right to enter into partnerships with the latter or to employ them in order to perform conveyances (82 *LSG* 1636 and 1645–6, 1985; 83 *LSG* 27, 1986). Two large retailers launched estate agencies in their numerous stores, offering conveyancing at fixed prices through contacts with independent solicitors. Woolworths opened 39 property shops in ten weeks in 1985, and Debenhams opened Home Centres in 12 of its stores. If these operations become widespread, they will be able to use their market power to negotiate low fees from solicitors. But Woolworths apparently found the franchise unprofitable and closed it after a few months (135 *NLJ* 672, 1985; *Financial Times*, 17 August 1985). W. P. Insurance Consultants Ltd. of Portsmouth, a brokerage and accounting office, also proposed to offer conveyancing (134 *NLJ* 1078, 1984). Finally, the one certainty that emerged from legislation was that a new occupation of licensed conveyancers would be created, who could compete with solicitors, though they could offer no other services connected to land transfers (Administration of Justice Act 1985 s. 12).

Solicitors responded to these threats in several ways. They mobilized their considerable rhetorical forces to attack the notion that anyone else should perform conveyances. Their argument that conveyancing required legal training was undercut by the fact that many firms used legal executives and other unadmitted staff to perform much of the work. Furthermore, the Halifax Building Society disclosed that it employed a staff of 40 to check the conveyances performed by independent solicitors, and it found serious errors requiring a new or corrected deed in 5 per cent of the transactions, essential documents missing in 3 per cent, erroneous deeds of assignment of life insurance policies in 25 per cent and applications lodged outside the official priority period of search in 40 per cent (134 *NLJ* 492, 1984). Solicitors argued that the market power of building societies threatened the free market. But there was little price competition among solicitors. Their own survey showed that more than two-thirds of purchasers received no estimates of the cost of the service from their solicitors (81 *LSG* 1817, 1984). And another survey found considerable variation in the fees charged, which would have been narrowed by meaningful competition (*Which*? 67, February 1985).

Solicitors harped on the potential conflict of interest, particularly between a building society eager to lend and a potential purchaser needing independent advice (81 *LSG* 1010–11, 1485–96 and 2195, 1984). But this argument was also unpersuasive. First, the Consumers' Association found that more than two-thirds of all home buyers and four-fifths of first buyers at present arrange their mortgages with a building society before consulting a solicitor, so that the latter offers little protection to the client (Warman, 1985). Second, solicitors had their own conflict of interest in seeking to retain the conveyancing market (quite apart from the profits they earned from conveyancing charges). The National Consumer Council (1984) estimated that solicitors' firms derived about 10 percent of their pretax profits from interest on client accounts, most of which represented the 10 percent deposit by purchasers at the exchange of contracts and held for about a month until the completion of the sale.

While the Law Society was arguing, solicitors were acting to safeguard their market from the attacks described above. They pursued three main initiatives. First, they proposed to form their own building society and compete with existing lenders – a common practice in the eighteenth century, although the Law Society was sceptical of its contemporary practicability (81 *LSG* 1259 and 1263–5, 1984; Miles, 1981). William Heath & Co., a London firm with a large conveyancing practice, floated the idea and claimed that 10 per cent of respondents were favourable (81 *LSG* 338–41 and 3219, 1984). But solicitors were unable to raise the large initial capital investment, and eventually just 200 of the initial organizers joined the Surrey Building Society in a co-operative scheme (83 *LSG* 2961, 1986).

Second, solicitors decided to emulate their colleagues in Scotland and set up their own estate agencies. Since this is the first professional contact for most vendors and purchasers and requires far less capital and expertise than a building society, it seemed an ideal solution (134 *NLJ* 899, 1984), although it did risk antagonizing the estate agents and provoking retaliation. Although the Law Society was concerned about solicitors running an estate agency, it saw no major problems with solicitors selling property, either as individual firms or co-operatively (81 *LSG* 1261–3, 1984; 82 *LSG* 257 and 673–4, 1985; 134 *NLJ* 847 and 1051, 1984; 135 *NLJ* 94–5 and 107–9, 1985). Solicitors seem quite eager to take advantage of such schemes. The first Solicitors' Property Centre opened at Berwick-on-Tweed on 17 September 1984, serving all three local firms. Within the next twelve months centres opened in Northumberland, Wrexham, Clwyd and Crawley. They engendered considerable opposition. In Crawley, the estate agents boycotted the seven member firms, and non-member firms formed a 'fast sell house scheme' in cooperation with local estate agents. Nevertheless, the National Association of Solicitors' Property Centres claimed in 1986 that the centres at Berwick-on-Tweed, Wrexham and Crawley had captured 25–40 per cent of the market (83 *LSG* 1383, 1986). Individual firms – Langley in Lincoln and Picton in Watford and seven other towns – also offered estate agency and conveyancing services for a fixed percentage of the sale price (Bennett, 1985; *Sunday Times* 47, 28 April 1985; 82 *LSG* 165–6, 1294–5, 1757 and 1902, 1985; Bennett, 1985). Most local law societies responding to the Council's consultative paper on changes in the solicitors' rules of conduct endorsed the idea of Solicitors' Property Centres (82 *LSG* 2893, 1985). And the Young Solicitors' Group has urged more liberal guidelines (83 *LSG* 2013–15, 1986).

The third major initiative is co-operative schemes to publicize solicitors' conveyancing services, often at fixed and competitive prices. The Homebuyers Group, launched on 1 October 1984, claimed 300 member firms by the end of 1985. It grants territorial exclusivity by admitting only one firm for every 25,000–35,000 local population; it expected to start advertising at the beginning of 1986, with an annual budget of £750,000–£1,000,000 (82 *LSG* 3153, 1985). The Conveyancing Exchange also planned to limit the number of member firms and to grant territorial exclusivity. It claimed that its initial advertising budget would be £3.5 million (81 *LSG* 1090, 1984; 134 *NLJ* 691–2 1984; 135 *NLJ* 218–19, 1985).

In addition to these major initiatives, the threat of competition stimulated other changes in the conveyancing practices of solicitors. It undoubtedly accelerated interest in and use of computers to simplify and accelerate conveyancing and reduce its cost. Although the Royal Commission (1979, vol. 2: 401–5) had rejected the idea that solicitors' firms adopt the company form, competition with other occupations organized as companies revived the notion (82 *LSG* 246, 1985). In response to solicitor requests, the Council of the Law Society authorized them to accept payment by credit card (82 *LSG* 886, 1985). And solicitors began advertising low fixed fees for conveyancing (134 *NLJ* 1077–8, 1984). A private enterprise, Comparative Business Information Ltd., offered to provide solicitors' firms with data that would allow them to calculate their relative profitability, which elicited considerable interest (81 *LSG* 397, 1984). At the same time, the Law Society continued to prosecute 'unqualified conveyancers', although it consistently lost because the conveyances were performed by a barrister or notary (80 *LSG* 1458, 1983). And it sought greater penalties and an independent prosecutorial body for unauthorized practice (82 *LSG* 246, 1985), garnering some support from the Lord Chancellor's Department (1983: 21).

The end of this story remains in doubt. No one knows how much business the new occupation of licensed conveyancers will attract or how they will be organized, when the first examinees qualify in the spring of 1987. The Building Societies Act 1986 allowed building societies to perform conveyances only for non-borrowers, a meaningless concession, but they may be able to circumvent the restriction by establishing subsidiaries to act for borrowers. Yet this compromise between the building societies and solicitors is unlikely to last. The Committee of the West London Law Society has urged solicitors to boycott banks and building societies that perform conveyances (83 *LSG* 2385, 1986). The outcome of competition between solicitors and estate agents is uncertain. The only prediction I can advance with confidence is that competition will intensify among solicitors and between them and others involved in the transfer of property.

## Other jurisdictional boundaries

If the fight over conveyancing has been the most important jurisdictional struggle for solicitors, it has not been the only one. The boundaries of the solicitors' monopoly have always been much less clear and therefore more difficult to police than those of the barristers' exclusive rights of audience in the higher courts. By contrast with the United States, laypersons in England and Wales have never been prohibited from giving legal advice for pay or drafting legal documents without remuneration. Therefore solicitors, even more than most professionals, continually have had to fight rearguard actions against a host of other occupations that intrude on their turf. As early as 1729, legislation prohibited anyone other than an attorney or a solicitor from prosecuting or defending an action, under penalty of fine, and provided that an attorney or solicitor who allowed another to act in his name would be struck off the Roll (Holdsworth, 1938: 55). Yet at least until the end of the nineteenth century the boundaries surrounding the solicitor's domain remained quite unclear. As late as 1861, a wholly unqualified layperson publicly advertised his readiness to perform the services of a solicitor (Abel-Smith and Stevens, 1967: 62). Legislation in 1860 and 1874 increased the penalties for such behaviour. Between 1886 and 1913 the Law Society obtained convictions against 279 laypersons for unauthorized practice, an average of ten a year; between 1902 and 1913 it secured similar convictions against 56 solicitors who either had been struck from the Roll or were assisting laypersons to practise, an average of five a year (Law Society, Annual Reports; see also Abbott, 1986). Between 1943 and 1963, it was still bringing five to ten actions a year and was successful in 87 of those prosecutions (ibid.; Johnstone and Hopson, 1967: 486). In the next eight years it issued 46 warning letters (Law Society, Annual Reports).

The adversaries in these skirmishes were quite diverse (see generally Abbott, 1986: 213–18). In the nineteenth and early twentieth centuries, London solicitors sought to prevent London law stationers from preparing documents for the probate of wills on behalf of provincial solicitors (Proceedings and Resolutions of a Special General Meeting, 9 June 1882, in Law Society, Annual Report, 1882: 33–4; Law Society, Annual Report, 1909: 38–9; Abel-Smith and Stevens, 1967: 206). Solicitors objected to laypersons who drafted contracts not under seal (Law Society,

Annual Report, 1909: 38–9). They complained about trade protection societies (ibid., 1859: 10) and others who represented or assisted creditors in county court or otherwise helped them recover debts (ibid., 1848: 23; 1861: 15–18; 1909: 38–9; Kirk, 1976: 157). They deplored the practice of Poor Law guardians appointing non-solicitor agents to remove the poor to another jurisdiction (Law Society, Annual Report, 1847: 5). They claimed the right to perform the functions of notaries (ibid., 1844: 14; 1888: 33–4). They asserted exclusive authority to register joint stock companies and limited partnerships (ibid., 1909: 38–9). And they challenged the right of others to act as agents for inventors seeking to protect their patents (ibid., 1848: 23). They even objected to laypersons acting on behalf of poor people unable to afford a solicitor's fee (ibid., 1887: 29–32). One practice that particularly aroused professional ire was the solicitor who allowed a layperson to practise under cover of the solicitor's name, in exchange for a share of the fee (ibid., 1861: 15–18; 1888: 8–10) – an offer made to David Copperfield after he had qualified as a proctor in Doctors' Commons (Dickens, 1850). This was one reason for the rule promulgated in 1847 requiring that the solicitor and his clerk be located in the same office (Law Society, Annual Report, 1847: 11).

In recent years solicitors have tried to restrict the ability of banks and trust companies to draft wills and codicils and to probate them (Abel-Smith and Stevens, 1967: 401; 1968: 135). Although the Royal Commission (1979, vol. 1: 228–9) recommended that trust companies be able to probate wills without the intervention of a solicitor, the Lord Chancellor's Department (1983: 20) rejected this. During the committee stage of the Administration of Justice Bill, the Attorney General indicated his intention to reconsider the solicitors' monopoly of applications for probate (135 *NLJ* 671, 1985). But the legislation as enacted prohibits probate and letters of administration by laypersons (Administration of Justice Act 1985, s.7; 83 *LSG* 742, 1986). Austin Mitchell and Ken Weetch have introduced a Freedom of Probate Bill, supported by the National Consumer Council, to allow trust companies to probate wills without the intervention of a solicitor, but it died for lack of government support (135 *NLJ* 144, 1985). Thus the probate monopoly appears safe for the moment.

The Law Society opposed the creation, in 1906, of the Office of the Public Trustee, which had administered 10,000 trusts worth £10 million by 1919 (Abel-Smith and Stevens, 1967: 207). The Society negotiated market divisions with accountants (who agreed not to draft memoranda or articles of association of companies) and estate agents (who refrain from executing sales contracts) (Abel-Smith and Stevens, 1968: 155; Zander, 1968: 181 n. 5). Indeed, the Royal Commission recommended that the execution of contracts for the sale of land formally become part of the solicitors' monopoly (1979, vol. 1: 266). On the other hand, the Society failed to prevent companies from conducting their own proceedings in county court, often through non-lawyer officers (Zander, 1968: 169–70) or to restrain trade unions from negotiating the injury claims of their members, either under the Industrial Tribunals Act (10,000 a year) or in tort (50,000 in 1971) (Latta and Lewis, 1974; Royal Commission, 1979, vol. 1: 12). In 1985, county courts resolved 45,000 cases under the small claims procedure, with only 48 per cent of large plaintiffs and 16 per cent of small plaintiffs represented by solicitors, and the Lord Chancellor's Department (1986) is considering raising the jurisdictional limit from £500 to £1000. And solicitors have suffered some major losses in their jurisdictional squabbles; accountants, for instance, have taken over much of the task of giving tax advice (Abel-Smith and Stevens, 1967: 402; Kirk, 1976: 157). Solicitors are also threatened by foreign law firms from the United States, Canada, Australia, Italy and Finland, which have opened London offices and are competing for commercial business (Davies, 1985).

In discussing the control that barristers exercise over production by producers I adverted to some of the tensions between the two branches, especially the anger of barristers at the late payment of fees (see chapter 5). On the other side of the divide, solicitors also have their complaints: the threat of conveyancing by barristers and of direct access by barristers to lay clients, late return of briefs and rights of audience. Barristers clearly relinquished their claim to do conveyancing only in 1903. In 1949, the Bar Council asserted that employed barristers could perform conveyances and backed down under pressure from the Law Society only in 1955 (Zander, 1968: 178–9). The Society is unable successfully to prosecute the rare barrister who conveys property (see 'The conveyancing monopoly', p. 184).

Although the convention that solicitors must act as intermediaries between barristers and clients was widely accepted and observed throughout the nineteenth century, the Bar Council formally conceded it in contentious matters only in 1888, promulgating a rule to that effect in 1902–3 and extending it to non-contentious matters ten years later (Kirk, 1976: 136; Hazell, 1978b: 19; Abel-Smith and Stevens, 1967: 122). The only exceptions were patent agents and parliamentary agents (Kirk, 1976: 174 n. 35). Yet this issue continues to surface. Barristers asked the Royal Commission to allow them to receive briefs directly from other professionals, such as accountants and employed barristers, who often are far more knowledgeable about the legal issues involved than generalist solicitors (Senate, 1978c: B.3). The Commission rejected this, though they did recommend that the approximately 25 London notaries public be able to brief barristers directly (1979, vol. 1: 224–5). Solicitors, on the other hand, have sought to circumvent the rule that they cannot brief other solicitors; although this can be done if the first withdraws from the matter, county courts often allow a solicitor who specializes in litigation to handle judgement summonses for others (National Board for Incomes and Prices, 1968: 20). Interestingly, when the Law Society's Contentious Business Committee (1986) made its frontal attack on the Bar's exclusive rights of audience, it also conceded that barristers should be able to contact clients directly, and Austin Mitchell's Legal Profession Reform Bill would authorize this (136 *NLJ* 837, 1986). And barristers have responded to Law Society expansionism by arguing that they should be able to appear without solicitors in Crown court in committals for sentence, appeals against sentence, guilty pleas, appeals against conviction and some trials (136 *NLJ* 455, 1986). The Law Society's subsequent consultative document 'Direct access to the Bar', however, returns to the position that solicitors must remain essential and exclusive intermediaries, at least until solicitors obtain full rights of audience (83 *LSG* 3481–2, 1986; 136 *NLJ* 1080, 1986).

Solicitors' complaints about barristers' late return of briefs are a muted counterpart of the Bar's anger at late payment of fees. The Bar asserts that the problem is minor and that solicitors made fewer than six complaints a year to the Bar Council's Professional Conduct Committee between 1972 and 1976 (Senate, 1977b: XIV.4). Yet the Senate's own evidence to the Royal Commission found late returns in a quarter of a sample of briefs and discovered that a barrister other than the one originally instructed handled the matter in more than a third of all cases (Senate, 1978c: E.7).

But this dispute is minor compared with the recently revived claim by solicitors to expanded rights of audience. Solicitors at present have rights of audience in all matters in magistrates' and county courts, before industrial tribunals, lands tribunals and employment appeals tribunals, in planning enquiries, in the Chancery Division court in bank, in chambers in the High Court and in some Crown Court proceedings. The Law Society had sought only minor increases in its evidence to the Royal Commission (see chapter 5, p. 87), and even these had been rejected by the Commission (1979, vol. 1: 209, 220) and by the Lord Chancellor's Department (1983: 19). At the same time, the Lord Chancellor's Department did enlarge the jurisdiction of county courts from £2000 to £5000 in 1981 (ibid.: 22). Yet the threat to the conveyancing monopoly and the Government's lack of sympathy for the solicitors' case led the Law Society to declare in March 1984 that it sought greatly expanded rights of audience (134 *NLJ* 302–3, 1984). The Prime Minister promptly rejected the claim. But the Law Society's Contentious Business Committee (1986) has now advanced the case for what is virtually fusion. Although this has little likelihood of quick success, the dividing line between barristers and solicitors is certain to remain in flux.

## Self-promotion

If solicitors spend considerable energy fighting off extraprofessional competitors, they must also control competition among their own members. A number of rules and practices serve to prevent one solicitor from gaining competitive advantage over another. A relatively trivial example shows that restrictive practices were virtually contemporaneous with the formation of professional associations. In the early nineteenth century, it was customary for solicitors' offices to remain open on Saturdays (Slinn, 1984: 99); in 1844, solicitors in Leeds, Manchester, Liverpool and Newcastle agreed to close their offices at 2 p.m. on Saturday, and this spread to 22 of the 60 provincial cities by 1854 (Kirk, 1976: 119).

Solicitors derive a substantial proportion of their business from referrals by other occupations and professions: the 1978 Users' Survey found that 10 per cent of those who consulted a solicitor had been recommended to the firm by an estate agent, building society or bank manager (Royal Commission, 1979, vol. 2: 212); a 1983 survey of conveyancing confirmed this (81 *LSG* 1817, 1984); and a 1986 survey found that 18 per cent of clients had been recommended by a bank, estate agent or other professional (83 *LSG* 1113–14, 1986). Consequently, the Law Society prohibits partnerships or even office sharing between solicitors and other professionals (Zander, 1968: 216–17, 229; Royal Commission, 1979, vol. 1: 399). The Farrand Committee recommended in favour of associations between solicitors and estate agents, and the Royal Institute of Chartered Surveyors eventually agreed (136 *NLJ* 833–4, 1986). The Law Society recently indicated that it is considering allowing interprofessional partnerships; some solicitors favour the idea, but local law societies remain strongly opposed (82 *LSG* 1225 and 2893–902, 1985). And when the Office of Fair Trading recommended an end to prohibitions on partnerships or fee sharing between solicitors and others, the Law Society indicated its opposition (83 *LSG* 2530, 1986).

The focus of the controversy over intraprofessional competition has been the solicitor's own efforts at self-promotion. Although, until recently, all professions proscribed self-promotion, this was not always the case. In 1843, a solicitor advertised in *The Times*, offering to recover debts for a commission of 10 per cent (thereby also violating the prohibition on contingent fees) (Manchester, 1980: 66). Though the Law Society complained about such practices, it did not punish them (Law Society, Annual Report, 1861: 15–18). Nevertheless, by the twentieth century the rule against self-promotion was explicit and enforced with increasing stringency (Abel-Smith and Stevens, 1967: 196; Zander, 1968: 222). Responding to threats from building societies seeking conveyancing business in the mid 1930s, the Law Society prohibited 'touting' in 1934 and defined this to include the undercutting of fees (Abel-Smith and Stevens, 1967: 386). It required a vendor of realty, who offered free or cut-rate conveyancing as an inducement to potential purchasers, to allow the latter to choose their own solicitors (ibid.: 203; Zander, 1968: 216–17). It prohibited a solicitor who offered free legal advice from accepting the recipient as a fee-paying client (Zander, 1968: 239), though an exception has been made for lawyers who serve on the rota of citizens' advice bureaux. It prohibited a solicitor employed in commerce or industry from accepting as clients employees recommended by their common employer (ibid.: 216–17). Similarly, it prohibited a trade union from recommending its solicitor to members who needed personal legal services (ibid.). The hostility the Law Society displayed toward the law centres, when they first appeared in the 1970s, reflected the fear that the latter would capture a significant share of legal aid work (Monopolies and Mergers Commission, 1976b: 19–20). When solicitors discovered that the centres actually stimulated work for private practitioners, the attitude of the profession changed considerably (Royal Commission, 1979, vol. 1: 79; Garth, 1980: 70–6; Cooper, 1983: ch. 2, 6, 7).

When the Monopolies and Mergers Commission considered the ban against advertising in the 1970s, almost all professional lawyer associations strongly supported the existing rule, which was the basis of seven prosecutions before the disciplinary tribunal between 1971 and 1974 (1976b: 12, 16–17; but see Johnstone and Hopson, 1967: 483). Although that Commission recommended relaxation of the rule (1976b: 40; see also Monopolies Commission, 1970), and even the Royal Commission favoured limited individual advertising (1979, vol. 1: 376), the Law Society made no change. All these measures seem to have been quite successful in dampening price competition: only 2 per cent of respondents to a 1982 Consumers' Association survey (a category that should be unusually careful in making purchases) sought a quotation from a second solicitor (*LAG Bulletin* 10, February 1983).

Once again, the stimulus for change appears to have been the threat to the conveyancing monopoly: if solicitors were going to have to compete with other occupations for half of their work, they were determined to do so on equal terms. The abruptness of this turnaround is indicated by the following incident. Since 1978, the Law Society steadfastly had resisted a campaign by Peter Browne, a Bristol solicitor, who sought to advertise a do-it-yourself service he provided to consumers at little or no cost. In September 1983, when the European Court for Human Rights declined to review his petition until he had exhausted his domestic remedies, the Law Society refused to fund his appeal, thereby effectively quashing his challenge (33 *NLJ* 858 and 1028, 1983). Yet just two months later, in the wake of Austin Mitchell's bill to eliminate the conveyancing monopoly, the Council of the Law Society indicated its intention to liberalize the rules on advertising (80 *LSG* 2962, 1983). At first it was very cautious: solicitors could not disclose their fees; the size of the advertisement was limited; it could appear only once a week; and solicitors could use only local newspapers, not the national press (80 *LSG* 2961, 1983). Clearly the Council hoped to prevent advertising from fostering the concentration of business.

Indeed, it continued to urge forms of collective advertising designed to enhance the reputation of the profession and to generate demand for all solicitors. The College of Presidents and Secretaries of Local Law Societies considered spending £1 million pounds a year on institutional advertising (134 *NLJ* 465–6, 1984). And the Law Society negotiated an exclusive agreement with Waterlow to produce its directory in exchange for publishing 30,000 regional directories and distributing them to citizens' advice bureaux, town halls, social service offices and police stations in place of the legal aid list of the Lord Chancellor's Department (134 *NLJ* 468 and 776, 1984). The *Law Society's Gazette* started providing subscribers with a newsletter describing recent changes in the law, which they could send to existing clients, thereby promoting business without redistributing it among solicitors (134 *NLJ* 24–5, 1984).

Yet subsequent discussions within the national and local law societies rapidly led to a relaxation of these restrictions. The new practice rule, effective 1 October 1984, allowed advertising in the press or on the radio (but not on television) and by direct mail only to present or former clients or in response to inquiries. It permitted solicitors to list prices but not to make claims about specialization or quality (81 *LSG* 1802–3 and 2194, 1984). In fact, the Society was doing little more than bowing to the inevitable. Lord Benson, who had chaired the Royal Commission on Legal Services, endorsed price advertising in his Keith Tucker Memorial Lecture on 2 May 1984; and his own profession, accountancy, permitted advertising, even on television, from October of that year (134 *NLJ* 465–6 and 692, 1984).

Still, the atttitude of solicitors remained ambivalent. The Society brought disciplinary proceedings against a member of its own Council, William Heath, for advertising after the Council had decided to allow the practice but before it had issued guidelines (135 *NLJ* 70, 1985). And most solicitors were in no rush to exercise their privileges (134 *NLJ* 777, 1984). Larger firms thought advertising undignified. Smaller firms feared the additional expense and doubted whether advertising would be effective. There were empirical data to support such scepticism: a 1973 survey of 102 divorce petitioners (70 per cent response rate) found that half used a solicitor recommended by friends of relatives, 13 per cent had used the solicitor previously, 9 per cent were referred by a citizen's advice bureau, and 8 per cent used the legal aid list and 4 per cent a telephone book (Murch, 1980: 12); the 1978 users' survey found that half of all clients chose their solicitors on the basis of prior acquaintance or the recommendations of friends, neighbours or relatives, whereas only 3 per cent used an impersonal source such as a telephone book (Royal Commission, 1979, vol. 2: 212); and a 1986 survey found that 60 per cent of clients had relied on personal recommendations, 26 per cent on prior use and only 2 per cent on advertising (83 *LSG* 1113–14, 1986; see also Blacksell et al., 1986: table 36; Watkins, 1986d: 7–8). Responding to the discomfort among smaller firms, Stanley Best, chairman of the British Legal Association, consistently opposed individual advertising and successfully forced the Law Society to submit the issue to a postal ballot. The result was approval of the innovation by a vote of 13,529 to 11,246 but rejection of any further liberalization by a vote of 16,291 to 5288 (134 *NLJ* 44, 1984; 135 *NLJ* 670, 1985; 82 *LSG* 1985–6, 2893 and 3502, 1985). In 1985, only 1 per cent of solicitors in Devon and Cornwall definitely planned to advertise, and 48 per cent were certain they would not do so. Although 28 per cent thought they would if other firms advertised, firms in north Devon had agreed among themselves not to do so (Blacksell et al., 1986: 25–6 and table 39). A rural Norfolk solicitor, who made house calls, wanted to leaflet prospective clients, a marketing mechanism he thought was far more cost-effective than advertising, but he feared complaints from local practitioners (Slatter and Moseley, 1986: 23–4). Yet in England, as elsewhere, attitudes toward advertising divided along generational lines: the Young Solicitors' Group recommended voluntary specialization, the accreditation of specialization and permission to advertise specialities (81 *LSG* 3146, 1984) – reforms that the Law Society's Education and Training Committee has endorsed (83 LSG 2380 and 2818–25, 1986). And provincial solicitors now seem to have been won round: the law societies of Birmingham, Manchester and Liverpool jointly issued a call for further liberalization of the advertising rules (83 *LSG* 2402–5, 1986).

If individuals were unlikely to be strongly swayed by advertising, market research suggested that large commercial consumers might be influenced. A 1984 survey of 200 public and private sector organizations with annual turnovers of at least £10 million found that half had changed their solicitors or thought of doing so during the previous year, mainly in search of specialist expertise. Among the half who had not considered changing, two-thirds would do so if the quality of their present services deteriorated and a quarter if they could reduce their legal costs. Only a third of the 200 organizations could name *any* of the top three City firms (134 *NLJ* 1100, 1984). Another survey of directors and high level managers of 57 commercial enterprises found that two-thirds did not know the hourly rates charged by their solicitors, and nine-tenths had not shopped around for a firm (134 *NLJ* 874, 1984). Yet a survey of 150 leading London firms (12 per cent response) suggested that they remained reluctant even to explore promotional avenues (134 *NLJ* 774, 1984). Still, three major City firms hired public relations organizations in early 1985 (Campbell-Smith, 1985b). And an expansionist Northampton firm holds seminars and sends out brochures advising commercial clients about current legal issues (Berlins and Rice, 1986).

Recently, the Law Society's Contingency Planning Working Party has proposed a comprehensive revision of the practice rules and advertising code (1986). These retain very vague restrictions on efforts to obtain business and reciprocal referrals of business. However, they authorize advertising in any medium, including television, while continuing to prohibit unsolicited telephone calls or visits and direct mail. Advertisements must be in 'good taste' and refrain from comparisons of quality and success and claims of specialization.

## Price fixing

Like all professionals (indeed, all entrepreneurs), solicitors fear and seek to avoid price competition, which can alter market shares and reduce profits. The regulation of fees, therefore, is always a central concern of the attempts by producers to control production. Some form of regulation can be traced back as far as the fifteenth century, and by the eighteenth century virtually all fees for contentious matters were set by the courts (Abel-Smith and Stevens, 1967: 19). In 1843, conveyancing fees, which had been subjected to regulation much earlier, were proportioned to the length of the document (Christian, 1896: 156–9; Birks, 1960: 224; Abel-Smith and Stevens, 1967: 197; Kirk, 1976: 145; Offer, 1981: 24).

Although this allowed solicitors to inflate fees by elaborate drafting, they were unhappy with the scheme because clients were unwilling to pay the mandatory fee for small parcels and might have been willing to pay more than the stipulated fee for large ones (Birks, 1960: 224; Offer, 1981: 31). Consequently, an *ad valorem* scale was introduced as an alternative and quickly replaced the older schedule, immediately increasing the profitability of larger conveyances by a factor of two or three (Christian, 1896: 199; Birks, 1960: 224; Kirk, 1976: 137; Offer, 1981: 39).

During the succeeding 90 years there were constant struggles to raise the scale fees (e.g. Law Society, Annual Report, 1893: app. A, pp. 173–211). They rose by a third in 1925 and again in 1944, bringing the total increase to 50 per cent since 1883 (there were other minor changes in 1919, 1931, 1936, 1963 and 1970) (Abel-Smith and Stevens, 1967: 200, 377–9; Kirk, 1976: 145; Bowles and Phillips, 1977: 640). Although the Law Society described scale fees as maxima intended to protect the client against unscrupulous solicitors, they tended to operate as minima as well, with the strong encouragement of the professional association (Anderson, 1984: 71). When the Law Society outlawed touting in 1934, it also proscribed the undercutting of fees (Abel-Smith and Stevens, 1967: 386). Two years later the Council promulgated a practice rule prohibiting solicitors from performing conveyances for less than the scales established by local law societies (Kirk, 1976: 146). These usually were set at 85 per cent of the Remuneration Order scale but tended to approach the latter (ibid.). In 1964, virtually all of the more than 100 local law societies had set their minimum fees at 100 per cent of the Remuneration Order (Abel-Smith and Stevens, 1967: 386; Kirk, 1976: 146).

Scale fees came under attack from two sources. Consumers believed they artificially inflated conveyancing costs. Solicitors felt they established a ceiling; although the scale could be waived with the consent of the client, this required a certificate from the Law Society, which was backlogged with applications. In 1972, the Society abolished the scale, substituting eight criteria to guide the setting of fees in the future (Bowles and Phillips, 1977: 640). Yet this formal change had little effect: fees remained tied to property values, moving down with the recession of 1973–4 but upwards thereafter, and judicial decisions continued to approve this relationship (ibid.: 647; Bowles, 1981; Royal Commission, 1979, vol. 1: 274–6). Although the amount of time required by a conveyance varies, the most expensive properties demand no more than twice as much work as the least expensive (Royal Commission, 1979, vol. 2: 124). A 1971 study revealed that the amount of time per conveyance ranged from an average of 230 minutes for a parcel worth less than £1000 to an average of 911 minutes for one worth more than £20,000 (a ratio of 4:1); the conveyancing fees, by contrast, ranged from an average of £17.6 to £228.6 (a ratio of 13:1) (National Board for Prices and Incomes, 1971: 56–7). Hence it is not surprising that the Royal Commission reported that solicitors earned twice as much an hour when conveying properties over £30,000 as they did when conveying those under £5000 (1979, vol. 2: 131; see also vol. 1: 274–5). The Law Society also continued to insist on other restrictive practices: a solicitor should not act for both parties in a conveyance (Kirk, 1976: 152); and any solicitor who does so must charge the full fee to each party (National Board for Prices and Incomes, 1971: 2; Royal Commission, 1979, vol. 1: 266–7).

It seems clear that there has been little price competition in conveyancing. The 1978 users' survey found that 61 per cent of domestic conveyancing clients did not have a clear idea in advance what the fees would be, though 49 per cent also did not ask (ibid.: vol. 2: 249–50). Studies by the Consumers' Association in the 1970s found that fees charged by different solicitors for conveying the same parcel varied by a ratio of 2.5:1 (quoted in Zander, 1980: 24; cf. Cox, 1982–3). In 1983, private solicitors were charging approximately twice as much as local authorities to convey comparable houses (*LAG Bulletin* 5, August 1983). In October 1984, when the Law Society first allowed price advertising, conveyancing fees for properties of the same worth varied by more than 100 percent within a single town (*Which?* 66–7, February 1985; see also Taylor, 1984). Yet the extraprofessional competition caused by the breach in the solicitors' conveyancing monopoly and the intraprofessional competition this has induced will inevitably lower prices. It also will lead to concentration, which in the short run should increase economies of scale (although in the long run it may facilitate a return to cartelized pricing). The hours invested per conveyance declined as the proportion of income a firm earned from conveyancing rose, with the result that specialist firms charged less than generalist, at least for properties worth more than £30,000 (Royal Commission, 1979, vol. 2: 124, 464).

Conveyancing is not the only non-contentious matter in which the Law Society sought to regulate fees, if it is the most important by far. Although a fixed schedule for other non-contentious services was abandoned in 1953, seven factors were substituted to guide solicitors (Abel-Smith and Stevens, 1967: 382). The Law Society proposed in 1959 that probate fees should be proportioned to the value of the estate, although this was never formally adopted (ibid.: 395). The absence of price competition is strongly suggested by the fact that 91 per cent of clients consulting a solicitor about the settling of an estate did not have a clear idea in advance how much the solicitor would charge (Royal Commission, 1979, vol. 2: 250). In contentious matters, fees remain fixed by the courts. Consequently, it was estimated in 1968 that solicitors derived two-thirds of their income from fees set by the profession or the courts (National Board for Prices and Incomes, 1968: 14). Legal aid also determines fee levels, although it is far less important for solicitors than barristers; but solicitors often fail to inform clients that they may be liable for a contribution or a statutory charge or only eligible for legal aid for part of the services rendered (Davis and Bader, 1985a; 1985b).

Several remedial devices are intended to protect the client against the absence of effective competition, though none is very satisfactory. A client dissatisfied with a solicitor's fee may obtain a remuneration certificate from the Law Society free of charge. But this remedy is little used; between 1953 and 1962, only about 200 clients a year sought certificates (Johnstone and Hopson, 1967: 500). Between 1974 and 1976 the number of requests varied between 1021 and 2010 (about half of which involved conveyancing), or 1000 for every one or 2000 of the estimated 2 million bills a year (Law Society, 1977: 165; Royal Commission, 1979, vol. 1: 545). One reason for the lack of interest in this procedure is that only a small proportion of bills are reduced as a result – between 17 and 26 per cent (ibid.). Alternatively, a client can ask the court to tax the client's own solicitor's fees (although the client will pay for the taxation unless there is a significant reduction). But once again the numbers are inconsequential: 89 out of 11,135 cases in 1966 (0.5 per cent) (Zander, 1968: 207 n. 61), between 107 and 164 instances a year in both Queen's Bench and Chancery Divisions combined between 1975 and 1978, out of an estimated 5 million bills annually (Zander, 1980: 25; Royal Commission, 1979, vol. 1: 544). On the other hand, the fact that the losing party must pay the adversary's taxed costs tends to set a limit on what that party's own solicitor can charge.

# 13

# The structures of production

## Geographic distribution

Whereas the Bar long was concentrated almost exclusively in London, and provincial chambers only began to expand in the twentieth century, solicitors always have been dispersed throughout England and Wales. The establishment of the county courts in the early nineteenth century, together with the roles of solicitors in performing conveyances and acting as intermediaries for London barristers (and solicitors), provided strong incentives for solicitors to establish practices throughout the country. Fragmentary nineteenth-century data suggest that two-thirds of solicitors consistently have practised in the provinces. In 1900, a third of all solicitors practised within 10 miles of the central post office in London (Offer, 1981: 12). Between 1919 and 1947 two-thirds of solicitors with practising certificates worked in the provinces; the 1951 census confirmed this, as did the distribution of Law Society members from 1948 to 1959, who by then were fairly representative of the profession (see table 2.41). Although the proportion of solicitors practising in London may have declined folllowing World War II (Johnstone and Hopson, 1967: 361; National Board for Prices and Incomes, 1968: 34), in the 1980s a third of solicitors practised in Greater London and half within the metropolitan counties (Watkins et al., 1986b: 9; see table 2.19). In the 20 years 1961–81, the proportion of all lawyers in the London area increased at the expense of rural regions (see table 4.8).

If solicitors are not as concentrated in London as are barristers, neither are they distributed in proportion to the population. First, they are overrepresented in the central cities and underrepresented in the suburbs and countryside (K. Foster, 1973: 155–7). In 1967, a fifth of all London solicitors were located in the square mile of the City (Abel-Smith and

Stevens, 1967: 436); 1140 of the 1624 solicitors' firms in greater London (70 per cent) were found in just 6 of the 118 postal districts (5 per cent); of the remaining 112, 13 districts had no firms, 18 had only one, and 19 had two each (Zander, 1968: 212 n. 70). In Birmingham in 1971, 136 out of 171 solicitors were located in the city centre, where the ratio of solicitors to population was one and a half to three and a half times the ratio in the surrounding towns (Bridges et al., 1975: 11, 16–17).

Provincial cities may contain the fastest growing sector of the profession. Between 1823 and 1901, when the total number of solicitors in England and Wales increased about 230 per cent, the increase was 483 per cent in Liverpool and 729 per cent in Birmingham (Kirk, 1976: 109). Between 1951 and 1971, the number of solicitors grew twice as fast in Birmingham as in the nation as a whole, even though the city lost 9 per cent of its population (Bridges et al., 1975: 18). Yet the concentration in commercial centres tends to be at the expense of poor residential areas and suburbs, not rural areas: the counties (outside Greater London) with the lowest ratio of population to solicitors were rural (Watkins et al., 1986b: 16, 27).

Enormous differences in the ratio of population to solicitors can be found not only between cities, suburbs and countryside but also among cities and regions. The population per solicitor for the UK as a whole was 4700 in 1971, but it ranged from 2000 in Guildford and Bournemouth to 16,500 in Tower Hamlets, 26,000 in Salford, 37,000 in Bootle and 66,000 in Huyton (K. Foster, 1973: 158). In England and Wales in 1971 it varied regionally from 3704 in the East Midlands to 1754 in London and the South-east; 14 years later the disparity had increased (see table 2.19). Several variables appear to influence this distribution. It is correlated with the proportion of freehold housing. This is not surprising, given that a third of solicitors' clients consult them about real property, and homeowners are twice as likely to consult lawyers as are renters. It is also correlated with the proportion of the population who are retired, perhaps a surrogate index for wills, trusts and probate, which constitute more than a fifth of the matters about which clients consult solicitors. Finally, it is correlated with the level of retail sales, a general index of economic activity. Studies disagree whether indices of class other than property ownership are correlated with the concentration of solicitors (K. Foster, 1973: 161; Watkins et al., 1986b: 33; Royal Commission, 1979, vol. 2: 189, 191, 198; cf. Mayhew and Reiss, 1969).

The amount and kind of business that a local population generates also affects the profitability of practice, thereby influencing the location of solicitors. The average profits of principals in 1969 ranged from £7984 in firms with one to four principals in Central London to £13,388 for all Midland solicitors and £18,454 for all firms in Central London; and the disparities have been growing in recent years (National Board for Prices and Incomes, 1969: 31). In 1985, sole practitioners in central London, the South and the Midlands earned gross incomes 50 per cent higher than those in the North and 23 per cent higher than those in Wales. Partners in firms with two to four principals earned 37 per cent more in London than in the North, the South or Wales. And partners in firms with five principals or more earned nearly two and a half times as much as those in Wales, two and a third times as much as those in the North, twice as much as those in the Midlands and two-thirds again as much as those in the South (Marks, 1986: 3261). The salaries offered to solicitors by firms advertising in the *Law Society's Gazette* declined progressively from central London to provincial cities to suburban London to the country (see table 2.39). In the light of this, it is not surprising that the Royal Commission expressed concern about the inaccessibility of solicitors to people in the countryside, suburbs and poorer sections of cities (1979, vol. 1: 181–2).

## Firm size

The movement toward larger units of production, which characterized the Bar (see chapter 5, p. 103), is also visible among solicitors, although the causes and effects differ. The reason is not scarcity of space but economies of scale, the need to specialize and the size and complexity of the problems of corporate clients. The outcome is a truly collective productive unit rather than the pretence maintained by barristers that a set is simply an aggregation of individuals who happen to find themselves sharing office space and a clerk. But whereas virtually all chambers have grown, and most contain 10–15 barristers, many solicitors continue to practise in very small units; however, a few firms are far larger than any barristers' set.

This growth is a very recent phenomenon. Freshfields, one of the best-known City firms, contained fewer than four partners for much of the nineteenth century. As late as 1938, it contained three profit-sharing and three salaried partners (Slinn, 1984: 32, 156). Until well after World War II, the vast majority of solicitors practised alone or with one or two partners, often a son, brother or other relative (Williams, 1980: 191–203; see table 2.20). The mean number of partners did not reach 2.0 until 1930 and was only 2.5 as late as 1950 (see table 2.20). Thereafter, the proportion of firms containing one or two solicitors declined dramatically: from nearly three-quarters of all firms (containing half of all solicitors) in 1966 to just over half of all firms (containing slightly more than a quarter of all solicitors) 13 years later (see table 2.21). Since then, the proportions seem to have remained quite stable: a third of firms are solo practices (containing a tenth of all solicitors), and another quarter contain two solicitors (representing 15 per cent of practitioners) (see table 2.22). On the other hand, the number of practising certificates held by sole practitioners increased 48 per cent between 1979 and 1983, while the total number of practising certificates increased only 26 per cent, suggesting that a growing number of those who have completed their three years as assistant solicitors cannot find satisfactory positions in firms (compare tables 2.14 and 2.30; see also 135 *NLJ* 195, 1985).

As one might expect, the tendency toward concentration has been more pronounced in London, where the mean firm size in 1969 was slightly higher than it was in the rest of the country because London contained significantly fewer two-partner firms and more with at least five partners (see table 2.23). And provincial cities, like Birmingham, may resemble London: between 1951 and 1971, the number of Birmingham solicitors increased 55 per cent, but the number of firms actually dropped 6 percent (Bridges et al., 1975: 26–9; see table 2.23). But mergers have begun to occur in the provinces: in the spring of 1987 two firms with offices in Norwich, Great Yarmouth and Amsterdam joined to form the largest regional solicitors' firm, with 36 principals and 200 staff (83 *LSG* 3203, 1986). Howes Percival, a Northampton firm, increased its gross revenues tenfold between 1977 and 1986, growing from 7 to 22 partners, and has established offices in Wellingborough and Nottingham; they are frequently approached by firms seeking to merge and expect to expand to Birmingham and Leicester, with 20 solicitors and 45 staff outside the home office (Berlins and Rice, 1986). London and Wales may represent the extremes: in 1985, 14 per cent of London principals were in firms with five principals or fewer, compared with 80 per cent of Welsh principals; but 72 per cent of London principals were in firms with ten principals or more, compared with 11 per cent of Welsh principals (see table 2.22; see also Thomas, 1986: 21–2).

Firms in Devon and Cornwall, another rural setting, also remain small. In 1985, 38.5 percent contained one or two principals, another 38.5 per cent contained three to five, and only 21.7 per cent contained more (Blacksell et al., 1986: table 19). These firms show striking stability and continuity: 17 per cent date from the eighteenth century or earlier, 29 per cent from the nineteenth century and another 18 percent from before World War II. On the other hand, 23 per cent have been established since 1975, an indication of the rapid growth of the profession (ibid.:

table 14). More than two-thirds of Devon and Cornwall firms had experienced neither a merger nor a breakup within the memory of a living member (ibid.: table 16). The solicitors themselves are equally immobile: three-quarters have worked for the same firm for more than five years, a fifth never worked for any other firm, and more than half had worked for only two (ibid.: tables 6, 9). They are also local people: more than half were born in the South-west, more than a third in the same county and a sixth in the same town; within Cornwall, two-thirds were born in the South-west, half in the same county and a third in the same town (ibid.: table 7). Yet it is regionalism rather than kinship that provides the glue: only 14.5 per cent of the firms had any family connections (ibid.: 6).

As the proportion of solicitors practising in smaller firms has declined, large firms have begun to emerge. This, too, is a recent phenomenon (cf. Smigel, 1969). I found no firms with ten partners before World War II (see table 2.24) and very few with more than five (see table 2.20). The two largest City firms in 1946, Linklaters & Paine and Slaughter & May, each had 12 partners (Slinn, 1984: 159). In Birmingham in 1875, the largest firm had four partners; 50 years later the ceiling was seven; in the City of London that year, the largest firm had eight partners and the three largest a total of only 19 (Kirk, 1976: 116). Most of the change has occurred since 1950. Using as a population the 15 firms with the largest number of partners in 1983, we can see that their median size grew very slowly from 1849 to 1930, then increased 47 per cent in the 1930s, 20 per cent in the 1940s, 57 per cent in the 1950s, 56 per cent in the 1960s and 113 per cent between 1970 and 1983 (see table 2.24).

One critical event was the 1967 decision to lift the 20-partner limit originally imposed in 1862, because the four largest City firms had reached or were approaching that ceiling by 1964 (Abel-Smith and Stevens, 1967: 403). By 1973, there were 50 firms in London with more than ten partners and 5 with more than 30; Birmingham contained 6 firms with more than ten partners, Manchester had 5, and Leeds and Liverpool each had 3 (Kirk, 1976: 116). The proportion of firms with five or more principals doubled from 9 per cent in 1966 to 18 per cent in 1979; the proportion of solicitors in those firms grew almost fourfold, from 12 to 46 per cent (see table 2.21). By 1985, the proportion of firms with five or more principals had risen to 19 per cent, but the proportion of principals in those firms had grown to more than half (see table 2.22). The proportion of firms with more than ten principals increased from 3 to 4 per cent between 1977 and 1985, but the proportion of principals in firms with at least ten principals increased from 16 per cent in 1976 to 24 per cent in 1985 (see tables 2.21, 2.22). The number of firms with at least 20 principals increased from none in the 1960s to 25 in 1977 and 66 in 1985 (see tables 2.22, 2.24).

As firms have grown they have developed branch offices. In the late 1970s, more than a third of all firms had them; 9 per cent had three offices, and 5 per cent had more (Royal Commission, 1979, vol. 2: 459). In 1985, the 38 firms in Bristol had 83 branches; the 18 firms in Brighton and Hove had 37, and the 14 firms in Oxford had 39; most of the firms were established by two- to ten-person partnerships (Reeves, 1986: 144). By contrast, half the firms in Devon and Cornwall in 1985 had only one office, a quarter had two, 15 per cent three, and only 13 per cent had more (Blacksell et al., 1986: table 15A).

In the last few years, this growth has led to the emergence of 'megafirms', which, if not as large as those in the United States (cf. Galanter, 1983), still differ qualitatively from the rest of the profession. In 1984, one City firm had 200 lawyers, another eight had at least 100, and 13 had 50–100 (as did five West End firms); seven City firms, ten West End firms and four provincial firms had 30–50 lawyers (see table 2.25). Qualified staff at the 11 largest City firms grew an average of 30 per cent in 1982–6, while Clifford-Turner grew 86 per cent and Lovell, White & King grew 63 percent (83 *LSG* 3471, 1986). The first profile of such a firm (itself a measure of the new interest in self-promotion) confirms the rapidity of growth. Richards Butler, founded in 1920, had only 3 partners until after World War II, 9 in 1948 and 11 in 1956; then it doubled to 22 by 1970 and more than trebled to 39 by 1980. The pace of expansion has increased since then: it added 14 new partners in the 1980s and another 10 in May 1985, resulting in a 70 per cent increase in six years (136 *NLJ* 384–90, 1985).

A subset of the megafirms is distinguished by the work they do. The status and prosperity of Freshfields, for instance, is largely a function of its long relationship with the Bank of England, dating back to the eighteenth century; but Freshfields has also worked for the P and O Company, Lloyd's, banks and companies and generations of nobility and gentry (Slinn, 1984: 11–12, 127–9). Ten City firms represented 55 percent of the 1456 companies listed in Crawford's Directory of City Connections 1984–5; 23 City firms had an average of 63.3 such clients each (Campbell-Smith, 1985b; Hermann, 1985). There seems to be considerable consensus about who these firms are: a survey of 500 national and international clients identified and ranked 11 favourites (135 *NLJ* 975, 1985). In the late 1970s, 54 firms had offices in European Community countries (Law Society, 1977: 158). In 1984, all 16 City firms with more than 60 lawyers had offices abroad; in 1986, English solicitors' firms had 18 offices in Paris, 17 in Hong Kong, 13 in New York, 11 in Singapore, 9 in Brussels and 3 in Tokyo (Lichtig, 1986).

Despite the high rate of growth, these firms have found it difficult to expand rapidly enough to keep up with the business and are relying increasingly on lateral hiring, though rarely of partners (Campbell-Smith, 1985a; 135 *NLJ* 975, 1985; 136 *NLJ* 384–90, 1986). The hiring of recent entrants has also changed: the proportion of non-graduates has dropped significantly but so has the proportion drawn from Oxford and Cambridge (see table 2.27). Richards Butler, which used to recruit articled clerks only at Oxbridge, now interviews undergraduates at Nottingham, Durham, Exeter and Bristol (136 *NLJ* 384–90, 1986).

## Composition of solicitors' firms

Solicitors' firms not only have more partners; they also have grown and changed in other ways. Principals have always relied heavily on a wide variety of subordinated personnel. In the nineteenth century these included law writers and engrossers, copying clerks and managing clerks, as well as articled clerks and salaried solicitors (Birks, 1960: 232–3; Offer, 1981: 21). The ratio of clerks to solicitors appears to have increased in the last half of the nineteenth century, from 0.86 in 1850 to 2.09 in 1900 (see tables 4.1, 4.2). In 1900, it was estimated that 50,000 people were employed in law; since there were only 16,000 solicitors (and many fewer barristers), there must have been at least two employees per solicitor; in 1914, each solicitor was assisted by 2.5 employees (Offer, 1981: 20).

Unfortunately, we have no record of what changes occurred during the next half century. But the last three decades clearly have seen important shifts in employment patterns. In the late 1970s, it was estimated that there were more than 100,000 subordinated personnel in solicitors' firms, or perhaps four per principal (Royal Commission, 1979, vol. 1: 27; vol. 2: 461). In 1985, a Peat Marwick study estimated that there were 127,000 people in solicitors' firms: 21,590 principals, 31,750 other fee earners and 73,660 other staff, or a ratio of almost five employees per principal (83 *LSG* 246, 1986). Between 1957 and 1982, the number of principals holding practising certificates increased 97 per cent, but the number of assistant solicitors and consultants increased 395 per cent – four times as fast (see table 2.31). The number of new articles registered grew 221 per cent (see table 2.14), but the number of articled clerks must have grown a great deal less rapidly because the average length of articles dropped by about half. A 1985 study of firms in Devon and Cornwall found that during the previous ten years 36 per cent of firms had seen an increase in the number of assistant solicitors and only 22 per cent a decrease, while 6 per cent had seen an increase in the number of articled clerks and 31 per cent a decrease (Blacksell et al., 1986: table 20). In a 1983–4 survey of East Midlands firms, half had no articled clerks, and few had more than two (Saunders and Faulkner, 1985). Membership in the Institute of Legal Executives actually declined (see table 2.32).

The more reliable figures for the period 1966–76 show that the number of principals grew less rapidly than the number of assistant solicitors but more rapidly than the number of articled clerks, legal executives and clerical staff (see table 2.26). As a result, the ratio of employees to principals remained fairly constant, but assistant solicitors have displaced legal executives and, to a lesser degree, articled clerks (see table 2.29; Glasser, 1979: 203). There seem to be several reasons for this shift. The number of articled clerks declined, despite the increasing rate of entry, because articles are much shorter. The number of legal executives fell because the greater availability of higher education made the position less attractive than other careers open to graduates and because assistant solicitors could perform many of the same services for firms at lower cost (Slinn, 1984: 169). And the number of assistant solicitors grew because of the rapid expansion of the profession and the reluctance of principals to share partnership profits.

Although all firms have increased their subordinated labour force, the expansion of this category is also a function of the growth of firm size and the greater number of employees per principal in the larger firms. Although the ratio is higher for sole practitioners than for two-partner firms (because the former cannot share responsibilities with a partner), thereafter it increases steadily with the number of partners (see table 2.29). This variation is most pronounced for the ratio of assistant solicitors to principals, and it has increased over time (ibid.). In 1984, the ratio of employed fee earners to profit-sharing partners was 0.9 for firms with two to four partners but 2.1 for firms with more than 15 (136 *NLJ* 59, 1986). There are also geographic variations (which similarly increase over time), but these probably reflect regional differences in firm size (National Board for Prices and Incomes, 1968: 35; 1969: 30).

Firms grow largely by increasing their subordinate labour force. In 1963–4, the largest City firm had 20 partners (the statutory limit), 50 assistant solicitors, 25 articled clerks and 30 managing and junior clerks – more than five employees per partner (excluding clerical staff) (Johnstone and Hopson, 1967: 365–6). In 1967, the larger City firms had nine employees per principal (Abel-Smith and Stevens, 1968: 144–5). In 1983, the leading City firm of Freshfields had 50 partners and more than 350 employees (Slinn, 1984: 159). More recently, firms have begun to replace clerical staff with computers, and there is a strong relationship between firm size and reliance on computers (Saunders and Faulkner, 1985; Blacksell et al., 1986: 15). The correlation between firm size and ratio of assistant solicitors to principals becomes stronger among the firms with at least 20 principals (see table 2.28), ranging from 2.35 for Linklaters & Paine (the largest, with 60 principals and 141 assistants) to 0.29 for Bartletts De Reya (with 21 principals and only 6 assistants) (see table 2.25).

One way in which large firms augment that ratio is by postponing the date at which they will consider assistants for partnership. (In the nineteenth century some firms, such as Freshfields, never offered partnerships to salaried solicitors) (Slinn, 1984: 133). Law Society rules require a minimum of three years, and smaller firms must offer some assistants partnerships at that point. But Richards Butler makes assistants wait six to seven years (136 *NLJ* 384–90, 1986). At Allen & Overy, 18 per cent of the assistants had been admitted more than six years; 14 per cent at Linklaters & Paine (Solicitors' and Barristers' Directory and Diary, 1985). A 1985 Peat Marwick study found that assistant solicitors became partners in 3.5 years in firms with two to four principals, but they waited 5.7 years in firms with 15 principals or more (83 *LSG* 246, 1986).

As firms grow they are compelled to adopt more bureaucratic forms of management. The executive partner of Richards Butler is virtually a full-time manager (136 *NLJ* 384–90, 1986). Freshfields hired a chartered accountant in 1970, created a managing partner in 1972 and established a partnership board of ten in 1978 (Slinn, 1984: 170–1). Linklaters & Paine hired a non-solicitor as director of administration in 1983 (Campbell-Smith, 1985b). And even the small but fast-growing Northampton firm of Howes Percival has appointed a full-time managing director with extensive powers over partnership shares (Berlins and Rice, 1986).

A major reason for the growth of employees is partner profits. The exploitation of labour is not a recent innovation in solicitors' firms. In the late nineteenth century, the leading City firm of Freshfields allowed its unadmitted staff to take home copying work: it paid the clerk three and a half pence per folio but charged the client four pence; since there was no additional overhead, the firm reaped a 12.5 per cent profit (Slinn, 1984: 121). Although legal secretaries formed an association in 1977 and established courses and credentials, they have had little success in raising their wages. Using the data generated by the Royal Commission together with more recent figures on the number of chargeable hours by each category of fee earner, I calculated that articled clerks, assistant solicitors and legal executives generated between 2.5 and 4.8 times as much income for their firms as they were paid in salary (Abel, 1982: 26; Hiley, 1984). Even making a generous allowance for the overhead consumed by their work (probably about a third of their gross earnings), they produced substantial income for their employers. The gap between gross earnings and net salary (a crude measure of surplus value extracted) increases with firm size (except for articled clerks), even though larger firms pay somewhat better (see table 2.38).

This, and the fact that the ratio of employees to principals is greater in larger firms, undoubtedly goes far to explain the fact that partner income varies with firm size. Surveys by the National Board for Prices and Incomes (1968: 39; 1969: 31) found a direct relationship between size and profits. The 1985 Peat Marwick study commissioned by the Law Society also found that median net 1984 profits per principal varied from £17,900 in firms with two to four principals to £81,300 in London firms with at least 15 principals (83 *LSG* 169–70, 1986). Middle-ranking partners in the larger City firms earned £150,000 to £200,000 in 1985, and several earned considerably more (135 *NLJ* 975, 1985; Campbell-Smith, 1985b).

We can explore several other possible explanations for this variation. Large firms are not significantly more efficient than small: net profits were 33–5 per cent of gross income, although they were only 27 per cent for sole practitioners (83 *LSG* 246, 1986). Partners work *shorter* hours than employees. A 1976 survey found that partners billed 985–1080 hours a year compared with 1044–100 for assistant solicitors and legal advisers; a 1980 survey found that junior partners billed the most hours (1229) but that senior partners (947) billed less than senior assistant solicitors (1064), junior assistant solicitors (1085) and legal executives (1081). The most recent study (1983) found that senior assistant solicitors billed more hours (1055) than senior partners (1046), though less than junior partners (1142) (Hiley, 1984). And though the capital investment per principal varies directly with firm size (from £14,000 for two to four partner firms to £48,300 for those with at least 15 partners), most of this represents profits retained for retirement rather than investment, and in any case the amount is too small to explain the disparity in earnings (83 *LSG* 335, 1986).

Thus the growth in the size of solicitors' firms represents a transformation in the productive unit from an independent professional (perhaps associated with a relative and assisted by a small clerical staff) to a large, much more bureaucratic enterprise, in which employed lawyers and paraprofessionals outnumber partners and, in turn, are outnumbered by clerical staff. We no longer see a professional exchanging expertise for fees but a new form of capitalist (whose capital is a professional credential) extracting surplus value from workers who must sell their labour because the state has granted the professional a monopoly over the market for legal services.

## Managing clerks/legal executives

The managing clerk (retitled the legal executive in 1963 in an effort to upgrade the status) has been a central figure in the production of legal services. Throughout the nineteenth century solicitors relied heavily on unadmitted staff to perform virtually every function except court appearances. In 1732, no more than 5000 solicitors employed an estimated 45,000 clerks (though many clerks were very junior) (Kirk, 1976: 114). A hundred years later there were said to be about two clerks for every solicitor, although most London solicitors had four, and some had as many as 20 (ibid.: 114–15). We have seen that the ratio of unadmitted staff to principals was approximately 2:1 around the turn of the century. The census lists 36,967 unadmitted staff in 1901, 33,468 in 1911 and 48,495 in 1921. A 1939 Law Society survey found that the 9633 practices responding employed 46,183 law clerks; since the median firm contained two to three principals, the ratio was still about 2:1 (Kirk, 1976: 114–15). The number of clerks was said to have declined in the 1940s and 1950s (Johnstone and Hopson, 1967: 401), which is consistent with the 1965 estimate by the Institute of Legal Executives (ILEX), shortly after its formation, that 30,000 were eligible for membership (Abel-Smith and Stevens, 1967: 396). Johnstone and Hopson (1967: 401) estimated that each principal employed a managing clerk, who was assisted by a junior clerk. Between 1966 and 1976, the number of legal executives (belonging to ILEX) employed in private practice dropped from 17,200 to 16,208 (Royal Commission, 1979, vol. 1: 408). It seems likely that the number of legal executives actually remained constant; but since the number of solicitors holding practising certificates increased by half during this period, the ratio of legal executives to principals declined, most markedly in the larger firms (which, as we saw above, have a higher ratio of assistant solicitors to principals) (see tables 2.26, 2.29 and 2.32).

We may be able to understand the diminished role of the managing clerk by examining the clerk's relationship with other producers of legal services. Clerks repeatedly have tried to improve their status and just as consistently have failed. In 1832 they formed the United Law Clerks' Society and invited membership from clerks within a 25-mile radius of London (Kirk, 1976: 120–1). One goal was to improve salaries, which then averaged £150 a year, although clerks could earn considerably more through the commissions they received for bringing business into the firm (ibid.). This estimate seems high, since junior clerks at Freshfields earned £60–70 toward the end of the nineteenth century, though they could increase this to £100 by working as much as 15 hours a week overtime (after a six-day, 51-hour week) (Slinn, 1984: 120). In 1892 a second organization was created, the Solicitors' Managing Clerks' Association (SMCA), but it was no more successful (Royal Commission, 1979, vol. 1: 406; Johnstone and Flood, 1982: 173). In 1919, yet a third organization, the National Confederation of Law Clerks, sought to negotiate with the Law Society over minimum salaries, which then ranged between 25 and 30 shillings a week (Abel-Smith and Stevens, 1967: 194; Kirk, 1976: 121–2; Offer, 1981: 58–60).

The insuperable problem for clerks was their inability to control the supply of producers: not only was it easy to become a clerk but in 1939, when the economy had largely recovered from the depression, 2500 qualified solicitors were still employed as managing clerks (Kirk, 1976: 114–15). In 1945, when membership of the SMCA reached 500 for the first time (no more than a few per cent of all clerks), it made another effort, in co-operation with the Law Society, to enhance the status and emoluments of clerks by initiating an examination. But employers refused to recognize the qualification, and fewer than 50 clerks took it each year (ibid.: 121, 123). Finally, in 1963, the SMCA and the Law Society created the Institute of Legal Executives to establish standards for students, associates and fellows (ibid.: 124). The change in name was significant – an attempt to shed the Victorian image of the lowly clerk. Criteria for admission were fairly rigorous: students had to pass four O-level examinations with a minimum grade of C; associates had to be at least 20 years old, have worked in a solicitor's office for at least three years and pass four examinations roughly equivalent to A-levels; and fellows had to be more than 25 years old, have worked in a solicitor's office for at least eight years and pass three papers comparable to those on the Law Society's final (Royal Commission, 1979, vol. 1: 409–10). These hurdles are substantial: approximately two-thirds of candidates pass the associates' examination, and only half pass the fellows' (see table 2.32; Wilson and Marsh, 1975: 308).

Yet despite these persistent and energetic efforts, legal executives have failed to professionalize, at least as measured against the success of the professional project among barristers and solicitors. First, ILEX has not required that its members obtain post-secondary educational credentials; as the proportion of solicitors graduating from university increased in the 1960s and 1970s, this absence of formal credentials weakened the campaign by legal executives for improved status and income. Second, legal executives cannot control supply: they cannot prevent firms from hiring managing clerks who lack ILEX credentials or replacing legal executives with assistant solicitors, articled clerks or other unadmitted clerical personnel. As some legal executives secured higher salaries, firms seem to have done just this. The salaries of managing clerks averaged £1500 in the 1950s and £2000 in the 1960s (Kirk, 1976: 124). In 1964 an experienced clerk earned £1300–1700 a year in London (£3000 in the top firms), though much less in the provinces (Abel-Smith and Stevens, 1967: 397; Johnstone and Hopson, 1967: 410). In 1976, the median salary for a legal executive was £3692 (£4238 in firms with ten or more partners) (Royal Commission, 1979, vol. 2: 465, 468). Salaries were considerably better in both government and industry (ILEX, Third Memorandum to the Royal Commission, cited in Johnstone and Flood, 1982: 176).

In response to rising labour costs, the Law Society consciously decided to replace legal executives (Abel-Smith and Stevens, 1967: 398; Kirk, 1976: 124). Two alternatives were readily available. With the rapid growth of the profession, increasing numbers of assistant solicitors were seeking employment. They lacked whatever class consciousness might have characterized managing clerks, both because they were from the middle rather than the working class and because they aspired to become solicitors. Collective action is extremely difficult (if not impossible) for an exploited category whose transitory membership is defined solely by age. Assistant solicitors also tend to be a cheaper form of labour because they turn over rapidly before acquiring the seniority that might justify higher salaries.

The other way of driving down the wages of legal executives was to replace men by the increasing numbers of well-educated women entering the workforce in the 1960s and 1970s. Solicitors then could take advantage of the prevailing sexism to deny women clerical workers comparable pay and opportunities for advancement. In 1976, 47 per cent of those studying for ILEX examinations were women (ILEX, Second Memorandum to the Royal Commission, cited in Johnstone and Flood, 1982: 174–5). Between November 1983 and October 1984, 49 per cent of the new fellows admitted to ILEX were women (23 *Legal Executive* 10–12, 1985). In 1976, women members of ILEX earned 66–91 per cent of the salaries of their male counterparts; discrimination increased with seniority and was most pronounced among those employed in commerce and industry

(Royal Commission, 1979, vol. 2: 445). Other strategies further undermined the collective strength of legal executives. They were given ever more specialized tasks to perform, thereby reinforcing their subordination (Johnstone and Hopson, 1967: 410; Johnstone and Flood, 1982: 177). And a small number of the most ambitious were co-opted by being admitted into the profession through the special provision for 'ten-year men' (*sic*).

Consequently, when ILEX repeated its earlier request that legal executives share in profits, enjoy greater rights of audience and be allowed to administer oaths and practise on their own, the Royal Commission flatly turned them down (1979, vol. 1: 410–12; cf. Johnstone and Flood, 1982: 183–6). And their subordination is further symbolized by the fact that, although ILEX is nominally self-regulating, the Law Society actually exercises disciplinary power, punishing an average of 14 managing clerks a year between 1953 and 1963, an average of 16 a year between 1948 and 1979 (Johnstone and Hopson, 1967: 407–8, 485; Johnstone and Flood, 1982: 186–7; Law Society, Annual Reports). And though ILEX and the Law Society now issue joint recommendations for legal executive salaries, these have no binding force, and more experienced legal executives earn less than assistant solicitors. In 1984, an ILEX associate over the age of 21 was supposed to be paid £6500–8500, compared with the minimum of £3375–4300 recommended for articled clerks (about the same age and legal knowledge); but an ILEX fellow more than 25 years old was supposed to be paid £8500–9500, compared with the £8320–9670 that a sample of assistant solicitors earned in their first six months after admission (compare 80 *LSG* 1905, 1983; 81 *LSG* 1829, 1984; 83 *LSG* 1868, 1986 and Law Society Committee on Education and Training, 1985: 6, with table 2.38). Yet the fact that legal executives now can qualify as licensed conveyancers and compete directly with their former employers may lead to an improvement in their status and income.

## The distribution of solicitors among practice settings

Another way of exploring changes in the structure of production is to examine the distribution of solicitors among the various settings in which they practise: self-employed versus employees and private practice versus government and industry and commerce. Except for an isolated survey in 1939, we have no accurate data until 1957, when the Law Society began keeping records of those holding practising certificates. But these data tell us nothing about the many solicitors who fail to take out certificates – probably few in private practice but many in public or private employment. Several commentators have hazarded guesses about qualified solicitors without certificates, but these are based on little more than the number enrolled (many of whom no longer practise at all) and speculations about their distribution among practice settings. Kirk (1976: 114) estimated that in 1853 there were 5000 more solicitors than the 10,000 who held practising certificates. The Council of the Law Society (1944) estimated the number at 3000–4000 in 1939 (in addition to the 17,102 practising certificates). Gower and Price (1957: 324) estimated that 4000 practised without certificates in addition to the 18,344 who held them; Wheatcroft (1962: 15) thought there were only 1500 in 1962, in addition to the 19,790 certificates; Johnstone and Hopson (1967: 350 n. 13) suggested 2000 in 1967 in addition to the 22,223 certificates; and Kirk (1976: 114) noted that there were 7260 names on the Roll in 1974 in addition to the 28,741 certificates.

It seems unlikely that the number of practitioners without certificates varied historically between 7 per cent and 33 per cent of those holding certificates, so these estimates are of dubious value. Indeed, the proportion of solicitors on the Roll without practising certificates has been strikingly constant: 23 per cent in 1973 and 22 per cent in 1984 (Marks, 1984: 2607; 1985). In 1985, it was estimated that 3800 of the 8550 solicitors on the Roll without certificates were over 65, so that most were probably retired, and many had died (135 *NLJ* 71, 1985).

The best we can do is trace changes in the relative size of the various categories of certificate holders, recognizing that abrupt variation may be due to rulings that practitioners must or need not take out certificates – as apparently occurred in central government in 1974 and again in 1980 and 1981 (see tables 2.30, 2.31). I will begin with private practice. The number of partners grew more rapidly than the total number of certificates between 1939 and 1957, probably because of the small number of new solicitors admitted during the war. This pattern was reversed between 1957 and 1982, when the number of partners grew at a fairly steady 4 per cent a year, somewhat more slowly than the total number of certificates. This may reflect the difficulties that confronted a young solicitor seeking to open a practice and also, perhaps, the effect of the 1970 rule prohibiting a solicitor from practising on his own or in partnership for three years after qualifying. But throughout these 40 years, partners remained about half of those holding certificates.

During most of this period the number of sole practitioners declined, not just as a proportion of the profession but even absolutely (23 per cent) between 1957 and 1978 – two decades in which the number of certificates grew 85 per cent. Between 1978 and 1985 the category expanded, both absolutely (58 per cent) and relative to the total number of certificates (which increased 41 per cent). This presumably reflects the number of assistant solicitors who have served the requisite three years and who either are being laid off in preference to less expensive new admittees or are leaving because they are not offered partnerships. Nevertheless, during these 40 years sole practitioners have declined from a quarter of all certificates to less than a tenth.

The third category in private practice, assistant solicitors, remained a constant proportion of certificates between 1939 and 1957. But since then it has doubled (from 14 to 28 per cent of certificates). At the same time, consultants holding certificates have multiplied rapidly, perhaps because of new retirement schemes as well as a change in the requirement of a certificate in 1974. Consequently, those employed within private practice grew from 14 per cent of all certificates in 1957 to a third in 1984.

Outside private practice, public sector employment showed a decline between 1939 and 1957, perhaps merely an artifact of changing rules about who must hold a certificate; thereafter, this category paralleled the overall growth of the profession. Employment in private industry remained constant in the first two decades of this period but almost doubled its proportion of practising certificates in the second.

Summing up these changes, we see that the category of self-employed solicitors (partners and sole practitioners) declined from three-quarters of the total to two-thirds between 1939 and 1957 and to just over half in 1984. The category of employed solicitors (assistant solicitors and consultants in private practice and solicitors in government and industry) grew from a third to nearly half of all certificates – and this significantly understates its real growth because many solicitors employed by public and private enterprises do not take out practising certificates. Consequently, at least half of the members of a profession that prides itself on its independence are now employed. Employment, particularly outside private practice, represents a safety valve for a profession that has lost significant control over supply. But private practitioners rightly fear that employed solicitors constitute potential competitors, and in 1982 the Law Society's Professional Purposes Committee proposed that salaried solicitors be required to obtain experience in private practice before setting up on their own, no matter how many years they had worked since being admitted. Predictably, this was criticized by the Local Government Group, the Commerce and Industry Group, the prosecuting solicitors and the law centre solicitors; even the Master of the Rolls opposed it, and the proposal died (133 *NLJ* 411, 1983).

## Solicitors employed in commerce and industry

We have seen that the number of solicitors holding practising certificates and employed in commerce, industry, nationalized enterprises or other full-time employment increased fourfold between 1957 and 1984, nearly doubling their proportion of all practising certificates. Other evidence suggests that this category grew even more rapidly. Johnstone and Hopson (1967: 376–7 n. 55) estimated that all lawyers employed in the private sector had doubled between 1950 and 1960 and totalled 350–400 in 1961, two-thirds of whom were solicitors (cf. Wheatcroft, 1962: 15). Abel-Smith and Stevens (1967: 44) thought there were 600 privately employed solicitors in 1964. The Commerce and Industry Group of the Law Society had 1150 members in 1977, but many privately employed solicitors did not join; the Royal Commission estimated the total at 1000–2000 (1979, vol. 1: 232; vol. 2: 566). This suggests an increase of tenfold or twentyfold in 30 years.

Such rapid growth is attributable to both pushes and pulls. Newly qualified solicitors have multiplied so quickly that there are not enough jobs for them in private practice. At the same time, industry has sought to expand its in-house staff in response to the high and rapidly increasing fees charged by private firms (Imperial Chemical Industries, 1976). In order to attract talent, industry offered higher starting salaries and more rapid advancement than private practice. In 1971, the median income of employed solicitors was estimated to be £5000, the lower quartile £3700 and the upper quartile £6400; by contrast, the median income of all solicitors that year was little more than £2000; over a quarter made less than £1500, and only slightly more than a quarter made more than £3000 (compare *Solicitors' Journal*, 1972 with table 2.36). In 1976, articled clerks in commerce and industry earned a median of £3350, and 20 per cent earned more than £5000 – two to three times what clerks were earning in private practice (Royal Commission, 1979, vol. 2: 466, 572; Winyard, 1976). The income differences between assistant solicitors in private practice and employed solicitors with comparable experience remain substantial. In the late 1970s, those who had qualified for less than two years earned a median of £3980 in private practice and £5340 in industry; for those who had practised two to four years the difference was £5108 and £6837 (Royal Commission, 1979, vol. 2: 466, 569). Between 1980 and 1986, solicitors with at least three and a half years experience employed in industry consistently earned 25–40 per cent more than those in firms with fewer than eight partners and about the same as those in firms with more than 20 partners (see table 2.38). As careers progress, employed solicitors fall behind those in private practice: the median income of solicitors employed in industry in 1976 ranged from £7920 to £10,385, depending on age, compared with a median profit of £13,581 for all principals in private practice (Royal Commission, 1979, vol. 2: 478, 569). Yet relatively few solicitors leave commerce for private practice at this stage in their careers.

Legal departments in industry and commerce, like private firms, have been growing in size and complexity. In 1961, the largest establishment was that of the Prudential Assurance Company, with 23 solicitors (Johnstone and Hopson, 1967: 376–7 n. 55). Imperial Chemical Industries (1976) had 60 employed lawyers within the UK 15 years later, half of them solicitors. A 1977 survey of the members of the Commerce and Industry Group of the Law Society (38 per cent response rate) revealed an average establishment of three solicitors and three other legal staff, but 15 per cent of the enterprises had five to nine solicitors, and 6 per cent had ten or more (Royal Commission, 1979, vol. 2: 567–8).

## Solicitors in government

### *Local government*

Solicitors occupy virtually all the positions held by legally qualified employees in local government. This is largely a historical artifact: in the eighteenth century, when barristers were unavailable outside London except during the brief sittings of the assizes, solicitors eagerly sought and gained offices as clerks to the board of guardians and to navigation, turnpike and enclosure commissions and as clerks of the peace, town clerks, county court clerks and justices' clerks (Christian, 1896: 231 n. 1; Miles, 1984). Such offices were worth hundreds or even thousands of pounds a year (Williams, 1980: 221–2). They appear to be relatively unimportant today: only 5 per cent of solicitors in Devon and Cornwall in 1985 were clerks to the tax commissioners, 2 per cent sat on social security appeals tribunals, and 1 per cent were coroners (Blacksell et al., 1986: 7).

Until recently solicitors monopolized the role of chief executive in local government. In 1955 there were 1375 solicitors in local government, half of whom were clerks or deputy clerks and the rest assistant solicitors; by contrast, there were only eight barristers (Hobson and Stewart, 1969: 201, 212). In 1956, 80 per cent of local authorities serving populations over 5000 had a solicitor as clerk. This dominance diminished somewhat in the 1960s, as local governments hired clerks with business backgrounds, but 82 per cent of all town clerks were still solicitors in 1962 (Wheatcroft, 1962: 15; Johnstone and Hopson, 1967: 376–7 n. 55; Zander, 1968: 179; Kirk, 1976: 197). And in 1978 there were 2500 solicitors in local government and only 60 barristers, partly because the latter could not execute conveyances (Royal Commission, 1979, vol. 1: 232). Some of these establishments are enormous: in the early 1960s, the London County Council was the largest solicitors' firm in the country, with 56 solicitors and 132 unadmitted clerks (Johnstone and Hopson, 1967: 448–9). Some 425 prosecuting solicitors were also employed by 29 out of the 41 police authorities in the late 1970s (Prosecuting Solicitors, 1977); in 1980, the Metropolitan Police Solicitor's Department employed 62 solicitors, and provincial prosecuting solicitors' departments employed 602 (Royal Commission on Criminal Procedure, 1981b: 201–2). However, the Crown Prosecution Service, established in 1986, expected to hire most of the 900 solicitors then employed by local police authorities and to need perhaps another 800 lawyers, though many of these will be barristers (133 *NLJ* 988, 1983; 135 *NLJ* 1131, 1985).

We have seen that though the number of local government solicitors with practising certificates doubled between 1957 and 1984, it increased less rapidly than the total number of certificates. One reason may have been the displacement of solicitors by professional city managers (Abel-Smith and Stevens, 1967: 401). Another may have been the relatively low salaries. The local authority pay scale in 1977 provided a starting salary of £5001 for solicitors 25 years old, rising to £7719 – considerably more than the £3980 paid to assistant solicitors starting in private practice (Royal Commission, 1979, vol. 2: 466, 686). But the gap quickly narrowed with age and soon reversed. The Local Government Group (1977: 16) estimated that chief officers earned about £13,000, deputies about £10,000 and other solicitors £5000–9000. That year, nearly a quarter of solicitors earned more than £8000 (see table 2.35). And advertisements for government solicitors (both central and local) consistently offered less than positions in private practice in London, though more than those in the suburbs or countryside (see table 2.39). In order to retain their solicitors in the 1960s, the London County Council (CLCC) had to allow them to maintain outside practices, and about a third did so (Johnstone and Hopson, 1967: 450). In addition, the LCC pioneered substantial salaries for articled clerks, offering £800–1000 in 1960 when most clerks still were paying premiums and earning little or no salary (ibid.). In 1984, the Law Society offered a local government diploma course to those with two years' experience in local government, creating an incentive for them to remain (Annual Report, 1983–4).

*Central government*

If solicitors dominate local government, barristers dominate central government (see chapter 6, p. 112). Many central government departments did not offer articles until recently. But solicitors have increased their share of central government positions, partly because they enjoy expanding rights of audience, whereas employed barristers could not appear at all and cannot brief private barristers (Drewry, 1981: 40). At the end of the nineteenth century there were only 20–30 solicitors in central government (Incorporated Law Society, Calendar, 1885: 1481; 1891: 1386–7; 1892: 1269–70; 1893: 1308–9). There were about 400 solicitors in central government in 1968, 412 in 1976, about 450 in 1978 and 420 in 1983 (Royal Commission, 1979, vol. 2: 52; Zander, 1980: 5; see tables 2.30, 4.4). They tend to be concentrated in certain departments: the General Post Office, the Departments of Agriculture and Energy, the Treasury Solicitor (which acts for many other departments), the Welsh Office, the Office of Fair Trading, the Official Solicitor, the Public Trustee and the Land Registry (Johnstone and Hopson, 1967: 376–7 n. 55; Drewry, 1981: 30; see table 4.4). They are also found in public and private corporations: the Central Electricity Generating Board, the British Railways Board, British Telecom, the National Coal Board and the BBC (Solicitors' and Barristers' Directory and Diary, 1985). As the titles of the departments suggest, central government solicitors tend to provide fairly routine services or to be involved in matters concerning property rather than to engage in policy making (Drewry, 1981: 30). Furthermore, they head only 8 out of 31 departments, even though they are 54 per cent of all central government lawyers and a majority in more than 15 (and about 80 per cent of all lawyers) (see table 4.4).

Since 1918, solicitors in central government have been career civil servants (Drewry, 1981: 20–1). This means that they are governed by Civil Service salary scales, which in 1976 began at £4289 for a 25-year-old legal assistant (about a third of the total) and rose to £14,000 for the 13 (2 per cent) who held the title 'solicitor' (Royal Commission, 1979, vol. 2: 687; Equal Opportunities Commission, 1978: 25). In 1976–7, the median after-tax income of the civil service legal class (both barristers and solicitors) (£7904) compared favourably with that of principals in private practice (£7643), but only because they are paid better in the first five years of practice; thereafter the positions are reversed (Royal Commission, 1979, vol. 2: 692–5). The Crown Prosecution Service, which began operation in 1986, paid Crown prosecutors £10,500–15,000 and senior Crown prosecutors £16,500. But it was concerned that it would not attract qualified applicants, since in 1985 the Civil Service could fill only 40 out of 93 vacancies for lawyers with even better offers (135 *NLJ* 1131, 1985). This is not surprising, since the median net income of principals in 1984 (even excluding those in London firms with more than 14 partners) was £21,300 (83 *LSG* 169–70, 1985). In 1986 the Treasury Solicitor advertised 48 vacancies at salaries up to £25,000 but found few applicants (Hughes, 1986).

# 14

# The work of solicitors

## The private market

The basic contours of solicitors' work have remained fairly constant for the last century and a half, despite changes in emphasis and in some of the more marginal functions they perform. The core has been conveyancing and litigation. Attorneys and solicitors displaced barristers in the execution of conveyances by the end of the seventeenth century. In the latter half of the eighteenth century conveyancing already produced a third to a half of their income (Miles, 1984; Robson, 1959: 54). The other staple of a solicitor's work was litigation. In the nineteenth century, solicitors specializing in county court litigation sometimes were 'briefed' by other solicitors (Forbes, 1979: 15). This practice violated professional rules but still persists, although the specialist may have to file a change of solicitor form (Zander, 1968: 165–6; Kirk, 1976: 159). In the provinces most litigation concerned petty debts and therefore paid poorly unless it was mass produced. Because the higher courts were concentrated in London, provincial solicitors could do little more than the preparatory work and forwarded most cases to London agents (Miles, 1984; Reader, 1966: 162–3). In the mid 1960s, some 70 of the latter belonged to the London Agents' Association and paid commissions of 5–25 per cent to the forwarding firms (Johnstone and Hopson, 1967: 371).

The nineteenth century saw a decline in contentious work and an increase in non-contentious, principally conveyancing but also wills, trusts and probate, the formation and dissolution of partnerships and companies, election agency and the promotion of railway bills (Reader, 1966: 162–3; Offer, 1981: 12; Miles, 1984). Following the passage of the Limited Liability Act of 1855 and the Joint Stock Companies Act of 1856, the number of new companies formed rapidly climbed to a high of 689 in 1863 (Slinn, 1984: 109, 113–14). But if this was a period of expansion, solicitors were also threatened by competitors. They earlier had been displaced by banks as negotiators of loans or money lenders (Miles, 1981). Specialized estate agents took over their role of managing the estates of landowners (D. Spring, 1963: 58, 67). They lost bankruptcy and company liquidations to the Board of Trade in 1890 (Offer, 1981: 46) and the administration of trusts to banks and trust companies and to the Office of the Public Trustee, established over their protests in 1906. They were forced to share the work of land transfers with estate agents, auctioneers and surveyors; taxation and some company law was taken over by accountants; many commercial matters went to arbitration, where solicitors might be unnecessary; industrial tribunals were intended to render solicitors superfluous; electoral work was taken over by professional agents (ibid.: 54–5); the introduction of banking supplanted the functions of solicitors in drafting bills of exchange (Birks, 1960: 229); and patent agents monopolized most patent work (Van Zyl Smit, 1985). But as solicitors lost some subjects, they found others to replace them. For instance, with the entry of Britain into the European Community, the net income of solicitors from overseas work increased from £19 million in 1975 to £40 million in 1977 and £79 million in 1983 (Central Statistical Office, 1976–7: 43; Campbell-Smith, 1985b).

Several studies have been conducted in the last two decades that give us a fairly accurate and consistent picture of the income generated by different kinds of work. Non-contentious matters still dominate, and conveyancing remains the single largest category. In 1966, solicitors earned half their income from residential conveyancing, two-thirds from conveyancing and probate and less than 3 per cent from county court litigation (National Board for Prices and Incomes, 1968: 10). A 1971 survey of Birmingham solicitors also found that non-contentious work generated two-thirds of solicitor income; most litigation involved family matters (7 per cent of total income) or crime (6 per cent) (Bridges et al., 1975: 34). The comprehensive study conducted by the Law Society for the Royal Commission found that non-contentious work produced three-quarters of solicitor income – almost half from conveyancing and the remaining quarter shared about equally by probate and company work. Matrimonial, criminal and personal injury litigation constituted about 5, 4 and 3 per cent respectively (Royal Commission, 1979, vol. 2: 489, 494). The most recent Peat Marwick study for the Law Society found that conveyancing accounted for 30 per cent of gross fee income in 1983–4, but since it is more profitable than other subjects its contribution to net income may have been higher (83 *LSG* 169–70, 1986). In the last ten years, contentious work seems to have increased and non-contentious work to have declined – particularly probate, wills and trusts (136 *NLJ* 59, 1986).

We get a similar picture if we look at the work of solicitors from the perspective of individual clients (unfortunately, none of the surveys examines the use of solicitors by business). The 1978 users' survey found that 35 per cent of the consultations concerned residential property, 21 per cent involved wills and estates, 12 per cent family litigation, 7 per cent crimes and 7 per cent personal injuries (Royal Commission, 1979, vol. 2: 198). A 1982 survey by the Consumers' Association found that, after conveyancing, its members used solicitors to make wills and probate them, for divorce, for consumer problems and property damage and for disputes over property (in descending order) (*LAG Bulletin* 10, February 1983). A 1986 survey found that among those who had ever used a solicitor, 70 per cent had done so for conveyancing, 27 per cent for wills and trusts, 14 per cent for divorce or separation and 7 per cent for motoring offences (multiple responses permitted). Not surprisingly, the general public's image of solicitors mirrors this pattern: 67 per cent associate solicitors with domestic conveyancing and property, 42 per cent with family matters, 37 per cent with wills and trusts, 28 per cent with criminal cases, 12 per cent with disputes and 9 per cent with claims and compensation (multiple responses permitted) (83 *LSG* 1113, 1986).

Individual firms differ widely from this aggregate distribution. Firm size is the most important determinant. In 1966, sole practitioners spent 37 per cent of their time on conveyancing and 9.7 per cent on probate, whereas London firms with more than four solicitors spent 22 and 6.8 per cent respectively; for other non-contentious work (mainly company law), the proportions were reversed (10.6 and 25.6 per cent) (National Board for Prices and Incomes, 1968: 47; see also Bridges et al., 1975: 29, 32). In 1975–6, sole practitioners derived almost twice as great a proportion of their income from conveyancing as did firms with ten or more lawyers (59.9 per cent compared with 32.4 per cent) but little more than a tenth as much from company work (3.7 per cent versus 32.2 per cent) (Royal Commission, 1979, vol. 2: 489). Despite the overall decline in the importance of conveyancing, solicitors in rural Devon and Cornwall still derived 85.7 per cent of their income from such work in 1985 (Blacksell et al., 1986: 18–19). Nationwide in 1983–4, 45 per cent of sole practitioners derived more than half their income from conveyancing, compared with 30 per cent of firms with 2–4 partners, 26 per cent of firms with 5–14 partners and only 2 per cent of firms with at least 15 partners. On the other hand, 73 per cent of firms with at least 15 partners derived a quarter of their income or less from conveyancing, compared with 27 per cent of firms with 5–14 partners, 24 per cent of firms with 2–4 partners and 14 per cent of sole practitioners (83 *LSG* 169–70, 1986). It seems clear that it is the large firm (at least 10 partners in 1975, 15 in 1983) that is the aberration.

The distinctions just noted suggest that solicitors' firms are somewhat specialized. But with the exception of the very largest, most firms still feel the need to provide a full range of services, at least for established clients (Bridges et al., 1975: 37). A survey of solicitors' firms in the mid 1970s found that three-quarters performed services in each of the eight major subject-matter categories, and virtually all engaged in conveyancing and probate (Royal Commission, 1979, vol. 2: 489). In 1983, almost all firms in Devon and Cornwall practised in the areas of residential conveyancing, wills and trusts, housing, commercial law, property, family and general litigation (Watkins et al., 1986a: 17). Despite the pressures to remain generalists, firms do specialize for a variety of reasons. Some subjects are highly technical and esoteric, such as air law, shipping and banking. Some subjects fit together because they tend to serve the same categories of client. Solicitors performing matrimonial, personal injury, criminal and other litigation serve the general public; 78 per cent of Devon and Cornwall firms in 1983 said that more than 70 per cent of their clients were individuals (Blacksell et al., 1986: table 40). Solicitors who draft and probate wills and advise about taxation serve wealthy individuals; until after World War II, Freshfields derived most of its work from such a clientele (Slinn, 1984: 159). Finally, most larger firms advise business enterprises about company and commercial law, international trade and taxation (Podmore, 1977b: 636; Bridges et al., 1975: 37–8; cf. Heinz and Laumann, 1982).

The increasing involvement of the state in the market for legal services also encourages and sometimes requires specialization. At present, only specialist members of panels can provide legal aid before mental health tribunals or in cases involving children in care (the latter panel contains about 1000 names) (Law Society, Annual Report, 1985–6: 12), and the recent Legal Aid Scrutiny report by the Lord Chancellor's Department recommended that this be extended generally (83 *LSG* 2050–6 1986). At about the same time, the Lord Chancellor's Civil Justice Review recommended that personal injury solicitors retained by paying clients also be required to obtain a specialist certification – a proposal opposed by the President of the Law Society (83 *LSG* 2057, 1986). On the other hand, the Law Society can now certify solicitors as specialist insolvency practitioners under the Insolvency Act 1985 (83 *LSG* 2202 and 2459, 1986).

Sometimes specialization is a function of aversion. In 1966, 15 percent of all solicitors' firms did no county court work; three years later the percentage had doubled (National Board for Prices and Incomes, 1969: 11). It is not surprising, therefore, that such litigation accounted for less than 3 per cent of solicitor income in 1966 (National Board for Prices and Incomes, 1968: 10). In 1971, almost half of all Birmingham firms did no criminal work; they also avoided debt collection, which is very unprofitable, performing it only as a favour to an established client or to obtain other business (Bridges et al., 1975: 36–7; Blacksell et al., 1986: 20). In 1983, most solicitors in Devon and Cornwall (86 per cent) acknowledged that they had less experience handling welfare benefits than any other legal matter (Watkins et al., 1986a: 21).

But some firms profitably handle these and other categories of unpopular work by engaging in mass production. In the 1960s, a few firms bought up debt claims and consequently accounted for as much as 40 per cent of all county court litigation (Zander, 1968: 182). Litigation becomes more profitable (or at least less unprofitable) the higher the proportion of total income it represents. Thus, firms that derived 2.5 per cent of their income from litigation incurred 5.9 per cent of their expenses in that field, but those that derived 9.3 per cent of their income from litigation incurred only 11.8 per cent of their expenses there (National Board for Prices and Incomes, 1968: 21). Among the Birmingham solicitors studied in 1971, litigation represented 72 per cent of all bills for the 11 firms (6 per cent) that specialized but only 26 per cent of the bills for the 133 (77 per cent) that did not (Bridges et al., 1975: 33). Specialist litigators had a higher staff/solicitor ratio and delegated more work in order to achieve the volume that permitted economies of scale sufficient to generate profits (ibid.: 39–43).

Differences in the profitability of various categories of work help to explain its distribution. For instance, few City firms were interested in doing commercial conveyancing until the £100 ceiling on fees was lifted in 1953 (Abel-Smith and Stevens, 1967: 435). The great divide in profitability has been between contentious and non-contentious matters. In 1969, contentious work produced 20 per cent of solicitors' earnings but accounted for 30 per cent of their expenses (National Board for Prices and Incomes, 1969: 10). Conveyancing, on the other hand, produced 56 per cent of total revenue but represented only 41 per cent of expenses (ibid.: 14). In 1971, solicitors charged an average of £57.20 for a conveyance but incurred expenses of only £31.70, a profit of 45 per cent; the profit for executing a purchaser's mortgage was 68 per cent (National Board for Prices and Incomes, 1971: 18–19). In 1983, a Peat Marwick study found that all categories of fee earners consistently billed fewer hours if they did conveyancing work rather than other non-contentious work, fewer hours if they did any kind of non-contentious work rather than litigation and fewer hours if they did civil litigation rather than criminal (Hiley, 1984).

The 1975–6 study confirmed this general picture but suggested some nuances. Among non-contentious matters, company work was the most profitable, followed by conveyancing; probate appeared to be only moderately profitable. As the proportion of non-contentious work increased, so did its profitability; but as the proportion of conveyancing work increased, profitability declined sharply (Royal Commission, 1979, vol. 2: 496, 498–9). The latter correlation appears to be a function of firm size rather than subject-matter specialization; smaller firms, which derive the highest proportion of their income from conveyancing, are also less profitable, either because they are inefficient or because they make less use of subordinated personnel. Indeed, partners seem to spend a disproportionate amount of time on conveyancing. They performed 55–7 per cent of the work although they constituted only 43 per cent of legal personnel in 1976; articled clerks and assistant solicitors were underutilized (compare table 2.26 with Royal Commission, 1979, vol. 2: 129). Nevertheless, Devon and Cornwall firms, though small, derived 85.7 per cent of their income from conveyancing while devoting only 76.7 per cent of their time to it (Blacksell et al., 1986: 18–19).

Sometimes solicitors find so few private clients that they are forced to take other work merely to subsist. In the eighteenth and nineteenth centuries they occupied official positions, acted as intermediaries between the Overseers of the Poor and the local JP, or clerked for the JP (Miles, 1984). They were also general business agents and property managers for large landowners (Spring, 1963: ch. 3). In the early twentieth century they combined practice with selling insurance, collecting rents and debts and acting as house agents or accountants (Offer, 1981: 13; cf. Carlin, 1962). And in the 1970s, 12 per cent of West Midlands solicitors had another occupation: 3 per cent were farmers and 9 per cent public officials (Podmore, 1977b: 611).

Both of the principal categories of solicitors' work – conveyancing and litigation – constantly fluctuate in response to factors over which solicitors exercise very little control. The value of property transferred has risen rapidly for at least the last 100 years (see chapter 10, p. 167). Avner Offer (1981: 50–1) calculated that the total value of sales, leases and mortgages of real property in 1898 was £393 million (at a time when all British exports were worth only £233 million); assuming that clients paid scale fees, solicitors earned £5.4 million from conveyancing in 1905, about half their total earnings that year and £328 for every solicitor. During this period, solicitors' conveyancing income perfectly tracked fluctuations in the number of conveyances, leases and mortgages (ibid.:

52–3). Gross advances on building society mortgages rose from £9.3 million to £955.4 million (more than a hundredfold) between 1910 and 1965, while the *Statist* price index rose from 78 to 404 (fivefold) (compare tables 5.7 and 4.7). Although these estimates ignore commercial conveyancing, the latter accounts for only 10 per cent of the conveyancing income of private practitioners, both because almost seven times as many residential as commercial parcels change hands each year and because commercial transactions are often handled by solicitors employed by the buyer or seller (Royal Commission, 1979, vol. 1: 248; vol. 2: 106, 108; Bowles and Phillips, 1977: 648).

One reason why solicitor conveyancing income outpaced inflation is that only about one dwelling in ten was owner occupied in 1901, but half were in 1978 (Royal Commission, 1979, vol. 1: 39). Furthermore, property values have outrun inflation since the 1960s. Both the number and value of conveyances rose between 1965 and 1969 (National Board for Prices and Incomes, 1969: 22). The average house price jumped from £5000 in 1970 to £13,712 in 1977; the total value of residential properties transferred rose from £760 million in October 1973 to £1286 million in November 1977; and the annual value of all land sales increased from £11,920 million in 1973 to £18,990 million in 1978 (Royal Commission, 1979, vol. 2: 106, 108–9, 114; see tables 5.8, 5.9). The average solicitor's fee for a residential sale in November 1978 was £184 for a buyer and £337 for a seller (ibid.: 119). Solicitors thus earned approximately £66.6 million from conveying 127,829 properties that month (see table 5.8). The recession of 1973–4 did dampen sales (by a sixth), which may explain why conveyancing fell from 56 per cent of all solicitor income in 1966 to 46 per cent in 1976 (Royal Commission, 1979, vol. 2: 109; Glasser, 1979: 202). But the number and value of conveyances and net and gross advances on mortgages by building societies have increased rapdily since then (see tables 5.7–5.9).

Contentious work is also affected by several variables over which solicitors have only limited influence. The first is the jurisdiction of those courts in which solicitors have a right of audience. The creation of the county courts in 1846 increased the annual number of cases filed by solicitors more than fourfold, from about 100,000 to an average of 433,000 in the succeeding five years (Abel-Smith and Stevens, 1967: 35). This tripled by 1910 and exceeded 2 million by the 1980s (see table 5.1). These increases reflected not only the growth of the population and the economy but also expansion of the jurisdictional limit from an initial £40 in 1846 to £50 in 1850, £100 in 1903, £200 in 1938, £400 in 1955, £750 in 1970, £1000 in 1974 and £5000 in 1986 (£30,000 in equity)

(Kirk, 1976: 158). The criminal jurisdiction of magistrates' courts has also expanded.

Nevertheless, litigation remained unattractive. The maximum fees were low (5 shillings when the county courts were first established); most civil cases involved petty debts, which solicitors bought from creditors at a discount and then prosecuted on their own behalf (Kirk, 1976: 156; cf. Friedman, 1973: 265); and many potential clients lacked the capacity to pay even minimal fees. We saw earlier that solicitors were very timid in pressing for expanded rights of audience, until they were threatened with loss of the conveyancing monopoly (see chapter 5, p. 87). The incredible growth of tribunals since the 1930s has created relatively little work for solicitors: although 49 per cent of respondents and 33 per cent of applicants were represented by lawyers before industrial tribunals in October 1977, most solicitors still do very little tribunal work (Royal Commission, 1979, vol. 1: 168; Bridges et al., 1975: 51). Between 1978 and 1982, the proportion of applicants represented by lawyers before the industrial tribunals varied between 26 and 38 per cent and the proportion of respondents between 37 and 47 per cent (McFadyen, 1984).

Solicitors have not been entirely passive in the face of fluctuations in market demand. In the 1970s they took two initiatives, perhaps responding to concerns about the rapidly expanding supply of solicitors. First, they engaged in collective advertising, seeking to alert the public to hidden legal problems, overcome the widespread fear of law and lawyers and publicize the advantages of solicitors over other service providers. The most notable effort was the 'Mr Whatsisname' campaign of 1977–8, which cost £300,000; despite its lack of tangible results, it led to the expenditure of another £390,000 the following year (Podmore, 1980: 73 n. 12; Fennell, 1982; cf. Zander, 1968: 213–14). More recently, the Law Society's Professional and Public Relations Committee collaborated with the Schools Curriculum Development Committee to study the teaching of law in secondary schools, which might encourage the assertion of legal rights and the use of lawyers (81 *LSG* 1194, 1984). Second, solicitors participated in schemes of private insurance for legal expenses, very widespread in Germany but unknown in England until 1974, when Lloyd's wrote the first policy. Although the initial market targeted was business enterprises (with respect to employment and tax disputes), the principal effort to stimulate demand was an agreement between the Law Society and Sun Alliance to launch a family legal expenses insurance policy in 1982. Despite considerable publicity, it seems to have attracted few buyers and generated little business (Vann, 1985; 133 *NLJ* 217, 1983). Only 5 per cent of a sample of Devon and

Cornwall solicitors in 1985 thought legal insurance very important, and only another 8 per cent thought it important (Blacksell et al., 1986: table 54). In 1984–5 the Law Society also arranged to allow clients to pay for legal services with credit cards, and 850 firms had signed up with Access by late 1985 (134 *NLJ* 1079, 1984; 135 *NLJ* 1097, 1985). Perhaps the most dramatic break with tradition is the willingness of solicitors to consider contingent fees in personal injury cases. The First National Conference of Civil Litigation Solicitors in May 1986 endorsed a proposal for a contingency fund, though they continued to oppose contingent fees (83 *LSG* 1861–2, 1986). And the Law Society itself appears to be reconsidering the matter (136 *NLJ* 647–8, 1986).

## Demand creation through public subsidy

One reason why solicitors have devoted limited energy to stimulating demand from individual paying clients is the secure income they have derived from conveyancing, at least until recently. Another may be the rising demand for solicitors' services fostered by the creation of legal aid in 1950 and its constant expansion since then (Abel, 1985). Prior to 1950, solicitors represented indigents without any fee under the Poor Person's Procedure, but few were served. From 1928 to 1937 the number of applications granted (only half of those made) rose from about 2000 to about 3000 a year; if these had been spread evenly over the entire profession, each solicitor would have been handling less than one case every five years. As applications increased, a number of provincial law societies refused to accept even this minimal burden. During World War II, when the divorce rate jumped and threatened the morale of the troops, the armed forces created staffs of salaried solicitors who handled many times the number of clients represented under the Poor Person's Procedure. However, these services were disbanded shortly after the war, and by 1949 the annual caseload of the Poor Person's Procedure had dropped to about 6600 (Law Society, Annual Reports).

By contrast, 37,700 certificates were issued in 1951 – the first full year under the Legal Aid Act. Though the number declined somewhat during the 1950s, there were 77,530 legal aid certificates and 46,284 instances of legal advice in 1961; and the numbers have risen steadily ever since (Lord Chancellor's Department, Legal Aid Annual Reports; see table 5.10). The advent of the legal aid scheme appears to have curtailed the altruism of solicitors. In response to a 1966 survey, half of all firms acknowledged that they offered no free legal advice at all, another third offered an hour a week or less, and only 2–3 per cent offered more than

5 hours a week (National Board for Prices and Incomes, 1968: 19).

The impact of legal aid on contentious work cannot be exaggerated: solicitors earned £40 million from legal aid in 1979–80 and four and a half times as much in 1983–4 (Lord Chancellor's Department, Legal Aid Annual Reports; see table 2.33). The Legal Aid Scrutiny by the Lord Chancellor's Department in 1986 stated that £281 million was paid to solicitors by legal aid in 1984–5 and expected the total budget of the programme to rise to £400 million in 1986–7 (83 *LSG* 2050–6, 1986). Because barristers monopolize major civil matters, solicitors engage in relatively little litigation outside the areas dominated by legal aid – criminal defence, matrimonial cases and personal injuries (Bridges et al., 1975: 50). In 1975–6, sole practitioners derived 80 per cent of their income in contentious matters from legal aid, and even firms with ten or more partners derived 60–70 per cent of such income from that source. Between 60 and 80 per cent of all criminal and matrimonial litigation was paid by legal aid (Royal Commission, 1979, vol. 2: 492; see also Murch, 1977; 1978). Nevertheless, because contentious matters generate a much smaller proportion of total income for solicitors than they do for barristers, legal aid is far less salient to the former. Although legal aid paid for 28 per cent of all contentious matters in 1975–6, it represented only 6 per cent of solicitors' gross fees (ibid., vol. 1: 529), compared with half the income of the Bar. In 1984, criminal legal aid accounted for only 3 per cent of solicitors' gross fees (136 *NLJ* 59, 1986).

Yet these figures do not accurately indicate the significance of legal aid to solicitors, for the income is very unequally distributed. And whereas the large majority of beginning barristers rely heavily on legal aid, many solicitors never have much to do with the programme. A 1975–6 survey of 1480 firms revealed that two-thirds received no more than 10 per cent of their income from legal aid, and 87 per cent received no more than 20 per cent; only 2 per cent received more than half of their income from this source and only 1 per cent more than 70 per cent (ibid., vol. 2: 491). In both 1975–6 and 1980–1, half of all solicitors' firms received a total of only 6 per cent of all payments, whereas the 5 per cent of firms specializing in legal aid accounted for a third of all payments (Lord Chancellor's Department, Legal Aid Annual Reports, 1975–6: app. p. 13; 1980–1: app. p.16; for a description of a legal aid firm, see Morton, 1986). This distribution is strikingly constant: in both 1979–80 and 1983–4, nearly three-fifths of solicitors' firms received a tenth of all payments, whereas a tenth received half, and a quarter 1983–4 received three-quarters (see table 2.33). There is a suspicion that a few of the firms heavily dependent on legal aid may be exploiting the system: the 1985–6 Report of the House of Commons Committee on Public Accounts found that one firm, consisting of a sole principal, a consultant, three assistant solicitors and their staff, received £231,987.71 for 4677 bills (*Legal Action* 3, August 1986).

A survey of all firms earning more than £10,000 from criminal legal aid work in magistrates' courts (22 per cent response) found that they earned 13 per cent of their gross income from this source (a median of £48,000). Yet even within this group there was substantial variation: 6 firms (2 per cent of respondents) earned more than 75 per cent of their income from this source, and another 15 (5 per cent) earned more than 50 per cent; 294 of the 2725 fee earners (10.8 per cent) obtained more than 60 per cent of their income from this source, and 96 (3.5 per cent) earned more than 95 per cent of their income from criminal legal aid (82 *LSG* 3425–9, 1985). Among 161 firms studied in Birmingham in 1972, 11 did a high volume of legal aid work, and 30 did a significant volume, whereas the remaining 120 did little or none; specialist firms submitted three times as many legal aid bills per solicitor as those that did not specialize (Bridges et al., 1975: 12, 39–43). In Devon and Cornwall in 1985, 35 per cent of firms derived less than 20 per cent of their income from legal aid, whereas 10 per cent derived at least 40 per cent from that source (Blacksell et al., 1986: table 44). And just as smaller firms were more dependent on conveyancing, so legal aid as a proportion of firm income varies inversely with firm size (Royal Commission, 1979, vol. 2: 503–4).

Legal aid has become increasingly important to solicitors in the last two decades, and this trend is likely to continue, especially if solicitors lose a significant amount of conveyancing. Consequently, the Law Society has been concerned with questions of subject-matter coverage, client eligibility and fee levels. Although the Royal Commission recommended major expansions of the legal aid scheme (Abel, 1982: 16–19), the Lord Chancellor's Department rejected virtually all of them, either on substantive grounds or because of lack of funds (1983: 11, 13, 15, 19). It agreed in principle that legal aid ought to be available for both lay and legal representation before tribunals (ibid.: 18). Indeed, representation appears significantly to enhance the applicant's chances of success: 46 per cent of represented applicants before social security appeals tribunals won, compared with 27 per cent of those unrepresented (Alexander, 1986). Such representation could greatly enlarge demand for solicitors' services, since between 1978 and 1982, 30–40 per cent of both applicants and respondents before the industrial tribunals appeared without representation; but nothing has been done to implement this proposal. A minor victory has been the appointment of an independent solicitor to represent children in child care proceedings (parents are already represented) (ibid.: 17). But, just as important, this has concentrated such work in a national panel of qualified solicitors who have handled more than five contested cases – a form of government-mandated specialization that also applies to representation before the mental health review tribunal (134 *NLJ* 445, 1984).

Overshadowing changes in the definition of subject matter coverage has been the progressive decline in financial eligibility as a result of the failure of the Lord Chancellor's Department to adjust guidelines for inflation. Whereas 80 per cent of the population was eligible for legal aid when it was introduced in 1950, only 40 per cent remained eligible by the mid 1970s – and just 20 per cent of families with children. Notwithstanding reviews of financial eligibility in 1979, 1982 and 1983, a single man earning the average male income, who would have been eligible in 1980, became ineligible at £700 less than the average male income six years later; and families with children fared even worse. Then, in 1986, the Lord Chancellor's Department made the first reduction in eligibility since the creation of legal aid – a cut of a sixth in the allowance for dependents – through which it hoped to save £7.5 million a year (Lord Chancellor's Department, 1983: 10; Glasser, 1986; 136 *NLJ* 156, 1986). At the same time, the government has failed to provide continuing funding for law centres, which had multiplied from 1 in 1970 to 44 in 1981, with the result that Southall cut its services by half, Paddington closed, and Hillingdon and Liverpool 8 were expected to close soon (83 *LSG* 1022, 1986).

Despite the Government's determination to cut legal aid costs – which had increased threefold between 1979 and 1986, overran the budget by £30 million in the last of those years and were expected to rise five times as fast as the total government budget between 1986 and 1990 (Glasser, 1986; Dean, 1986a) – the Law Society has pressed vigorously for an increase in fee levels. The inadequacy of those fees was suggested by the withdrawal from criminal legal aid and Green Form work by the largest legal aid firm in the country, Bowling & Co. of Stratford, East London, in 1985, and the withdrawal from criminal legal aid in 1986 by Messrs Peter Soar of Cambridge, whose senior partner was chairman of the Legal Aid Practitioners' Group (135 *NLJ* 975, 1985; 83 *LSG* 1022, 1986). In 1986, a West London firm with 3 partners and 13 fee earners deriving 85 per cent of their business from legal aid dissolved, and another London firm was seeking 8 redundancies in a staff of 27 because legal aid owed them more than £70,000 (*Legal Action* 6, May 1986; 5, June 1986). A *Legal Action* survey in July 1986 elicited responses from 206 readers: 29 per cent said that legal aid work was becoming less profitable, another 16 per cent complained that payments were becoming slower, and 12 per cent voiced both grievances; but because they were committed to serving the poor and had no alternative sources of revenue none was withdrawing from legal aid practice, and 68 per cent were not cutting back such work at all (*Legal Action* 8–9, October 1986).

At the instance of the Law Society, Peat Marwick surveyed 313 firms containing 2725 fee earners – a 22 per cent response from all firms earning more than £10,000 a year from magistrates' court criminal legal aid work (an earlier study had elicited too few responses) (134 *NLJ* 875 and 1052, 1984). It found that among those earning more than 60 per cent of their income from criminal legal aid, profits from that work were 13 per cent lower than profits from other subjects (22 per cent less in London). Principals in firms deriving more than 30 per cent of their income from criminal legal aid made about half as much as principals doing no criminal legal aid (even when the analysts controlled for firm size and location). Principals who earned more than 60 per cent of their income from criminal legal aid made a significantly smaller contribution to firm profits than those earning less than 60 per cent; indeed, in London those earning more than 60 per cent of their income from criminal legal aid represented a net loss to their firms.

On the basis of these findings, the Law Society sought an increase of 26–34 per cent in criminal legal aid fees in order to make earnings comparable with those of senior legal assistants in the civil service or solicitors employed in commerce and industry. When the Lord Chancellor awarded only 5 per cent, the Law Society joined the Bar in litigation that led to a reconsideration (Peat Marwick, 1985; 82 *LSG* 3425–9, 1985; 83 *LSG* 246, 606 and 1022, 1986; Duffy, 1986). In the end, solicitors obtained 4.5 per cent on top of the original 5 per cent offer, plus a 2 per cent London weighting and another 2 per cent for all solicitors if the Law Society agreed to join a standing committee on efficiency in the criminal courts (83 *LSG* 2050 and 2282–7, 1986). Clearly the Law Society, like the Senate, increasingly will be involved in activities that closely resemble collective bargaining with the government. Indeed, it was the perception by those practitioners heavily dependent on legal aid that their professional associations were not acting sufficiently like trade unions that led to the emergence of the Legal Aid Practitioners, Group, the Campaign for the Bar and some of the support for the British Legal Association.

But the present government's determination to cut costs seems certain to triumph over the Law Society's efforts to increase the legal aid budget. The total budget rose from £49 million in 1975–6 to £257 million in

1985–6, both because demand expanded and because unit costs rose faster than inflation; it was expected to reach £400 million in 1986–7. In response, the Lord Chancellor's Department conducted a Legal Aid Scrutiny, which made a number of radical proposals. In order to control unit costs, it recommended paying standard fees for standardized services rather than reimbursing lawyers on the basis of the time expended. And it sought to eliminate legal advice under the Green Form scheme, whose numbers had increased from 180,000 in 1974–5 to 950,000 in 1984–5. The Scrutiny found that citizens' advice bureaux could assess a claimant's benefit entitlement for £4, which would pay for only 9 minutes of solicitor time. Consequently, it recommended that the bureaux replace solicitor advice except in criminal and family matters and when litigation was required, hiring an additional 200 lawyers and 800 advice workers. Not surprisingly, the Legal Aid Practitioners' Group vehemently protested this curtailment of solicitor advice (83 *LSG* 2050–6 and 2202, 1986; *Legal Action* 4, May 1986; 136 *NLJ* 622, 1986). The government has abandoned the idea of abolishing the Green Form scheme, but others of the recommended changes may be implemented (136 *NLJ* 1051–2, 1986).

The legal aid scheme created in 1950 relies on potential clients taking the initiative to consult solicitors, thereby reproducing existing patterns of lawyer use. Although the Law Society developed lists of solicitors willing to take legally aided clients and distributed millions of them, this did not significantly change patterns of use (Monopolies and Mergers Commission, 1976b: 12–13; Royal Commission, 1979, vol. 1: 363). In recent years, solicitors have turned to other devices – principally duty solicitor schemes and citizens' advice bureaux – to encourage the public to use legal services in new ways, thereby increasing demand. Duty solicitor schemes have been tried at prisons, tribunals and police stations. Although the Lord Chancellor's Department (1983: 9) rejected the Royal Commission's recommendation (1979, vol. 1: 99) that legal aid be extended to prison disciplinary proceedings, a court has ruled that legal aid is available (133 *NLJ* 1007, 1983). The Greater Manchester Legal Services Committee established a rota of solicitors who made weekly visits to Manchester Prison to determine the demand for civil legal representation. Although the Home Office refused to fund a similar proposal for Wandsworth Prison, a scheme did operate at Strangeways Prison between 1983 and 1985 (133 *NLJ* 774, 1983; *Legal Action* 3, August 1985). The Birmingham Duty Advocate Scheme studied the social security appeals tribunals in January 1985, finding that only 52 out of 112 appellants appeared, 14 of whom were represented; among the other 38, 25 per cent did not know they could be represented, and

83 per cent would have preferred representation (*Legal Action* 5, April 1985).

But though duty solicitors in prisons and tribunals might generate substantial business, the largest experiment thus far has been the attempt to provide legal services to those arrested. Starting in the 1970s, solicitors volunteered time to staff schemes in criminal courts, providing immediate advice and accepting clients for representation under legal aid (Royal Commission, 1979, vol. 1: 92). Statutory authority for such schemes took effect in 1983, and, by 1986, 80 per cent of the 224 busiest magistrates' courts had them, though only 10 per cent of the other 400 courts. The Royal Commission on Criminal Procedure (1981a) recommended the extension of duty solicitors to police stations, and pilot schemes were established in several locations starting in 1984. Despite the fact that solicitors were on call 24 hours a day, the early results were disappointing. In Northampton and Birmingham, only 20 per cent of those detained asked to see a solicitor, and two-thirds of them wanted their regular solicitor, not the duty solicitor; in London only 13 per cent sought representation. At one scheme in south London there was only one call for a solicitor in 24 hours (134 *NLJ* 847, 1984; 135 *NLJ* 195–6, 997–8, 1024, 1041 and 1072, 1985; 81 *LSG* 1731, 1984; 82 *LSG* 3214, 1985; *Legal Action* 4, April 1985).

When the Lord Chancellor's Department decided to extend the service nationwide in 1985, it encountered severe opposition from the Law Society to its proposed remuneration levels for both solicitors and administrative staff (135 *NLJ* 878 and 997–8, 1985). But the Law Society eventually capitulated and even decided to spend £50,000 to publicize the scheme when it began in December 1985, targeting the population between 15 and 24 years of age. During May 1986, when 24-hour solicitors were available in three-quarters of the country, 6600 calls were made (26–33 percent of all suspects), an annualized rate of 80,000; when fully operational the scheme is expected to produce 110,000 calls a year. However, by July 1986 only about a third of London magistrates' courts were covered (*Legal Action* 4–5, August 1985; Dean, 1986b; 83 *LSG* 1289, 1961 and 2295–6, 1986). And the experience of the first eight months has been disappointing: nationwide, the service produced 6000 requests per month for a duty solicitor instead of the expected 8300 (*Legal Action* 3, November 1986).

Yet the problem with successful duty solicitor schemes, like most mechanisms for stimulating demand, is that they also tend to redistribute that demand. Thus the schemes were supported by younger solicitors eager to break into the market and resisted by older solicitors anxious to avoid competition. Indeed, the Law Society initially sought to require clients to sign a statement that they had been given an opportunity to consult their previous solicitors (133 *NLJ* 814, 1983). The views of two solicitors in Devon and Cornwall epitomize this dilemma:

> [The town] is so small, we have a number of regular offenders and regular solicitors, so we don't get much call for this [the duty solicitor scheme].
>
> The duty solicitor scheme results in competition for clients. It is totally wrong because criminals have no loyalty and as a result the quality of advocacy has gone down. Previously two firms dealt with the lot, now we have twenty firms doing it.
>
> (Blacksell et al., 1986: 31)

Citizens' advice bureaux (CABx) raise a somewhat different set of problems. Because they receive millions of enquiries a year – 4.8 million in 1981–2, 6 million in 1985–6 (National Association, 1981–2: 3; 1985–6) – and refer about a third of them to solicitors under the legal aid scheme, some 3000 solicitors were volunteering their time to staff advice rotas at CABx in the 1970s (Royal Commission, 1979, vol. 1: 12, 16). Other solicitors also staffed 120 free legal advice centres, from which they often obtained legal aid work (ibid.: 12, 76–7). More than half the solicitors in Devon and Cornwall served on such rotas, even though few obtained lucrative work as a result (Blacksell et al., 1986: 8 and table 13). Conflict can arise over the allocation of work among solicitors and the exclusion of those who turn out to be incompetent (Watkins et al., 1986c: 18). The real danger of the CABx, however, is that they not only refer work to private practitioners but also threaten to supplant them. A government working party suggested in mid 1986 that legal aid costs could be substantially reduced by delivering legal advice through salaried solicitors employed by CABx and then referring particularly complex matters to national panels of specialist lawyers, as already occurs with child care and mental health cases (Dean, 1986a).

The use of public subsidies to create demand for solicitors thus introduces several new problems. First, it may be ineffective – people may not want to use lawyers, even if they are free and accessible. Second, solicitors become dependent on a government paymaster, creating conflicts between their loyalties to their clients and their economic interests. Third, public subsidies inevitably affect the distribution of business. On the one hand, all beneficiaries of government largess seem to feel entitled to share it equally. Thus, legal aid lists do not discriminate among practitioners, rota schemes are open to all, and referral services distribute business randomly, even though this may not serve the interests of clients. On the other hand, various forces tend to concentrate business.

The Law Society recently opposed a proposal to allow applicants to seek Green Form legal advice by post and to receive it by post or telephone, fearing that private solicitors would lose business to salaried services (such as the Child Poverty Action Group) or to specialist solicitors who advertised (*Legal Action* 1–2, May 1986). The fact that legal aid fees are always lower than those paid by private clients means that solicitors must mass produce legal aid work in order to make comparable profits. And the government's desire to control and reduce expenditures leads it to prefer salaried staff to private practitioners. In either case, legal aid becomes the primary source of income for a small number of solicitors but increasingly irrelevant to most of the profession.

# 15

# Solicitor income

Until after World War II, solicitors appear to have done very well economically, enjoying a median income higher than barristers and other professionals, such as doctors and dentists (see table 2.34; Kirk, 1976: 94). In 1956, they had fallen behind medical professionals, although principals in private practice continued to earn more than any other category of professional (ibid.). By 1976, even principals earned less than physicians and salaried solicitors and little more than civil servants or middle management in industry, although the highest decile continued to outperform any category except middle and upper management (Royal Commission, 1979, vol. 1: 541). Several factors may have contributed to this erosion in the relative earnings of solicitors: the loss of supply control as a result of the expansion of academic legal education, leading to an increase in sole practitioners and small-firm principals; the recession of 1973–4, which cut housing prices and sales and thus conveyancing income; the greater salience of health over law, especially as the technical abilities of medicine advanced; and the increasing dependence of solicitors on legal aid. Whatever the reason, the trend is not likely to be reversed.

Although it seems likely that similar criteria were used to compare professional incomes at a given time, it is much more hazardous to assume that figures purporting to represent solicitor income at different times employed the same method. Nevertheless, solicitor income seems to have risen steadily throughout this century, increasing fivefold or sixfold by the mid 1950s, during a period when the *Statist* price index rose at about the same rate (compare tables 2.37 and 4.7). Assistant solicitor salaries declined from the mid 1920s to 1930–1 as a result of the depression and were no higher in 1939 than they had been in 1919 (Kirk, 1976: 112; see table 2.39), suggesting that the gains of principals during this period may be attributable, in part, to greater exploitation of subordinate labour. The more rapid rise of assistant solicitor salaries after World War II (see tables 2.37, 2.39), when the effects of the war compounded by the efficacy of supply control led to labour shortages, may have contributed to the worsening position of principals.

Fragmentary evidence on earnings from conveyancing (which accounted for half the total income of the profession) generally confirms this picture. In 1926–7, immediately following a one-third increase in scale fees, earnings from conveyancing alone totalled £653, the highest level (in normalized pounds) previously recorded (Offer, 1981: 82). Between 1958 and 1968, income from conveyancing rose by a factor of two and a half to three, during a period when overall inflation rates were much lower (National Board for Prices and Incomes, 1968: 8; see table 4.7). Thereafter, conveyancing income grew somewhat more slowly (National Board for Prices and Incomes, 1971: 73). Nevertheless, there was a 7 per cent increase in the number of owner-occupied houses between 1966 and 1976, a threefold increase in the average price and a steep increase in the number and value of mortgages, with the result that the gross income of solicitors rose from £167 million to £703 million during this period, an average of 5 per cent a year (Glasser, 1979: 202).

Yet when these figures are normalized to account for the overall rate of inflation, solicitors appear to have made no gains and actually lost ground. Routh (1980: 60, 63) argues that solicitor income rose 282 per cent between 1913–14 and 1955–6, while the cost of living increased 425 percent to 1960. However, Abel-Smith and Stevens (1967: 400) contend that solicitor income increased from £400 in 1939 to £3,000 in 1964, more than sevenfold during a period when prices only tripled. Between 1955–6 and 1966 the income of principals rose at almost exactly the same rate as that of all manual or salaried workers (National Board of Prices and Incomes, 1968: 7). In the period 1974–5 to 1976–7, solicitor net profits rose only 26 per cent, while the retail price index jumped 44 per cent (Royal Commission, 1979, vol. 1: 517). The Peat Marwick survey found that the net median income of principals in firms with fewer than 16 partners increased 82 per cent from 1977 to 1984 and the median salaries of assistant solicitors and salaried partners increased 123 per cent, but the earnings of all workers increased 147 per cent (83 *LSG* 169–70, 1986). A survey of 250 firms by the Centre for Interfirm Comparison found that their gross revenues (but not their profits) increased 7 per cent in 1985 after accounting for inflation (Moffatt, 1986). Even when we acknowledge all the problems with these figures (including the fact that the Law Society has a stake in underestimating income), they seem at least consistent with the view that solicitors improved their financial position during the first half of the century (the period of most effective supply control) and have lost ground since the early 1970s (when such control eroded).

As was the case with barristers (see chapter 8), medians conceal more than they disclose, for there are very significant income differences among solicitors. Between 1816 and 1821, the three partners at Freshfields, a leading City firm, were sharing annual profits of £10,000–20,000, at a time when fewer than 200 solicitors were earning even £300 and most less than £75 (Slinn, 1984: 37; Birks, 1960: 208). When Charles Freshfield died in 1891, he left an estate of £256,089; his brother and partner, Henry, died four years later, leaving an estate of £338,630 (Slinn, 1984: 118–19). In 1913–14, the upper quartile of solicitors made more than four times as much as the lower quartile and the highest decile almost four times as much as the median (Routh, 1980: 60–1). Many solicitors were unable to establish their own practices, either alone or with others, and became managing clerks at £150 a year; perhaps 5000 London solicitors made as much as £1000 a year; but a few hundred partners in City firms with four or five principals earned £5000 (Offer, 1981: 13). These disparities were smaller than those among barristers, and they declined significantly in the succeeding four decades, but in 1955–6 the upper quartile still made two and a half times as much as the lower and the upper decile almost that much more than the median (Routh, 1980: 60–1; cf. Doctors and Dentists, 1960: 284). That year two-fifths of solicitors made less than £2000 and almost two-thirds less than £3000, but 2.8 per cent made at least £10,000 (Kirk, 1976: 93; Gower and Price, 1957: 334–5; Abel-Smith and Stevens, 1967: 384; Doctors and Dentists, 1960: 284). In 1966, the ratio of the upper quartile of principals to the lower was 2.3:1 (National Board for Prices and Incomes, 1968: 7). And in 1976/7 the highest decile of principals earned 1.6 times as much as the median (Royal Commission, 1979, vol. 2: 692, 697).

Between 1973 and 1979 there seems to have been a divergence of the extremes for all lawyers, which probably also reflects the situation of solicitors, who were at least 80 per cent of the total (see table 4.6). This would be consistent with the erosion of supply control leading to the entry of large numbers of low-paid assistant solicitors and younger principals with insufficient work or highly dependent on legal aid. Between 1967 and 1979, the proportion of lawyers earning less than £500 a year remained a remarkably constant one fifth, although the proportion earning more than £15,000 grew from 1 per cent to 11.2 per cent and the proportion earning £6000–15,000 grew from 8.1 per cent to 22.7 per cent (see table 2.35). Similarly, the proportion earning less than £20 a week hardly declined at all between 1970 and 1972 (from

18.3 per cent to 16.8 per cent), but the proportion earning more than £50 increased from 30.8 per cent to 43.5 per cent (see table 2.36). Thus, the bottom of the professional income pyramid failed to keep up with inflation, while earnings at the top rose faster than inflation. Yet the ratio of the upper quartile to the lower and of the highest decile to the median was only about half what it had been at the beginning of the century.

A number of variables appear to be associated with income differences among solicitors. One that is of declining (perhaps even negligible) significance is capital investment. At the turn of the century, partnership in a firm required a substantial investment: £1000–5000 or the equivalent of three to ten years' profits (Offer, 1981: 18; but see Slinn, 1984: 117, 170). When a sole practitioner retired, he could expect to receive three times the annual net income of the practice as payment for goodwill. By 1939, such payments had declined to two times annual net income (Birks, 1960: 287). In 1955, the average capital outlay for partnership in a sample of 586 principals was £3844, just 1.7 times the annual average income; furthermore, 15 per cent paid nothing, and another 22 per cent paid less than a year's income (Doctors and Dentists, 1960: 284–5). The average capital investment had increased to £7060 in 1966 and £7081 in 1968, but earnings grew faster (National Board for Prices and Incomes, 1968: 11; 1969: 36). In 1976, the average capital investment was £12,660 (just about a year's income) – somewhat lower in firms with fewer than five partners but almost twice as high in those with more than ten (Royal Commission, 1979, vol. 2: 485, 487). Fewer than a third of all firms required a partner to make an out-of-pocket contribution on becoming a member (only 14 per cent of firms with more than nine partners), so that any investment today comes from undistributed profits (ibid.: 462). By 1984, median net assets per principal were £17,800, ranging from £14,100 in 2–4 partner firms to £48,300 in firms with more than 14 partners – substantially less than a year's profits (83 *LSG* 335, 1986). Retirement is handled no longer by sale of partnership shares but through pension funds. Consequently, capital investment cannot explain the huge income disparities between solicitors.

Not surprisingly, the most powerful determinant of income is status, particularly the difference between salaried solicitors and principals. The very unsatisfactory data for the period before World War II suggest that assistant solicitors earned only a fifth to a fourth as much as principals (see table 2.37). In 1955–6 and 1966 the median income of salaried solicitors was a third that of principals (Doctors and Dentists, 1960: 284; National Board for Prices and Incomes, 1968: 7). In 1976, the ratio ranged from half for sole practitioners to a third in firms with more than nine principals (see table 2.40). And in 1984, the median income of all assistant solicitors and salaried partners was £9600, almost half the £21,300 income enjoyed by all principals except those in London firms with more than 15 partners (83 *LSG* 169–70, 1986). One reason for the gradual convergence may actually have been the efficacy of supply control; the small number of assistant solicitors admitted in the 1950s and 1960s were able to command higher salaries as firms sought to expand in response to the rapidly growing economy and the rise in conveyancing income. Advertised salaries for positions offered in the *Law Society's Gazette* confirm this view: assistant solicitor salaries doubled during the 1960s, doubled again during the 1970s and again by the mid 1980s (see tables 2.38, 2.39). In 1984, sole practitioners earned little more than salaried lawyers in industry with at least three and a half years experience (£20,400 versus £18,370) (compare 136 *NLJ* 59, 1986 with table 2.38). As the production of new solicitors has risen, the rate of increase in starting salaries has declined: Reuter Simkin (1981–5) placed 33 articled clerks in first jobs at an average starting salary of £9020 between April and September 1983; two years later the average for 71 such placements had risen to only £11,220; and during the next six months 45 articled clerks in central London started at an average of £11,690 (83 *LSG* 2227–8 1986). Perhaps partly because of these increasing labour costs, the net profit of all firms declined from 36 per cent of total income in 1977 to 33 per cent in 1984 (83 *LSG* 246, 1986).

The effects of diminished supply control may also be visible in the convergence between the incomes of self-employed solicitors and those employed in the public or private sectors. In 1955–6 and again in 1966, salaried solicitors outside law firms earned almost three-quarters as much as principals in private practice (Doctors and Dentists, 1960: 284; National Board of Prices and Incomes, 1968: 7). And by 1976–7, the after-tax earnings of both salaried solicitors in commerce and industry and the civil service legal class (which includes barristers as well as solicitors in central government) were virtually equivalent to those of principals in private practice (Royal Commission, 1979, vol. 1: 536). In 1984, the salaries of solicitors with more than three and a half years experience in industry again were almost equivalent to those of all principals (compare table 2.38 with 83 *LSG* 169–70, 1986).

Income also varies strongly with age, though of course this is closely associated with the status differences just discussed. In 1955–6, income increased steadily up to 65 years: solicitors 55–64 years old made three times as much as those under 35 (Doctors and Dentists, 1960: 284). But income also increases with age within each status category. For principals, it reached its highest level among those 46–50 (when partners earn twice as much as those under 31) and was only about half as high among those 65 (Royal Commission, 1979, vol. 2: 478). Interestingly, the large City firm of Richards Butler distributes profits entirely in proportion to years with the firm rather than contribution to earnings – a practice that may change as competition among firms intensifies (136 *NLJ* 384–90, 1986). For assistant solicitors, salaries increased a third during the initial four years and then levelled off for those not offered partnerships (Royal Commission, 1979, vol. 2: 466). This remained true in the 1980s (see table 2.38). The salaries of articled clerks increased only 17 per cent between their first and second years (Royal Commission, 1979, vol. 2: 467). And beginning legal executives earned half as much as those in their late 40s, while legal executives in their 60s earned a quarter less (ibid.: 468). Salaried solicitors in commerce and industry enjoyed a 75 per cent increase between the age groups 25–29 and 40–65 and the civil service legal class an increase of 80 per cent (ibid.: vol. 1: 537, 539).

The steeper earnings curve of principals is related to the fact that income varies with firm size (see chapter 13, p. 206; see also Moffatt, 1986). This correlation was noted in 1966 (National Board for Prices and Incomes, 1968: 10) and reconfirmed and elaborated in 1976–7. The net profit per principal in firms with more than 9 partners was almost twice that of sole practitioners (see table 2.40); the median income of principals in firms with more than 19 partners was five times that of sole practitioners (Zander, 1980: 36; cf. 75 *LSG* 422–8, 1978). In 1984, all principals (excluding London firms with more than 15 partners) made more than twice as much as sole practitioners (£21,300 versus £9500) (83 *LSG* 169–70, 1986). Another survey the following year found that sole practitioners earned a median of £20,400, principals in firms with 5–14 partners earned £28,400, principals in firms with more than 14 partners earned £38,200, and principals in central London firms with more than 14 partners earned £81,300 (136 *NLJ* 58, 1986). Indeed, a significant proportion of the partners in the largest City firms earned more than £100,000, and a few earned several times as much (135 *NLJ* 975, 1985; Campbell-Smith, 1985b).

One reason for the higher earnings of principals in larger firms is that they are able to charge their clients more for the labour of subordinate employees without paying those workers proportionally higher salaries (National Board for Prices and Incomes, 1968: 44). The ratio between the hourly fees charged by firms with more than nine partners and those charged by sole practitioners was 2:1 for assistant solicitors, 2.3:1 for legal executives and 1.4:1 for articled clerks. The ratio of salaries paid by those two categories of firm was 1.25:1 for assistant solicitors, 1.22:1 for legal executives and 1.5:1 for articled clerks (see table 2.40). In 1984, firms with more than 14 partners paid their assistant solicitors 1.45 times as much as did sole practitioners (£13,800 versus £9500); even central London firms with more than 14 partners paid their assistant solicitors only 1.62 times as much as did sole practitioners. The ratio of the salaries of articled clerks was even smaller: 1.26:1 (£6300 versus £5000) (83 *LSG* 169–70, 1986; 136 *NLJ* 58, 1986). Between 1980 and 1985, firms with more than 20 partners paid their assistant solicitors only about 10 per cent more than firms with fewer than 8 partners (see table 2.38).

These income data are fragmentary, discontinuous, of dubious accuracy and difficult to compare. Nevertheless, they do cast important light on the theories of the professions introduced in the initial chapter. First, variation in income between professions, across time and within the profession strongly support the view that solicitors enjoyed fluctuating market control. Solicitors were the highest paid profession as long as they exercised market control, and their incomes were relatively clustered around the mean; as control eroded in the 1970s, incomes dispersed because those at the bottom of the income pyramid lost ground, and differences between private practice and employment converged. Second, much of the difference among solicitors expresses the proliferation of capitalist relations of production, in which principals can extract surplus value from employees not because principals have made a capital investment in the firm but because they possess formal credentials and control networks of clients. Third, these differences constitute a system of stratification within the profession, necessitating mechanisms to distribute solicitors (and others) across strata, justify the resulting inequality and exercise authority over it.

# 16

# Governance and self-regulation

## The Law Society

A Society of Gentlemen Practisers in the Courts of Law and Equity was founded in London in 1739 for the purpose of controlling the number of attorneys and solicitors, striking from the Rolls those who committed egregious misconduct and protecting the monopolies the two groups enjoyed (Abel-Smith and Stevens, 1967: 20–1). It never enrolled more than 200 members and had become largely moribund by the 1820s (Holdsworth, 1938: 63–7). A new organization, the Incorporated Law Society, was formed in 1825 (Christian, 1896: 176, 178; Kirk, 1976: 25–8). This continued to pursue similar aims – the economic betterment and enhanced social status of solicitors – although sometimes it may have misconstrued solicitor self-interest, as when it agitated (unsuccessfully) until 1853 for a reduction in the stamp duty on practising certificates, despite the fact that these fees had been the quid pro quo of the original grant of the conveyancing monopoly (Abel-Smith and Stevens, 1967: 54).

Until very recently it has been an association of London practitioners more than a national institution, for its physical location in the capital made it far more useful to those who practised there. It grew rapidly from the initial 292 subscribers to about 1000 a decade later, but 90 per cent of these practised in London, even though the capital then contained only a third of the profession (a ratio that has remained constant for the next 150 years) (see table 2.41). It took another 40 years for the membership to reach 25 per cent of the profession, and two-thirds of the members were still London solicitors. In 1871, half of all London practitioners belonged to the Law Society but only a tenth of provincial practitioners (Law Society, Annual Report, 1871: 17). Representation was even lower within the major provincial cities, for these had their own societies, many of which antedated the Law Society: in 1871, only 13 out of 295 solicitors in Manchester were members, 16 out of 283 in Liverpool, 24 out of 193 in Birmingham, 10 out of 189 in Bristol and 5 out of 104 in Leeds (Kirk, 1976: 39). The 1880s witnessed rapid growth, and by the 1890s half of all practitioners were members, equally divided between London and the provinces. By the 1920s, two-thirds of those holding practising certificates were members, and provincial solicitors were three-fifths of this total. A major push for membership in the 1950s persuaded 90 per cent of those holding practising certificates in both London and the provinces to join, and these figures have remained constant to the present (see table 2.41).

However, membership is much lower among solicitors employed in commerce and industry and in government, many of whom do not hold practising certificates (Johnstone and Hopson, 1967: 461 n. 8; Podmore, 1980: 103–4). The proportion of enrolled solicitors who belong to the Society is much lower – 71 per cent in 1973, 65 per cent in 1984 – although it is important to recognize that some solicitors on the Roll are retired or deceased (Marks, 1985). That proportion also varies by age: it is lowest among solicitors under 30 and over 64 and highest among those 40–44 and 50–59 (Marks, 1984).

If the Society's membership did not mirror that of the profession until the 1950s, its structure of governance was even more unrepresentative, and it remains so today. Although gerontocracy is less extreme in the Law Society than at the Bar (see chapter 9), it is still pronounced. In 1895, half the members of the Council were over 60; four years later the average age remained 60 (Kirk, 1976: 44). In 1963–4, Council members had practised an average of 32 years since qualifying; by contrast, 47 per cent of all solicitors were less than 40 years old in 1969 and thus presumably had practised less than 15 years (National Board for Prices and Incomes, 1969: 6). Furthermore, it was understood that a Council member would be re-elected indefinitely until he died or resigned (Johnstone and Hopson, 1967: 462–3). In 1985, only 5 of the 68 Council members (7 percent) were under 40, compared with 55 per cent of all solicitors (Law Society Bye-Laws Revision Committee, 1985). Among the 58 Council members for whom data are available, 36 (62 per cent) had practised for more than 25 years and thus presumably were at least 50 years old, and two past presidents who served on the Council each had practised for 37 years; but only 27.5 per cent of solicitors *on the Roll* were 50 or older (Solicitors' and Barristers' Directory and Diary, 1985; Marks, 1984). There were no Council members under 35 in 1984 and only one in 1985 to represent the 37.4 per cent of solicitors on the

Roll who were that young; the average age of Council members was 54, although the median age of those on the Roll was under 40 (Marks, 1984; 82 *LSG* 208, 1985; Solicitors' and Barristers' Directory and Diary, 1985). (The fact that the President of the Law Society for 1986–7 was a 48-year-old suburban Croydon practitioner who was elected to the Council at the age of 31 does not alter this generalization.) The tension between London and provincial practitioners was resolved by alternating the office of president betweem them and allocating a number of Council seats to the provinces (35 out of 65 in 1963–4), chosen by the constituent organizations of the Association of Provincial Law Societies until 1954 and by local constituencies since then (Kirk, 1976: 40; Johnstone and Hopson, 1967: 463; Royal Commission, 1979, vol. 1: 384). Thus, London practitioners retain about half the positions, although they represent only a third of the membership. In 1984, London solicitors actually occupied slightly fewer than a third of the Council seats.

Other constituencies are also underrepresented. There was only one woman on the Council and only eight women on standing committees, although women were over 20 per cent of the profession and nearly 40 per cent of new admissions (Brougham, 1984; see table 2.16). There were no ethnic minorities. Only 7 of the 68 Council members in 1985 were not in private practice (10 per cent), compared with the 28 per cent of those holding practising certificates and the even higher percentage of those on the Roll (Law Society Bye-Laws Revision Committee, 1985). Large firms were overrepresented and small firms underrepresented. In 1979, no sole practitioner sat on the Council, although that category contained 11 per cent of principals; and only 3 out of 70 Council members (4 per cent) were principals from two-partner firms, although the latter constituted 16 per cent of principals (Royal Commission, 1979, vol. 1: 389; see table 2.21; cf. Podmore, 1980: 116). In 1985, 9 out of the 53 Council members in private practice (17 per cent) were in the 0.9 per cent of firms with more than 19 principals; 42 per cent of the Council members in private practice were in firms with more than nine partners, which contained only 24.4 per cent of all principals. Small firms remained underrepresented: there was only one sole practitioner to speak for the 10.1 per cent of all principals in solo practice; and there were only 12 (23 per cent of the private practitioners on the Council) to represent the 39.2 per cent of all principals in two- to four-partner firms (compare Solicitors' and Barristers' Directory and Diary, 1985 with table 2.22; cf. 80 *LSG* 3221, 1983; 133 *NLJ* 897, 1983).

The unrepresentative composition of the Council reflects the lack of democratic structures and mass participation in governance. Between 1945 and 1967, only 6 out of the nearly 300 members elected to the

Council faced an opponent; in the single contested election of 1967, only 15 per cent of members voted (Abel-Smith and Stevens, 1968: 126). There were no contested elections for president and only one for vice-president in the 30 years preceding the Royal Commission (1979, vol. 1: 396–7). Attendance at annual general meetings is low (Johnstone and Hopson, 1967: 464). In recent years, growing dissatisfaction has increased the pressure for democratization. The British Legal Association (BLA; discussed below) called a special general meeting of the Law Society in 1984, which approved proxy voting at future general meetings (134 *NLJ* 92, 1984; 81 *LSG* 476, 1984). The BLA then sought, unsuccessfully, to use its proxies to secure nomination of officers and election of the president by the membership, a reduction in the size of the Council and the length of members' terms and the elimination of geographic constituencies for members (81 *LSG* 1642, 1984; 134 *NLJ* 419 and 614, 1984). Several local law societies expressed their dissatisfaction with the organization of the Society (134 *NLJ* 468, 1984; 135 *NLJ* 307, 1985; 81 *LSG* 1091–2 and 1914, 1984).

In response, the Council commissioned a study of governance by Coopers & Lybrand (82 *LSG* 2, 1985). This led the Council to propose eliminating postal ballots following a general meeting (itself defeated by a postal ballot) and to reduce the terms of Council members from five years to four (rather than the one year proposed by the BLA). Although the Council refused to open its meetings to members, it was overruled by a postal ballot (83 *LSG* 167–9 and 826, 1986). The fact that the Law Society Bye-Laws Revision Committee produced a vigorous minority dissent renewing the call for direct election of the president (among other proposals) is evidence that pressure for change will continue (135 *NLJ* 863–4, 1985).

Perhaps the most difficult question confronting the Society is whether it can continue to perform the numerous functions in which the public interest should be paramount – such as administering the legal aid scheme and disciplining solicitors – while vigorously advocating the interests of solicitors. One indication of the rate at which the responsibilities of the Law Society have been growing is the fee for the practising certificate, which rose from £60 in 1982 to £125 in 1985 and then to £225 in 1987 (82 *LSG* 1833, 1985; 83 *LSG* 2210–11, 2380 and 2455, 1986). Several local law societies have urged that the Law Society cease administering legal aid and disciplining solicitors and concentrate on representing the profession (134 *NLJ* 468, 1984; 81 *LSG* 1914, 1984).

## Local law societies

The present hegemony of the Law Society should not blind us to the fact that local law societies antedated its founding and continue to command strong loyalties. Law societies that survive today were established in Bristol in 1770, Yorkshire in 1786, Somerset in 1796, Sunderland in 1800, Leeds in 1805, Plymouth in 1815, Gloucester in 1817 and Birmingham, Hull and Kent in 1818 – all prior to the Incorporated Law Society (Christian, 1896: 176; Robson, 1959: ch. 4; Kirk, 1976: 36). Over the next 20 years, societies were founded in Bolton (1826), Liverpool (1827), Newcastle-upon-Tyne (1827), Carlisle (1834), Preston (1834), Dorset (1835), Lancaster (1838), Manchester (1838), Worcestershire (1841) and Wolverhampton (1847) (Christian, 1896: 242–3; Manchester, 1980: 67). At a time when the Incorporated Law Society enrolled perhaps 5 per cent of solicitors, almost all of whom practised in London, more than a third of Liverpool solicitors joined to found its law society (Williams, 1980: 184, 186, 188). Seeking a national voice – especially against the threatened loss of business to public officials and the restrictive taxation of fees – provincial solicitors founded the Metropolitan and Provincial Law Association in 1847, which enrolled 10 per cent of provincial solicitors in its first two years (Birks, 1960: 212–14; Kirk, 1976: 38). For the next 25 years it functioned alongside, and to some extent in rivalry with, the Law Society. During that period additional societies were established in Bath (1858), Leicester (1860), Sunderland (1860), Sussex (1860), Bristol (1871) and Cambridge (1871). Although the Metropolitan and Provincial Law Association merged with the Law Society in 1872, two years later the largest local law societies – Birmingham, Manchester, Liverpool, Newcastle and Leeds – organized the Associated Provincial Law Societies to unite the 35 existing local groups, and between 1871 and 1900 another 36 local law societies were launched (Parker, 1987; Christian, 1896: 242–3; Birks, 1960: 212–13; Abel-Smith and Stevens, 1967: 54, 62; Kirk, 1976: 40).

In 1887, the 60 local law societies contained 3233 members (compared with the 2251 provincial members of the Law Society); by 1894, the 62 local societies had increased their enrolment to 4538 (compared with the 4132 provincial members of the Law Society) (Incorporated Law Society, Calendar, 1887: 1148–9; 1894: 1322–4; Law Society, Annual Report, 1887; 1894). In the 1950s, additional groups emerged in suburban London, largely in order to police the minimum fee schedules for conveyancing proposed by the Law Society, and by 1962 the country was covered by 117 local societies (Abel-Smith and Stevens, 1967: 386–7).

In 1979, 24,405 solicitors belonged to 121 local law societies, ranging in size from 10 to 1200 members (Royal Commission, 1979, vol. 1: 384). In Devon and Cornwall in 1985, roughly equal proportions of solicitors belonged to the Law Society (92 per cent) and to local law societies (90 per cent) (Blacksell et al., 1986: 7).

Tensions between London and provincial practitioners persist, fuelled by differences in the content of their work and the structure of their practices. Conveyancing remains the staple of provincial practice, whereas solicitors in central London depend far more on other non-contentious matters and on litigation (Kirk, 1976: 155). In 1899, the Yorkshire Law Society broke away from the Associated Provincial Law Societies when the latter failed to oppose land registration with sufficient vigour (Kirk, 1976: 142). This divergence was manifest again in 1967, when the Council of the Law Society (dominated by London solicitors) favoured the abolition of conveyancing scale fees (by one vote), although 110 of the 112 local law societies had urged its retention (Zander, 1968: 204). More recently, the geographic division has been significant in the controversy over malpractice insurance premiums, which pitted smaller firms (dominant outside London) against the larger firms in central London (see 'Malpractice', p. 259).

## Other organizations

As the profession has become more heterogeneous in background and more diverse in structure and function, new groupings have emerged to represent particular interests. Sometimes their goal has been exclusivity, to foster social interaction or assert status. During the nineteenth century, an elite of London solicitors created a private club within the precincts of the Law Society; not surprisingly, it aroused the ire of those not invited to join and was finally abolished in 1900 (Kirk, 1976: 34). But other men's clubs survive from that period, including the City Law Club and the Lowtonian Society (Slinn, 1984: 45). As early as 1844, the younger members of the Law Society formed their own Legal Protective Association (Kirk, 1976: 42). Today there are associations of women lawyers, minority lawyers and younger lawyers (the Trainee Solicitors' Group for articled clerks and assistant solicitors and the Young Solicitors' Group).

Many organizations unite solicitors by subject-matter specialization: the Solicitors' London Agents' Association (who handle litigation for provincial firms), the London (Criminal Courts) Solicitors' Association, the Local Government Legal Society and the Commerce and Industry

Group of the Law Society (Johnstone and Hopson, 1967: 361, 474). The Solicitors' Family Law Association was founded in 1982, attracting more than 400 members within two years (134 *NLJ* 198, 1984). The Legal Aid Practitioners' Group was founded in 1981 to advance the distinctive interests of those doing substantial amounts of legally aided work; a year later it had 500 member firms containing more than 2000 solicitors (*LAG Bulletin* 4, June 1982). One of its more outspoken members urged it to seek a 1 per cent tax on the fees earned by solicitors representing paying clients in order to increase legal aid fees (133 *NLJ* 336, 1983). The National Association of Civil Litigation Solicitors was established in June 1986 (83 *LSG* 2203, 1986). Another category of organizations is based on political affiliation or social activism, such as the Society of Labour Lawyers, the Society of Conservative Lawyers, the Haldane Society, the Legal Action Group and the National Council for Civil Liberties.

Dissent within the Law Society by those who felt it was not representing younger solicitors, provincial solicitors or smaller firms or acting with sufficient vigour led them to found the British Legal Association in 1964. It quickly enrolled 10 per cent of the profession within its first two years, although membership has declined since then. And it actually adopted the legal form of a trade union in 1970 (Kirk, 1976: 44, 46, 150; Royal Commission, 1979, vol. 1: 385). In recent years it has operated more as a ginger group within the Law Society. Finally, some solicitors in the public sector or in legal aid firms have joined trade unions and contemplated or engaged in industrial action, although the Law Society has warned that this may lead to discipline (*Haldane Bulletin*, 1983; 81 *LSG* 2992–3, 1984).

## Discipline

The power to engage in self-regulation is one of the goals that motivates an occupation to seek professional status. The efficacy of self-regulation is one of the measures by which outsiders judge whether a profession deserves that status. It is noteworthy, therefore, that solicitors did not become fully self-regulating until 1920, long after they claimed to be a profession and almost 100 years after they established the Law Society. Throughout the early nineteenth century discipline was sporadic and ineffective, at least partly because each court maintained its own Roll of authorized practitioners, and a solicitor or attorney struck from one Roll could seek admission to another. (This problem still troubles the 50 American jurisdictions; American Bar Association, 1970.) A first step toward centralization was taken in 1839, when a national registrar created a single Roll of attorneys and another of solicitors (Abel-Smith and Stevens, 1967: 24 n. 2). But for another half century discipline was very infrequent (see table 2.42); in the 1870s, only about 0.05 per cent of all solicitors were disciplined a year (Kirk, 1976: 80). Furthermore, many of those punished were suspended only briefly, and even those struck off the Roll were soon readmitted (Law Society, Annual Report, 1857: 16). The inefficacy of discipline was dramatically illustrated in 1877, when the Law Society discovered that its chief clerk had been systematically embezzling its funds for 33 years! (Law Society, Annual Report, 1877: 27)

One problem was that the Supreme Court remained responsible for disciplining solicitors. Only in 1873 did the Law Society obtain even the right to be heard by the Court in disciplinary proceedings (Kirk, 1976: 78; cf. Holdsworth, 1965: 225). At that time, the Council of the Law Society was reviewing two or three complaints of solicitor misconduct each week, but this level of grievances was not reflected in the number of formal proceedings. The Council heard 428 complaints in the nine months between November 1887 and August 1888. Nearly a quarter (102) concerned unauthorized practice by laypersons – evidence that considerable professional energy was still being devoted to protecting the solicitors' monopoly; more than a quarter of these led to formal proceedings. Barristers lodged 26 complaints seeking payment of their fees by solicitors, none of which led to proceedings. There were 178 complaints about misconduct, only 11 of which (6 per cent) led to proceedings, and 130 about misapplication of money, only 10 per cent of which led to formal action (Proceedings and Resolutions of the Annual Provincial Meeting of the Members of the Society, 1888: 52–3). Thus, from the outset, it seems clear that the Law Society was more concerned to protect its own interests than those of its clients.

Despite this indifferent record, the Society sought authority to hear and dispose of complaints in the first instance. Its president, Benjamin Greene, argued that its procedures would be more effective and efficient than those of the Court. But the real motive for the Society's claim may have been Greene's assurance that 'any accused solicitor will...come before a tribunal composed of members of his own profession, to whom, if at all, he should be able to justify himself' (ibid.: 52). By contrast, the judges of the Supreme Court were all barristers, who were unlikely to be sympathetic to solicitors. The Society was persuasive; in 1888 it obtained authority to conduct a preliminary hearing of all complaints and recommend action to the Court (Kirk, 1976: 78; Abel-Smith and Stevens, 1967: 188). The Master of the Rolls appointed a disciplinary committee from among the Council members.

Greene's promise that solicitors would look after their own was amply fulfilled. Between 1889 and 1913, the disciplinary committee dismissed 73 per cent of the 2178 complaints it heard (see table 2.42; cf. Christian, 1896: 232). Indeed, during the two decades 1893–1913, almost as many solicitors were struck off the Roll after conviction of a crime (an average of seven a year), even though that was not automatic, as were struck off following a disciplinary proceeding (Law Society, Annual Reports; Kirk, 1976: 77). One reason for the survival of two uncoordinated procedures may have been the fact that the Society had jurisdiction over only the half of all solicitors who were members (see table 2.41). In 1919, the Society finally gained authority to conduct its own disciplinary proceedings following the preliminary hearing, although solicitors retained a right of appeal to the Court (Kirk, 1976: 79). The High Court reserved the power to discipline *sua sponte* but did so only once between 1919 and 1950 (Johnstone and Hopson, 1967: 481 n. 72). When a litigant sought to apply directly to the High Court in 1985 to strike a solicitor off the Roll, he was confronted by the catch-22 that he had to be represented by a barrister – who had to be briefed by a solicitor! (*Re* McKernan's Application, 135 *NLJ* Rep. 1164, 1985.)

Acquisition by the Law Society of full powers of self-regulation, like the earlier grant of limited jurisdiction, again rendered discipline more lenient. In the period 1892–1913, the Court imposed punishment in 83 per cent of the 543 matters it heard. Most of the sanctions were severe: 56 per cent of those whose punishment is specified were struck off the Roll, and another 15 per cent were suspended (see table 2.42). But in the interwar period, when the Society first acquired decision-making authority, only 36 per cent of solicitors tried were punished, and even in the 18 years 1940–58 the proportion reached only 68 per cent, significantly below the level of severity that had characterized judicial discipline. Furthermore, during this last period many of the suspensions were brief (an average of 15 months in the decade 1953–63); those suspended or struck off the Roll were allowed to continue working as managing clerks; and an increasing proportion of the punishments (30 per cent of the total between 1948 and 1958) were fines, whose amount averaged £230 (Johnstone and Hopson, 1967: 484–5 and nn. 78–9; but see Abel-Smith and Stevens, 1967: 190). Between 1967 and 1970, an average of 3.75 solicitors who had been struck off the Roll applied for readmission, and 2.25 were admitted (Law Society, Annual Reports).

In recent decades the disciplinary process has operated as follows. A complaint made to the Law Society is screened by the staff of its Professional Purposes Department. Unless the staff find there is no case to answer they send the matter to the Professional Purposes Committee (composed of Council members), which itself can reprimand and withhold a practising certificate but which forwards more serious cases to the disciplinary tribunal. In the 1960s, the tribunal consisted of panels drawn from a list of 12 solicitors; then it was reorganized into panels of two solicitors and a layperson appointed by the Master of the Rolls. It can strike off the Roll, suspend, fine, reprimand or make an order as to costs (Johnstone and Hopson, 1967: 479–81; Royal Commission, 1979, vol. 1: 348). There is an appeal to the Queen's Bench Division. Since 1975, a complainant who feels that the Professional Purposes Committee has dismissed the complaint without cause can seek review by the Lay Observer. Under the Solicitors Act 1974 the Law Society also has summary power to seize files, cut telephone lines and close practices without a hearing or any of the other requirements of natural justice, though in theory this does not prevent a solicitor from continuing to practise elsewhere (132 *NLJ* 525, 1982). The Administration of Justice Act 1985 gave the Law Society authority to order a solicitor to produce files and to impose conditions on a current practising certificate if solicitors fail to deliver their client account reports (83 *LSG* 742, 1986).

The actual disciplinary process bears little resemblance to this elaborate formal apparatus. It relies almost exclusively on complaints by laypersons; beween 1973 and 1978, only 14 per cent of all complaints were filed by solicitors (Royal Commission, 1979, vol. 1: 315). Laypersons have many grievances. The 1978 users' survey found that, though 67 per cent were completely satisfied, 17 per cent were only fairly satisfied, 7 per cent somewhat dissatisfied and 6 per cent very dissatisfied (ibid.: 311). A 1982 survey by the Consumers' Association found that 80 per cent of solicitors' clients were satisfied (ranging from 92 per cent of those seeking wills to 73 per cent of those seeking a divorce), but fewer than two-thirds said they would use the same solicitor again (*LAG Bulletin* 10, February 1983). A 1986 survey commissioned by the Law Society found that 90 per cent of clients were satisfied but only 72 per cent of those accused of motoring offences; 10 per cent probably would not use the same solicitor again, and 9 per cent definitely would not (83 *LSG* 1113–14, 1986; see also Watkins et al., 1986d: 9–11).

Although solicitors should take pride in the high proportion of clients who are satisfied, discontent among even 10 per cent represents at least half a million grievances a year. Few of these are expressed to the Law Society. One reason is ignorance: the users' survey found that only 17 per cent of former clients knew that the Law Society handled complaints (Royal Commission, 1979, vol. 1: 292; vol. 2: 263). Laypersons are also reluctant to complain: only a third of those clients who believed they had cause for complaint actually complained to *anyone*; of these, 69 per cent complained directly to the solicitor; only 6 per cent complained to the Law Society (ibid., vol. 2: 255–6). Thus, only 2 per cent of aggrieved clients file complaints with the Law Society. Even so, clients file about five times as many complaints per solicitor as they file per barrister (compare tables 2.43 and 1.47).

One reason for client passivity may be that the Law Society will not discipline most of the behaviour that produces client dissatisfaction (see Joseph, 1984: 32–3). Clients complain about delay, inefficiency, incompetence, negligence, lack of interest, discourtesy and cost (Royal Commission, 1979, vol. 1: 312–14; vol. 2: 233, 244, 254; Law Society, 1977: 54; see table 2.44). An analysis of 142 complaints about solicitors made to ten citizens' advice bureaux during three months in 1982 found that the causes were delay, lack of information and communication and overcharging (132 *NLJ* 891, 1982). Individual clients in particular feel that solicitors are unfriendly and aloof, fail to answer calls and create work for themselves (82 *LSG* 1469–70, 1985). Among the 8 per cent who expressed dissatisfaction in the 1986 survey, the reasons given were slowness (35 per cent), inefficiency and incompetence (28 per cent), excessive cost (22 per cent), lack of consideration (19 per cent) and lack of communication (10 per cent) (83 *LSG* 1113–14, 1986). But the grounds on which the disciplinary tribunal punished solicitors between 1961 and 1963 were very different: violation of accounts regulations, misappropriation of client funds, false statements in applying for a practising certificate, criminal convictions, acting as a solicitor without holding a current practising certificate and failing to account for money. Delay (which constituted 67 per cent of *justified* complaints a decade later) was the basis for punishment in only 8 per cent of the cases punished (Johnstone and Hopson, 1967: 482–3 n. 77; Royal Commission, 1979, vol. 1: 314).

Given the divergent concerns of the grievants and the disciplinary process, it is not surprising that most lay complaints are rejected. In the early 1960s, the staff of the Professional Purposes Department disposed of 85 per cent of the 1200–1500 complaints a year without further action (Johnstone and Hopson, 1967: 479–80). The same pattern prevails today: 70 percent of complaints are found either to be unjustified or to concern negligence, over which the Society disclaims jurisdiction; in a sample of 6321 complaints, it found only one instance of negligence worthy of further consideration (Law Society, 1977: 53). Of the 1694 complaints filed between June and August 1978, the Professional Purposes Department dismissed 200 because they involved negligence (12 per cent), 1294 as unsubstantiated (76 per cent) and 43 as frivolous (3 per cent) (Royal Commission, 1979, vol. 1: 340). Of the 8750 complaints to the Law Society in 1984, the Professional Purposes Committee took action in only 463 (5 per cent) (83 *LSG* 583 and 608, 1986).

But getting a complaint to the Professional Purposes Committee is only the first step. In 1963, 205 cases were sent to the Committee; between 1953 and 1963 it withheld or qualified the solicitor's practising certificate in an average of 11 cases a year, and the displinary tribunal imposed punishment in an average of 41 cases a year (this was unusually high; in the last three years of this period an average of only 24 solicitors were punished annually) (Johnstone and Hopson, 1967: 479–80, 481 n. 70, 484 nn. 78–9). If we combine these figures, 75–83 per cent of all hearings led to no punishment. In 1978, the Committee dismissed 5 cases, issued 23 reprimands, imposed conditions on 8 practising certificates and sent 17 cases (32 per cent) to the disciplinary tribunal (Royal Commission, 1979, vol. 1: 344). Of the 463 cases in which the Professional Purposes Committee took action in 1984, it intervened in 48 instances for violations of the account rules (10 per cent), made 44 orders (to pay fees, produce an accountant's report) (10 per cent), issued 289 rebukes and conditions on practising certificates (62 per cent) and sent only 82 matters to the Disciplinary Tribunal (18 per cent) (83 *LSG* 583 and 608, 1986).

At this final (and more visible) stage there is less attrition, but only because the vast majority of complaints have already disappeared. Even so, a significant fraction of those tried are let off with minor penalties. Of the 73 solicitors punished between 1961 and 1963, 33 (45 per cent) were struck off the Roll, 20 (27 per cent) were suspended for an average of 15 months, 18 (25 per cent) were fined an average of £230, and 2 (3 per cent) were merely reprimanded (Johnstone and Hopson, 1967: 484 nn. 78–9). In the 12 months following 25 April 1977, the tribunal struck off 14 solicitors (31 per cent of those punished), suspended 6 for up to five years (13 per cent), fined 17 up to £750 (38 per cent) and reprimanded 8 (18 per cent) (Royal Commission, 1979, vol. 1: 248–9). Thus, as the number penalized increased, the severity of penalties declined (cf. Steele and Nimmer, 1976). Although the number struck off the Roll or suspended varied considerably from year to year (see table 2.42), there is no evidence that it has increased in proportion to the rapid expansion of the profession in the last two decades. Between 1973 and 1979, the Law Society received 43,041 complaints but punished only 333 solicitors, or 0.8 per cent (see table 2.42). It is not surprising that only a third of those who complained to the Law Society were satisfied with the outcome (Royal Commission, 1979, vol. 2: 256).

Nor has the oversight of the Lay Observer significantly altered the reluctance of the Professional Purposes Committee to forward cases to the tribunal. In the first decade of its operation, the Lay Observer also dismissed without examination 1627 of the 3130 complaints received (52 per cent), criticized the Law Society in only 118 of the 1359 complaints investigated (9 per cent) and recommended that the Law Society reconsider only 36 cases, which represented 31 per cent of the cases criticized, 3 per cent of the cases investigated and 1 per cent of the complaints filed (see table 2.44; see also Royal Commission, 1979, vol. 1: 247). If we cumulate the attrition at each stage of the disciplinary process, we see that out of every 100 grievances experienced by clients, 2 are reported to the Law Society, 0.2 are investigated, 0.002 are tried and fewer than 0.001 result in serious punishment (Abel, 1982: 43).

The Law Society has not been oblivious to the inadequacies of its disciplinary procedures. It has begun to take seriously client complaints about forms of negligence and discourtesy that are not sufficiently weighty to justify formal discipline. In response to recommendations by the Royal Commission (1979, vol. 1: 304–5, 351, 546–7), it drafted professional standards requiring solicitors to communicate regularly with clients, inform clients which solicitor is responsible and provide the client with information about costs (81 *LSG* 1182, 1984; 82 *LSG* 1606–7, 1985). The Council approved in principle a scheme to arbitrate complaints of negligence against solicitors, although the latter must agree to submit to arbitration (82 *LSG* 15, 1985). It also sought the power to punish negligence (80 *LSG* 2354, 1983), and the Administration of Justice Act 1985 gave the Council authority to discipline solicitors for inadequate professional services, impose costs and limit the solicitor's practising certificate (s. 1) and to exclude from legal aid work a solicitor who commits an offence against a legally aided client (s. 44). It also belatedly followed the recommendation of the Royal Commission that laypersons should be involved in the investigation of complaints (1979, vol. 1: 351) by adding laypersons and solicitors not on the Council to the Professional Purposes Committee (81 *LSG* 2974, 1984; 82 *LSG* 15, 1985; 134 *NLJ* 350–1, 1984). On the other hand, its receptivity to complaints does not seem to have increased. It still refuses to hear complaints brought against a solicitor by a layperson who is not the solicitor's client (*Legal Action* 5, February 1985; 136 *NLJ* 106–7, 1986). And though it plans to interview complainants in person (rather than requiring them to submit their complaints in writing), its motives seem mixed:

> Not only could it save the Office substantial time and wasted effort in examining and summarising the real issues in many complaints at the outset, it could provide some complainants with what they really require

> – a sympathetic ear into which to pour their troubles. Certain complaints could well turn out in the interview to be unfounded at the outset.
>
> (134 *NLJ* 851, 1984)

Thus the goal appears to be to pacify complainants rather than help them express legitimate grievances.

Pressure for change in the disciplinary process was brought to a head by the Glanville Davies affair. Without going into the details of this complex and lengthy matter, it is sufficient to note that Leslie Parsons filed a complaint of overcharging against his solicitor, Glanville Davies, a member of the Council of the Law Society from 1967 to 1982. Despite the fact that Davies's bill was reduced on taxation from £197,000 to £67,736, the Law Society took no disciplinary action and allowed Davies to resign from the Council on grounds of ill health. Further complaints to the Lay Observer provided no greater satisfaction. When Parsons finally took judicial proceedings, one judge found that Davies had been guilty of at least gross and persistent misconduct, and ultimately he was struck off the Roll in 1983. The Law Society's own internal enquiry concluded that the disciplinary proceedings had fallen far short of the necessary standard; there were administrative failures, wrong decisions, mistakes, errors of judgement, failures in communication, highhandedness and insensitivity; the whole affair was a disgrace to the Society (80 *LSG* 3202–10, 1983; 81 *LSG* supplement, 22 February 1984; 81 *LSG* 938–46, 1984; Law Society Council's Commission of Enquiry, 1984). The Society paid compensation to Leslie Parsons for its inadequate handling of the case, establishing that it will be liable in the future for the failure to exercise reasonable care in the investigation of complaints (136 *NLJ* 835–7, 1986).

As a result of this judgement, which followed a long accumulation of criticism, the Society commissioned a study by Coopers & Lybrand, which included discipline among its many topics (82 *LSG* 2, 1985). The Coopers draft report (1985b: paras 73–4) clearly came as a shock to the Council, for it recommended transferring all disciplinary powers from the Law Society to an independent statutory Solicitors' Complaints Board (though this would preserve a solicitor majority). Soon thereafter the National Consumer Council (1985) published a survey it had commissioned the previous year, showing that only 15 per cent of the 1992 respondents thought that either solicitors or the Law Society should be investigating complaints. If a new body were to be created, only 5 per cent of respondents wanted a solicitor majority, 36 per cent wanted equal representation of solicitors and others, and 55 per cent favoured a majority for non-solicitors. At about the same time (12 February 1985),

Alf Dubs, the Labour MP for Battersea, introduced a private members bill, cosponsored by five others (including Austin Mitchell, the instigator of the attack on the conveyancing monopoly) and supported by the Legal Action Group and the National Consumer Council (*Legal Action* 4, March 1985; 135 *NLJ* 143–4, 1985). This Solicitors (Independent Complaints Procedure) Bill would create an independent General Legal Council with a bare majority of solicitors and the power to investigate and correct both misconduct and negligence as well as to arbitrate malpractice claims.

Reaction to these initiatives was mixed. Some local law societies, notably the larger ones in or around London (Holborn, City of London, City of Westminster, Central and South Middlesex, Croydon and District) supported the Coopers proposal, but large provincial societies like Manchester, Liverpool and Birmingham opposed it (135 *NLJ* 1071–2, 1985; 82 *LSG* 3222, 1985). The Young Solicitors' Group and the local government solicitors also supported the proposal (82 *LSG* 2091–2, 1985; 83 *LSG* 583 and 590–1, 1986). But the Council of the Law Society was adamantly opposed – indeed, it persuaded Coopers & Lybrand to include an alternative proposal that would preserve Law Society responsibility for discipline but increase internal separation of functions and give laypersons a majority on the investigating body. Not surprisingly, the Law Society's Council, its Management and Consultation Steering Committee and its Professional Purposes Committee all applauded the second alternative (83 *LSG* 580–3 and 826–7, 1986).

The reform implemented on 31 August 1986 eliminated the Professional Purposes Committee and Department, shifting responsibility for practising certificates and accounts reports to the Finance and Administration Department and creating an Ethics and Guidance Committee to draft and modify rules of professional conduct and advise solicitors. It established a physically separate Solicitors' Complaints Bureau, consisting of an Investigation Committee with a lay chairperson, six other lay members, two solicitors not on the Council and two Council members, and an Adjudication Committee with nine Council members, three other solicitors not on the Council and six lay members (all non-Council members to be appointed by the Master of the Rolls). The Bureau was given a £4 million annual budget and twice the staff of its predecessor. But prosecutions are still heard by the Solicitors' Disciplinary Tribunal (83 *LSG* 2450, 1986). It is far from clear whether these changes will increase either the effectiveness of social control or the degree of public confidence.

## Financial misconduct

If the Law Society has dragged its feet in disciplining solicitors, the problem of financial misconduct has been harder to ignore. Solicitors who failed to account for client moneys, misapplied them and ultimately defaulted and declared bankruptcy were a recurrent problem well into the twentieth century. Between 1861 and 1877, 942 solicitors declared bankruptcy – 130 of them more than once – and one solicitor did so a staggering 12 times in those 16 years (Kirk, 1976: 100). In 1900, a former president of the Law Society was convicted of defrauding his clients (Offer, 1981: 56). In the single year 1901, 55 solicitors declared bankruptcy, and at least 42 did so each year until 1905, depriving clients of a total of £1.5 million (Birks, 1960: 271; Kirk, 1976: 104). In 1904, 76 undischarged bankrupts were still in practice (Kirk, 1976: 100). The Law Society could do little about this problem. A solicitor who speculated with his client's money committed no crime until passage of the Larceny Act in 1901 (ibid.: 101; Birks, 1960: 271). Until 1906, the Society could not refuse to renew the annual certificate of a solicitor who declared bankruptcy, and only in 1957 did it gain the authority to suspend a certificate in mid-year (Kirk, 1976: 100).

Measures to correct this situation were taken very slowly and only against the strong opposition of many solicitors. The Society required all entrants to pass an examination in accounts starting in 1906 and began making *ex gratia* payments to the clients of defaulting solicitors in 1912, although the total amounts paid were very small given the number and magnitude of defaults (see table 2.45). The Solicitors Act of 1933 required the Society to adopt rules about client accounts, which it did with reluctance in 1935, but large numbers of solicitors consistently fail to comply with the reporting requirements (Birks, 1960: 273–5; Kirk, 1976: 103). In 1942 it established a compensation fund generated by mandatory contributions of £5 a year per practising certificate, and during the next decade and a half it made about 100 payments averaging £7000 each (Birks, 1960: 274–5; Abel-Smith and Stevens, 1967: 192; Kirk, 1976: 105). In 1945, the Society created an investigation department to examine solicitor accounts, and it contained three clerks and seven investigators by 1963–4 (Johnstone and Hopson, 1967: 479–80; Kirk, 1976: 103). Between 1949 and 1970 the staff examined an average of 64 accounts a year; since 1971 the number has more than doubled (Law Society, Annual Reports).

As a result of all these measures, solicitor bankruptcies dropped to about ten a year in 1970 (Kirk, 1976: 104). Because sole practitioners are overrepresented among bankrupts (92 per cent in 1957, when they were only 26 per cent of principals), the decline in bankruptcies may reflect the decline in solo practice and may reverse as the latter did in 1979 (Birks, 1960: 274; see table 2.30). Nevertheless, the contributions required to maintain the compensation fund had to be doubled in 1956, and in 1975 the Council was given discretion to raise the level as needed. Contributions were set at £15 that year, £20 the next and £30 the following year; but though they subsequently rose to £40, they returned to £30 in 1984–5 (Kirk, 1976: 105; Podmore, 1980: 98 n. 3; Law Society, Annual Report, 1983–4: 31; 82 *LSG* 1833, 1985). Although the number of defaulting solicitors may have declined, the fund still paid an average of £927,000 a year in the decade ending 1984 (see table 2.45). And solicitors are still unenthusiastic about submitting their accounts to the Law Society: an average of 1385 a year submitted inadequate or late accounts in the years 1977, 1978, 1980 and 1982 – about 10 per cent of those required to report – and the Society is starting to impose fines as well as suspend certificates (Law Society, Annual Reports; 82 *LSG* 13, 1985).

## Malpractice

The last form of regulation is an external control over which the profession has little influence: claims for damages by clients injured by solicitor negligence. Unlike barristers, solicitors have always been liable for malpractice (although they share the Bar's immunity in the course of litigation). Nevertheless, successful claims seem to have been rare until recently. In 1963–4, little more than half of all solicitors carried malpractice insurance; only 8 per cent of solicitors were the subject of negligence claims that year; only half of these paid any damages; and only half of the latter were the result of judgements (Johnstone and Hopson, 1967: 503). The low level of claims is not evidence of a high level of quality. In response to a 1986 survey, 28 out of 45 citizens' advice bureaux in South Wales expressed their lack of confidence in referring clients to solicitors, particularly with respect to employment matters (12 bureaux), housing (10), matrimonial disputes (8), welfare benefits (8) and applications to tribunals (7) (Beale and Stow, 1986). And the notorious solicitor gadfly Michael Joseph has recently documented several cases of solicitor incompetence in personal injury matters (Joseph, 1984: 151–247).

Indemnity insurance became compulsory in 1976. The master policy negotiated by the Law Society established premiums at £435 for sole practitioners and £348 per partner. These were subject to a surcharge based on claims experience, ranging from 125 per cent for those whose claims were between one and two times their premium to 200 per cent for those whose claims were more than four times their premium. Premiums rose rapidly thereafter: £888 per principal in inner London and £658 elsewhere in 1978–9, £933 and £718 in 1979–80, £1083 and £833 in 1981–2, £1361 and £1047 in 1982–3 and £1532 and £1179 in 1983–4 (Royal Commission, 1979, vol. 1: 327; Podmore, 1980: 98 n. 3; 80 *LSG* 2035 and 2042, 1983).

This tripling of premiums in seven years upset many solicitors, fueling historical tensions within the profession (Law Society, 1982). The British Legal Association, claiming to speak on behalf of smaller firms against a Law Society establishment controlled by the larger City firms, advocated basing premiums on gross fees instead of the number of principals. In November 1982, a poll of 64 local law societies found that 48 favoured such a change and 8 opposed it; not surprisingly, the City of London Solicitors' Company flatly rejected the proposal (80 *LSG* 2035, 2042 and 2044, 1983). The BLA forced the Society to conduct a postal ballot of its members. There were 11,534 valid responses (of the 42,396 members and 24,149 premium payers). Asked whether gross fees should be taken into account in setting the premium, 73.5 per cent agreed and 21 per cent preferred the existing system. Approximately equal proportions thought that the premium should be based exclusively on gross fees (46.5 per cent) and on both the fees and the number of principals (45.1 per cent). Asked whether they thought the present system was unfair, 55.1 per cent agreed, but the proportion was much higher in the provinces (68 per cent) than in London (35 per cent) and in smaller firms than in larger (ranging from 71 per cent in two-partner firms to 12 per cent in firms with more than 20 principals). Solicitors split along similar lines when asked whether the premium should be based on gross fees without a cutoff (80 *LSG* 2484–94, 1983).

Because the framing of the questions left membership preferences ambiguous, the BLA demanded a new ballot on its motion that the premium should be calculated solely on the basis of gross fees with no upward ceiling or tapering. The motion was carried 9846 to 7041 (45 per cent of the membership voting) (81 *LSG* 322, 1984; 133 *NLJ* 967, 1983). Although the Council denied that it was bound by such votes, it decided to base premiums exclusively on gross fees. The 1984–5 premium of £31.5 million was equivalent to 1.86 per cent of gross fees, which would represent an increased premium for partners earning more than £63,000 (£82,000 in inner London) and a decrease for the rest (134 *NLJ* 419, 1984; 81 *LSG* 1170, 1984). The City firms naturally were furious and appealed to the Master of the Rolls, who rejected the Council's action as unfair to the larger firms (81 *LSG* 1571–4, 1984). This dramatically illustrated the limited autonomy enjoyed by solicitors, since the Master of the Rolls, of course, is a judge and former barrister. Declining to challenge his authority, the Council adopted a premium schedule proportioned to gross fees but tapering from 2.0 to 0.2 per cent, with a ceiling at £200,000 – an annual change of no more than £90 per partner from the previous year (81 *LSG* 1804, 1984; cf. Law Society, 1985). The following year the tapering was even greater, from 2.0 to 0.1 per cent, with adjustments for the ratio of staff to partners and discounts for rural and for criminal practice (82 *LSG* 1678–9, 1985). At the same time, the global premium continued to increase, by 6 per cent in 1984–5 and 24 per cent in 1985–6 (8 per cent of which represented an increase in coverage from £100,000 a claim to £250,000) (ibid.). In 1986–7, tapering was increased further (from 2.4 per cent for partners earning less than £50,000 gross to 0.1 per cent for those earning more than £220,000), and coverage rose to £500,000 per claim (83 *LSG* 2126, 1986). Premiums were individualized further: a 10 per cent discount for firms with two staff per principal or fewer and a similar surcharge for those with five staff per principal or more; a 10 per cent discount for firms located in towns with fewer than 10,000 people; and a discount ranging from 10 to 30 per cent for firms doing substantial amounts of criminal law or small debt collection (83 *LSG* 2466–74, 1986). Yet even these changes were not sufficient to resolve the problems, and in 1986 the president announced that the Law Society intended to become a self-insurer, hoping to preserve solvency with annual 15 per cent premium increases until 1991, when claims were expected to range between £94.4 million and £111.4 million a year (83 *LSG* 2960 and 3047–53, 1986). Although the economic and psychological costs of malpractice liability remain much lower in England than in the United States, it is clear that premiums will continue to rise and tensions to intensify between base and elite within the profession. In order to settle claims more amicably (and cheaply), the Law Society recently created a voluntary arbitration scheme for claims of professional negligence (83 LSG 1876–7, 1986).

# IV

# Legal education

# 17

# The growth of academic institutions

Until recently, most solicitors were not university graduates, and most barristers were not law graduates; the change began after World War II and greatly accelerated in the 1970s. If we look at the quantity and quality of academic legal education we can see why this was so. The Civil War terminated the educational functions of the Inns of Court, and for the next two centuries formal education in the common law was virtually unavailable. Blackstone was appointed the first Vinerian Professor at Oxford in 1758, but after his resignation the chair was not filled. In 1800, Cambridge created the Downing Professorship. Yet very few students attended law lectures at either university in the nineteenth century. There were no examinations in law; the LLB simply was granted seven years after enrolment and the LLD five and a half years later. Whereas physicians were required to have a university degree in medicine in 1858, it was more than 100 years before lawyers began to think about a similar requirement (Ormrod Committee, 1971: 31).

The universities began to take increasing interest in legal studies in the mid-nineteenth century. Oxford offered a BA in law and history in 1850 and a BCL in 1852. Cambridge created a Board of Legal Studies in 1854, initiating the LLB the following year and the law tripos in 1858. But there were few takers. Between 1858 and 1871, only 135 students passed the Cambridge law tripos, about ten a year. Oxford separated law from history only in 1872, when it established the Honours School of Jurisprudence; but even then, professors taught only jurisprudence, Roman law and international law – *not* English law. The number of candidates varied between 35 and 80 a year until the end of the century, about a third of whom obtained a fourth class degree or worse (Ormrod Committee, 1971: 4–7; Abel-Smith and Stevens, 1967: 71, 165; Lawson, 1968: 31, 33, 35, 55 n.5, 259). Other universities also introduced legal studies during this period. University College London opened a law faculty in 1826, although examinations remained voluntary. Because faculty were paid a percentage of student fees and attracted few students (John Austin was the most notorious failure) it was hard to retain teachers. University College London awarded an LLB to its first three graduates in 1839 but conferred only one the following year and none in 1841; by the end of the nineteenth century, it had awarded only 135 degrees (Baker, 1977). In 1866, Roman law enrolled the most students – a total of eight – and other subjects had none; in 1888 only 13 students enrolled in the department (Keeton, 1939: 126, 128). Academic legal education offered few advantages to those seeking to practise: those who passed in Roman law were excused from that subject on part 1 of the Bar final after 1891; those who took a law degree were exempted from the Law Society's intermediate examination after 1895 (Lawson, 1968: 121, 134–5).

Towards the end of the century, a number of provincial universities began teaching law, although most of their faculty were practitioners teaching part time to prepare articled clerks for the solicitors' examinations, an activity the Law Society subsidized. Manchester was the first in 1880, followed by Liverpool in 1886, Leeds (then still part of Manchester) in 1899, Aberystwyth in 1901, Swansea in 1905, Nottingham in 1907 and Sheffield in 1908 (Jenks, 1935: 163, 166). By 1910, legal instruction was offered at Bristol, Birmingham and Durham as well (Hazeltine, 1910: 19, 39). The Society of Public Teachers of Law (so named in order to exclude the 'private' crammers outside universities) was founded in 1908 by 45 teachers who met, significantly, at the Law Society's premises in Chancery Lane. The requirement by the Solicitors Act of 1922 that articled clerks complete a year of formal education constituted a major stimulus for the growth of provincial legal education. As a result, professional instruction was initiated at Newcastle, Exeter and Southampton (although students could no longer satisfy the requirement by studying at Dublin or Belfast), and law degrees were offered at Aberystwyth, Leeds, Birmingham, Bristol, Manchester, Sheffield and Liverpool (Jenks, 1935: 169; for enrolment in professional courses, see table 2.6). In the late 1920s, there were some 600–700 students reading law at Oxford and Cambridge (Anderson, 1984: 74). By World War II, Exeter, Hull and Nottingham also awarded law degrees. The law faculty at Oxford rose from 17 in 1914 to 25 in 1939 (Lawson, 1968: 150). The three colleges of the University of London (University, King's and the London School of Economics) expanded their joint law faculty to five professors, three readers and 21 others, and enrolment rose from 90 before World War I to 300–400 just before World War II (Jenks, 1935:

171–2; Keeton, 1939: 133; Anderson, 1984: 74). By 1934, there were about 100 instructors teaching some 2000 students throughout the country; but Oxbridge and London still contained about two-thirds, and the provincial universities still consisted primarily of practitioners preparing articled clerks for the Law Society's examinations (Manchester, 1980: 63–4; see tables 3.1, 3.2). Further incentive for law study was offered by the Bar in 1937, when those obtaining first or second class marks in contract and tort, land law and criminal law were exempted from those subjects on part 1 of the final (Lawson, 1968: 135).

World War II had a catastrophic effect on legal education, as it did on the production of lawyers generally (*JSPTL*, 1947). The 400 students at Oxford had disappeared by 1942, the 500 at Cambridge fell to 50, and the three London colleges dispersed to the countryside with drastically reduced numbers. Birmingham, which had 105 students (65 reading for the LLB), shrank to a quarter; Manchester, with 141 students (80 reading for the LLB), dropped to 44 in 1944; Sheffield fell to a third, Aberystwyth to 20 and Hull to fewer than five. The universities recovered very slowly after the war: in 1952, Bristol still had only nine students, Sheffield seven and even Manchester a mere 30 (Merricks, 1982).

Institutional growth commenced in the mid 1960s. In 1966 there were 17 law faculties in England and one in Wales (only three more than before the war): Oxford, Cambridge, the four London colleges (Queen Mary began teaching law in 1965), Aberystwyth, the older provincial universities (Birmingham, Bristol, Leeds, Liverpool, Manchester, Newcastle and Sheffield) and the newer ones (Exeter, Hull, Nottingham and Southampton) (Wilson, 1966: 5–6). Keele and Kent offered mixed degrees in law and other subjects, and Durham and Leicester initiated law degrees in 1966–7. By 1975, there were additional faculties at Reading, Warwick, Cardiff and the University of Wales Institute of Science and Technology (Wilson and Marsh, 1975: 243). The School of Oriental and African Studies of the University of London, which had offered postgraduate degrees in the laws of other countries, launched an undergraduate law degree that year, and East Anglia did so in 1977 (Wilson and Marsh, 1978: 1).

Equally important was the growth of the polytechnics, starting in the late 1960s. Previously, a number of educational institutions had prepared students for the external London LLB. But the Council for National Academic Awards (CNAA), created in 1964, established a Legal Studies Board in 1966, which authorized the first two polytechnics (Coventry and Manchester) to offer law degrees that year. Additional full-time programmes followed rapidly: two in 1967, one in 1969, two in 1970, one in 1971, three in 1972, three in 1973, four in 1974, four in 1975, one in 1977 and one in 1980 (Wilson and Marsh, 1975: 255; 1978: 2; 1981: 1, 3; Marsh, 1983: 74, 84, 87, 90; Green, 1976).

The cumulative effect of these changes was enormous. Prior to World War II, law degrees were offered by Oxford, Cambridge, London and ten provincial universities; Oxford and Cambridge enrolled almost two-thirds of all law students; together with London, the three universities enrolled three-quarters. By 1980, there were 34 university and 24 polytechnic law courses (including mixed degree programmes) – nearly a fourfold increase in the number of institutions. The Oxbridge law student body had grown by 50 per cent but now contained a mere 11 per cent of all students; the five London colleges enrolled five times as many students as three of them had done before the war, but they also had shrunk proportionately, so that the three oldest universities now contained only a fifth of all law students. The older provincial universities had increased fourfold, but they now contained only a fifth of all law students. The new provincial universities (all but one founded since the war) contained another fifth. But the most dramatic development was the founding of the polytechnics, which now taught two out of every five law students (see table 3.2).

Although I am interested primarily in the impact of these institutional changes on practitioners (see chapter 18), they also contributed to the emergence of a distinct category of legal professional – the academic lawyer. Prior to World War II, legal academics were numerically insignificant. Half of the 100 or so taught at Oxbridge or London; most of those teaching at provincial universities were practitioners (Jenks, 1935). Indeed, as late as 1963–4 Oxbridge and London contained an even higher proportion of full-time academics – nearly two-thirds (see table 3.1). By the 1980s, however, less than 10 percent taught at Oxbridge, another 10 per cent at London, 20 per cent at each of the older and the newer provincial universities and more than 40 per cent at the polytechnics (ibid.). In addition, 560 full-time and 877 part-time instructors at colleges of further education were teaching legal subjects in 1962, though not in degree programmes (Wilson, 1966: 59–60); in 1980, there were 832 full-time staff (Bailey and Marsh, 1981). The number of full-time university and polytechnic law teachers increased tenfold from 1933–4 to 1980–1 (during which time solicitors multiplied only two and a half times) – almost fivefold from 1963–64 to 1980–1.

Legal academics have not only increased numerically; they have also become differentiated, both internally and within the legal profession. Those who teach at universities are quite distinct from those who teach at polytechnics (and even more from those who teach at colleges of further education). The Society of Public Teachers of Law (SPTL) excluded polytechnic law teachers from membership, reaffirming this policy in 1966 and again in 1978 (Pettit, 1983: 234–5). There is little lateral mobility between institutions and even less across categories. In a 1982 sample of CNAA polytechnic law teachers (45 per cent response rate), 84 per cent had taught only at their present institution; of the 16 per cent who had taught elsewhere, 7 per cent had taught at another CNAA institution, 6 per cent at a college of further education and only 3 per cent at a university (Marsh, 1983: 75, 94). Because polytechnic law teachers were excluded from the Society of Public Teachers of Law they formed their own Association of Law Teachers (ALT) in 1965; although this welcomes university law teachers, few have joined. The SPTL had about 1000 domestic members in 1977 (plus another 500 from overseas) (SPTL, 1977); the ALT has about 700 members. The SPTL rejected the first application by a woman in 1938; when the next application was received in 1948 the Society changed its rules and admitted her (Pettit, 1983: 232–3). More women have entered law teaching, though none of the recent empirical studies has thought to describe this important change (Wilson, 1966; Wilson and Marsh, 1975; 1978; 1981; Bailey and Marsh, 1981; Marsh, 1983). Women law teachers felt sufficiently alienated from their male-dominated institutions to form a group in 1981 in order to offer support and encourage exchange concerning teaching and scholarship.

Despite the lack of lateral mobility among university law teachers, they are a strikingly homogeneous group. In 1966, two-thirds had degrees from Oxbridge, and another sixth had graduated from London; of the 28 per cent with first degrees from a provincial university, half had done postgraduate work at Oxbridge or London (Wilson, 1966: 29). My analysis of the 1981 directory of the SPTL confirmed the persistence of this pattern (although not all teachers belong to the Society). Among all the degrees held (both first and postgraduate), 260 were from Cambridge, 245 from Oxford and 186 from London – an institutional dominance similar to that found among barristers in the nineteenth and early twentieth centuries (see table 1.14). No other institution began to approach this level of influence, and those that produced significant numbers of law teachers – such as Birmingham (45), Manchester (32) and Sheffield (21) – tended to employ a disproportionate fraction of their own graduates. Similar insularity was visible at other institutions: 16 of the 38 teachers with degrees from Welsh faculties taught in Wales; 49 of the 62 who graduated from departments in Scotland taught there. Although polytechnic law teachers may be segregated from their university colleagues by institution and professional association, nearly three-quarters received their first degrees from a university (Marsh, 1983: 119). Notwithstanding this homogeneity of background, the internal structure of law faculties is intensely hierarchical; the one-eighth of instructors who are professors dominate governance, and many of the two-thirds who are lecturers will never receive promotions (see table 3.3).

Law teachers have also grown apart from practitioners. Even in 1966, three-quarters of university law teachers had obtained advanced degrees, and half had collected two or more, whereas virtually no practising lawyer had a higher degree in law (Wilson, 1966: 29). My own unsystematic review of the 1981 directory of the SPTL indicated that virtually all teachers had received some postgraduate education. Among CNAA law teachers, 19 per cent had a research degree and 29 per cent a taught master's degree (Sharman, 1983, cited in Marsh, 1983: 95 n. 18). Half of all university law teachers in 1966 had studied or taught abroad (Wilson, 1966: 29). In 1981, teachers listed in the SPTL directory had earned 146 degrees from universities outside Britain – only Oxford, Cambridge and London produced more British law teachers. In 1966, half of all university law teachers had practised, and 75 per cent were professionally qualified; but among those who had been teaching for less than five years, the proportions were only 20 and 40 per cent (Wilson, 1966: 32). The proportion with professional qualifications may have declined further when the Bar required all those sitting the final to take a year of vocational training. Yet the connection with practice seems to have remained higher outside university law faculties. In 1983, 56 per cent of CNAA teachers had a professional qualification (Sharman, 1983, cited in Marsh, 1983: 95 n. 18). Whereas only 40 per cent of law teachers at colleges of further education had a professional or university qualification in law in 1962, 67 per cent did in 1980, and they taught 79 per cent of all class hours (Bailey and Marsh, 1981: 88). In 1963–4, a quarter of university law faculty taught part time, devoting the rest of their energies to practice; in 1981, only a tenth still taught part time and less than a tenth of polytechnic teachers; at colleges of further education, part-time teachers taught 40 per cent of all classes in 1962 but only 10 per cent in 1980 (Bailey and Marsh, 1981: 87; but see table 3.1).

Yet if there has been increasing differentiation between academic and practising lawyers, the former are still primarily teachers rather than scholars (cf. Twining, 1980). Few, if any, have published at the time of apppointment; virtually all obtain security of employment after three years. Although publication is a prerequisite for a chair, there are so few professorships that this is not a realistic ambition for most academics.

Salary increments are granted for mere seniority. And teaching loads are heavy: an average of 8–10 hours a week at most universities, 11–15 at polytechnics and over 18 at colleges of further education (compared with 5–6 at most law schools in the United States). Although professors and department heads teach far less, their administrative obligations (roughly 20 hours a week) more than make up the difference (Wilson, 1966: 32, 100; Wilson and Marsh, 1975: 270; 1978: 21–2; 1981: 24–5; Bailey and Marsh, 1981: 89; Marsh, 1983: 91, 94).

# 18

# Law students

The emergence of academics as a significant category within the legal profession is important in its own right: they have had considerable influence on educational policy and have been persistent critics of legal rules and institutions. But here I am interested in legal education more as it affects the production of lawyers – both their numbers and their characteristics. The last two decades have witnessed one of the most rapid expansions of formal legal education ever experienced in any country; the only parallels are other Commonwealth countries, such as Canada, Australia and New Zealand, which also switched from apprenticeship to academic education after World War II (Arthurs et al., 1988; Weisbrot, 1988; Murray, 1988). Immediately prior to World War II there were about 1500 undergraduate law students; in 1983–4 there were over 14,000, more than a ninefold increase. Most of this growth occurred very recently. In the almost three decades between 1933–4 and 1961–2, the number of law students increased only 75 percent. In the next decade they increased 107 per cent; and from 1971–2 to 1983–4 they increased 118 per cent (see table 3.2). The number of law graduates also increased dramatically, from 576 in 1948 (already inflated by returning veterans) to 4006 in 1983 – almost sevenfold (see table 3.5).

We can understand these increases better by comparing them with changes in the society and the profession. Some of the expansion of legal education is simply the expansion of higher education: between 1962–3 and 1980–1, full-time university enrolment increased from 87,000 to 246,000; between 1962–3 and 1979–0, full-time and part-time enrolment in other public sector tertiary education (excluding teacher training and the Open University) increased from 133,000 to 276,000 (Farrant, 1981: table 2.1 in that work). But part represents growing interest in law as a career. Between 1971–2 and 1980–1, the enrolment of undergraduate law students increased 92 per cent, while the number of home entrants under 21 to British public higher education increased only 64 per cent (see tables 3.2, 3.4). The impact of this expansion of academic legal education on the profession is profound, as we have seen already. In 1933–4, there were 1804 undergraduate law students, or about 10 per cent of the 18,743 barristers and solicitors listed in the 1931 census (see tables 3.2 and 4.1). In 1953–4, there were 2640 undergraduate law students, or 13 per cent of the 19,594 solicitors and barristers practising in 1953 (excluding employed barristers and solicitors who did not take out practising certificates) (see tables 3.2, 1.16 and 2.14). In 1961–2, there were 3169 undergraduate law students, or about 15 per cent of the 21,356 barristers and solicitors. In 1971–2 there were 6574 undergraduate law students, or 23 per cent of the 28,080 barristers and solicitors. And in 1983–4 there were 14,362 undergraduate law students, or 30 per cent of the 48,016 barristers and solicitors. If all these students graduate and enter the profession, it will double again in a decade. Thus, the influence of academic legal education on the size of the profession cannot be exaggerated.

At the same time, neither the profession nor the academic institutions (individually or collectively) control enrolments. In 1975, for instance, the Board of Legal Studies of the CNNA informed the Department of Education and Science that it opposed further expansion and received assurances from the Department that none was intended. Nevertheless, the Department approved two new university law schools the following year (Marsh, 1983: 92). In 1981, the central government cut the budget for all universities, which responded by eliminating 10,000 places in order to maintain the level of expenditure per student. The result was an increase of more than 20 per cent in polytechnic intake that year and a rise in enrolment from 30,000 to 37,500 between 1980 and 1985 (reducing polytechnic expenditure per student to £2500, compared with £3000 in universities). Recently, the Secretary of State's National Advisory Board for Public Sector Higher Education announced a plan to cut the budget for polytechnics by 15 million in the autumn of 1987, resulting in the elimination of 18,000 places. Furthermore, whereas law previously was grouped with business studies as a protected subject, it will exchange places with economics in social and administrative studies, which are not protected, with the result that polytechnic law departments expect enrolments to decline more than 7 per cent. It is noteworthy that the Law Society *protested* these cuts (135 *NLJ* 1224, 1985; 74 *New Society* 463, 13 December 1985; Wilby, 1985b).

If enrolment in law departments has grown, the demand for places has grown even faster. Consequently, undergraduate admissions have become the central mechanism for selecting who may become a lawyer. The ratio of applications to places increased by about half between the early 1960s and the late 1970s, though it varied considerably between institutions (see table 3.6). On the other hand, the ratio appears to have declined somewhat at the newer provincial universities and the polytechnics, which were expanding during this period. But this ratio is distorted by multiple applications. Total admissions as a percentage of total applications gives a better picture of the pressure for places. This has dropped fairly steadily since the early 1960s (ibid.). The slow decline in applications to university law departments in the early 1980s has been reversed; there was an increase of 11.8 per cent in 1983–4. More than 1500 candidates apply for the 60 places at South Bank Polytechnic (Duncan and Wojciechowski-Kibble, 1986: 36). In 1984, there were about 10,000 applications for 2800 places in university law departments (Wojciechowski-Kibble and Duncan, 1985). In the end, about two-fifths of domestic applicants and a quarter of overseas applicants find places (ibid.; Lee, 1984: 165).

Competition for entry is visible in the rising qualifications of those admitted. Between 1980 and 1983, nearly three-quarters of domestic entrants to university law departments had at least three A-levels, and another 3–5 per cent had two (UGC, 1984). Among full-time students accepted to polytechnic law departments, the proportion with A-levels rose from 77 to 83 per cent between 1980 and 1983 (Marsh, 1983: 101). In 1983–4, 70 per cent of university law departments required three A-levels, although 75 per cent of polytechnic law departments accepted two (Lee, 1984: 167). In 1970, 88 per cent of domestic students admitted to university law departments had three A-levels with a total score of at least 9; ten years later the proportion was 98 per cent (Wojciechowski-Kibble and Duncan, 1985). (In the points system, A grades are worth 5, B grades 4, and so on.) In both years, this was the highest proportion of any subject, including medicine (Farrant, 1981: table 2.1 in that work). All university law departments required a minimum of 10 points on A-levels, 16 required 11, and some even required 12, although only one polytechnic required 10 points on three A-levels, and the rest required 6–9 points on two (ibid.: 168–9). By contrast, the average A-level score of university entrants in all subjects in 1983 was 11.0 (up from 9.9 in 1980); among polytechnic entrants in all subjects it was 5.4 (up from 4.9) (Wilby, 1985a). In 1981, the A-level grades of entering university law students were exceeded only by those entering in medicine and veterinary science (UCCA, 1981). In 1983, the scores of entering university law students (an average of 12.0) were exceeded only by those in medicine (13.2), biological and physical sciences (12.5), general engineering (12.4) and maths (12.3) (ibid., 1984: table 6.6). A fifth of all university law departments accepted only those applicants who listed them first; and in 1984, 95 per cent of men and 97 per cent of women admitted to law departments had made law their first choice (Lee, 1984: 166; UCCA, 1985: table 4).

Among university law departments, 12 per cent admitted *no* students after their A-levels, and two-thirds admitted less than 5 per cent; at polytechnics, by contrast, more than half admitted a quarter of their students after A-levels, and a fifth admitted more than half of their students at this time (Lee, 1984: 171). Half of university law departments required formal entry qualifications from mature students, compared with only 10 per cent of polytechnics; 30 per cent of university law departments enrolled less than 5 per cent mature students, compared with 15 per cent of polytechnics; 15 per cent of university law departments enrolled 10–20 per cent mature students, compared with 45 percent of polytechnics (ibid.: 169). Thus, it seems clear that admission to university law departments is intensely competitive, whereas polytechnic departments are less demanding and more flexible.

If prior academic credentials are the greatest obstacle to gaining admission to a law department, cost is a significant problem in staying the course. We saw above that the rise of academic legal education appears to have lowered the cost of qualifying, since tuition is free for domestic students, and local authorities offer means-tested grants for maintenance. In 1966, more than 80 per cent of all undergraduates held such grants, and most of the 13 per cent who registered as private students were from overseas (Wilson, 1966: 20). In 1973, 90 per cent of university and 88 per cent of polytechnic undergraduate law students received grants, and private students at university had fallen to 8 per cent; these proportions have remained fairly constant since then (Wilson and Marsh, 1975: 253, 257; 1978: 8, 11; 1981: 8, 12).

Financial burdens are also eased by part-time degree programmes for those students who must support families or are ineligible for local authority grants. Here, again, the creation of polytechnic law departments has been critical for, unlike the universities, they offer sandwich courses (intensive instruction for employees released from work – introduced at Trent in 1967) and part-time day and evening courses (two began in 1972, two in 1974, three in 1977, one each in 1978 and 1979, two in 1980 and one in 1981) (see table 3.7; Marsh, 1983: 84–5, 87, 90). Students are accepted to these courses with lower academic credentials; only 32 percent had A-levels (compared with 81 per cent of full-time students), and the proportion appears to be declining (Marsh, 1983:

101–2). Whereas 18 per cent of polytechnic law students were studying part time in 1983–4, only 2 per cent of university undergraduate law students were doing so (compare tables 3.2 and 3.3). Furthermore, whereas many universities are situated in settings inaccessible to most of the population, polytechnics are within commuting distance in inner cities. At 35 per cent of polytechnics, more than half the law students lived at home; at none of them did less than 5 per cent live at home, though this was the case at 36 per cent of universities (Lee, 1984: 169). Thus polytechnics are more accessible in terms of cost as well as academic qualifications.

The growing prominence of academic education as the principal route through which most lawyers qualify has affected the composition of the legal profession as well as its size. But despite the fact that law departments admit students on the basis of criteria that are considerably more universalistic than those guiding the selection of articled clerks and assistant solicitors, pupils and tenants, and that law students are subsidized far more heavily than apprentices ever were, there has been little change (if any) in the class composition of entrants. Indeed, intense competition for places in undergraduate law departments actually may have narrowed class recruitment.

University students have always come from privileged backgrounds. Between 1928 and 1961, only about a quarter were the children of fathers in manual occupations (Robbins Committee, 1963: app. II-B, table 6). A 1961–2 survey of the cohort born in 1940–1 found that only 4 per cent were studying full time for a university degree, but the proportions ranged from 33 per cent of those in social class I and 11 per cent of those in social class II to 1 per cent in social classes IV and V. On the other hand, only 7 per cent of those in social class I were not in any educational programme, compared with 65 per cent of those in classes IV and V (ibid.: app. 1, part. 2, s. 2, table 2). Among the men who completed an internal degree in 1960, 12 per cent were from social class I (compared with 2.4 per cent of the population), whereas only 26 per cent were from classes IV-VI (compared with 64.9 per cent of the population) (Kelsall et al., 1972: tables 1, 3). These disparities were even greater at the elite universities: only 13 per cent of Oxbridge men were working class, compared with 24 per cent at London, 30–5 per cent at provincial universities and 43 per cent in Wales (ibid.: table 22).

The situation did not change significantly in the next two decades, despite the expansion of provincial universities (Farrant, 1981: tables 2.17, 2.18 in that work). Indeed, class bias intensified. In 1970, 30 percent of university entrants were from class I, compared with 9 per cent of the population; seven years later the proportions were 36 and 10 per cent. At the other end of the spectrum, 28 per cent of university entrants in 1970 were from classes IV-VI, compared with 63 per cent of the population; seven years later the proportions were 24 and 61 per cent (Edwards and Roberts, 1980: table 6). Nor were the polytechnics significantly more representative, though this was one of their explicit purposes. In 1976, 46 per cent of the male students were from classes I and II (compared with 19 per cent of the general population), and only 26 per cent were in classes III(M), IV or V (compared with more than 60 per cent of the general population) (Whitburn et al., 1976: tables 4.12, 4.A, 4.B).

If undergraduates are privileged, law students are still more privileged. In 1955, a staggering 84 per cent of all entrants to law faculties were from social classes I or II (Wedderburn, 1956: 15–16). In the late 1970s, 50 per cent of those 20–24 years old in full-time education and 54 per cent of university law students had professional or managerial fathers (compared with 21 per cent of the general population 16–19 years old); on the other hand, 30 per cent of those 20–24 years old in full-time education and 16 per cent of university law students had working class fathers (compared with 66 per cent of the general population 16–19 years old) (Royal Commission, 1979, vol. 2: 59). A 1978–9 survey of 592 first-year law students (excluding Oxbridge) found that 47 per cent came from social class I and only 13 per cent from working class backgrounds. Indeed, the inheritance of status was even more direct: 34 per cent of the male law students had salaried professional fathers, 15 per cent had lawyer relatives, and 5 per cent had lawyer fathers (McDonald, 1982: 268–9).

There are few data concerning the proportion of ethnic minorities in law departments. Several institutions admitted significant numbers of overseas students in the 1980s, when the Thatcher government cut back the funding of universities and polytechnics and simultaneously raised the tuition charged to non-residents (Marsh, 1983: 101). The number of overseas students studying all subjects rose from 26,000 in 1971–2 (5.6 per cent of total enrolment) to 58,000 in 1978–9 (11.4 per cent) (Woodhall, 1981: table 7.2). The proportion of overseas male law applicants admitted rose from 1978 to 1984, and overseas students as a proportion of undergraduate law enrolment increased from 5.9 per cent in 1980–1 to 9.4 per cent in 1983–4 – from 6.1 to 11.1 per cent of entrants (see tables 3.3, 3.6). Overseas students are very unequally distributed, being concentrated at Oxbridge and London (which have always been attractive to the elite from overseas) as well as at some of the more innovative faculties like Kent, Warwick and Cardiff (see table

3.9). Thirty-six per cent of a sample of university law departments and 10 per cent of a sample of 22 polytechnics admitted student bodies composed of more than 10 per cent overseas students, and the universities acknowledged that they were engaging in reverse discrimination (Lee, 1984: 166). Nevertheless, this is a very unusual group of minorities – predominantly wealthy students from Hong Kong, Singapore, Malaysia, the Persian Gulf states and Nigeria (as well as non-minorities from North America) – and almost all return home after graduating. On the other hand, a number of London polytechnics (South Bank, North London and Central London) and colleges (Vauxhall, Kingsway-Princeton and Merton) have co-operated in access programmes for minority residents lacking the usual academic credentials, with the result that minority enrolment at the Polytechnic of the South Bank rose from 2.5 per cent to 40 percent in 1984 (Wojciechowski-Kibble and Duncan, 1985; 135 *NLJ* 522, 1985). There are 300 applicants for the 24 places at Vauxhall; 18 completed the first course (1983–4) and 15 the second; most of these have performed well in the law degree courses (Duncan and Wojciechowski-Kibble, 1986: 46–9).

The growth of academic legal education has had one unambiguous effect: it opened the profession to women. The academy, as an ostensibly meritocratic institution, has always been somewhat more cautious about engaging in explicit discrimination. The first woman was admitted to read law at University College London in 1873, although it did not grant a degree to a woman until 1917, and Oxford did not do so until 1921 (Baker, 1977: 7; Lawson, 1968: 133). But the gender composition of the undergraduate law student body has changed significantly only since the late 1960s. At first, much smaller proportions of women applicants than of men seem to have been accepted by university law departments, which is surprising, since women usually have better secondary school credentials; but the gap between the two has virtually disappeared (see table 3.6). Women quickly rose from 17 per cent of incoming university law students in 1967 to 39 per cent in 1978 (Department of Education and Science, Education Statistics for the UK), an average of 42 per cent among students entering between 1979 and 1981 (Marsh, 1983: 101) and 45 per cent of 1983–4 entrants (see table 3.3). They were 11 per cent of full-time polytechnic law students in 1967 but 37 per cent in 1978 and 46 per cent in 1983; 11 per cent of part-time polytechnic law students in 1967 but 29 per cent in 1978 and 1983 (CNAA, Annual Reports; Marsh, 1983: 101). Women were 44 per cent of university law graduates and 43 per cent of polytechnic law graduates in 1985 (Marks, 1986: 3259). These changes closely parallel the entry of women into higher education generally. Women increased from 32 to 44 per cent of qualified school leavers between 1971–2 and 1983–4 and from 43 to 49 per cent of home entrants to higher education during the same period (see table 3.4).

Indeed, it is only a slight exaggeration to say that the expansion of legal academic institutions is largely attributable to the enrolment of significant numbers of women for the first time. Male entrants to university law departments increased 27 per cent between 1967 and 1978, whereas female entrants increased 297 per cent; male students in full-time polytechnic courses increased 47 per cent, whereas female students increased 611 per cent; and male students in part-time polytechnic courses increased 37 per cent, whereas female students increased 301 per cent. The number of male entrants to university law departments peaked in 1975 and has declined since then, whereas the number of female entrants has grown steadily; the number of full-time male students at polytechnics fluctuated erratically between 1968 and 1975 and only increased thereafter, whereas the number of female students increased fairly steadily (see tables 3.7 and 3.8). Here, again, we can see the distinctive contribution of the polytechnics to changing the composition of the profession – in this case the proportion of women. By contrast, women are less well represented within the most elite institutions, such as Cambridge (18 per cent) and Oxford (25 per cent) (see table 3.9).

The greater obstacles confronting women are visible in the fact that they come from more privileged class backgrounds. All women undergraduates are more likely than men to belong to classes I and II and less likely than men to belong to classes IV-VI (Whitburn et al., 1976: tables 4.12, 4.A, 4.B; Kelsall et al., 1972: tables 1, 3, 22). In a 1978–9 survey of 592 undergraduate law students (excluding Oxbridge), 60 per cent of the women were from class I (compared with only 38 per cent of men), and 21 per cent of the women were from classes III and IV (compared with 33 per cent of men); higher percentages of women had salaried professional fathers and lawyer relatives (McDonald, 1982: 268–9). Thus, the entry of women has also signified a narrowing of class recruitment.

Law is taught in settings other than first degree programmes at universities and polytechnics. In 1973, some 5000 secondary school students took their O-levels in law, and 5400 took their A-levels (up from 243 in 1960 and 1864 in 1965) (Wilson and Marsh, 1975: 246; Marsh, 1983: 76, 78). This experience may strengthen their interest in reading law for a degree: 7 per cent of full-time and 11 per cent of part-time polytechnic law students in 1982 gave 'enjoyment of previous legal studies' as the reason for beginning a law degree course (Marsh, 1983:

104). Colleges of further education offer instruction in law to students preparing for careers in accounting, banking and insurance: 5814 class hours in 1962, 9505 in 1965 and 13,776 in 1980 (Wilson, 1966: 119; Bailey and Marsh, 1981: 84).

The University of London long has offered an external LLB, for which students prepare either on their own or at a variety of public and private institutions (Marsh, 1980: 6; Wilson, 1966: 61). Not surprisingly, the success rate of such students has been low – a good deal lower than that achieved by internal students, as we will see below. Wilson and Marsh (1975: 262) calculated that only 22 per cent of those who registered between 1959 and 1970 graduated between 1962 and 1973, although most of this attrition was due to the failure of students to take the examination, for the pass rate of examinees varied between 54 and 80 per cent and exceeded 70 per cent throughout the 1970s (see table 3.10). But the numbers graduated were too small to have a significant impact on the production of lawyers; many students were from overseas and expected to return home; and in any case the University of London excluded both full-time and overseas students in 1977, reserving the degree for part-time domestic students, with the result that registrations declined to less than a third of what they had been (Wilson and Marsh, 1975: 245; see table 3.10).

Finally, there are a substantial number of postgraduate students, concentrated at Oxbridge and London but with increasing numbers at provincial universities and polytechnics. Until recently, most have been overseas students who expect to return home to practise or teach. But this dominance has been declining: overseas students were 70 per cent of postgraduates in 1966, 57 per cent in 1974, 54 per cent in 1980 and 44 per cent in 1983 (Wilson, 1966: 22; Wilson and Marsh, 1975: 263; 1981: 19; see table 3.3).

Not all entrants to degree programmes complete them or obtain the same credentials. How does the winnowing process affect the numbers and characteristics of lawyers? First, there are differences in the success rates of university and polytechnic students, just as we found differential pass rates on the professional examinations among graduates of these institutions (see chapter 10, p. 145). At least nine out of every ten entrants to university law departments graduate – perhaps as many as 19 out of 20 – and this proportion was relatively constant throughout the 1970s and 1980s (CHULS, 1984: table 5; see tables 3.3 and 3.8). The completion rate at polytechnics is significantly lower – somewhere between two-thirds and three-quarters – and for part-time students it is only 30 per cent (Marsh, 1983: 103; see table 3.11). At the Polytechnic of the South Bank, nearly a third of entering students withdraw before their first-year examinations, though the proportion is no higher among mature students than others (see table 3.12). We saw above that only about 20 per cent of those enrolled for the external London LLB ever obtain the degree. To the extent that there are class differences between those in university and polytechnic law departments or in full-time and part-time courses, these differences in completion rates reproduce the narrowly restricted class composition of the profession.

The quality of degree attained appears to be associated with two variables, both of which may reflect class background. Polytechnic students consistently obtain a lower class of degree than their university counterparts. Among those who graduated between 1971 and 1981, 15 per cent of polytechnic students obtained an upper second, compared with 32 per cent of a sample of 2000 graduates of 19 university law departments (excluding Oxbridge) in 1981 (Marsh, 1983: 108). Between 1978 and 1983, 3.2 per cent of university law graduates obtained a first class degree, compared with 0.8 percent of polytechnic law graduates, and 32.8 per cent obtained an upper second, compared with 16.1 per cent (Marks, 1985: 2913). More than half of all polytechnic law teachers felt that their graduates were disadvantaged in their future careers compared with those holding university degrees (Marsh, 1983: 109). The other variable correlated with academic performance is gender. Although men and women complete their courses in equal proportions (see table 3.8; but see Rule, 1980: 33), women obtain a higher proportion of firsts and seconds and a lower proportion of third class degrees or passes than men in both university and polytechnic law departments (see tables 3.8 and 3.3; Rule, 1980: 39–40; Marks, 1985: 2913). Thus, to the extent that women lawyers fail to attain the same professional rewards as men, the obstacles must be located in the post-academic stages of their careers (see chapter 4, p. 81 and chapter 11, p. 174).

A very high proportion of those becoming lawyers today complete an undergraduate law degree, though this is a development of the last two decades (see chapter 2, p. 47 and chapter 10, p. 143). About nine out of ten university graduates expecting to sit their professional examinations have read law, and so have a similar percentage of polytechnic graduates actually sitting those exams (see tables 3.15, 3.17). To what extent is the reverse true: what proportion of law graduates ultimately become lawyers? Once again the linkage between academic education and professional careers, which used to be quite loose, has tightened considerably. In the early 1950s, only 52 per cent of Oxbridge law graduates who took first class degrees and 52 per cent of Cambridge law graduates with upper seconds entered law practice; in 1977, the proportions were 73 and 62 per cent (Senate, Annual Statement, 1981–2:

48). An analysis of the 139 men who read part II of the law tripos under F. J. Odgers at Emmanuel College, Cambridge, in the 1950s provides further detail. As of 1959, only three were practising barristers; another nine had been called to the Bar, but three of them had left practice (to teach, become a solicitor or work in the War Office); two more were academics, and one was in the Church. Ten were called to foreign bars, 42 were solicitors, 19 were chartered accountants, and 56 were in business, commerce, the civil service or the colonial administration (minutes of a meeting of the Legal Education Committee of the Bar Council, 10 February 1959). Thus, only about a third were practising lawyers. Of the 2343 students who received law degrees between 1961 and 1963, only 559 (24 per cent) were known to have joined the legal profession; 188 foreign students presumably returned to their home countries; 192 were engaged in further degrees and 517 in specialized courses (Abel-Smith and Stevens, 1967: 370 n. 5).

Since the 1970s, two-thirds to three-quarters of law graduates consistently have expected to enter private practice, and another 5–10 per cent have expected to work in the public or private sector, presumably as employed lawyers (Marks, 1985: 2913; see tables 3.14, 3.15). Although a smaller proportion of entering law students anticipate professional careers, about a third of all law students change their plans during those three years; some abandon the idea of practice because they fear they cannot afford the long period of financial dependency or lack the necessary contacts; but more come to embrace the idea of a legal career (McDonald, 1982: 270–1). The only marked difference between university and polytechnic graduates is that the latter are less oriented towards the Bar, perhaps anticipating the particularistic selection of pupils and tenants. A higher proportion of women than men become solicitors, and a lower proportion of women than men become barristers – choices that are consistent with recruitment practices in the two branches and their flexibility in accommodating family responsibilities (Wilson and Marsh, 1978: 25; Marks, 1985: 2913). A higher proportion of polytechnic than university law graduates sit the professional examinations, suggesting either that the training of the former is more vocational or that the credential opens fewer other doors; there is a similar difference between part-time and full-time polytechnic law graduates (compare tables 3.15–3.17). But if a higher proportion of law graduates are becoming lawyers, those with the best degrees seem to have shifted their allegiance from the Bar to the solicitors' branch. Whereas 27 per cent of those with first class degrees in law from Oxford became barristers between 1973 and 1977, only 18–19 per cent did so in 1978 and 1979 (80 *LSG* 220–1, 1983). Among those university law graduates with first class degrees who immediately prepared for and sat the professional examinations between 1981 and 1985, 92 passed the Bar final (4.6 per cent of all passing) and 347 passed the solicitors' final (3.6 per cent of all passing) (83 *LSG* 2531–2, 1986). Indeed, the Bar Council's Working Party on the Quality of Entry is thinking of recommending mini-pupillages and substantial awards to the best law graduates to woo them away from the larger solicitors' firms (135 *NLJ* 1041, 1985).

What difference does it make that academic legal education has rapidly become almost the exclusive route to the legal profession and almost the exclusive means of preparing for a legal career? Unfortunately, my quantitative data cannot answer this central question. Yet it is clear that the curriculum in most law departments is strongly influenced by the professional associations. In order to ensure that their graduates are exempt from part I of the Bar final and the solicitors' CPE, all departments must require the six core subjects (contract, torts, criminal law, land law, trusts and constitutional and administrative law), which occupy about two-thirds of the students' coursework (Marsh, 1983: 96–8). Only a small number of institutions have been markedly innovative in their curricula (for example, Kent, Warwick, Edinburgh, Sheffield, Cardiff and LSE among universities and the South Bank and Liverpool Polytechnics). Recently, there has been some thought of extending the law degree for another year (in emulation of the honours degree in Scotland and mixed degrees in England and Wales) and of increasing the number of required subjects (Northern Ireland has added evidence and company law), though the academic institutions are resisting the latter (CHULS, 1984). Given the central role that undergraduate legal education now plays in determining how many become lawyers, who they are and how they think, the professional associations are certain to demand a significant say in shaping that experience.

# V

# Conclusion

# 19

# The trajectories of professionalism

The history of barristers and solicitors during the last two centuries offers invaluable insights into the phenomenon of professionalism. In this concluding chapter I will summarize the transformations in the professional configuration and speculate about the future of the legal professions, making more explicit the contrasts between the two branches. And I will return to the theories of professionalism with which I began – Weberian and economic theories of lawyers in the marketplace, Marxist theories of the productive relations within lawyering, and structural functional theories of lawyers in the social order – showing how they illuminate the data presented in this book and how they might be refined.

## Controlling the production of producers

Both Weberian and economic theories define the professions in terms of their control over entry. The history of the legal professions vividly illustrates the power of this approach. First, there can be no doubt that solicitors and barristers consciously sought to limit entry. Professional associations in both branches emerged expressly to control supply; that was the purpose of both the local and the national law societies from the end of the eighteenth century and the stimulus for founding the Bar Council at the end of the nineteenth. Complaints about overcrowding were voiced repeatedly in both branches. Entry requirements proliferated and were formalized and raised, including examinations, academic and professional education, apprenticeship and fees. The Law Society sometimes acknowledged that it increased the passing grade in order to reduce entry. In both branches the sharp fluctuations in pass rates after the wars, during the depression and in the 1980s, as well as the long-term secular decline through the 1950s, strongly suggest such manipulation.

Second, there was no more than a loose connection between entry barriers and the standards of technical competence by which they were justified. This is most apparent at the Bar, which began the nineteenth century with traditional requirements of 'character' rather than expertise. But both branches reduced the length of training for those with degrees from universities, although these taught no English law until the end of the nineteenth century. Both branches chose to *examine* entrants rather than train them, content to leave education to private crammers. They took virtually no interest in the content or quality of apprenticeship. And contemporary restrictions on the amount of space available to tenants in the Inns or to Bar students in the vocational course do not even purport to be related to quality. I am arguing not that entry requirements were irrelevant to practice (for then they would be too hard to justify), only that they cannot be understood entirely in such instrumental terms.

Third, although control never was complete, entry barriers clearly affected the number of practitioners. The profession failed to recover from adventitious tragedies like the two world wars. It failed to respond to the economic boom of the 1950s and 1960s. There was only a weak association between supply and demand. And both median income and the dispersion of income varied with the degree of supply control. Thus, there is ample evidence that lawyers engaged in efforts to control the production of producers and were increasingly effective until the 1960s.

The two branches differed, however, in their strategies of control. The Bar entered the nineteenth century with barriers validated by tradition and framed in terms of ascribed traits that purported to ensure good character. Applicants for admission to the Inns had to state their condition in life, secure recommendations and keep terms, and they were encouraged to attend university – none of which had anything to do with technical competence. The first mandatory examination introduced tested only general knowledge, and when legal knowledge finally was examined the standard was, and remained, lower than that for solicitors. The high cost of training and of surviving the early years of practice restricted entry to those with independent means. And the decision by chambers to accept pupils and tenants remained intensely particularistic. Because the Bar was ancient, small, homogeneous and geographically concentrated, it could rely on informal understandings and individual low-visibility decisions to control who entered and how many.

Solicitors differed in every respect. They had been unable to enforce their only entry barrier – articles – without invoking state power in the early eighteenth century (whereas pupillage remained optional until the 1960s). Cost was much less of an obstacle (although not insignificant) because articled clerks could live at home and solicitors could hope to support themselves as soon as they qualified. The Law Society introduced professional examinations before the Inns did so; it tested legal knowledge before insisting on general knowledge; and its examinations consistently were much harder than those taken by barristers. Few solicitors attended university until after World War II, but when they began doing so most read law. Thus, solicitors clearly framed their entry requirements in terms of achievements, if these were only loosely tied to technical competence.

These differences are not merely a historical accident. They also reflect the fact, emphasized by Weberian theory but overlooked by economists, that the professional project seeks status as well as material rewards. Indeed, the two goals often conflict: aggressive pursuit of material self-interest is inconsistent with status pretensions (thus the Bar tolerates its inability to sue for fees in order to preserve the fiction that they are honorariums). We can see this concern with collective mobility more clearly by reviewing the long-standing rivalry between the branches as an expression of status competition. Barristers sought to preserve the status conferred by birth, whereas solicitors sought to acquire status through association with wealthy and powerful clients. The Bar encouraged and then required a university degree and subsequently a minimum of lower second class honours, whereas solicitors sought a more democratic image by admitting school leavers (though few actually enter). The Bar retains such traditional anachronisms as keeping terms (having ejected solicitors from the Inns) and court dress (which solicitors are forbidden to wear). Barristers jealously insist that solicitors show respect by attending chambers for conferences. Barristers benefit from their concentration in the capital, whereas most solicitors are dispersed in provincial urban and rural settings. The prohibition against partnerships at the Bar may enhance the status of barristers by strengthening their claim to greater 'independence' (notwithstanding the increasingly collective structure of chambers). The Bar's historical immunity from state regulation (of fees, malpractice and discipline) reinforces this image of autonomy. I noted earlier that conflict over limitations on transfer between the branches largely expressed status concerns, since few members of either branch actually sought to transfer. Barristers protect their status by keeping clients (and thus contagion with social disorder) at a distance. In order to do this, they sacrifice the economic advantages that might be gained if clients had direct access to barristers; and chambers are prepared to pay a lower status clerk more money than most of their tenants make to deal with the dirty work of getting business and negotiating fees. The Bar's obsession with retaining its exclusive rights of audience reflects not only economic fears but also the superior status associated with performing the highly visible and symbolically powerful function of High Court advocacy. This advantage is significantly strengthened by the Bar's monopoly of appointment to the higher judiciary. Barristers also derive status advantages from appearing to be the specialists (compared with generalist solicitors) and from their dominance of many central government legal offices.

If the legal professions sought to control the production of producers in order to enhance both their material situation and their social status, that project had inherent limitations. First, professions can only modify market forces, not suspend them. Entry barriers slowed the production of lawyers after wars and during the early years of the economic boom following World War II; but eventually the imbalance between supply and demand created irresistible pressures. Second, the single largest ascriptive barrier – gender – could not withstand the advance of feminism and the critique of all forms of inequality. Third, the costs of producing lawyers were gradually socialized: stamp duties were repealed, premiums abolished, undergraduates and those studying for the professional examination supported by means-tested grants, articled clerks (if not pupils) paid salaries and beginning practitioners enabled to earn income through the legal aid scheme. Finally, the emergence of the academy as the principal institution bestowing credentials significantly reduced the importance of professional examinations as an entry barrier. Undergraduate law enrolments increased at a rate unprecedented in England and Wales and unequalled in any other country: ninefold between 1939 and 1983, twice as fast as the increase in the number of all undergraduates between 1962–3 and 1979–80.

How fast will the legal professions continue to grow, and what control will they exercise over the production of producers? Several things are clear. To the extent that growth reflected the determination of women to attain equality, the rate will stabilize, since women are now almost half of all law students. If the academy undermined the profession's control over entry, the academy itself has become the principal bottleneck, attracting twice as many applicants as it accepts. Undergraduate law enrolments are not likely either to expand (because of limited state resources and opposition by teachers to increasing class size or teaching hours) or to contract (because of resistance by academic institutions and, paradoxically, the profession itself). However, the total number of law graduates will continue to grow, if at a decreasing rate, until the cohort retiring is a large as the cohort entering, which will take another generation.

This will have a differential impact on the two branches, reflecting their divergent strategies of supply control. One might expect that solicitors would have been more successful in preserving control since they embraced modern concepts of achievement as the justification for entry barriers earlier than the Bar and more enthusiastically. But the flaw inherent in any requirement of an examination or an academic credential is that it can and will be attained if the reward is sufficient. Thus, it is the Bar that has retained greater supply control through the institutions of pupillage and tenancy, which allow particularistic decisions shielded from public scrutiny. Yet the Bar has had to moderate its reliance on ascription, with the result that those entering the two branches are similar in background and education (which may be why the struggle over trivial status inequalities has become so intense). The residual capacity of private practitioners to influence their numbers (barristers through their control over tenancies, principals in solicitors' firms through their control over employment and partnerships) has forced increasing numbers of law graduates into public and private employment, which simultaneously offers a safety valve for pressures to eliminate such control. Thus, supply control has been re-established through new mechanisms (the academy and the productive unit) and at a higher level.

## Allocating lawyers to roles

Because professions are privileged enclaves, entry barriers influence who enjoy those privileges as well as how many do so. Because professions are also internally differentiated in terms of structure and function and heterogeneous in social composition, mechanisms are necessary to allocate entrants to roles and to justify that allocation. Liberal capitalism explains both who become professionals and the positions they attain by reference to the ideology of meritocracy: rewards reflect ability and effort. Structural functional theory critically examines that claim: to what extent are ascriptive differences – particularly class background, gender and race – associated with membership in or position within the profession? The answer to this question will determine the legitimacy of major forms of social inequality. These issues have become even more significant as the erosion of supply control has accentuated the internal differentiation of the legal profession and increased the heterogeneity of entrants. Furthermore, the degree to which the legal profession mirrors the larger society is particularly salient (as contrasted, for instance, with the representativeness of accountants) because the identity of lawyers may affect the access to law of deprived social categories.

We saw above that entry barriers to the legal profession underwent a radical transformation after World War II, as out-of-pocket costs declined and particularistic decisions (to take on apprentices, grant tenancies or hire assistant solicitors) became more universalistic under the influence of academic education. This appears to have been a necessary condition for the entry of women (if it was not sufficient; academic education had been the gateway to the legal profession in continental Europe and America for decades before women entered in significant numbers). But otherwise the change in entry barriers had little effect on the composition of the profession. Class background, which had always been privileged, remained unchanged or even narrowed further. Although an explicit purpose of the dramatic expansion of polytechnics was to make higher education more broadly accessible, their law graduates were virtually indistinguishable in terms of class origin from those of the universities. Furthermore, women entrants came from even more privileged backgrounds than men, presumably because they still had to overcome substantial social and cultural impediments; and the men they displaced, who had the worst credentials of the male applicant pool, generally came from the least privileged backgrounds. All this simply illustrates once again the capacity of privilege to reproduce itself under liberal capitalism. To the extent that privilege is also associated with race, the shift to academic entry admitted few blacks, and the number enrolled in access courses designed to correct this remains very small. Perhaps the greatest significance of higher education, besides facilitating the entry of women, was to translate ascribed privilege into academic achievement, thereby offering a meritocratic legitimation for the distinction between legal professionals and lay people.

The internal structural and functional differentiation of the legal professions simultaneously stratifies lawyers in terms of material rewards, power and status. Many of these distinctions are formalized and thus presumably legitimated by reference to tradition. Barristers enjoy higher status than solicitors but lower median income. Private practitioners enjoy higher status than lawyers employed in the public or private sectors, but the latter start at higher salaries and have greater security; these differences appear to be greater among barristers. Employed lawyers reflect the wealth and power of their employers. Compared with the single distinction between principals and assistant solicitors, the Bar appears to have a multiplicity of formal divisions: silks and juniors, benchers and others, heads and tenants, tenants and floaters; and only the Bar leads to the crowning achievement of the higher judiciary. On the other hand, differences between solicitors' firms appear to be more momentous than those between barristers' chambers. Within private practice, specialists enjoy greater income and prestige than generalists, and specialities themselves can be ranked in terms of the wealth and status of the clients served. A new, but vitally important, difference is the degree of dependence on public funds, which generally varies inversely with income; at the Bar, dependence tends to decline with increasing experience, but among solicitors it is more permanent – a function of firm size and clientele. Finally, there is greater variation in income within the Bar, both because beginners are not salaried and because the most successful are formally distinguished as silks.

A wide range of criteria and mechanisms distribute lawyers among these divisions. The least problematic is age: it is widely accepted that the salaries, authority and prestige of lawyers employed in the public and private sectors and in academia should increase with seniority. The centrality of undergraduate legal education and the greatly increased diversity of institutions conferring law degrees mean that the law department to which an applicant gains admission and the quality of degree the student attains strongly influence the graduate's future career. I noted above that educational institutions transform accidents of birth (parental income, occupation and education) into academic achievements. Barristers' chambers, solicitors' firms and public and private employers select apprentices and newly qualified lawyers largely on the basis of their academic performance. Perhaps because chambers continue to place more weight on ascribed characteristics, university graduates (who tend to be more privileged) go to the Bar in higher proportions than polytechnic graduates. The consequences of this initial selection seem to be most momentous for solicitors: starting salaries for articled clerks are three times as high in City firms as in rural practices, and income continues to vary dramatically with firm size. Solicitors' firms make a further selection when they take an assistant into partnership, and gender seems to play a greater role at that time. Careers at the Bar appear to be the most fluid: financial success seems to be a function of the technical competence of an advocate as judged by market forces, and further status rewards (silk, a judgeship) occur at widely spaced intervals. Once a lawyer is established in employment or private practice, there is surprisingly little lateral mobility between categories or structures of practice, although this may be changing.

This variety of mechanisms allocating lawyers to roles suggests several generalizations. First, the more universalistic selection processes are highly visible and occur earlier, whereas the more particularistic decisions are much less visible and occur later (compare undergraduate admissions with the selection of tenants). Second, the firm that takes on an articled clerk, hires an assistant solicitor or adds a partner clearly plays a central role in determining rewards and does so early in the lawyer's career. At the Bar, by contrast, success or failure appears to be the product of impersonal forces operating on the individual barrister and to remain an open question much longer in the lawyer's career.

The last observation applies exclusively to white males: the paradox that the Bar appears to be more meritocratic may be explained by the fact that it is more homogeneous because the barriers to entry are more ascriptive. Neither branch has offered a satisfactory answer to the persistent inequalities of race and gender. Blacks are a higher proportion of the Bar, despite its greater emphasis on ascription, for reasons that are largely historical (the tradition that aspiring barristers from the new Commonwealth trained at the Inns of Court, the fact that the Bar examination is easier). But black lawyers are more segregated at the Bar than in solicitors' firms, and the resulting 'ghetto' chambers are disproportionately dependent on public funds and specialize in criminal and family law, which severely limits the income and prestige their tenants can attain. The reliance by chambers on educational credentials to select pupils and tenants will only reinforce this inequality as long as blacks remain disadvantaged by reason of class background and prior education.

The position of women is almost a mirror image of that of blacks: they are a higher proportion of entering solicitors than of barristers, and they are integrated within solicitors' firms. The reason for the smaller numbers at the Bar is both the fear that it is more difficult to combine a barrister's practice with family responsibilities and explicit prejudice by barristers' clerks, who believe that women will earn less (for themselves and thus for the clerk), whether or not they have families. But the fact that women are taken on as articled clerks and assistant solicitors in the proportions that their (superior) academic credentials warrant has not ensured their continued success as solicitors. First, they have been channelled to traditional women's work: conveyancing, wills and trusts and family matters. Second, few firms have made adequate provision for maternity leave, childcare and part-time work. And third, even those that have tried to do so inevitably favour the male solicitor who shows greater commitment to practice by leaving childcare to his wife. In the absence of a structural solution to these problems (such as the equal sharing of childcare responsibilities by both sexes), women will never reach the same levels of income, power and prestige within the legal profession as men. The unanswered question is how long racial and sexual inequality can be legitimated in terms of the inferior academic 'achievements' of blacks and the 'choices' of branch, subject matter and motherhood by women.

## Restricting competition

Professions seek to restrict competition for obvious economic reasons; but they also do so to enhance status, because even capitalist societies display considerable ambivalence about the explicit pursuit of material gain. Although a profession can define and defend its monopoly at the same time that it constructs entry barriers, both projects must be well advanced before the profession can limit internal competition, for it would be economic suicide to surrender competitive advantage to outsiders who are not similarly restrained. Barristers and solicitors differ significantly in their need to restrict competition and the resources they can mobilize to do so. Barristers are more exposed to market forces: their performance is relatively public; winning or losing is an obvious (if often erroneous) measure of quality; and the immediate consumers – solicitors – are sophisticated and often endowed with considerable market power (because they are repeat players). Solicitors, by contrast, generally perform in private (offices); it is hard to evaluate the quality of their facilitative activities; and their individual consumers are relatively ignorant about law and lawyers and lacking in market power (because demand is infrequent and unpredictable); even businesses tend to be less knowledgeable about solicitors than solicitors are about barristers. Consumers can choose among thousands of barristers in London and hundreds in the larger provincial cities, whereas many solicitors enjoy a 'natural' geographic monopoly or oligopoly. Thus, the actual market situation of the two branches inverts the ideological claim that barristers are more 'independent'; indeed, the purpose of the ideology may be to mystify this reality. For instance, the 'cab-rank' rule that obliges a barrister to accept each potential client in the queue may seek to mask the fact that most barristers already are financially compelled to do so.

If barristers are more exposed to competition, they are also better placed to protect themselves. Their monopoly (rights of audience in the higher courts) represents the core function of the legal profession (compared with the solicitors' more peripheral function of conveyancing); their actions (like those of surgeons) are enormously consequential; and their performance is highly ritualized. The structure of the Bar also makes it easier to enforce restrictive practices informally. Compared with solicitors, barristers are less numerous, more homogeneous, geographically far more concentrated and grouped into a few hundred chambers, each with a single head and senior clerk. Hierarchic authority is preserved by the lengthy career ladder: pupils are subordinate to everyone, younger barristers are subordinate to older tenants and the senior clerk, experienced barristers are subordinate to the head, and barristers seeking silk or judgeships are subordinate to judges and the Lord Chancellor. Among solicitors, by contrast, authority tends to be bounded by the firm; since this is the competitive unit, such authority intensifies competition rather than moderates it. Finally, the Bar entered the nineteenth century with an effective system of supply control and traditional warrants for its restrictive practices, whereas solicitors spent much of the nineteenth century constructing both.

Each branch has suffered major attacks on its restrictive practices in recent years. The erosion of control over the production of producers increased the size and heterogeneity of the profession, intensifying internal competition and reducing the efficacy of informal regulation. As the Bar grew, it was compelled to formalize its restrictive practices, thereby exposing them to external criticism. Even the Conservative government has attacked the restrictive practices of barristers and solicitors, who are its natural supporters, nicely illustrating the 'relative autonomy' of *laissez-faire* ideology. These developments suggest another apparent paradox: the legal profession was able to preserve its restrictive practices while operating within the 'free market' of atomistic consumers; but when the professional monopoly confronted the monopsony of the state as consumer (under the legal aid scheme or the new Crown Prosecution Service), many of these restrictions collapsed.

Solicitors have been considerably more vulnerable to these new competitive forces. Because many of their activities are too technical and insufficiently indeterminate (in the terminology of Jamous and Peloille), they constantly are exposed to external competition: from the state ('officialism'), large private enterprises (trust companies and now building societies) and other professions and occupations (such as accounting). These threats have proliferated with the emergence of multipurpose service firms catering to the needs of business. At the same time, individual consumers have become increasingly critical of what they perceive to be the excessive fees of solicitors, particularly for conveyancing. Solicitors in private practice are also more vulnerable to competition from employed solicitors, who share the same monopoly, whereas employed barristers cannot invade the exclusive rights of audience of privately practising barristers. It is only these cumulative threats to the economic base of solicitors that has led them, reluctantly, to challenge the Bar on its own turf – advocacy – and even to talk about fusion. The similarity in education and background of the two branches and even in the structures of practice (as chambers come to resemble solicitors' firms) will make this difficult to resist.

Many restrictive practices have been eliminated or weakened by these internal and external assaults. The Bar repealed the rules requiring that a silk be assisted by a junior paid two-thirds of the silk's fee. The formal submonopolies of the circuits have been eliminated, and the 'natural' monopolies enjoyed by many solicitors are endangered by the growth of branch offices and regional if not yet national firms. The Law Society has allowed solicitors considerable freedom to engage in self-promotion, and even the Bar may relax its prohibition. Solicitors have abandoned the rigidity of scale fees. Employed barristers can compete with solicitors in conveying property and briefing the privately practising Bar. Solicitors are getting a foot in the door of higher court advocacy. At the same time, they now must share the conveyancing monopoly with licensed conveyancers and soon, perhaps, with the employees of building societies. There is talk of allowing partnerships between solicitors and other professionals, if not yet among barristers.

But it is essential not to exaggerate the 'freedom' of the contemporary market for lawyers' services. Many older restrictions survive, if in altered form, and many new ones have emerged. Barristers remain more protected from competition than solicitors. Their exclusive rights of audience are virtually intact, whereas the solicitors' conveyancing monopoly is seriously endangered. The symbiotic relationship between the two branches persists: most solicitors are not really interested in High Court advocacy and would capture only a small part of that market were they allowed to do so; on the other hand, barristers are more than content to allow solicitors to continue acting as intermediaries with lay clients. The characteristics of the Bar described above have allowed them to preserve the two-counsel and two-thirds rules in practice; barristers' clerks still engage in parallel if not conspiratorial pricing; and the market division between silks and juniors formally survives. Barristers have responded to their dependence on solicitor intermediaries by using their clerks to construct ongoing relationships with solicitors' firms and government departments as well as return circuits with other chambers.

Because solicitors were more dependent on the state to regulate their market, the withdrawal of formal support has left them more exposed. Yet most solicitors have remained reluctant to use their new freedom to advertise, particularly to engage in price competition, preferring collective promotional schemes by law societies or private initiatives that purport to stimulate demand without redistributing it. Even individual advertising has been of dubious value to consumers, since most solicitors claim competence in all subjects. Members of both branches have sought insulation from market forces through employment in the public or private sectors, although they have had to sacrifice some of their claim to being professionals.

Perhaps the most important form of protection is simply the further elaboration of the phenomenon that originally gave birth to the professions, namely specialization. Nineteenth-century specialization by court has been replaced by specialization in terms of substantive area and even client. Barristers have always been able to specialize substantively because generalist solicitors performed the function of referring lay clients. The growth in size of solicitors' firms (discussed in 'Transforming the productive unit', p. 298) has allowed their members to specialize as well, confident that large business clients will look to the firm for a wide variety of services. These firms have the same enduring relationship with business clients (and wealthy individuals) that chambers have with their solicitor intermediaries. As firms continue to expand and merge, the market may become increasingly oligopolistic. The state, which eliminated some of the older restrictive practices, now regulates the market in important ways, setting prices for legally aided matters (thereby influencing the price structure of the private market) and creating formal specializations through its reimbursement policies. Certainly the political confrontation between the Lord Chancellor and the Bar Council and Law Society over the level of legal aid fees could not be further removed from the classical model of a free market. The persistence and variety of restrictive practices is a salutary reminder of the mythic nature of that ideal.

## Responding to demand and creating it

Although the number and distribution of legal professionals reflect the demand for their services very imperfectly, major changes in demand inevitably have important consequences. The fortuity of the increase in home ownership, mobility and housing prices is largely responsible for the rise in the number of privately practising solicitors. But ownership and mobility are growing slowly today, if at all, and inflation has also declined; in any case, solicitors may lose considerable conveyancing work to building societies. On the other hand, demand from business clients is likely to continue growing, fuelled by economic expansion, international competition, concentration and continued government regulation. The recent doubling of the Bar has been even more dependent on a single source of demand: legal aid. But here, too, the brakes have been applied: fiscal conservatism dominates state expenditure (although the legal aid scheme, unlike law centres, remains demand fed), and the social behaviour for which most legal aid is rendered – crime and divorce – seems to have stabilized. The failure of lawyers to diversify their market may be catastrophic, particularly for the Bar.

The legal profession initially was very cool toward actions that might stimulate demand. Because legal aid was introduced at a time when the demand generated by the postwar boom exceeded the restricted supply, driving up lawyer incomes, the profession perceived the innovation primarily as a threat of state interference and control. Private efforts at self-promotion were inconsistent with the status pretensions of legal professionals. Only the erosion of supply control, the decline of other restrictive practices and the dramatic expansion of the welfare state persuaded lawyers to embrace demand creation. The fervour with which the Law Society and the Senate, narrower constituencies like the Legal Aid Practitioners' Group, the British Legal Association and the Campaign for the Bar, and rank-and-file lawyers now demand dramatic increases in legal aid fee levels is indicative of the enthusiasm for – indeed dependence on – that scheme. Similarly, a Law Society that until recently condemned advertising in unequivocal terms, now permits and actually encourages it.

Yet strategies of demand creation confront inescapable limitations and contradictions. Perhaps most fundamental is the fact that few individuals or businesses can be convinced they need legal services. They will use lawyers when compelled: to defend against a criminal charge or a civil suit or obtain a divorce. But law as a facilitative mechanism is alien and frightening to most, which may be one reason why so few have enrolled in prepaid plans. Even if individuals could be persuaded that they need lawyers, the state is unwilling to pay. Several decades of effort to expand eligibility and extend coverage to tribunals have come to naught. Finally, efforts to create demand inevitably concentrate it – a tendency the profession opposes. This must be one reason why lawyers can advertise but not solicit business in person or by telephone or letter, although the latter are far more efficient ways of communicating with potential consumers (loss of status is another consideration). It also explains the continuing interest in collective advertising despite the absence of any demonstrable results. Recent innovations in public demand creation, such as the expansion of the services of citizens' advice bureaux in civil matters and duty solicitor schemes in courts, prisons and police stations, all take great pains to distribute the business equally, more concerned to prevent some lawyers from gaining a competitive advantage than to enhance the quality of services provided to clients. But these efforts inevitably fail because the profit margin of publicly subsidized work is so low that a solicitor can make a living only by increasing volume. Effective demand creation, public or private, thus seems inextricably linked to the self-interest of individual professionals and hence to further concentration in the market for legal services.

## Transforming the productive unit

Each of the three major theoretical frameworks with which I began is deeply concerned with the structure of the unit within which professionals produce legal services. Neoclassical economics is primarily interested in horizontal market relationships among producers and between producers and consumers. It sees a connection between the kind and degree of market competition and the structure of the productive unit. Marxist theory focuses on the distribution of power and the extraction of value within vertical relations of production. It sees class struggle between exploiters and exploited as determining the structure of the productive unit. Structural functionalism begins with an idealized notion of the 'independence' of the individual professional. It sees this threatened by the growing size, hierarchy and rigidity of the productive unit – usually epitomized in the concept of bureaucracy. Although these three theories often fail to engage each other, the transformations they address are intimately connected in fact. When the professional project is at its height and the profession enjoys significant control over the production of and by producers, it secures material gain and status at the expense of consumers, who pay monopoly rents. There is less exploitation of younger professionals and paraprofessionals, and the productive unit remains small. When market control is weakened, allowing greater competition within the profession and between it and other producers, professionals increasingly must extract value and achieve status at the expense of subordinates; consequently, the productive unit grows larger and more hierarchic and bureaucratic. In addition, an increasing proportion of professionals become employees of their clients, as house counsel or civil servants, relinquishing the fiction of independence and losing status, if not pay.

Neoclassical economics attributes the growth of the productive unit to the need to become more efficient and thus more competitive in response to the erosion of supply control and the elimination of many restrictive practices. Indeed, the comfortable market niche long guaranteed by the conveyancing monopoly is a major reason for the continued survival of small solicitors' firms (which are particularly endangered by its breach).

Increased size ensures a steadier flow of business from individual consumers (whose needs are sporadic), thereby ensuring that the professional's most valuable resource – time – is not wasted. Greater volume allows productive units to cut costs, which is essential to achieving profitability in legally aided matters. A high continuous volume can be sought by the productive unit itself or delivered by some referral agency: solicitors' firms and government departments for barristers, citizens' advice bureaux and legal insurance plans for solicitors. Increased size also ensures that the productive unit can satisfy the numerous and diverse needs of clients, which are growing ever larger (businesses for solicitors, larger solicitors' firms for barristers), without running the risk of losing the client to a competitor. Greater size can enhance productivity by routinizing repetitive tasks, achieving economies of scale (capital investment in computers, for instance, or expenditures on advertising) and permitting specialization. Solicitors' firms grow in order to increase the internal division of labour horizontally across substantive areas. Because solicitors refer work from lay clients to barristers, entire chambers can be substantively specialized; but all sets seek a vertical division of labour by seniority so that barristers are available to handle matters of varying weightiness. Firms also grow because solicitors increasingly are competing with outsiders. Competition for conveyancing work has led both to vertical integration with building societies, estate agents and chartered surveyors, as well as horizontal integration through branch offices and collective advertising and estate agency schemes (in order to compete with the horizontally integrated building societies and major retailers). Competition with major accounting firms may also lead to joint partnerships. These moves are prompted by status considerations as well: solicitors wish to retain their superiority to other occupations and professions and avoid subordination as employees. Indeed, size and continuing growth themselves become marks of status, as well as input measures of 'quality' that must substitute for the unavailable process and outcome measures. The net result is the transformation of the market from one dominated by exchanges between individual producers and consumers to one in which large institutions organize both producers and consumers and mediate the transaction between them.

Marxist theory attributes the growth of the productive unit to the need to increase the exploitation of labour. The bourgeoisie use their control over productive capital to extract surplus value from workers whose labour they purchase. Legal professionals rarely make a significant capital investment in their firms today, and, when they do, it is through retained profits rather than initial investments or the purchase of goodwill from a predecessor. Instead, professionals use their ownership of a formal credential to extract surplus from lay workers whose labour they purchase. In each case, the state constructs and protects the owner's title. Thus, paraprofessionals cannot set up independent practices in competition with their former employers, even though they would be doing exactly the same work they do as employees. More senior professionals also use the network of clients they have attracted to exploit the labour of recent entrants, who are prevented from competing effectively by restrictive practices and starting costs.

The direct economic interest in increasing the number of fee earners obviously shapes the relationship of the barristers' clerk to chambers' tenants (though not the relationship among tenants). To the extent that barristers bill clients for services actually performed by solicitors but whose value solicitors cannot capture because they are denied rights of audience, the Bar also exploits solicitors. But the most patently exploitative relationship is that between principals and employees in solicitors' firms, for we know that partner profits are directly proportional to firm size and the ratio of subordinated employees to principals. Such subordination is legitimated in several ways. Legal executives differ in training from solicitors, cannot work without a supervising solicitor and can become solicitors only with great difficulty (few do so). They do not control their own numbers (since the credentials of the Institute of Legal Executives are not required by all firms) or engage in self-regulation (the province of the Law Society). But with the expansion of higher education and the declining legitimacy of class, it has become difficult to obtain enough qualified men for these positions and to retain the more experienced. Their places have been taken by women, who are now about half of all new ILEX diploma holders. The persistence of patriarchal attitudes (including expectations that the position is only a resting-place before marriage and a family) offer additional justification for the subordination of women legal executives.

At the same time, legal executives themselves have been displaced by articled clerks (with the rapid expansion of new entrants) and especially assistant solicitors (the Law Society has required three years in this status only since World War II). These positions are filled almost equally by men and women. Subordination is facilitated by two characteristics. First, firms purport to offer essential training (hence, despite protestations to the contrary, it is in the interest of the profession that undergraduate legal education remain 'academic'). Second, these positions are transitory; endurance will be rewarded by full membership in the profession. As the rewards (both material and status) become greater, they call for and justify greater sacrifice. This may explain why the length of time to partnership increases with firm size. Thus the traditional warrant of subordination – class – has been replaced by others: gender (showing the enduring power of patriarchy), age and inexperience. If salaried partner becomes a permanent status and is filled disproportionately by women, gender (signifying divided loyalties between family and career) will justify that form of subordination as well. And of course the subordination of those not earning fees is justified by both gender and class (as well as lack of formal credentials). At the same time that solicitors increase their reliance on subordinated labour, they break down work into ever smaller units, allowing it to be performed by unadmitted staff. Evidence that intensified horizontal competition (with both professionals and other occupations) compels a shift from the exploitation of clients (through market control) to the exploitation of subordinates (through what might be called professional capitalism) can be found in the fact that partners, who traditionally did a disproportionate amount of conveyancing work, increasingly are delegating it to subordinates.

Structural functional theories are concerned less with the genesis of changes in the productive unit than with the consequence. Such theories seek to justify the professional configuration by deploring the alternative of mass production, hyperspecialization, hierarchy and bureaucratization. There is ample evidence of such trends. We have seen that the size of both barristers' chambers and solicitors' firms has increased greatly in the last two decades. Within chambers, this has had less effect on relations among barristers (who ostensibly remain independent practitioners despite pupillage awards and guaranteed incomes for new tenants that strongly resemble employment), although mechanisms are needed to decide whether to grow and whom to admit to tenancy. But growth certainly has altered the role of the barristers' clerk. The senior clerk is becoming less of an entrepreneur (since ongoing relationships with other large institutions tend to provide a steady flow of clients, and many fees are now set by the state) and more of an administrator, ensuring the orderly performance of work by the tenants. This change is symbolized by the elimination of the clerk's separate fee, the criticism by many barristers of the percentage commission, and the increasing use of formal contracts between clerks and heads. The consequences are even more pronounced in the larger solicitors' firms, some of which now have more than 500 principals and employees and numerous branch offices, both domestic and international. Here bureaucratization is symbolized by the emergence of the unadmitted chief administrator, which effectively severs management from control in the professional firm, much as it did a century ago in the limited companies such firms represent. And of course the solicitor or barrister employed by (mostly large) private enterprises and government departments is subjected most strongly to bureaucratic authority.

What is the future of the unit for producing legal services? Entry to academic legal education now controls the number of lawyers (and tenancies control the number of privately practising barristers), though at levels that ensure continued growth. Solicitors have encountered particular difficulties preserving restrictive practices and fending off external competitors. Thus, competitive pressures will intensify. Growth in the unit of production will be fostered by the public sector's determination to cut costs (compelling economies of scale) and the continued growth of private sector clients (encouraging further specialization). Solicitors' firms will increase both the intensive and extensive exploitation of subordinated labour, justifying this by differences of age, experience, educational credentials and gender between the small number of profit-sharing principals and the large number of employees. Although the work of solicitors will remain technically demanding, unadmitted staff will experience both deskilling and displacement by information technology. The increasing size, internal differentiation and hierarchy within the productive unit will require its further bureaucratization. Solicitors' firms in which management is separated from control, capital investments of retained profits are made in labour-saving equipment, and a significant portion of partnership income is generated by surplus value extracted from employees will become structurally indistinguishable from capitalist enterprises. Larger clients, both public and private, increasingly will employ lawyers rather than retain private practitioners, in order to cut costs and enhance loyalty. Barristers' chambers will be somewhat insulated from these pressures by the intermediation of solicitors' firms. But I see nothing to hinder the proliferation and expansion of large solicitors' firms, resulting in the progressive concentration of that profession, although small firms may retain a market niche in rural areas. Thus market control will shift from the profession as a whole, acting through its associations, to a small number of large productive units, which may be tempted by the attractions of cartelization. Most lawyers (even beginning barristers) will have to accept employee status for at least some of their careers; many will remain in that status permanently. Few will perceive this as exploitation, gladly trading the mythic 'independence' of professionalism for protection from market forces.

## Reconstructing the professional community

Collective action through voluntary associations always has been a necessary counterweight to the strongly developed individualism of the professions. Weberian theories attribute such action to the desire for material gain and status enhancement, epitomized in the professional project. Economic theories direct attention to the free-rider problem. Structural functionalism sees the ideals of community and democracy endangered by heterogeneity and oligarchy. Marxist theories predict that professionals who are also workers will struggle against exploitation through collective, usually syndicalist, action, notwithstanding their privileges both within the workplace (autonomy) and outside (income and status).

Community took very different forms in the two branches of the legal profession. The Bar entered the nineteenth century as a small, homogeneous, geographically concentrated profession. *All* barristers belonged to the significant professional organizations: one of the four Inns of Court and one of the eight circuits. These traditional decentralized institutions served primarily to express and foster collegiality, allowing social control to be exercised informally. Gerontocratic oligarchy appears to have been the mode of governance, accepted by young as well as old. But this structure was inadequate to defend, much less aggressively pursue, professional self-interest. Consequently, when younger barristers felt threatened by solicitors at the end of the nineteenth century, they formed a centralized, modern voluntary association, the Bar Council. The endemic problems of voluntary organizations were accentuated by the fact that the Inns retained most of the profession's authority and resources, with the result that the Bar Council remained a minority organization until after World War II. Yet the willingness of barristers to tolerate this situation for so long is evidence of the security of the Bar's professional privileges.

At the beginning of the nineteenth century solicitors, by contrast, possessed none of the traits of a profession other than the conveyancing monopoly (acquired almost by accident) and the requirement of apprenticeship (poorly enforced). Their efforts to construct a profession were hampered by larger numbers, geographic dispersion and greater functional heterogeneity. Starting from scratch, elites in provincial cities and later in London created formal, modern organizations whose explicit purpose was to secure the material benefits and social status of professionalism. There was a conscious distinction between organizations pursuing the professional project (the Law Society in London and federations of provincial law societies) and those more concerned with collegiality (London clubs, both within the Law Society and outside, and local law societies in smaller cities). For solicitors, the endemic problems of voluntary associations were compounded by the fundamental division between the minority of London solicitors, who dominated the

Law Society, and the majority of provincial solicitors, whose interests often diverged, with the result that the Law Society, like the Bar Council, remained a minority organization until after World War II.

Both branches have had to reconstruct their communities in response to the postwar transformation of the profession. Barristers slowly transferred the locus of collective action from the four Inns, with their traditional decentralized, secretive, gerontocratic governance, to a single modern, more democratic institution – the Senate and the Bar Council in various combinations, and now the General Council of the Bar. Both branches have encountered substantial difficulties in enrolling members who are increasingly heterogeneous in personal background (age, gender, race) and work situation. Although each branch has persuaded almost all private practitioners to join the national organization (indeed, the Bar recently abandoned voluntarism for compulsion), neither has attracted a majority of the growing number of lawyers employed in the public or private sector, who constitute as many as half of all those qualified. Each has made limited moves toward greater democracy, leading to more frequent electoral contests and agitation for direct election of the chief executive. But the governance of both branches remains unrepresentative in terms of age, gender, race and employment; the Law Society is still dominated by London practitioners from larger firms; and membership of the General Council certainly does not reflect the fact that half the income of the Bar derives from public funds (furthermore, the Bar recently debated disenfranchising those outside private practice). The failure of both official bodies to represent the interests of all lawyers is evidenced by the proliferation of voluntary organizations. Unlike their predecessors, these are not based on geographic proximity (which is of decreasing relevance in an age when communication is instantaneous, transportation rapid and the economy national) but on subject-matter specialities, work situation (employment in the public or private sector), age, race, dependence on public funds and political orientation. Some of these (such as the British Legal Association and the Campaign for the Bar) clearly would like the Law Society and the General Council to adopt a more adversarial stance toward the government, abandoning the pretence of disinterested professionalism for the aggressive pursuit of sectarian advantage. And the recent confrontation over legal aid payments between the Bar Council and the Law Society, representing legal aid practitioners, and the Lord Chancellor acting for their governmental paymaster, suggests that this form of syndicalism is likely to become more common (as well as the unionization of employed lawyers and unadmitted staff). Finally, the growth in the size of productive units (barristers' chambers, solicitors' firms and public and private employers) may lead them to become important loci of collective action. It is ironic that just when the two principal associations have finally acquired the organizational structure and resources that might allow them seriously to pursue the ideals of community and democracy, they must cope with severe internal dissension, competition with rivals, confrontation with the central government and loyalties to productive units.

Professional associations are founded or activated in order to seek or defend material benefits and social status. But all of them eventually aspire to the privilege of self-regulation. Here, again, the two branches diverge markedly. The Bar has always wielded complete control over its members. Discipline, largely informal for centuries, was exercised by the Inns (and earlier the circuits) until after World War II, when it was transferred to the Senate. The high visibility of most barrister activity to the rest of the Bar, the bench and solicitors continues to facilitate informal control, although the greater number of barristers limits its efficacy. Barristers are now subject to liability for malpractice outside advocacy and have had to obtain insurance, but the number and size of the claims and the amount of the premium remain insignificant.

By contrast, the Law Society had to work hard to persuade the courts to grant it control over misconduct (just as it successfully sought to control entry examinations, the Roll and restrictive practices). Because informal controls clearly were insufficient to cope with the embarrassing problem of financial misconduct (which barristers did not share), the Law Society established a qualifying examination in accounting, elaborate reporting procedures and a fund to reimburse client losses (recently the problem seems to have been contained by the decline in solo practice). Because solicitors have so much more contact with lay clients, they are the object of proportionally many more grievances than barristers. The level of discontent is not ameliorated by the failure of self-regulation to respond to the majority of complaints, which deal with discourtesy and incompetence rather than ethical violations. Fearing pressure for greater public accountability, the Law Society instituted a Lay Observer and recently added lay participants to the disciplinary process. But solicitors still dominate, with the result that only a tiny fraction of complaints lead to serious punishment. Change occurs only in response to scandals exposed by outsiders, as in the Glanville Davies affair, or internal dissension, as in the struggle over allocating malpractice insurance premiums. Yet notwithstanding their energetic efforts, solicitors seem increasingly subject to external control, as evidenced by the increase in the size, magnitude and success of malpractice claims and the exposure of the Law Society to liability for failure to exercise effective discipline. Thus, the far greater autonomy of the Bar may have been attained at the expense of greater external control over solicitors, a classic illustration of the moral division of labour.

## The future of the legal professions

It would be presumptuous for me as an outsider to predict the future of the legal professions, much less advise them about how they should respond. But it may be useful to conclude by summarizing the challenges they confront at the end of the twentieth century.

If we make the conservative assumption that academic law departments will remain at about their present size, the number of qualified lawyers will continue to grow for two more decades. The Law Society and the General Council of the Bar will have to decide whether to try to impose additional limits on entry to private practice. Even if they do not (or cannot), the proportion of qualified lawyers in employment is likely to increase significantly (particularly in the private sector), potentially marginalizing private practice, which traditionally has been the core of the profession. This will also raise questions about the appropriateness of legal education as training for what are essentially managerial tasks (just as classics eventually was displaced as the training for civil servants). Employment will also increase within private practice, particularly within large solicitors' firms but perhaps also among younger barristers. The ideals of professionalism may be harder to preserve when a majority of lawyers are employees.

Both branches will continue to experience a simultaneous increase in their internal stratification and the heterogeneity of entrants. For the Bar the principal inequalities will be the underrepresentation of women and the segregation of blacks; for solicitors they will be the underrepresentation of blacks and the relegation of women to inferior positions. Senior private practitioners – heads of chambers and principals in firms – will face the task of changing or explaining these inequalities. Solicitors will experience increased competition: within private practice (through advertising), from employed lawyers (performing conveyances in building societies) and from other occupations (such as accounting). This inevitably will compel the substitution of unadmitted staff for professionals and of information technology for both. Solicitors may well persist in challenging the Bar's monopoly of advocacy, at least in lesser matters, impelled by status rivalry as well as material interest. But the threat to the Bar's market control will come less from competitors than from the principal consumer – the state – which at present accounts for half its income. Because both branches must anticipate continued growth of supply combined with little or no growth in their single largest categories of demand – conveyancing and legal aid – they will have to seek new markets.

Competition and concern to enhance profitability will promote further concentration, particularly among solicitors, with the concomitant proliferation of capitalist relations of production and bureaucratic authority within productive units and the tendency towards oligopoly among them. Professional associations will encounter great difficulty containing the increasingly numerous and deep divisions within each branch and accommodating each in governance. At the same time, their own jurisdictions may be squeezed between an increasingly interventionist state (acting on behalf of consumers) and ever larger productive units jealous of their authority over their members.

The social phenomena that we recognize as legal professions are the product of a historically specific environment that found its clearest expression in the last half of the nineteenth and the first half of the twentieth centuries. Both producers of legal services (barristers and solicitors) and consumers functioned for the most part as private individuals. The similarity in producers' background and working environment allowed them to take collective action, both informally and formally, to regulate how many entered the profession, who did so, and relations among themselves and between them and consumers.

I believe that a qualitative change in the professional configuration has been occurring during the last two decades. If we cannot predict its outcome with any confidence, at least we can identify some of its causes. Units of production have become far more collective: solicitors' firms of course, but also barristers' chambers (even if they do not share profits), and certainly public and private employers. Consumers also have been collectivized: private companies, central and local government, and perhaps most importantly individual clients under the aegis of the state that pays for their legal aid. Caught between these new forms of organization, an increasing proportion of the profession is employed. Significant control over entry – numbers, background and technical competence – is in the hands of large institutions external to the profession: universities and polytechnics and the state that pays for them and supports their students. The greater heterogeneity of both the background and the work environment of lawyers has led to the proliferation of voluntary associations, which often pursue divergent agendas. Because at least some of these groups find themselves opposing the state and large private employers, they assume progressively more syndicalist or corporatist forms. A legal services market in which the principal actors are no longer private individuals and their professional associations but collective producers, collective consumers, academic institutions, and a deeply involved state will diverge more and more visibly from the self-image of the legal profession, which remains strongly coloured by an idealization of its nineteenth-century traditions. The transformation of the legal profession is just beginning.

# Tables and figures

## Appendix 1

## Barristers

## Entry

**Table 1.1** Bar examination pass rates, 1873–1974

| | Roman law | | | Constitutional law and legal history[k] | | | Contracts and torts | | | Criminal law | | | Real property | | | Final (pt 2) | | | Final (pt 2) (*The Times*) | | |
|---|---|---|---|---|---|---|---|---|---|---|---|---|---|---|---|---|---|---|---|---|---|
| Year[a] | Taking | Passing | % | Taking | Passing | % | Taking | Passing | % | Taking | Passing | % | Taking | Passing | % | Taking | Passing | % | Taking | Passing | % |
| 1873[b] | | | | 121 | 95 | 79 | | | | | | | | | | | | | | | |
| 1874[c] | | | | | 57 | | | | | | | | | | | | | | | | |
| 1875 | | | | | 158 | | | | | | | | | | | | | | | | |
| 1876 | | 159 | | | 170 | | | | | | | | | | | | | | | | |
| 1877[c] | | 180 | | | 155 | | | | | | | | | | | | | | | | |
| 1878[c] | 319 | 250 | 78 | 256 | 138 | 54 | | | | | | | | | | | | | | | |
| 1879 | 310 | 246 | 79 | 457 | 287 | 63 | | | | | | | | | | | | | | | |
| 1880 | 314 | 250 | 80 | 388 | 280 | 72 | | | | | | | | | | | | | | | |
| 1881 | 314 | 230 | 73 | 387 | 242 | 63 | | | | | | | | | | | | | | | |
| 1882 | 320 | 232 | 72 | 362 | 269 | 74 | | | | | | | | | | | | | | | |
| 1883 | 396 | 297 | 75 | 363 | 240 | 66 | | | | | | | | | | | | | | | |
| 1884 | 331 | 240 | 73 | 420 | 259 | 62 | | | | | | | | | | | | | | | |
| 1885 | 305 | 238 | 78 | 451 | 269 | 60 | | | | | | | | | | | | | | | |
| 1886 | 319 | 248 | 78 | 399 | 274 | 69 | | | | | | | | | | | | | | | |
| 1887 | 262 | 210 | 80 | 378 | 289 | 76 | | | | | | | | | | | | | | | |
| 1888 | 304 | 258 | 85 | 339 | 275 | 81 | | | | | | | | | | | | | | | |
| 1889 | 253 | 220 | 87 | 343 | 251 | 73 | | | | | | | | | | | | | | | |
| 1890 | 278 | 251 | 90 | 368 | 273 | 74 | | | | | | | | | | | | | | | |
| 1891 | 292 | 264 | 90 | 396 | 300 | 76 | | | | | | | | | | | | | | | |
| 1892[d] | 85 | 79 | 93 | 130 | 109 | 84 | | | | | | | | | | | | | | | |
| 1894 | | | | | | | | | | | | | | | | | | | 566 | 355 | 63 |
| 1895 | | | | | | | | | | | | | | | | | | | 347 | 198 | 57 |
| 1896 | | | | | | | | | | | | | | | | | | | | | |
| 1897 | | | | | | | | | | | | | | | | | | | 199[b] | 111[b] | 56 |
| 1898 | | | | | | | | | | | | | | | | | | | 450 | 315 | 70 |
| 1899 | | | | | | | | | | | | | | | | | | | 379 | 240 | 63 |
| 1900 | | | | | | | | | | | | | | | | | | | 258 | 179 | 69 |

| | | | | | | | | | | | | | | | | | | | | |
|---|---|---|---|---|---|---|---|---|---|---|---|---|---|---|---|---|---|---|---|---|---|
| 1901 | | | | | | | | | | | | | | | | | | | 345 | 237 | 69 |
| 1902 | | | | | | | | | | | | | | | | | | | 361 | 282 | 78 |
| 1903 | | | | | | | | | | | | | | | | | | | 329 | 262 | 80 |
| 1904 | | | | | | | | | | | | | | | | | | | 383 | 304 | 79 |
| 1905 | | | | | | | | | | | | | | | | | | | 408 | 315 | 77 |
| 1906 | | | | | | | | | | | | | | | | | | | 454 | 326 | 72 |
| 1907 | | | | | | | | | | | | | | | | | | | 413 | 344 | 83 |
| 1908 | | | | | | | | | | | | | | | | | | | 444 | 296 | 67 |
| 1909 | | | | | | | | | | | | | | | | | | | 491 | 339 | 69 |
| 1910[e] | 171[d] | 119[d] | 70[d] | 316[b] | 207[b] | 66[b] | | | | 307[b] | 234[b] | 76[b] | 244[b] | 176[b] | 72[b] | 270[b] | 194[b] | 72[b] | 520 | 366 | 70 |
| 1911[e] | 707 | 494 | 70 | 869 | 587 | 68 | | | | 838 | 608 | 73 | 685 | 477 | 70 | 588 | 410 | 70 | 558 | 393 | 70 |
| 1912[c] | 448 | 294 | 66 | 513 | 346 | 67 | | | | 465 | 321 | 69 | 529 | 351 | 66 | 521 | 355 | 68 | 681 | 479 | 70 |
| 1913[c] | 393 | 200 | 51 | 403 | 273 | 68 | | | | 391 | 286 | 73 | 421 | 253 | 60 | 577 | 320 | 55 | 720 | 415 | 58 |
| 1914 | 263[c] | 157[c] | 60[c] | 311[c] | 181[c] | 58[c] | | | | 269[c] | 196[c] | 73 | 269[c] | 168[c] | 62[c] | 524 | 301 | 57 | 638 | 355 | 56 |
| 1915 | 207 | 122 | 59 | 220 | 138 | 63 | | | | 193 | 146 | 76 | 224 | 121 | 54 | 302 | 191 | 63 | 316 | 194 | 61 |
| 1916 | 164 | 99 | 60 | 160 | 107 | 67 | | | | 111[c] | 88[c] | 79 | 96 | 82 | 85 | 191 | 145 | 76 | 216 | 156 | 72 |
| 1917[c] | 95 | 60 | 63 | 88 | 62 | 70 | | | | 83 | 68 | 82 | 70 | 48 | 69 | 84 | 60 | 71 | 140 | 95 | 68 |
| 1918 | 127 | | | | | | | | | 108 | 93 | 86 | | | 69 | 105 | 72 | 69 | 117 | 80 | 68 |
| 1919[c] | 194 | 86 | 68 | 141 | 94 | 67 | | | | 202 | 187 | 93 | 104 | 72 | 77 | 137 | 108 | 79 | 183 | 144 | 79 |
| 1920[b] | 218 | 128 | 66 | 179 | 135 | 75 | | | | 269 | 227 | 84 | 149 | 115 | 86 | 202 | 160 | 79 | 301 | 231 | 77 |
| 1921 | 527 | 127 | 58 | 217 | 154 | 71 | | | | 556 | 448 | 81 | 186 | 160 | 79 | 425 | 355 | 84 | 395 | 326 | 83 |
| 1922 | 471[c] | 254 | 48 | 547 | 295 | 54 | | | | 571[c] | 489[c] | 86[c] | 372 | 295 | 79[c] | 244[b] | 212[b] | 87[b] | 500 | 425 | 85 |
| 1923 | 259[b] | 301[c] | 64[c] | 557[c] | 396[c] | 71[c] | | | | 279[b] | 245[b] | 88[b] | 442[c] | 349[c] | 80[b] | 228[b] | 193[b] | 85[b] | 478 | 404 | 85 |
| 1924 | 103[d] | 164[b] | 63[b] | 302[b] | 215[b] | 71[b] | | | | 107[d] | 90[d] | 84[d] | 217[b] | 174[b] | 76[d] | 271[b] | 198[b] | 73[b] | 517 | 411 | 79 |
| 1925 | | 79[d] | 77[d] | 256[b] | 179[b] | 70[b] | | | | 145[d] | 92[d] | 63[d] | 84[d] | 64[d] | (60)[d] | 130[d] | 89[d] | 68[d] | 535 | 376 | 70 |
| 1926 | | | (50)[d] | | | (50)[d] | | | | | | (60)[d] | | | (50)[d] | 348[c] | 265[c] | 76[c] | 456 | 349 | 76 |
| 1927 | | | (72)[d] | 170 | 96 | 56[d] | | | | | | (72)[d] | | | (60)[b] | 420 | 339 | 81 | 449 | 359 | 80 |
| 1928 | | | | | | (50)[d] | | | | | | | | | (50)[d] | 424 | 367 | 87 | 455 | 323 | 71 |
| 1929 | | | (55)[b] | | | (55)[b] | | | | 204[d] | 94[d] | 46[d] | 186[d] | 129[d] | 69[d] | 283[b] | 246[b] | 87[b] | 551 | 352 | 64 |
| 1930 | | | | | | | | | | | | | | | | 205[d] | 102[d] | 50[d] | 607 | 391 | 64 |
| 1931 | | | | 182[d] | 117[d] | 64[d] | 372[b] | 281[b] | 76[b] | | | | 221[d] | 134[d] | 61[d] | 449[i] | 246[i] | 55[i] | 610 | 311 | 51 |
| 1932 | | | (50)[d] | | | (50)[d] | 390[b] | 195[b] | 50[b] | | | | | | (50)[d] | 312[b,j] | 159[b,j] | 51[b,j] | 659 | 363 | 55 |
| 1933 | 140[d] | 61[d] | 44[d] | 190[d] | 123[d] | 65[d] | | | | | | | | | | 507[j] | 245[j] | 48[j] | 554 | 262 | 47 |
| 1934 | 392 | 249 | 64 | 472[b] | 240[b] | 51[b] | 346[b] | 232[b] | 67[b] | | | | 412[b] | 224[b] | 54[b] | 492[j] | 258[j] | 52[j] | 558 | 302 | 54 |
| 1935 | | | | | | | | | | | | | | | | 537[j] | 266[j] | 50[j] | 544 | 273 | 50 |
| 1936 | 253[b] | 198[b] | 78 | | | (70)[d] | | | (55)[d] | | | | | | (70)[d] | 540[j] | 294[j] | 54[j] | 540 | 263 | 49 |
| 1937 | | | (60)[d] | 221[d] | 124[d] | 56[d] | | | | | | | | | | 251 | 127 | 51 | 437 | 232 | 53 |

*continued*

**Table 1.1** (*cont'd*)

| Year[a] | Roman law | | | Constitutional law and legal history[k] | | | Contracts and torts | | | Criminal law | | | Real property | | | Final (Pt 2) | | | | | Final (Pt 2) (*The Times*) | | |
|---|---|---|---|---|---|---|---|---|---|---|---|---|---|---|---|---|---|---|---|---|---|---|---|
| | Taking | Passing | % | Taking | Passing | % | Taking | Passing | % | Taking | Passing | % | Taking | Passing | % | Taking | Passing All | % | Passing Part | % | Taking | Passing | % |
| 1938 | 140 | 109 | 78[d] | | | | | | (70)[b] | | | | 196 | 135 | 60[b] | 520 | 263 | 51 | 30 | 6 | 456 | 239 | 52 |
| 1939 | 57 | 38 | 67[d] | 98 | 56 | 57[d] | 57 | 34 | 60[d] | | | | | | | 495 | 260 | 53 | | | 565 | 284 | 50 |
| 1940 | | | (55)[b] | 35 | 21 | (60)[d] | | | | | | | 20 | 11 | 55[d] | 258 | 103 | 40 | | | 323 | 130 | 40 |
| 1941 | 28 | 24 | 86[d] | 36 | 22 | 61[d] | 125 | 81 | 65 | | | | 56 | 35 | 62[b] | 167 | 66 | 40 | 25 | 15 | 193 | 81 | 42 |
| 1942 | 95 | 73 | 77 | | | (55)[b] | 30 | 17 | 57[d] | | | | | | (55)[b] | 144 | 53 | 37 | 6 | 4 | 129 | 45 | 35 |
| 1943 | 82 | 68 | 83[b] | 102 | 66 | 65[b] | | | | | | | 62 | 28 | 45[b] | 164 | 73 | 45 | 18 | 11 | 162 | 67 | 41 |
| 1944 | 51 | 43 | 84[d] | 35 | 21 | 60[d] | | | (70)[b] | | | | 63 | 34 | 54[d] | 204 | 89 | 44 | 30 | 15 | 184 | 81 | 52 |
| 1945 | | | | | | | 58 | 39 | 67[d] | | | | | | | 212 | 109 | 51[b] | 28 | 13 | 265 | 137 | 52 |
| 1946 | 158 | 112 | 71[d] | 326 | 205 | 63[b] | 117 | 96 | 82 | | | | 215 | 136 | 63[b] | 516 | 297 | 58 | 44 | 9 | 448 | 262 | 59 |
| 1947 | 569 | 398 | 70 | 729 | 351 | 48 | 554 | 494 | 89 | 489 | 369 | 75[d] | 499 | 328 | 66 | 802 | 365 | 46 | 114 | 14 | | | |
| 1948 | 589 | 370 | 63 | 697 | 482 | 69 | 402 | 313 | 78[b] | 1142 | 712 | 62 | 471 | 324 | 69 | 914 | 454 | 50 | 106 | 12 | | | |
| 1949 | 667 | 384 | 58 | 751 | 418 | 56 | 619 | 455 | 74 | 987 | 633 | 64 | 494 | 311 | 63 | 1251 | 598 | 48 | 93 | 7 | | | |
| 1950 | 728 | 393 | 54 | 814 | 397 | 49 | 642 | 355 | 55 | 881 | 483 | 55 | 595 | 356 | 60 | 1338 | 415 | 31 | 125 | 9 | | | |
| 1951 | 685 | 388 | 57 | 842 | 357 | 42 | 612 | 434 | 71 | 863 | 490 | 57 | 516 | 339 | 66 | 1470 | 527 | 36 | 135 | 9 | | | |
| 1952 | 764 | 447 | 59 | 942 | 493 | 52 | 739 | 432 | 58 | 882 | 501 | 57 | 565 | 323 | 57 | 1286 | 586 | 46 | 108 | 8 | | | |
| 1953 | 769 | 454 | 59 | 910 | 472 | 52 | 958 | 441 | 46 | 982 | 651 | 66 | 806 | 484 | 60 | 1268 | 504 | 40 | 148 | 12 | | | |
| 1954 | 730 | 436 | 60 | 988 | 466 | 47 | 986 | 573 | 58 | 901 | 586 | 65 | 739 | 417 | 56 | 1391 | 545 | 39 | 163 | 12 | | | |
| 1955 | 745 | 364 | 49 | 997 | 467 | 47 | 882 | 513 | 58 | 852 | 621 | 73 | 789 | 434 | 55 | 1542 | 544 | 35 | 151 | 10 | | | |

|  |  |  |  |  |  |  |  |  |  |  |  |  |  |  |  |  |  |  |  |  |
|---|---|---|---|---|---|---|---|---|---|---|---|---|---|---|---|---|---|---|---|---|
| 1956 | 819 | 439 | 54 | 1035 | 494 | 48 | 882 | 523 | 59 | 866 | 590 | 68 | 806 | 371 | 46 | 1534 | 501 | 33 | 100 | 7 |
| 1957 | 788 | 414 | 53 | 955 | 495 | 52 | 952 | 559 | 59 | 935 | 561 | 60 | 930 | 482 | 52 | 1746 | 599 | 34 | 141 | 8 |
| 1958 | 842 | 471 | 56 | 893 | 502 | 56 | 1061 | 548 | 52 | 1079 | 458 | 42 | 971 | 452 | 47 | 1782 | 629 | 35 | 204 | 11 |
| 1959 | 846 | 506 | 60 | 985 | 465 | 47 | 1155 | 590 | 51 | 1413 | 563 | 40 | 995 | 566 | 57 | 1622 | 704 | 43 | 221 | 14 |
| 1960 | 984 | 549 | 56 | 1106 | 560 | 51 | 1283 | 724 | 56 | 1696 | 563 | 33 | 1136 | 491 | 43 | 1586 | 603 | 38 | 241 | 15 |
| 1961 | 1145 | 672 | 59 | 1258 | 666 | 53 | 1429 | 658 | 46 | 1924 | 789 | 41 | 1175 | 527 | 45 | 1677 | 697 | 42 | 217 | 13 |
| 1962 | 1248 | 631 | 51 | 1338 | 702 | 52 | 1884 | 762 | 40 | 1745 | 906 | 52 | 1378 | 588 | 43 | 1919 | 794 | 41 | 299 | 16 |
| 1963 | 1487 | 713 | 50 | 1376 | 692 | 50 | 1899 | 829 | 44 | 2067 | 825 | 40 | 1629 | 647 | 40 | 2039 | 832 | 41 | 303 | 15 |
| 1964 | 929 | 443 | 48 | 935 | 504 | 54 | 1425 | 640 | 45 | 1260 | 639 | 51 | 1206 | 486 | 40 | 2007 | 650 | 32 | 273 | 14 |
| 1965 | 1116 | 545 | 49 | 1080 | 550 | 51 |  |  |  | 1392 | 797 | 57 | 1249 | 517 | 41 | 1451 | 417 | 29 | 219 | 15 |
| 1966[g] | 1087 | 571 | 53 | 995 | 574 | 58 |  |  |  | 1237 | 732 | 59 | 639 | 305 | 48[d] | 1187 | 372 | 31 | 175 | 15 |
| 1967[g] | 1044 | 582 | 56 | 1015 | 588 | 58 |  |  |  | 1234 | 610 | 49 | 1084 | 523 | 48 | 1225 | 413 | 34 | 225 | 18 |
| 1968[g] | 546 | 301 | 55 | 441 | 188 | 43 |  |  | 42[d] | 899 | 330 | 37 | 816 | 423 | 52 | 1329 | 397 | 30 | 260 | 20 |
| 1969[g] | 157 | 73 | 46[d] | 176 | 97 |  |  |  | 36[d] | 362 | 235 | 65[d] | 394 | 291 | 74[d] | 1393 | 480 | 34 | 244 | 18 |
| 1970[g] |  |  |  |  |  |  |  |  | 63[d] | 173 | 96 | 55[d] | 223 | 109 | 49[d] | 1756 | 708 | 40 | 283 | 16 |
| 1971[d] old |  |  |  |  |  |  |  |  |  |  |  |  |  |  |  | 327 | 103 | 31 | 58 | 18 |
| transitional |  |  |  |  |  |  |  |  |  |  |  |  |  |  |  | 405 | 176 | 43 | 39 | 10 |
| new |  |  |  |  |  |  |  |  |  |  |  |  |  |  |  | 74 | 53 | 72 | 3 | 4 |
| 1972 old |  |  |  |  |  |  |  |  |  |  |  |  |  |  |  | 364 | 135 | 37 | 54 | 15 |
| transitional |  |  |  |  |  |  |  |  |  |  |  |  |  |  |  | 529 | 259 | 49 | 50 | 9 |
| new |  |  |  |  |  |  |  |  |  |  |  |  |  |  |  | 521 | 363 | 70 | 48 | 9 |
| 1973 old |  |  |  |  |  |  |  |  |  |  |  |  |  |  |  | 1020 | 490 | 48 | 96 | 9 |
| 1974 old[d] |  |  |  |  |  |  |  |  |  |  |  |  |  |  |  | 867 | 565[h] | 65[h] |  |  |

*continued*

**Table 1.1** (*cont'd*)

[a] Composite of four examinations each year 1873–1927;
three a year 1928–63; two a year 1964–74 (1965–74 for part 2).
[b] Two terms.
[c] Three terms.
[d] One term.
[e] These years also report results for Roman-Dutch law (4 took, 3 passed Hilary term 1910; 3/3 Trinity term 1912) and Hindu and Mohammedan law (14/8 Hilary term 1910; 23/13 Easter term 1911; 17/10 Trinity term 1911; 20/14 Trinity term 1912).
[f] Figures in parentheses are estimates.
[g] The figures for part 2 only describe first-takers.
Pass rates on part 2 for those with partial passes were:
Michaelmas term 1968: 152/143, 94%; Trinity term 1969; 124/100, 81%; Michaelmas term 1969: 147/137, 93%;
Trinity term 1970: 142/130, 92%; Michaelmas term 1970: 162/150, 93%; Trinity term 1971: 137/121, 88%.
[h] Combines those who passed all and those who passed part.
[i] New final introduced this year: 181 took, 87 passed (48%).
[j] Old final administered 1932–6:
1932: 93 took, 53 passed (57%) (two terms)
1933: 48 took, 20 passed (42%)
1934: 38 took, 22 passed (58%)
1935: 8 took, 6 passed (75%) (one term)
1936: 12 took, 5 passed (42%).
[k] English law 1873–92.

*Sources*: *Law Notes*; *Bar Examination Journal*; *The Times*

**Table 1.2** Bar examination pass rates, 1966–76
(a) Part 1

| | | Group A | | | | | | | | Group B | | | | | | | |
|---|---|---|---|---|---|---|---|---|---|---|---|---|---|---|---|---|---|
| | | Taking all | | | | | Retaking part | | | Taking all | | | | | Retaking part | | |
| | | Tak-ing | Passing all | | Passing 2/3 | | Pass-ing | Complet-ing % | Passing 2/3 % | Taking | Passing all | | Passing 2/3 | | Pass-ing | Complet-ing % | Passing 2/3 % |
| | | no. | no. | % | no. | % | no. | | | no. | no. | % | no. | % | no. | | |
| 1968 | T | 177 | 34 | 19 | 42 | 24 | | | | | | | | | | | |
| | M | 163 | 47 | 29 | 21 | 13 | | | | | | | | | | | |
| 1969 | T | 478 | 127 | 27 | 107 | 22 | 27 | 62 | 7 | 91 | 53 | 58 | 19 | 21 | 8 | 80 | 10 |
| | M | 286 | 55 | 19 | 62 | 22 | 79 | 59 | 5 | 43 | 19 | 44 | 8 | 19 | 25 | 64 | 3 |
| 1970 | T | 483 | 166 | 34 | 103 | 21 | 113 | 91 | | 265 | 94 | 35 | 62 | 23 | 34 | 63 | |
| | M | 247 | 50 | 20 | 38 | 15 | 96 | 75 | | 155 | 53 | 34 | 40 | 26 | 95 | 69 | |
| 1971 | T | 364 | 164 | 45 | | | 83 | 81 | | 271 | 157 | 58 | | | 106 | 74 | |
| | M | 261 | 94 | 36 | | | 81 | 80 | | 181 | 94 | 52 | | | 171 | 66 | |
| 1972 | T | 304 | 144 | 47 | 47 | 15 | 44 | 74 | | 186 | 102 | 55 | 28 | 15 | 70 | 62 | |
| | M | 151 | 35 | 23 | 28 | 19 | 57 | 58 | | 119 | 49 | 41 | 16 | 13 | 135 | 69 | |
| 1973 | T | 423 | 182 | 43 | | | 67 | 73 | | 298 | 131 | 44 | | | 82 | 49 | |
| | M | 167 | 40 | 24 | 23 | 14 | 59 | 60 | | 155 | 101 | 65 | | | 87 | 69 | |
| 1974 | T | 441 | 163 | 37 | 66 | 15 | 38 | 52 | 10 | 176 | 118 | 67 | | | 47 | 69 | |
| | M | 66 | 40 | 61 | 7 | 10 | 83 | 88 | | 155 | 127 | 82 | | | 72 | 75 | |
| 1975 | T | 451 | 239 | 53 | 59 | 13 | 52 | 52 | 4 | 186 | 134 | 72 | 28 | 15 | 41 | 75 | 2 |
| | M | 190 | 59 | 31 | 25 | 13 | 68 | 84 | 2 | 159 | 108 | 68 | 32 | 20 | 66 | 56 | 2 |
| 1976 | T | 794 | 246 | 31 | 111 | 14 | 57 | 65 | 4 | 210 | 168 | 80 | 38 | 18 | 26 | 50 | 2 |
| | M | 259 | 44 | 17 | 44 | 17 | 83 | 66 | 2 | 225 | 142 | 63 | 52 | 23 | 69 | 71 | |

T: Trinity; M: Michaelmas.

(b) Part 2

| | Taking all | | | | Retaking part | | | |
|---|---|---|---|---|---|---|---|---|
| | Trinity | | Michaelmas | | Trinity | | Michaelmas | |
| | Taking no. | Passing % | Taking no. | Passing % | Taking no. | Passing % | Taking no. | Passing % |
| 1966 | 209 | 32 | 163 | 31 | 114 | 85 | 90 | 89 |
| 1967 | 200 | 31 | 111 | 19 | 100 | 98 | 102 | 95 |
| 1968 | 214 | 30 | 185 | 32 | 96 | 87 | 141 | 94 |
| 1969 | 257 | 35 | 243 | 36 | 100 | 81 | 137 | 93 |
| 1970 | 397 | 46 | 311 | 30 | 130 | 91 | 150 | 90 |
| 1971 | 332 | 41 | 215 | 51 | 121 | 88 | 104 | 76 |
| 1972 | 543 | 59 | 150 | 37 | 39 | 95 | 61 | 74 |
| 1973 | 464 | 66 | 128 | 41 | 64 | 77 | 60 | 78 |
| 1974 | 470 | 54 | 182 | 51 | 36 | 72 | 97 | 91 |
| 1975 | 668 | 73 | 139 | 51 | 38 | 68 | 67 | 83 |
| 1976 | 591 | 67 | 111 | 42 | 28 | 68 | 86 | 87 |
| Average | | 47 | | 38 | | 87 | | 88 |

Pass rates include conditional passes.
*Sources*: Senate, 1977a: XI.29, XI.32; *Law Notes*

| Year | Term | Intending practitioners | | | | | Non-intending practitioners | | | | |
|---|---|---|---|---|---|---|---|---|---|---|---|
| | | Entered | Sat | Passed | Passed as % of Sat | No. sitting MT /no. sitting TT (%) | Entered | Sat | Passed | Passed as % of Sat | No. sitting MT /no. sitting TT (%) |
| 1973 | Trinity | 525 | 478 | 263 | 55.0 | | 324 | 252 | 121 | 48.0 | |
| | Michaelmas | 190 | 161 | 92 | 57.1 | 34 | 243 | 210 | 81 | 38.6 | 83 |
| 1974 | Trinity | 646 | 598 | 380 | 63.5 | | 377 | 319 | 126 | 39.5 | |
| | Michaelmas | 261 | 240 | 159 | 66.3 | 40 | 260 | 224 | 120 | 53.6 | 70 |
| 1975 | Trinity | 733 | 682 | 537 | 78.7 | | 328 | 287 | 169 | 58.9 | |
| | Michaelmas | 210 | 188 | 112 | 59.6 | 28 | 207 | 167 | 95 | 56.9 | 58 |
| 1976 | Trinity | 688 | 653 | 485 | 74.3 | | 328 | 266 | 150 | 56.4 | |
| | Michaelmas | 214 | 184 | 110 | 59.8 | 28 | 227 | 176 | 87 | 49.4 | 66 |
| 1977 | Trinity | 681 | 632 | 506 | 80.1 | | 322 | 269 | 139 | 51.7 | |
| | Michaelmas | 152 | 133 | 93 | 69.9 | 21 | 214 | 182 | 104 | 57.1 | 68 |
| 1978 | Trinity | 668 | 619 | 509 | 82.3 | | 413 | 359 | 232 | 64.6 | |
| | Michaelmas | 151 | 129 | 90 | 69.8 | 21 | 198 | 172 | 96 | 55.8 | 48 |
| 1979 | Trinity | 647 | 599 | 477 | 79.6 | | 427 | 369 | 218 | 59.1 | |
| | Michaelmas | 139 | 125 | 77 | 61.6 | 21 | 236 | 194 | 91 | 46.9 | 53 |
| 1980 | Trinity | 578 | 519 | 451 | 86.9 | | 422 | 364 | 253 | 69.5 | |
| | Michaelmas | 112 | 97 | 66 | 68.0 | 19 | 185 | 148 | 78 | 52.7 | 41 |
| 1981 | Trinity | 642 | 600 | 514 | 85.7 | | 385 | 323 | 223 | 69.0 | |
| | Michaelmas | 100 | 77 | 44 | 57.1 | 13 | 156 | 124 | 60 | 48.4 | 38 |
| 1982 | Trinity | 746 | 686 | 565 | 82.4 | | 509 | 443 | 298 | 67.3 | |
| | Michaelmas | 152 | 117 | 62 | 53.0 | 17 | 190 | 153 | 85 | 55.6 | 35 |
| 1983 | Trinity | 873 | 798 | 625 | 78.9 | | 524 | 454 | 284 | 62.5 | |
| | Michaelmas | 186 | 152 | 87 | 57.2 | 14 | 239 | 191 | 79 | 41.3 | 28 |
| 1984 | Trinity | 786 | 747 | 511 | 68.5 | | 454 | 380 | 174 | 45.8 | |
| | Michaelmas | 185 | 153 | 61 | 40.0 | 12 | 223 | 179 | 48 | 26.8 | 28 |
| Total 1973–84: | | | | | | | | | | | |
| | Trinity | 8213 | 7611 | 5823 | 76.5 | | 4813 | 4085 | 2387 | 58.4 | |
| | Michaelmas | 2052 | 1756 | 1053 | 60.0 | | 2578 | 2120 | 1024 | 48.3 | |

The Trinity examination is given in May/June; the Michaelmas examination in September is taken mainly by those who failed all or part of the Trinity examination.
*Sources*: Council of Legal Education, 1976; Senate, Annual Statement, 1983–4: 26

**Table 1.4** Proportion of those passing Bar examination, part 2, who were first-takers and repeaters, 1949–71

| Year | Proportion of passing who: | | | | No. who passed part previous year |
|---|---|---|---|---|---|
| | were first-takers | | had partial pass | | |
| | no. | % | no. | % | |
| 1949 | 450 | 75 | 148 | 25 | 106 |
| 1950[a] | 99 | 72 | 39 | 28 | 93 |
| 1951 | | | | | 125 |
| 1952 | | | | | 135 |
| 1953 | | | | | 108 |
| 1954 | 398 | 73 | 147 | 27 | 148 |
| 1955[b] | 266 | 71 | 107 | 29 | 163 |
| 1956[b] | 235 | 74 | 83 | 26 | 151 |
| 1957 | 462 | 77 | 137 | 23 | 100 |
| 1958[b] | 353 | 72 | 136 | 28 | 141 |
| 1959 | 504 | 72 | 200 | 28 | 204 |
| 1960 | 367 | 61 | 236 | 39 | 221 |
| 1961 | 461 | 66 | 236 | 34 | 241 |
| 1962 | 526 | 66 | 268 | 34 | 217 |
| 1963 | 564 | 68 | 268 | 32 | 299 |
| 1964 | 405 | 62 | 245 | 38 | 303 |
| 1965 | 260 | 62 | 157 | 38 | 273 |
| 1966 | 372 | 64 | 206 | 36 | 219 |
| 1967 | 413 | 66 | 211 | 34 | 175 |
| 1968 | 397 | 62 | 246 | 38 | 225 |
| 1969 | 480 | 67 | 237 | 33 | 260 |
| 1970 | 708 | 72 | 280 | 28 | 244 |
| 1971 | 103 | 46 | 121 | 54 | 283 |

[a] One term.
[b] Two terms.
*Source*: *Law Notes*

(a) Proportion of entrants with university degree

| | Year | | | | | | | | | | | | | | | | | | | |
|---|---|---|---|---|---|---|---|---|---|---|---|---|---|---|---|---|---|---|---|---|
| | 83 | 80 | 79 | 78 | 77 | 76 | 75 | 74 | 73 | 72 | 71 | 70 | 69 | 68 | 67 | 66 | 65 | 64 | 63 | 49 |
| % called with university degree[a] | 98 | 93 | 90 | 89 | 87 | 91 | 87 | 86 | 85 | 77 | 76 | 79 | 81 | 78 | 72 | 80 | 78 | 76 | | 57 |
| % called with law degree[a] | 84 | 78 | 71 | 67 | 67 | 73 | 70 | 63 | 73 | 62 | 64 | 70 | 71 | 66 | 58 | 65 | 62 | 60 | | 40 |
| % starting practice with law degree | | | | 70 | | | | | | | | 64 | | | | | | | | |
| % practising Bar with university degree | | | | | | | | | | | | | | | | | 93 | | | |
| % practising Bar with mixed or law degree | | | | | | | | | | | | | | | | | 70 | | | |
| % admitted to Gray's Inn with university degree | | | | | | | 20 | 28 | 26 | 26 | 11 | | | | | | | | | |
| % UK students admitted to Inns with university degree[c] | | | | | | | 11 | 16 | 9 | 11 | 5 | | | | | | | | | |
| % UK students admitted to Inns with law or mixed degree | | | | | | | 39 | 80 | 82 | 84 | 84 | | | | | | | | | |
| % overseas students admitted to Inns with university degree[c] | | | | | | | 17 | 51 | 55 | 57 | 63 | | | | | | | | | |
| % overseas students admitted to Inns with mixed degree[b] | | | | | | | 43 | 54 | 48 | 62 | 64 | | | | | | | | | |
| 1967 practitioners called: | | | | | | | | | | | | | | | | | | | | |
| 1963–67[d] (by year called): | | | | | | | | | | | | | | | 14 | 10 | 5 | 15 | 16 | |
| % with university degree | | | | | | | | | | | | | | | 88 | 88 | 88 | 82 | 93 | |
| % with law degree | | | | | | | | | | | | | | | 79 | 70 | 61 | 68 | 71 | |
| % university degrees from Oxbridge | | | | | | | | | | | | | | | 76 | | | | | |

[a] UK residents intending to practise.
[b] No law degree from any non-UK admission.
[c] Many non-graduates (about half) are currently undergraduates, some of whom are reading law.
[d] 1967 figure is average for all call dates;
1963–6 figures are for barristers called in those years.

*Sources*: Layton et al., 1978a: 76; Gower, 1950: 151 n. 42; Royal Commission, 1979, vol. 1: 609–10; Wilson, 1966: 7, 67; Zander, 1968: 41 n. 28; Ormrod Committee, 1971: 114; Wilson and Marsh, 1975: 297; 1978: 3; 1981: 36; Senate, 1977a: XI.33–4; Bolton Report, 1967; CHULS, 1984: table 13

(b) Course enrolments for parts 1 and 2 of the Bar final

| | Part 1 | | | | | Part 2 (ICSL) | | |
|---|---|---|---|---|---|---|---|---|
| | | | Polytechnic of Central London | | | | | |
| | ICSL | City University | 1-year | 2-year | Total | Intending practitioners | Non-intending practitioners | Total |
| 1973–74 | 326 | | | | | | | 597 |
| 1974–75 | 320 | | | | | | | 551 |
| 1975–76 | 453 | | | | | | | 458 |
| 1976–77 | 295 | | | | | | | 499 |
| 1977–78 | 61 | 150 | | | 211 | | | 641 |
| 1978–79 | | n.a. | | | | 575 | 307 | 882 |
| 1979–80 | | 75 | 67 | 12 | 154 | 528 | 263 | 791 |
| 1980–81 | | 80 | 69 | 13 | 162 | 589 | 251 | 840 |
| 1981–82 | | 83 | 79 | 7 | 169 | | | 1060 |
| 1982–83 | | 90 | 85 | | 175 | 804 | 230 | 1034 |
| 1983–84 | | 91 | 96 | | 187 | 733 | 207 | 940 |
| 1984–85 | | 287 | | 15 | | 765 | 137 | 902 |
| 1985–86 | | 289 | | 14 | | 737 | 195 | 932 |

ICSL: Inns of Court School of Law
*Source*: Senate, Annual Statements

**Table 1.6** Class of degrees of Oxbridge law graduates who became barristers and solicitors, 1950–83

| | Firsts | | Cambridge upper seconds | |
|---|---|---|---|---|
| Year of graduation | % practising as barristers | % practising as solicitors | % practising as barristers | % practising as solicitors |
| Early 1950s | 38 | 14 | 29 | 21 |
| Late 1950s | 28 | 23 | 16 | 27 |
| Early 1960s | 28 | 22 | 22 | 38 |
| Late 1960s | 33 | 18 | 19 | 41 |
| Early 1970s | 32 | 21 | 17 | 33 |
| 1976 | 15 | 35 | 16 | 29 |
| 1977 | 28 | 45 | 20 | 42 |
| 1978 | 15 | 14 | 13 | 22 |
| 1982[a] | 17 | 52 | 9 | 51 |
| 1983[a] | 6 | 58 | 15 | 47 |

[a] Percentage of Cambridge law graduates stating intent to become barristers or solicitors.

*Sources*: Senate, Annual Statement, 1981–2: 48; 79 *LSG* 232, 1982; Reeves, 1986: 102

**Table 1.7** Pupillages and tenancies, 1969–84

| | Year | | | | | | | | | | | | | | | | | | | |
|---|---|---|---|---|---|---|---|---|---|---|---|---|---|---|---|---|---|---|---|---|
| | 1965 | 69–70 | 70–1 | 71–2 | 72–3 | 73–4 | Dec. 74 | 75 | March 76 | Nov. 76 | Spring 76 | 76 | 77 | 78 | 79 | 80 | 81 | 82 | 83 | 84 |
| Questionnaire response rate (%): | | | | | | | | | | | | | | | | | | | | |
| London | | | | | | | | | | | 92 | 74 | 72 | 62 | 69 | 66 | 70 | 68 | 63 | 81 |
| Provinces | | | | | | | | | | | 60 | 72 | 65 | 59 | 65 | 53 | 52 | 60 | 66 | 83 |
| Pupils in chambers: | | | | | | | | | | | | | | | | | | | | |
| London | | | | | | | 404 | | | | 433 | 386 | 407 | 351 | 354 | 360 | 394 | 437 | 365 | 590 |
| Provinces | | | | | | | | | | | 63 | 68 | 71 | 57 | 72 | 61 | 58 | 74 | 71 | 85 |
| Floaters: | | | | | | | | | | | | | | | | | | | | |
| London | | | | | | | 102 | 102 | 94 | 103 | 103 | 94 | 110 | 80 | 106 | 98 | 136 | 134 | 83 | 132 |
| Provinces | | | | | | | | 1 | 4 | 12 | 12 | 9 | 9 | 11 | 3 | 5 | 10 | 10 | 8 | 11 |
| Total | 47 | | | | | | 102 | 103 | 98 | 115 | 115 | 103 | 119 | 91 | 109 | 103 | 146 | 144 | 91 | 143 |
| Pupillage available next year: | | | | | | | | | | | | | | | | | | | | |
| London | | | | | | | | | | | 471 | 345 | 353 | 290 | 303 | 245 | 296 | 155 | 555 | 630 |
| Provinces | | | | | | | | | | | 72 | 74 | 60 | 58 | 63 | 52 | 52 | 24 | 86 | 106 |
| Floaters, years since call: | | | | | | | | | | | | | | | | | | | | |
| < 1 | | | | | | | | | | | | 8 | 30 | 22 | | | | | | 127 |
| 1–2 | | | | | | | | | | | | 79 | 63 | 40 | | | | | | |
| 2–3 | | | | | | | | | | | | 6 | 17 | 15 | | | | | | |
| 3–4 | | | | | | | | | | | | 4 | 7 | 7 | | | | | | 16 |
| 4–5 | | | | | | | | | | | | 1 | | 2 | | | | | | |
| 5–6 | | | | | | | | | | | | 1 | | | | | | | | |
| ⩾ 7 | | | | | | | | | | | | 1 | | | | | | | | |

| | | | | | | | | | | | | | | | | |
|---|---|---|---|---|---|---|---|---|---|---|---|---|---|---|---|---|
| Net increase in practitioners | 46 | | | 205 | 218 | 231 | 278 | 235 | 195 | 187 | 149 | 177 | 96 | 179 | 168 | 171 |
| Seats vacated | | | | 70 | 103 | 68 | 86 | 147 | 131 | 98 | | | | | | |
| Seats available | | 107 | 126 | 176 | 175 | 211 | 267 | | | | | | | | | |
| Starting practice | | 241 | 222 | 275 | 321 | 299 | 364 | 382 | 326 | 285 | | | | | | |
| Chambers with no pupils: | | | | | | | | | | | | | | | | |
| London | | | | | | | | | | 21 | 19 | 18 | 12 | 12 | 28 | 30 |
| Provinces | | | | | | | | | | 27 | 24 | 16 | 14 | 12 | 31 | 43 |
| No. of pupillages available | | | | | | | 595 | 622 | 693 | 665 | 630 | 623 | 736 | 802 | | |
| No. intending practitioners passing Bar final | | | | | | | 649 | 595 | 599 | 599 | 554 | 517 | 558 | 627 | 712 | |
| Pupillages as % of no. passing final | | | | | | | 92 | 105 | 116 | 111 | 114 | 121 | 132 | 128 | | |

*Sources*: Senate, 1978d: 5; Senate, 1978c: D.16; Senate, Annual Statement, 1982–3; 1983–4; 1984–5; Royal Commission, 1979, vol. 1: 458

**Table 1.8** Departures from practice expressed as a proportion of cohort beginning practice, 1956–85

| Year | Number starting practice in that and preceding nine years | Number from that cohort ceasing practice that year | Percentage ceasing practice |
|---|---|---|---|
| 1985 | 3139 | 68 | 2.2 |
| 1984 | 3166 | 55 | 1.7 |
| 1983 | 3140 | 60 | 1.9 |
| 1982 | 3138 | 52 | 1.7 |
| 1981 | 3131 | 72 | 2.3 |
| 1980 | 3083 | 82 | 2.7 |
| 1979 | 3015 | 82 | 2.7 |
| 1978 | 2850 | 70 | 2.5 |
| 1977 | 2704 | 79 | 2.9 |
| 1976 | 2584 | 41 | 1.6 |
| 1975 | 2331 | 49 | 2.1 |
| 1974 | 2105 | 38 | 1.8 |
| 1973 | 1886 | 15 | 0.8 |
| 1972 | 1723 | 26 | 1.5 |
| 1971 | 1560 | 12 | 0.8 |
| 1970 | 1446 | 33 | 2.3 |
| 1969 | 1290 | 20 | 1.6 |
| 1968 | 1241 | 31 | 2.5 |
| 1967 | 1193 | 25 | 2.1 |
| 1966 | 1084 | 16 | 1.5 |
| 1965 | 1066 | 27 | 2.5 |
| 1964 | 1042 | 11 | 1.1 |
| 1963 | 1098 | 16 | 1.5 |
| 1962 | 1095 | | |
| 1961 | 1150 | | |
| 1960 | 1216 | 27 | 2.2 |
| 1959 | 1287 | 68 | 5.3 |
| 1958 | 1395 | 66 | 4.7 |
| 1957 | 1481 | 61 | 4.1 |
| 1956 | 1515 | 64 | 4.2 |

**Table 1.9** Applications by solicitors to have name removed from Roll with a view to being called to the Bar, 1912–58

| Year | Number | Year | Number |
|---|---|---|---|
| 1957–58 | 4 | 1933–34 | 3 |
| 1956–57 | 7 | 1932–33 | 4 |
| 1955–56 | 1 | 1931–32 | 4 |
| 1954–55 | 6 | 1930–31 | 4 |
| 1953–54 | 9 | 1929–30 | 3 |
| 1952–53 | 5 | 1928–29 | 6 |
| 1951–52 | 8 | 1927–28 | 1 |
| 1950–51 | 5 | 1926–27 | 1 |
| 1949–50 | 10 | 1925–26 | 2 |
| 1948–49 | 12 | 1924–25 | 4 |
| 1947–48 | 15 | 1923–24 | 5 |
| 1946–47 | | 1922–23 | 8 |
| 1945–46 | 20 | 1921–22 | 8 |
| 1944–45 | 14 | 1920–21 | 10 |
| 1943–44 | 4 | 1919–20 | 11 |
| 1942–43 | 2 | 1918–19 | 17 |
| 1941–42 | 4 | 1917–18 | 4 |
| 1940–41 | 2 | 1916–17 | 4 |
| 1939–40 | 2 | 1915–16 | 2 |
| 1938–39 | 3 | 1914–15 | 4 |
| 1937–38 | 6 | 1913–14 | 8 |
| 1936–37 | 7 | 1912–13 | 16 |
| 1935–36 | 5 | | |
| 1934–35 | 4 | 1889–90 | 22 |

*Source*: Law Society, Annual Reports

**Table 1.10** Admissions to the Inns of Court, 1800–90

| Year(s) | Gray's Inn[e] | | Lincoln's Inn | | Middle Temple | | Total (excluding Inner Temple) | |
|---|---|---|---|---|---|---|---|---|
| | Annual (actual or average) | Decade[d] | Annual | Decade | Annual | Decade | Annual | Decade average |
| 1890 | 8[a] | | 69 | | 71 | | 148 | |
| 1880–89 | 26 | 264 | | | 128[b] | 128[c] | | |
| 1880 | 11 | | 78 | | 72 | | 161 | |
| 1870–79 | 23 | 231 | 98 | 981 | 108[b] | 1083[c] | | 239 |
| 1870 | 10 | | 114 | | 66 | | 190 | |
| 1860–69 | 16 | 165 | 88 | 880 | 129[b] | 1287[c] | | 233 |
| 1860 | 11 | | 93 | | 24 | | 128 | |
| 1850–59 | 18 | 181 | 86 | 858 | 51[b] | 511[c] | | 155 |
| 1850 | 15 | | 76 | | 45 | | 136 | |
| 1840–49 | 40 | 396 | 91 | 914 | 91[b] | 907[c] | | 222 |
| 1840 | 40 | | 95 | | 102 | | 237 | |
| 1830–39 | 72 | 717 | 103 | 1029 | 81[b] | 812[c] | | 256 |
| 1830 | 60 | | 79 | | 62 | | 201 | |
| 1820–29 | 54 | 539 | 90 | 901 | 56[b] | 561[c] | | 200 |
| 1820 | 58 | | 92 | | 45 | | 195 | |
| 1810–19 | 35 | 346 | 86 | 856 | 51[b] | 506[c] | | 172 |
| 1810 | 38 | | 68 | | 41 | | 147 | |
| 1800–09 | 26 | 264 | 67 | 670 | 36[b] | 363[c] | | 129 |
| 1800 | 16 | | 62 | | 24 | | 102 | |

[a] 1889.
[b] Ten-year average based on decade estimate.
[c] Decade estimate.
[d] Estimates.
[e] [illegible] during much of the century (Napier and Stephenson, 1888: 19).

**Table 1.11** Calls to the Bar, 1821–41

| Year | | Number | |
|---|---|---|---|
| 1841 | Michaelmas term | | |
| | Trinity term | 37 | |
| | Easter term | 36 | |
| | Hilary term | 50 | |
| | Total | | 123 |
| 1840 | Michaelmas term | 52 | |
| | Trinity term | 33 | |
| | Easter term | 42 | |
| | Hilary term | 30 | |
| | Total | | 157 |
| 1839 | Michaelmas term | 42 | |
| | Trinity term | 42 | |
| | Easter term | 50 | |
| | Hilary term | 43 | |
| | Total | | 177 |
| 1838 | Michaelmas term | 49 | |
| 1834 | | | 111 |
| 1833 | | | 103 |
| 1832 | | | 120 |
| 1831 | | | 103 |
| 1830 | | | 117 |
| 1829 | | | 122 |
| 1828 | | | 85 |
| 1827 | | | 104 |
| 1826 | | | 78 |
| 1825 | | | 90 |
| 1824 | | | 88 |
| 1823 | | | 76 |
| 1822 | | | 60 |
| 1821 | | | 75 |

*Sources*: 1821–34: Whishaw, 1835: 162–233 (underestimated because calculated from barristers still in practice in 1835); 1838–41: *The Legal Observer*

**Table 1.12** Admissions and calls by Inn, men/women called and calls as percentage of admissions, 1841–1984

| Year | Admissions | | | | | Calls | | | | | Calls | | Calls as % of admissions 3 yrs earlier[a] |
|---|---|---|---|---|---|---|---|---|---|---|---|---|---|
| | IT | MT | LI | GI | Total | IT | MT | LI | GI | Total | M | F | |
| 1984 | 222 | 412 | 342 | 287 | 1263 | 173 | 289 | 247 | 236 | 945 | | | |
| 1983 | 222 | 342 | 380 | 303 | 1247 | 157 | 298 | 308 | 311 | 1074 | | | |
| 1982 | 238 | 376 | 385 | 382 | 1381 | 126 | 287 | 266 | 308 | 987 | | | |
| 1981 | 161 | 357 | 371 | 390 | 1279 | 143 | 238 | 196 | 253 | 830 | | | |
| 1980 | 145 | 266 | 314 | 327 | 1052 | 148 | 206 | 245 | 241 | 840 | | | |
| 1979 | 162 | 261 | 266 | 300 | 989 | 159 | 215 | 199 | 300 | 873 | | | |
| 1978 | 159 | 219 | 213 | 277 | 868 | 173 | 265 | 240 | 265 | 943 | | | |
| 1977 | 146 | 239 | 174 | 281 | 840 | 191 | 286 | 196 | 207 | 880 | | | |
| 1976 | 193 | 315 | 224 | 320 | 1052 | 159 | 251 | 157 | 215 | 782 | | | |
| 1975 | 322 | 467 | 609 | 443 | 1419 | 227 | 304 | 185 | 227 | 943 | | | |
| 1974 | 290 | 412 | 314 | 316 | 1332 | 185 | 247 | 167 | 201 | 800 | | | |
| 1973 | 274 | 412 | 303 | 294 | 1283 | 220 | 247 | 172 | 181 | 820 | | | |
| 1972 | 225 | 358 | 241 | 309 | 1133 | 259 | 289 | 242 | 229 | 1019 | | | |
| 1971 | 227 | 292 | 252 | 261 | 1032 | 200 | 212 | 217 | 224 | 930 | | | |
| 1970 | 195 | 218 | 231 | 215 | 859 | 261 | 211 | 242 | 276 | 990 | | | |
| 1969 | 269 | 336 | 334 | 323 | 1262 | 196 | 171 | 200 | 190 | 757 | | | |
| 1968 | 307 | 409 | 340 | 345 | 1401 | 194 | 144 | 155 | 146 | 639 | | | 36 |
| 1967 | 391 | 398 | 443 | 504 | 1736 | 162 | 114 | 154 | 111 | 541 | | | 39 |
| 1966 | 356 | 314 | 399 | 372 | 1441 | 154 | 136 | 172 | 116 | 578 | | | 42 |
| 1965 | 438 | 339 | 546 | 381 | 1704 | 196 | 231 | 198 | 156 | 781 | | | 47 |
| 1964 | 529 | 310 | 464 | 324 | 1627 | 164 | 179 | 192 | 155 | 690 | | | 52 |
| 1963 | 484 | 316 | 385 | 329 | 1514 | 172 | 203 | 196 | 155 | 726 | | | 58 |
| 1962 | 522 | 445 | 490 | 324 | 1781 | 113 | 222 | 237 | 165 | 737 | | | 63 |
| 1961 | 422 | 370 | 478 | 276 | 1546 | 72 | 175 | 277 | 162 | 686 | | | 66 |
| 1960 | 349 | 331 | 369 | 284 | 1333 | 75 | 221 | 231 | 149 | 676 | | | 68 |

| | | | | | | | | | | | | | |
|---|---|---|---|---|---|---|---|---|---|---|---|---|---|
| 1959 | 243 | 342 | 377 | 292 | 1254 | 86 | 200 | 269 | 139 | 694 | | | 62 |
| 1958 | 169 | 251 | 392 | 278 | 1090 | 77 | 174 | 250 | 172 | 673 | | | 59 |
| 1957 | 136 | 288 | 336 | 254 | 1014 | 65 | 115 | 179 | 151 | 510 | | | 57 |
| 1956 | 121 | 293 | 359 | 238 | 1011 | 74 | 158 | 188 | 140 | 560 | | | 60 |
| 1955 | 85 | 284 | 388 | 239 | 996 | 79 | 173 | 177 | 151 | 580 | | | 59 |
| 1954 | 101 | 277 | 333 | 286 | 997 | 86 | 140 | 175 | 135 | 536 | | | 61 |
| 1953 | 109 | 231 | 334 | 244 | 959 | 92 | 146 | 135 | 136 | 509 | | | 60 |
| 1952 | 138 | 194 | 334 | 285 | 951 | 108 | 164 | 161 | 183 | 616 | | | 60 |
| 1951 | 106 | 251 | 253 | 259 | 869 | 98 | 141 | 135 | 145 | 519 | | | 54 |
| 1950 | 160 | 246 | 279 | 254 | 939 | 92 | 148 | 137 | 143 | 520 | | | 56 |
| 1949 | 166 | 229 | 244 | 263 | 902 | 99 | 158 | 127 | 141 | 525 | | | 61 |
| 1948 | 152 | 244 | 263 | 222 | 881 | 117 | 169 | 129 | 87 | 502 | | | 74 |
| 1947 | 168 | 273 | 292 | 234 | 967 | 88 | 108 | 84 | 90 | 370 | | | 76 |
| 1946 | 207 | 291 | 306 | 242 | 1046 | 77 | 84 | 55 | 92 | 308 | 295 | 7 | 71 |
| 1945 | 150 | 175 | 203 | 210 | 738 | 38 | 56 | 22 | 53 | 169 | 162 | 0 | 69 |
| 1944 | 83 | 117 | 153 | 139 | 492 | 15 | 29 | 20 | 28 | 92 | 90 | 0 | 50 |
| 1943 | 65 | 95 | 78 | 119 | 357 | 21 | 43 | 10 | 31 | 105 | 124 | 1 | 41 |
| 1942 | 47 | 64 | 56 | 94 | 261 | 9 | 43 | 16 | 29 | 97 | 95 | 0 | 37 |
| 1941 | 32 | 53 | 34 | 66 | 185 | 29 | 61 | 34 | 32 | 156 | 158 | 6 | 47 |
| 1940 | 28 | 47 | 21 | 36 | 132 | 39 | 78 | 35 | 40 | 192 | 129 | 5 | 53 |
| 1939 | 55 | 98 | 43 | 74 | 270 | 84 | 121 | 47 | 67 | 319 | 308 | 11 | 59 |
| 1938 | 126 | 165 | 69 | 103 | 463 | 80 | 95 | 45 | 74 | 294 | 276 | 12 | 59 |
| 1937 | 119 | 162 | 85 | 106 | 472 | 74 | 106 | 49 | 61 | 290 | 286 | 5 | 60 |
| 1936 | 109 | 184 | 75 | 124 | 492 | 94 | 106 | 51 | 61 | 312 | 298 | 12 | 64 |
| 1935 | 127 | 180 | 90 | 144 | 541 | 83 | 74 | 59 | 77 | 293 | 269 | 11 | 64 |
| 1934 | 128 | 163 | 78 | 125 | 494 | 88 | 121 | 57 | 66 | 332 | 305 | 13 | 65 |
| 1933 | 119 | 177 | 74 | 115 | 485 | 94 | 105 | 57 | 63 | 319 | 296 | 22 | 62 |
| 1932 | 133 | 155 | 87 | 130 | 505 | 99 | 119 | 63 | 64 | 345 | 329 | 14 | 63 |
| 1931 | 131 | 136 | 98 | 103 | 468 | 105 | 89 | 52 | 75 | 321 | 265 | 8 | 64 |
| 1930 | 127 | 171 | 80 | 115 | 493 | 120 | 86 | 71 | 77 | 354 | 325 | 14 | 67 |
| 1929 | 171 | 192 | 104 | 97 | 564 | 91 | 97 | 69 | 85 | 342 | 316 | 13 | 66 |

*continued*

**Table 1.12** *(cont'd)*

| Year | Admissions | | | | | Calls | | | | | Calls | | Calls as % of admissions 3 yrs earlier[a] |
|---|---|---|---|---|---|---|---|---|---|---|---|---|---|
| | IT | MT | LI | GI | Total | IT | MT | LI | GI | Total | M | F | |
| 1928 | 168 | 170 | 97 | 108 | 543 | 121 | 90 | 53 | 78 | 342 | 324 | 16 | 67 |
| 1927 | 172 | 117 | 105 | 119 | 513 | 99 | 103 | 65 | 69 | 336 | 317 | 15 | 66 |
| 1926 | 186 | 134 | 96 | 120 | 536 | 102 | 93 | 53 | 84 | 332 | 323 | 10 | 67 |
| 1925 | 183 | 142 | 71 | 105 | 501 | 116 | 128 | 70 | 75 | 389 | 361 | 9 | 61 |
| 1924 | 158 | 140 | 101 | 108 | 507 | 108 | 112 | 74 | 72 | 366 | 334 | 18 | 61 |
| 1923 | 169 | 128 | 88 | 125 | 510 | 89 | 164 | 66 | 103 | 422 | 382 | 10 | 73 |
| 1922 | 185 | 146 | 121 | 137 | 589 | 85 | 170 | 53 | 87 | 395 | 377 | 10 | 112 |
| 1921 | 161 | 139 | 94 | 139 | 533 | 86 | 100 | 50 | 79 | 315 | 304 | | 216 |
| 1920 | 163 | 361 | 113 | 161 | 798 | 90 | 86 | 22 | 56 | 254 | 251 | | 171 |
| 1919 | 160 | 258 | 54 | 122 | 594 | 115 | 92 | 29 | 62 | 298 | 300 | | 98 |
| 1918 | 37 | 73 | 21 | 29 | 160 | 48 | 43 | 21 | 37 | 149 | 151 | | 51 |
| 1917 | 33 | 39 | 8 | 29 | 109 | 34 | 52 | 20 | 30 | 136 | 140 | | 44 |
| 1916 | 35 | 48 | 4 | 45 | 132 | 36 | 60 | 38 | 42 | 176 | 176 | | 55 |
| 1915 | 52 | 51 | 20 | 45 | 168 | 37 | 62 | 63 | 41 | 203 | 200 | | 63 |
| 1914 | 108 | 89 | 30 | 67 | 294 | 87 | 114 | 80 | 63 | 344 | 344 | | 72 |
| 1913 | 161 | 106 | 87 | 81 | 435 | 125 | 166 | 130 | 82 | 503 | 495 | | 68 |
| 1912 | 146 | 150 | 80 | 64 | 440 | 108 | 125 | 109 | 72 | 414 | 412 | | 70 |
| 1911 | 156 | 135 | 62 | 82 | 435 | 120 | 108 | 76 | 53 | 357 | 355 | | 68 |
| 1910 | 172 | 269 | 227 | 113 | 781 | 101 | 109 | 66 | 80 | 356 | 333 | | 69 |
| 1909 | 171 | 167 | 129 | 74 | 541 | 108 | 116 | 66 | 55 | 345 | 344 | | 71 |
| 1908 | 179 | 159 | 118 | 86 | 542 | 98 | 84 | 68 | 54 | 304 | 299 | | 70 |
| 1907 | 177 | 170 | 93 | 90 | 530 | 117 | 90 | 66 | 49 | 322 | 297 | | 74 |
| 1906 | 173 | 142 | 82 | 91 | 488 | 110 | 87 | 57 | 44 | 298 | 302 | | 73 |
| 1905 | 157 | 128 | 86 | 70 | 441 | 120 | 94 | 60 | 48 | 322 | 322 | | 76 |
| 1904 | 168 | 108 | 100 | 66 | 442 | 106 | 79 | 56 | 35 | 276 | 272 | | 74 |

|  |  |  |  |  |  |  |  |  |  |  |  |  |
|---|---|---|---|---|---|---|---|---|---|---|---|---|
| 1903 | 151 | 128 | 89 | 60 | 428 | 101 | 72 | 61 | 26 | 260 | 261 | 69 |
| 1902 | 160 | 122 | 68 | 61 | 411 | 107 | 82 | 60 | 41 | 290 | 287 | 66 |
| 1901 | 140 | 112 | 76 | 54 | 382 | 92 | 57 | 44 | 52 | 245 | 248 | 68 |
| 1900 | 136 | 98 | 74 | 34 | 342 | 60 | 47 | 51 | 52 | 210 | 217 | 75 |
| 1899 | 166 | 86 | 82 | 64 | 398 | 106 | 70 | 77 | 38 | 291 | 292 | 75 |
| 1898 | 151 | 97 | 85 | 72 | 405 | 93 | 56 | 80 | 31 | 260 | 260 | 72 |
| 1897 | 111 | 71 | 66 | 75 | 323 | 103 | 65 | 48 | 25 | 241 |  | 69 |
| 1896 | 151 | 70 | 87 | 60 | 368 | 102 | 84 | 51 | 27 | 264 | 261 | 74 |
| 1895 | 120 | 78 | 80 | 42 | 320 | 112 | 85 | 52 | 21 | 270 |  | 77 |
| 1894 | 155 | 94 | 80 | 43 | 372 | 133 | 102 | 50 | 14 | 299 | 304 | 78 |
| 1893 | 144 | 127 | 74 | 29 | 374 | 123 | 103 | 57 | 20 | 303 | 306 | 76 |
| 1892 | 144 | 127 | 68 | 34 | 373 | 124 | 91 | 36 | 19 | 270 | 273 | 75 |
| 1891 | 179 | 125 | 72 |  | 376 | 134 | 87 | 54 |  | 275 | 291 | 70 |
| 1890 | 176 | 115 | 72 | 21 | 384 | 124 | 86 | 49 | 12 | 271 | 266 | 71 |
| 1889 | 185 | 117 | 49 |  | 351 | 95 | 85 | 50 |  | 230 | 252 | 70 |
| 1888 | 186 | 121 | 71 |  | 378 | 113 | 82 | 64 |  | 259 |  | 73 |
| 1887 | 171 | 125 | 63 |  | 359 | 128 | 96 | 42 |  | 266 | 272 | 68 |
| 1886 | 172 | 121 | 81 |  | 374 | 134 | 82 | 41 |  | 257 | 275 | 66 |
| 1885 | 143 | 127 | 65 |  | 335 | 122 | 78 | 56 |  | 251 | 274 | 63 |
| 1884 | 168 | 148 | 50 |  | 366 | 124 | 71 | 51 |  | 246 | 252 | 67 |
| 1883 | 184 | 124 | 55 |  | 363 | 113 | 80 | 40 |  | 233 | 237 | 64 |
| 1882 | 193 | 147 | 73 |  | 413 | 147 | 69 | 52 |  | 268 | 270 | 70 |
| 1881 | 176 | 116 | 77 |  | 369 | 134 | 59 | 63 |  | 256 | 280 | 67 |
| 1880 | 188 | 124 | 76 |  | 381 | 135 | 66 | 71 |  | 272 | 281 | 65 |
| 1879 | 183 | 114 | 73 |  | 370 | 124 | 66 | 72 |  | 261 | 266 | 63 |
| 1878 | 214 | 126 | 85 |  | 425 | 84 | 47 | 56 |  | 187 | 200 | 61 |
| 1877 | 182 | 89 | 75 |  | 346 | 113 | 65 | 74 |  | 252 | 241 | 66 |
| 1876 | 186 | 113 | 99 |  | 398 | 92 | 54 | 58 |  | 204 | 204 | 66 |
| 1875 | 161 | 111 | 87 |  | 359 | 125 | 65 | 69 |  | 259 | 272 | 68 |
| 1874 | 148 | 110 | 89 |  | 347 | 113 | 79 | 78 |  | 270 | 272 | 70 |

*continued*

**Table 1.12** (*cont'd*)

| Year | Admissions | | | | | Calls | | | | | Calls | | Calls as % of admissions 3 yrs earlier[a] |
|---|---|---|---|---|---|---|---|---|---|---|---|---|---|
| | IT | MT | LI | GI | Total | IT | MT | LI | GI | Total | M | F | |
| 1873 | 154 | 99 | 92 | | 345 | 102 | 83 | 95 | | 280 | 273 | | 70 |
| 1872 | 172 | 119 | 105 | | 396 | 105 | 70 | 84 | | 259 | 265 | | 73 |
| 1871 | 128 | 126 | 116 | | 370 | | 67 | 76 | | 244 | 249 | | 71 |
| 1870 | 172 | 130 | 114 | | 416 | 101 | 75 | 57 | | 227 | 229 | | 69 |
| 1869 | 136 | 118 | 112 | | 366 | 95 | 70 | 64 | | 220 | 234 | | 65 |
| 1868 | 141 | 106 | 84 | | 331 | 86 | 63 | 55 | | 203 | 212 | | 66 |
| 1867 | 127 | 98 | 81 | | 306 | 85 | 66 | 56 | | 182 | 183 | | 65 |
| 1866 | 127 | 116 | 87 | | 330 | 60 | 68 | 69 | | 211 | 220 | | 68 |
| 1865 | 111 | 119 | 79 | | 309 | 74 | 60 | 52 | | 189 | 197 | | 69 |
| 1864 | 104 | 102 | 80 | | 286 | 77 | 36 | 65 | | 178 | 187 | | 72 |
| 1863 | 100 | 113 | 89 | | 302 | 77 | 29 | 62 | | 165 | 170 | | 69 |
| 1862 | 103 | 109 | 93 | | 305 | 68 | 37 | 74 | | 173 | 185 | | 66 |
| 1861 | 103 | 74 | 70 | | 247 | 43 | 17 | 61 | | 121 | 130 | | 68 |
| 1860 | 75 | 47 | 93 | | 215 | 35 | 21 | 64 | | 120 | 126 | | 76 |
| 1859 | 101 | 59 | 92 | | 252 | 50 | 28 | 59 | | 137 | 142 | | 73 |
| 1858 | 70 | 33 | 100 | | 203 | 44 | 30 | 58 | | 132 | 135 | | 71 |
| 1857 | 58 | 30 | 81 | | 169 | 42 | 16 | 55 | | 113 | 113 | | 63[b] |

| | | | | | | | | | | |
|---|---|---|---|---|---|---|---|---|---|---|
| 1856 | 59 | 42 | 86 | 187 | 38 | 24 | 51 | 113 | 125 | 65[b] |
| 1855 | 57 | 26 | 72 | 155 | 44 | 26 | 49 | 119 | 105 | |
| 1854 | 65 | 39 | 75 | 179 | 60 | 31 | 49 | 140 | 132 | |
| 1853 | 63 | 32 | 78 | 173 | 74 | 45 | 38 | 157 | 106 | |
| 1852 | | | | | | | | | 103 | |
| 1851 | | | | | | | | | 54 | |
| 1850 | | | | | | | | | 153 | |
| 1849 | | | | | | | | | 110 | |
| 1848 | | | | | | | | | | |
| 1847 | | | | | | | | | 181 | |
| 1846 | | | | | | | | | 182 | |
| 1845 | | | | | | | | | 121 | |
| 1844 | | | | | | | | | 126 | |
| 1843 | | | | | | | | | 108 | |
| 1842 | | | | | | | | | 73 | |
| 1842 | | | | | | | | | 118 | |

IT: Inner Temple
MT: Middle Temple
LI: Lincoln's Inn
GI: Gray's Inn
M,F: male, female
[a] Three-year running totals (of admissions and calls) are used to calculate % in order to dampen effect of short-term fluctuation.
[b] Single-year figures.
*Sources*: Inner Temple Treasurer's Office, admissions and calls by Inn, 1853–1984; *The Times* (second set of figures with male/female)

**Table 1.13** Admissions and calls in Middle Temple, UK and overseas, and percentage called in Middle Temple and Lincoln's Inn with university degree, 1800–1930

| | England | | | | Colonies[a] | | | | Lincoln's Inn |
|---|---|---|---|---|---|---|---|---|---|
| Year | Admitted | Ever called[b] | Called as % of admitted | University degree as % of called | Admitted | Ever called | Called as % of admitted | University degree as % of called | University degree as % of called |
| 1930 | 69 | 53 | 77 | 79 | 106 | 77 | 72 | 74 | |
| 1920 | 180 | 131 | 73 | 31 | 181 | 132 | 73 | 27 | |
| 1910 | 103 | 78 | 76 | 24 | 166 | 137 | 83 | 8 | |
| 1900 | 64 | 54 | 84 | 48 | 34 | 30 | 88 | 21 | |
| 1890 | 71 | 54 | 76 | 61 | 44 | 34 | 77 | 53 | 77 |
| 1880 | 72 | 50 | 69 | 52 | 51 | 37 | 73 | 51 | 88 |
| 1870 | 66 | 57 | 86 | 35 | 56 | 25 | 45 | 52 | 80 |
| 1860 | 24 | 19 | 79 | 37 | 26 | 13 | 50 | 23 | 84 |
| 1850 | 45 | 41 | 91 | | 9 | 3 | 33 | | 88 |
| 1849 | 66 | 49 | 74 | | | | | | |
| 1848 | 52 | 37 | 71 | | | | | | |
| 1847 | 68 | 47 | 69 | | | | | | |
| 1846 | 90 | 65 | 72 | | | | | | |
| 1845 | 73 | 46 | 63 | | | | | | |

| | | | | |
|---|---|---|---|---|
| 1844 | 109 | 81 | 74 | |
| 1843 | 98 | 72 | 73 | |
| 1842 | 94 | 70 | 74 | |
| 1841 | 89 | 67 | 75 | |
| 1840 | 102 | 65 | 64 | 77 |
| 1839 | 103 | 68 | 66 | |
| 1838 | 128 | 78 | 61 | |
| 1837 | 101 | 60 | 59 | |
| 1836 | 78 | 57 | 73 | |
| 1835 | 81 | 51 | 63 | |
| 1834 | 65 | 36 | 55 | |
| 1833 | 49 | 31 | 63 | |
| 1832 | 51 | 25 | 49 | |
| 1831 | 61 | 35 | 57 | |
| 1830 | 62 | 22 | 35 | 53 |
| 1820 | 45 | 26 | 58 | 63 |
| 1810 | 41 | 19 | 46 | 76 |
| 1800 | 24 | 12 | 50 | 44 |

[a] In the late nineteenth century students from the colonies came mostly from Ireland. Before 1850, Irish students are included under the heading of England. Because Irish students were called to the Bar in Ireland, the total called is significantly understated. After 1900 most of the colonial students are from India and increasingly from the new Commonwealth countries.

[b] Increase in admissions and calls 1837–41 may reflect the decline of Gray's Inn.

*Sources*: Sturges, 1949; Lincoln's Inn, 1896

**Table 1.14** Barristers called, by Inns: overseas and UK, men and women, graduates (Oxford, Cambridge, London) and non-graduates
(a) Middle Temple, 1932–52, 1970[c]

| | Overseas[a] | | | United Kingdom | | | | | | | | | |
|---|---|---|---|---|---|---|---|---|---|---|---|---|---|
| | | | | Non-graduates | | | Graduates[b] | | | | | | |
| Year | No. | % of total | % women | No. | % of UK | % women | No. | % of UK | % women | % from Oxford | % from Cam-bridge | % from London | % from Oxbridge and London |
| 1970 | 73 | 43 | 10 | 22 | 23 | 14 | 73 | 77 | 19 | 25 | 27 | 5 | 57 |
| 1952 | 74 | 46 | 3 | 18 | 21 | 6 | 69 | 79 | 10 | 22 | 36 | 22 | 80 |
| 1951 | 49 | 43 | 2 | 11 | 17 | 9 | 53 | 83 | 2 | 34 | 30 | 21 | 85 |
| 1950 | 53 | 38 | 2 | 25 | 30 | 4 | 59 | 70 | 7 | 46 | 25 | 15 | 86 |
| 1949 | 60 | 44 | 3 | 22 | 29 | 14 | 54 | 71 | 6 | 35 | 41 | 9 | 85 |
| 1948 | 70 | 41 | 1 | 28 | 28 | 7 | 71 | 72 | 4 | 37 | 34 | 14 | 85 |
| 1947 | 43 | 39 | 2 | 14 | 21 | 0 | 52 | 79 | 2 | 38 | 46 | 12 | 96 |
| 1946 | 38 | 45 | 3 | 13 | 28 | 8 | 34 | 72 | 3 | 21 | 47 | 18 | 86 |
| 1945 | 28 | 55 | 4 | 13 | 57 | 8 | 10 | 43 | 10 | 30 | 30 | 30 | 90 |
| 1944 | 12 | 44 | 0 | 2 | 13 | 0 | 13 | 87 | 8 | 8 | 23 | 15 | 46 |
| 1943 | 32 | 68 | 0 | 9 | 60 | 0 | 6 | 40 | 0 | 17 | 17 | 0 | 34 |
| 1942 | 30 | 73 | 0 | 2 | 18 | 0 | 9 | 82 | 0 | 22 | 22 | 33 | 77 |
| 1941 | 49 | 79 | 2 | 6 | 46 | 0 | 7 | 54 | 0 | 43 | 29 | 0 | 72 |
| 1940 | 49 | 63 | 0 | 9 | 31 | 0 | 20 | 69 | 10 | 25 | 15 | 35 | 75 |
| 1939 | 58 | 49 | 5 | 17 | 28 | 0 | 43 | 72 | 5 | 35 | 23 | 26 | 84 |
| 1938 | 43 | 44 | 0 | 9 | 17 | 0 | 45 | 83 | 11 | 42 | 31 | 13 | 86 |
| 1937 | 47 | 48 | 0 | 13 | 25 | 8 | 38 | 75 | 0 | 37 | 42 | 13 | 92 |
| 1936 | 51 | 49 | 2 | 14 | 26 | 7 | 39 | 74 | 0 | 36 | 44 | 15 | 95 |
| 1935 | 38 | 52 | 0 | 11 | 31 | 9 | 24 | 69 | 0 | 33 | 46 | 8 | 87 |
| 1934 | 52 | 46 | 2 | 7 | 12 | 0 | 53 | 88 | 6 | 34 | 28 | 9 | 71 |
| 1933 | 62 | 69 | 5 | 9 | 32 | 22 | 19 | 68 | 0 | 53 | 11 | 21 | 85 |
| 1932 | 35 | 60 | 0 | 6 | 26 | 50 | 17 | 74 | 6 | 65 | 12 | 0 | 77 |

[a] Categorized by residence and/or employment. Some overseas may enter practice in UK and vice versa.
[b] Degrees are not all first degrees.
[c] Excludes transfers of barristers previously called at another Inn and honorary barristers. Since the register is kept by year of admission rather than call, some barristers called may have been omitted from 1970 calls if admitted before 1964 and from early 1930s calls if admitted before 1929.

(b) Gray's Inn, 1913–53, 1984

| Year | Overseas[a] | | | United Kingdom | | | | | | | | | |
|---|---|---|---|---|---|---|---|---|---|---|---|---|---|
| | | | | Non-graduates | | | Graduates[b] | | | | | | |
| | No. | % of total | % women | No. | % of UK | % women | No. | % of UK | % women | % from Oxford | % from Cam-bridge | % from London | % from Oxbridge and London |
| 1984 | 42 | 18 | 38 | 0 | 0 | 0 | 193 | 100 | 39 | 7 | 8 | 23 | 38 |
| 1953 | 32 | 24 | 6 | 17 | 17 | 18 | 84 | 83 | 13 | 29 | 25 | 29 | 83 |
| 1952 | 55 | 30 | 0 | 30 | 23 | 3 | 98 | 77 | 17 | 19 | 22 | 29 | 70 |
| 1951 | 58 | 40 | 2 | 14 | 16 | 14 | 72 | 84 | 12 | 17 | 25 | 29 | 71 |
| 1950 | 58 | 41 | 0 | 19 | 22 | 11 | 66 | 78 | 15 | 20 | 26 | 26 | 72 |
| 1949 | 63 | 44 | 0 | 17 | 22 | 6 | 62 | 78 | 11 | 24 | 27 | 29 | 80 |
| 1948 | 48 | 55 | 4 | 10 | 25 | 0 | 30 | 75 | 7 | 27 | 23 | 33 | 83 |
| 1947 | 29 | 32 | 0 | 25 | 40 | 0 | 38 | 60 | 3 | 21 | 32 | 21 | 74 |
| 1946 | 36 | 37 | 3 | 20 | 33 | 0 | 41 | 67 | 2 | 20 | 24 | 22 | 66 |
| 1945 | 19 | 36 | 0 | 14 | 41 | 0 | 20 | 59 | 10 | 10 | 15 | 35 | 60 |
| 1944 | 10 | 36 | 0 | 11 | 61 | 0 | 7 | 39 | 0 | 14 | 14 | 28 | 56 |
| 1943 | 11 | 35 | 0 | 7 | 35 | 14 | 13 | 65 | 0 | 38 | 15 | 15 | 68 |
| 1942 | 10 | 33 | 0 | 11 | 55 | 0 | 9 | 45 | 0 | 0 | 0 | 67 | 67 |
| 1941 | 14 | 44 | 7 | 5 | 28 | 0 | 13 | 72 | 0 | 8 | 23 | 46 | 77 |
| 1940 | 18 | 45 | 0 | 6 | 27 | 0 | 16 | 73 | 12 | 19 | 12 | 44 | 75 |
| 1939 | 22 | 33 | 0 | 16 | 36 | 12 | 29 | 64 | 3 | 21 | 28 | 31 | 80 |
| 1938 | 26 | 35 | 0 | 12 | 25 | 25 | 36 | 75 | 8 | 42 | 22 | 22 | 86 |
| 1937 | 23 | 38 | 13 | 3 | 8 | 33 | 35 | 92 | 6 | 17 | 23 | 26 | 66 |
| 1936 | 20 | 33 | 10 | 7 | 17 | 14 | 34 | 83 | 3 | 35 | 12 | 26 | 73 |
| 1935 | 32 | 42 | 0 | 6 | 14 | 17 | 38 | 86 | 5 | 13 | 21 | 39 | 73 |

*continued*

**Table 1.14** *(cont'd)*

(b) Gray's Inn, 1913–53, 1984

| | Overseas[a] | | | United Kingdom | | | | | | | | | |
|---|---|---|---|---|---|---|---|---|---|---|---|---|---|
| | | | | Non-graduates | | | Graduates[b] | | | | | | |
| Year | No. | % of total | % women | No. | % of UK | % women | No. | % of UK | % women | % from Oxford | % from Cam-bridge | % from London | % from Oxbridge and London |
| 1934 | 24 | 36 | 0 | 5 | 12 | 0 | 37 | 88 | 5 | 19 | 32 | 30 | 81 |
| 1933 | 28 | 44 | 0 | 8 | 23 | 12 | 27 | 77 | 4 | 33 | 30 | 22 | 85 |
| 1932 | 24 | 38 | 4 | 9 | 22 | 11 | 31 | 78 | 6 | 23 | 19 | 32 | 74 |
| 1931 | 23 | 31 | 0 | 14 | 27 | 7 | 37 | 73 | 5 | 30 | 22 | 35 | 87 |
| 1930 | 21 | 28 | 0 | 10 | 19 | 30 | 44 | 81 | 2 | 23 | 20 | 23 | 66 |
| 1929 | 27 | 33 | 0 | 12 | 21 | 0 | 44 | 79 | 5 | 18 | 30 | 43 | 91 |
| 1928 | 26 | 33 | 0 | 13 | 25 | 8 | 40 | 75 | 5 | 25 | 45 | 18 | 88 |
| 1927 | 20 | 29 | 0 | 10 | 21 | 10 | 38 | 79 | 8 | 24 | 32 | 18 | 74 |
| 1926 | 31 | 37 | 0 | 17 | 33 | 0 | 35 | 67 | 3 | 23 | 37 | 26 | 86 |
| 1925 | 15 | 20 | 0 | 22 | 37 | 0 | 38 | 63 | 5 | 23 | 37 | 21 | 81 |
| 1924 | 23 | 32 | 4 | 21 | 42 | 10 | 29 | 58 | 3 | 17 | 31 | 38 | 86 |
| 1923 | 28 | 27 | 0 | 33 | 43 | 0 | 43 | 57 | 2 | 23 | 23 | 28 | 74 |
| 1922 | 35 | 41 | 0 | 19 | 37 | 0 | 32 | 63 | 0 | 19 | 38 | 16 | 73 |
| 1921 | 45 | 56 | 0 | 18 | 51 | 0 | 17 | 49 | 0 | 24 | 65 | 6 | 95 |
| 1920 | 24 | 43 | 0 | 9 | 28 | 0 | 23 | 72 | 0 | 22 | 22 | 26 | 70 |
| 1919 | 25 | 41 | 0 | 17 | 47 | 0 | 19 | 53 | 0 | 16 | 16 | 32 | 64 |
| 1918 | 22 | 58 | 0 | 8 | 50 | 0 | 8 | 50 | 0 | 0 | 50 | 25 | 75 |
| 1917 | 19 | 61 | 0 | 4 | 33 | 0 | 8 | 67 | 0 | 0 | 25 | 25 | 50 |
| 1916 | 34 | 79 | 0 | 3 | 33 | 0 | 6 | 67 | 0 | 0 | 50 | 33 | 83 |
| 1915 | 25 | 61 | 0 | 9 | 56 | 0 | 7 | 44 | 0 | 0 | 14 | 43 | 57 |
| 1914 | 36 | 58 | 0 | 16 | 62 | 0 | 10 | 38 | 0 | 30 | 50 | 20 | 100 |
| 1913 | 35 | 54 | 0 | 20 | 67 | 0 | 10 | 33 | 0 | 20 | 30 | 50 | 100 |

[a] Overseas includes those with residences overseas (including Ireland and Northern Ireland), unless the student's father is retired or deceased.
[b] Degrees are not all first degrees.
*Source*: Gray's Inn list of students desirous of being called to the Bar this term

| | Overseas[a] | | | United Kingdom | | | | | | | | | |
|---|---|---|---|---|---|---|---|---|---|---|---|---|---|
| | | | | Non-graduates | | | Graduates[b] | | | | | | |
| Year | No. | % of total | % women | No. | % of UK | % women | No. | % of UK | % women | % from Oxford | % from Cam-bridge | % from London | % from Oxbridge and London |
| 1984 | | | | | | | 102 | 100 | 38 | | | | |
| 1952 | 91 | 59 | 6 | 7 | 11 | 0 | 55 | 89 | 7 | | | | |
| 1951 | | | | | | 13[c] | | | 13[c] | | | | |
| 1950 | | | | | | 15[c] | | | 15[c] | | | | |
| 1949 | | | | | | 8[c] | | | 8[c] | | | | |
| 1948 | | | | | | 8[c] | | | 8[c] | | | | |
| 1947 | | | | | | 9[c] | | | 9[c] | | | | |
| 1946 | 21 | 39 | 10 | 8 | 24 | 0 | 25 | 76 | 0 | 36 | 28 | 4 | 68 |
| 1945 | 9 | 41 | 0 | 1 | 8 | 0 | 12 | 92 | 17 | 33 | 25 | 42 | 100 |
| 1944 | 13 | 62 | 0 | 2 | 25 | 0 | 6 | 75 | 17 | 50 | 33 | 17 | 100 |
| 1943 | 9 | 82 | 0 | 0 | 0 | 0 | 2 | 100 | 0 | 0 | 100 | 0 | 100 |
| 1942[d] | 14 | 88 | 0 | 0 | 0 | 0 | 2 | 100 | 0 | 50 | 50 | 0 | 100 |
| 1941 | 24 | 75 | 0 | 2 | 25 | 0 | 6 | 75 | 0 | 17 | 50 | 33 | 100 |
| 1940 | 37 | 77 | 0 | 4 | 36 | 25 | 7 | 64 | 0 | 14 | 58 | 14 | 85 |
| 1939 | 34 | 72 | 3 | 4 | 31 | 50 | 9 | 69 | 11 | 44 | 33 | 0 | 77 |
| 1938 | 26 | 58 | 4 | 2 | 11 | 0 | 17 | 89 | 0 | 24 | 24 | 24 | 72 |
| 1937 | 26 | 55 | 4 | 1 | 5 | 0 | 20 | 95 | 5 | 20 | 65 | 15 | 100 |
| 1936[d] | 20 | 61 | 0 | 1 | 8 | 0 | 12 | 92 | 0 | 42 | 33 | 25 | 100 |
| 1935 | 30 | 51 | 3 | 4 | 14 | 0 | 25 | 86 | 0 | 48 | 32 | 20 | 100 |
| 1934[e] | 8 | 62 | 12 | 1 | 20 | 100 | 4 | 80 | 0 | 25 | 50 | 25 | 100 |
| 1933 | 28 | 49 | 7 | 7 | 24 | 29 | 22 | 76 | 5 | 41 | 50 | 9 | 100 |
| 1932 | 34 | 71 | 6 | 4 | 29 | 25 | 10 | 71 | 0 | 30 | 50 | 10 | 90 |
| 1931 | 26 | 52 | 0 | 1 | 4 | 0 | 23 | 96 | 4 | 52 | 39 | 9 | 100 |
| 1930 | 40 | 56 | 0 | 3 | 10 | 33 | 28 | 90 | 0 | 57 | 25 | 4 | 86 |
| 1929 | 30 | 68 | 0 | 0 | 0 | 0 | 14 | 100 | 14 | 36 | 43 | 14 | 93 |
| 1928[f] | 23 | 55 | 0 | 2 | 11 | 0 | 17 | 89 | 6 | 71 | 24 | 6 | 100 |

[a] Categorized by residence and/or employment.
[b] Degrees are not all first degrees.
[c] Percentage applies to all UK calls.
[d] Only two terms.
[e] Only one term.
[f] Only three terms.

*Source:* Lincoln's Inn call list

**Table 1.14** (*Cont'd*)
(d) Inner Temple (admissions), 1867, 1886, 1907, 1927

| | Overseas[a] | | United Kingdom | | | | | | | |
|---|---|---|---|---|---|---|---|---|---|---|
| | | | Non-graduates | | Graduates[b] | | | | | |
| Year | No. | % of total | No. | % of UK | No. | % of UK | % from Oxford | % from Cam-bridge | % from London | % from Oxbridge and London |
| 1927 | 54 | 45 | 21 | 32 | 44 | 68 | 55 | 32 | 5 | 82 |
| 1907 | 31 | 18 | 13 | 9 | 133 | 91 | 53 | 39 | 5 | 97 |
| 1886 | 35 | 20 | 23 | 17 | 115 | 83 | 57 | 37 | 3 | 97 |
| 1867 | 7 | 5 | 17 | 13 | 109 | 87 | 50 | 39 | 4 | 93 |

[a] Categorized by residence and/or employment.
[b] Degrees are not all first degrees.
[c] Some may matriculate at university later, since many are only 18 years old.
*Source*: Inner Temple Treasurer's Office, Inner Temple warrants for admission

**Table 1.15** Undergraduate education of barristers in Gray's Inn, 1984: numbers called

| *University* | | *Polytechnic* | |
|---|---|---|---|
| Aberystwyth | 1 | Birmingham | 1 |
| Aston | 1 | Bristol | 3 |
| Birmingham | 5 | City of London | 2 |
| Bradford | 1 | Kingston | 4 |
| Bristol | 7 | Leeds | 2 |
| Brunel | 2 | Leicester | 1 |
| Buckingham | 2 | Liverpool | 5 |
| Cambridge | 15 | Manchester | 7 |
| Cardiff | 6 | Middlesex | 5 |
| Durham | 2 | Newcastle | 1 |
| East Anglia | 5 | North London | 2 |
| Essex | 1 | Portsmouth | 1 |
| Exeter | 2 | Teesside | 1 |
| Keele | 8 | Wolverhampton | 3 |
| Kent | 5 | | |
| Lancaster | 1 | *Other* | |
| Leeds | 2 | Chelmer Inst. of Higher Educ. | 3 |
| Leicester | 5 | Ealing CHE | 5 |
| Liverpool | 6 | Wimbledon School of Art | 1 |
| London | 45 | | |
| Manchester | 11 | *Non-graduates* | 7 |
| Newcastle | 2 | | |
| Nottingham | 5 | *Total* | 229 |
| Oxford | 14 | | |
| Queen's (Belfast) | 1 | | |
| Reading | 4 | | |
| Rhodes (S. Af.) | 1 | | |
| Sheffield | 1 | | |
| Southampton | 2 | | |
| St Andrews (Scotland) | 1 | | |
| Sussex | 1 | | |
| Trinity (Dublin) | 1 | | |
| UWIST | 2 | | |
| Warwick | 5 | | |
| Witwatersrand (S. Af.) | 1 | | |
| York | 1 | | |

*Source*: Gray's Inn list of students desirous of being called to the Bar this term

**Table 1.16** Number of barristers, 1947–85

| | | Change in previous year | | | | | Called to Bar | | | | | | Admitted to Inns[a] | | | |
|---|---|---|---|---|---|---|---|---|---|---|---|---|---|---|---|---|
| | Number in private practice 30 Sept. | No. starting practice | No. ceasing practice | | Net gain | Gain as % of prior year's total | Total | British domicile | Overseas domicile | | Women barristers | | Total | UK | Overseas domicile | |
| | | | over 10 years | under 10 years | | | | | no. | % | number | % of Bar | | | no. | % |
| 1985 | 5367 | 335 | 103 | 68 | 164 | 3.2 | 945 | 694 | 251 | 27 | 696 | 13.0 | 1147 | 836 | 311 | 27 |
| 1984 | 5203 | 325 | 99 | 55 | 171 | 3.4 | 902 | 670 | 232 | 26 | 641 | 12.3 | 1227 | 869 | 358 | 29 |
| 1983 | 5032 | 323 | 95 | 60 | 168 | 3.5 | 1052 | 758 | 294 | 28 | 573 | 11.4 | 1263 | 883 | 380 | 30 |
| 1982 | 4864 | 282 | 51 | 52 | 179 | 3.8 | 936 | 682 | 254 | 27 | 524 | 10.8 | 1357 | 873 | 484 | 36 |
| 1981 | 4685 | 270 | 102 | 72 | 96 | 2.1 | 904 | 657 | 247 | 27 | 472 | 10.1 | 1247 | 849 | 398 | 32 |
| 1980 | 4589 | 309 | 50 | 82 | 177 | 4.0 | 862 | 624 | 238 | 28 | 447 | 9.7 | 1007 | 722 | 285 | 28 |
| 1979 | 4412 | 302 | 71 | 82 | 149 | 3.5 | 896 | 670 | 226 | 25 | 409 | 9.3 | 951 | 684 | 276 | 29 |
| 1978 | 4263 | 285 | 28 | 70 | 187 | 4.6 | 954 | 671 | 283 | 29 | 370 | 8.7 | 842 | 596 | 246 | 29 |
| 1977 | 4076 | 326 | 52 | 79 | 195 | 5.0 | 843 | 654 | 189 | 22 | 336 | 8.7 | 794 | 616 | 183 | 23 |
| 1976 | 3881 | 382 | 106 | 41 | 235 | 6.4 | 857 | 628 | 229 | 27 | 313 | 8.1 | 1059 | 827 | 232 | 22 |
| 1975 | 3646 | 364 | 27 | 49 | 278 | 8.3 | 902 | 663 | 239 | 27 | 258 | 7.1 | 1817 | 1023 | 794 | 44 |
| 1974 | 3368 | 299 | 30 | 38 | 231 | 7.4 | 741 | 529 | 212 | 29 | 252 | 7.5 | 1322 | 840 | 482 | 36 |
| 1973 | 3137 | 321 | 88 | 15 | 218 | 7.5 | 913 | 561 | 352 | 38 | 239 | 7.6 | 1255 | 838 | 417 | 33 |
| 1972 | 2919 | 275 | 44 | 26 | 200 | 7.4 | 1011 | 586 | 425 | 42 | 196 | 6.7 | 1133 | 745 | 388 | 34 |
| 1971 | 2714 | 222 | 80 | 12 | 130 | 5.0 | 979 | 556 | 423 | 43 | 167 | 6.2 | 1022 | 659 | 363 | 36 |
| 1970 | 2584 | 241 | 72 | 33 | 136 | 5.6 | 935 | 471 | 464 | 50 | 147 | 5.7 | 857 | 537 | 320 | 37 |
| 1969 | 2448 | 137 | 48 | 20 | 69 | 2.9 | 688 | 370 | 318 | 46 | 133 | 5.4 | 1258 | 692 | 566 | 45 |
| | | | | | | | | | | | | | 1255 | 674 | 581 | 46 |

| | | | | | | | | | | | | | | | | |
|---|---|---|---|---|---|---|---|---|---|---|---|---|---|---|---|---|
| 1968 | 2379 | 139 | 62 | | 31 | 46 | 2.0 | 525 | 246 | 279 | 53 | 138 | 5.8 | 1389 | 705 | 684 | 49 |
| | | | | | | | | | | | | | | 1401 | 759 | 642 | 46 |
| 1967 | 2333 | 206 | 87 | | 25 | 94 | 4.2 | 559 | 247 | 312 | 56 | 127 | 5.4 | 1739 | 931 | 805 | 46 |
| | | | | | | | | | | | | | | 1737 | 931 | 806 | 46 |
| 1966 | 2239 | 129 | 38 | | 16 | 75 | 3.5 | 528 | 236 | 292 | 55 | 117 | 5.2 | 1444 | 683 | 761 | 53 |
| | | | | | | | | | | | | | | 1440 | 699 | 741 | 51 |
| 1965 | 2164 | 138 | 65 | | 27 | 46 | 2.2 | 751 | 283 | 466 | 63 | 99 | 4.6 | 1708 | 663 | 1045 | 61 |
| 1964 | 2118 | 80 | 24 | | 11 | 45 | 2.2 | 729 | 237 | 492 | 67 | 98 | 4.6 | 1630 | 578 | 1052 | 65 |
| 1963 | 2073 | 158 | 33 | | 16 | 109 | 5.5 | 792 | 198 | 594 | 75 | 103 | 5.0 | 1514 | 541 | 973 | 64 |
| 1962 | 1964 | 110 | | 81 | | 46 | 2.4 | 737 | 205 | 532 | 72 | 97 | 4.9 | 1782 | | | |
| 1961 | 1918 | 108 | | 92 | | −1 | −0.1 | 687 | 211 | 476 | 69 | 91 | 4.7 | 1566 | | | |
| 1960 | 1919 | 85 | 62 | | 27 | −4 | −0.2 | 682 | 192 | 490 | 72 | 84 | 4.4 | | | | |
| 1959 | 1923 | 88 | 44 | | 68 | −24 | −1.2 | 692 | 252 | 440 | 64 | 81 | 4.2 | | | | |
| 1958 | 1947 | 91 | 46 | | 66 | −21 | −1.1 | 626 | 234 | 392 | 62 | 80 | 4.1 | | | | |
| 1957 | 1968 | 97 | 41 | | 61 | −5 | −0.3 | 546 | 241 | 305 | 56 | 78 | 4.0 | | | | |
| 1956 | 1973 | 111 | 82 | | 64 | −35 | −1.7 | 523 | 265 | 258 | 50 | 68 | 3.4 | | | | |
| 1955 | 2008 | 114 | 54 | | 62 | −2 | −0.1 | 601 | 288 | 313 | 52 | 64 | 3.2 | | | | |
| 1954 | 2010 | 136 | | | | 103 | 5.4 | 513 | 303 | 210 | 41 | 71 | 3.5 | | | | |
| | | | | | | | | | | | | 73 | | | | | |
| 1953 | 1907 | 155 | | | | | | 536 | 328 | 208 | 40 | | | | | | |
| 1952 | | 165 | | | | | | 597 | 350 | 247 | 41 | | | | | | |
| 1951 | | 174 | | | | | | 501 | 340 | 161 | 33 | | | | | | |
| 1950 | | 156 | | | | | | 551 | 336 | 215 | 39 | | | | | | |
| 1949 | | 196 | | | | | | 514 | 317 | 197 | 39 | | | | | | |
| 1948 | | 177 | | | | | | 481 | 322 | 159 | 33 | | | | | | |
| 1947 | | 131 | | | | | | 372 | 253 | 119 | 32 | | | | | | |

[a] Where two figures are given for a single year, sources differ.

*Sources*: Senate, Annual Statements; Ormrod Committee, 1971: 114–15; Royal Commission, 1979, vol. 2: 53; Senate, 1977a: I.3; Layton et al., 1978b: 30

**Table 1.17** Calls as proportion of admissions (UK/overseas) and starts as proportion of calls (UK), 1947–84

(a) Number called as % of number admitted, three-year running total

| | Years between admission and call | | | |
|---|---|---|---|---|
| | UK | | Overseas | |
| | 2 | 3 | 2 | 3 |
| 1983 | 93 | 105 | 83 | 99 |
| 1982 | 98 | 104 | 92 | 105 |
| 1981 | 103 | 96 | 101 | 108 |
| 1980 | 96 | 80 | 113 | 62 |
| 1979 | 82 | 74 | 58 | 46 |
| 1978 | 73 | 72 | 46 | 41 |
| 1977 | 72 | 80 | 39 | 51 |
| 1976 | 75 | 81 | 53 | 58 |
| 1975 | 78 | 90 | 69 | 75 |
| 1974 | 86 | 89 | 92 | 79 |
| 1973 | 91 | 87 | 96 | 77 |
| 1972 | 83 | 69 | 84 | 64 |
| 1971 | 60 | 59 | 59 | 54 |
| 1970 | 46 | 48 | 48 | 41 |
| 1969 | 38 | 45 | 35 | 32 |
| 1968 | 38 | 41 | 31 | 29 |
| 1967 | 43 | | 35 | |
| 1982–66 | 73 | 74 | 56 | 52 |
| 1982–72 | 86 | 86 | 73 | 68 |
| 1971–66 | 50 | 50 | 43 | 39 |

(b) Number starting practice as % of UK calls

| Year | Year starting practice: Same as call | Year starting practice: Next year | Year | Year starting practice: Same as call | Year starting practice: Next year |
|---|---|---|---|---|---|
| 1984 | 49 | 43 | 1958 | 39 | 38 |
| 1983 | 43 | 47 | 1957 | 40 | 32 |
| 1982 | 41 | 43 | 1956 | 42 | 39 |
| 1981 | 41 | 43 | 1955 | 40 | 38 |
| 1980 | 50 | 46 | 1954 | 45 | 41 |
| 1979 | 45 | 45 | 1953 | 47 | 44 |
| 1978 | 42 | 44 | 1952 | 47 | 49 |
| 1977 | 50 | 52 | 1951 | 51 | 52 |
| 1976 | 61 | 58 | 1950 | 46 | 49 |
| 1975 | 55 | 69 | 1949 | 62 | 61 |
| 1974 | 57 | 53 | 1948 | 55 | 70 |
| 1973 | 57 | 55 | 1947 | 52 | |
| 1972 | 47 | 49 | | | |
| 1971 | 40 | 47 | 1982–47 | 49 | 50 |
| 1970 | 51 | 65 | | | |
| 1969 | 37 | 56 | 1982–78 | 44 | |
| 1968 | 57 | 56 | 1977–69 | 51 | |
| 1967 | 83 | 87 | 1968–62 | 58 | |
| 1966 | 55 | 46 | 1961–55 | 41 | |
| 1965 | 49 | 58 | 1954–47 | 51 | |
| 1964 | 34 | 40 | | | |
| 1963 | 80 | 77 | | | |
| 1962 | 54 | 52 | | | |
| 1961 | 51 | 56 | | | |
| 1960 | 44 | 34 | | | |
| 1959 | 35 | 38 | | | |

Layton et al. (1978a: 73–4 and nn. 10–11) make similar calculations assuming 1.5–2 and 2.5–3 years between admission and call for UK students and 3.5–4 years for

**Table 1.18** Proportion of barristers admitted to Middle Temple (1950, 1960 and 1970) ever called, UK and Overseas

| | Overseas | | | UK | | |
|---|---|---|---|---|---|---|
| Year admitted | Number admitted | Number ever called | Calls as % of admissions | Number admitted | Number ever called | Calls as % of admissions |
| 1970[a] | 74 | 23 | 31 | 144 | 103 | 72 |
| 1960 | 236 | 141 | 60 | 83 | 45 | 54 |
| 1950 | 90 | 66 | 73 | 171 | 70 | 41 |

[a] Includes only calls before 1 January 1976.
*Source*: Middle Temple, 1977

**Table 1.19** Inns of Court School of Law: applications, registrations, tuition and financial support, 1973–85

| | | Registrations | | | Tuition (£) | | No. of LEAs granting | | | % of intending practitioners receiving grants | |
|---|---|---|---|---|---|---|---|---|---|---|---|
| Year (autumn) | Applications | Total | Intending | Non-intending | Intending | Non-intending | Full support | Partial support | None | UK | Non-UK |
| 1986 | | | | | 1225 | 1124 | | | | | |
| 1985 | 1230 | 932 | 737 | 195 | 1035 | 950 | 41 | 57 | 4 | 74.5 | 48.8 |
| 1984 | 1409 | 887 | 754 | 133 | 963 | 883 | 42 | 52 | 3 | 80.1 | 62.0 |
| 1983 | 1404 | 929 | 725 | 204 | 860 | 788 | 46 | 52 | 3 | 86 | 42 |
| 1982 | 1418 | 1026 | 800 | 226 | 860 | 788 | | | | 81 | 45 |
| 1981 | 1240 | 1053 | 688 | 365 | 822 | | | | | 84 | |
| 1980 | 966 | 840 | 589 | 251 | | | | | | | |
| 1979 | 957 | 779 | 521 | 258 | | | | | | | |
| 1978 | 1023 | 882 | 575 | 307 | | | | | | | |
| 1977 | | 921 | | | | | | | | | |
| 1976 | | 799 | | | | | | | | | |
| 1975 | | 826 | | | | | | | | | |
| 1974 | | 860 | | | | | | | | | |
| 1973 | | 833 | | | | | | | | | |

*Sources*: Senate, Annual Statement, 1983–4: 26, 42; 1984–5: 39; 1985–6: 60–2; Whitfield and Walker Report, 1985; AGCAS, 1981b: 3

## Composition

**Table 1.20** Age at call of UK barristers called to Bar in Middle Temple, 1970

| Age | Number | Per cent |
|---|---|---|
| 21 | 8 | 9 |
| 22 | 22 | 24 |
| 23 | 32 | 34 |
| 24 | 7 | 8 |
| 25 | 6 | 6 |
| 26 | 5 | 5 |
| 27 | 4 | 4 |
| 28 | 1 | 1 |
| 29 | 2 | 2 |
| 30–9 | 3 | 3 |
| 40–9 | 2 | 2 |
| Over 49 | 1 | 1 |
| Total | 93 | 100 |
| Median | 22–3 | |
| Mean | 23.0 | |

*Source*: Middle Temple, 1977

**Table 1.21** Occupations of fathers of barristers (UK residents) at time of call
(a) Gray's Inn, 1984, 1953

| Category | No. | Occupations (no. if more than one) |
|---|---|---|
| *1984* | | |
| Professional | 67 | engineer (16); management consultant (5); accountant (4); barrister (7); physician (10); schoolmaster/teacher (5); nurse; university teacher (6); architect; surveyor (4); solicitor; dentist; ophthalmic optician; physicist; tax consultant; financial consultant; pharmacist (2); MP |
| Business executive | 26 | company director (14); marketing executive; sales and marketing director (2); banker (2); sales manager (2); administrator (2); contracts manager; business executive; engineering director |
| Entrepreneur | 14 | farmer (2); businessman (2); dairy contractor; contract furnisher; property developer; building contractor (3); antique dealer; display manufacturer; freight forwarder; grocer |
| White-collar employee | 34 | probation officer (2); civil servant (4); forestry consultant; projects manager; local government (2); metallurgist; schools inspector; head mill representative; clerk (3); media (3); litigation clerk; diplomatic service; secretary (3); office manager; chair, industrial tribunal; polytechnic administrator (2); data processor; military systems analyst; insurance broker; inspector; technical information manager; airline pilot |
| Blue-collar employee | 19 | master mariner; postman; National Trust custodian; school caretaker (2); steelworker; police (3); miner (2); factory worker; butcher; driver; storeman; joiner; construction foreman; electrician; refrigerator plant operator |
| Total | 160 | |
| *1953* | | |
| Professional | 44 | engineer (17); architect (3); military (3); barrister (4); clergy (4); judge (4); physician (6); MP (2); author (3); headmaster; accountant (2); solicitor; professor; newspaper editor; teacher (2) |
| Gentleman | 1 | |
| Business executive | 15 | manager (3); bank officer; company director (9); insurance manager; publisher |
| Entrepreneur | 9 | farmer (2); military outfitter; merchant (3); insurance broker; ship broker; boat builder; stockbroker |
| White-collar employee | 20 | civil servant (9); journalist (3); sub-postmaster; local government; railway clerk; solicitor's managing clerk; shipping surveyor; tax inspector; clerk; insurance underwriter |
| Blue-collar employee | 3 | tailor; police (2) |
| Total | 92 | |

(b) Middle Temple, 1970, 1952

| Category | No. | Occupations (no. if more than one) |
| --- | --- | --- |
| *1970* | | |
| Professional | 49 | vice-principal CFE; military (7); schoolmaster (6); physician (11); accountant (2); engineer (8); clergy; architect; patent agent; solicitor (2); lecturer (2); chartered surveyor (2); forensic pathologist; barrister (4) |
| Business executive | 15 | company director (8); bank manager (3); advertising director; chief executive officer; BOAC manager; sales executive |
| Entrepreneur | 7 | wine shipper; clothing manufacturer; businessman (2); farmer; off-licensee |
| White-collar employee | 21 | stockbroker clerk; maintenance supervisor; diplomat (2); chartered land agent; insurance clerk; optician; garage director (2); civil servant (2); commercial traveller; factory manager; solicitor's clerk; secretary; nutritionist; bank official; inspector of taxes; actuary; salesman; company representative |
| Blue-collar employee | 2 | porter; cotton spinner |
| Total | 84 | |
| *1952* | | |
| Professional | 31 | MP; solicitor (7); military (3); physician (7); stock exchange member; accountant (2); clergy (2); architect; barrister; college principal; schoolmaster; engineer (3); county court registrar |
| Business executive | 8 | company director (8) |
| Entrepreneur | 11 | fruit broker; manufacturer (3); merchant; builder; furniture dealer; farmer (2); linen draper; jeweller |
| White-collar employee | 12 | commercial traveller; journal editor; civil servant (4); motor agent; purchasing agent; journalist; colliery official; surveyor; diplomat |
| Blue-collar employee | 4 | tailor; police (2); British Rail |
| Total | 66 | |

(c) Lincoln's Inn, 1945–6, 1936–44, 1927–35

| Category | No. | Occupations (no. if more than one) |
|---|---|---|
| *1945–6* | | |
| Professional | 16 | solicitor (5); barrister (3); JP; pharmacist; military; MP; physician (2); agricultural engineer; minister |
| Gentleman | 4 | |
| Business executive | 5 | shipping manager; commercial manager; managing director (2); banker |
| Entrepreneur | 8 | timber merchant; shipping broker; paper merchant; merchant (3); furniture manufacturer |
| White-collar employee | 6 | solicitor's managing clerk; clerk (2); civil servant (2); accountant's clerk |
| Blue-collar employee | 0 | |
| Total | 39 | |
| *1936–44* | | |
| Professional | 41 | quantity surveyor; solicitor (4); barrister (9); hospital matron; military (4); university teacher (3); chartered accountant; headmaster (2); physician (4); bank accountant; surveyor; engineer (3); minister (4); scientist; playwright; singing teacher |
| Gentleman | 6 | |
| Business executive | 8 | company director (6); manager; bank manager |
| Entrepreneur | 13 | jeweller; merchant (2); mill owner; grain merchant; master builder; grocer; merchant tailor; mine owner; farmer (2); stockbroker; furniture manufacturer |
| White-collar employee | 9 | civil servant (3); teacher; solicitor's managing clerk; savings bank actuary; local government official; company secretary; commercial traveller |
| Blue-collar employee | 1 | worsted spinner |
| Total | 78 | |
| *1927–35* | | |
| Professional | 89 | barrister (29); engineer (3); judge (3); physician (10); magistrate; military (10); university teacher (2); MP (2); author; Privy Councillor; schoolmaster (4); minister (5); solicitor (10); dentist; engineer (3); pharmacist; Speaker, House of Commons; naturalist; conveyancing counsel |
| Gentleman | 36 | |
| Business executive | 9 | company director (6); general manager; co-operative society manager; insurance manager |
| Entrepreneur | 19 | leather merchant; cotton broker (2); ship broker; chemical manufacturer; produce broker; stock jobber; merchant (8); stockbroker (2); manufacturer; farmer |
| White-collar employee | 9 | civil servant (6); police superintendent; schools inspector; solicitor's managing clerk |
| Blue-collar employee | 2 | silk thrower; silk spinner |
| Total | 164 | |

(d) Inner Temple (admissions), 1907, 1886, 1867

| Category | No. | Occupations (no. if more than one) |
|---|---|---|
| *1907* | | |
| Professional | 76 | JP (7); barrister (13); military (10); accountant; judge (2); Inspector-General in bankruptcy; solicitor (9); engineer (6); university teacher; MP (3); clergy (10); physician (8); schoolmaster (2); stockbroker (3) |
| Gentleman | 1 | |
| Business executive | 2 | company director; banker |
| Entrepreneur | 21 | merchant (11); manufacturer (6); brewer (2); publisher; ship owner |
| White-collar employee | 4 | school inspector; diplomatic corps; actuary; civil servant |
| Blue-collar employee | 0 | |
| Total | 104 | |
| *1886* | | |
| Professional | 51 | military (5); physician (2); clergy (15); barrister (6); solicitor (10); JP (4); judge (2); Attorney-General; engineer (3); MP (2); schoolmaster |
| Gentleman | 23 | |
| Business executive | 1 | company director |
| Entrepreneur | 23 | merchant (14); manufacturer (15); landowner; publisher; contractor; farmer; brewer |
| White-collar employee | 9 | civil servant (5); schools inspector; bank manager (2); cashier |
| Blue-collar employee | 0 | |
| Total | 107 | |
| *1867* | | |
| Professional | 52 | university teacher; physician (3); stockbroker (3); clergy (16); judge (2); JP (3); barrister (8); MP (2); solicitor (8); military (4); police magistrate; engineer |
| Gentleman | 43 | |
| Business executive | 0 | |
| Entrepreneur | 3 | merchant (3) |
| White-collar employee | 15 | civil service (6); land agent; clerk (4); diplomatic corps (2); postmaster; company secretary |
| Blue-collar employee | 0 | |
| Total | 113 | |

**Table 1.22** Women at the Bar: proportions of calls, QCs and benchers, 1960–85

| | Women as % of calls | New Queen's Counsel | | | Women as % of QCs | Women as % of benchers |
|---|---|---|---|---|---|---|
| | | Total | Women | % | | |
| 1985 | | 48 | 5 | 10 | 2 | |
| 1984 | | 42 | 0 | 0 | 2 | |
| 1983 | | 40 | 2 | 5 | 2 | |
| 1982 | | 56 | 4 | 7 | | |
| 1981 | | 52 | 0 | 0 | | |
| 1980 | | 53 | 1 | 2 | | 1.7 |
| 1979 | | 52 | 3 | 6 | | |
| 1978 | | 40 | 0 | 0 | 1 | |
| 1977 | | 29 | 1 | 3 | | 1 |
| 1976 | | 30 | 1 | 3 | 1 | 0.5 |
| 1975 | 17 | 34 | 1 | 3 | | |
| 1974 | 19 | 32 | 0 | 0 | | |
| 1973 | 17 | 46 | 1 | 2 | | |
| 1972 | 15 | 44 | 0 | 0 | | |
| 1971 | *c*.16 | 37 | 0 | 0 | | |
| 1970 | 19 | 32 | 1 | 3 | | |
| 1969 | 25 | 38 | 0 | 0 | | |
| 1968 | | 32 | 0 | 0 | | |
| 1967 | | 31 | 0 | 0 | | |
| 1966 | | 22 | 0 | 0 | | |
| 1965 | 15 | 40 | 0 | 0 | | |
| 1964 | | 18 | 0 | 0 | | |
| 1963 | | 17 | 0 | 0 | | |
| 1962 | | 18 | 0 | 0 | | |
| 1961 | | 34 | 0 | 0 | | |
| 1960 | 17 | 22 | 1 | 5 | | |

*Sources*: Knightly and Colton Report, 1971; Bar List, 1981: 132–7; 1984; Royal Commission, 1979, vol. 2: 443; Equal Opportunities Commission, 1978: 14; Sachs and Wilson, 1978: 175; Podmore and Spencer, 1982: 21; Kennedy, 1978: 150; Solicitors'

**Table 1.23** Number of chambers with women tenants, London and provinces, 1967–84

| | London Number of women | | | | | | Provinces Number of women | | | | | | Total Number of women | | | | | | London chambers with woman as: | |
|---|---|---|---|---|---|---|---|---|---|---|---|---|---|---|---|---|---|---|---|---|
| | 0 | 1 | 2 | 3 | 4 | 5 | 0 | 1 | 2 | 3 | 4 | 5 | 0 | 1 | 2 | 3 | 4 | 5 | Clerk | Head |
| 1984 | 124 | 64 | 27 | 3 | 1 | 0 | 68 | 40 | 4 | 3 | 1 | 0 | 192 | 104 | 31 | 6 | 2 | 0 | 15 | 9[b] |
| 1977, Oct. | | | | | | | | | | | | | 97 | 106 | | | 87 | | | |
| 1976 | 63 | 68 | 31 | 18 | 7 | 4 | 34 | 38 | 17 | 8 | 2 | 0 | 97 | 106 | 48 | 26 | 9 | 4 | 42[a] | |
| 1975 | 74 | 57 | 25 | 16 | 6 | 3 | | | | | | | | | | | | | 14 | 5 |
| 1972 | 94 | 54 | 21 | 6 | 4 | 1 | | | | | | | | | | | | | 12 | 4 |
| 1970 | 92 | | | 68 | | | 39 | | 31 | | | | 151 | 62 | 26 | 11 | 0 | 0 | | |
| 1967 | 115 | 37 | 18 | 4 | 1 | 0 | 41 | | 29 | | | | 148 | | 87 | | | | 4 | 1 |

[a] London and provinces.
[b] One of these is a sole practitioner.
*Sources*: Equal Opportunities Commission, 1978: 16; Royal Commission, 1979, vol. 2: 443; Kennedy, 1978: 152; Knightly and Colton Report, 1971; Solicitors' and Barristers' Directory and Diary, 1985

**Table 1.24** Silks: numbers (absolute and proportion of Bar) and appointments (absolute and proportion of applicants), 1800–1985

| Year | Number of living silks[a] | Number appointed this year[b] | Number of barristers | Silks as % of Bar | Number of applications to take silk | Year | Number of living silks | Number appointed this year | Number of barristers | Silks as % of Bar |
|---|---|---|---|---|---|---|---|---|---|---|
| 1985 | 553 | | | | | 1929 | 284 | 11 | | |
| 1984 | 545 | 42 | | | | 1928 | | (9)[10] | | |
| 1983 | | 40 | | | | 1927 | | (11)[12] | 2966 | |
| 1982 | 512 | 56 | | | | 1926 | | (9)[10] | | 9.6 |
| 1981 | 482 | 52 | 4685 | 10.29 | | 1925 | | 16 | | |
| 1980 | | 53 | 4589 | | | 1924 | 303 | (13)[15] | | |
| 1979 | | 52 | 4412 | | | 1923 | | (16)[21] | | |
| 1978 | 404 | 40 | 4263 | 9.48 | 151 | 1922 | | (13)[14] | | |
| 1977 | 384 | 29 | 4076 | 9.42 | 134 | 1921 | | (10)[11] | | |
| 1976 | 372 | 30 | 3881 | 9.59 | 140 | 1920 | | 19[18] | | |
| 1975 | 370 | | | | | 1919 | 297 | 43[38] | | |
| 1974 | 365 | 34 | 3646 | 10.01 | 110 | 1918 | | 1 | | |
| | 345 | 32 | 3368 | 10.24 | 110 | 1917 | | 4 | 2953 | |
| 1973 | 329 | 40 | 3137 | 10.49 | 156 | 1916 | 248 | 0 | | 10.1 |
| 1972 | | 39 | | | 153 | 1915 | | 0 | | |
| 1971 | | 37 | | | | 1914 | | 15[0] | | |
| 1970 | | 32 | | | | 1913 | | 26[25] | | |
| 1969 | | 38 | | | | 1912 | 236 | 21[0] | | |
| 1968 | | 32 | | | | 1911 | | 0 | | |
| 1967 | | 31 | | | | 1910 | | 19[0] | | |
| 1966 | | 22 | | | | 1909 | 255 | 9[0] | | |
| 1965 | | 40 | | | | 1908 | | 15[14] | 4733 | |
| 1964 | | 18 | | | 180 | 1907 | | 0 | | |
| 1963 | | 17 | | | | 1906 | | 15[0] | | |
| 1962 | 300? | 18 | | | | 1905 | | 11[0] | | |
| 1961 | | 34 | | | | 1904 | | 13 | | |

| | | | | | | | | | | |
|---|---|---|---|---|---|---|---|---|---|---|
| 1960 | (345) | 22 | | | 61 | 1903 | | 9[0] | | |
| 1959 | | 16 | | | | 1902 | 259 | 13 | | |
| 1958 | | 16 | | | | 1901 | | 16 | | 5.3 |
| 1957 | 180 | 16 | 1968 | 9.1 | | 1900 | 245 | (8)[2] | | |
| 1956 | | 11 | | | | 1899 | | (14)[8] | | |
| 1955 | | 21 | | | | 1898 | | (9)[0] | | |
| 1954 | | 22 | | | | 1897 | | (21)[12] | | |
| 1953 | | 17 | | | | 1896 | | (14)[8] | | |
| 1952 | | 20 | | | | 1895 | 209 | (14)[3] | | |
| 1951 | | 16 | | | | 1894 | 213 | (12)[4] | | |
| 1950 | 312 | 16 | | | | 1893 | 210 | 11[0] | 4823 | |
| 1949 | | 19 | | | | 1892 | 209 | 19[16] | | |
| 1948 | | 15 | | | | 1891 | 201 | 12[13] | | 4.2 |
| 1947 | | 23 | | | | 1890 | 197 | 9 | | |
| 1946 | | 23[1] | | | | | 200 | 11 | | |
| 1945 | | 26[0] | | | | 1889 | 198 | 1 | | |
| 1944 | | 0 | | | | 1888 | 174 | 15 | | |
| 1943 | | 23 | | | | 1887 | 183 | 0 | | |
| 1942 | | 0 | | | | 1886 | 167 | 17 | | |
| 1941 | | 0 | | | | 1885 | 189 | 20 | | |
| 1940 | | 0 | | | | 1884 | | 0 | | |
| 1939 | 279 | 16 | | | | 1883 | | 6 | | |
| 1938 | | (16)[17] | | | | 1882 | | (19)[9] | | |
| 1937 | | (16)[14] | | | | 1881 | | (10)[12] | 4792 | |
| 1936 | | (13)[16] | | | | 1880 | 174 | (20)[19] | | 3.6 |
| 1935 | | (15)[16] | | | | 1879 | | 0 | | |
| 1934 | | (8) | | | | 1878 | | 2 | | |
| 1933 | | (10)[13] | | | | 1877 | 191 | (21)[15] | | |
| 1932 | | (8)[10] | | | | 1876 | 180 | (1)[2] | | |
| 1931 | | (12)[11] | | | | 1875 | | 15 | | |
| 1930 | | 18 | | | | 1874 | | (24)[26] | | |

*continued*

**Table 1.24** *(cont'd)*

| Year | Number of living silks[a] | Number appointed this year[b] | Number of barristers | Silks as % of Bar | Number of applications to take silk |
|---|---|---|---|---|---|
| 1873 | | 8 | | | |
| 1872 | | (18)[19] | | | |
| 1871 | | 0 | | | |
| 1870 | 171 | 0 | | | |
| 1869 | | (14)[15] | | | |
| 1868 | | (21)[16] | | | |
| 1867 | | 0 | | | |
| 1866 | | (28)[24] | | | |
| 1865 | | 9 | | | |
| 1864 | | (4)[3] | | | |
| 1863 | 129 | (5)[4] | 4360 | 3.0 | |
| 1862 | | (7)[0] | | | |
| 1861 | | (14)[18] | 3071 | | |
| 1860 | 116 | (0)[8] | | 3.8 | |
| 1859 | | (3)[0] | | | |
| 1858 | | (16)[1] | | | |
| 1857 | | (8)[3] | | | |
| 1856 | 69 | (2)[3] | | | |
| 1855 | 65 | (5)[0] | | | |
| 1854 | 66 | (5)[0] | | | |
| 1853 | 62 | 6 | | | |
| 1852 | | 0 | | | |

| Year | Number of living silks | Number appointed this year | Number of barristers | Silks as % of Bar |
|---|---|---|---|---|
| 1851 | | (19)[22] | 2816 | |
| 1850 | 71 | (7)[12] | | 2.5 |
| 1849 | | 8 | | |
| 1848 | | 0 | | |
| 1847 | | 6 | | |
| 1846 | | 0 | | |
| 1845 | 69 | 9 | 2317 | 3.0 |
| 1844 | | 7 | | |
| 1843 | | 0 | | |
| 1842 | 65 | 8[0] | | |
| 1841 | 66 | 3[7] | 2088 | 3.2 |
| 1840 | 76 | 0 | | |
| 1835 | 60<br>53 | | 1300 | 4.3 |
| 1834 | | 16 | | |
| 1833 | | 5 | | |
| 1832 | | 4 | 1130 | |
| 1830 | 51 | | | 4.5 |
| 1820 | 33 | | *c.*750 | |
| 1802 | 22 | | | |
| 1800 | 25 | | 598 | 4.2 |

[a] Figure in parentheses is overestimate, since some have been appointed to the bench or retired.
[b] Figures in parentheses are underestimates based on silks still in practice in a later year, when some would have died, retired, or been appointed to the bench. Figures in brackets are those from *The Times*, which differ from other sources.

*Sources*: Law List; Odgers, 1901; Incorporated Law Society, Calendar; *The Legal Almanac, Remembrancer and Diary*; Waterlow Bros & Layton's *Legal Almanac*, 1903–10; Waterlow's *The Legal Pocket Book and Calendar*, 1911–20; Shaw, 1877: 22–6; Senate, Annual Statements; Bar List, 1981; Monopolies and Mergers Commission, 1976a: 5; Royal Commission, 1979, vol. 1: 479; Cocks, 1983: 122–3, 218 n. 42; Abel-Smith and Stevens, 1967: 242; Megarry 1962: 89–90; Abel-Smith and Stevens, 1968: 119; Gower and Price, 1957: 332 n. 59, 333; Solicitors' and Barristers' Directory and Diary, 1984; 1985; *The Times*.

... and number of women barristers,[a] 1785–1980

| | South-eastern | Midland | Oxford | Northern | North-eastern | Western | Wales and Chester | |
|---|---|---|---|---|---|---|---|---|
| 1980 | 1208 (91) | 620 (38) | | 514 (53) | 331 (33) | 521 (34) | 199 (14) | |
| 1970 | 706 (42) | 267 (11) | 215 (5) | 292 (21) | 176 (9) | 247 (14) | 101 (3) | |
| 1960 | 585 (24) | 248 (10) | 260 (5) | 375 (27) | 204 (5) | 338 (22) | 119 (9) | |
| 1950 | 795 (22) | 192 (9) | 217 (7) | 319 (16) | 229 (6) | 267 (5) | 139 (10) | |
| | | | | | | | N. Wales and Chester | S. Wales and Chester |
| 1940 | 708 (20) | 222 (3) | 164 (5) | 300 (12) | 227 (6) | 242 (2) | 21 (0) | 93 (7) |
| 1930 | 605 (10) | 198 (4) | 169 (4) | 360 (2) | 302 (2) | 183 (2) | 52 (0) | |
| 1920 | 447 | 266 | 119 | 296 | 282 | 202 | 45 | |
| 1910 | 485 | 247 | 140 | 391 | 309 | 241 | 42 | |
| 1906 | 673 | 222 | 201 | 335 | 274 | 227 | 45 | |
| 1890 | 572 | 154 | 181 | 314 | 201 | 191 | 37 | |
| 1880 | 572 | 191 | 173 | 247 | 205 | 198 | 29 | |

| | Home | Midland | Oxford | Northern | Norfolk | Western | N. Wales and Chester | | S. Wales and Chester | |
|---|---|---|---|---|---|---|---|---|---|---|
| 1870 | 372 | 122 | 108 | 210 | 62 | 136 | 27 | | 33 | |
| 1860 | 289 | 63 | 121 | 271 | 51 | 120 | 22 | | 16 | |
| 1850 | 196 | 64 | 131 | 240 | 48 | 133 | 23 | | 26 | |
| 1844 | | | | 221 | | | | | | |
| 1840 | 139 | 54 | 99 | 166 | 42 | 112 | 16 | | 22 | |
| | | | | | | | N. Wales | S. Wales | Chester | Brecon |
| 1830 | 78 | 42 | 80 | 110 | 25<br>34 | 96 | 5 | 13 | 20 | 16 |
| 1820 | 69 | 24 | 62 | 82 | 20 | 58 | 6 | 9 | 24 | 11 |
| 1800 | | | | 63 | | | | | | |
| 1785 | 30 | | | 19 | 14 | | | | | |

[a] Figures in parentheses are women barristers, included in total.

*Sources*: Clarke's New Law List, 1820–40; Law List, 1850–1970; Bar List, 1980; Duman, 1980: 620; 1981: 97; Cocks, 1983: ch. 2 and p. 214

**Table 1.26** Growth of provincial Bar: number of barristers in principal cities, 1894–1985

| | | | | | | | | | | | | | 1976 | | 1979 | | 1985 | | |
|---|---|---|---|---|---|---|---|---|---|---|---|---|---|---|---|---|---|---|---|
| | | | | | | | | | | | | | | | | | Barristers | | |
| | 1894 | 1904 | 1910 | 1914 | 1920 | 1930 | 1940 | 1950 | 1960 | 1962 | 1964 | 1970 | Barr. | Pupils | Barr. | Sets | Total | Women | Sets |
| Birmingham | 27 | 28 | 29 | 37 | 34 | 41 | 49 | 59 | 78 | 80 | 75 | 99 | 153 | 12 | 165 | 12 | 213 | 5 | 14 |
| Bournemouth | | | 0 | | 0 | 0 | 0 | 1 | 6 | 5 | | 3 | 7 | 0 | 5 | 2 | 5 | 0 | 1 |
| Bradford | | | 11 | | 11 | 10 | 9 | 13 | 9 | | | 13 | 16 | 2 | 14 | 1 | 18 | 1 | 1 |
| Brighton | | | 1 | | 1 | 1 | 1 | 0 | 2 | | | 5 | 12 | 0 | 15 | 2 | 11 | 0 | 2 |
| Bristol | | | 16 | | 14 | 18 | 28 | 22 | 24 | | 20 | 34 | 52 | 9 | 65 | 5 | 86 | 4 | 6 |
| Cambridge | | | 2 | | 1 | 1 | | 0 | 2 | | | 0 | 10 | 0 | 11 | 1 | 16 | 1 | 1 |
| Cardiff | | | 16 | | 17 | 23 | 24 | 27 | 27 | | 20 | 31 | 69 | 15 | 75 | 4 | 88 | 0 | 4 |
| Chester | | | 4 | | 3 | 3 | 4 | 5 | 10 | | 10–20 | 17 | 30 | 2 | 36 | 3 | 38 | 2 | 4 |
| Colchester | | | 0 | | 0 | 0 | 0 | 1 | 3 | | | 6 | 15 | 0 | 13 | 1 | 25 | 1 | 1 |
| Exeter | | | 4 | | 4 | 5 | 5 | 4 | 0 | | | 0 | 17 | 0 | 29 | 4 | 22 | 0 | 3 |
| Hull | | | 2 | | 3 | 3 | 1 | 2 | 6 | 6 | | 7 | 11 | 1 | 13 | 1 | 14 | 1 | 1 |

| | | | | | | | | | | | | | | | | | | | |
|---|---|---|---|---|---|---|---|---|---|---|---|---|---|---|---|---|---|---|---|
| Leeds | 23 | 20 | 25 | | 20 | 18 | 26 | 35 | 54 | | 50 | 62 | 95 | 8 | 129 | 8 | 162 | 7 | 11 |
| Leicester | | | 0 | | 0 | 2 | 7 | 8 | 10 | | 10 | 19 | 25 | 4 | 37 | 4 | 40 | 2 | 3 |
| Liverpool | 70 | 79 | 83 | | 70 | 63 | 77 | 69 | 104 | 95 | 85 | 102 | 155 | 10 | 179 | 14 | 198 | 9 | 15 |
| Manchester | 75 | 97 | 103 | | 84 | 77 | 99 | 99 | 127 | | 110 | 142 | 221 | 17 | 249 | 19 | 301 | 16 | 21 |
| Middlesbrough | | | 0 | | 0 | 1 | 2 | 0 | 0 | | | 0 | 8 | 0 | 11 | 1 | 18 | 0 | 2 |
| Newcastle-upon-Tyne | | | 11 | | 8 | 9 | 14 | 18 | 22 | | 20 | 28 | 57 | 5 | 64 | 5 | 82 | 4 | 5 |
| Newport | | | 1 | | 1 | 1 | 4 | 6 | 5 | | | 8 | 0 | 0 | 2 | 1 | 3 | 0 | 1 |
| Norwich | | | 6 | | 3 | 5 | 4 | 7 | 7 | | | 9 | 24 | 2 | 10 | 1 | 35 | 1 | 2 |
| Nottingham | | | 3 | | 1 | 4 | 8 | 8 | 11 | | 20 | 31 | 46 | 8 | 55 | 3 | 60 | 1 | 3 |
| Plymouth | | | 3 | | 4 | 3 | 1 | 3 | 1 | | | 0 | 4 | 0 | 8 | 1 | 15 | 0 | 2 |
| Preston | | | 5 | | 5 | 7 | 12 | 13 | 11 | | | 2 | 1 | 0 | 0 | 0 | 52 | 11 | 3 |
| Sheffield | | | 7 | | 6 | 6 | 5 | 7 | 10 | | | 13 | 22 | 3 | 28 | 3 | 35 | 0 | 3 |
| Southampton | | | 0 | | 0 | 0 | 0 | 6 | 4 | | 10–20 | 7 | 15 | 3 | 26 | 2 | 30 | 1 | 2 |
| Swansea | | | 1 | | 5 | 12 | 15 | 17 | 20 | | | 18 | 24 | 3 | 30 | 2 | 36 | 1 | 2 |
| Wolverhampton | | | | 0 | 5 | 4 | 3 | 1 | 0 | | | 0 | 0 | 0 | 0 | 0 | 0 | 0 | 0 |
| Other | | | | 43 | 41 | 30 | 21 | 13 | 16 | | | 4 | 3 | 0 | 14 | 4 | 53 | 1 | 4 |
| Total | | 309 | 373 | 376 | 340 | 346 | 415 | 444 | 556 | | | 660 | 1092 | 104 | 1283 | 104 | 1656 | 69 | 117 |

*Sources*: Incorporated Law Society, Calendar, 1894: 25–4; Waterlow Bros & Layton's *Legal Almanac*, 1904: 122–8; Senate, 1978d: 1; Zander, 1968: 72 n.15; Abel-Smith and Stevens, 1967: 428–9; Royal Commission, 1979, vol. 1: 448; Law List, 1910, 1920, 1930, 1940, 1950, 1960, 1970; Megarry, 1962: 7–8; Solicitors' and Barristers' Directory and Diary, 1985

**Table 1.27** Distribution of barristers between London and provinces and average size of sets, 1953–84

| | Number of sets | | | Number of barristers | | Size of average set | | |
|---|---|---|---|---|---|---|---|---|
| | London | Provinces | Total | London | Provinces | London | Provinces | Provincial Bar as percentage of total |
| 1984 | 222 | 119 | 341 | 3698 | 1505 | 16.7 | 12.6 | 29 |
| 1983 | 215 | 115 | 330 | 3589 | 1443 | 16.7 | 12.5 | 29 |
| 1982 | 207 | 113 | 320 | 3461 | 1403 | 16.7 | 12.4 | 29 |
| 1981 | 203 | 111 | 314 | 3307 | 1378 | 16.3 | 12.4 | 29 |
| 1980 | 202 | 109 | 311 | 3227 | 1362 | 16.0 | 12.5 | 30 |
| 1979 | 197 | 109 | 306 | 3125 | 1287 | 15.9 | 11.8 | 29 |
| 1978 | 197 | 105 | 302 | 2990 | 1273 | 15.2 | 12.1 | 30 |
| 1977 | 193 | 102 | 295 | 2894 | 1182 | 14.9 | 11.6 | 29 |
| 1976 | 188 | 99 | 287 | 2754 | 1127 | 14.6 | 11.4 | 29 |
| 1975 | 181 | 93 | 274 | 2598 | 1048 | 14.4 | 11.3 | 29 |
| 1974 | 174 | 94 | 268 | 2427 | 941 | 13.9 | 10.0 | 28 |
| 1973 | 173 | 90 | 263 | 2254 | 883 | 13.0 | 9.8 | 28 |
| 1972 | 171 | 85 | 256 | 2108 | 811 | 12.3 | 9.5 | 28 |

| | | | | | | | | |
|---|---|---|---|---|---|---|---|---|
| 1971 | 168 | 83 | 251 | 1981 | 733 | 11.8 | 8.8 | 27 |
| 1970 | 169 | 74 | 243 | 1898 | 686 | 11.2 | 9.3 | 27 |
| 1969 | 172 | 76 | 248 | 1811 | 637 | 10.5 | 8.4 | 26 |
| 1968 | 170 | 75 | 245 | 1773 | 606 | 10.4 | 8.1 | 25 |
| 1967 | 171 | 74 | 245 | 1738 | 595 | 10.2 | 8.1 | 26 |
| 1966 | 177 | 76 | 253 | 1696 | 543 | 9.6 | 7.1 | 24 |
| 1965 | 181 | 75 | 256 | 1631 | 533 | 9.0 | 7.1 | 25 |
| 1964 | 181 | 75 | 256 | 1598 | 520 | 8.8 | 6.9 | 25 |
| 1963 | 183 | 76 | 259 | 1568 | 505 | 8.6 | 6.6 | 24 |
| 1962 | 182 | 81 | 263 | 1468 | 496 | 8.1 | 6.1 | 25 |
| 1961 | 190 | 77 | 267 | 1463 | 472 | 7.7 | 6.1 | 25 |
| 1960 | 189 | 80 | 269 | 1458 | 461 | 7.7 | 5.8 | 24 |
| 1959 | 193 | 84 | 277 | 1456 | 467 | 7.5 | 5.6 | 24 |
| 1958 | | | | 1483 | 464 | | | 24 |
| 1957 | | | | 1502 | 466 | | | 24 |
| 1956 | | | | 1463 | 474 | | | 24 |
| 1955 | | | | 1530 | 478 | | | 24 |
| 1954 | | | | 1530 | 480 | | | 24 |
| 1953 | | | | 1456 | 451 | | | 24 |

*Source*: Senate, Annual Statements

**Table 1.28** Distribution of sets and barristers by size of set, 1960–79, 1984

| | London | | | | | | | | Provinces | | | | | | | |
|---|---|---|---|---|---|---|---|---|---|---|---|---|---|---|---|---|
| | % of sets by number of members | | | | % of barristers by size of set | | | | % of sets by number of members | | | | % of barristers by size of set | | | |
| | ⩽ 5 | 6–10 | 11–15 | ⩾ 16 | ⩽ 5 | 6–10 | 11–15 | ⩾ 16 | ⩽ 5 | 6–10 | 11–15 | ⩾ 16 | ⩽ 5 | 6–10 | 11–15 | ⩾ 16 |
| 1960 | 25 | 55 | 19 | 2 | 10 | 56 | 31 | 3 | 50 | 41 | 9 | 0 | 24 | 58 | 18 | 0 |
| 1961 | 26 | 53 | 20 | 2 | | | | | | | | | | | | |
| 1962 | 21 | 58 | 18 | 3 | | | | | | | | | | | | |
| 1963 | 19 | 55 | 23 | 3 | | | | | | | | | | | | |
| 1964 | 18 | 52 | 25 | 4 | | | | | | | | | | | | |
| 1965 | 19 | 43 | 28 | 5 | | | | | | | | | | | | |
| 1966 | 18 | 45 | 31 | 7 | | | | | | | | | | | | |
| 1967 | 13 | 41 | 33 | 13 | | | | | | | | | | | | |
| 1968 | 14 | 37 | 38 | 12 | | | | | 28 | 37 | 29 | 5 | 8 | 35 | 46 | 12 |
| 1970 | 15 | 26 | 36 | 20 | | | | | 23 | 36 | 27 | 14 | | | | |
| 1976 | 6 | 20 | 26 | 50 | | | | | 22 | 25 | 30 | 24 | | | | |
| 1979 | 3 | 18 | 28 | 51 | 0.4[a] | 9[a] | 23[a] | 67[a] | 19 | 19 | 29 | 32 | 6[a] | 15[a] | 39[a] | 40[a] |
| | 1–9 | 10–19 | 20–29 | ⩾ 30 | | | | | 1–9 | 10–19 | 20–29 | ⩾ 30 | | | | |
| 1984 | 14 | 48 | 37 | 0.5 | | | | | 28 | 45 | 25 | 2 | | | | |
| | ⩽ 4 | 5–9 | 10–14 | ⩾ 15 | | | | | ⩽ 4 | 5–9 | 10–14 | ⩾ 15 | | | | |
| 1984 | 3 | 10 | 22 | 65 | | | | | 8 | 17 | 17 | 52 | | | | |

[a] The 1979 figures for distribution of sets by number of barristers group sets with more than five barristers by aggregates of five (i.e. 6–10). I calculated the number of barristers in these categories by assuming that all barristers were in a set in the middle of the range (i.e. 8). The assumption seems to have been fairly accurate because the London total calculated in this way, 3112, was very close to the actual total of 3080; in the provinces the assumption seems less justified; there the estimated total was 1041 and the actual 1287.

*Sources*: Senate, Annual Statements; Royal Commission, 1979, vol. 1: 449; Senate 1977a: III.2–3; Chambers for Young Barristers Subcommittee, 1973; Solicitors' and Barristers' Directory and Diary, 1985

**Table 1.29** Internal composition of chambers (size and gender) in London (by Inn) and provinces, 1984

| | Number (percentage) of barristers per set | | | | Number (percentage) of women barristers per set | | | | | |
|---|---|---|---|---|---|---|---|---|---|---|
| Inn/location | 1–9 | 10–19 | 20–29 | ⩾ 30 | 0 | 1 | 2 | 3 | 4 | Mean |
| Temple | 14 (9) | 67 (44) | 70 (46) | 1 (1) | 83 (55) | 41 (27) | 22 (15) | 3 (2) | 1 (1) | 0.65 |
| Lincoln's | 10 (23) | 29 (67) | 4 (9) | 0 (0) | 23 (53) | 19 (44) | 1 (2) | 0 | 0 | 0.67 |
| Gray's | 6 (27) | 9 (41) | 7 (32) | 0 (0) | 14 (64) | 3 (14) | 4 (18) | 0 | 1 (5) | 0.68 |
| Rest of London | 2 (40) | 2 (40) | 1 (20) | 0 (0) | 4 (80) | 1 (20) | 0 | 0 | 0 | 0.20 |
| Provinces | 32 (28) | 52 (45) | 29 (25) | 2 (2) | 68 (59) | 40 (35) | 4 (3) | 3 (3) | 1 (1) | 0.53 |
| Total | 64 (19) | 159 (47) | 111 (33) | 3 (1) | 192 (57) | 104 (31) | 31 (9) | 6 (2) | 2 (1) | 0.57 |

*Source*: Solicitors' and Barristers' Directory and Diary, 1985

**Table 1.30** Income of barristers (QCs and juniors) from civil and criminal work, 1974–5

| | QCs | | Juniors | | All barristers | |
|---|---|---|---|---|---|---|
| | £ | % | £ | % | £ | % |
| Civil | 3,300,000 | 72 | 7,000,000 | 47 | 10,300,000 | 53 |
| Criminal | 1,300,000 | 28 | 7,800,000 | 53 | 9,100,000 | 47 |

*Source*: Senate, 1977b: XVI.12

**Table 1.31** Source of barrister income: public/private, QCs/juniors, 1974–5

| | QCs | | Juniors | | All barristers | |
|---|---|---|---|---|---|---|
| Source of fees | £000 | % | £000 | % | £000 | % |
| *Public funds* | 1300 | 24 | 7900 | 49 | 9200 | 43 |
| Prosecution (London) | 40 | 1 | 1300 | 8 | 1340 | 6 |
| Prosecution (circuit) | 370 | 7 | 1700 | 11 | 2070 | 10 |
| Criminal legal aid | 770 | 14 | 3300 | 20 | 4070 | 19 |
| Civil legal aid | 120 | 2 | 1600 | 10 | 1720 | 8 |
| *Private funds* | 3300 | 62 | 6900 | 43 | 10,200 | 48 |
| Private criminal | 120 | 2 | 700 | 4 | 820 | 4 |
| Private civil and arbitrator fees | 3180 | 60 | 6200 | 39 | 9380 | 44 |
| *Other* | 750 | 14 | 1200 | 8 | 1950 | 9 |
| Judicial | 170 | 3 | 200 | 1 | 370 | 2 |
| Overseas | 300 | 6 | 250 | 2 | 550 | 2 |
| Miscellaneous | 280 | 5 | 750 | 5 | 1030 | 5 |
| *Totals* | 5350 | 100 | 16,000 | 100 | 21,350 | 100 |

*Source*: Senate, 1977b: XVI.12

| Total payments (£) | 1975–6 Counsel no. | Paid % | % total payment | 1976–7 Counsel no. | Paid % | % total payment | 1977–8 Counsel no. | Paid % | % total payment | 1979–80 Counsel no. | Paid % | % total payment | 1980–1 Counsel no. | Paid % | % total payment |
|---|---|---|---|---|---|---|---|---|---|---|---|---|---|---|---|
| 1–250 | 1594 | 41.8 | 4.7 | 1552 | 38.5 | 3.8 | 1609 | 37.6 | 3.4 | 1326 | 27.5 | 2.0 | 1149 | 22.8 | 1.2 |
| 251–1000 | 1294 | 33.9 | 23.9 | 1347 | 33.4 | 20.4 | 1342 | 31.4 | 17.7 | 1427 | 29.6 | 13.8 | 1169 | 23.2 | 7.2 |
| 1001–2000 | 561 | 14.7 | 26.6 | 630 | 15.6 | 24.2 | 689 | 16.1 | 22.5 | 1098 | 22.8 | 26.1 | 898 | 17.8 | 14.0 |
| 2001–4000 | 265 | 7.0 | 23.9 | 351 | 8.7 | 25.6 | 459 | 10.7 | 29.8 | 714 | 14.8 | 31.7 | 1169 | 23.2 | 35.0 |
| 4001–6000 | 68 | 1.8 | 11.0 | 93 | 2.3 | 12.1 | 102 | 2.4 | 11.4 | 152 | 3.2 | 12.0 | 420 | 8.3 | 21.5 |
| 6001–8000 | 19 | 0.5 | 4.3 | 26 | 0.6 | 4.8 | 34 | 0.8 | 5.4 | 61 | 1.3 | 6.7 | 145 | 2.9 | 10.5 |
| 8000 | 15 | 0.4 | 5.7 | 32 | 0.8 | 9.1 | 39 | 0.9 | 9.9 | 42 | 0.8 | 7.7 | 97 | 1.9 | 10.7 |
| Total | 3816 | £2,996,859 | | 4031 | £3,718,549 | | 4274 | £4,319,012 | | 4820 | £6,161,526 | | 5047 | £9,484,833 | |

| Total payments (£) | 1982–3 Counsel no. | Paid % | % total payment | 1983–4 Counsel no. | Paid % | % total payment | 1984–5 Total payment |
|---|---|---|---|---|---|---|---|
| 1–250 | 1526 | 28.8 | 2.1 | 2113 | 38.0 | 4.2 | |
| 501–1000 | 624 | 11.8 | 3.4 | | | | |
| 1001–1500 | 490 | 9.3 | 4.6 | 815 | 14.5 | 6.8 | |
| 1501–2000 | 385 | 7.3 | 5.1 | | | | |
| 2001–4000 | 1162 | 22.0 | 25.3 | 1101 | 19.6 | 18.5 | |
| 4001–6000 | 537 | 10.1 | 19.7 | 681 | 12.1 | 19.0 | |
| 6001–8000 | 279 | 5.3 | 14.5 | 366 | 6.5 | 14.5 | |
| 8000 | 291 | 5.5 | 25.4 | 516 | 9.2 | 27.0 | |
| Total | 5294 | £14,376,033 | | 5612 | £17,459,409 | | £63,000,000 |

*Source*: Lord Chancellor's Department, Legal Aid Annual Reports, 1975–6, 1976–7, 1977–8, 1979–80, 1980–1, 1982–3, 1983–4; 83 *LSG* 2050–6, 1986

**Table 1.33** Percentage of barristers' gross fees derived from public funds, by status and speciality, 1974–5, 1976–7

<table>
<tr><th></th><th colspan="2">1974–5</th><th colspan="2">1976–7</th></tr>
<tr><th></th><th>QCs</th><th>Juniors</th><th>QCs</th><th>Juniors</th></tr>
<tr><td>London Chancery and specialist</td><td>2</td><td>4</td><td>1.5</td><td>2.8</td></tr>
<tr><td>London family and common law</td><td rowspan="2">31</td><td rowspan="2">55</td><td>23.5</td><td>40.6</td></tr>
<tr><td>London criminal</td><td>77.2</td><td>91.7</td></tr>
<tr><td>Circuit</td><td>61</td><td>65</td><td>62.8</td><td>69.4</td></tr>
</table>

*Sources*: Senate, 1977b: XIX.6; Royal Commission, 1979, vol. 1: 520

**Table 1.34** Percentage of barristers' gross fees derived from public funds, by status and experience, London and circuit, 1974–5, 1976–7

| | 1974–5: London | | | | 1974–5: circuit | | | | 1976–7 | | | |
|---|---|---|---|---|---|---|---|---|---|---|---|---|
| | | Legal aid | | | | Legal aid | | | | Legal aid | | |
| | Prosecution | Criminal | Civil | Total | Prosecution | Criminal | Civil | Total | Prosecution | Criminal | Civil | Total |
| *Queen's Counsel* | | | | | | | | | | | | |
| More than 2 years | 9 | 21 | 3 | 33 | 21 | 36 | 3 | 60 | 7 | 14 | 2 | 23 |
| 2 years or less | 3 | 14 | 7 | 24 | 25 | 32 | 4 | 61 | 14 | 15 | 5 | 34 |
| *Juniors* | | | | | | | | | | | | |
| More than 15 years | 27 | 13 | 10 | 50 | 26 | 17 | 14 | 57 | 18 | 13 | 10 | 41 |
| 9–15 years | 26 | 14 | 10 | 50 | 25 | 24 | 14 | 63 | 19 | 17 | 10 | 46 |
| 4–8 years | 22 | 31 | 11 | 64 | 22 | 33 | 16 | 71 | 19 | 27 | 13 | 59 |
| 3 years or less | 13 | 36 | 10 | 59 | 19 | 33 | 15 | 67 | 15 | 37 | 14 | 66 |

**Table 1.35** Percentage of barristers' gross fees derived from public funds, by speciality, status and experience, 1974–5

| Category and seniority | Public funds | Private sources | Judicial fees | Overseas fees | Misc. fees | Total | No. in sample |
|---|---|---|---|---|---|---|---|
| *London Chancery and specialist* | | | | | | | |
| QC | | | | | | | |
| before 1972 | 1 | 81 | 1 | 12 | 5 | 100 | 54 |
| 1972 and after | 4 | 75 | 1 | 7 | 13 | 100 | 27 |
| Junior | | | | | | | |
| over 15 years | 4 | 77 | 1 | 3 | 15 | 100 | 68 |
| 9–15 years | 2 | 82 | 0 | 8 | 8 | 100 | 78 |
| 4–8 years | 4 | 73 | 0 | 9 | 14 | 100 | 77 |
| 0–3 years | 7 | 77 | 0 | 5 | 11 | 100 | 91 |
| *London family, common law and criminal* | | | | | | | |
| QC | | | | | | | |
| before 1972 | 33 | 56 | 4 | 3 | 4 | 100 | 51 |
| 1972 and after | 23 | 59 | 3 | 6 | 9 | 100 | 17 |
| Junior | | | | | | | |
| over 15 years | 49 | 46 | 2 | — | 3 | 100 | 112 |
| 9–15 years | 50 | 44 | 1 | 1 | 4 | 100 | 134 |
| 4–8 years | 62 | 35 | — | 1 | 2 | 100 | 190 |
| 0–3 years | 59 | 26 | 1 | 6 | 8 | 100 | 292 |
| *Circuit* | | | | | | | |
| QC | | | | | | | |
| before 1972 | 60 | 28 | 8 | 1 | 3 | 100 | 26 |
| 1972 and after | 62 | 32 | 5 | — | 1 | 100 | 32 |
| Junior | | | | | | | |
| over 15 years | 57 | 35 | 6 | — | 2 | 100 | 128 |
| 9–15 years | 64 | 35 | — | — | 1 | 100 | 155 |
| 4–8 years | 72 | 25 | 1 | — | 2 | 100 | 212 |
| 0–3 years | 68 | 22 | — | — | 10 | 100 | 343 |

*Source*: Semate. 1977c: addendum p. 9

**Table 1.36** Earnings of barristers compared with other professionals, 1908 to 1981–2

| | Barristers | Solicitors | Accountants | Architects | Engineers | Doctors | Dentists |
|---|---|---|---|---|---|---|---|
| 1981–2 | 17,700 | | | | | | |
| 1976[a] | 8,338 | 10,093 | 8,708 | 8,840 | 7,693 | 7,605 | 7,963 |
| 1975[a] | 7,627 | 9,451 | 7,699 | 8,411 | 6,659 | 6,710 | 7,555 |
| 1974[a] | 7,420 | 8,483 | 6,879 | 8,532 | 5,565 | 5,577 | 6,170 |
| 1972 | 3,733 | 6,582 | 3,323 | 3,786 | 2,326 | 3,440 | 3,616 |
| 1971 | 3,681 | 5,286 | 3,117 | 2,969 | 2,095 | 3,560 | 3,840 |
| 1955–6 | 1,251 | 1,688 | | | | 2,300 | 2,090 |
| 1954–5 | 1,210 | | | | | | |
| 1939 | 390 | | | | | | |
| 1922–3 | 580 | 811 | | | | 723 | 514 |
| 1913–14 | 210 | 390 | | | | 370 | 310 |
| 1908 | 390 | | | | | | |

[a] Excludes those earning less than £2000 per year.

*Sources*: Abel-Smith and Stevens, 1967: 243; Hazell, 1978c: 99; Routh, 1980: 60–1; Royal Commission, 1979, vol. 2: 682; Bar Council, n.d.a

**Table 1.37** Percentage increase in barrister earnings, 1969–70 to 1975–6

| | 1969–70 to 1971–2 | 1972–3 to 1973–4 | 1973–4 to 1974–5 | 1974–5 to 1975–6 | 1972–3 to 1975–6 |
|---|---|---|---|---|---|
| QC | | | | | |
| Gross | 42.8 | 16.3 | 16.0 | 12.8 | 45.1 |
| Net | 43.5 | 9.3 | 19.4 | 11.5 | 40.2 |
| Junior[a] | | | | | |
| Gross | 33.3 | 11.4 | 11.6 | 20.7 | 43.7 |
| Net | 43.3 | 10.9 | 9.8 | 20.5 | 51.2 |

[a] More than 15 years experience.
*Source*: Office of Manpower Economics, 1974: 154–5; Review Body, 1978: 112

**Table 1.38** Percentage increase in CPI and income of all barristers, QCs and juniors, 1974–5 to 1981–2

| | | All barristers | | QCs | | Juniors | |
|---|---|---|---|---|---|---|---|
| | CPI | Gross | Net | Gross | Net | Gross | Net |
| 1974–5 to 1976–7 | 45 | 22 | 16 | 18 | 8 | 23 | 18 |
| 1976–7 to 1981–2 | 81 | 125 | 121 | 137 | 136 | 108 | 104 |
| 1974–5 to 1981–2 | 163 | 175 | 157 | 179 | 156 | 157 | 140 |

CPI: Consumer price index
*Source*: Bar Council, n.d.a: table B

**Table 1.39** Percentage increase in barrister income by seniority and specialization, 1976–7 to 1981–2[a]

| | | QCs | | | Juniors | | | | |
|---|---|---|---|---|---|---|---|---|---|
| | All barristers | All | Post April 1974 | Pre April 1979 | All | 3 years | 4–8 years | 9–15 years | ⩾ 16 years |
| All barristers | 121 | 136 | 113 | 153 | 104 | 114 | 72 | 88 | 72 |
| Criminal | 115 | 86 | — | 95 | 115 | 142 | 91 | 69 | 40 |
| Family and common law | 123 | 143 | 136 | 119 | 117 | 178 | 96 | 90 | 87 |
| Chancery and specialist | 142 | 142 | 94 | 166 | 122 | 182 | 96 | 124 | 76 |

[a] Consumer price index rose 81 per cent during the period.
*Source*: Bar Council, n.d.a: table C

**Table 1.40** Adjusted net-of-tax earnings of barristers and other professions, differences by age and between median and highest earners, 1976–7 (£)

| Profession | Median | Highest quartile | Highest decile | Age | | | Median as % of highest decile | 25–29 as % of 40–65 |
|---|---|---|---|---|---|---|---|---|
| | | | | 25–29 | 30–39 | 40–65 | | |
| Barristers | 5,218 | 7,968 | 11,443 | 3,317 | 6,910 | 9,296 | 46 | 36 |
| Salaried barristers industry | 8,754 | 10,950 | | 6,093 | 7,782 | 10,584 | | 58 |
| Solicitors | 7,643 | 9,413 | 12,417 | 5,809 | 8,323 | 9,560 | 62 | 60 |
| Salaried solicitors industry | 8,754 | 8,988 | 10,651 | 6,252 | 8,256 | 9,453 | 82 | 66 |
| Asst solicitors and salaried partners | 4,183 | 4,797 | 6,387 | 4,317 | 5,850 | 4,790 | 65 | 90 |
| Civil service legal class | 7,904 | 8,087 | 9,294 | 4,642 | 6,275 | 8,414 | 85 | 55 |
| Local authority solicitors | | | | 5,372 | | | | |
| Civil service administration | 7,278 | 8,652 | 9,944 | 4,616 | 6,434 | 8,374 | 73 | 55 |
| Hospital doctors | 9,183 | 10,363 | 11,813 | 5,148 | 7,051 | 10,792 | 78 | 48 |
| General medical practitioners | 8,078 | 9,014 | 9,836 | | 8,030 | 8,254 | 82 | |
| Industry – middle management and above | 7,624 | 10,246 | 13,486 | | | | | 57 |

*Source*: Royal Commission, 1979, vol. 1: 536–41

**Table 1.41** Barrister net income before taxes, by status, speciality and age 1974–5, 1975–6, 1976–7, 1981–2 (median unless otherwise specified) (£)

| | 1974–5 | 1975–6 | 1976–7 | | 1981–2 |
|---|---|---|---|---|---|
| *Queen's Counsel* | | | | | |
| Upper quartile | | 26,500 | 23,700 | | 60,859 |
| Median | 18,000 | 19,400 | 17,200 | | 36,474 |
| Lower quartile | | 14,200 | 11,600 | | 25,809 |
| London Chancery and specialist | | | 23,905 | | 55,773 |
| London family and common law | | | 18,093 | | 34,229 |
| London criminal | | | 17,610 | | 25,651 |
| Circuit | | | 15,645 | | |
| 2 years or more | 19,405 | | 20,058 | 22,168 | 39,235 |
| Less than 2 years | 18,690 | | 17,382 | 18,048 | 32,457 |
| *Juniors* | | | | | |
| Upper quartile | | 9,500 | 9,100 | | 17,414 |
| Median | 5,700 | 6,100 | 5,700 | | 11,555 |
| Lower quartile | | 3,500 | 3,100 | | 6,834 |
| London Chancery and specialist | | | 8,463 | | 17,700 |
| London family and common law | | | 4,940 | | 10,971 |
| London criminal | | | 4,785 | | 11,100 |
| Circuit | | | 6,258 | | |
| Over 15 years | 8,612 | | 9,466 | 10,376 | 14,828 |
| 9–15 | 8,607 | | 9,507 | 10,553 | 15,968 |
| 4–8 | 5,675 | | 6,616 | 7,190 | 10,228 |
| ⩽ 3 | 2,753 | | 2,648 | 3,025 | 5,361 |

*Sources*: Royal Commission, 1979, vol. 1: 487; vol. 2: 597, 601; Zander, 1980: 30–1; Bar Council, n.d.a: tables 24, 28

**Table 1.42** Barrister net income (including pension) before taxes, highest and lowest earners by speciality, status and experience, 1974–5

| | Upper decile £ | Upper quartile £ | Median £ | Lower quartile £ | Lower decile £ |
|---|---|---|---|---|---|
| Juniors up to 3 years from call | | | | | |
| Group 1 (87) | 5,909 | 3,690 | 1,931 | 627 | 293 |
| Group 2 (270) | 4,883 | 3,046 | 1,572 | 545 | 229 |
| Group 3 (334) | 6,544 | 4,404 | 2,717 | 1,316 | 541 |
| Juniors, 4–8 years from call | | | | | |
| Group 1 (77) | 11,767 | 8,400 | 6,485 | 4,254 | 1,764 |
| Group 2 (190) | 8,655 | 6,599 | 4,811 | 3,542 | 2,418 |
| Group 3 (211) | 10,374 | 7,767 | 5,956 | 4,108 | 2,802 |
| Juniors over 15 years from call | | | | | |
| Group 1 (66) | 17,423 | 13,467 | 9,112 | 5,026 | 1,882 |
| Group 2 (111) | 17,925 | 12,107 | 8,089 | 5,387 | 2,264 |
| Group 3 (128) | 14,398 | 10,585 | 7,458 | 5,044 | 3,814 |
| QCs appointed after 1972 | | | | | |
| Group 1 (27) | 35,477 | 28,297 | 23,152 | 19,164 | 14,712 |
| Group 2 (17) | —[a] | 20,185 | 16,411 | 13,057 | —[a] |
| Group 3 (32) | 20,289 | 18,263 | 14,158 | 10,089 | 8,420 |
| QCs appointed before 1972 | | | | | |
| Group 1 (54) | 49,933 | 31,006 | 22,229 | 14,868 | 8,110 |
| Group 2 (61) | 24,180 | 20,659 | 14,555 | 11,401 | 8,934 |
| Group 3 (26) | 23,140 | 20,340 | 16,316 | 12,682 | 10,853 |

Group 1: London Chancery and London specialist
Group 2: London family, London common law, Middlesex (London criminal)
Group 3: circuiteers
[a] Numbers too small to justify a figure.
*Source*: Zander, 1980: 32 from INBUCON, 1977: tables 14, 15

**Table 1.43** Distribution of net[a] barrister income, 1967–79

| | Per cent earning net income (£) | | | | | | | | | | | | | |
|---|---|---|---|---|---|---|---|---|---|---|---|---|---|---|
| Year | 0–249 | 250–449 | 500–999 | 1000–1999 | 2000–2999 | 3000–3999 | 4000–4999 | 5000–5999 | 6000–7999 | 8000–9999 | 10,000–11,999 | 12,000–14,999 | 15,000–19,999 | ≥ 20,000 | Number |
| 1967 | 8.4 | 9.7 | 17.4 | 30.9 | 9.5 | 6.0 | 6.2 | 3.8 | 3.8 | 1.9 | 1.4 | 1.0 | | | 3750 |
| 1968 | 7.0 | 5.6 | 14.3 | 23.0 | 24.3 | 6.3 | 5.6 | 4.3 | 4.1 | 2.2 | 1.2 | 1.0 | 0.6 | 0.2 | 4330 |
| 1969 | 10.7 | 4.4 | 8.5 | 18.1 | 16.0 | 11.0 | 8.6 | 12.2[b] | | 5.0[c] | 4.4 | | 1.2[d] | | 2756 |
| 1970 | 9.5 | 5.5 | 10.6 | 18.0 | 14.8 | 10.2 | 8.1 | 12.6[b] | | 5.4[c] | 3.8 | | 0.9 | 0.4 | 2761 |
| 1971 | 10.1 | 2.5 | 11.9 | 22.5 | 8.8 | 9.3 | 9.1 | 12.5[b] | | 5.9[c] | 5.0 | | 1.6 | 0.7 | 3226 |
| 1972 | 11.5 | 9.0 | 10.2 | 13.4 | 11.4 | 7.2 | 7.7 | 15.7[b] | | 4.4[c] | 6.3 | | 1.2 | 2.0 | 3664 |
| 1973 | | | | | | | | | | | | | | | |
| 1974 | 17.8 | | 10.6 | 15.3 | 9.1 | 5.6 | 5.9 | 8.3 | 8.5 | 5.2 | 4.1 | 3.3 | 2.7 | 3.7 | 4258 |
| 1975 | 18.8 | | 9.3 | 10.1 | 8.1 | 12.9 | 5.4 | 5.1 | 10.5 | 8.1 | 2.8 | 2.7 | 3.6 | 2.8 | 4410 |
| 1976 | 12.0 | | 7.2 | 11.5 | 10.2 | 8.0 | 10.0 | 7.3 | 10.0 | 6.5 | 5.1 | 4.0 | 3.8 | 4.5 | 4442 |
| 1977 | 12.2 | | 7.3 | 14.0 | 9.0 | 9.6 | 8.5 | 6.0 | 12.5 | 8.5 | 4.0 | 5.0 | 3.5 | 4.3 | 4805 |
| 1978 | 17.4 | | 5.5 | 9.4 | 7.5 | 6.3 | 10.3 | 5.7 | 13.6 | 5.3 | 5.2 | 4.9 | 3.5 | 5.3 | 5168 |
| 1979 | 13.5 | | 5.0 | 12.1 | 7.9 | 6.3 | 7.0 | 5.8 | 10.9 | 8.5 | 5.3 | 5.1 | 4.7 | 8.3 | 5068 |

[a] Excludes capital allowances.
[b] 5000–7499.
[c] 7500–9999.
[d] ≥ 15,000

*Source*: Inland Revenue Statistics, 1971–82: professional earnings

**Table 1.44** Dispersion of net barrister income, QCs and juniors, 1974–5, 1976–7, 1981–2

| | All barristers | | QC | | Juniors | |
|---|---|---|---|---|---|---|
| | Highest decile /median | Lowest decile /median | Highest decile /median | Lowest decile /median | Highest decile /median | Lowest decile /median |
| 1974–5 | 2.8 | 0.2 | 1.8 | 0.5 | 2.3 | 0.2 |
| 1976–7 | 2.5 | 0.2 | 1.8 | 0.5 | 2.2 | 0.2 |
| 1981–2 | 2.7 | 0.3 | 2.4 | 0.4 | 2.2 | 0.3 |

*Source*: Bar Council, n.d.a: table 9

**Table 1.45** Median income of criminal practitioners, by location, degree of specialization and experience, 1982–3, 1983–4

| | Years since call | | | | | | | | |
|---|---|---|---|---|---|---|---|---|---|
| | 1982–3: gross | | | 1983–4: gross | | | 1983–4: net | | |
| | 5–9 | 10–15 | ⩾ 16 | 5–9 | 10–15 | ⩾ 16 | 5–9 | 10–15 | ⩾ 16 |
| London | | | | | | | | | |
| specialist[a] | 18,400 | 20,700 | 27,500 | 19,400 | 18,000 | 25,000 | 9,390 | 8,620 | 12,860 |
| mixed[b] | 12,900 | 23,200 | 27,300 | 13,900 | 26,700 | 31,700 | 7,750 | 15,700 | 17,980 |
| Provincial[c] | 17,700 | 32,400 | 30,400 | 20,300 | 29,600 | 31,000 | 13,020 | 19,270 | 19,620 |

[a] Chambers derives > 90 per cent income from criminal work.
[b] Chambers derives 50–90 per cent income from criminal work.
[c] Chambers derives < 50 per cent income from criminal work.
*Source*: Coopers & Lybrand, 1985a: 17, 23

**Table 1.46** Disposition of disciplinary complaints, 1957–84
(a) Bar Council, 1957–74

| Year | Number of complaints | Dismissed; no evidence; miscellaneous | Referred to Inns or Senate | Pending |
|---|---|---|---|---|
| 1973–74 | 100 | 76 | 11 | 4 |
| 1972–73 | 89 | 73 | 5 | 7 |
| 1971–72 | 90 | 61 | 13 | 4 |
| 1970–71 | 69 | 50 | 7 | 6 |
| 1969–70 | 63 | 45 | 6 | 7 |
| 1968–69 | 41 | 7 | 3 | 7 |
| 1967–68 | 50 | 31 | 7 | 3 |
| 1966–67 | 25 | 19 | 2 | 2 |
| 1965–66 | 37 | 32 | 4 | |
| 1964–65 | 46 | 43 | 2 | |
| 1963–64 | 43 | 37 | 6 | |
| 1962–63 | 38 | 34 | | 2 |
| 1961–62 | 43 | 30 | 2 | 2 |
| 1960–61 | 36 | 28 | 1 | 4 |
| 1959–60 | 35 | 21 | 3 | 7 |
| 1958–59 | | | | |
| 1957–58 | 39 | 30 | 3 | 3 |

*Source*: General Council of the Bar, Annual Statements

(b) Senate, 1968–9 to 1985

| Year | New complaints | Total reviewed | Dismissed; no evidence; misc. | With-drawn | Handled infor-mally | Summary proceed-ings | Sent to disci-plinary tribunal | Pending | Disciplinary tribunal | | | | |
|---|---|---|---|---|---|---|---|---|---|---|---|---|---|
| | | | | | | | | | Disbarred | Sus-pended | Repri-manded | Dis-missed | Pending |
| 1985 | 153 | 153 | 51 | 17 | 8 | 8 | 7 | 62 | 3 | 0 | 1 | 0 | |
| 1984 | 160 | 167 | 69 | 34 | 15 | 1 | 7 | 41 | 2 | 1 | 0 | 0 | |
| 1983 | 150 | 161 | 76 | 27 | 11 | 4 | 7 | 36 | 2 | 4 | 3 | 1 | |
| 1982 | 148 | 157 | 77 | 23 | 25 | 4 | 5 | 23 | 5 | 1 | 3 | 1 | |
| 1981 | 154 | 160 | 78 | 28 | 19 | 5 | 10 | 20 | 3 | 3 | 5 | 2 | 4 |
| 1980 | 137 | 143 | 75 | 26 | 10 | 15 | 15 | 2 | 2 | 2 | 1 | 3 | |
| 1979 | 118 | 178 | 91 | 26 | 12 | 7 | 10 | 32 | 3 | | 1 | 1 | 1 |
| 1978 | 127 | 179 | 80 | 13 | 15 | 14 | 14 | 43 | 5 | 1 | 4 | 1 | 1 |
| 1977 | 155 | 177 | 105 | 4 | | 15 | 14 | 39 | 4 | 4 | 4 | 2 | 1 |
| 1976 | 109 | 125 | 86 | 3 | 14 | | 10 | 12 | 4 | 2 | 1 | 3 | |
| 1975 | 98 | 116 | 70 | 1 | 8 | | 12 | 25 | 1 | | 2 | | |
| 1974 | 75 | | 20 | | | | | | 4 | | | 1 | 3 |
| 1974[a] | 34 | | 48 | | 7 | | 8 | 12 | 2 | 1 | 1 | | 9 |
| 1972–73 | 23 | 26 | 14 | 2 | 1 | | 3 | 3 | 2 | | 1 | 1 | |
| 1971–72 | 21 | 24 | 8 | | 5 | | 8 | 1 | | 2 | | 2 | 2 |
| 1970–71 | 11 | 20 | 9 | | 3 | | 5 | 3 | 3 | 1 | | 3 | |
| 1969–70 | 14 | 20 | 7 | | 1 | | 5 | 6 | 3 | | | | 1 |
| 1968–69 | 19 | | 6 | | 4 | | 3 | 6 | | | | | |
| Total | 1706 | | 970 | 178 | 223 | | | 143 | 48 | 21 | 27 | 21 | |

[a] Senate reconstituted in 1974; this is old procedure.
*Source*: Senate, Annual Statements

**Table 1.47** Origin of disciplinary complaints, 1972–8

| Source of complaint | 1972 | 1973 | 1974 | 1975 | 1976 | 1977 | 1978 | 1972–8 Total | % |
|---|---|---|---|---|---|---|---|---|---|
| Prisoners | 21 | 26 | 21 | 18 | 20 | 31 | 23 | 160 | 22 |
| Other lay clients | 28 | 34 | 40 | 31 | 40 | 51 | 46 | 270 | 36 |
| Courts | 4 | 7 | 13 | 17 | 15 | 20 | 25 | 101 | 14 |
| Solicitors | 8 | 17 | 13 | 11 | 16 | 15 | 13 | 93 | 13 |
| Barristers | 4 | 6 | 3 | 9 | 5 | 10 | 19 | 56 | 8 |
| Professional Conduct Committee | 4 | 3 | 4 | 6 | 9 | 3 | 1 | 30 | 4 |
| Law Society | — | 2 | 2 | 3 | 1 | 2 | 2 | 12 | 2 |
| Others | 5 | 2 | — | 6 | 1 | 4 | 4 | 22 | 3 |
| Total | 74 | 97 | 96 | 101 | 107 | 136 | 133 | 744 | |

*Source*: Royal Commission, 1979, vol. 1: 316

**Table 1.48** Substance of disciplinary complaints, 1972–8

| Nature of complaint | 1972 | 1973 | 1974 | 1975 | 1976 | 1977 | 1978 | 1972–8 Total | % |
|---|---|---|---|---|---|---|---|---|---|
| Advertising, touting | 8 | 5 | 2 | 10 | 7 | 5 | 6 | 43 | 6 |
| Conflict of interest | 3 | 1 | 1 | 4 | 3 | 1 | 1 | 14 | 2 |
| Bad advice | 2 | 4 | 10 | 4 | 7 | 9 | 6 | 42 | 6 |
| Abuse of qualification | 2 | 3 | 2 | 4 | 1 | 11 | 15 | 38 | 5 |
| Acting without instructions | 3 | 9 | 5 | 5 | 6 | 10 | 18 | 56 | 8 |
| Acting contrary to instructions | 3 | 2 | 2 | 5 | 2 | 8 | 1 | 23 | 3 |
| Lack of courtesy | 5 | 5 | 5 | 7 | 3 | 11 | 6 | 42 | 6 |
| Unrelated to practice | 6 | 4 | 14 | 8 | 9 | 11 | 11 | 63 | 8 |
| Withholding information | 7 | 10 | 6 | 8 | 8 | — | 1 | 40 | 5 |
| Refusing to act | 2 | 4 | 2 | 3 | 2 | — | 1 | 14 | 2 |
| Inadequate representation | 20 | 24 | 19 | 17 | 34 | 27 | 20 | 161 | 22 |
| Undue influence | 5 | 8 | 10 | 4 | 7 | 8 | 6 | 48 | 6 |
| Conduct of proceedings | 2 | 2 | 8 | 12 | 8 | 19 | 19 | 70 | 9 |
| Fees | 2 | 1 | 3 | — | — | 7 | 4 | 17 | 2 |
| Late returns | 4 | 5 | 1 | 3 | 3 | — | 3 | 19 | 3 |
| Delay | — | 6 | 4 | 4 | 5 | 4 | 6 | 29 | 4 |
| Chambers practice | — | 1 | — | 3 | 2 | 2 | 4 | 12 | 2 |
| Absence | — | 3 | 2 | — | — | 3 | 5 | 13 | 2 |
| Total | 74 | 97 | 96 | 101 | 107 | 136 | 133 | 744 | |

*Source*: Royal Commission, 1979, vol. 1: 315

**Table 1.49** Disciplinary complaints per 100 privately practising barristers, 1957–8 to 1985

| Year | Number of complaints[a] | Number of barristers in private practice[b] | Complaints per 100 barristers |
|---|---|---|---|
| 1985 | 153 | 5367 | 2.9 |
| 1984 | 160 | 5203 | 3.1 |
| 1983 | 150 | 5032 | 3.0 |
| 1982 | 148 | 4864 | 3.0 |
| 1981 | 154 | 4685 | 3.3 |
| 1980 | 137 | 4589 | 3.0 |
| 1979 | 118 | 4412 | 2.7 |
| 1978 | 127 | 4263 | 3.0 |
| 1977 | 155 | 4076 | 3.8 |
| 1976 | 109 | 3881 | 2.8 |
| 1975 | 98 | 3646 | 2.7 |
| 1974 | 75 | 3368 | 2.2 |
| 1973–74 | 100 | 3137 | 3.0 |
| 1972–73 | 89 | 2919 | 3.0 |
| 1971–72 | 90 | 2714 | 3.3 |
| 1970–71 | 69 | 2584 | 2.7 |
| 1969–70 | 63 | 2448 | 2.6 |
| 1968–69 | 41 | 2379 | 1.7 |
| 1967–68 | 50 | 2333 | 2.1 |
| 1966–67 | 25 | 2239 | 1.1 |
| 1965–66 | 37 | 2164 | 1.7 |
| 1964–65 | 46 | 2118 | 2.2 |
| 1963–64 | 43 | 2073 | 2.1 |
| 1962–63 | 38 | 1964 | 1.9 |
| 1961–62 | 43 | 1918 | 2.2 |
| 1960–61 | 36 | 1919 | 1.9 |
| 1959–60 | 35 | 1923 | 1.8 |
| 1957–58 | 39 | 1968 | 2.0 |

[a] To Bar Council until 1974; to Senate thereafter.
[b] Year ending September after 1974; year beginning September before then.
*Sources*: tables 1.16, 1.46

**Table 1.50** Senate membership as proportion of practitioners, 1975–6 to 1985–6

| | 1975–6 | 1976–7 | 1977–8 | 1978–9 | 1979–80 | 1980–1 | 1981–2 | 1982–3 | 1983–4 | 1984–5 | 1985–6 |
|---|---|---|---|---|---|---|---|---|---|---|---|
| *Queen's Counsel* | | | | | | | | | | | |
| No. | 370 | 372 | 384 | 404 | 423 | 453 | 482 | 512 | 526 | 545 | 532 |
| % paid | 91.9 | 96.5 | 98.2 | 97.0 | 95.7 | 84.1 | 95.6 | 95.1 | 94.1 | 95.0 | 95.3 |
| % underpaid | 6.8 | 2.4 | 1.0 | 2.2 | 2.6 | 14.6 | 2.9 | 3.1 | 4.0 | 3.3 | 2.3 |
| % not paying | 1.4 | 1.1 | 0.8 | 0.7 | 1.7 | 1.3 | 1.5 | 1.8 | 1.9 | 1.7 | 2.4 |
| *Juniors* | | | | | | | | | | | |
| Over 15 yrs: | | | | | | | | | | | |
| No. | 780 | 809 | 804 | 801 | 849 | 942 | 990 | 993 | 954 | 836 | 1140 |
| % paid | 77.6 | 80.6 | 81.3 | 81.3 | 82.2 | 62.5 | 74.0 | 80.5 | 82.4 | 76.2 | 82.2 |
| % underpaid | 17.9 | 10.6 | 8.7 | 9.5 | 9.4 | 26.9 | 15.9 | 10.4 | 8.6 | 12.4 | 9.7 |
| % not paying | 4.5 | 8.8 | 10.0 | 9.2 | 8.4 | 10.6 | 10.1 | 9.1 | 9.0 | 11.4 | 8.1 |
| 11–15 yrs: | | | | | | | | | | | |
| No. | 580 | 550 | 557 | 541 | 622 | 888 | 1009 | 992 | 1185 | 1243 | 1309 |
| % paid | 86.2 | 86.0 | 83.5 | 82.4 | 84.7 | 67.7 | 85.1 | 82.2 | 80.0 | 79.7 | 80.6 |
| % underpaid | 12.1 | 8.7 | 8.4 | 9.4 | 8.0 | 25.3 | 10.0 | 9.9 | 10.5 | 11.2 | 9.5 |
| % not paying | 1.7 | 5.3 | 8.1 | 8.1 | 7.2 | 7.0 | 4.9 | 8.0 | 9.5 | 9.1 | 9.9 |
| 6–10 yrs: | | | | | | | | | | | |
| No. | 950 | 1100 | 1278 | 1243 | 1385 | 1449 | 1439 | 1436 | 1423 | 1429 | 1365 |
| % paid | 77.9 | 82.5 | 82.8 | 78.9 | 80.2 | 59.4 | 77.4 | 78.1 | 79.1 | 78.1 | 81.0 |
| % underpaid | 19.5 | 10.0 | 7.5 | 10.8 | 8.0 | 24.5 | 10.1 | 8.4 | 6.6 | 8.3 | 7.8 |
| % not paying | 2.6 | 7.5 | 9.7 | 10.3 | 11.8 | 16.1 | 12.4 | 13.6 | 14.3 | 13.6 | 11.2 |
| 0–5 yrs: | | | | | | | | | | | |
| No. | 1050 | 1050 | 1053 | 1274 | 1133 | 857 | 765 | 991 | 944 | 1150 | 1021 |
| % paid | 55.2 | 83.0 | 83.8 | 84.4 | 81.1 | 68.6 | 76.9 | 86.4 | 85.6 | 87.0 | 73.2 |
| % underpaid | 8.6 | 3.3 | 1.1 | 0.8 | 0 | 11.3 | 4.1 | 1.6 | 0.6 | 0 | 0.6 |
| % not paying | 36.2 | 13.6 | 15.1 | 14.8 | 19.9 | 20.1 | 19.1 | 12.0 | 13.8 | 13.0 | 26.2 |
| *All private practitioners* | | | | | | | | | | | |
| No. | 3730 | 3881 | 4076 | 4263 | 4412 | 4589 | 4685 | 4864 | 5032 | 5203 | 5367 |
| % paid | 74.1 | 84.1 | 84.3 | 83.2 | 82.7 | 65.8 | 80.1 | 82.9 | 82.7 | 81.7 | 77.2 |
| % underpaid | 13.7 | 7.4 | 5.6 | 6.6 | 5.7 | 21.7 | 9.6 | 7.1 | 6.5 | 7.3 | 6.3 |
| % not paying | 12.2 | 8.5 | 10.1 | 10.3 | 11.6 | 12.5 | 10.3 | 10.0 | 10.8 | 11.0 | 12.6 |
| *Judges* | | | | | 250 | | 304 | 333 | 338 | 372 | 371 |
| *Employed barristers* | | 2600 | | | 1300 | | 1865 | 1953 | 2022 | 2514 | 1839 |
| *Retired* | | | | | 670 | | 765 | 750 | 663 | 629 | 483 |
| *Total membership* | | | | | 6406 | | 7138 | 7413 | 7512 | 8146 | 8060 |

*Source*: Senate, Annual Statements

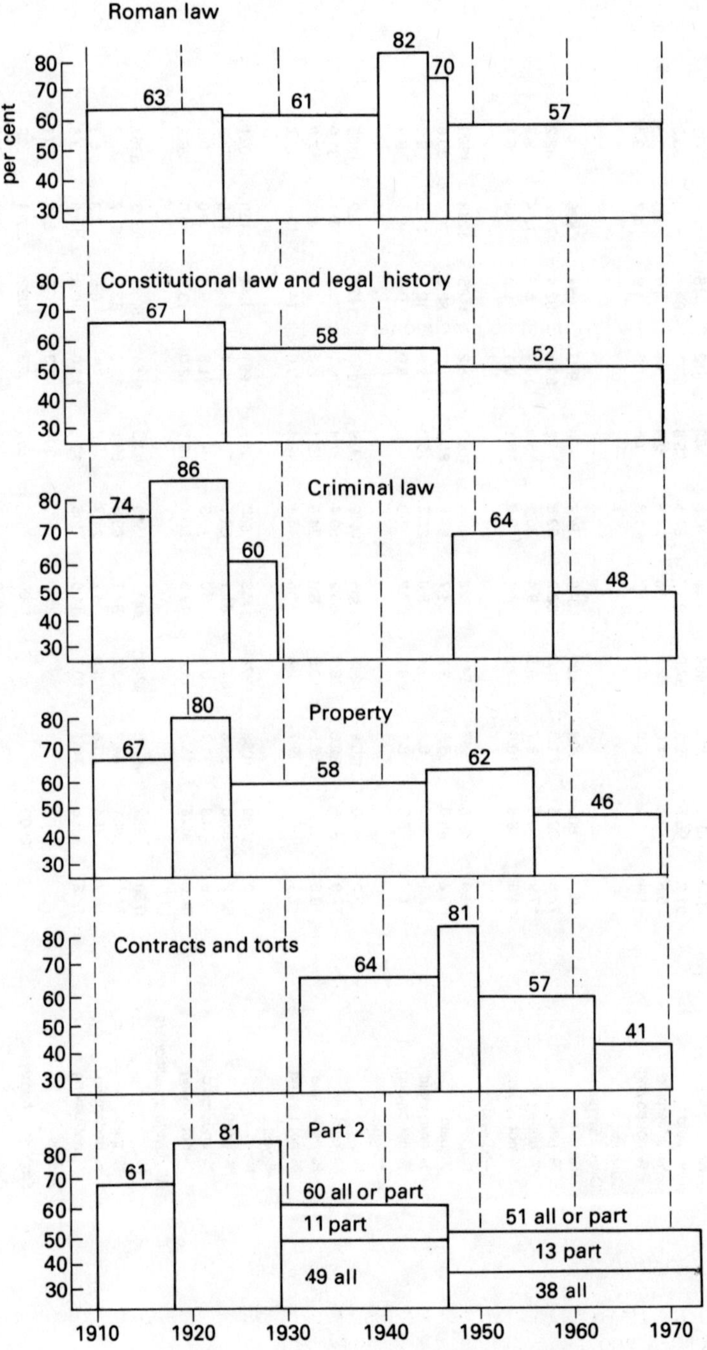


**Figure 1.1** Bar final pass rates, 1910–72

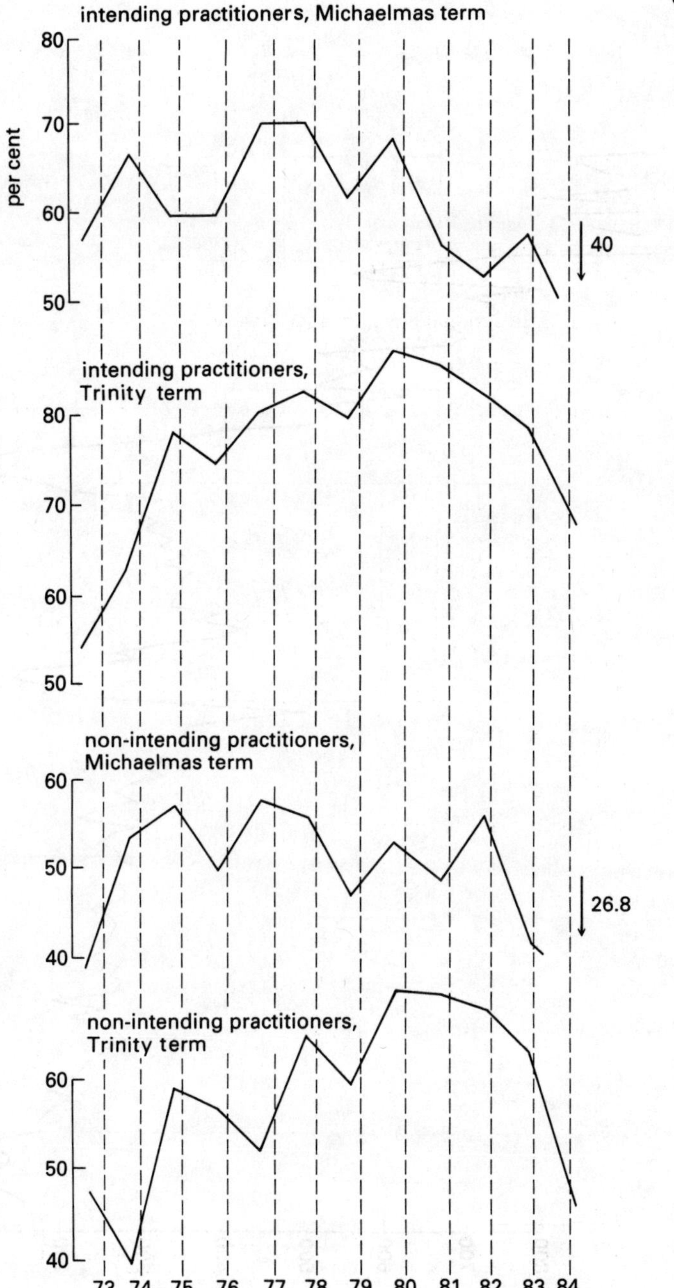


**Figure 1.2** Bar final, part 2, pass rates, intending/non-intending practitioners, Michaelmas and Trinity terms, 1973–84

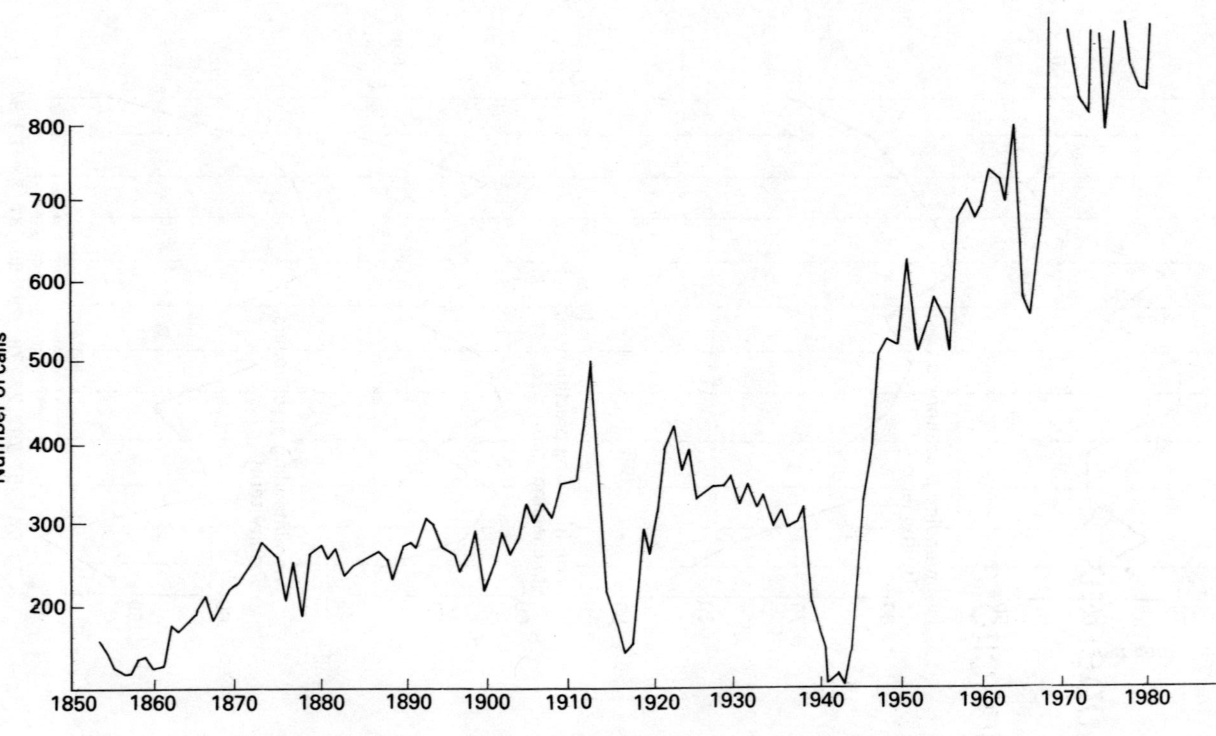


**Figure 1.3** Calls to the Bar: all barristers, 1853–1984; UK domiciliaries, 1947–84

# Appendix 2

# Solicitors

## Entry

**Table 2.1** Proportion seeking to become solicitors without completing secondary school, 1861–1979

| Passing preliminary examination | | Taking intermediate examination[a] following year | | |
|---|---|---|---|---|
| Years | Number | Years | Number | Per cent[b] |
| 1861–2 to 1869 | 3,470 | 1862–3 to 1870 | 3,841 | 90 |
| 1871–79 | 5,776 | 1872–80 | 7,909 | 75 |
| 1880–89 | 5,967 | 1881–90 | 10,750 | 56 |
| 1890–99 | 3,819 | 1891–1900 | 7,858 | 49 |
| 1900–09 | 3,019 | 1901–10 | 7,863 | 38 |
| 1910–19 | 1,184 | 1911–20 | 4,207 | 28 |
| 1920–29 | 1,692 | 1921–30 | 7,670 | 22 |
| 1930–39 | 1,836 | 1931–40 | 10,071 | 18 |
| 1940–49 | 715 | 1941–50 | 7,677 | 9 |
| 1950–59 | 690 | 1951–60 | 13,460 | 5 |
| 1965–71 | 184 | 1966–72 | 20,211 | 1 |
| 1973–78 | 133 | 1974–79 | 15,818 | 1 |

[a] Trust accounts, 1910–60; final part 1, 1966–79.

[b] Because the denominator includes those repeating the intermediate examination, the ratio is artificially deflated.

*Source*: table 2.10

**Table 2.2** Educational background of new articled clerks, 1881–5, 1903–7

| | Number (percentage) in year | | | | | | | | | |
|---|---|---|---|---|---|---|---|---|---|---|
| | 1881 | 1882 | 1883 | 1884 | 1885 | 1903 | 1904 | 1905 | 1906 | 1907 |
| Number of articles | 965 | 947 | 930 | 787 | 819 | 701 | 594 | 621 | 531 | 531 |
| Passed Law Society preliminary exam | 634 (66) | 618 (65) | 593 (64) | 496 (63) | 495 (60) | 327 (47) | 290 (49) | 296 (48) | 243 (46) | 242 (46) |
| Excused from preliminary exam | 331 | 329 | 337 | 291 | 324 | 374 | 304 | 325 | 288 | 289 |
| University degree: | 103 (31) | 112 (34) | 106 (31) | 101 (35) | 119 (37) | 103 (28) | 95 (31) | 105 (32) | 84 (24) | 86 (30) |
| Oxford | | | | | | | 46 | 56 | 43 | 40 |
| Cambridge | | | | | | | 47 | 48 | 35 | 38 |
| Other | | | | | | | 2 | 1 | 6 | 8 |
| Matriculation | 58 | 48 | 49 | 55 | 62 | 78 | 50 | 52 | 50 | 55 |
| Previous moderations: | | | | | | | | | | |
| Cambridge | 3 | 5 | 7 | 1 | 6 | 10 | 7 | 6 | 8 | 9 |
| Oxford | 0 | 5 | 2 | 1 | 3 | 2 | 4 | 3 | 3 | 2 |
| Oxford and Cambridge schools exam board | 5 | 7 | 5 | 4 | 7 | 17 | 15 | 13 | 6 | 7 |
| College of preceptors | | 8 | 8 | 3 | 10 | 5 | 6 | 6 | 8 | 7 |
| Cambridge local | 97 | 90 | 105 | 87 | 86 | 87 | 63 | 66 | 62 | 52 |
| Oxford local | 29 | 31 | 38 | 20 | 26 | 64 | 56 | 57 | 38 | 57 |
| Dispensation order | 27 | 20 | 22 | 11 | 10 | 4 | 7 | 12 | 11 | 5 |

[a] Percentage represents university degree holders as proportion of those excused from preliminary examination.
*Source*: Law Society, Annual Report, 1908: appendix to report of Examinations Committee, pp. 83–4

**Table 2.3** Educational background of solicitors, 1880–1984

| Year | Graduates as % of solicitors admitted[a] | Graduates as % of new articles | Graduates as % of enrolment in Law Society College of Law | Law graduates as % of solicitors admitted | Law graduates as % of enrolment in Law Society College of Law | Graduates as % of those passing Law Society examination | |
|---|---|---|---|---|---|---|---|
| | | | | | | Inter-mediate | Final |
| 1984 | 87 | | | | | | |
| 1983 | 83 | | 99 | | | | |
| 1982 | 85 | | 98 | 90 | | | |
| 1981 | 84 | | | | | | |
| 1980 | 82(85) | | | | | | |
| 1979 | 82(84) | | | | | | |
| 1978 | 79(74) | 91 | | 60 | 63 | | |
| 1977 | 75(80) | | 91? | | 67 | | |
| 1976 | 71(86) | 89 | 66 | | 60 | | |
| 1975 | 67(73) | 86 | 61 | | | | |
| 1974 | 69(65) | 84 | 70 | | 70 | | |
| 1973 | 64(68) | 79 | 64 | | 64 | | |
| 1972 | 62(64) | 84 | 61 | | 61 | | |
| 1971 | 57(55) | 70 | 58 | | 58 | | |
| 1970 | (44) | | | 40 | | | |
| 1969 | 47(52) | | | 41 | | | |
| 1968 | 45(41) | | | 39 | | | |
| 1967 | 45(47) | | | 40 | | | |
| 1966 | 44(47) | | | 38 | | | |
| 1965 | 56 | | | 51 | | | |
| 1964 | 45 | | | 39 | | | |
| 1963 | 44(49) | 44 | | | | | |
| 1962 | (53) | | | | | | |

| | | | | |
|---|---|---|---|---|
| 1961 | 60(53) | | | |
| 1960 | 60(49) | >50 | | |
| 1959 | (48) | | | |
| 1958 | (50) | | | |
| 1957 | (49) | | | |
| 1956 | (44) | | | |
| 1955 | (47) | | | |
| 1954 | (46) | | | |
| 1953 | (50) | | | |
| 1952 | (58) | | | |
| 1951 | (43) | | | |
| 1950 | 37 | 35 | | |
| 1949 | 36 | | 26 | |
| 1930 | 29 | 29 | | |
| 1925 | 18 | | 14 | |
| 1922 | 18 | | 14 | |
| 1921 | 16.5 | | | |
| 1907 | | 16 | | |
| 1906 | | 16 | | |
| 1905 | | 17 | | |
| 1904 | | 16 | | |
| 1903 | | 15 | | |
| 1900 | 17 | | | |
| 1892–7 | 16 | | | |
| 1886 | 13 | | | |
| 1885 | | 15 | | |
| Nov. 1885 | | | | 14 |
| June 1885 | | | | 14 |
| April 1885 | | | | 11 |
| Jan. 1885 | | | | 15 |
| 1884 | | 13 | | |

*continued*

**Table 2.3** *(cont'd)*

| Year | Graduates as % of solicitors admitted[a] | Graduates as % of new articles | Graduates as % of enrolment in Law Society College of Law | Law graduates as % of solicitors admitted | Law graduates as % of enrolment in Law Society College of Law | Graduates as % of those passing Law Society examination | |
|---|---|---|---|---|---|---|---|
| | | | | | | Inter-mediate | Final |
| 1883 | | 11 | | | | | |
| Nov. 1883 | | | | | | 11 | 11 |
| June 1883 | | | | | | 9 | 9 |
| April 1883 | | | | | | 18 | 13 |
| Jan. 1883 | | | | | | 12 | 14 |
| 1882 | 11 | 12 | | | | | |
| Nov. 1882 | | | | | | 9 | 8 |
| June 1882 | | | | | | 10 | 9 |
| April 1882 | | | | | | 7 | 11 |
| June 1882 | | | | | | 7 | 12 |
| 1881 | 16 | 11 | | | | | |
| Nov. 1881 | | | | | | 7 | 8 |
| June 1881 | | | | | | 6 | 8 |
| April 1881 | | | | | | 7 | 9 |
| Jan. 1881 | | | | | | 7 | 6 |
| Nov. 1880 | | | | | | 9 | 7 |
| June 1880 | | | | | | 6 | 8 |
| April 1880 | | | | | | 10 | 19 |
| Jan. 1880 | | | | | | 14 | 15 |

[a] Figures in parentheses are calculations from final examination pass lists and admissions to Roll in *Law Society's Gazette*; complete listing 1950–63, approximately one-quarter sample 1966–80

*Sources*: Law Society, 1977: 82, 85, X.2; Ormrod Committee, 1971: 112; Abel-Smith and Stevens, 1967: 398; 1968: 130; Wilson and Marsh, 1981: 38; Johnstone and Hopson, 1967: 414 n. 28; Wilson, 1966: 5,7; Zander, 1961; 1968: 22 n. 1; Royal Commission, 1979, vol. 1: 609–10, 613; vol. 2: 47–8; Gower, 1950: 151 n. 92; Gower and Price, 1957: 323; Kirk, 1976: 57–8, 64; Law Society, Annual Report, 1908; 1983–4; Incorporated Law Society, Calendar; *Law Society's Gazette*

**Table 2.4** Education and experience of new admissions, 1969, 1980–5

| | Law graduates | | Non-law graduates | | Mature students | | School leavers | | Overseas solicitors | | Barristers | | Scots and N. Ireland solicitors | | Total |
|---|---|---|---|---|---|---|---|---|---|---|---|---|---|---|---|
| | no. | % | no. | % | no. | % | no. | % | no. | % | no. | % | no. | % | |
| 1969 | 553 | 40.5 | 86 | 6.3 | | | | | | | | | | | |
| 1980 | 2267 | 64 | 618 | 17 | 102 | 3 | 406 | 11 | 73 | 2 | 65 | 2 | 7 | 0.2 | 3538 |
| 1981 | 2217 | 69 | 483 | 15 | 92 | 3 | 278 | 9 | 96 | 3 | 50 | 2 | 7 | 0.2 | 3223 |
| 1982 | 1608 | 72 | 299 | 13 | 41 | 2 | 192 | 9 | 73 | 3 | 21 | 1 | 2 | 0 | 2237 |
| 1983 | 1822 | 70 | 344 | 13 | 56 | 2 | 191 | 7 | 138 | 5 | 42 | 2 | 3 | 0 | 2596 |
| 1984 | 1979 | 73 | 383 | 14 | 80 | 3 | 144 | 5 | 102 | 4 | 35 | 1 | 5 | 0.2 | 2728 |
| 1985 | 2014 | 75 | 408 | 15 | 87[a] | 3[a] | [a] | [a] | 174[b] | 6[b] | [b] | [b] | [b] | [b] | 2683 |

[a] Mature students and school leavers.
[b] Overseas solicitors and barristers.
*Sources*: *Law Society's Gazette*; Marks, 1985; 1986; Law Society, Annual Report, 1983–4; 1984–5

**Table 2.6** Enrolment in Law Society College of Law and professional courses in provincial universities, 1864–5 to 1982

| | Law Society | | | | Law Society | | | Law Society | | |
|---|---|---|---|---|---|---|---|---|---|---|
| Year | New Enrolment | Total Enrolment | Year | Provincial universities | Total | Women students | Year | Lectures | Classes | Examination classes |
| 1982 | 3,372 | | 1939–40 | 168 | | | 1883–84 | 98 | 34 | 82 |
| 1981 | | | 1938–39 | 984 | | | 1882–83 | 83 | 38 | 82 |
| 1980 | | | 1937–38 | 937 | | | 1881–82 | 76 | 0 | 102 |
| 1979 | 5,643 | | 1936–37 | 972 | | | 1880–81 | 81 | 0 | 120 |
| 1978 | 5,298 | | 1935–36 | 1,132 | | | 1879–80 | 85 | 0 | 87 |
| 1977 | 4,120 | | 1934–35 | 1,191 | | | | | | |
| 1976 | 3,950 | 12,985 | 1933–34 | 1,207 | 600 | | 1876–77 | 146 | 65 | |
| 1975 | 3,639 | 12,153 | 1932–33 | 1,085 | | | 1875–76 | 157 | 54 | |
| 1974 | 3,235 | 11,374 | 1931–32 | 1,053 | | | 1874–75 | 180 | 69 | |
| 1973 | 3,182 | 10,230 | 1930–31 | 1,037 | | | 1873–34 | 207 | 78 | |
| 1972 | 3,086 | 10,269 | 1929–30 | 985 | | | 1872–73 | 244 | 94 | |
| 1971 | 2,721 | 8,778 | 1928–29 | 1,025 | 496 | | 1871–72 | 229 | 75 | |
| 1970 | 2,442 | 8,730 | 1927–28 | 931 | 486 | | 1870–71 | 252 | 95 | |
| 1969 | 2,286 | 8,920 | 1926–27 | 931 | 463 | | 1869–70 | 210 | 75 | |
| 1968 | 2,244 | 8,972 | 1925–26 | 594 | 391 | 14 | 1868–69 | 171 | 63 | |
| 1967 | 2,034 | 8,251 | 1924–25 | 489 | 297 | 10 | 1867–68 | 152 | 70 | |
| 1966 | 1,908 | 7,558 | 1923–24 | 325 | 226 | 10 | 1866–67 | 76 | 95 | |

| | | | | | | | | | |
|---|---|---|---|---|---|---|---|---|---|
| 1965 | 1,792 | 7,027 | 1922–23 | 291 | 206 | 13 | 1865–66 | 118 | 162 |
| 1964 | 2,080 | 6,010 | 1921–22 | | 243 | 18 | 1864–65 | 187 | |
| 1963 | 1,923 | 4,544 | 1920–21 | | 262 | 9 | | | |
| 1962 | 1,989 | | 1919–20 | | 295 | 7 | 1846 | 300 | |
| 1961 | 1,574 | | 1918–19 | | 208 | | 1836 | 200 | |
| 1960 | 1,183 | | 1917–18 | | 62 | | | | |
| 1959 | 1,051 | | 1916–17 | | 69 | | | | |
| 1958 | 972 | | 1915–16 | | 87 | | | | |
| 1957 | 915 | | 1914–15 | | 138 | | | | |
| 1956 | 782 | | 1913–14 | | 283 | | | | |
| 1955 | 899 | | 1912–13 | | 274 | | | | |
| 1954 | | | 1911–12 | | 249 | | | | |
| 1953 | | | 1910–11 | | 247 | | | | |
| 1952 | 942 | | 1909–10 | | 271 | | | | |
| 1951 | 842 | | 1908–09 | | 277 | | | | |
| 1950 | 1,016 | | 1907–08 | | 300 | | | | |
| 1949 | 848 | | 1906–07 | | 276 | | | | |
| 1948 | 800 | | 1905–06 | | 235 | | | | |
| | | | | | (214) | | | | |
| | | | 1904–05 | | 132 | | | | |
| | | | | | (212) | | | | |
| | | | 1903–04 | | 135 | | | | |

*Sources*: Law Society, Annual Reports; Kirk, 1976: 55–6, 61; Law Society, 1977: 6

**Table 2.5** Proportion seeking to become solicitors without an undergraduate law degree, 1880–1976

| Passing intermediate law examination | | Taking final examination two years later | | |
|---|---|---|---|---|
| Years | Number | Years | Number | Per cent[a] |
| 1880–89 | 8,085 | 1882–91 | 10,257 | 79 |
| 1890–99 | 6,018 | 1892–1901 | 7,966 | 76 |
| 1900–09 | 5,882 | 1902–11 | 8,442 | 70 |
| 1910–19 | 2,459 | 1912–21 | 3,786 | 65 |
| 1920–29 | 4,541 | 1922–31 | 6,016 | 75 |
| 1930–39 | 5,862 | 1932–41 | 10,013 | 59 |
| 1940–49 | 1,317 | 1942–51 | 8,303 | 16 |
| 1950–59 | 4,584 | 1952–61 | 12,118 | 38 |
| 1963–65 | 4,786 | 1965–67 | 10,121 | 47 |
| 1966–68 | 5,346 | 1968–70 | 15,368 | 35 |
| 1969–71 | 4,793 | 1971–73 | 20,590 | 23 |
| 1972–74 | 4,392 | 1974–76 | 26,886 | 16 |
| 1975–76 | 3,033 | 1977–78 | 22,366 | 14 |

[a] Because the denominator includes those repeating the final examination, the ratio is artificially deflated.
*Source*: table 2.9

**Table 2.7** Minimum salaries for articled clerks (£), 1980–1 to 1987–8

| | | *In lodgings:* | |
|---|---|---|---|
| *Year* | *In parental home* | *London* | *Provinces* |
| 1980–1 | 1781 | 3016 | 2442 |
| 1981–2 | 1933 | 3349 | 2711 |
| | *London* | | *Provinces* |
| 1982–3 | 3728 | | 2998 |
| | *Inner London* | *Outer London* | *Provinces* |
| 1983–4 | 3900 | 3650 | 3150 |
| 1984–5 | 4300 | 4000 | 3375 |
| 1985–6 | 4850 | 4550 | 3850 |
| 1986–7 | 5550 | 5250 | 4450 |
| 1987–8 | 6400 | 6100 | 5200 |

*Sources*: Law Society Standing Committee on Entry and Training, 1983: app. 10; Law Society Committee on Education and Training, 1985; Law Society, Annual Report, 1985–6: 13

| | 1962 | 1961 | 1960 | 1959 | 1958 | 1957 | 1956 | 1955 | 1954 | 1953 | 1952 | 1951 | 1950 | 1949 | 1948 |
|---|---|---|---|---|---|---|---|---|---|---|---|---|---|---|---|
| Positions found by introduction: | | | | | | | | | | | | | | | |
| Solicitors | 204 | 204 | 220 | 237 | 247 | 223 | 203 | | 173 | 209 | 190 | | | 199 | |
| Clerks | 186 | 112 | 96 | 44 | 36 | 40 | 21 | | 16 | 14 | | | | | |
| Partnerships wanted: | | | | | | | | | | | | | | | |
| Ads | | | | | | 299 | 266 | | 331 | 406 | 423 | 397 | 326 | 307 | 313 |
| Replies | | | | | | 969 | 1,078 | | 929 | 849 | 867 | 1,055 | 824 | 722 | 724 |
| Ratio replies/ads | | 3 | | | | 3.2 | 4.1 | | 3.6 | 2.1 | 2.0 | 2.7 | 2.5 | 2.4 | 2.3 |
| Partnerships offered: | | | | | | | | | | | | | | | |
| Ads | | | | | | 193 | 210 | | 205 | 130 | 180 | 188 | 183 | 174 | 164 |
| Replies | | | | | | 2,299 | 1,830 | | 1,881 | 1,612 | 1,844 | 1,674 | 1,366 | 1,213 | 1,160 |
| ratio replies/ads | | 3.5 | | | | 11.9 | 8.7 | | 9.2 | 12.4 | 10.2 | 8.9 | 7.5 | 7.0 | 7.1 |
| Situations wanted admitted: | | | | | | | | | | | | | | | |
| Ads | | | | | | 360 | 324 | | 333 | 431 | 371 | 335 | 468 | 254 | 195 |
| Replies | | | | | | 1,598 | 1,515 | | 1,867 | 1,458 | 1,240 | 1,417 | 1,714 | 1,401 | 1,116 |
| Ratio replies/ads | 7.5 | 7.5 | 9.5 | 8 | | 4.4 | 4.7 | | 5.6 | 3.4 | 3.3 | 4.2 | 3.7 | 5.5 | 5.7 |
| Situations wanted unadmitted: | | | | | | | | | | | | | | | |
| Ads | | | | | | 205 | 213 | | 221 | 264 | 247 | 298 | 235 | 189 | 162 |
| Replies | | | | | | 596 | 569 | | 630 | 824 | 593 | 694 | 620 | 496 | 517 |
| Ratio replies/ads | 4 | 7 | 5 | | | 2.9 | 2.7 | | 2.9 | 3.1 | 2.4 | 2.3 | 2.6 | 2.6 | 3.2 |
| Situations vacant: | | | | | | | | | | | | | | | |
| Ads | | | | | | 864 | 896 | | 800 | 707 | 678 | 839 | 995 | 1,124 | 1,072 |
| Replies | | | | | | 5,473 | 5,809 | | 4,952 | 5,254 | 4,305 | 4,164 | 4,186 | 3,842 | 3,272 |
| Ratio replies/ads | | | 1.5 | | | 6.3 | 6.5 | | 6.2 | 7.4 | 6.3 | 5.0 | 4.2 | 3.4 | 3.1 |
| Articles vacant: | | | | | | | | | | | | | | | |
| Ads | | | | | | 45 | 76 | | 93 | 92 | 52 | 67 | 42 | 67 | 68 |
| Replies | | | | | | 129 | 276 | | 243 | 220 | 180 | 192 | 98 | 95 | 99 |
| Ratio replies/ads | | | | | | 2.9 | 3.6 | | 2.6 | 2.4 | 3.5 | 2.9 | 2.3 | 1.4 | 1.5 |
| Articles wanted: | | | | | | | | | | | | | | | |
| Ads | | | | | | 95 | 46 | | 51 | 43 | 44 | 54 | 43 | 42 | 41 |
| Replies | | | | | | 305 | 233 | | 214 | 160 | 227 | 253 | 218 | 133 | 166 |
| Ratio replies/ads | | | | | | 3.2 | 5.1 | | 4.2 | 3.7 | 5.2 | 4.7 | 5.1 | 3.2 | 4.0 |
| Total | | | | | | | | | | | | | | | |
| Ads | 4,862 | 4,894 | 4,914 | 4,222 | 2,959 | 2,353 | 2,366 | | 2,362 | 2,365 | 2,336 | 3,451 | 2,369 | 2,233 | 2,042 |
| Replies | 13,453 | 11,912 | 11,994 | 13,461 | 12,482 | 11,940 | 12,024 | | 11,358 | 10,885 | 10,171 | 10,388 | 9,209 | 7,973 | 7,084 |

*Source*: Law Society, Annual Reports

**Table 2.9** Articled clerks in large City firms, by degree, 1976

| Firm | Oxbridge graduates % | Graduates of other universities % | Non-graduates % |
|---|---|---|---|
| Slaughter & May | 42 | 32 | 26 |
| Linklaters & Paine | 40 | 26 | 34 |
| Allen & Overy | 66 | 13 | 21 |
| Freshfields | 44 | 31 | 25 |

*Source*: Podmore, 1980: 33 n. 18

**Table 2.10** Number taking and passing and percentage passing Law Society examinations, 1836–1986

| | Preliminary | | | Final: part I/CPE | | | Final: part II | | | | |
|---|---|---|---|---|---|---|---|---|---|---|---|
| | | Passing | | | Passing | | | Passing all | | Passing part | |
| | Taking | no. | % | Taking | no. | % | Taking | no. | % | no. | % |
| 1986 August | | | | | | | 3,242 | 1,948 | 60.1 | 401 | 12.4 |
| 1986 February | | | | | | | 811 | 530 | 63.4 | 76 | 9.4 |
| 1985 August | | | | | | | 5,068 | 2,539 | 50.1 | 531 | 10.5 |
| 1985 August[e] | | | | | | | 4,826 | 2,540 | 52.2 | 531 | 11.6 |
| | | | | | | | 3,181 | 1,869 | 58.8 | 331 | 10.4 |
| February[f] | | | | | | | 726 | 497 | 68.5 | 65 | 9.0 |
| 1984 August[e] | | | | | | | 4,547 | 2,396 | 52.7 | 523 | 11.5 |
| | | | | | | | 3,225 | 1,774 | 55.0 | 352 | 10.9 |

| | | | | | | | | | | | | |
|---|---|---|---|---|---|---|---|---|---|---|---|---|
| | February[f] | | | | | | | 660 | 408 | 61.8 | 79 | 12.0 |
| 1983 | August[e] | | | | | | | 4,547 | 2,417 | 53.2 | 478 | 10.5 |
| | | | | | | | | 3,163 | 1,891 | 59.8 | 329 | 10.4 |
| | February[f] | | | | | | | 643 | 399 | 62.1 | 80 | 12.4 |
| 1982 | August[e] | | | | 5,241[g] | 3,447[g] | 66[g] | 4,353 | 2,467 | 56.7 | 466 | 10.7 |
| | | | | | | | | 3,187 | 1,826 | 57.3 | 293 | 9.2 |
| | February[f] | | | | | | | 572 | 341 | 59.6 | 101 | 17.7 |
| 1981 | August | | | | 4,658[h] | 3,010[h] | 65[h] | 4,457 | 2,116 | 47.5 | NA | NA |
| | | | | | | | | 3,150 | 1,641 | 52.1 | 340 | 10.8 |
| | February | | | | | | | 2,040 | 1,267[i] | 62.1[i] | | |
| 1980 | August[e] | | | | 1,008[j] | 350[j] | 35[j] | 3,679 | 2,509[i] | 68.2[i] | | |
| | | | | | | | | 2,729 | 1,487 | 54.5 | 238 | 8.7 |
| | February | | | | | | | 5,623 | 3,895[i] | 68.7[i] | | |
| 1979 | August | | | | 1,855[j] | 780[j] | 42[j] | 7,173 | 4,710[i] | 65.7[i] | | |
| | February | | | | | | | 7,368 | 4,858[i] | 65.9[i] | | |
| | | | | | | | | Taking | Passing | | | |
| | | | | | | | | | no. | % | | |
| 1978 | | 42 | 13 | 31 | 2,912 | 1,493 | 51 | 11,700 | 7,936 | 68 | | |
| 1977 | | 63 | 14 | 22 | 2,805 | 1,535 | 55 | 10,666 | 7,904 | 74 | | |
| 1976 | | 77 | 21 | 27 | 2,799 | 1,510 | 54 | 9,722 | 6,667 | 69 | | |
| 1975 | | 101 | 30 | 30 | 2,697 | 1,523 | 56 | 8,839 | 6,307 | 71 | | |
| 1974 | | 82 | 23 | 28 | 2,750 | 1,657 | 60 | 8,325 | 5,549 | 67 | | |
| 1973 | | 84 | 32 | 38 | 2.725 | 1,464 | 54 | 7,167 | 4,701 | 66 | | |
| 1972 | | | | | 2.340 | 1,271 | 54 | 7,009 | 4,630 | 66 | | |
| 1971 | | 73 | 25 | 34 | 2,002 | 1,296 | 65 | 6,414 | 4,818 | 75 | | |
| 1970 | | 69 | 30 | 43 | 2,912 | 1,754 | 60 | 6,050 | 4,529 | 75 | | |
| 1969 | | 59 | 24 | 41 | 3,049 | 1,743 | 57 | 5,002 | 3,295 | 66 | | |
| 1968 | | 65 | 22 | 34 | 2,938 | 1,566 | 53 | 4,316 | 2,797 | 65 | | |
| 1967 | | 55 | 21 | 38 | 3,269 | 1,964 | 60 | 3,916 | 2,508 | 64 | | |
| 1966 | | 80 | 29 | 36 | 3,701 | 1,816 | 49 | 3,476 | 1,926 | 55 | | |
| 1965 | | 86 | 33 | 38 | 3,712 | 1,926 | 52 | 2,729 | 1,816 | 66 | | |
| 1964 | | | | | 3,324 | 1,870 | 56 | 2,309 | 1,606 | 70 | | |
| 1963 | | | | | 1,648 | 990 | 60 | 1,740 | 1,260 | 72 | | |

*continued*

**Table 2.10** (*cont'd*)

| | Preliminary | | | Intermediate | | | | | | Final | | | Honours | | |
|---|---|---|---|---|---|---|---|---|---|---|---|---|---|---|---|
| | | | | Law | | | Trust accounts | | | | | | | | |
| | Taking | Passing no. | % | Taking | Passing no. | % | Taking | Passing no. | % | Taking | Passing no. | % | Taking | Passing no. | % |
| 1962 | | | | 1,623 | 823 | 51 | 2,350 | 1,103 | 47 | 1,408 | 743 | 53 | 472 | 203 | 43 |
| 1961 | 121 | 50 | 41 | 953 | 575 | 60 | 1,343 | 764 | 57 | 1,205 | 708 | 59 | 475 | 233 | 49 |
| 1960 | 115 | 52 | 45 | 817 | 467 | 57 | 1,505 | 798 | 53 | 1,145 | 684 | 58 | 481 | 252 | 52 |
| 1959 | 113 | 44 | 39 | 769 | 434 | 56 | 1,413 | 781 | 55 | 1,186 | 760 | 64 | 491 | 289 | 59 |
| 1958 | 144 | 59 | 41 | 718 | 444 | 62 | 1,381 | 722 | 52 | 1,239 | 666 | 54 | 358 | 197 | 55 |
| 1957 | 66 | 27 | 41 | 693 | 417 | 60 | 1,373 | 747 | 54 | 1,159 | 667 | 58 | 424 | 208 | 49 |
| 1956 | 84 | 38 | 45 | 734 | 435 | 59 | 1,378 | 720 | 52 | 1,250 | 733 | 59 | 282[d] | 164[d] | 58[d] |
| 1955 | 96 | 40 | 42 | 688 | 418 | 61 | 1,293 | 699 | 54 | 1,265 | 693 | 55 | 302[d] | 159[d] | 53[d] |
| 1954 | 151 | 45 | 30 | 715 | 471 | 66 | 1,310 | 772 | 59 | 1,172 | 641 | 55 | 226 | 131 | 58 |
| 1953 | 176 | 61 | 35 | 832 | 526 | 63 | 1,180 | 738 | 63 | 1,258 | 601 | 48 | 226 | 56 | 25 |
| 1952 | 345 | 123 | 36 | 821 | 474 | 58 | 885 | 633 | 72 | 1,239 | 592 | 48 | 291 | 57 | 20 |
| 1951 | 320 | 142 | 44 | 735 | 494 | 67 | 839 | 626 | 75 | 1,184 | 680 | 57 | 278 | 105 | 38 |
| 1950 | 286 | 111 | 39 | 688 | 471 | 68 | 903 | 723 | 80 | 1,406 | 818 | 58 | 267 | 85 | 32 |
| 1949 | 228 | 95 | 42 | 657 | 471 | 72 | 1,024 | 714 | 70 | 1,528 | 882 | 58 | 313 | 92 | 29 |
| 1948 | 288 | 131 | 45 | 348 | 246 | 71 | 1,567 | 966 | 62 | 1,397 | 844 | 60 | 317 | 73 | 23 |
| 1947 | 267 | 136 | 51 | 225 | 145 | 64 | 1,805 | 1,219 | 68 | 1,446 | 890 | 62 | 274 | 75 | 27 |
| 1946 | 171 | 88 | 51 | 122 | 83 | 68 | 1,224 | 980 | 80 | 791 | 560 | 71 | | 101 | 13 |
| 1945 | 95 | 46 | 48 | 106 | 72 | 68 | 228 | 164 | 72 | 163 | 113 | 69 | | 22 | 13 |
| 1944 | 66 | 37 | 56 | 126 | 97 | 77 | 197 | 130 | 66 | 165 | 84 | 51 | | 18 | 11 |
| 1943 | 57 | 25 | 44 | 148 | 125 | 84 | 193 | 123 | 64 | 109 | 77 | 71 | | 5 | 5 |
| 1942 | 90 | 43 | 48 | 157 | 119 | 76 | 203 | 134 | 66 | 114 | 75 | 66 | | 10 | 9 |
| 1941 | 110 | 52 | 47 | 247 | 165 | 67 | 333 | 159 | 48 | 215 | 150 | 70 | | 21 | 10 |

| | | | | | | | | | | | | | | |
|---|---|---|---|---|---|---|---|---|---|---|---|---|---|---|
| 1940 | 132 | 62 | 47 | 368 | 265 | 72 | 438 | 267 | 61 | 682 | 394 | 58 | 486 | 47 | 10 |
| 1939 | 195 | 112 | 57 | 687 | 411 | 60 | 742 | 498 | 67 | 1,197 | 648 | 54 | 475 | 90 | 19 |
| 1938 | 246 | 130 | 53 | 824 | 450 | 55 | 1,043 | 716 | 69 | 1,278 | 819 | 64 | 641 | 192 | 30 |
| 1937 | 267 | 119 | 45 | 1,190 | 721 | 61 | 1,291 | 986 | 76 | 1,382 | 930 | 67 | 619 | 209 | 34 |
| 1936 | 295 | 136 | 46 | 1,273 | 802 | 63 | 1,358 | 977 | 72 | 1,224 | 741 | 61 | 585 | 130 | 22 |
| 1935 | 381 | 161 | 42 | 1,182 | 676 | 57 | 1,273 | 808 | 63 | 1,104 | 776 | 70 | 497 | 133 | 27 |
| 1934 | 452 | 233 | 52 | 1,203 | 739 | 61 | 1,251 | 882 | 71 | 1,074 | 640 | 60 | 489 | 133 | 27 |
| 1933 | 550 | 236 | 43 | 1,062 | 478 | 45 | 1,118 | 699 | 63 | 984 | 590 | 60 | 486 | 135 | 28 |
| 1932 | 504 | 229 | 45 | 817 | 525 | 64 | 1,024 | 690 | 67 | 873 | 693 | 79 | 503 | 153 | 30 |
| 1931 | 477 | 258 | 54 | 782 | 512 | 65 | 949 | 658 | 69 | 461 | 355 | 77 | 96[c] | 34[c] | 35[c] |
| 1930 | 487 | 222 | 46 | 769 | 548 | 71 | 942 | 703 | 75 | 765 | 606 | 84 | 419 | 148 | 35 |
| 1929 | 416 | 220 | 53 | 929 | 671 | 72 | 934 | 696 | 75 | 772 | 646 | 83 | 355 | 171 | 48 |
| 1928 | 404 | 189 | 47 | 863 | 560 | 65 | 915 | 711 | 78 | 738 | 616 | 82 | 310 | 131 | 42 |
| 1927 | 271 | 168 | 62 | 802 | 547 | 68 | 868 | 701 | 81 | 605 | 496 | 93 | 290 | 126 | 43 |
| 1926 | 255 | 135 | 53 | 811 | 553 | 68 | 752 | 532 | 70 | 455 | 422 | 90 | 205 | 106 | 52 |
| 1925 | 283 | 163 | 58 | 644 | 414 | 64 | 638 | 516 | 81 | 547 | 490 | 82 | 203 | 91 | 45 |
| 1924 | 315 | 179 | 57 | 672 | 451 | 67 | 577 | 480 | 83 | 584 | 479 | 83 | 97 | 56 | 58 |
| 1923 | 275 | 164 | 60 | 536 | 273 | 51 | 592 | 473 | 80 | 561 | 468 | 82 | 85 | 54 | 64 |
| 1922 | 287 | 150 | 52 | 738 | 437 | 59 | 761 | 574 | 75 | 528 | 431 | 82 | | 72 | 14 |
| 1921 | 271 | 137 | 51 | 653 | 409 | 63 | 691 | 586 | 85 | 414 | 341 | 92 | | 79 | 19 |
| 1920 | 310 | 187 | 60 | 388 | 226 | 58 | 603 | 541 | 90 | 579 | 534 | 97 | | 128 | 22 |
| 1919 | 168 | 108 | 64 | 109 | 76 | 70 | 376 | 363 | 97 | 388 | 377 | | | 97 | 25 |
| 1918 | 84 | 48 | 57 | 68 | 42 | 62 | 59 | 51 | 86 | 87 | 80 | 92 | | 14 | 16 |
| 1917 | 55 | 31 | 56 | 53 | 35 | 66 | 48 | 38 | 79 | 43 | 38 | 88 | | 3 | 7 |
| 1916 | 93 | 48 | 52 | 133 | 91 | 68 | 118 | 97 | 82 | 166 | 130 | 78 | | 19 | 11 |
| 1915 | 109 | 56 | 51 | 203 | 122 | 60 | 209 | 161 | 77 | 300 | 218 | 73 | 145 | 28 | 19 |
| 1914 | 267 | 132 | 49 | 718 | 426 | 59 | 568 | 372 | 65 | 553 | 408 | 74 | 237 | 44 | 19 |
| 1913 | 266 | 145 | 55 | 658 | 406 | 62 | 611 | 418 | 68 | 605 | 457 | 76 | 285 | 35 | 12 |
| 1912 | 310 | 174 | 56 | 690 | 434 | 63 | 835 | 501 | 60 | 651 | 508 | 78 | 326 | 66 | 20 |
| 1911 | 365 | 227 | 62 | 660 | 419 | 63 | 780 | 456 | 58 | 661 | 478 | 72 | 316 | 69 | 22 |
| 1910 | 357 | 215 | 60 | 607 | 408 | 67 | 829 | 482 | 58 | 724 | 537 | 74 | 341 | 107 | 31 |

continued

**Table 2.10** *(cont'd)*

| | Preliminary | | | Intermediate | | | | | | Final | | | Honours | | |
|---|---|---|---|---|---|---|---|---|---|---|---|---|---|---|---|
| | | | | Law | | | Trust accounts | | | | | | | | |
| | Taking | Passing no. | % | Taking | Passing no. | % | Taking | Passing no. | % | Taking | Passing no. | % | Taking | Passing no. | % |
| 1909 | 366 | 235 | 64 | 646 | 431 | 67 | 573 | 320 | 56 | 772 | 549 | 71 | 337 | 90 | 27 |
| 1908 | 424 | 265 | 62 | 651 | 460 | 71 | 87 | 69 | 79 | 886 | 575 | 65 | 373 | 106 | 28 |
| 1907 | 424 | 252 | 59 | 676 | 503 | 74 | 143 | 124 | 87 | 841 | 522 | 62 | 380 | 107 | 28 |
| 1906 | 464 | 259 | 56 | 655 | 480 | 73 | 26 | 22 | 85 | 891 | 619 | 69 | 418 | 99 | 24 |
| 1905 | 546 | 301 | 55 | 663 | 444 | 67 | | | | 867 | 568 | 66 | 358 | 115 | 32 |
| 1904 | 581 | 330 | 57 | 1,017 | 771 | 76 | | | | 964 | 656 | 68 | 392 | 128 | 33 |
| 1903 | 557 | 367 | 66 | 883 | 648 | 73 | | | | 900 | 579 | 64 | 368 | 121 | 33 |
| 1902 | 536 | 370 | 69 | 1,166 | 924 | 79 | | | | 936 | 626 | 67 | 327 | 75 | 23 |
| 1901 | 503 | 282 | 56 | 899 | 674 | 75 | | | | 838 | 573 | 68 | 345 | 89 | 26 |
| 1900 | 506 | 358 | 71 | 791 | 547 | 69 | | | | 848 | 568 | 67 | 162 | 49 | 30 |
| 1899 | 613 | 442 | 72 | 801 | 622 | 78 | | | | 844 | 647 | 77 | | | |
| 1898 | 575 | 415 | 72 | 812 | 602 | 74 | | | | 824 | 640 | 78 | | | |
| 1897 | 531 | 362 | 68 | 834 | 668 | 80 | | | | 794 | 581 | 73 | | | |
| 1896 | 499 | 347 | 70 | 852 | 634 | 74 | | | | 728 | 567 | 78 | | | |
| 1895 | 520 | 377 | 72 | 837 | 568 | 68 | | | | 655 | 527 | 80 | | | |
| 1894 | 588 | 421 | 72 | 792 | 554 | 70 | | | | 696 | 446 | 64 | | | |
| 1893 | 583 | 404 | 69 | 679 | 552 | 81 | | | | 849 | 623 | 73 | | | |
| 1892 | 538 | 359 | 67 | 699 | 566 | 81 | | | | 890 | 613 | 69 | | | |
| 1891 | 590 | 380 | 64 | 761 | 616 | 81 | | | | 929 | 638 | 69 | | | |
| 1890 | 545 | 312 | 57 | 856 | 636 | 74 | | | | 933 | 644 | 69 | | | |
| 1889 | 549 | 328 | 60 | 861 | 626 | 73 | | | | 979 | 706 | 72 | | | |
| 1888 | 525 | 338 | 64 | 949 | 698 | 74 | | | | 988 | 672 | 68 | | | |
| 1887 | 746 | 568 | 76 | 989 | 742 | 75 | | | | 1,037 | 594 | 57 | | | |
| 1886 | 649 | 439 | 68 | 1,050 | 773 | 74 | | | | 1,147 | 852 | 74 | | | |

| | | | | | | | | | |
|---|---|---|---|---|---|---|---|---|---|
| [illegible] | [illegible] | [illegible] | [illegible] | [illegible] | [illegible] | [illegible] | [illegible] | [illegible] | 77 |
| 1883 | 770 | 625 | 81 | 1,250 | 907 | 73 | 1,033 | 808 | 78 |
| 1882 | 952 | 793 | 83 | 1,267 | 947 | 75 | 944 | 709 | 75 |
| 1881 | 980 | 798 | 81 | 1,250 | 890 | 71 | 913 | 760 | 83 |
| 1880 | 1,041 | 844 | 81 | 912 | 698 | 77 | 919 | 609 | 66 |
| 1879 | 979 | 759 | 76 | 980 | 774 | 79 | 847 | 660 | 78 |
| 1878 | 1,009 | 736 | 73 | 875 | 715 | 82 | 845 | 693 | 82 |
| 1877 | 936 | 652 | 70 | 800 | 703 | 88 | 797 | 645 | 81 |
| 1876 | 802 | 607 | 76 | 607 | 492 | 81 | 758 | 624 | 82 |
| 1875 | 921 | 694 | 75 | 973 | 746 | 77 | 1,012 | 718 | 71 |
| 1874 | 685 | 544 | 79 | 791 | 660 | 83 | 715 | 616 | 86 |
| 1873 | 825 | 652 | 79 | 861 | 768 | 89 | 650 | 560 | 86 |
| 1872 | 762 | 597 | 78 | 910 | 781 | 86 | 662 | 569 | 86 |
| 1871 | 898 | 710 | 79 | 540[a] | 419[a] | 78[a] | 551 | 490 | 89 |
| 1870 | 895 | 720 | 80 | 688 | 610 | 89 | 520 | 471 | 91 |
| 1869 | 800 | 612 | 76 | 633 | 567 | 90 | 492 | 428 | 87 |
| 1868 | 739 | 557 | 75 | 476 | 428 | 90 | 422 | 350 | 83 |
| 1867 | 694 | 530 | 76 | 527 | 476 | 83 | 461 | 393 | 85 |
| 1866 | 633 | 512 | 81 | 464 | 439 | 95 | 475 | 436 | 92 |
| 1864–65 | 444 | 380 | 86 | 412 | 383 | 93 | 544 | 493 | 91 |
| 1863–64 | 535 | 449 | 84 | 516 | 485 | 94 | 845 | 440 | 91 |
| 1862–63 | 407 | 333 | 82 | 125 | 121 | 97 | 439 | 374 | 85 |
| 1861–62 | 135 | 97 | 72 | 16 | 15 | 94 | 398 | 359 | 90 |
| 1860–61 | | | | | | | 477 | 417 | 87 |
| 1859–60 | | | | | | | 383 | 344 | 90 |
| 1858–59 | | | | | | | 443 | 392 | 88 |
| 1857–58 | | | | | | | 361 | 293 | 81 |
| 1856–57 | | | | | | | | | |
| 1855–56 | | | | | | | | | |
| 1854–55 | | | | | | | 393 | 355 | 90 |
| 1853–54 | | | | | | | 391 | 347 | 89 |
| 1852–53 | | | | | | | | | |
| 1851–52 | | | | | | | 394 | 352 | 90 |
| 1850–51 | | | | | | | 471 | 445 | 94 |

*continued*

**Table 2.10** (*cont'd*)

| | Preliminary | | | Intermediate | | | | | | Final | | | Honours | | |
|---|---|---|---|---|---|---|---|---|---|---|---|---|---|---|---|
| | | | | Law | | | Trust accounts | | | | | | | | |
| | Taking | Passing no. | % | Taking | Passing no. | % | Taking | Passing no. | % | Taking | Passing no. | % | Taking | Passing no. | % |
| 1849–50 | | | | | | | | | | | | | | | |
| 1848–49 | | | | | | | | | | 417 | 391 | 94 | | | |
| 1847–48 | | | | | | | | | | 429 | 400 | 96 | | | |
| 1846–47 | | | | | | | | | | | | | | | |
| 1845–46 | | | | | | | | | | 346 | 309 | 89 | | | |
| 1845 | | | | | | | | | | 347 | 318 | 92 | | | |
| 1844 | | | | | | | | | | 392 | 378 | 96 | | | |
| 1843 | | | | | | | | | | 410 | 382 | 93 | | | |
| 1842 | | | | | | | | | | 394 | 376 | 95 | | | |
| 1841 | | | | | | | | | | 415 | 395 | 95 | | | |
| 1840 | | | | | | | | | | 497 | 486 | 98 | | | |
| 1839 | | | | | | | | | | 440 | 415 | 94 | | | |
| 1838 | | | | | | | | | | 465 | 445 | 96 | | | |
| 1837 | | | | | | | | | | 439 | 424 | 97 | | | |
| 1836 | | | | | | | | | | 207 | 207 | 100 | | | |

[a] Trinity term examination results missing.
[b] No separate honours examination. Percentage calculated on base of those taking final.
[c] Results available for only one of the three exams this year.
[d] Results available for only two of the three exams this year.
[e] First row(s) represent those who sat all or part; last row sat all.
[f] Virtually all those sitting the February examination are repeaters.
[g] CPE for all of 1982; 145 took the old part I, 51 passed (35 per cent).
[h] CPE for all of of 1981; according to one source, 479 took old part I, 137 passed (29 per cent); according to another, 412 took old part I, 145 passed (35 per cent).
[i] Does not distinguish between those who passed all or part.
[j] Final part I for entire year.

*Sources*: *Law Notes*; Law Society Printed Lists of those passing part II qualifying examinations in whole or part; Law Society manuscripts; 82 *LSG* 3430, 1985; 83 *LSG* 3499–500, 1986; AGCAS, 1980a: 2; Law Society, Annual Reports

**Table 2.11** Pass rates on examinations carrying exemptions from Law Society preliminary examination, 1906–7

| | | | |
|---|---|---|---|
| *Oxford and Cambridge Schools Examination Board (July 1907)* | | | |
| Higher certificate | | 58% | (765/1315) |
| Lower certificate | | 45% | (386/867) |
| *Cambridge local examination (Dec. 1906)* | | | |
| Junior boys: | under 16 | 74% | (2557/3456) |
| | over 16 | 46% | (475/1033) |
| Senior boys: | under 19 | 78% | (1076/1380) |
| | over 19 | 31% | (72/232) |
| *Oxford local examination (Dec. 1906)* | | | |
| Junior boys: | under 16 | 71% | (5911/8369) |
| | over 16 | 63% | (1390/2208) |
| Senior boys: | under 19 | 64% | (4058/6387) |
| | over 19 | 37% | (525/1438) |

*Source*: Law Society, Annual Report, 1908: appendix to report of the Examinations Committee, pp. 83–4

**Table 2.12** Pass rates on Law Society final examination, by university and polytechnic graduates and class of degree, 1980–6

| | 1980 | | | 1981 | | | 1982 | | | 1980–82 | 1984 | 1985[a] | | | 1986[a] | | |
|---|---|---|---|---|---|---|---|---|---|---|---|---|---|---|---|---|---|
| | Sat | Passed or referred | % | Sat | Passed or referred | % | Sat | Passed or referred | % | % Passed or referred | % Passed or referred[a] | Sat | Passed or referred | % | Sat | Passed or referred | % |
| Univ. I and II (1) | 559 | 552 | 93 | 794 | 696 | 88 | | | | 90 | | | | | | | |
| CNAA I and II (1) | 112 | 95 | 85 | 108 | 79 | 73 | | | | 80 | | | | | | | |
| Univ. II (2) | 183 | 108 | 59 | 843 | 505 | 60 | | | | 63 | | | | | | | |
| CNAA II (2) | 373 | 184 | 43 | 411 | 162 | 39 | | | | 44 | | | | | | | |
| Univ. III and unclassed | 164 | 57 | 35 | 128 | 31 | 24 | | | | 32 | | | | | | | |
| CNAA III and unclassed | 129 | 30 | 23 | 135 | 26 | 19 | | | | 20 | | | | | | | |
| All univ. | 906 | 687 | 76 | 1765 | 1227 | 70 | | | | 72 | 73 | | | 75 | | | 79.9 |
| All CNAA | 614 | 309 | 50 | 654 | 267 | 41 | | | | 46 | 47 | | | 50 | | | 54.0 |
| All I and II (1) degrees | 671 | 617 | 92 | 902 | 775 | 86 | 862 | 758 | 88 | | 88–97[b] | 865[b] | 771[b] | 89[b] | 1131[b] | 1031[b] | 91.2[b] |
| All II (2) degrees | 1081 | 659 | 61 | 1254 | 667 | 53 | 1321 | 784 | 59 | | 54 | 1084 | 646 | 60 | 1271 | 778 | 61.2 |
| All III and unclassed degrees | 293 | 87 | 30 | 263 | 57 | 22 | 272 | 81 | 30 | | 51 | 615 | 315 | 51 | 263 | 91 | 34.6 |
| Law graduates | 2045 | 1362 | 67 | 2419 | 1499 | 62 | 2455 | 1623 | 66 | | | 2564 | 1732 | 68 | | | 59.5 |
| All first-time candidates | 2633 | 1702 | 65 | 3150 | 1985 | 63 | 3187 | 2104 | 66 | | | | | | | | 60.1 |

[a] Only law degrees.
[b] Includes unclassified second.
*Sources*: Marsh, 1983: 110; Law Society Standing Committee on Entry and Training, 1983: app. 3; 80 *LSG* 586, 1983; 82 *LSG* 3433, 1985; 83 *LSG* 3499–500, 1986

**Table 2.13** Pass rates on CPE, by those studying at College of Law and polytechnics, 1979–82

| | 1979 | | 1980 | | 1981 | | 1982 | |
|---|---|---|---|---|---|---|---|---|
| | Passed | Referred | Passed | Referred | Passed | Referred | Passed | Referred |
| College of Law | 74.8 | 6.3 | 78.0 | 3.9 | 82.0 | 4.1 | 80.9 | 4.3 |
| Polytechnics | 60.7 | 18.7 | 64.5 | 15.0 | 75.5 | 12.2 | 68.8 | 16.9 |

*Source*: Law Society Standing Committee on Entry and Training, 1983: app. 4

**Table 2.14** Changes in the size of the profession: practising certificates, annual change (absolute and percentage), solicitors admitted, new articles registered and solicitor deaths, 1730–1879 (fragmentary), 1879–1985 (complete)[f]

| Year | Practising certificates[e] | Annual change Absolute | % | Solicitors admitted[b] | New articles registered | Solicitor deaths |
|---|---|---|---|---|---|---|
| 1985 | 46,490 | 1653 | 3.7 | 2687 | 2889 | |
| 1984 | 44,837 | 1853 | 4.3 | 2728 | 2803 | |
| 1983 | 42,984 | 1336 | 3.2 | 2596 | 2623 | |
| 1982 | 41,738 | 1943 | 4.9 | 2241 | 2414 | |
| 1981 | 39,795 | 1963 | 5.2 | 3223 | 3149 | |
| 1980 | 37,832 | 3742 | 11.0 | 3538 | (1667)<br>1353[d]<br>1711 | |
| 1979 | (35,461)<br>34,090 | 1226 | 3.7 | (2723)<br>2552 | 3445<br>2814 | |
| 1978 | 32,864 | 56 | 0.2 | (2448)<br>2538 | 2983 | |
| 1977 | 32,812 | 1562 | 5.0 | 2480 | 2535 | |
| 1976 | 31,250 | 1400 | 4.7 | 2184 | 2730 | |
| 1975 | 29,850 | 1109 | 3.9 | 2203 | 2412 | 328 |
| 1974 | 28,741 | 1362 | 5.0 | 1849 | 2481 | 278 |
| 1973 | 27,379 | 1052 | 4.0 | 1764 | 2423 | 286 |
| 1972 | 26,327 | 961 | 3.8 | 1713 | 1914 | 318 |
| 1971 | 25,366 | 959 | 3.9 | 1682 | 1856 | 302 |
| 1970 | 24,407 | 833 | 3.5 | 1877 | 1739 | 336 |
| 1969 | 23,574 | 787 | 3.5 | 1365 | 1707 | 319 |
| 1968 | 22,787 | 564 | 2.5 | 997[a] | 1531 | 344 |
| 1967 | 22,223 | 551 | 2.5 | 1107 | 1613 | 324 |

| | | | | | | |
|---|---|---|---|---|---|---|
| 1966 | 21,672 | 417 | 2.0 | 1123 | 1520 | 319 |
| 1965 | 21,255 | 572 | 2.8 | 1009 | 1630 | 328 |
| 1964 | 20,683 | 414 | 2.0 | 663 | 1495 | 312 |
| 1963 | 20,269 | 479 | 2.5 | 805 | 1680 | 336 |
| 1962 | 19,790 | 352 | 1.8 | 766 | 1351 | 344 |
| 1961 | 19,438 | 369 | 1.9 | 685 | 1408 | 386 |
| 1960 | 19,069 | 329 | 1.8 | 711 | 954 | 398 |
| 1959 | 18,740 | 218 | 1.1 | 784 | 982 | 368 |
| 1958 | 18,522 | 178 | 1.0 | 673 | 906 | 401 |
| 1957 | 18,344 | 179 | 1.0 | 734 | 980 | 349 |
| 1956 | 18,165 | 22 | 0.1 | 745 | 985 | 383 |
| 1955 | 18,143 | 312 | 1.7 | 695 | 937 | 395 |
| 1954 | 17,831 | 144 | 0.8 | 603 | 1020 | 438 |
| 1953 | 17,687 | 59 | 0.3 | 649 | 982 | 422 |
| 1952 | 17,628 | 232 | 1.3 | 588 | 998 | 418 |
| 1951 | 17,396 | 361 | 2.1 | 717 | 1105 | 459 |
| 1950 | 17,035 | 717 | 4.4 | 926 | 937 | |
| 1949 | 16,318 | 751 | 4.8 | 895 | 873 | 404 |
| 1948 | 15,567 | 219 | 1.4 | 877 | 1137 | 411 |
| 1947 | 15,348 | 494 | 3.3 | 904 | 1263 | 447 |
| 1946 | 14,854 | 1875 | 14.4 | 441 | 1048 | 438 |
| 1945 | 12,979 | −84 | −0.6 | 180 | 222 | 480 |
| 1944 | 13,063 | −277 | −2.1 | 117 | 179 | 505 |
| 1943 | 13,340 | −495 | −3.6 | 122 | 186 | 480 |
| 1942 | 13,835 | −595 | −4.1 | 104 | 237 | 527 |
| 1941 | 14,430 | −1454 | −9.1 | 194 | 262 | 408 |
| 1940 | 15,884 | −1218 | −7.1 | 323 | 314 | 480 |
| 1939 | 17,102 | 203 | 1.2 | 567 | 512 | 462 |
| 1938 | 16,899 | 421 | 2.6 | 932 | 735 | 450 |
| 1937 | 16,478 | 179 | 1.1 | 831 | 568 | 456 |

*continued*

**Table 2.14** (*cont'd*)

| Year | Practising certificates[e] | Annual change Absolute | % | Solicitors admitted[b] | New articles registered | Solicitor deaths |
|---|---|---|---|---|---|---|
| 1936 | 16,299 | 167 | 1.0 | 751 | 847 | 536 |
| 1935 | 16,132 | 191 | 1.2 | 630 | 837 | 459 |
| 1934 | 15,941 | 158 | 1.0 | 655 | 964 | 472 |
| 1933 | 15,783 | 167 | 1.0 | 595 | 1007 | 504 |
| 1932 | 15,616 | −52 | −0.3 | 695 | 930 | 494 |
| 1931 | 15,668 | 220 | 1.4 | 615 | 861 | 488 |
| 1930 | 15,418 | 122 | 0.8 | 680 | 719 | 423 |
| 1929 | 15,297 | 129 | 0.9 | 610 | 742 | 440 |
| 1928 | 15,168 | 25 | 0.2 | 580 | 731 | 385 |
| 1927 | 15,143 | −9 | −0.1 | 440 | 789 | 314 |
| 1926 | 15,152 | 20 | 0.1 | 455 | 707 | 293 |
| 1925 | 15,132 | 61 | 0.4 | 455 | 903 | 279 |
| 1924 | 15,071 | 45 | 0.3 | 455 | 649 | 279 |
| 1923 | 15,026 | 137 | 0.9 | 444 | 637 | 291 |
| 1922 | 14,889 | 266 | 1.8 | 446 | 697 | 247 |
| 1921 | 14,623 | −114 | −1.0 | 383 | 611 | 268 |
| 1920 | (15,205)<br>14,747 | 387 | 2.7 | 606 | 747 | 296 |
| 1919 | (15,063)<br>14,380 | 1083 | +7.3 | 335 | 637 | 256 |
| 1918 | (14,040) | 194 | 1.4 | 81 | 137 | 305 |
| 1917 | (13,846) | −516 | −3.6 | 95 | 103 | 247 |

| | | | | | | |
|---|---|---|---|---|---|---|
| 1916 | (14,362) | −626 | −4.2 | 111 | 110 | 261 |
| 1915 | (14,988) | −889 | −5.7 | 158 | 188 | 262 |
| 1914 | (15,887) | −852 | −5.1 | 351 | 313 | |
| 1913 | (16,739)<br>16,788 | −20 | −0.1 | 485 | 428 | |
| 1912 | (16,759) | 20 | 0.1 | 494 | 459 | |
| 1911 | 17,259<br>(16,739) | −102 | 0.6 | 489 | 554 | |
| 1910 | (16,841) | −4 | 0 | 501 | 507 | |
| 1909 | (16,845)<br>16,797 | 120 | 0.7 | 561 | 529 | |
| 1908 | (16,725) | −16 | 0.1 | 512 | 524 | |
| 1907 | (16,741) | 117 | 0.7 | 590 | 538 | |
| 1906 | (16,624) | 116 | 0.7 | 591 | 538 | |
| 1905 | (16,508) | 53 | 0.3 | 593 | 632 | |
| 1904 | (16,455) | 93 | 0.6 | 637 | 597 | |
| 1903 | 16,265<br>(16,362) | 97 | 0.6 | 558 | 701 | |
| 1902 | (16,265) | 129 | 0.8 | 557 | 676 | |
| 1901 | 16,265<br>(16,136) | 130 | 0.8 | 584 | 674 | |
| 1900 | (16,006) | 56 | 0.4 | 593 | 667 | |
| 1899 | (15,950) | 140 | 0.9 | 633 | 718 | |
| 1898 | (15,810) | 181 | 1.1 | 581 | 696 | |
| 1897 | (15,629) | 111 | 0.7 | 556 | 718 | |
| 1896 | (15,518) | 94 | 0.6 | 533 | 707 | |

*continued*

**Table 2.14** (*cont'd*)

| Year | Practising certificates[e] | Annual change Absolute | % | Solicitors admitted[b] | New articles registered | Solicitor deaths |
|---|---|---|---|---|---|---|
| 1895 | (15,424) | 22 | 0.1 | 535 | 707 | |
| 1894 | (15,402) | 121 | 0.8 | 541 | 747 | |
| 1893 | (15,281) | 116 | 0.8 | 575 | 682 | |
| 1892 | (15,165) | −2 | 0 | 592 | 641 | |
| 1891 | (15,167) | 77 | 0.5 | 645 | 647 | |
| 1890 | (15,090) | 94 | 0.6 | 662 | 565 | |
| 1889 | (14,896) | 108 | 0.7 | 716 | 764 | |
| 1888 | (14,788) | 477 | 3.3 | 842 | 666 | |
| 1887 | (14,311) | 418 | 3.0 | 829 | 661 | |
| 1886 | (13,893) | 301 | 2.2 | 882 | 757 | |
| 1885 | (13,592) | 202 | 1.5 | | 824 | |
| 1884 | (13,390) | 324 | 2.5 | | 787 | |
| 1883 | (13,066) | 105 | 0.8 | | 930 | |
| 1882 | (12,961) | 396 | 3.2 | 808 | 947 | |
| 1881 | (12,565) | −123 | −1.0 | | 965 | |
| 1880 | 12,688 | 425 | 3.5 | | | |
| 1879 | 12,263 | | | | | |
| 1878 | | | | 656 | | |
| 1877 | | | | 594 | | |
| 1876 | | | | 306[c] | | |
| 1871 | 10,576 | | | | | |
| 1865 | *c.*10,200 | | | | | |
| 1864 | | | | | 466 | |
| 1863 | 10,418 | | | | 365 | |
| 1862 | | | | | 477 | |

| | | | | | |
|---|---|---|---|---|---|
| 1861 | 10,029 | | | | 606 |
| 1860 | | | | | 535 |
| 1859 | 10,047 | | | | 539 |
| 1858 | | | | | 479 |
| 1857 | | | | | 425 |
| 1856 | | | | | 419 |
| 1855 | | | | 347 | 575[9] |
| 1854 | | | | | 500[9] |
| 1853 | 10,200 | | | | 374[9] |
| 1852 | | | | | 548[9] |
| 1851 | 9,957 | | | | 532[9] |
| 1850 | 10,087 | | | | 585[9] |
| 1849 | | | | | 540[9] |
| 1848 | 9,943 | | | | 576[9] |
| 1847 | | | | | 647[9] |
| 1846 | | | | | 637[9] |
| 1845 | 10,188 | | | | 523 |
| 1844 | 10,120 | −64 | −0.6 | | |
| | 9,942 | | | | 483 |
| 1843 | 10,184 | 186 | 1.9 | | 498 |
| | 9,939 | | | av. 391 | |
| 1842 | 9,998 | −75 | −0.7 | | 469 |
| 1841 | (11,684) | | | | |
| | 10,073 | 40 | 0.4 | | 486 |
| 1840 | 10,033 | 124 | 1.3 | | 457 |
| 1839 | 9,909 | 36 | 0.4 | | 469 |
| 1838 | 9,873 | 138 | 1.4 | | 463 |
| 1837 | 9,735 | 16 | 0.2 | | 518 |

*continued*

**Table 2.14** (*cont'd*)

| Year | Practising certificates[e] | Annual change | | Solicitors admitted[b] | New articles registered | Solicitor deaths |
|---|---|---|---|---|---|---|
| | | Absolute | % | | | |
| 1836 | 9,719 | 6 | 0.1 | av. 5–600 | 558 | |
| 1835 | 9,713<br>10,436 | 233 | 2.5 | | 577 | |
| 1834 | 9,480 | 30 | 0.3 | | 585 | |
| 1833 | 9,450 | 229 | 2.5 | | 540 | |
| 1832 | 9,221<br>8,061 | 138 | 1.5 | | 522 | |
| 1831 | 9,083 | 67 | 0.7 | | 467 | |
| 1830 | 9,016 | 108 | 1.2 | | 634 | |
| 1829 | 8,908 | 284 | 3.3 | | 601 | |
| 1828 | 8,624 | 194 | 2.3 | | 587 | |
| 1827 | 8,430 | 237 | 2.9 | | 642 | |
| 1826 | 8,193 | 265 | 3.3 | | 576 | |
| 1825 | 7,928 | 34 | 0.4 | | 625 | |
| 1824 | 7,894 | 276 | 3.6 | | 638 | |
| 1823 | 7,618 | 265 | 3.6 | | 685 | |
| 1822 | 7,353 | 263 | 3.7 | | 583 | |
| 1821 | 7,090 | 160 | 2.3 | | 610 | |
| 1820 | 6,930 | 166 | 2.5 | | 557 | |
| 1819 | 6,764 | 406 | 6.4 | | 303 | |
| 1818 | 6,358 | −21 | −0.3 | | 646 | |

| | | | | |
|---|---|---|---|---|
| 1817 | 6,379 | 185 | 3.0 | 584 |
| 1816 | 6,194 | 106 | 1.7 | 407 |
| 1815 | 6,088 | 30 | 0.5 | 532 |
| 1814 | 6,058 | 130 | 2.2 | 434 |
| 1813 | 5,928 | 177 | 3.1 | 451 |
| 1812 | 5,751 | −8 | −0.1 | 452 |
| 1811 | 5,763 | 55 | 1.0 | 413 |
| 1810 | 5,712 | 6 | 0.1 | 373 |
| 1809 | 5,706 | 82 | 1.5 | 317 |
| 1808 | 5,624 | 76 | 1.4 | 350 |
| 1807 | 5,548 | | | 299 |
| 1806 | | | | 285 |
| 1805 | | | | 223 |
| 1800 | 4,969<br>5,300 | | | |
| 1784 | 4,400 | | | |
| 1775 | 3,127 | | | |
| 1730 | 4,829 | | | |

[a] Results of August examination published late, preventing admission of successful candidates.
[b] Figures for 1924–34 inclusive are estimates.
[c] Half year.
[d] New date for registering articles this year.
[e] Figures in parentheses 1881–1920 from HM Commissioners of Inland Revenue.
[f] Figures in parentheses represent alternative data for given year, thought to be less accurate.
[g] These figures include further articles registered, which typically is about 20 per cent of the total.

*Sources*: Law Society, Annual Reports; Proceedings at a Special General Meeting of the Law Society, 12 January 1872, p. 2; *The Legal Observer*, 1840–1; S. Warren, 1845: 2; 1863, vol. 1: 2–3; Hall, 1962: 28; Reader, 1966: 211; Offer, 1981: 64; Millerson, 1964: 268; Kirk, 1976: 30, 42, 58, 108; Odgers, 1901: 30; Law Society, manuscript records

**Table 2.15** Change in size of profession, by periods

| Period | Annualized change in number of practising certificates (%) |
|---|---|
| 1962–84 | 5.8 |
| 1970–84 | 7.0 |
| 1962–70 | 2.9 |
| 1952–62 | 1.2 |
| 1939–52 | 0.2 |
| 1947–52 | 2.7 |
| 1939–45 | −4.0 |
| 1920–39 | 0.8 |
| 1913–20 | −1.7 |
| 1918–20 | 4.1 |
| 1913–18 | −3.2 |
| 1889–1913 | 0.5 |
| 1879–1888 | 2.3 |
| 1871–1879 | 1.9 |
| 1835–1871 | 0.03 |
| 1800–1835 | 3.1 |

*Source*: table 2.14

## Composition

**Table 2.16** Women as a percentage of practising certificates and solicitors admitted, 1920–85

| | Practising certificates | | | Solicitors admitted | | | |
|---|---|---|---|---|---|---|---|
| Year | Total | Women | % women | Total | Men | Women | % women |
| 1985 | | | | 2,683 | 1,572 | 1,111 | 41.4 |
| 1984 | | | | 2,728 | 1,656 | 1,072 | 39.3 |
| 1983 | 42,984 | 8,703 | 20.2 | 2,596 | 1,638 | 958 | 36.9 |
| 1982 | | | | 2,241 | 1,466 | 775 | 34.6 |
| 1981 | | | | 3,223 | 2,244 | 979 | 30.4 |
| 1980 | 37,852 | 3,700 | 9.8 | 3,538 | 2,560 | 978 | 27.6 |
| 1979 | | | | 2,552 | 1,816 | 736 | 28.8 |
| 1978 | | | | 2,538 | 1,905 | 633 | 24.9 |
| 1977 | 32,812 | 2,132 | 6.5 | 2,480 | 1,950 | 530 | 21.2 |
| 1976 | 31,250 | 1,779 | 5.7 | 2,184 | 1,741 | 443 | 20.3 |
| 1975 | 29,850 | 1,563 | 5.2 | 2,203 | 1,871 | 332 | 15.1 |
| 1974 | 28,741 | 1,299 | 4.5 | 1,849 | 1,566 | 283 | 15.3 |
| 1973 | 27,379 | 1,185 | 4.3 | 1,764 | 1,542 | 222 | 12.6 |
| 1972 | 26,327 | 906 | 3.5 | 1,713 | 1,515 | 198 | 11.6 |
| 1971 | 25,366 | 803 | 3.2 | 1,682 | 1,516 | 166 | 9.9 |
| 1970 | 24,407 | 743 | 3.0 | 1,877 | 1,712 | 165 | 8.8 |
| 1969 | 23,574 | 681 | 2.9 | 1,365 | 1,265 | 100 | 7.3 |
| 1968 | 22,787 | 619 | 2.7 | 997 | 908 | 89 | 8.9 |
| 1967 | | | | 1,107 | 1,023 | 84 | 7.6 |
| 1966 | | | | 1,123 | 1,054 | 69 | 6.1 |
| 1965 | | | | 1,009 | 947 | 62 | 6.1 |
| 1964 | | | | | | | |
| 1963 | 20,269 | 440 | 2.2 | | | | |
| 1959 | | | | | | | 6.7 |
| 1957 | 18,344 | 337 | 1.8 | 734 | 694 | 40 | 5.4 |
| 1951 | 19,689 | 526 | 2.7 | | | | |
| 1950s[a] | | | | 711 | 681 | 30 | 4.2 |
| 1940s[a] | | | | 416 | 404 | 12 | 2.9 |
| 1931 | 15,777 | 116 | 0.7 | | | | |
| 1930s[a] | | | | 695 | 679 | 16 | 2.3 |
| 1920s[a] | | | | 489 | 480 | 8.5 | 1.7 |

Annualized average

*Sources*: census; Royal Commission, 1979, vol. 1: 496; vol. 2: 439, 442, 446; Equal Opportunities Commission, 1978: 19; Birks, 1960: 277–8; 120 *Solicitors' Journal* 682–3, 1976; Johnstone and Hopson, 1967: 360 n. 13; Kirk, 1976: 110–12; Sachs and Wilson, 1978: 174, 231; Law Society, personal communication; Marks, 1986: 3258

**Table 2.17** Women as proportion of solicitors on the Roll, by private practice/employment and age, 1983

| | Private practice | | | | | Other | | | | | All solicitors | | | | | Solicitors in private practice as % of all enrolled | |
|---|---|---|---|---|---|---|---|---|---|---|---|---|---|---|---|---|---|
| | Men | | Women | | | Men | | Women | | | Men | | Women | | | | |
| Age | no. | % in cohort | no. | % in cohort | % of cohort who are women | no. | % in cohort | no. | % in cohort | % of cohort who are women | no. | % in cohort | no. | % in cohort | % of cohort who are women | Men | Women |
| < 30 | 5,400 | 18 | 2,500 | 48 | 32 | 1,400 | 14 | 900 | 30 | 39 | 6,700 | 17 | 3,400 | 41 | 34 | 81 | 74 |
| 30–34 | 6,600 | 22 | 1,300 | 25 | 17 | 1,700 | 17 | 1,000 | 33 | 38 | 8,300 | 21 | 2,400 | 29 | 22 | 80 | 54 |
| 35–39 | 6,100 | 21 | 700 | 13 | 11 | 2,200 | 22 | 800 | 27 | 26 | 8,300 | 21 | 1,500 | 18 | 16 | 73 | 47 |
| 40–44 | 4,100 | 14 | 300 | 6 | 7 | 1,100 | 11 | 100 | 3 | 9 | 5,200 | 13 | 400 | 5 | 7 | 79 | 75 |
| 45–64 | 7,200 | 24 | 300 | 6 | 4 | 3,700 | 37 | 100 | 3 | 4 | 10,900 | 28 | 400 | 5 | 4 | 66 | 75 |
| Total | 29,400 | | 5,200 | | 15 | 10,100 | | 3,000 | | 23 | 39,500 | | 8,200 | | 17 | | |

*Source*: Marks, 1984: table 6

**Table 2.18** Distribution among practice categories of men and women solicitors holding practising certificates, 1983, 1984–5

| | 1983 | | | | | 1984–5 |
|---|---|---|---|---|---|---|
| | Men | | Women | | | |
| Category | no. | % in category | no. | % in category | Women as % of category | Women as % of category |
| Partnership | 18,580 | 49.2 | 887 | 16.9 | 4.6 | 6.7 |
| Assistant solicitor | 7,659 | 20.3 | 2,932 | 56.0 | 27.8 | 32.3 |
| Own account | 3,571 | 9.5 | 337 | 6.4 | 8.6 | 11.6 |
| Consultant | 1,817 | 4.8 | 89 | 1.7 | 4.7 | |
| Local government | 2,492 | 6.6 | 377 | 7.2 | 13.1 | |
| Commerce, industry, nationalized undertaking | 1,735 | 4.6 | 196 | 3.7 | 10.2 | |
| Full-time government service | 95 | 0.3 | 11 | 0.2 | 10.4 | |
| Other full-time employment | 1,335 | 3.5 | 344 | 6.6 | 20.5 | |
| Unemployed | 13 | 0 | 27 | 0.5 | 67.5 | |
| Retired | 36 | 0.1 | 10 | 0.2 | 21.7 | |
| Abroad | 13 | 0 | 6 | 0.1 | 31.6 | |
| Own account and partnership | 50 | 0.1 | 2 | 0 | 4.0 | |
| Own account and assistant solicitor | 28 | 0.1 | 4 | 0.1 | 12.5 | |
| Own account and other employment | 325 | 0.9 | 13 | 0.2 | 3.8 | |
| Total | 37,749 | | 5,235 | | 13.9 | |

*Sources*: Law Society; Marks, 1986: 3258

**Table 2.19** Geographic distribution of solicitors, 1971, 1983 and 1985

| | 1983 (Roll) | | | 1971 (practising certificate) | 1985 (Solicitors' and Barristers' Directory) | |
|---|---|---|---|---|---|---|
| | Private practice | | Other | | | |
| | Number | Pop./solic. | Number | Pop./solic. | Number | Pop./solic. |
| London and SE | 14,900 | 1,149 | 5,100 | 1,754 | 17,912 | 924 |
| SW | 3,500 | 1,250 | | 2,326 | 3,371 | 1,261 |
| Wales | 1,700 | 1,639 | | 2,941 | 1,588 | 1,731 |
| W. Midlands | 2,600 | 1,961 | | 3,226 | 2,792 | 1,826 |
| E. Midlands | 1,600 | 2,326 | | 3,704 | 1,893 | 1,998 |
| E. Anglia | 1,100 | 1,695 | | 2,941 | 1,190 | 1,551 |
| Yorks and Humber. | 2,100 | 2,273 | | 3,448 | 2,564 | 1,876 |
| NW | 3,900 | 1,639 | | 2,857 | 3,884 | 1,638 |
| N | 1,400 | 2,222 | | 3,571 | 1,447 | 2,120 |
| England and Wales | 32,900 | 1,515 | 8,700 | 2,439 | 36,641 | 1,324 |
| Outside England and Wales | 1,700 | | 600 | | | |

*Sources*: K. Foster, 1973; Marks, 1984: tables 7, 8; Watkins et al., 1986b: 10

**Table 2.20** Size of London solicitors' firms (number of principals), 1802–1950

| Year | 1 | | 2 | | 3 | | 4 | | 5 | | 6 | | 7 | | 8 | | 9 | | 10 | | Total | Mean |
|---|---|---|---|---|---|---|---|---|---|---|---|---|---|---|---|---|---|---|---|---|---|---|
| | no. | % | no. | % | no. | % | no. | % | no. | % | no. | % | no. | % | no. | % | no. | % | no. | % | | |
| 1950 | 26 | 37 | 20 | 28 | 7 | 10 | 6 | 8 | 7 | 10 | 1 | 1 | 2 | 3 | 1 | 1 | | | 1 | 1 | 71 | 2.5 |
| 1940 | 26 | 52 | 7 | 14 | 6 | 12 | 3 | 6 | 3 | 6 | 2 | 4 | 2 | 4 | 1 | 2 | | | | | 50 | 2.4 |
| 1930 | 26 | 47 | 14 | 25 | 9 | 16 | 1 | 2 | 2 | 4 | 1 | 2 | 1 | 2 | | | 2 | 4 | | | 55 | 2.0 |
| 1920 | 21 | 44 | 16 | 25 | 6 | 12 | 2 | 4 | 1 | 2 | 1 | 2 | | | 1 | 2 | | | | | 48 | 1.9 |
| 1910 | 23 | 46 | 17 | 34 | 5 | 10 | 4 | 8 | | | | | | | 1 | 2 | | | | | 50 | 1.8 |
| 1900 | 23 | 42 | 21 | 38 | 6 | 11 | 2 | 4 | 1 | 2 | | | | | | | 2 | 4 | | | 55 | 1.7 |
| 1890 | 23 | 50 | 15 | 33 | 5 | 11 | 1 | 2 | 1 | 2 | | | | | | | 1 | 2 | | | 46 | 1.7 |
| 1880 | 27 | 64 | 10 | 24 | 4 | 10 | 1 | 2 | | | | | | | | | | | | | 42 | 1.5 |
| 1870 | 27 | 64 | 9 | 21 | 2 | 5 | 4 | 9 | | | | | | | | | | | | | 42 | 1.6 |
| 1860 | 28 | 54 | 18 | 35 | 4 | 8 | 2 | 4 | | | | | | | | | | | | | 52 | 1.6 |
| 1850 | 35 | 71 | 8 | 16 | 4 | 8 | 2 | 4 | | | | | | | | | | | | | 49 | 1.4 |
| 1840 | 30 | 62 | 11 | 23 | 6 | 12 | 1 | 2 | | | | | | | | | | | | | 48 | 1.5 |
| 1830 | 35 | 60 | 19 | 33 | 4 | 7 | | | | | | | | | | | | | | | 58 | 1.5 |
| 1820 | 30 | 61 | 16 | 33 | 3 | 6 | | | | | | | | | | | | | | | 49 | 1.4 |
| 1802 | 31 | 82 | 7 | 18 | | | | | | | | | | | | | | | | | 38 | 1.2 |

A sample was drawn from the Law List by picking the first principal on each page and recording the size of firm in which the principal practised.
*Source*: Law List

**Table 2.21** Distribution of principals and firms by firm size (number of principals) and average number of principals per firm, 1825, 1881, 1925, 1966, 1971, 1976 and 1979

| Year | 1 | 2 | 3 | 4 | 5–9 | 10–14 | ≥ 15 | Average principals per firm |
|---|---|---|---|---|---|---|---|---|
| 1979 | | | | | | | | |
| Principals | 11 | 16 | 26 | | 29 | 17 | | 3.0 |
| Firms | 34 | 24 | 24 | | 14 | 4 | | |
| 1976 | | | | | | | | |
| Principals | 11 | 18 | 27 | | 29 | 16 | | 3.6 |
| Firms | 32 | 27 | 24 | | 14 | 2 | 1 | |
| 1971, Birmingham | | | | | | | | |
| Principals | 11 | 15 | 10 | 19 | | ← 46 → | | |
| Firms | 36 | 28 | 20 | | | ← 16 → | | |
| 1969 | | | | | | | | |
| Firms | 40 | 30 | 21 | | | ← 10 → | | 2.4 |
| 1966 | | | | | | | | |
| Principals | 19 | 26 | 30 | | | ← 12 → | | 2.2 |
| Firms | 42 | 30 | 20 | | | ← 9 → | | |
| 1925, Birmingham | | | | | | | | |
| Firms | 67 | | | | | | | |
| 1881, firms[a] | | | | | | | | |
| London | 9 | 57 | 23 | 8 | 3 | | | |
| Provinces | 10 | 63 | 26 | 1 | 1 | | | |
| 1825, Birmingham | | | | | | | | |
| Firms | 80 | | | | | | | |

[a] Estimated from alphabetic listing of all firms containing Law Society member, letters A to E.

*Sources*: National Board for Prices and Incomes, 1968: 33; 1969: 28; Bridges et al., 1975: 27–8; Incorporated Law Society, Calendar, 1881; Royal Commission, 1979, vol. 1: 187

**Table 2.22** Firm size by number of principals and location, 1977, 1983 and 1985

| | January 1977 | | December 1983 | | March 1985[c] | | | | | | |
|---|---|---|---|---|---|---|---|---|---|---|---|
| | | | | | | | | London | | Wales | |
| Principals | Number of firms | % | Number of firms | % | Number of firms | % | % of principals | % firms | % principals | % firms | % principals |
| 1 | 2054 | 32.0 | 2809 | 37.5 | 2506 | 33.1 | 10.1 | 21.6 | 2.3 | 36.8 | 14.6 |
| 2 | 1699 | 26.5 | 1774 | 23.7 | 1868 | 24.7 | 15.1 | 17.1 | 3.0 | 29.6 | 23.4 |
| 3 | 932 | 14.5 | 1001 | 13.4 | 1082 | 14.3 | 13.1 | 11.3 | 3.7 | 14.4 | 17.1 |
| 4 | 603 | 9.4 | 624 | 8.3 | 683 | 9.0 | 11.0 | 9.3 | 2.2 | 8.8 | 13.9 |
| 5 | 352 | 5.5 | 396 | 5.3 | 427 | 5.6 | 8.6 | 4.1 | 2.8 | 5.4 | 10.7 |
| 6 | 217 | 3.4 | 212 | 2.8 | 250 | 3.3 | 6.1 | 4.1 | 3.8 | 2.0 | 4.8 |
| 7 | 148 | 2.3 | 172 | 2.3 | 200 | 2.6 | 5.7 | 4.7 | 2.5 | 0.2 | 0.6 |
| 8 | 107 | 1.7 | 111 | 1.5 | 115 | 1.5 | 3.7 | 2.7 | 1.5 | 0.2 | 0.7 |
| 9 | 73 | 1.1 | 66 | 0.9 | 63 | 0.8 | 2.2 | 1.4 | 3.3 | 0.2 | 0.8 |
| 10 | 50 | 0.8 | 75 | 1.0 | 83 | 1.1 | 3.4 | 2.5 | 3.3 | 0.7 | 2.7 |
| 11–15 | 128 | 2.0 | 158 | 2.1 | 167[a] | 2.2 | } | 7.2[a] | } | 0.7[a] | } |
| 16–19 | 32 | 0.5 | 39 | 0.5 | 65[b] | 0.9 | } 21.0 | 4.9[b] | } 71.6 | 0.9[b] | } 10.7 |
| ⩾ 20 | 25 | 0.4 | 55 | 0.7 | 66 | 0.9 | } | 9.1 | } | 0 | } |
| Total | 6420 | | 7492 | | 7575 | | | (no.= 486) | (no. = 3630) | (no. = 443) | (no. = 1120) |

[a] 11–14.
[b] 15–19.
[c] Excludes low fee earners (⩽ £15,000 per year).
*Sources*: Marks, 1984: table 9 (from London Insurance Brokers); 1985: table 13

**Table 2.23** Regional distribution of firms by number of principals, 1969

| | 1 | | 2 | | 3–4 | | $\geqslant 5$ | | |
|---|---|---|---|---|---|---|---|---|---|
| Area | no. | % | no. | % | no. | % | no. | % | Average |
| Central London | 440 | 35 | 260 | 21 | 280 | 22 | 280 | 22 | 3.1 |
| North | 560 | 36 | 510 | 32 | 380 | 24 | 120 | 8 | 2.2 |
| Midlands | 260 | 36 | 240 | 33 | 160 | 22 | 60 | 8 | 2.2 |
| Central and South-east | 920 | 48 | 520 | 27 | 320 | 17 | 140 | 7 | 2.0 |
| West and Wales | 460 | 40 | 420 | 37 | 220 | 19 | 40 | 4 | 1.8 |
| Birmingham 1971 | | 36 | | 28 | | 20 | | 16 | |

*Sources*: National Board for Prices and Incomes, 1969: 28, 35; Bridges et al., 1975: 27

**Table 2.24** Growth in number of principals, 1830–1985, among 15 largest solicitors' firms in 1983

| Firm | 1985 | 1983 | 1970 | 1960 | 1950 | 1940 | 1930 | 1920 | 1910 | 1900 | 1890 | 1880 | 1870 | 1860 | 1850 | 1840 | 1830 |
|---|---|---|---|---|---|---|---|---|---|---|---|---|---|---|---|---|---|
| Allen & Overy | 48 | 47 | 18 | 16 | 11 | 8 | 2 | | | | | | | | | | |
| Clifford-Turner | | 53 | 24 | 15 | 11 | 8 | 5 | | | | | | | | | | |
| Coward Chance | 43 | 42 | 18 | 8 | 9 | 7 | 6 | 4 | | | | | | | | | |
| Frere Cholmeley | 22 | 32 | 14 | 11 | 7 | 8 | 5 | 5 | 5 | 6 | 6 | 3 | 4 | 4 | 3 | 3 | 2 |
| Freshfields | 46 | 43 | 20 | 10 | 8 | 6 | 5 | 5 | 4 | 3 | 3 | 3 | 4 | 5 | 3 | 3 | 3 |
| Theodore Goddard | 36 | 30 | 22 | 16 | 8 | 5 | 3 | 2 | | | | | | | | | |
| Linklaters & Paine | 60 | 62 | 27 | 18 | 10 | 11 | 9 | 9 | 6 | 3 | 3 | 2 | 4 | 3 | 2 | 2 | |
| Lovell White & King | 43 | 49 | 20 | 15 | 10 | 7 | 4 | 2 | | | | | | | | | |
| McKenna | 29 | 33 | 12 | 9 | 6 | 5 | 2 | 5 | 3 | 2 | 1 | | | | | | |
| Norton Rose | 57 | 56 | 23 | 7 | 5 | 6 | 5 | 5 | 5 | 4 | 4 | 4 | 3 | 3 | 3 | 2 | |
| Oppenheimer Nathan & Vandyck | 31 | 29 | 21 | 14 | 8 | 7 | 3 | 3 | | | | | | | | | |
| Richards Butler | 35 | 32 | 17 | 11 | 8 | 3 | 4 | | | | | | | | | | |
| Simmons | 47 | 50 | 23 | 11 | 3 | 4 | 2 | 2 | | | | | | | | | |
| Slaughter & May | 61 | 55 | 27 | 20 | 14 | 11 | 9 | 3 | | | | | | | | | |
| Herbert Smith & Co. | 56 | 54 | 27 | 14 | 6 | 8 | 7 | | | | | | | | | | |
| Median | 46 | 44.5 | 20.9 | 13 | 8.3 | 6.9 | 4.7 | 4.1 | 4.6 | 3.6 | 3.4 | 3 | 3.8 | 3.8 | 2.8 | 2.5 | 2.5 |

*Sources*: Law List; Solicitors' and Barristers' Directory and Diary

**Table 2.25** Composition of solicitors' firms with at least 20 principals, 1984
(a) City firms

| Name | Total lawyers | Principals | Assistant solicitors | Ratio AS/P | Consultants | Women | | Branch offices | |
|---|---|---|---|---|---|---|---|---|---|
| | | | | | | Principals | AS | UK | Abroad |
| Linklaters & Paine | 201 | 60 | 141 | 2.35 | 0 | 4(8%) | 34(24%) | 0 | 0 |
| Clifford-Turner | 169 | 54 | 114 | 2.11 | 1 | 3(6) | 34(30) | 0 | 9 |
| Herbert Smith & Co. | 164 | 56 | 103 | 1.84 | 5 | 3(5) | 34(33) | 0 | 2 |
| Slaughter & May | 162 | 61 | 101 | 1.66 | 0 | 0(0) | 17(17) | 0 | 2 |
| Norton Rose Bottrell & Roche | 153 | 57 | 90 | 1.58 | 6 | 1(2) | 36(40) | 0 | 2 |
| Coward Chance | 137 | 43 | 93 | 2.16 | 1 | 2(5) | 26(28) | 0 | 8 |
| Lovell White & King | 137 | 43 | 94 | 2.19 | 0 | 2(5) | 27(29) | 0 | 3 |
| Allen & Overy | 135 | 48 | 87 | 1.81 | 0 | 0(0) | 17(20) | 0 | 2 |
| Simmons & Simmons | 100 | 47 | 50 | 1.06 | 3 | 2(4) | 9(18) | 0 | 2 |
| Richards Butler & Co. | 83 | 35 | 46 | 1.31 | 2 | 0(0) | 11(24) | 0 | 2 |
| Stephenson Harwood | 79 | 39 | 39 | 1.00 | 1 | 1(3) | 14(36) | 0 | 1 |
| Cameron Markby | 74 | 37 | 37 | 1.00 | 0 | 1(3) | 16(43) | 0 | 2 |

| | | | | | | | | | |
|---|---|---|---|---|---|---|---|---|---|
| Wilde Sapte | 73 | 31 | 40 | 1.29 | 2 | 1(3) | 9(22) | 2 | 4 |
| Freshfields | 70 | 46 | 24 | 0.52 | 0 | 2(4) | 4(16) | 0 | 3 |
| Herbert Oppenheimer Nathan & Vandyck | 68 | 31 | 37 | 1.19 | 0 | 6(9) | 11(30) | 0 | 1 |
| Theodore Goddard & Co. | 64 | 36 | 28 | 0.78 | 0 | 7(19) | 10(36) | 0 | 3 |
| Macfarlanes | 60 | 25 | 32 | 1.28 | 3 | 0(0) | 11(34) | 0 | 0 |
| Turner Kenneth Brown | 57 | 33 | 22 | 0.67 | 2 | 2(6) | 12(55) | 0 | 0 |
| Holman Fenwick & Willan | 57 | 35 | 22 | 0.63 | 0 | 1(3) | 3(14) | 0 | 0 |
| Barlow Lyde & Gilbert | 56 | 25 | 29 | 1.16 | 2 | 0(0) | 8(28) | 0 | 0 |
| Ashurst Morris Crisp & Co. | 53 | 20 | 33 | 1.65 | 0 | 0(0) | 7(21) | 0 | 1 |
| Berwin Leighton | 52 | 26 | 26 | 1.00 | 0 | 1(4) | 11(42) | 0 | 1 |
| Titmuss, Sainer & Webb | 49 | 25 | 20 | 0.80 | 4 | 2(8) | 7(35) | 0 | 0 |
| Ince & Co. | 49 | 26 | 20 | 0.77 | 3 | 0(0) | 0 (0) | 0 | 2 |
| Durrant Piesse | 45 | 26 | 19 | 0.73 | 0 | 1(4) | 8(42) | 0 | 0 |
| (D.J.) Freeman & Co. | 44 | 30 | 13 | 0.43 | 1 | 4(13) | 6(46) | 0 | 0 |
| Paisner & Co. | 40 | 22 | 16 | 0.73 | 2 | 0(0) | 0 (0) | 0 | 0 |
| Clyde & Co. | 35 | 23 | 11 | 0.48 | 1 | 2(9) | 4(36) | 1 | 1 |
| Taylor Garrett | 34 | 24 | 10 | 0.42 | 0 | 2(8) | 5(50) | 0 | 0 |

(b) West End firms

| Name | Total lawyers | Principals | Assistant solicitors | Ratio AS/P | Consultants | Women | | Branch offices | |
|---|---|---|---|---|---|---|---|---|---|
| | | | | | | Principals | AS | UK | Abroad |
| McKenna & Co. | 78 | 9 | 49 | 1.69 | 0 | 0(0) | 15(31) | 0 | 3 |
| Nabarro Nathanson | 73 | 39 | 31 | 0.79 | 3 | 5(13) | 4(13) | 0 | 0 |
| Jaques & Lewis | 60 | 34 | 21 | 0.62 | 5 | 5(15) | 9(43) | 0 | 2 |
| Denton, Hall & Burgin | 57 | 32 | 23 | 0.72 | 2 | 3(9) | 9(39) | 1 | 2 |
| Rowe & Maw | 49 | 28 | 20 | 0.71 | 1 | 3(11) | 4(20) | 0 | 0 |
| Baker & McKenzie | 41 | 19 | 21 | 1.11 | 1 | 1(5) | 4(19) | 0 | 28 |
| Boodle Hatfield & Co. | 40 | 23 | 16 | 0.70 | 1 | 1(4) | 8(50) | 1 | 0 |
| Farrer & Co. | 37 | 22 | 15 | 0.68 | 0 | 2(9) | 3(20) | 0 | 0 |
| Frere Cholmeley | 37 | 22 | 11 | 0.50 | 4 | 0(0) | 2(36) | 0 | 2 |
| Reynolds Porter Chamberlain | 37 | 22 | 14 | 0.64 | 1 | 4(18) | 9(64) | 0 | 0 |
| Field Fisher & Martineau | 35 | 21 | 14 | 0.67 | 0 | 1(5) | 7(50) | 1 | 0 |
| Lawrence Graham | 32 | 21 | 9 | 0.43 | 0 | 5(24) | 7(78) | 2 | 1 |
| Bartletts De Reya | 30 | 21 | 6 | 0.29 | 3 | 2(9) | 3(50) | 0 | 0 |
| Joynson-Hicks & Co. | 30 | 22 | 7 | 0.32 | 1 | 1(5) | 1(14) | 0 | 0 |

(c) Provincial firms

| Name | Total lawyers | Principals | Assistant solicitors | Ratio AS/P | Consultants | Women | | Branch offices | |
|---|---|---|---|---|---|---|---|---|---|
| | | | | | | Principals | AS | UK | Abroad |
| Edge & Ellison Hatwell Pritchett & Co. (B'ham) | 45 | 26 | 19 | 0.73 | 0 | 2(18) | 10(53) | 0 | 0 |
| Pinsent & Co. (B'ham) | 43 | 22 | 21 | 0.95 | 0 | 1(5) | 5(24) | 0 | 0 |
| Booth & Co. (Leeds) | 37 | 20 | 17 | 0.85 | 0 | 0(0) | 5(29) | 0 | 0 |
| Dickinson Dees (Newcastle) | 33 | 20 | 10 | 0.50 | 3 | 0(0) | 2(20) | 0 | 0 |

*Source*: Solicitors' and Barristers' Directory and Diary, 1985

**Table 2.26** Change in the number and ratio of principals, assistant solicitors, articled clerks, legal executives and clerical staff, 1966–76 and 1985

| | | Assistant solicitors | | Articled clerks | | Legal executives | | Clerical staff | |
|---|---|---|---|---|---|---|---|---|---|
| | Number of principals | Number | Per principal | Number | Per principal | Number | Per principal | Number | Per principal |
| Devon and Cornwall, 1985 | 333 | 152 | 0.46 | 38 | 0.11 | 241 | 0.73 | 1,193 | 3.58 |
| England and Wales, 1976 | 23,275 | 6,611 | 0.28 | 6,846 | 0.29 | 17,647 | 0.75 | 68,857 | 2.95 |
| Birmingham, 1971 | 450 | 123 | 0.27 | 187 | 0.42 | 467 | 1.04 | 1,816 | 4.04 |
| England and Wales, 1969 | 15,810 | 4,020 | 0.25 | 5,810 | 0.37 | 14,420 | 0.91 | 57,790 | 3.66 |
| England and Wales, 1966 | 15,100 | 3,500 | 0.23 | 5,100 | 0.34 | 17,200 | 1.14 | 52,500 | 3.48 |
| Percentage change England and Wales, 1966–76 | 55 | 89 | | 34 | | 3 | | 31 | |

*Sources*: National Board for Prices and Incomes, 1968: 34; 1969: 8, 29; Bridges et al., 1975: 28; Law Society, 1978: 6; Blacksell et al., 1986: table 19

**Table 2.27** Educational background of assistant solicitors and principals in large City firms, 1984

| | Assistant solicitors | | | | Principals | | | |
|---|---|---|---|---|---|---|---|---|
| Firm | Number | % from Oxford | % from Cambridge | % without degree | Number | % from Oxford | % from Cambridge | % without degree |
| Allen & Overy | 87 | 24 | 29 | 9 | 48 | 33 | 19 | 15 |
| Freshfields | 24 | 17 | 33 | 29 | 46 | 35 | 28 | 11 |
| Lovell White & King | 94 | 16 | 21 | 14 | 43 | 26 | 23 | 26 |
| Theodore Goddard & Co. | 28 | 14 | 18 | 0 | 36 | 19 | 8 | 17 |
| Ashurst Morris Crisp & Co. | 33 | 9 | 15 | 21 | 20 | 25 | 25 | 30 |
| Linklaters & Paine | 141 | 18 | 28 | 10 | 60 | 15 | 27 | 20 |
| Cameron Markby | 37 | 16 | 8 | 19 | 37 | 22 | 14 | 35 |

*Source*: Solicitors' and Barristers' Directory and Diary, 1985

**Table 2.28** Ratio of assistant solicitors to principals in firms with 20 principals or more, 1984

| Number of principals | Ratio | Mean for category | Number of principals | Ratio | Mean for category |
|---|---|---|---|---|---|
| 61 | 1.7 | | 29 | 1.7 | |
| 60 | 2.4 | | 28 | 0.7 | |
| ⩾60 | | 2.05 | 26 | 1.0 | |
| 57 | 1.6 | | 26 | 0.8 | |
| 56 | 1.8 | | 26 | 0.7 | |
| 54 | 2.1 | | 26 | 0.7 | |
| 50–9 | | 1.83 | 25 | 1.2 | |
| 48 | 1.8 | | 25 | 1.3 | |
| 47 | 1.1 | | 25 | 1.2 | |
| 46 | 0.5 | | 24 | 0.4 | |
| 43 | 2.2 | | 23 | 0.5 | |
| 43 | 2.2 | | 23 | 0.7 | |
| 40–9 | | 1.56 | 22 | 0.7 | |
| 39 | 1 | | 22 | 0.7 | |
| 39 | 1.3 | | 22 | 0.7 | |
| 37 | 1 | | 22 | 0.5 | |
| 36 | 0.8 | | 22 | 0.3 | |
| 35 | 1.3 | | 22 | 1.0 | |
| 35 | 0.6 | | 21 | 0.7 | |
| 34 | 0.6 | | 21 | 0.3 | |
| 33 | 0.7 | | 21 | 0.4 | |
| 32 | 0.7 | | 20 | 1.6 | |
| 31 | 0.8 | | 20 | 0.5 | |
| 31 | 1.2 | | 20 | 0.8 | |
| 30 | 0.4 | | 20–9 | | 0.80 |
| 30–9 | | 0.87 | | | |

*Source*: Solicitors' and Barristers' Directory and Diary, 1985

**Table 2.29** Ratio of employees to principals by size of firm (number of principals) and category of employee, 1966, 1968, 1971 and 1976

| | Year and number of principals | Assistant solicitors[a] | Articled clerks | Legal executives | Clerical staff | All fee earners | All employees |
|---|---|---|---|---|---|---|---|
| 1976 | 1 | 0.4 | 0.3 | 0.9 | 3.5 | 1.6 | 5.1 |
| | 2 | 0.3 | 0.25 | 0.7 | 3.1 | 1.25 | 4.35 |
| | 3–4 | 0.3 | 0.3 | 0.8 | 3.3 | 1.4 | 4.7 |
| | 5–9 | 0.4 | 0.3 | 0.9 | 3.4 | 1.6 | 5.0 |
| | ⩾10 | 0.7 | 0.5 | 1.0 | 3.6 | 2.2 | 5.8 |
| 1971 Birmingham | 1 | 0.10 | 0.49 | 0.82 | 3.59 | 1.41 | 5.00 |
| | 2 | 0.32 | 0.19 | 0.71 | 5.42 | 1.22 | 6.64 |
| | 3 | 0.26 | 0.77 | 1.41 | 4.14 | 2.44 | 6.58 |
| | 4 | 0.13 | 0.26 | 1.10 | 3.28 | 1.49 | 4.77 |
| | ⩾5 | 0.27 | 0.42 | 1.11 | 4.05 | 1.80 | 5.85 |
| 1968 | 1 | 0.27 | 0.27 | 0.94 | 3.71 | 1.48 | 5.19 |
| | 2 | 0.20 | 0.26 | 0.91 | 3.71 | 1.37 | 5.08 |
| | 3–4 | 0.18 | 0.37 | 0.82 | 3.22 | 1.37 | 4.59 |
| London | ⩾5 | 0.49 | 0.55 | 1.06 | 3.96 | 2.10 | 6.06 |
| Provinces | ⩾5 | 0.24 | 0.46 | 0.91 | 4.01 | 1.61 | 5.62 |
| 1966 | 1 | 0.29 | 0.27 | 0.91 | 3.66 | 1.47 | 5.13 |
| | 2 | 0.18 | 0.24 | 0.98 | 4.55 | 1.40 | 5.95 |
| | 3–4 | 0.20 | 0.32 | 1.13 | 3.24 | 1.65 | 4.89 |
| London | ⩾5 | 0.34 | 0.56 | 1.80 | 4.07 | 2.70 | 6.77 |
| Provinces | ⩾5 | 0.23 | 0.46 | 1.11 | 3.74 | 1.80 | 5.54 |

[a] Includes salaried partners in 1976.

*Sources*: National Board for Prices and Incomes, 1968: 34; 1969: 29; Bridges et al., 1975: 28; Royal Commission, 1979, vol. 1: 458; vol. 2: 460

...stribution across practice categories of solicitors holding practising certificates 1939, 1955, 1957–85

| Year (ends 31 Oct.) | Partnership | Assistant solicitor | Sole practitioner | Sole practitioner and other employment | Sole practitioner and assistant solicitor | Sole practitioner and partnership | Partnership and assistant solicitor | Partnership and other employ ment | Commissioner for oaths | Consultant | HM forces | Not in active practice, retired, unemployed | Commerce, industry and nationalized enterprises | Central government[a] | Local government | Other full-time employment | Practising abroad |
|---|---|---|---|---|---|---|---|---|---|---|---|---|---|---|---|---|---|
| 1985 | 22,053 | 11,793 | 4,031 | 121 | 80 | 58 | b | b | b | 2,057 | b | 114 | 1,989 | 163 | 2,896 | 1.037 | 98 |
| 1984 | 19,875 | 12,610 | 3,840 | 209 | 24 | 60 | b | b | b | 2,034 | b | 22 | 1,829 | 100 | 3,000 | 1,175 | 12 |
| 1983 | 19,467 | 10,591 | 3,908 | 338 | 32 | 52 | b | b | b | 1,906 | b | 46 | 1,931 | 106 | 2,869 | 1,679 | 19 |
| 1982 | 19,065 | 10,860 | 3,398 | 337 | 46 | 117 | 18 | 166 | 2 | 1,773 | 1 | 44 | 1,799 | 66 | 2,899 | 1,005 | 102 |
| 1981 | 18,377 | 10,701 | 3,060 | 239 | 41 | 100 | 18 | 42 | 4 | 1,673 | 2 | 28 | 1,715 | 68 | 2,746 | 873 | 108 |
| 1980 | 17,922 | 9,580 | 2,815 | 305 | 16 | 96 | 16 | 92 | 6 | 1,590 | 3 | 15 | 1,636 | 166 | 2,627 | 869 | 78 |
| 1979 | 17,419 | 8,537 | 2,634 | 343 | 27 | 89 | 15 | 98 | 5 | 1,484 | 2 | 33 | 1,513 | 215 | 2,594 | 761 | 21 |
| 1978 | 17,061 | 7,645 | 2,478 | 184 | 16 | 89 | 14 | 66 | 4 | 1,382 | 2 | 32 | 1,238 | 258 | 2,520 | 771 | 104 |
| 1977 | 16,808 | 6,989 | 2,691 | 135 | 56 | 109 | 29 | 48 | 4 | 1,280 | 3 | 86 | 1,092 | 296 | 2,465 | 702 | 82 |
| 1976 | 16,400 | 6,223 | 2,895 | 131 | 65 | 153 | 22 | 39 | 2 | 1,031 | 1 | 33 | 952 | 336 | 2,370 | 561 | 36 |
| 1975 | 15,956 | 5,775 | 2,894 | 123 | 48 | 64 | 30 | 39 | 6 | 1,001 | 1 | 68 | 985 | 353 | 1,710 | 746 | 51 |
| 1974 | 15,387 | 5,226 | 2,778 | 163 | 66 | 89 | 24 | 69 | 9 | 965 | 2 | 49 | 1,143 | 428 | 1,965 | 344 | 34 |
| 1973 | 14,670 | 5,712 | 2,773 | 108 | 56 | 73 | 8 | 15 | 9 | 392 | 2 | 50 | 983 | 48 | 1,883 | 574 | 23 |
| 1972 | 13,657 | 5,860 | 2,719 | 143 | 131 | 139 | 11 | 11 | 7 | 381 | 1 | 42 | 851 | 48 | 1,804 | 484 | 38 |
| 1971 | 13,585 | 5,015 | 2,725 | 139 | 131 | 142 | 12 | 10 | 11 | 385 | 1 | 47 | 822 | 48 | 1,785 | 475 | 33 |
| 1970 | 13,401 | 4,252 | 2,738 | 127 | 128 | 133 | 12 | 10 | 8 | 391 | 1 | 52 | 795 | 49 | 1,776 | 501 | 33 |
| 1969 | 13,077 | 3,825 | 2,754 | 127 | 112 | 129 | 12 | 10 | 6 | 398 | 1 | 50 | 773 | 49 | 1,748 | 472 | 33 |
| 1968 | 12,784 | 3,474 | 2,769 | 112 | 95 | 119 | 12 | 9 | 6 | 380 | 1 | 50 | 745 | 47 | 1,721 | 430 | 31 |
| 1967 | 12,184 | 3,428 | 2,874 | 149 | 105 | 113 | 12 | 7 | 8 | 342 | 1 | 63 | 732 | 49 | 1,667 | 408 | 33 |
| 1966 | 11,686 | 3,367 | 2,987 | 181 | 122 | 120 | 17 | 28 | 7 | 296 | 1 | 71 | 677 | 47 | 1,672 | 363 | 28 |
| 1965 | 11,377 | 3,274 | 3,006 | 196 | 131 | 147 | 18 | 35 | 13 | 274 | 1 | 66 | 657 | 48 | 1,635 | 344 | 30 |
| 1964 | 11,099 | 3,142 | 3,014 | 161 | 135 | 141 | 15 | 43 | 8 | 230 | 2 | 62 | 632 | 49 | 1,592 | 327 | 31 |
| 1963 | 10,851 | 3,017 | 3,045 | 138 | 151 | 156 | 20 | 52 | 12 | 201 | 2 | 65 | 581 | 55 | 1,566 | 320 | 37 |
| 1962 | 10,539 | 2,943 | 3,057 | 124 | 139 | 167 | 12 | 53 | 8 | 198 | 7 | 47 | 523 | 54 | 1,544 | 336 | 39 |
| 1961 | 10,192 | 3,044 | 3,138 | 155 | 98 | 149 | 15 | 45 | 3 | 147 | 19 | 54 | 470 | 57 | 1,507 | 310 | 25 |
| 1960 | 9,897 | 2,887 | 3,289 | 163 | 104 | 122 | 17 | 43 | 7 | 122 | 28 | 57 | 458 | 46 | 1,464 | 351 | 14 |
| 1959 | 9,760 | 2,785 | 3,277 | 140 | 115 | 128 | 18 | 45 | 10 | 86 | 12 | 46 | 452 | 34 | 1,446 | 361 | 19 |
| 1958 | 9,717 | 2,704 | 3,245 | 138 | 113 | 117 | 18 | 43 | 5 | 68 | 40 | 48 | 407 | 35 | 1,413 | 347 | 18 |
| 1957 | 9,661 | 2,520 | 3,207 | 143 | 149 | 125 | 19 | 42 | 10 | 39 | 31 | 67 | 430 | 26 | 1,409 | 328 | 14 |
| 1955 | 9,500 | 2,500 | 3,500 | | | | | | | | | | 404 | 37 | 1,375 | 309 | |
| 1939 | 6,937 | 2,256 | 3,986 | | | | | | | | | | 512 | 1,991 | | | |

[a] Central government obviously made two abrupt changes in its policies concerning whether solicitor employees had to take out practising certificates, in 1974 and in 1981.
[b] No longer separately identified.
*Sources*: Law Society, Annual Reports; Gower and Price, 1957: 325; Abel-Smith and Stevens, 1968: 144; 36 *LSG* 285–8, 1939

**Table 2.31** Change in distribution across practice categories of solicitors holding practising certificates, 1939–57, 1957–82 and 1984

| | Partnership | | Sole practitioner | | Total self-employed | | Assistant solicitor or consultant | | Public sector[a] | | Private employment[b] | | Total employed | | Total practising certificates |
|---|---|---|---|---|---|---|---|---|---|---|---|---|---|---|---|
| | % of total | % change | % of total | % change | % of total | % change | % of total | % change | % of total | % change | % of total | % change | % of total | % change | % change |
| 1984 | 45 | 106 | 9 | 18 | 54 | | 33 | | 7 | | 7 | | 46 | | |
| 1982 | 47 | 97 | 8 | 6 | 55 | 75 | 31 | 395 | 7 | 107 | 7 | 270 | 45 | 287 | 128 |
| 1957 | 55 | 39 | 18 | −20 | 73 | 18 | 14 | 11 | 8 | −77 | 4 | 9 | 27 | 0 | 12 |
| 1939 | 44 | | 25 | | 69 | | 14 | | 13 | | 3 | | 31 | | |

[a] Local and central government.
[b] Commerce and industry and other full-time employment.
*Source*: table 2.30.

**Table 2.32** Legal executive examination results and ILEX membership, 1963–85

| Year[a] | Fellows | | | | Associates | | | | Students | |
|---|---|---|---|---|---|---|---|---|---|---|
| | | Part II examination | | | | Part I examination | | | | |
| | Total | Taking | Passing | % | Total | Taking | Passing | % | Total | New |
| 1985 autumn | | 689 | 333 | 48 | | 896 | 579 | 65 | | |
| 1984 autumn | | 426 | 196 | 46 | | 736 | 473 | 64 | | |
| summer | | 1152 | 629 | 55 | | 3518 | 2481 | 71 | | |
| 1983 autumn | | | | 40 | | | | 69 | | |
| summer | | 1307 | 693 | 53 | | 2576 | 1768 | 69 | | |
| 1982 autumn | | 450 | 252 | 56 | | 519 | 343 | 66 | | |
| summer | | 1275 | 677 | 53 | | 2163 | 1642 | 76 | | |
| 1981 autumn | | 437 | 189 | 43 | | 450 | 337 | 75 | | |
| summer | | 1288 | 683 | 53 | | 2185 | 1638 | 75 | | |
| 1980 autumn | | 464 | 218 | 47 | | 508 | 310 | 61 | | |
| summer | | 1683 | 928 | 55 | | 2227 | 1538 | 69 | | |
| 1979 autumn | | | | | | 593 | 387 | 65 | | 777 |
| summer | | | | | | | 569 | | | |
| 1978 | 5724 | | 296 | | 3949 | 607 | 366 | 59 | 3438 | 702 |
| 1977 | 5801 | | 195 | | 3968 | | 537 | | 3930 | 1759 |
| 1976 | 6126 | | 242 | | 4070 | | 726 | | 4809 | 1182 |
| 1975 | | | | | | | | | 4538 | |
| | 6627 | | 173 | | 3631 | | 357 | | 4500 | 1334 |
| 1974 | 6477 | | 192 | | 3714 | | 588 | | 4218 | 1333 |
| 1973 | 6563 | | | | 3430 | | | | 3902 | |
| | 6523 | | 201 | | 3444 | | 301 | | 3968 | 1164 |
| 1972 | 6570 | | 197 | | 3448 | | 346 | | 3317 | 836 |
| 1971 | 6623 | | | | 3464 | | | | 3007 | |
| | 6590 | | 157 | | 3451 | | 344 | | 2963 | 819 |

*continued*

**Table 2.32** (*cont'd*)

| | Fellows | | | | Associates | | | | Students | |
|---|---|---|---|---|---|---|---|---|---|---|
| | | Part II examination | | | | Part I examination | | | | |
| Year[a] | Total | Taking | Passing | % | Total | Taking | Passing | % | Total | New |
| 1970 | 6733 | | 130 | | 3514 | | 372 | | 2900 | 853 |
| 1969 | 6984 | 1404 | 140 | | 3430 | 2674 | 416 | | 2935 | |
| 1968 | 7126 | | 112 | | 3315 | | 497 | | 2974 | 837 |
| 1967 | 7218 | | 81 | | 3018 | | 488 | | 3024 | 903 |
| 1966 | 7344 | | 45 | | 2690 | | 340 | | 3114 | 890 |
| 1965 | 7459 | | 43 | | 2469 | | | | 3020 | |
| 1964 | 7206 | | 4 | | 1968 | | | | 2395 | |
| 1963[b] | 6530 | | | | 1500 | | | | 1470 | |
| | 6190 | 253 | 100 | 40 | 1305 | 1780 | 1356 | 76 | 1446 | |

[a] Autumn is a resit for summer.
[b] Existing managing clerks admitted under grandfather clause.
*Sources*: *Legal Executive*; Ormrod Committee, 1971: 113; Wilson and Marsh, 1975: 307; Zander, 1980: 10; Royal Commission, 1979, vol. 1: 408; National Board for Prices and Incomes, 1969: 8; Johnstone and Hopson, 1967: 405 n. 10; Kirk, 1976: 124

**Table 2.33** Distribution of legal aid payments among solicitors' firms, 1975–6 to 1984–5

| | 1975–6 | | | 1976–7 | | | 1977–8 | | | 1979–80 | | |
|---|---|---|---|---|---|---|---|---|---|---|---|---|
| Amount received (£) | No. of firms | % of firms | % of total payments | No. of firms | % of firms | % of total payments | No. of firms | % of firms | % of total payments | No. of firms | % of firms | % of total payments |
| 1–500 | 2,228 | 27.3 | 0.9 | 1,928 | 23.5 | 0.7 | 1,836 | 21.8 | 0.5 | 1,872 | 21.0 | 0.4 |
| 501–1,000 | 1,945 | 23.8 | 5.6 | 1,832 | 22.3 | 4.3 | 1,756 | 20.8 | 3.5 | 727 | 8.2 | 0.7 |
| 1,001–2,000 | 1,640 | 20.1 | 13.5 | 1,712 | 20.8 | 11.6 | 1,711 | 20.3 | 10.4 | 935 | 10.5 | 1.9 |
| 2,001–5,000 | 1,207 | 14.8 | 21.3 | 1,296 | 15.8 | 18.9 | 1,389 | 16.5 | 17.3 | 1,680 | 18.9 | 7.6 |
| 5,001–10,000 | 734 | 9.0 | 25.6 | 876 | 10.7 | 25.1 | 1,043 | 12.4 | 25.6 | 1,464 | 16.5 | 14.2 |
| 10,001–20,000 | 332 | 4.1 | 22.2 | 453 | 5.5 | 25.1 | 504 | 6.0 | 24.1 | 1,218 | 13.7 | 23.1 |
| 20,001–40,000 | 51 | 0.6 | 6.1 | 87 | 1.1 | 8.6 | 126 | 1.5 | 10.4 | 705 | 7.9 | 26.6 |
| 40,001–60,000 | 22 | 0.3 | 4.9 | 31 | 0.4 | 5.7 | 56 | 0.7 | 8.6 | 180 | 2.0 | 11.7 |
| >60,000 | | | | | | | | | | 113 | 1.3 | 13.8 |
| Total | 8,159 | £40,046,927 | | 8,215 | £48,886,126 | | 8,421 | £57,562,410 | | 8,894 | £74,083,910 | |

| | 1980–1 | | | 1982–3 | | | 1983–4 | | | 1984–5 |
|---|---|---|---|---|---|---|---|---|---|---|
| Amount received (£) | No. of firms | % of firms | % of total payments | No. of firms | % of firms | % of total payments | No. of firms | % of firms | % of total payments | Total payments |
| 1–500 | 1,688 | 18.3 | 0.3 | 1,403 | 14.4 | 0.2 | | | | |
| 501–1,000 | 1,466 | | | 579 | 5.9 | 0.3 | | | | |
| 1,001–2,000 | | 15.9 | 1.7 | 808 | 8.3 | 0.8 | 4,704 | 43.4 | 3.6 | |
| 2,001–5,000 | 1,636 | 17.8 | 5.4 | 1,502 | 15.4 | 3.6 | | | | |
| 5,001–10,000 | 1,537 | 16.7 | 11.1 | 1,577 | 16.2 | 8.0 | 1,541 | 14.2 | 6.2 | |
| 10,001–20,000 | 1,416 | 15.4 | 20.0 | 1,706 | 17.5 | 17.1 | 1,834 | 16.9 | 14.5 | |
| 20,001–40,000 | 942 | 10.2 | 26.2 | 1,254 | 12.9 | 24.4 | 1,507 | 13.9 | 23.3 | |
| 40,001–60,000 | 305 | 3.3 | 14.8 | 464 | 4.8 | 15.8 | 587 | 5.4 | 15.7 | |
| >60,000 | 224 | 2.4 | 20.6 | 446 | 4.6 | 30.0 | 663 | 6.1 | 36.8 | |
| Total | 9,214 | £100,607,850 | | 9,739 | £156,018,611 | | 10,836 | £183,020,571 | | £281,000,000 |

*Sources*: Legal Aid Annual Reports Lord Chancellor's Department, 83 *LSG* 2050–6, 1986

**Table 2.34** Solicitor income (£) compared with that of other professions, 1913–14 to 1976–7

| | 1913–14 | 1922–3 | 1955–6 | 1974[a] | 1975[a] | 1976[a] | 1976–7[b] |
|---|---|---|---|---|---|---|---|
| Barristers | 210 | 580 | 1,251 | 7,420 | 7,627 | 8,338 | 5,218 |
| Solicitors | 390 | 811 | 1,688 | 8,483 | 9,451 | 10,093 | 7,643[c] |
| Doctors | 370 | 723 | 2,300 | 5,577 | 6,710 | 7,605 | |
| General practitioners | | | | | | | 8,078 |
| Hospital doctors and consultants | | | | | | | 9,183 |
| Dentists | 310 | 514 | 2,090 | 6,170 | 7,555 | 7,963 | |
| Accountants | | | | 6,879 | 7,699 | 8,708 | |
| Architects | | | | 8,532 | 8,411 | 8,840 | |
| Engineers | | | | 5,515 | 6,659 | 7,693 | |
| Civil service | | | | | | | 7,278 |
| Industry middle management | | | | | | | 7,624 |

[a] Excludes those earning less than £2000.
[b] After tax.
[c] Principals.
*Sources*: Routh, 1980: 60; Royal Commission, 1979, vol. 2: 682, 692

**Table 2.35** Distribution of net[a] income of sole practitioners, assistant solicitors and consultants, 1967–79.

| | Percentage earning net income (£) | | | | | | | | | | | | | |
|---|---|---|---|---|---|---|---|---|---|---|---|---|---|---|
| | 0–249 | 250–499 | 500–999 | 1000–1999 | 2000–2999 | 3000–3999 | 4000–4999 | 5000–5999 | 6000–7999 | 8000–9999 | 10,000–11,999 | 12,000–14,999 | 15,000–19,999 | ⩾ 20,000 | Number |
| 1967 | 18.7 | 9.6 | 11.4 | 22.7 | 12.3 | 7.0 | 5.2 | 4.1 | 4.0 | 2.4 | 1.0 | 0.7 | 0.4 | 0.5 | 5671 |
| 1968 | 16.0 | 5.0 | 10.0 | 22.2 | 22.8 | 7.7 | 5.0 | 4.3 | 3.5 | 1.7 | 0.8 | 0.4 | 0.6[d] | | 5970 |
| 1969 | 18.3 | 9.5 | 11.6 | 8.6 | 15.8 | 12.2 | 7.4 | 9.7[b] | | 3.6[c] | 2.6 | | 0.8[d] | | 4659 |
| 1970 | 18.2 | 5.4 | 11.8 | 12.4 | 16.4 | 9.7 | 7.9 | 9.7[b] | | 4.2[c] | 3.0 | | 1.2[d] | | 4790 |
| 1971 | 13.0 | 6.4 | 8.9 | 12.4 | 19.3 | 9.4 | 9.6 | 10.6[b] | | 5.0[c] | 3.4 | | 2.1[d] | | 5126 |
| 1972 | 20.7 | 4.8 | 7.9 | 10.2 | 11.6 | 7.1 | 6.5 | 14.2[b] | | 4.5[c] | 8.1 | | 4.2[d] | | 4883 |
| 1973 | | | | | | | | | | | | | | | |
| 1974 | 26.1 | | 8.5 | 14.4 | 11.1 | 8.0 | 5.1 | 5.0 | 6.8 | 4.4 | 3.7 | 2.7 | 2.2 | 1.9 | 5149 |
| 1975 | 33.1 | | 2.3 | 11.3 | 11.0 | 9.2 | 6.1 | 3.6[e] | 6.9[f] | 5.4 | 3.1 | 3.8 | 2.5 | 1.8 | 5463 |
| 1976 | 28.9 | | 7.6 | 9.3 | 7.9 | 6.1 | 4.5 | 9.0 | 8.9 | 4.7 | 4.0 | 2.6 | 3.5 | 3.0 | 5364 |
| 1977 | 24.7 | | 8.3 | 10.6 | 6.8 | 6.6 | 6.5 | 3.4 | 9.7 | 6.6 | 5.3 | 4.2 | 3.3 | 3.9 | 5362 |
| 1978 | 25.3 | | 7.7 | 11.7 | 5.6 | 6.3 | 5.9 | 3.8 | 5.7 | 5.8 | 6.2 | 4.6 | 4.5 | 5.3 | 5907 |
| 1979 | 21.8 | | 4.5 | 14.2 | 10.3 | 4.6 | 5.3 | 3.6 | 7.9 | 4.2 | 4.6 | 6.0 | 3.7 | 7.5 | 5897 |

[a] Excludes capital allowances.
[b] 5000–7499.
[c] 7500–9999.
[d] ⩾ 15,000.
[e] 5000–6999.
[f] 7000–7999.
*Source*: Inland Revenue Statistics, 1971–80: professional earnings

**Table 2.36** Distribution of solicitor income, 1970–2

| | Per cent of male solicitors with weekly earnings (£) in each category | | | | | | | | | | | | | |
|---|---|---|---|---|---|---|---|---|---|---|---|---|---|---|
| | 0–11.99 | 12–14.99 | 15–16.99 | 17–19.99 | 20–24.99 | 25–29.99 | 30–34.99 | 35–39.99 | 40–44.99 | 45–49.99 | 50–59.99 | 60–69.99 | 70–79.99 | ⩾ 80 | Number |
| 1970 | 10.6 | 4.8 | 1.9 | 1.0 | 5.7[a] | 13.5[b] | 10.6 | 6.7 | 8.0 | 6.4 | 9.7 | 21.1[c] | | | 104 |
| 1971 | 9.7 | | 1.8 | 3.5 | 7.1 | 5.3 | 14.2 | 4.4 | 9.8 | | 15.0 | 7.1 | 7.1 | 15.0 | 113 |
| 1972 | | | 16.0[d] | 0.8[e] | 5.3 | 5.4 | 8.4 | 11.4 | 5.4 | 3.8 | 13.0 | 12.2 | | 18.3 | 131 |

[a] 20–23.99
[b] 24–29.99
[c] ⩾ 60
[d] < 18
[e] 18–19.99
*Source*: Department of Employment, 1970–2

**Table 2.37** Changes in income over time, all solicitors and assistant solicitors, 1859–1976

| | All solicitors (£) | Assistant solicitors (£) |
|---|---|---|
| 1976 | 10,093[a] | |
| 1975 | 9,451[a] | |
| 1974 | 8,483[a] | |
| 1966 | 3,176–4,300 | 1,500 |
| 1964 | | 1,000–1,250 |
| 1961 | | 850–1,000 |
| 1956–57 | 1,755 | 600–800 |
| 1955–56 | 1,688 | |
| | 1,750 | |
| 1954–55 | 1,652 | |
| 1949–50 | 2,432 | 600 |
| 1938–39 | 1,180 | 200 |
| 1928 | | 250 |
| 1922–23 | 1,096 | |
| | 811 | |
| 1913–14 | 568 | |
| | 390 | |
| 1900 | 300 | |
| 1892 | 200 | |
| 1861 | 200 | |
| 1859 | 300 | |

[a] Excludes incomes under £1000.

*Sources*: Abel-Smith and Stevens, 1967: 58, 210, 399; Offer, 1981: 15; Routh, 1980: 60; Royal Commission, 1979, vol. 2: 682; Kirk, 1976: 92, 95; Zander, 1968: 54; Gower and Price, 1957: 334–5; Doctors and Dentists, 1960: 284

**Table 2.38** Salaries (£) of assistant solicitors, by firm size and experience, and of solicitors employed in industry, 1980–6

| Months since admission | Law firms, no. of partners | | | Industry | Law firms, no. of partners | | | Industry | Law firms, no of partners | | | Industry |
|---|---|---|---|---|---|---|---|---|---|---|---|---|
| | ⩾ 21 | 8–20 | ⩽ 7 | | ⩾ 21 | 8–20 | ⩽ 7 | | ⩾ 21 | 8–20 | ⩽ 7 | |
| | *Oct. 1980 to March 1981* | | | | *Oct. 1981 to March 1982* | | | | *Oct. 1982 to March 1983* | | | |
| ⩽ 6 | 7,500 | 6,470 | 6,250 | | 6,724 | 6,190 | 6,610 | | 7,740 | 7,760 | 7,750 | |
| 7–18 | | | | | 8,170 | 6,890 | 7,010 | | 10,030 | 8,560 | 8,040 | |
| 19–30 | 8,760 | 7,090 | 7,260 | | 9,200 | 8,480 | 7,700 | | 10,820 | 9,650 | 8,160 | |
| 31–42 | 8,670 | 8,300 | 7,720 | 7,910[a] | 10,130 | 8,870 | 8,000 | | 11,810 | 10,450 | 9,360 | |
| > 42 | 11,410 | 8,490 | 9,790 | 13,790 | 13,370 | 11,940 | 10,660 | 14,060 | 14,940 | 12,350 | 11,510 | 14,420 |
| Number[b] | 101 | 115 | 87 | 45 | 96 | 136 | 152 | 16 | 165 | 140 | 140 | 55 |
| | *April to Sept. 1983* | | | | *Oct. 1983 to March 1984* | | | | *April to Sept. 1984* | | | |
| ⩽ 6 | 8,070 | 7,470 | 7,540 | | 9,600 | 8,550 | 7,750 | | 9,670 | 8,910 | 8,320 | |
| 7–18 | 10,040 | 8,000 | 8,510 | | 10,080 | 9,400 | 8,660 | | 11,330 | 9,100 | 9,250 | |
| 19–30 | 11,110 | 9,780 | 8,680 | | 11,700 | 10,130 | 8,920 | | 11,510 | 10,230 | 9,310 | |
| 31–42 | 12,060 | 9,820 | 9,930 | | 12,060 | 11,920 | 10,360 | | 13,990 | 12,070 | 11,220 | |
| > 42 | 15,810 | 15,880 | 11,650 | 16,680 | 16,200 | 14,430 | 13,410 | 18,580 | 18,470 | 14,420 | 14,720 | 18,370 |
| Number[b] | 180 | 156 | 150 | 114 | 188 | 188 | 162 | 110 | 170 | 177 | 218 | 116 |
| | *Oct. 1984 to March 1985* | | | | *April to Sept. 1985* | | | | *Oct. 1985 to March 1986* | | | |
| ⩽ 6 | 10,720 | 9,430 | 9,030 | | 10,727 | 10,079 | 9,995 | | 11,800 | 10,850 | 10,170 | |
| 7–18 | 11,430 | 10,060 | 9,360 | | 12,346 | 10,595 | 10,324 | | 12,560 | 11,610 | 10,660 | |
| 19–30 | 12,910 | 12,230 | 10,950 | | 14,165 | 12,678 | 10,736 | | 15,300 | 13,540 | 10,500 | |
| 31–42 | 14,680 | 12,760 | 12,440 | | 13,850 | 12,833 | 12,589 | | 16,720 | 14,710 | 13,550 | |
| > 42 | 18,600 | 15,890 | 13,530 | 17,200 | 19,022 | 18,537 | 16,666 | 19,783 | 21,740 | 19,460 | 16,010 | 20,530 |
| Number[b] | 156 | 252 | 150 | 42 | 140 | 259 | 210 | 91 | n.a. | n.a. | n.a. | n.a. |

[a] All solicitors with 42 months experience or less.
[b] Estimates.
*Source*: Reuter Simkin, 1981–5; 1986

**Table 2.39** Salaries (£) for positions offered in *Law Society's Gazette*, average and range, 1925–84

| Year | | London | Suburbs | Government | Country | Provincial cities | Total |
|---|---|---|---|---|---|---|---|
| 1984 | Average[a] | 13,155 (42) | 10,667 (9) | 12,055 (9) | 9,756 (39) | 12,100 (5) | 11,418 (104) |
| | Range | 9,500–25,000 | 7,500–18,000 | 10,500–19,000 | 7,000–15,000 | 11,000–14,000 | 7,000–25,000 |
| 1983 | Average | 11,270 (48) | 12,250 (8) | 10,730 (13) | 8,782 (33) | 13,500 (8) | 10,693 (110) |
| | Range | 8,000–25,000 | 10,000–16,000 | 10,000–12,500 | 6,000–13,000 | 8,000–25,000 | 6,000–25,000 |
| 1982 | Average | 10,561 (49) | 9,091 (11) | 8,417 (6) | 8,731 (26) | 9,062 (8) | 9,675 (100) |
| | Range | 6,000–17,500 | 7,500–12,000 | 7,500–10,000 | 6,500–16,000 | 6,500–12,000 | 6,500–17,500 |
| 1981 | Average | 9,683 (41) | 7,913 (23) | 8,537 (8) | 7,710 (29) | 9,417 (6) | 8,667 (107) |
| | Range | 6,500–17,000 | 5,500–17,000 | 5,500–12,000 | 6,000–13,000 | 7,000–13,000 | 5,500–17,000 |
| 1980 | Average | 8,705 (37) | 6,535 (14) | 9,090 (21) | 6,071 (28) | 8,062 (8) | 7,768 (108) |
| | Range | 5,000–15,000 | 5,000–8,000 | 6,500–15,500 | 4,750–9,000 | 6,000–10,500 | 4,750–15,500 |
| 1979 | Average | 7,588 (45) | 5,900 (15) | 6,700 (23) | 6,152 (23) | 6,800 (10) | 6,841 (116) |
| | Range | 5,000–15,000 | 4,000–8,000 | 5,400–8,500 | 5,000–12,000 | 4,000–10,000 | 4,000–15,000 |
| 1978 | Average | 6,204 (38) | 5,882 (14) | 6,155 (18) | 4,717 (24) | 5,333 (9) | 5,729 (103) |
| | Range | 3,700–11,000 | 5,000–8,000 | 4,900–9,000 | 3,000–7,000 | 4,500–6,000 | 3,700–11,000 |
| 1977 | Average | 5,875 (44) | 5,083 (6) | 5,762 (8) | 4,508 (31) | 5,018 (14) | 5,292 (103) |
| | Range | 3,500–9,000 | 4,000–6,000 | 4,800–6,500 | 3,000–6,000 | 3,500–7,750 | 3,000–9,000 |
| 1976 | Average | 6,032 (37) | 4,881 (21) | 5,493 (7) | 4,367 (30) | 5,212 (13) | 5,203 (108) |
| | Range | 3,000–10,000 | 3,500–10,000 | 4,900–6,200 | 3,000–9,000 | 4,250–12,000 | 3,000–12,000 |
| 1975 | Average | 4,623 (35) | 3,898 (22) | 4,537 (20) | 3,919 (13) | 3,625 (16) | 4,219 (106) |
| | Range | 3,250–6,000 | 3,000–5,500 | 3,750–5,600 | 3,500–5,000 | 2,500–6,000 | 2,500–6,000 |
| 1974 | Average | 4,253 (29) | 3,577 (11) | 4,022 (26) | 3,541 (22) | 3,604 (14) | 3,879 (102) |
| | Range | 2,500–8,000 | 2,500–4,500 | 3,000–5,000 | 2,500–6,000 | 3,000–4,500 | 2,500–8,000 |

*continued*

**Table 2.39** *(cont'd)*

| *Year* | | *London* | *Suburbs* | *Government* | *Country* | *Provincial cities* | *Total* |
|---|---|---|---|---|---|---|---|
| 1973 | Average | 4,077 (42) | 3,250 (14) | 3,946 (12) | 2,917 (21) | 3,514 (14) | 3,636 (103) |
| | Range | 2,500–6,000 | 2,500–5,000 | 3,200–6,000 | 2,500–4,000 | 2,250–5,000 | 2,250–6,000 |
| 1972 | Average | 3,148 (44) | 2,876 (19) | 3,200 (6) | 2,361 (28) | 2,911 (14) | 2,876 (111) |
| | Range | 2,000–6,000 | 2,000–4,000 | 2,400–3,700 | 2,000–3,000 | 2,000–4,500 | 2,000–6,000 |
| 1970 | Average | 2,784 (38) | 2,443 (14) | 2,245 (11) | 2,109 (34) | 2,603 (16) | 2,461 (113) |
| | Range | 1,600–4,000 | 1,700–3,500 | 1,900–2800 | 1,500–3,000 | 2,000–4,000 | 1,500–4,000 |
| 1969 | Average | 2,618 (8) | 1,980 (15) | 2,367 (6) | 1,998 (28) | 2,075 (14) | 2,222 (91) |
| | Range | 1,550–5,000 | 1,450–2,500 | 2,100–2,800 | 1,500–2750 | 1,500–3,000 | 1,450–5,000 |
| 1968 | Average | 2,528 (16) | 1,894 (24) | 2,325 (8) | 1,821 (29) | 2,003 (16) | 2,036 (93) |
| | Range | 2,000–4,200 | 1,400–2,500 | 1,700–3,000 | 1,500–2,500 | 1,650–3,000 | 1,400–4,200 |
| 1961–2 | Average | 1,321 (31) | 1,068 (23) | 1,320 (5) | 1,140 (34) | 1,300 (15) | 1,207 (108) |
| | Range | 900–2,000 | 850–1,350 | 1,100–1,500 | 800–2,000 | 950–2,000 | 800–2,000 |
| 1950–2 | Average | 781 (35) | 579 (6) | 682 (11) | 640 (11) | 800 (4) | 725 (67) |
| | Range | 425–1,250 | 450–800 | 600–800 | 450–900 | 600–1,250 | 425–1,250 |
| 1945–6 | Average | | | | | | |
| | Range | | | | | | 450–500 |
| 1930–1[b] | Average | | | | | | 295 (46) |
| | Range | | | | | | 200–500 |
| 1925–6[b] | Average | 325 (29) | | | 268 (22) | | |
| | Range | 250–450 | | | 150–312 | | |

[a] Number of advertisements sampled indicated in parentheses.
[b] Salaries requested by recently admitted solicitors seeking employment.
*Source*: *Law Society's Gazette*

**Table 2.40** Income and hourly fees (£) for partners, salaried partners and assistant solicitors, legal executives and articled clerks, by firm size, 1976–7

| | Partners | | Salaried partners and assistant solicitors | | Legal executives | | Articled clerks | |
|---|---|---|---|---|---|---|---|---|
| Number of principals | Hourly fee | Net profit per principal | Hourly fee | Salary | Hourly fee | Salary | Hourly fee | Salary |
| 1 | 13 | 8,261 | 12 | 4,200 | 9 | 3,482 | 7 | 1,548 |
| 2 | 14 | 9,887 | 12 | 3,990 | 10 | 3,481 | 7 | 1,482 |
| 3–4 | 15 | 11,129 | 12 | 4,028 | 10 | 3,542 | 7 | 1,516 |
| 5–9 | 17 | 12,444 | 13 | 4,166 | 11 | 3,738 | 7 | 1,561 |
| 10–14 | 21 | 15,769[a] | 16 | 5,262[a] | 13 | 4,238[a] | 9 | 2,276[a] |
| 15–19 | 23 | | 18 | | 12 | | 9 | |
| ⩾ 20 | 38 | | 24 | | 21 | | 10 | |

[a] All firms with ten or more principals.
*Source*: Royal Commission, 1979, vol. 2: 464–8, 478

**Table 2.41** Law Society membership and number of practising certificates, London and provinces, 1825–1985

| | Law Society membership | | | Practising certificates | | |
|---|---|---|---|---|---|---|
| | Total | London | Provinces | Total | London | Provinces |
| 1985 | 39,406 | | | 46,490 | | |
| 1984 | 37,998 | | | 44,837 | | |
| 1983 | 37,624 | | | 42,984 | | |
| 1982 | 37,529 | | | 41,738 | | |
| 1981 | 35,430 | | | 39,795 | | |
| 1980 | 33,461 | | | 37,832 | | |
| 1979 | 31,737 | | | 34,090 | | |
| 1978 | 30,390 | | | 32,864 | | |
| 1977 | 29,473 | | | 32,812 | | |
| 1976 | 28,134 | | | 31,250 | | |
| 1975 | 16,833 | | | 29,850 | | |
| 1974 | 25,414 | | | 28,741 | | |
| 1973 | 24,557 | | | 27,379 | | |
| 1972 | 23,542 | | | 26,327 | | |
| 1971 | 22,480 | | | 25,366 | | |
| 1970 | 21,551 | | | 24,407 | | |
| 1969 | 20,987 | | | 23,574 | | |
| 1968 | 20,354 | | | 22,787 | | |
| 1967 | 19,811 | | | 22,223 | | |
| 1966 | 19,514 | | | 21,672 | | |
| 1965 | 19,081 | | | 21,255 | | |
| 1964 | 18,601 | | | 20,683 | | |
| 1963 | 18,287 | | | 20,269 | | |
| 1962 | 17,948 | | | 19,790 | | |
| 1961 | 17,350 | | | 19,438 | | |
| 1960 | 17,103 | | | 19,069 | | |
| 1959 | 16,891 | 5,552 | 11,339 | 18,740 | | |
| 1958 | 16,626 | 5,634 | 10,992 | 18,522 | | |
| 1957 | 16,930 | 5,706 | 11,224 | 18,344 | | |
| 1956 | 16,628 | 5,597 | 11,031 | 18,165 | | |
| 1955 | 16,509 | 5,573 | 10,936 | 18,143 | | |
| 1954 | 16,389 | 5,506 | 10,883 | 17,831 | | |
| 1953 | 16,225 | 5,440 | 10,785 | 17,687 | | |
| 1952 | 15,990 | 5,364 | 10,626 | 17,628 | | |
| 1951 | 15,590 | 5,243 | 10,347 | 17,396 | | |
| 1950 | 14,888 | 5,068 | 9,820 | 17,035 | | |
| 1949 | 14,015 | 4,837 | 9,178 | 16,318 | | |
| 1948 | 13,500 | 4,669 | 8,831 | 15,567 | | |

**Table 2.41** (*cont'd*)

| | Law Society membership | | | Practising certificates | | |
|---|---|---|---|---|---|---|
| | Total | London | Provinces | Total | London | Provinces |
| 1947 | 12,260 | 4,424 | 7,836 | 15,348 | 4,835 | 10,513 |
| 1946 | 11,589 | 4,067 | 7,552 | 14,854 | 4,685 | 10,169 |
| 1945 | 10,479 | 3,780 | 6,699 | 12,979 | 4,114 | 8,835 |
| 1944 | 10,379 | 3,776 | 6,603 | 13,063 | 4,175 | 8,888 |
| 1943 | 10,420 | 3,800 | 6,620 | 13,340 | 4,238 | 9,102 |
| 1942 | 10,486 | 3,841 | 6,645 | 13,835 | 4,355 | 9,480 |
| 1941 | 10,789 | 4,100 | 6,683 | 14,430 | 4,615 | 9,815 |
| 1940 | 11,156 | 4,298 | 6,858 | 15,884 | 5,181 | 10,703 |
| 1939 | 11,326 | 4,489 | 6,837 | 17,102 | 5,813 | 11,289 |
| 1938 | 11,124 | 4,449 | 6,675 | 16,899 | 5,750 | 11,149 |
| 1937 | 10,908 | 4,357 | 6,551 | 16,478 | 5,630 | 10,848 |
| 1936 | 10,753 | 4,305 | 6,448 | 16,299 | 5,488 | 10,811 |
| 1935 | 10,684 | 4,293 | 6,391 | 16,132 | 5,465 | 10,667 |
| 1934 | 10,578 | 4,259 | 6,319 | 15,941 | 5,378 | 10,563 |
| 1933 | 10,505 | 4,243 | 6,262 | 15,783 | 5,340 | 10,443 |
| 1932 | 10,336 | | | 15,616 | 5,322 | 10,294 |
| 1931 | 10,283 | 4,245 | 6,038 | 15,668 | 5,372 | 10,296 |
| 1930 | 10,252 | 4,218 | 6,034 | 15,418 | 5,241 | 10,177 |
| 1929 | 10,199 | 4,205 | 5,994 | 15,297 | 5,193 | 10,104 |
| 1928 | 10,178 | 4,174 | 6,004 | 15,168 | 5,143 | 10,025 |
| 1927 | 10,053 | 4,158 | 5,895 | 15,143 | 5,119 | 10,024 |
| 1926 | 10,023 | 4,150 | 5,873 | 15,152 | 5,165 | 9,987 |
| 1925 | 9,810 | 4,079 | 5,731 | 15,132 | 5,161 | 9,971 |
| 1924 | 9,557 | 4,045 | 5,512 | 15,071 | 5,133 | 9,938 |
| 1923 | 9,416 | 4,001 | 5,415 | 15,026 | 5,093 | 9,933 |
| 1922 | 9,360 | 3,984 | 5,376 | 14,889 | 5,055 | 9,834 |
| 1921 | 9,120 | 3,983 | 5,137 | 14,623 | 5,022 | 9,601 |
| 1920 | 8,876 | 3,943 | 4,933 | 14,767 | 5,035 | 9,732 |
| 1919 | 8,660 | 3,796 | 4,864 | 14,380 | 4,939 | 9,441 |
| 1918 | 8,588 | | | 14,040 | | |
| 1917 | 8,450 | 3,859 | 4,591 | 13,846 | | |
| 1916 | 8,729 | 3,965 | 4,764 | 14,362 | | |
| 1915 | 8,972 | 4,105 | 4,867 | 14,988 | | |
| 1914 | 9,073 | 4,165 | 4,908 | 15,887 | | |
| 1913 | 9,056 | 4,168 | 4,888 | 16,788 | | |
| 1912 | 9,051 | 4,140 | 4,911 | 16,759 | | |
| 1911 | 9,039 | 4,131 | 4,908 | 16,739 | | |
| 1910 | 8,794 | 4,070 | 4,724 | 16,841 | | |
| 1909 | 8,755 | 4,067 | 4,688 | 16,797 | | |
| 1908 | 8,611 | 4,005 | 4,606 | 16,725 | | |
| 1907 | 8,653 | 4,031 | 4,622 | 16,741 | | |
| 1906 | 8,590 | 4,010 | 4,580 | 16,624 | | |
| 1905 | 8,415 | 3,915 | 4,500 | 16,508 | | |

*continued*

**Table 2.41** (*cont'd*)

| | Law Society membership | | | Practising certificates | | |
|---|---|---|---|---|---|---|
| | Total | London | Provinces | Total | London | Provinces |
| 1904 | 8,067 | 3,759 | 4,308 | 16,455 | | |
| 1903 | 7,822 | 3,707 | 4,115 | 16,362 | | |
| 1902 | 7,819 | 3,675 | 4,144 | 16,265 | | |
| 1901 | 7,659 | 3,594 | 4,065 | 16,136 | | |
| 1900 | 7,860 | 3,630 | 4,230 | 15,948 | | |
| 1899 | 7,847 | 3,565 | 4,282 | 15,950 | | |
| 1898 | 7,882 | 3,570 | 4,312 | 15,810 | | |
| 1897 | 7,679 | 3,476 | 4,203 | 15,629 | | |
| 1896 | 7,769 | 3,500 | 4,269 | 15,518 | | |
| 1895 | 7,467 | 3,344 | 4,123 | 15,424 | | |
| 1894 | 7,490 | 3,358 | 4,132 | 15,402 | | |
| 1893 | 7,415 | 3,328 | 4,087 | 15,281 | | |
| 1892 | 7,002 | 3,206 | 3,796 | 15,165 | | |
| 1891 | 6,558 | 3,092 | 3,446 | 15,175 | | |
| 1890 | 6,350 | 3,020 | 3,330 | 15,090 | | |
| 1889 | 6,123 | 2,952 | 3,171 | 14,896 | | |
| 1888 | 5,120 | 2,735 | 2,385 | 14,788 | 5,800 | 9,000 |
| 1887 | 4,957 | 2,669 | 2,251 | 14,311 | | |
| 1886 | 4,675 | 2,606 | 2,039 | 13,893 | | |
| 1885 | 4,320 | | | 13,592 | | |
| 1884 | 4,220 | | | 13,390 | | |
| 1883 | 4,081 | | | 13,066 | | |
| 1882 | 3,890 | | | 12,961 | | |
| 1881 | 3,560 | 2,231 | 1,336 | 12,594 | | |
| 1880 | 3,235 | | | 12,688 | | |
| 1879 | | | | 12,263 | | |
| 1878 | 3,107 | 1,991 | 1,116 | | | |
| 1877 | 3,046 | | | | | |
| 1876 | 3,046 | 1,934 | 1,112 | | | |
| 1875 | 3,019 | 1,957 | 1,062 | | | |
| 1874 | 2,961 | 1,935 | 1,026 | | | |
| 1873 | 2,743 | 1,845 | 898 | | | |
| 1872 | | | | | | |
| 1871 | 2,451 | 1,774 | 677 | 10,576 | | |
| 1870 | 2,397 | 1,755 | 650 | | | |
| 1869 | 2,379 | 1,746 | 633 | | | |
| 1868 | 2,232 | | | | | |
| 1867 | 2,218 | 1,615 | 603 | | | |
| 1866 | 2,171 | 1,582 | 589 | | | |
| 1865 | 2,035 | 1,531 | 504 | *c.*10,200 | | |
| 1864 | 1,948 | 1,451 | 534 | | | |

**Table 2.41** (*cont'd*)

| | Law Society membership | | | Practising certificates | | |
|---|---|---|---|---|---|---|
| | Total | London | Provinces | Total | London | Provinces |
| 1863 | | | | 10,418 | | |
| 1862 | 1,869 | 1,407 | 462 | | | |
| 1861 | 1,802 | 1,370 | 432 | 10,029 | | |
| 1860 | 1,771 | 1,354 | 417 | | | |
| 1859 | 1,693 | 1,325 | 368 | 10,047 | | |
| 1858 | 1,642 | 1,292 | 350 | | | |
| 1857 | 1,600 | 1,273 | 327 | | | |
| 1856 | 1,551 | 1,234 | 317 | | | |
| 1855 | 1,504 | | | | | |
| 1854 | 1,457 | | | | | |
| 1853 | 1,301 | | | 10,200 | | |
| 1852 | 1,307 | 1,013 | 294 | | | |
| 1851 | 1,320 | 1,026 | 294 | 9,957 | | |
| 1850 | 1,329 | | | 10,087 | | |
| 1849 | 1,336 | 1,049 | 287 | | | |
| 1848 | 1,369 | 1,081 | 288 | 9,943 | | |
| 1847 | 1,371 | | | | | |
| 1846 | 1,363 | | | | | |
| 1845 | 1,352 | | | 10,188 | | |
| 1844 | | | | 9,942 | | |
| 1843 | 1,313 | | | 9,939 | 3,148 | 6,791 |
| 1842 | 1,291 | 1,048 | 243 | | | |
| 1841 | 1,205 | | | 10,073 | | |
| 1840 | | | | | | |
| 1839 | | | | | | |
| 1838 | 1,148 | | | | | |
| 1837 | 1,081 | 907 | 174 | | | |
| 1836 | 1,055 | | | | | |
| 1835 | 1,027 | 894 | 161 | 10,436 | | |
| 1834 | 965 | | | 8,061 | 2,555 | 5,506 |
| 1833 | 950 | 815 | 135 | 9,083 | | |
| 1832 | 836 | 724 | 112 | | | |
| 1831 | 695 | 607 | 88 | | | |
| 1830 | 673 | 594 | 79 | | | |
| 1829 | 566 | 508 | 58 | | | |
| 1828 | 438 | 397 | 41 | | | |
| 1827 | 407 | 365 | 42 | | | |
| 1826 | 407 | | | | | |
| 1825 | 292 | | | | | |

*Sources*: see table 2.14

**Table 2.42** Disciplinary proceedings, 1863–1985[b]

| | Complaints | No case to answer | Withdrawn etc. | No misconduct | Hearing filed This year | Hearing filed Last year | Total punished | Struck off Roll | Sus-pended | Fined | Costs | No order | Exonerated | Pending |
|---|---|---|---|---|---|---|---|---|---|---|---|---|---|---|
| 1984–85 | | | | | | | 67 | 22 | 6 | 28 | | | | |
| 1983–84 | 9000 | | | | | | 59 | 22 | 7 | 26 | 6 | | | |
| 1982–83 | | | | | | | 95 | | | | | | | |
| 1981–82 | | | | | | | | | | | | | | |
| 1980–81 | | | | | | | 55 | | | | | | | |
| 1979–80 | | | | | | | | | | | | | | |
| 1978–79 | 5915 | | | | | | 65 | 17 | 6 | 22 | 12 | | | |
| 1977–78 | 5815 | | | | | | 62 | | | | | | | |
| 1976–77 | 5834 | | | | | | 52 | | | | | | | |
| 1975–76 | 5752 | | | | | | 59 | | | | | | | |
| 1974–75 | 4742 | | | | | | 50 | | | | | | | |
| 1973–74 | 4853 | | | | | | 45 | 18 | 4 | 13 | 2 | | | |
| 1972–73 | 5270 | | | | | | | | | | | | | |
| 1971–72 | 4860 | | | | | | 45 | | | | | | | |
| 1970–71 | | | | | | | 33 | | | | | | | |
| 1969–70 | | | | | | | 25 | | | | | | | |
| 1968–69 | | | | | | | 51 | 10 | 6 | 8 | 5 | | | |
| 1967–68 | | | | | | | 40 | | | | | | | |
| 1966–67 | | | | | | | 24 | | | | | | | |
| 1965–66 | | | | | | | 30 | | | | | | | |
| 1964–65 | | | | | | | 36 | | | | | | | |
| 1963–64 | | | | | | | 26 | 10 | 8 | 12 | | | | |

| | | | | | | | |
|---|---|---|---|---|---|---|---|
| 1962–63 | | | 21 | | | | |
| 1961–62 | | | 19 | | | | |
| 1960–61 | | | 34 | | | | |
| 1959–60 | | | 54 | | | | |
| 1958–59 | | | 43 | 26 | 12 | 12 | 3 |
| 1957–58 | | | 57 | | | | |
| 1956–57 | 12 | 58 | 51 | 16 | 18 | 17 | |
| 1955–56 | 13 | 43 | 39 | 19 | 11 | 9 | |
| 1954–55 | 20 | 41 | 50 | 19 | 14 | 17 | |
| 1953–54 | 18 | 32 | 27 | 12 | 7 | 8 | |
| 1952–53 | 13 | 24 | 23 | 12 | 7 | 4 | |
| 1951–52 | 7 | 18 | 17 | 10 | 1 | 6 | |
| 1950–51 | 9 | 23 | 18 | 9 | 3 | 6 | |
| 1949–50 | 14 | 35 | 34 | 11 | 8 | 15 | |
| 1948–49 | 7 | 42 | 25 | 8 | 6 | 11 | |
| 1947–48 | 7 | 14 | 16 | 7 | 3 | 6 | |
| 1946–47 | | | | | | | |
| 1945–46 | 10 | 15 | 11 | 5 | 4 | 2 | |
| 1944–45 | 9 | 18 | 16 | 11 | 1 | 4 | |
| 1943–44 | 8 | 22 | 21 | 15 | 3 | 3 | |
| 1942–43 | 4 | 24 | 19 | 16 | 1 | 2 | |
| 1941–42 | 10 | 22 | 24 | 13 | 10 | 1 | |
| 1940–41 | 13 | 42 | 43 | 23 | 15 | 5 | |
| 1939–40 | 20 | 45 | 40 | 23 | 9 | 8 | |
| 1938–39 | 12 | 59 | 33 | 18 | 7 | 8 | |
| 1937–38 | 11 | 29 | 23 | 13 | 8 | 2 | |
| 1936–37 | 11 | 36 | 19 | 10 | 7 | 2 | |
| 1935–36 | | 10 | 28 | 18 | 10 | | |
| 1934–35 | | 44 | 18 | 13 | 5 | | |
| 1933–34 | | 68 | 27 | 24 | 3 | | |
| 1932–33 | | 63 | 28 | 22 | 6 | | |

*continued*

**Table 2.42** (*Cont'd*)

| | Complaints | No case to answer | Withdrawn etc. | No misconduct | Hearing filed: This year | Hearing filed: Last year | Total punished | Struck off Roll | Sus-pended | Fined | Costs | No order | Exonerated | Pending |
|---|---|---|---|---|---|---|---|---|---|---|---|---|---|---|
| 1931–32 | | | | | | 58 | 25 | 17 | 8 | | | | | |
| 1930–31 | | | | | | 72 | 23 | 17 | 6 | | | | | |
| 1929–30 | | | | | | 77 | 15 | 13 | 2 | | | | | |
| 1928–29 | | 31 | 10 | | | 69 | 22(10) | 16(5) | 6(5) | | 3 | | | |
| 1927–28 | | 43 | 8 | | | 84 | 29 | 24 | 5 | | 2 | | | |
| 1926–27 | | 37 | 1 | | | 60 | 17 | 11(12) | 6 | | 4 | | | |
| 1925–26 | | 39 | 4 | | | 70 | 19 | 11 | 8 | | 4 | | | |
| 1924–25 | | 37 | 1 | | | 59 | 16 | 10 | 6 | | 2 | | | |
| 1923–24 | | 43 | 0 | | | 72 | 24 | 16 | 8 | | 2 | | | |
| 1922–23 | | 40 | 3 | | | 62 | 11 | 6 | 5 | | 6 | | | |
| 1921–22 | | 32 | 0 | | | 51 | 12(13) | 8(9) | 4 | | 5 | | | |
| 1920–21 | | 40 | 1 | | | 54 | 6 | 4 | 2 | | 6 | | | |
| 1920[a] | | 11 | 2 | | | 20 | 5 | 5 | 0 | | 1 | | | |
| 1919[a] | 26 | 22 | 0 | 2 | | 13 | 1 | 0 | 1 | | 1 | | | |
| 1918–19 | 27 | 19 | 0 | 2 | | 30 | 4(3) | 0 | 4(3) | | 1 | | | |
| 1917–18 | 32 | 15 | 5 | 2 | | 37 | 8 | 4(5) | 4(3) | | 2 | | | |
| 1916–17 | 40 | 21 | 4 | 8 | | 27 | 5(7) | 2(4) | 3 | | 0 | | | |
| 1915–16 | 36 | 23 | 1 | 2 | | 42 | 8 | 4 | 4 | | 2 | | | |
| 1914–15 | 49 | 25 | 1 | 3 | | 38 | 9(18) | 7(13) | 2(5) | | 2 | | | |
| 1913–14 | 57 | 29 | 2 | 9 | | | 14 | 6 | 8 | | 3 | | | |
| 1913 | 47 | 25 | 6(3) | 7 | | 16 | 14(12) | 9(6) | 5(6) | | | | 2 | |
| 1912 | 57 | 33 | 9(4) | 7 | | 16 | 15(11) | 6(3) | 9(8) | | 2 | | 1 | |
| 1911 | 50 | 30 | 5(3) | 5 | | 12 | 10 | 3 | 7 | | 2 | | 2 | |

| | | | | | | | | | | | | | |
|---|---|---|---|---|---|---|---|---|---|---|---|---|---|
| 1910 | 60 | 33 | 9(4) | 15 | | 13 | 12 | 5 | 3 | | | 1 | |
| 1909 | 70 | 23 | 17(3) | 28 | | 22 | 15(13) | 7 | 6 | 3 | | 7 | |
| 1908 | 59 | 28 | 3(5) | 6 | | 22 | 19(15) | 11 | 4 | 5 | | 3 | |
| 1907 | 89 | 45 | 2 | | | 24 | 23 | | | | | 1 | |
| 1906 | 65 | 32 | 2 | | | 25 | 23 | | | | | 2 | |
| 1905 | 68 | 34 | 3 | | | 22 | 19 | | | | | 3 | |
| 1904 | 81 | 35 | 2 | | | 35 | 30 | 18 | 4 | 2 | 2 | 5 | 4 |
| 1903 | 87 | 39 | 4 | | | 32 | 26 | 12 | 6 | 3 | 2 | 6 | 3 |
| 1902 | 114 | 50 | 8 | | | 42 | 39 | 24 | 3 | 1 | | 3 | 10 |
| 1901 | 92 | 39 | 10 | | | 28 | 27 | 18 | 3 | | | 1 | 5 |
| 1900 | 70 | 28 | 9 | | | 25 | 18 | 13 | | 2 | | 7 | 3 |
| 1899 | 82 | 38 | 16 | | | 18 | 14 | 11 | | 1 | | 4 | 2 |
| 1898 | 94 | 47 | 12 | | | 20 | 18 | 15 | | 1 | | 2 | 2 |
| 1897 | 100 | 43 | 31 | | | 29 | 22 | 11 | 2 | 2 | | 7 | 4 |
| 1896 | 110 | 58 | 17 | | | 22 | 16 | 8 | 2 | | | 6 | 6 |
| 1895 | 122 | 73 | 17 | | | 28 | 21 | 9 | 3 | 1 | | 7 | 8 |
| 1894 | 143 | 74 | 21 | | | 36 | 32 | 10 | 5 | 2 | | 4 | 14 |
| 1893 | 132 | 74 | 22 | 4 | | 32 | | | | | | | |
| | 128 | 69 | 3 | | | 39 | 22 | | | | | 17 | |
| 1892 | 112 | 64 | 17 | 6 | 25 | | | | | | | | |
| | 111 | 65 | 0 | | 17 | 15 | | | | | | 2 | |
| 1891 | 115 | 68 | 21 | 10 | | 16 | | 19 | 7 | 2 | | | |
| 1890 | 110 | 57 | 24 | 8 | | 21 | | | | | | | |
| 1889 | 54 | 33 | 10 | 6 | | 5 | | 15 | 2 | 7 | | | |
| 1888 | | | | | | | 15 | 13 | 2 | | | | |
| 1887 | | | | | | | 29 | 22 | 6 | | | | |
| 1886 | | | | | | | 17 | 14 | 3 | | | | |
| 1885 | | | | | | | 14 | 10 | 4 | | | | |
| 1884 | | | | | | | 20 | 16 | 4 | | | | |
| 1883 | | | | | | | 25 | 19 | 6 | | | | |
| 1882 | | | | | | | 10 | 7 | 3 | | | | |

*continued*

**Table 2.42** (*Cont'd*)

| | Complaints | No case to answer | Withdrawn etc. | No misconduct | Hearing filed | | Total punished | Struck off Roll | Sus-pended | Fined | Costs | No order | Exonerated | Pending |
|---|---|---|---|---|---|---|---|---|---|---|---|---|---|---|
| | | | | | This year | Last year | | | | | | | | |
| 1881 | | | | | | | 8 | 5 | 3 | | | | | |
| 1880 | | | | | | | 10 | 5 | 5 | | | | | |
| 1879 | | | | | | | 8 | 6 | 2 | | | | | |
| 1878 | | | | | | | 12 | 8 | 4 | | | | | |
| 1877 | | | | | | | 3 | 3 | | | | | | |
| 1876 | | | | | | | 6 | 6 | | | | | | |
| 1875 | | | | | | | 7 | 7 | | | | | | |
| 1874 | | | | | | | 4 | 4 | | | | | | |
| 1873 | | | | | | | 4 | 2 | 2 | | | | | |
| 1872 | | | | | | | 5 | 4 | 1 | | | | | |
| 1871 | | | | | | | 6 | 2 | 4 | | | | | |
| 1870 | | | | | | | 7 | 7 | | | | | | |
| 1869 | | | | | | | 5 | 3 | 2 | | | | | |
| 1868 | | | | | | | 3 | 1 | 2 | | | | | |
| 1867 | | | | | | | 2 | 2 | | | | | | |
| 1866 | | | | | | | 1 | | 1 | | | | | |
| 1865 | | | | | | | 1 | 1 | | | | | | |
| 1864 | | | | | | | 4 | 4 | | | | | | |
| 1863 | | | | | | | 4 | 4 | | | | | | |
| 1850 | | | | | | | 2 | 2 | | | | | | |

[a] Solicitors Act 1919 initiated new procedure 1 January 1920; hence 1919 is last five months of that year and 1920 first seven months of year.
[b] Figures in parentheses are another source.
*Sources*: Proceedings and resolutions at the special general meeting of the Incorporated Law Society, 12 April 1889: 7; Law Society, Annual Report, 1901: 41 (appendix: 12th annual report of the committee appointed under the Solicitors Act 1888); Law Society, Annual Reports; *Law Society's Gazette*

**Table 2.43** Disciplinary complaints per 100 solicitors with practising certificates, 1971–2 to 1978–9

| Year | Number of complaints | Number of practising certificates | Complaints per 100 practising certificates |
|---|---|---|---|
| 1978–9 | 5,915 | 34,090 | 17.4 |
| 1977–8 | 5,815 | 32,865 | 17.7 |
| 1976–7 | 5,834 | 32,812 | 17.8 |
| 1975–6 | 5,752 | 31,250 | 18.4 |
| 1974–5 | 4,742 | 29,850 | 15.9 |
| 1973–4 | 4,853 | 28,741 | 16.9 |
| 1972–3 | 5,270 | 27,327 | 19.2 |
| 1971–2 | 4,860 | 26,327 | 18.5 |

*Source*: tables 2.14, 2.42

**Table 2.44** Actions of the Lay Observer, 1975–6 to 1985

| | 1975–6 | 1976–7 | 1977–8 | 1978 | 1979 | 1980 | 1981 | 1982 | 1983 | 1984 | Total 1975–84 | 1985 |
|---|---|---|---|---|---|---|---|---|---|---|---|---|
| *Actions* | | | | | | | | | | | | |
| New correspondence | 437 | 305 | 278 | 254 | 240 | 310 | 349 | 339 | 281 | 337 | 3130 | 340 |
| Allegations examined | 162 | 127 | 121 | 112 | 107 | 120 | 171 | 187 | 165 | 231 | 1503 | |
| Allegations disposed | 140 | 117 | 114 | 90 | 116 | 106 | 162 | 174 | 143 | 207 | 1359 | 209 |
| Criticisms of Law Society | 11 | 6 | 16 | 9 | 8 | 13 | 15 | 17 | 11 | 12 | 118 | 27 |
| Recommendations to Law Society to reconsider | 2 | 4 | 5 | 3 | 13 | 1 | 5 | 1 | 1 | 1 | 36 | |
| *Subject of complaint* | | | | | | | | | | | | |
| Delay/inaction | 82 | 31 | 31 | 28 | 16 | 17 | 14 | 3 | 7 | 6 | | |
| Withholding documents | 47 | 13 | 7 | 7 | 4 | 2 | 4 | 6 | 1 | 3 | | |
| Bills | 14 | 27 | 23 | 10 | 9 | 11 | 15 | 17 | 19 | 31 | | |
| Disclosing confidence | 13 | 7 | 7 | 5 | 3 | 1 | | 0 | 0 | 1 | | |
| Dissatisfaction with advice | | | 17 | 23 | 21 | 53 | 56 | 64 | 59 | 74 | | |
| Violating instructions | | | 9 | 7 | 3 | 1 | | 2 | 0 | 1 | | |
| Ethics | | | 23 | 22 | 35 | 20 | 50 | 66 | 59 | 69 | | |
| Financial loss | 35 | 49 | | | 5 | 1 | 4 | 1 | 0 | 3 | | |
| Legal aid | | | | | 3 | 5 | 5 | 8 | 6 | 8 | | |
| Miscellaneous | | | 10 | 10 | 15 | 11 | 25 | 21 | 20 | 34 | | |
| *Nature of legal problem* | | | | | | | | | | | | |
| Criminal | 3 | 4 | 7 | 13 | 6 | 5 | 7 | 9 | 4 | 12 | | |
| Matrimonial | 29 | 36 | 28 | 21 | 18 | 13 | 22 | 31 | 24 | 37 | | |
| Estates | 23 | 18 | 17 | 19 | 14 | 24 | 22 | 33 | 19 | 21 | | |
| Landlord–tenant | 16 | 3 | 5 | 3 | 2 | 1 | 4 | 7 | 4 | 7 | | |
| Conveyancing | 7 | 13 | 14 | 17 | 12 | 16 | 20 | 26 | 18 | 22 | | |
| Property | 62 | 26 | 21 | 11 | 10 | 18 | 18 | 26 | 40 | 45 | | |
| Contract | 3 | 7 | 7 | 3 | 1 | 3 | 3 | 3 | 5 | 7 | | |
| Personal injury | 3 | 3 | 4 | 10 | 11 | 7 | 4 | 4 | 2 | 7 | | |
| Employment | | 4 | 5 | 2 | 3 | 2 | 7 | 2 | 5 | 6 | | |
| Professional negligence | 4 | 2 | 4 | | 3 | 1 | 2 | 2 | 5 | 2 | | |
| Miscellaneous | 12 | 11 | 9 | 11 | 29 | 30 | 63 | 44 | 45 | 64 | | |

*Source*: Lay Observer, Annual Reports

**Table 2.45** Payments from the compensation fund, 1912–19, 1956–85

| | Number of claims | | Amount | | Amount paid net of recovery other sources | Amount rejected | Number of solicitors involved |
|---|---|---|---|---|---|---|---|
| | Made | Rejected | Claimed (£) | Paid (£) | (£) | (£) | |
| 1985 | | | | 1,008,000 | | | |
| 1984 | | | | 1,891,000 | | | |
| 1983 | | | | 666,000 | | | |
| 1982 | | | | 970,000 | | | |
| 1981 | | | | 534,000 | | | |
| 1980 | | | | 1,635,000 | | | |
| 1979 | | | | 625,000 | | | |
| 1978 | 85 | 5 | 844,508 | 837,110 | | 105,480 | 13 |
| 1977 | 99 | 4 | 889,184 | 528,238 | | 31,734 | 16 |
| 1976 | 265 | 7 | 1,697,749 | 829,573 | | 56,457 | 32 |
| 1975 | 296 | 8 | 1,135,080 | 655,863 | | 32,241 | 20 |
| 1974 | 236 | 11 | 585,643 | 439,451 | | 58,123 | 11 |
| 1973 | 102 | 5 | 848,362 | 195,950 | | 78,558 | 12 |
| 1972 | 74 | 19 | 557,493 | 205,809 | | 35,535 | 6 |
| 1971 | 147 | 11 | 496,444 | 142,569 | | 47,782 | 11 |
| 1970 | | | | 266,893 | | | |
| 1969 | | | | 136,948 | | | |
| 1968 | | | | 225,552 | | | |
| 1967 | | | | 264,019 | | | |
| 1966 | | | | 104,579 | | | |
| 1965 | | | | 57,842 | | | |
| 1964 | | | | 168,498 | | | |

*continued*

**Table 2.45** (*cont'd*)

| | Number of claims | | Amount | | Amount paid net of recovery other sources (£) | Amount rejected (£) | Number of solicitors involved |
|---|---|---|---|---|---|---|---|
| | Made | Rejected | Claimed (£) | Paid (£) | | | |
| 1963 | | | | | 195,268 | | |
| 1962 | | | | | 228,191 | 56,135 | |
| 1961 | | | | | 264,361 | 154,158 | |
| 1960 | | | | | 104,558 | 65,054 | |
| 1959 | | | | | 71,079 | 55,751 | |
| 1958 | | | | | 142,814 | 119,143 | |
| 1957 | | | | | 141,071 | 127,997 | |
| 1956 | | | | | 149,566 | 119,173 | |
| 1918–19[a] | 3 | | £ 149 17s 1d | £ 149 9s 5d | | | |
| 1917–18 | 6 | | £ 323 0s 5d | £ 297 18s 4d | | | |
| 1916–17 | 15 | | £ 620 14s 0d | £ 572 14s 0d | | | |
| 1914–15 | 7 | | £ 785 6s 0d | £ 729 3s 4d | | | |
| 1913–14 | 21 | | £1179 17s 7d | £1086 8s 7d | | | |
| 1912–13 | 13 | | £1463 2s 2d | £1319 3s 6d | | | |

[a] Last five months.

*Sources*: Law Society, Annual Reports; Royal Commission, 1979, vol. 1: 322–3; Law Society, 1977: 76–7

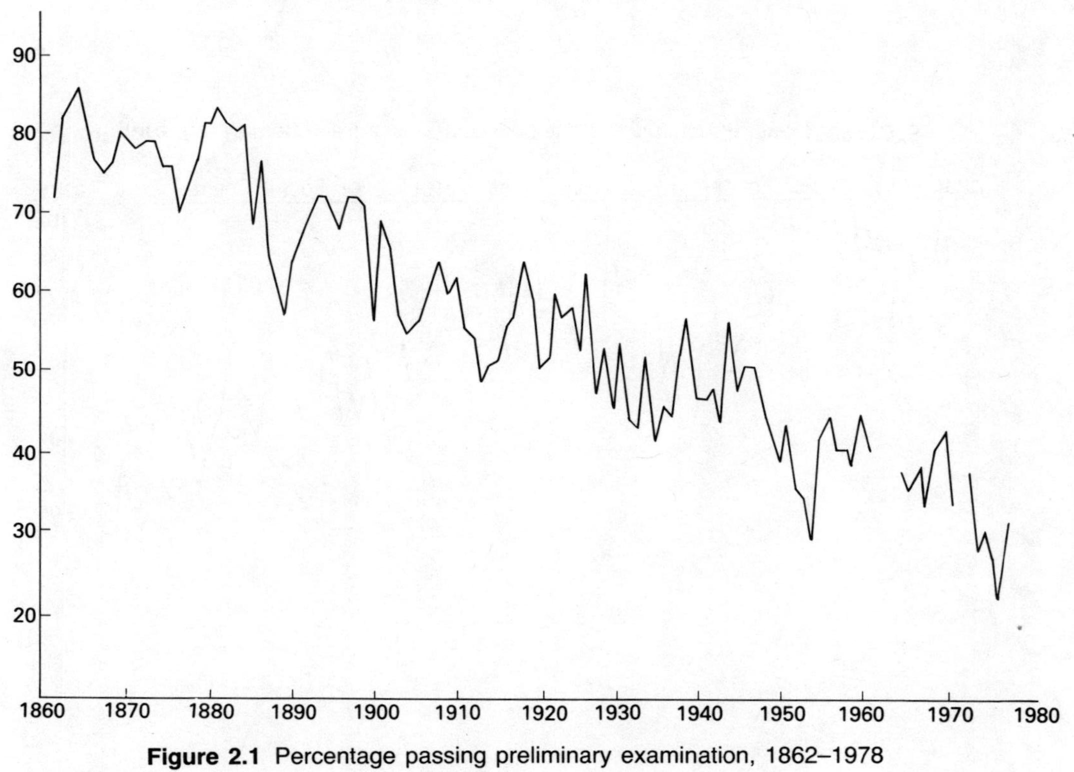


**Figure 2.1** Percentage passing preliminary examination, 1862–1978

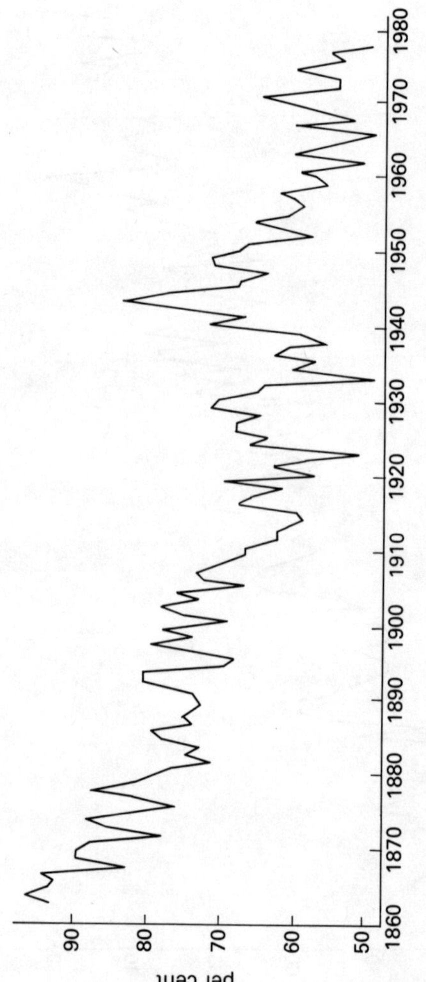


**Figure 2.2** Percentage passing intermediate examination in law, 1862–1978

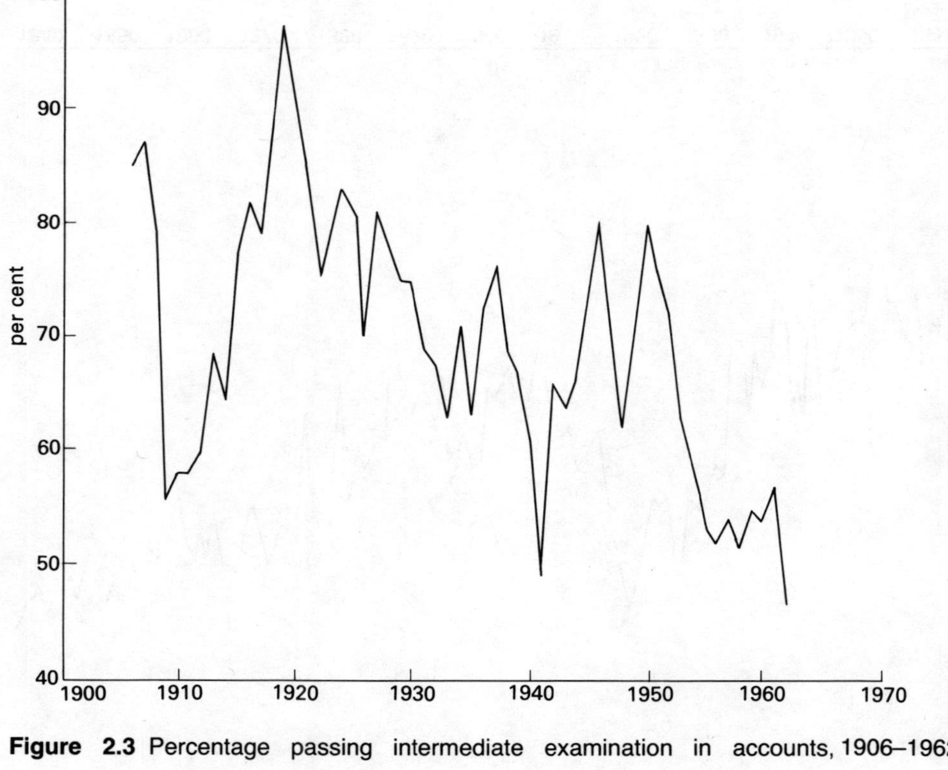


**Figure 2.3** Percentage passing intermediate examination in accounts, 1906–1962

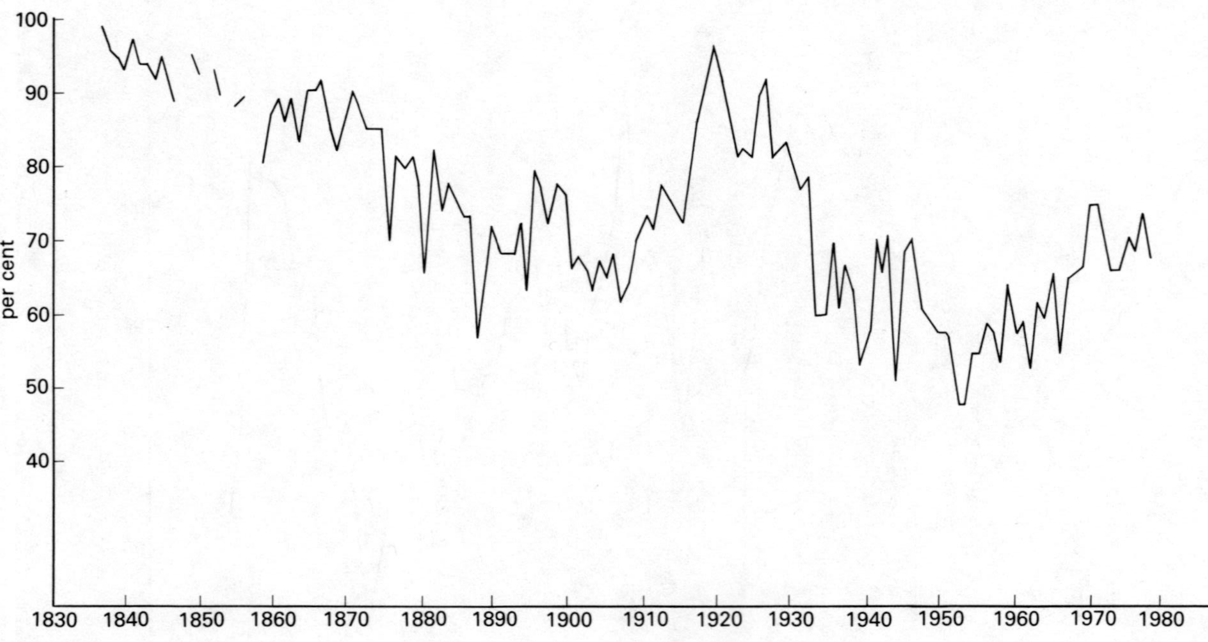


**Figure 2.4** Percentage passing final examination, 1836–1978

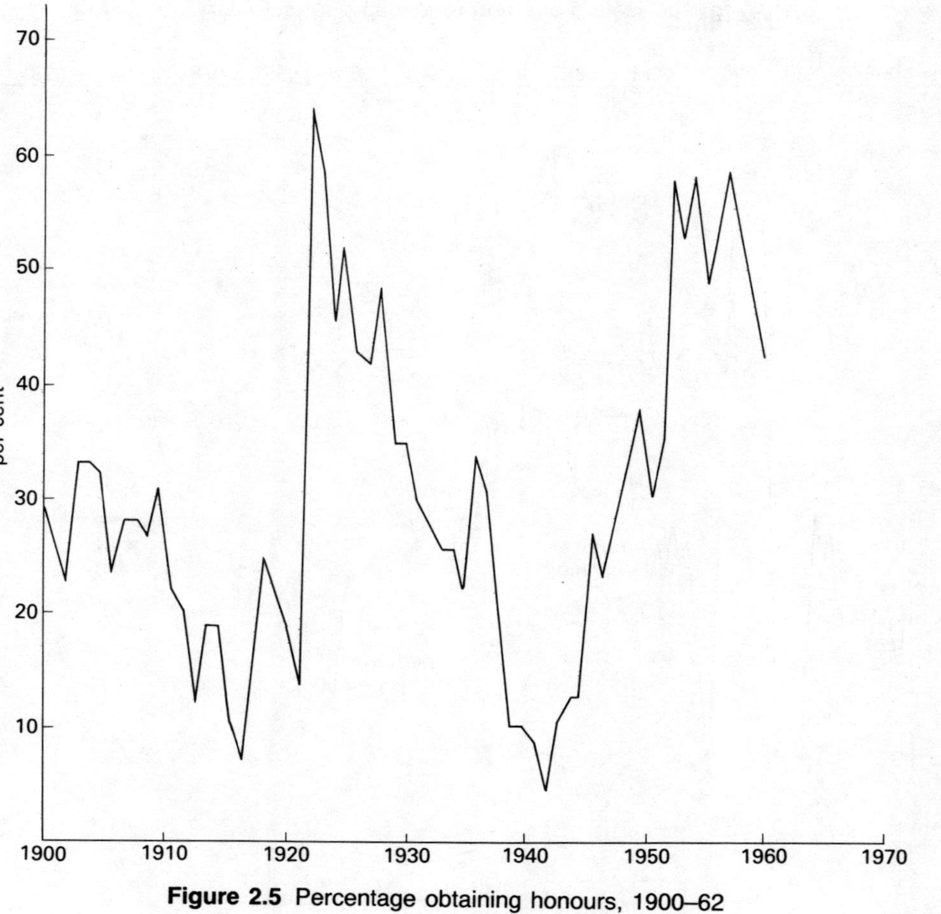


**Figure 2.5** Percentage obtaining honours, 1900–62

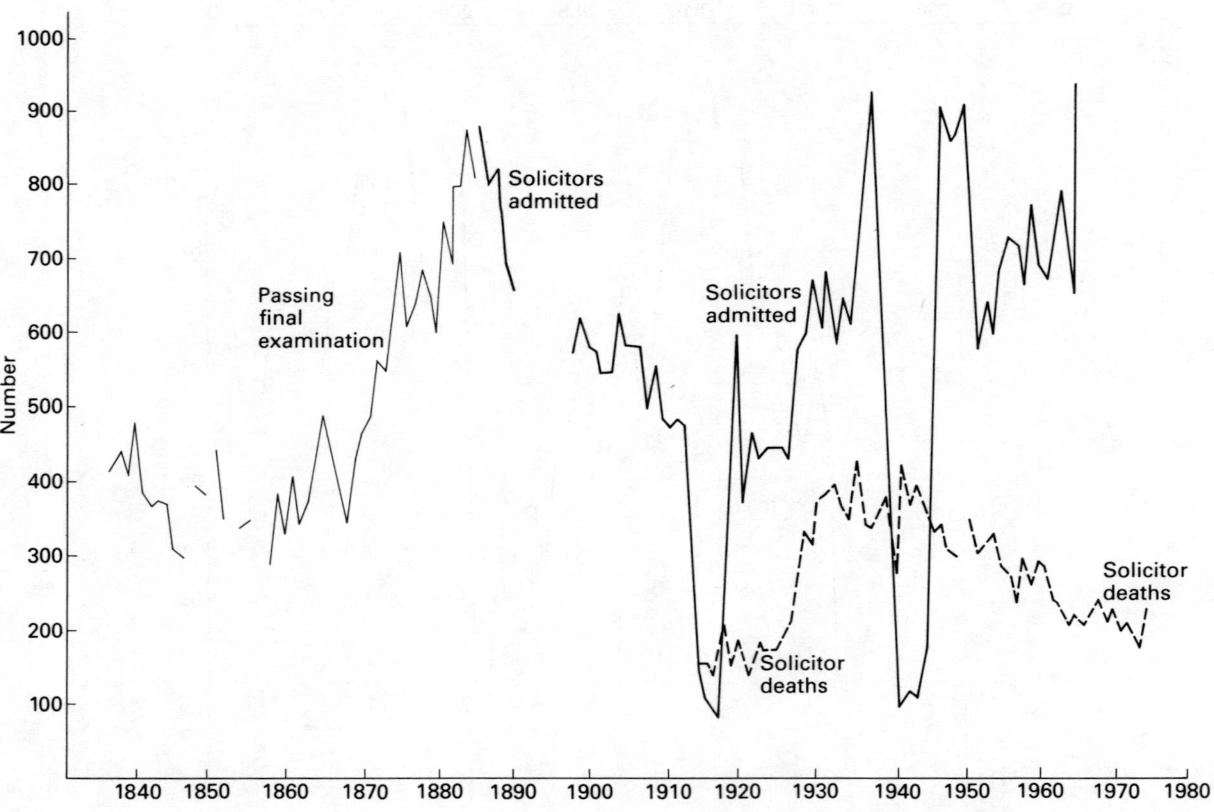


**Figure 2.6** Entry into and departure from the profession, 1837–1976

# Appendix 3

# Legal education

**Table 3.1** Law teaching staff at universities and polytechnics, 1909 to 1983–4

| | Full time: absolute number (% of full-time teachers) | | | | | | Part time | | |
|---|---|---|---|---|---|---|---|---|---|
| Year | Oxbridge | London | Older provincial | Newer provincial | Polytechnic | Total | University absolute (% of university) | Polytechnic absolute (% of polytechnic) | Mixed schools |
| 1909 | 44 (40) | 17 (16) | 48 (44) | | | | | | |
| 1910 | | 14 | 30 | | | | | | |
| 1933–4 | 41 (31) | 29 (22) | 40 (31) | 20 (15) | | 130 | | | |
| 1963–4 | 94 (35) | 73 (27) | 77 (28) | 28 (10) | | 272 | 91 (25) | | |
| 1965–6 | 88 (26) | 98 (29) | 99 (30) | 50 (15) | | 335 | 113 (25) | | |
| 1969 | | | | | 199 | | | | |
| 1974–5 | 121 (12) | 118 (12) | 168 (17) | 186 (19) | 381 (39) | 974 | 118 (17) | 108 (22) | 38 |
| 1977–8 | 113 (10) | 112 (10) | 217 (19) | 221 (19) | 486 (42) | 1149 | 159 (18) | 110[a] (18) | 44 |
| 1980–1 | 118 ( 9) | 113 ( 9) | 245 (19) | 250 (20) | 556 (43) | 1282 | 153 (11) | 113 (17) | 58 |
| 1983–4 | 100 | 117 | 236 | 275 | | | 91 (11) | | |
| % increase 1963–4 to 1983–4 | 6 | 60 | 206 | 882 | | | | | |

[a] 1976–7.
[b] Degree programme combining law and some other subject.
*Sources*: Wilson, 1966: 3, 98; Wilson and Marsh, 1975: 239, 268; 1978: 18; 1981: 21; Jenks, 1935; Hazeltine, 1909; 1910; CHULS, 1984: table 9

**Table 3.2** Law students at universities and polytechnics, 1933–4 to 1983–4: absolute numbers (percentage of full-time undergraduate internal law degree candidates)

| Year | Oxbridge | London | Older provincial | Newer provincial | Total university undergrad. | Annual % increase | Polytechnic | Annual % increase | Total undergrad. | Annual % increase | Univ. mixed degree | Poly. mixed degree | External London LLB | External poly. LLB | Part-time poly. | Postgrad. |
|---|---|---|---|---|---|---|---|---|---|---|---|---|---|---|---|---|
| 1933–34 | 1010 (56) | 307 (17) | 443 (25) | 44 (2) | 1804 (100) | | | | | | | | | | | |
| 1938–39 | 934 (62) | 203 (13) | 358 (24) | 20 (1) | 1515 (100) | | | | | | | | | | | 100 |
| 1953–54 | 1284 (49) | 476 (18) | 723 (27) | 157 (6) | 2640 (100) | | | | | | | | | | | 256 |
| 1958–59 | 1363 (45) | 556 (18) | 895 (29) | 227 (7) | 3041 (100) | | | | | | | | | | | |
| 1959–60 | 1279 (43) | 562 (19) | 923 (31) | 238 (8) | 3002 (100) | −1.3 | | | | | | | | | | |
| 1960–61 | 1232 (40) | 554 (18) | 1029 (34) | 255 (8) | 3070 (100) | 2.3 | | | | | | | | | | |
| 1961–62 | 1149 (36) | 569 (18) | 1167 (37) | 284 (9) | 3169 (100) | 3.2 | | | | | | | | | | |
| 1962–63 | 1096 (32) | 612 (18) | 1383 (41) | 310 (9) | 3401 (100) | 7.3 | | | | | | | | | | |
| 1963–64 | 1040 (29) | 636 (18) | 1524 (43) | 343 (10) | 3543 (100) | 4.2 | | | | | | | | | | 520 |
| 1964–65 | 1070 (28) | 657 (17) | 1699 (44) | 412 (11) | 3838 (100) | 8.3 | | | | | | | | | | 592 |
| 1965–66 | 1166 (28) | 755 (18) | 1776 (42) | 507 (12) | 4204 (100) | 9.5 | | | | | | | | | | 640 |
| 1970–71 | 1174 (19) | 855 (14) | 2124 (35) | 1182 (20) | 5335 (89) | | 663 (11) | | 5998 | | | | 1569 | | | |
| 1971–72 | 1321 (20) | 863 (13) | 2231 (34) | 1298 (20) | 5713 (87) | 7.1 | 861 (13) | 29.9 | 6574 | 9.6 | | | 1469 | | | |
| 1972–73 | 1394 (19) | 855 (12) | 2388 (33) | 1472 (20) | 6109 (83) | 6.9 | 1226 (17) | 42.4 | 7335 | 11.6 | | | 1289 | | 45 | |
| 1973–74 | 1508 (18) | 876 (11) | 2555 (31) | 1710 (21) | 6649 (81) | 8.8 | 1610 (19) | 31.3 | 8259 | 12.6 | | | 960 | 645 | 96 | 846 |
| 1974–75 | 1450 (16) | 907 (10) | 2671 (29) | 2044 (22) | 7072 (77) | 6.4 | 2151 (23) | 33.6 | 9223 | 11.7 | 877 | | 628 | | 245 | |
| 1976–76 | 1487 (14) | 952 (9) | 2755 (27) | 2290 (22) | 7484 (73) | 11.3 | 2789 (27) | 29.7 | 10273 | 11.4 | | | 387 | 718 | 318 | 1001 |
| 1976–77 | 1520 (14) | 1034 (9) | 2817 (25) | 2481 (22) | 7852 (71) | 4.9 | 3284 (29) | 17.7 | 11136 | 8.4 | | | 114 | 675 | 433 | 1039 |
| 1977–78 | 1426 (12) | 1063 (9) | 2856 (25) | 2552 (22) | 7897 (69) | 0.6 | 3533 (31) | 7.6 | 11430 | 2.6 | 1275 | | | 439 | 563 | |
| 1978–79 | 1532 (13) | 1090 (9) | 2871 (24) | 2590 (22) | 8083 (68) | 2.3 | 3734 (32) | 5.7 | 11817 | 3.4 | 1294 | 497 | | 450 | 702 | |
| 1979–80 | 1522 (13) | 1086 (9) | 2931 (24) | 2657 (22) | 8196 (68) | 1.4 | 3909 (32) | 4.7 | 12105 | 2.4 | | 496 | | 520 | 900 | |
| 1980–81 | 1510 (12) | 1121 (9) | 2987 (24) | 2780 (22) | 8398 (67) | 2.5 | 4205 (33) | 7.6 | 12603 | 4.1 | 1421 | 541 | | 352 | 1061 | 1137 |
| 1981–82 | 1533 (11) | 1186 (8) | 2729 (19) | 3077 (21) | 8525 (59) | | 5837 (41) | | 14362 | | 1863 | | | | 1253 | |
| % increase 1953–4 to 1983–4 | 19 | 149 | 277 | 1860 | 223 | | | | | | | | | | | |

*Sources*: Wilson, 1966; 13; Wilson and Marsh, 1975: 249–50, 255, 258–66; 1978: 4, 8, 11–17; 1981: 4, 9, 14–19; Marsh, 1983: 121–2; Jenks, 1935; CHULS, 1984: table 3

**Table 3.3** University law department enrolment, degrees and staff, 1971–2 to 1983–4

| | Full-time undergraduates | | | | | | | Postgraduates | | | | | | | Undergraduates | | New entrants | | | Degrees awarded | | | Staff | | |
|---|---|---|---|---|---|---|---|---|---|---|---|---|---|---|---|---|---|---|---|---|---|---|---|---|---|
| | | UK domicile | | | | Overseas | | | UK domicile | | | | Overseas | | | | | | | | | | | | |
| | | Men | | Women | | | | | Men | | Women | | | | | | | Other | | | | | | | |
| | Total | no. | % | no. | % | no. | % | Total | no. | % | no. | % | no. | % | Sandwich course | Part time | Home fees | no. | % | First | Ad-vanced | Total | Prof. | Reader/ s. lect. | lect. |
| 1983–84 | 10,609 | 5,330 | 55 | 4,287 | 45 | 992 | 9.4 | 1,385 | 459 | 59 | 320 | 41 | 606 | 44 | 111 | 118 | 3,085 | 383 | 11.1 | 3,420 | 514 | 848 | 118 | 136 | 588 |
| 1982–83 | 10,707 | 5,596 | 57 | 4,264 | 43 | 847 | 7.9 | 1,268 | 427 | 60 | 285 | 40 | 556 | 44 | 97 | 86 | 3,053 | 322 | 9.5 | 3,298 | 491 | 841 | 129 | 132 | 582 |
| 1981–82 | 10,757 | 5,838 | 58 | 4,188 | 42 | 731 | 6.8 | 1,248 | 468 | 64 | 265 | 36 | 515 | 41 | 87 | 90 | 3,286 | 258 | 7.3 | 3,365 | 447 | 862 | 123 | 136 | 593 |
| 1980–81 | 10,615 | 5,944 | 59 | 4,047 | 41 | 624 | 5.9 | 1,070 | 306 | 63 | 181 | 37 | 523 | 49 | 101 | 133 | 3,354 | 217 | 6.1 | 3,223 | 440 | 859 | 120 | 134 | 596 |
| 1979–80 | 10,331 | | | | | | | 812 | | | | | | | | | | | | | | | | | |
| 1978–79 | 10,203 | | | | | | | 847 | | | | | | | | | | | | | | | | | |
| 1977–78 | 10,053 | | | | | | | 771 | | | | | | | | | | | | | | | | | |
| 1976–77 | 9,874 | | | | | | | 708 | | | | | | | | | | | | | | | | | |
| 1975–76 | 9,412 | | | | | | | 674 | | | | | | | | | | | | | | | | | |
| 1974–75 | | | | | | | | | | | | | | | | | | | | | | | | | |
| 1973–74 | 8,162 | | | | | | | 612 | | | | | | | | | | | | | | | | | |
| 1972–73 | 7,469 | | | | | | | 599 | | | | | | | | | | | | | | | | | |
| 1971–72 | 6,934 | | | | | | | 640 | | | | | | | | | | | | | | | | | |

*Source*: UGC, University Statistics. Vol. 1: Students and staff

**Table 3.4** Growth of higher education, 1971–2 to 1982–3

| | Qualified school leavers (000) | | | Home entrants under 21 to British public higher educ. (000)[a] | | |
|---|---|---|---|---|---|---|
| | Men | Women | | Men | Women | |
| Year | no. | no. | % | no. | no. | % |
| 1982–83 | 64.2 | 60.6 | 49 | 31.8 | 25.1 | 44 |
| 1981–82 | 62.6 | 57.9 | 48 | 28.4 | 21.7 | 43 |
| 1980–81 | 60.2 | 53.2 | 47 | 24.2 | 18.4 | 43 |
| 1979–80 | 58.1 | 51.5 | 47 | 21.6 | 15.8 | 42 |
| 1978–79 | 58.1 | 48.5 | 45 | 20.8 | 14.5 | 41 |
| 1977–78 | 58.7 | 47.1 | 45 | 20.5 | 14.2 | 41 |
| 1976–77 | 56.8 | 45.2 | 44 | 20.3 | 13.6 | 40 |
| 1975–76 | 55.9 | 44.0 | 44 | 19.2 | 11.1 | 37 |
| 1974–75 | 52.1 | 40.9 | 44 | 17.9 | 10.3 | 37 |
| 1973–74 | 50.3 | 39.5 | 44 | 17.2 | 9.7 | 36 |
| 1972–73 | 49.3 | 39.0 | 44 | 17.3 | 8.9 | 34 |
| 1971–72 | 49.6 | 37.7 | 43 | 17.5 | 8.4 | 32 |

[a] Excluding teacher training.

*Source*: Department of Education and Science, 1984

**Table 3.5** Law degrees granted by universities and polytechnics and external London LLB degrees, 1948–84

| | First degrees | | | | | All degrees | | | | | |
|---|---|---|---|---|---|---|---|---|---|---|---|
| | Total internal | | | | | Total | | University | | Polytechnic | |
| | no. | Annual % increase | University | Polytechnic (CNAA) | External London LLB | no. | % increase | no. | % women | no. | % women |
| 1984 | | | | 1173 | | | | 2705 | 43 | | |
| 1983 | 3816 | | 2716 | 1100 | | 4006 | 3.6 | 2768 | 41 | 1238 | 41 |
| 1982 | | | | 1123 | | 3867 | −4.0 | 2739 | 40 | 1128 | 38 |
| 1981 | | | | 1312 | | 4028 | 11.3 | 2716 | 39 | 1312 | 39 |
| 1980 | 3564 | 4.5 | 2491 | 1073 | 142 | 3619 | 0.2 | 2649 | 37 | 970 | 36 |
| 1979 | 3411 | 2.5 | 2384 | 1027 | 145 | 3612 | 3.2 | 2573 | 33 | 1039 | 30 |
| 1978 | 3328 | 7.3 | 2405 | 923 | 166 | 3501 | 4.0 | 2577 | 30 | 924 | 28 |
| 1977 | 3102 | 17.7 | 2327 | 775 | 272 | 3365 | 13.7 | 2676 | 30 | 689 | |
| 1976 | 2635 | 11.0 | 2071 | 564 | 380 | 2959 | 6.6 | 2433 | 29 | 526 | |
| 1975 | 2374 | 8.9 | 1973 | 401 | 375 | 2775 | | 2340 | 26 | 435 | |
| 1974 | 2180 | 8.8 | 1882 | 298 | 435 | | | | | | |
| 1973 | 2004 | 10.3 | 1706 | 232 | 490 | | | | | | |
| 1972 | 1817 | 6.3 | 1663 | 154 | 524 | | | | | | |
| 1971 | 1709 | 9.7 | 1584 | 125 | 425 | | | | | | |
| 1970 | 1558 | 0 | 1449 | 109 | 463 | 1889 | | 1781 | | 108 | |
| 1969 | 1558 | 7.4 | 1521 | 37 | 457 | | | | | | |
| 1968 | | 11.1 | 1451 | | 373 | | | | | | |
| 1967 | | 12.5 | 1306 | | 250 | | | | | | |
| 1966 | | 8.3 | 1161 | | 319 | | | | | | |
| 1965 | | | 1072 | | 218 | | | | | | |
| 1962–3 | | | 929 | | | | | | | | |
| 1960 | | | 876 | | 87 | | | | | | |
| 1958 | | | 821 | | | | | | | | |
| 1948 | | | 576 | | | | | | | | |

*Sources*: Wilson and Marsh, 1975: 252; 1978: 7; 1981: 7; Marsh, 1983: 120–1; Ormrod Committee, 1971: 105; Abel-Smith and Stevens, 1967: 370 n. 3; CHULS, 1984: table 4; Read, 1984: 178; Marks, 1985: 2904

**Table 3.6** Difficulty of obtaining a place in university and polytechnic law departments, by gender, 1963 to 1984–5

| | Applications per place | | | | | University entrants as % of applicants | | | | |
|---|---|---|---|---|---|---|---|---|---|---|
| | | | | | | | Home | | Overseas | |
| | London Univ. | Older prov. univ. | Newer prov. univ. | Total univ. | Polytechnics | Total | Men | Women | Men | Women |
| 1984–5 | | | | | | | 39 | 36 | 23 | 27 |
| 1983–4 | 14.1 | 10.1 | 16.2 | 13.1 | | | 39 | | 26 | |
| 1982 | | | | | | | | | | |
| 1981 | | | | | | 44 | 43 | 23 | 20 | 38 |
| 1980–1 | 15.6 | 11.2 | 17.2 | 14.3 | 12 | 45 | 44 | 15 | 18 | |
| 1979 | 18.4 | 11.9 | 18.2 | 15.4 | | 46 | 43 | 13 | 13 | |
| 1978 | 16.5 | 12.0 | 17.5 | 14.9 | | 41 | 42 | 9 | 9 | 36 |
| 1977 | 15.2 | 13.3 | 18.6 | 15.7 | 13 | 40 | 43 | 10 | 15 | |
| 1976 | 15.8 | 13.6 | 17.8 | 15.7 | 13 | 38 | 41 | 9 | 12 | |
| 1975 | 15.7 | 12.5 | 16.4 | 14.7 | | 40 | 43 | 10 | 13 | 38 |
| 1974 | 14.7 | 14.0 | 16.4 | 15.2 | 14–15 | 42 | 47 | 18 | 15 | |
| 1973 | 14.3 | 14.1 | 19.0 | 15.9 | | 40 | 47 | 20 | 16 | |
| 1972 | | | | | | 38 | 46 | 15 | 14 | 36 |
| 1971 | | | | | | 39 | 47 | 19 | 17 | 45 |
| 1970 | | | | | | 42 | 48 | 18 | 13 | |
| 1969 | | | | | | 42 | 51 | 18 | 21 | 40 |
| 1968 | | | | | | 45 | 50 | 23 | 16 | |
| 1967 | | | | | | 50 | 54 | 17 | 19 | |
| 1966 | | | | | | 50 | 57 | 11 | 13 | 43 |
| 1965 | 12.4 | 11.8 | 24.6 | 14.3 | | 46 | 54 | 14 | 13 | 48 |
| 1964 | 11.4 | 9.2 | 18.5 | 12.5 | | | | | | 57 |
| 1963 | 10.3 | 7.8 | 17.5 | 10.0 | | | | | | |

*Sources*: Wilson, 1966: 14, 19; Wilson and Marsh, 1978: 6, 11; 1981: 6, 12; Marsh, 1983: 120; UCCA, Annual Reports; CHULS, 1984: table 2

**Table 3.7** Number of full-time and part-time students enrolled in law courses outside university, by gender, 1967–83

| | Full-time | | Sandwich | | Part-time day | | Evening | |
|---|---|---|---|---|---|---|---|---|
| | Men | Women | Men | Women | Men | Women | Men | Women |
| 1983 | | 5837 | | | | 1253 | | |
| 1982 | | 5603 | | | | 1158 | | |
| 1981 | | 5124 | | | | | | |
| 1980 | | 5052 | | | | | | |
| 1979 | | | | | | | | |
| 1978 | 2700 | 1160 | 100 | 100 | 1100 | 500 | 900 | 300 |
| 1977 | 2867 | 1447 | 97 | 38 | 530 | 254 | 1263 | 438 |
| 1976 | 3000 | 1173 | 116 | 30 | 463 | 242 | 1580 | 494 |
| 1975 | 2351 | 761 | 114 | 24 | 126 | 42 | 866 | 214 |
| 1974 | 2589 | 793 | 126 | 22 | 386 | 125 | 1444 | 338 |
| 1973 | 2398 | 683 | 110 | 17 | 306 | 73 | 1233 | 246 |
| 1972 | 2411 | 641 | 94 | 18 | 278 | 72 | 1230 | 202 |
| 1971 | 2456 | 547 | 79 | 17 | 290 | 49 | 1336 | 224 |
| 1970 | 2521 | 475 | 72 | 12 | 480 | 82 | 1328 | 196 |
| 1969 | 2353 | 403 | 54 | 11 | 220 | 19 | 1488 | 157 |
| 1968 | 2451 | 286 | 42 | 5 | 204 | 24 | 1376 | 159 |
| 1967 | 1842 | 225 | 22 | 1 | 1508 | 190 | [a] | [a] |

[a] Included in part-time day.
*Source*: CNAA, Annual Reports

**Table 3.8** University law students: entry, graduation and honours, by gender, 1967–78

| | Women | | | | | | Men | | | |
|---|---|---|---|---|---|---|---|---|---|---|
| | | | | | Women as % of | | | | | |
| | Entrants | Grads | Grads as % of entrants 3 years earlier | Hons as % grads | Entrants | Grads | Entrants | Grads | Grads as % of entrants 3 years earlier | Hons as % grads |
| 1978 | 1361 | 992 | 94 | 86 | 39 | 31 | 2120 | 2215 | 95 | 86 |
| 1977 | 1287 | 942 | 96 | 86 | 37 | 30 | 2169 | 2185 | 96 | 86 |
| 1976 | 1167 | 791 | 94 | 86 | 34 | 29 | 2224 | 1964 | 92 | 85 |
| 1975 | 1055 | 691 | 94 | 82 | 31 | 27 | 2341 | 1878 | 93 | 84 |
| 1974 | 986 | 558 | 95 | 86 | 30 | 23 | 2270 | 1872 | 96 | 86 |
| 1973 | 840 | 525 | 97 | 83 | 28 | 24 | 2142 | 1649 | 93 | 84 |
| 1972 | 735 | 401 | 90 | 84 | 27 | 19 | 2012 | 1680 | 91 | 86 |
| 1971 | 589 | 368 | 88 | 83 | 23 | 18 | 1954 | 1665 | 96 | 79 |
| 1970 | 542 | 319 | 93 | 84 | 23 | 18 | 177 | 1503 | 90 | 81 |
| 1969 | 446 | 304 | | 81 | 20 | 16 | 1840 | 1539 | | 79 |
| 1968 | 417 | 247 | | 79 | 19 | 14 | 1736 | 1496 | | 83 |
| 1967 | 343 | 224 | | 73 | 17 | 14 | 1670 | 1386 | | 80 |
| 1970–8 | | | 94 | | | | | | 94 | |

*Source*: Department of Education and Science, Education Statistics for the United Kingdom, tables 30, 35

**Table 3.9** University first law degrees, 1980: proportion women and overseas by institution

| | UK domicile | | Overseas | | |
|---|---|---|---|---|---|
| University | no. | % women | no. | % total enrolment | Total |
| Birmingham | 145 | 46 | 2 | 1 | 147 |
| Bristol | 96 | 50 | 4 | 4 | 100 |
| Brunel | 34 | 41 | 0 | 0 | 34 |
| Cambridge | 261 | 18 | 26 | 9 | 287 |
| Durham | 45 | 53 | 2 | 4 | 47 |
| East Anglia | 44 | 30 | 3 | 6 | 47 |
| Exeter | 83 | 43 | 0 | 0 | 83 |
| Hull | 75 | 40 | 3 | 4 | 78 |
| Kent | 71 | 41 | 10 | 12 | 81 |
| Leeds | 101 | 28 | 8 | 7 | 109 |
| Leicester | 113 | 35 | 1 | 1 | 114 |
| Liverpool | 100 | 35 | 0 | 0 | 100 |
| London | 448 | 39 | 87 | 16 | 535 |
| Manchester | 119 | 32 | 0 | 0 | 119 |
| Newcastle | 65 | 49 | 0 | 0 | 65 |
| Nottingham | 78 | 41 | 1 | 1 | 79 |
| Oxford | 227 | 25 | 22 | 9 | 249 |
| Reading | 49 | 47 | 3 | 6 | 52 |
| Sheffield | 115 | 42 | 1 | 1 | 116 |
| Southampton | 91 | 47 | 7 | 7 | 98 |
| Sussex | 26 | 42 | 0 | 0 | 26 |
| Warwick | 83 | 34 | 11 | 12 | 94 |
| Aberystwyth | 86 | 49 | 1 | 1 | 87 |
| Cardiff | 62 | 18 | 10 | 14 | 72 |
| UWIST | 44 | 45 | 3 | 6 | 47 |
| Total | 2661 | 36.5 | | | |

*Source*: Pickman, 1981: tables D2b, D2c, D3b, D3c

**Table 3.10** External London LLB, 1959–80

| | Registrations[a] | Exam cands | Grads | Grads as % of exam cands | Hons[b] | Hons as % of grads | % grads resident overseas | % grads studying in college |
|---|---|---|---|---|---|---|---|---|
| 1980 | 924 | 190 | 142 | 75 | 116 | | | 46 |
| 1979 | 987 | 207 | 145 | 70 | 113 | | | 28 |
| 1978 | 3984 | 239 | 166 | 69 | 130 | | | 21 |
| 1977 | 2710 | 381 | 272 | 71 | 213 | | | 54 |
| 1976 | 2687 | 514 | 380 | 74 | 309 | | | 72 |
| 1975 | 2463 | 507 | 375 | 74 | 300 | | | 73 |
| 1974 | 2634 | 576 | 435 | 76 | 334 | | | 83 |
| 1973 | 2240 | 649 | 490 | 76 | 385 | 79 | | 83 |
| 1972 | 2271 | 677 | 524 | 77 | 413 | 79 | *c.*57 | 84 |
| 1971 | 2124 | 617 | 425 | 69 | 313 | 74 | | 89 |
| 1970 | 2377 | 576 | 463 | 80 | 365 | 79 | 29 | 79 |
| 1969 | 2013 | 608 | 457 | 75 | 328 | 72 | 45 | 71 |
| 1968 | 1753 | 492 | 374 | 76 | 266 | 71 | 43 | 70 |
| 1967 | 2125 | 377 | 249 | 66 | 63 | 25 | 50 | 64 |
| 1966 | 1763 | 428 | 319 | 75 | 99 | 31 | 59 | 66 |
| 1965 | 966 | 306 | 218 | 71 | 53 | 24 | 67 | 65 |
| 1964 | 1765 | 269 | 184 | 68 | 50 | 27 | 63 | 61 |
| 1963 | 1483 | 268 | 181 | 68 | 54 | 30 | 59 | 60 |
| 1962 | 1486 | 266 | 155 | 58 | 41 | 26 | 52 | 50 |
| 1961 | 1325 | 265 | 160 | 60 | 38 | 24 | 44 | 46 |
| 1960 | 1247 | 167 | 100 | 58 | 25 | 25 | 36 | 46 |
| 1959 | | 160 | 87 | 54 | 26 | 30 | 31 | 44 |

[a] Year ending in March.
[b] Third class honours introduced in 1968.
*Sources*: Ormrod Committee, 1971: 108–9; Wilson and Marsh, 1975: 261: 261–2; 1978: 13; Marsh, 1983: 120

**Table 3.11** Graduates of polytechnics as percentage of entrants, 1966–83

| | Marsh[a] | | | Wilson[b] | | | CNAA[c] | | |
|---|---|---|---|---|---|---|---|---|---|
| | Entrants | Grads | Grads as % of entrants | Entrants | Grads | Grads as % of entrants | Entrants | Grads | Grads as % of entrants 3 years earlier |
| 1983 | | | | | | | 2341 | | |
| 1982 | | | | | | | 2342 | | |
| 1981 | | 1123 | 76 | 2156 | 1312 | 73 | | | |
| 1980 | 1701 | 1073 | 75 | 2135 | 1073 | 74 | | 970 | 59 |
| 1979 | 1572 | 1027 | 73 | 1975 | 1027 | 73 | | 1039 | 64 |
| 1978 | 1469 | 923 | 71 | 1809 | 923 | 72 | | 924 | 63 |
| 1977 | 1423 | 775 | 74 | 1440 | 775 | 75 | 1641 | 689 | 56 |
| 1976 | 1407 | 564 | 73 | 1405 | 564 | 73 | 1635 | 526 | 63 |
| 1975 | 1298 | 401 | 68 | 1287 | 401 | 68 | 1471 | 435 | 69 |
| 1974 | 1048 | 298 | 72 | 1039 | 298 | 71 | 1231 | 295 | 71 |
| 1973 | 769 | 232 | 75 | 775 | 232 | 72 | 830 | 231 | 74 |
| 1972 | 586 | 154 | 77 | 593 | 154 | 63 | 631 | 155 | 78 |
| 1971 | 415 | 125 | 64 | 418 | 125 | 65 | 415 | | |
| 1970 | 311 | 109 | 61 | 321 | 109 | 61 | 311 | | |
| 1969 | 200 | 37 | 40 | 243 | 39 | 42 | 200 | | |
| 1968 | 194 | | | 194 | | | | | |
| 1967 | 179 | | | 179 | | | | | |
| 1966 | 92 | | | 92 | | | | | |
| 1969–81 | | | 73 | | | 72 | (1972–80) | | 63 |

[a] The source for these columns is Marsh, 1983: 121.

[b] The sources for these columns are: Wilson and Marsh, 1978: 10; 1981: 11; Royal Commission, 1979, vol. 2: 47; Ormrod Committee, 1971: 107. They include part-time students.

[c] The source for these columns is the CNAA Annual Reports, 1970–81, which are also said to be the source for the data of Marsh, 1983 and Wilson and Marsh, 1978; 1981.

**Table 3.12** Entry and attrition of mature and other law students at Polytechnic of Central London, 1979–80 to 1984–5

| | | | Normal progress toward degree | | Withdrew before first-year exam | |
|---|---|---|---|---|---|---|
| | | Entrants[a] | Number | % of entrants | Number | % of entrants |
| 1979–80 | Mature | 25 (4) | 18 | 72 | 7 | 28 |
| | Other | 55 | 31 | 56 | 16 | 29 |
| 1980–81 | Mature | 33 (7) | 22 | 67 | 10 | 30 |
| | Other | 35 | 19 | 54 | 11 | 31 |
| 1981–82 | Mature | 33 (2) | 21 | 64 | 7 | 21 |
| | Other | 44 | 20 | 45 | 14 | 31 |
| 1982–83 | Mature | 38 (6) | 29 | 76 | n.a. | |
| | Other | 47 | 37 | 79 | n.a. | |
| 1983–84 | Mature | 27 (8) | 22 | 81 | 3 | 11 |
| | Other | 52 | 46 | 88 | 7 | 13 |

[a] Numbers in parentheses (included in total mature entrants) are those with less than two A-levels. Mature are 21 or older.
*Source*: Polytechnic of Central London, 1985: 175

**Table 3.13** Class of polytechnic first law degrees, by gender, 1971–83

| | First | | Upper second | | Lower second | | Third | | Unclassed degree, *aegrotat* | | |
|---|---|---|---|---|---|---|---|---|---|---|---|
| | no. | % | no. | % | no. | % | no. | % | no. | % | Total |
| 1983 men | 6 | 0.9 | 107 | 15.8 | 403 | 59.5 | 141 | 20.8 | 20 | 3.0 | 677 |
| women | 4 | 0.8 | 92 | 19.0 | 303 | 62.6 | 74 | 15.3 | 11 | 2.2 | 484 |
| 1981 men | 4 | 0.5 | 100 | 12.5 | 439 | 54.7 | 175 | 21.8 | 84 | 10.5 | 802 |
| women | 5 | 1.0 | 98 | 19.2 | 313 | 61.4 | 76 | 14.9 | 18 | 3.5 | 510 |
| 1980 men | 4 | 0.6 | 63 | 10.1 | 372 | 59.5 | 128 | 20.5 | 58 | 9.3 | 625 |
| women | 2 | 0.6 | 75 | 21.7 | 195 | 56.5 | 58 | 16.8 | 15 | 4.3 | 345 |
| 1979 men | 5 | 0.7 | 107 | 14.9 | 404 | 56.2 | 161 | 22.4 | 42 | 5.8 | 719 |
| women | 1 | 0.3 | 66 | 20.9 | 180 | 57.0 | 54 | 17.1 | 15 | 4.7 | 316 |
| 1978 men | 7 | 1.1 | 77 | 11.6 | 376 | 56.7 | 155 | 23.4 | 48 | 7.2 | 663 |
| women | 2 | 0.8 | 53 | 20.3 | 118 | 45.2 | 72 | 27.6 | 16 | 6.1 | 261 |
| 1977 | 6 | 0.9 | 97 | 14.1 | 354 | 52.0 | 179 | 26.0 | 53 | 7.7 | 689 |
| 1976 | 2 | 0.4 | 76 | 14.4 | 295 | 56.1 | 119 | 22.6 | 34 | 6.5 | 526 |
| 1975 | 1 | 0.2 | 58 | 13.4 | 240 | 55.4 | 93 | 21.5 | 41 | 9.5 | 433 |
| 1974 | 5 | 1.8 | 48 | 16.8 | 148 | 51.9 | 68 | 23.9 | 16 | 5.6 | 285 |
| 1973 | 3 | 1.3 | 36 | 15.6 | 119 | 51.5 | 63 | 27.3 | 10 | 4.3 | 231 |
| 1972 | 2 | 1.3 | 21 | 13.5 | 82 | 52.9 | 47 | 30.3 | 3 | 1.9 | 155 |
| 1971 | 1 | 0.8 | 21 | 16.7 | 62 | 49.2 | 42 | 33.3 | | | 126 |

*Source*: CNAA, Annual Reports

**Table 3.14** Career expectations of law graduates, 1962, 1972–9

| | University graduates (%) | | | | | | Polytechnic graduates (%) | | | | |
|---|---|---|---|---|---|---|---|---|---|---|---|
| | 1962 | 1972 | 1973 | 1974 | 1976 | 1979 | 1972 | 1973 | 1974 | 1976 | 1979 |
| Barrister | 10 | 12.5 | 12.5 | 14.5 | 11.5 | 10.5 | 16 | 17 | 8 | 6 | 18 |
| Solicitor | 50 | 57.5 | 59 | 56 | 60 | 60.5 | 53 | 58 | 63 | 63 | 48.5 |
| Further degree | | 6 | 7.5 | 5 | 4 | 4 | 7 | 6 | 6 | 6 | 4 |
| Teaching | | 1.5 | 1.5 | 1.5 | 1 | 1 | 4 | 4 | 2 | 1 | 1 |
| Civil service | | 0.5 | 0.5 | 1.5 | 1.5 | 1.5 | 3 | 3 | 1 | 1 | 2 |
| Local government | 5 | 1 | 1 | 2 | 1.5 | 1 | 2 | 0 | 1 | 1 | 1 |
| Industry/commerce | | 5 | 4 | 4 | 5.5 | 5.5 | 10 | 6 | 4 | 4 | 5 |

*Sources*: Wilson, 1966: 54–5; Wilson and Marsh, 1975: 288–9; 1978: 25; 1981: 28

**Table 3.15** Relationship between university legal education and professional careers, 1980–1 to 1982–3

| | First law degrees | | Expecting to do Bar or Law Society examinations | | | | |
|---|---|---|---|---|---|---|---|
| | (1) | (2) | (3) | (4) Law degree | (5) | | |
| | Total | UK domicile | Total | no. | % | (4) as % of (1) | (4) as % of (2) |
| 1982–83 | 3722 | 3366 | 2735 | 2362 | 86 | 63 | 70 |
| 1981–82 | 3605 | 3328 | 2662 | 2449[a] | 92 | 68 | 74 |
| 1980–81 | 3552 | 3320 | 2305 | 2148[a] | 93 | 60 | 65 |
| 1979–80 | 3485 | | 2164 | | | | |
| 1978–79 | 3419 | | 1227 | | | | |
| 1977–78 | | | 1262 | | | | |
| 1976–77 | | | 1366 | | | | |

[a] Administrative, business and social studies.
*Source*: UGC, University Statistics. Vol. 2: First destinations of university graduates

**Table 3.16** First destination of first degree university law graduates, 1980–2

| | 1980 | | 1981 | | 1982 | |
|---|---|---|---|---|---|---|
| | no. | % | no. | % | no. | % |
| Solicitors' examination | 1519 | 53.2 | 1524 | 51.8 | 1507 | 50.1 |
| Bar examination | 324 | 11.4 | 301 | 10.2 | 320 | 10.6 |
| Further education | 123 | 4.3 | 149 | 5.1 | 137 | 4.6 |
| Returned to home country | 138 | 4.8 | 170 | 5.8 | 192 | 6.4 |
| Employed/unavailable | 461 | 16.2 | 465 | 15.8 | 424 | 14.1 |
| Seeking employment | 92 | 3.2 | 100 | 3.4 | 145 | 4.8 |
| Unknown | 197 | 6.9 | 235 | 8.0 | 285 | 9.5 |
| Total | 2854 | | 2944 | | 3010 | |

*Source*: Universities Statistical Record

**Table 3.17** Relationship between polytechnic legal education and professional careers, 1975–83

| Year and course | | Proportion ot those doing professional exams who have read subject (%) | | | | | | | | | | | | Proportion of law graduates who do professional exams[a] | | | |
|---|---|---|---|---|---|---|---|---|---|---|---|---|---|---|---|---|---|
| | | Law | | Other admin, bus. or social studies | | Science | | Arts except lang. | | Lang. | | Number | | % | | Number | |
| | | M | F | M | F | M | F | M | F | M | F | M | F | M | F | M | F |
| 1983 | full time | 90 | 92 | 6 | 5 | 3 | 2 | 1 | 2 | 0 | 0 | 312 | 254 | 90 | 94 | 312 | 248 |
| | sandwich | 70 | 100 | 30 | 0 | 0 | 0 | 0 | 0 | 0 | 0 | 10 | 12 | 100 | 100 | 7 | 12 |
| 1982 | full time | 91 | 89 | 5 | 4 | 3 | 7 | 1 | 1 | 0 | 0 | 341 | 273 | 86 | 89 | 361 | 288 |
| | sandwich | 79 | 100 | 20 | 0 | 0 | 0 | 0 | 0 | 0 | 0 | 24 | 9 | 95 | 100 | 20 | 9 |
| 1981 | full time | 92 | 90 | 3 | 5 | 3 | 4 | 1 | 1 | 1 | 0 | 359 | 266 | 94 | 97 | 355 | 248 |
| | sandwich | 88 | 88 | 12 | 12 | 0 | 0 | 0 | 0 | 0 | 0 | 8 | 8 | 100 | 88 | 7 | 8 |
| 1980 | full time | 90 | 93 | 6 | 2 | 3 | 4 | 1 | 1 | 0 | 0 | 349 | 249 | 95 | 97 | 329 | 239 |
| | sandwich | 80 | 100 | 13 | 0 | 7 | 0 | 0 | 0 | 0 | | 15 | 3 | 100 | 100 | 12 | 3 |
| 1979 | full time | 92 | 97 | 2 | 1 | 5 | 2 | 1 | 0 | 0 | 0 | 372 | 151 | 92 | 86 | 377 | 170 |
| | sandwich | 90 | 100 | 10 | 0 | 0 | 0 | 0 | 0 | 0 | 0 | 21 | 4 | 94 | 62 | 18 | 8 |
| 1978 | full time | 96 | 95 | 2 | 2 | 1 | 3 | 1 | 1 | 0 | 0 | 324 | 133 | 91 | 87 | 343 | 145 |
| | sandwich | 100 | 80 | 0 | 20 | 0 | 0 | 0 | 0 | 0 | 0 | 13 | 5 | 100 | 100 | 12 | 4 |
| 1977 | | 95 | 91 | 2 | 6 | 2 | 3 | 1 | 0 | 0 | 0 | 343 | 101 | 89 | 88 | 366 | 105 |
| 1976 | | 94 | 83 | 4 | 10 | 1 | 0 | 1 | 7 | 0 | 0 | 300 | 101 | 93 | 89 | 303 | 94 |
| 1975 | | 96 | 94 | 2 | 1 | 0 | 0 | 1 | 3 | 0 | 1 | 272 | 67 | 91 | 88 | 289 | 72 |

[a] Of those whose career plans are known, excluding overseas students leaving the UK, those not available for employment, the unemployed and those who gained employment.

*Source*: AGCAS Polytechnic Statistics Working Group, 1984: table 1a

# Appendix 4

# Demographics

**Table 4.1** Growth of legal and medical professions, 1730–1981

| | Barristers | | | Solicitors | | | Barristers/solicitors | | | Physicians/surgeons | | |
|---|---|---|---|---|---|---|---|---|---|---|---|---|
| | M | F | Decennial % increase | M | F | Decennial % increase | M | F | Decennial % increase | M | F | Decennial % increase |
| 1730 | | | | *c.*4,000 | | | | | | | | |
| 1779 | 208 | | | 3,127 | | | | | | | | |
| 1780 | 257 | | | | | | | | | | | |
| 1785 | 379 | | | | | | | | | | | |
| 1790 | 424 | | | | | | | | | | | |
| 1800 | 598/577 | | | | | | | | | | | |
| 1802 | | | | 5,270 | | | | | | | | |
| 1810 | 880/708 | | | | | | | | | | | |
| 1814 | 821 | | | | | | | | | | | |
| 1816 | 747 | | | | | | | | | | | |
| 1820 | 840 | | | | | | | | | | | |
| 1830 | 1,129 | | | | | | | | | | | |
| 1832 | 1,130 | | | 8,702 | | | | | | | | |
| 1835 | 1,300 | | | | | | | | | | | |
| 1840 | 1,835 | | | | | | | | | | | |
| 1841 | 2,088 | | | 11,684[a] | | | 13,772 | | | 20,134[d] | | |
| 1843 | 2,484 | | | | | | | | | | | |
| 1845 | 2,317 | | | | | | | | | | | |
| 1850 | 3,268 | | | | | | | | | | | |

| | | | | | | | | | | | | |
|---|---|---|---|---|---|---|---|---|---|---|---|---|
| 1851 | 2,816 | | 34.9 | 11,350 | | −2.9 | 14,166 | | 2.9 | 17,491[d,e] | | |
| 1861 | 3,071 | | 9.1 | 11,386 | | 0.3 | 14,457 | | 2.1 | 14,415[f] | | |
| 1863 | 4,360 | | | | | | | | | | | |
| 1864 | 3,071 | | | | | | | | | | | |
| 1865 | 4,500 | | | | | | | | | | | |
| 1867 | 4,640 | | | | | | | | | | | |
| 1871 | 3,580 | | 16.6 | 12,314 | | 8.2 | 15,894 | | 9.9 | 14,684 | | 1.9 |
| 1881 | | | | | | | 17,386 | | 9.4 | 15,091 | 25 | 2.9 |
| 1891 | | | | | | | 19,978 | | 14.9 | 18,936 | 101 | 25.9 |
| 1893 | 4,000 | | | | | | | | | | | |
| 1901 | | | | | | | 20,998 | | 5.1 | 22,486 | 212 | 19.2 |
| 1911 | 4,121 | | | 17,259 | | | 21,380 | | 1.8 | 22,992 | 447 | 3.3 |
| 1921 | 2,953 | 20 | −27.9 | 14,956 | 17 | −13.2 | 17,909 | 37 | −16.1 | 22,965 | 1,253 | 3.3 |
| 1931 | 2,966 | 79 | −0.2 | 15,777 | 116 | 5.4 | 18,743 | | 4.4 | 22,647 | 2,123 | 2.3 |
| 1951 | 3,084 | 151 | 9.1 | 19,689 | 526 | 28.1 | 22,773 | 677 | 25.1 | 35,798 | 6,487 | 70.7 |
| 1961[b] | | | | | | | 32,050 | 1,290 | 42.2 | 51,020 | 9,680 | 43.5 |
| 1966 | | | | | | | 33,730 | 1,760 | 6.4 | 48,670[b] | 10,690[b] | −2.2 |
| 1971 | | | | | | | 36,050[b] | 2,470[b] | 8.5 | 50,800[c] | 11,100[c] | 4.3 |
| 1981 | | | | | | | 43,000[b] | 7,430[b] | 30.9 | 66,769[b,g] | 19,710[b,g] | 39.7 |

[a] Includes law writers and law students
[b] Ten per cent sample.
[c] One per cent sample.
[d] Includes medical students, apothecaries.
[e] Great Britain.
[f] Includes apothecaries.
[g] Includes dentists.

*Sources*: 1841, 1851, . . ., 1981 (and 1966) the source is the census. For other years the sources are: Odgers, 1901: 30; Law Society, Annual Report, 1865: 22; Cocks, 1983: 20 n. 28, 123, 216, 218 nn. 42–4; Reader, 1966:46, 211; S. Warren, 1845: 2; 1863, vol. 1: 1–2; Duman, 1973: 357; 1980: 619; 1981: 89; 1982: 8; Birks, 1960: 174; Christian, 1896: 116–17; Holdsworth, 1938: 8 n. 3

**Table 4.2** Legal professions other than barrister and solicitor, 1779–1920

| | Special pleaders | Serjeant | Conveyancers | Equity draughtsmen | King's/Queen's Serjeants | Queen's Ancient Sergeant | Law clerks[a] |
|---|---|---|---|---|---|---|---|
| 1779 | | 11 | | | | | |
| 1790 | | | 39 | | | | |
| 1797 | 54 | | 56 | | | | |
| 1800 | | 17 | | | | | |
| 1820 | 29 | 13 | 96 | | | | |
| 1830 | 45 | 22 | 80 | | 5 | | |
| 1835 | 20 | 24 | 20 | 34 | | | |
| 1840 | 77 | 19 | 42 | | 2 | | |
| 1841 | | 21 | | | | | |
| 1842 | | 23 | | | | | |
| 1845 | | 26 | | | | | |
| 1850 | 74 | 27 | 32 | | 1 | | 9,714[b] |
| 1860 | 19 | | 53 | | 2 | 1 | 16,605 |
| 1863 | | 29 | | | | | |
| 1870 | | 45 | 37 | | | 0 | 18,886 |
| 1877 | | 40 | | | | | |
| 1880 | | 34 | 10 | | | | 24,502 |
| 1881 | | | 17 | | | | |
| 1882 | | | 30 | | | | |
| 1883 | | | 43 | | | | |
| 1884 | | | 21 | | | | |
| 1886 | | | 16 | | | | |
| 1888 | | | 18 | | | | |
| 1890 | | 18 | 13 | | | | 27,374 |
| 1891 | | | 11 | | | | |
| 1900 | 1 | 2 | 3 | | | | 34,066 |
| 1910 | 1 | | 1 | | | | 34,106 |
| 1920 | | | 1 | | | | |

[a] Census years are 1851, 1861, etc.
[b] Excludes those under 20.
*Sources*: John Browne's General Law List for the Year 1797; Clarke's New Law List, 1820–40; Law List, 1850–1920; census; Kirk, 1976: 135; Law Society, Annual Report, 1936: 8; Holdsworth, 1938: 4

**Table 4.3** Comparison of growth of population and legal profession, 1851–1981

| | | 20–24 years old | | | | | 25–34 years old | | | | |
|---|---|---|---|---|---|---|---|---|---|---|---|
| | | Lawyers | | Population | | | Lawyers | | Population | | |
| | | no. | Decennial % increase | no. | Decennial % increase | Lawyers per 10,000 in age cohort | no. | Decennial % increase | no. | Decennial % increase | Lawyers per 10,000 in age cohort |
| 1851 | men | | | 795,455 | | | | | 1,317,234 | | |
| 1861 | men | 603 | | 860,210 | 8.1 | 7.0 | 3,458 | | 1,395,977 | 6.0 | 24.8 |
| 1871 | men | 844 | 40.0 | 951,917 | 10.7 | 8.9 | 3,024 | −12.6 | 1,589,598 | 13.9 | 19.0 |
| 1881 | men | 994 | 17.8 | 1,112,354 | 16.9 | 8.9 | 6,204[a] | 105.2 | 1,821,537 | 14.6 | 34.1 |
| 1891 | men | 971 | −2.3 | 1,247,346 | 12.1 | 7.8 | 6,897 | 11.2 | 2,089,010 | 14.7 | 33.0 |
| 1901 | men | 693 | −28.6 | 1,472,644 | 18.1 | 4.7 | 5,441 | −21.1 | 2,485,954 | 19.0 | 21.8 |
| 1911 | men | 645 | −6.9 | 1,502,652 | 2.0 | 4.3 | 4,999 | −8.1 | 2,831,655 | 13.9 | 17.7 |
| 1921 | men | 172 | −73.3 | 1,448,385 | −3.6 | 1.2 | 2,696 | −46.1 | 2,621,280 | −7.4 | 10.3 |
| 1931 | men | 748 | 334.8 | 1,699,141 | 17.3 | 4.4 | 3,120 | 15.7 | 3,062,282 | 16.8 | 10.2 |
| 1951 | men | 1,538 | 52.8 | 1,427,228 | −8.0 | 10.8 | 5,085 | 31.5 | 3,139,721 | 1.3 | 16.2 |
| 1961[c] | men | 2,080 | 35.2 | 1,593,744 | 11.7 | 13.1 | 7,200 | 41.6 | 3,271,422 | 6.8 | 22.0 |
| | women | 200 | | 1,617,548 | | 1.2 | 410 | | 3,218,533 | | 1.3 |
| 1966 | men | 4,090[b] | | 1,734,940[c] | | 25.6 | 7,620 | | 3,154,880[c] | | 24.2 |
| | women | 410[b] | | 1,733,490[c] | | 2.4 | 420 | | 3,101,070[c] | | 1.4 |
| 1971[c] | men | 4,510[b] | 116.8 | 2,072,700 | 30.1 | 21.8 | 9,880 | 37.2 | 3,378,900 | 3.3 | 29.2 |
| | women | 650[b] | 225.0 | 2,048,900 | 26.7 | 3.2 | 870 | 112.2 | 3,300,700 | 2.6 | 2.6 |
| 1981[c] | men | 3,220 | −28.6 | 3,520,465[d] | 69.8 | 9.1 | 17,800 | 80.2 | 3,519,426 | 4.2 | 50.6 |
| | women | 1,630 | 150.8 | 3,413,562[d] | 66.6 | 4.8 | 4,310 | 395.4 | 3,497,195 | 6.0 | 12.3 |

[a] 1881 census groups 25–44 together (9771 lawyers). I have apportioned this to the 25–34 category on the basis of the proportions in the 35–44 and the 45–54 categories in the 1891 census. Given the higher mortality in the older cohort, this overestimates the 25–34 category in 1881.
[b] 21–24.
[c] Based on 10 per cent sample.
[d] 16–24.
*Source*: census

**Table 4.4** Composition of central government legal services, 1983: head of department, proportion barristers and proportion women

| Department | Number | % barristers | % women | Head[a] |
|---|---|---|---|---|
| Ministry of Agriculture[b] | 28 | 29 | 14 | B |
| Charity Commissioner | 28 | 50 | 29 | B |
| Church Commissioners | 11 | 0 | 27 | S |
| HM Customs and Excise | 80 | 79 | 25 | B |
| Employment | 21 | 62 | 24 | B |
| Energy | 10 | 30 | 0 | S |
| Environment and Transport | 48 | 58 | 27 | B |
| Foreign and Commonwealth Office | 24 | 67 | 12 | B |
| Health and Safety Executive | 10 | 40 | 10 | S |
| Health and Social Services | 61 | 67 | 28 | B |
| Home Office | 14 | 79 | 14 | B |
| Industry and Trade | 59 | 49 | 25 | B |
| Inland Revenue | 54 | 56 | 20 | B |
| HM Land Registry | 90 | 11 | 9 | B |
| Law Commission | 28 | 61 | 21 | B |
| Law Offices Department | 10 | 90 | 0 | B |
| Metropolitan Police | 45 | 0 | 49 | B |
| Office of Fair Trading | 11 | 55 | 45 | B |
| Official Solicitor | 12 | 17 | 42 | S |
| Parliamentary Counsel's Office | 19 | 63 | 21 | B |
| Director of Public Prosecutions | 69 | 72 | 13 | B |
| Public Trustee | 9 | 11 | 0 | B |
| Procurator General and Treasury Solicitor | 133 | 27 | 17 | B |
| Welsh Office | 12 | 0 | 25 | S |
| Miscellaneous[c] | 28 | 39 | 18 | 4B/3S |
| Total | 914 | 46 | 21 | 23B/8S |

[a] Barrister/solicitor. All heads are men.
[b] Ministry of Agriculture, Fisheries and Food; Forestry Commission; EEC Intervention Board for Agricultural Produce.
[c] Commonwealth War Graves Commission, Council on Tribunals, Criminal Injuries Compensation Board, Crown Estate Commissioners, Department of Education and Science, General Synod of the Church of England, Registry of Friendly Societies
*Source*: Bar List, 1983

**Table 4.5** (a) Age distribution of barristers and solicitors, male and female, 1851–1981

| | | ≤ 24 | | 25–34 | | 35–44 | | 45–54 | | 55–64 | | 65–74 | | ≥ 75 | | Total |
|---|---|---|---|---|---|---|---|---|---|---|---|---|---|---|---|---|
| | | no. | % | no. | % | no. | % | no. | % | no. | % | no. | % | no. | % | |
| 1851[f] | Barr. | | 2.2 | | 30.8 | | 29.3 | | 23.0 | | 9.3 | | 3.8 | | 1.5 | |
| | Sol. | | 6.1 | | 25.4 | | 27.6 | | 36.7 | | 11.3 | | 4.0 | | 1.5 | |
| 1861 | Barr. | 64 | 2.1 | 765 | 24.9 | 880 | 28.7 | 690 | 22.5 | 467 | 15.2 | 155 | 5.0 | 50 | 1.6 | 3,071 |
| | Sol. | 539 | 4.7 | 2,693 | 23.7 | 2,712 | 23.8 | 2,585 | 22.7 | 1,957 | 17.2 | 708 | 6.2 | 192 | 1.7 | 11,386 |
| 1871 | Barr. | 95 | 2.7 | 995 | 27.8 | 842 | 23.5 | 746 | 20.8 | 538 | 15.0 | 300 | 8.4 | 64 | 1.8 | 3,850 |
| | Sol. | 749 | 6.1 | 2,929 | 23.8 | 2,820 | 22.9 | 2,292 | 18.6 | 2,003 | 16.3 | 1,203 | 9.7 | 318 | 2.6 | 12,314 |
| 1881 | Lawyers | 994 | 5.7 | 9,771[a] | 56.2[a] | | | 5,044[b] | 29.0[b] | | | 1,577[c] | 9.1[c] | | | 17.386 |
| 1891 | Lawyers | 982 | 4.9 | 6,897 | 34.5 | 5,529 | 27.7 | 3,179 | 15.9 | 1,971 | 9.9 | 1,420[c] | 7.1 | | | 19,978 |
| 1901 | Lawyers | 693 | 3.3 | 5,441 | 25.9 | 6,562 | 31.3 | 4,623 | 22.0 | 2,247 | 10.7 | 1,087 | 5.2 | 345 | 1.6 | 20,998 |
| 1911 | Barr. | 82 | 2.0 | 918 | 22.3 | 960 | 23.3 | 997 | 24.1 | 735 | 17.8 | 331 | 8.0 | 98 | 2.4 | 4,121 |
| | Sol. | 563 | 3.3 | 4,081 | 23.6 | 4,360 | 25.3 | 4,497 | 26.1 | 2,568 | 14.9 | 926 | 5.4 | 264 | 1.5 | 17,259 |
| 1921 | Barr. | 39 | 1.3 | 506 | 17.0 | 706 | 23.7 | 707 | 23.8 | 627 | 21.1 | 388[c] | 31.1[c] | | | 2,973 |
| | Sol. | 141 | 0.9 | 2,199 | 14.7 | 3,618 | 24.2 | 3,735 | 24.9 | 3,476 | 23.2 | 1,804[c] | 12.0[c] | | | 14,973 |
| 1931 | Male | 748 | 4.4 | 3,120 | 18.2 | 3,085 | 18.0 | 3,775 | 22.1 | 3,364 | 19.7 | 3,066[c] | 17.6[c] | | | 17,098 |
| 1951 | Barr.[d] | 91 | 2.8 | 861 | 26.6 | 864 | 26.7 | 630 | 19.5 | 453 | 14.0 | 265 | 8.2 | 71 | 2.2 | 3,235 |
| | Sol. | 2,231 | 11.0 | 4,388 | 21.7 | 5,834 | 28.9 | 3,049 | 15.1 | 2,263 | 11.2 | 1,753 | 8.7 | 687 | 3.4 | 20,215 |
| 1961[e] | Male | 3,790 | 11.8 | 7,200 | 22.5 | 6,960 | 21.7 | 7,880 | 24.6 | 3,670 | 11.5 | 1,640 | 5.1 | 910 | 2.8 | 32,050 |
| | Female | 30 | 2.3 | 410 | 31.8 | 190 | 14.7 | 210 | 16.3 | 150 | 11.6 | 30 | 2.3 | 0 | 0 | 1,290 |
| 1966[d] | Male | 5,690 | 16.9 | 7,620 | 22.6 | 6,800 | 20.2 | 6,440 | 19.1 | 5,040 | 14.9 | 2,140[c] | 6.3[c] | | | 33,730 |
| | Female | 620 | 35.2 | 420 | 23.9 | 310 | 17.6 | 220 | 12.5 | 140 | 8.0 | 50[c] | 2.8[c] | | | 1,760 |
| 1971[d,e] | Male | 497 | 13.8 | 988 | 27.4 | 684 | 19.0 | 584 | 16.2 | 615 | 17.1 | 237[c] | 6.6[c] | | | 3,605 |
| | Female | 73 | 29.6 | 87 | 35.2 | 40 | 16.2 | 24 | 9.7 | 18 | 7.3 | 5[c] | 2.0[c] | | | 247 |
| 1981[d,ε] | Male | 322 | 7.5 | 1,780 | 41.4 | 928 | 21.6 | 616 | 14.3 | 410 | 9.5 | 244[c] | 5.7[c] | | | 4,300 |
| | Female | 163 | 21.9 | 431 | 58.0 | 82 | 11.0 | 42 | 5.7 | 18 | 2.4 | 16[c] | 2.2[c] | | | 743 |

(b) Age distribution of male solicitors/male lawyers, 1851–1981

| Year | | Percentage in cohort | |
|---|---|---|---|
| | ≤ 34 | 35–54 | ≥ 55 |
| 1851[f] Solicitors | 31.5 | 64.3 | 16.8 |
| 1861 Solicitors | 28.4 | 46.5 | 25.1 |
| 1871 Solicitors | 30.5 | 44.3 | 25.2 |
| 1891 Lawyers | 39.5 | 43.6 | 17.0 |
| 1901 Lawyers | 29.2 | 53.3 | 17.5 |
| 1911 Solicitors | 26.9 | 51.4 | 21.8 |
| 1921 Solicitors | 15.6 | 49.1 | 35.2 |
| 1931 Lawyers | 22.6 | 40.1 | 37.3 |
| 1951 Solicitors | 32.7 | 44.0 | 23.3 |
| 1961 Lawyers | 34.3 | 46.3 | 19.4 |
| 1966 Lawyers | 39.5 | 39.3 | 21.2 |
| 1971 Lawyers | 41.2 | 35.2 | 23.7 |
| 1981 Lawyers | 48.9 | 35.9 | 17.2 |

[a] 25–45.
[b] 45–65.
[c] ≥ 65.
[d] Includes judges.
[e] Ten per cent sample.
[f] Great Britain.
*Source*: census

**Table 4.6** Distribution of gross weekly income of male judges, barristers and solicitors, 1973–9

| Year | no. | Per cent in income bracket (£) | | | | | | | | | | | | | | | | | |
|---|---|---|---|---|---|---|---|---|---|---|---|---|---|---|---|---|---|---|---|
| | | 0–<br>17.99 | 18–<br>19.99 | 20–<br>24.99 | 25–<br>29.99 | 30–<br>34.95 | 35–<br>39.99 | 40–<br>44.99 | 45–<br>49.99 | 50–<br>54.99 | 55–<br>59.99 | 60–<br>69.99 | 70–<br>79.99 | 80–<br>89.99 | 90–<br>99.99 | 100–<br>119.99 | 120–<br>149.99 | 150–<br>199.99 | ⩾ 200 |
| 1973 | 119 | 7.6 | 5.9 | 5.0 | 4.2 | 4.2 | 6.7 | 6.7 | 10.1 | 13.5 | | 19.3 | | 16.8[a] | | | | | |
| 1975 | 125 | | | | 14.4[b] | 2.4 | 4.8 | 1.6 | 8.8 | 5.6 | 7.2 | | | 11.2 | | 12.0[c] | 15.6[d] | | |
| 1976 | 151 | | | | | 7.9[e] | 4.0 | 3.3 | 2.7 | 6.6 | | | | | | 13.9 | 12.6 | 21.2[f] | |
| 1978 | 166 | | | | | | | 6.6[a] | 1.8 | 0.6 | 3.0 | 6.4 | 12.0 | 4.6 | 4.0 | 15.6 | 11.5 | 12.0 | 16.3 |
| 1979 | 149 | | | | | | | 6.7[g] | 2.0 | 2.0 | 2.1 | 8.6 | 10.6 | 10.9 | 6.0 | 17.4 | 13.4 | 15.5 | 18.1 |
| | | | | | | | | | | | | 6.1 | 9.6 | 6.7 | 8.1 | | | | |
| | | | | | | | | | | | | 2.0 | 6.9 | | | | | | |

[a] ⩾ 80
[b] < 30
[c] 100–129.99
[d] ⩾ 130
[e] < 35
[f] ⩾ 150
[g] < 45

| | Income in category (£) | | | | | | | |
|---|---|---|---|---|---|---|---|---|
| | Lowest decile | Lowest quartile | Median | Highest quartile | Highest decile | St. error of median | Highest decile/median | Highest quartile/lowest |
| 1973 | 32.3 | 40.4 | 51.8 | 67.9 | 90.6 | 0.3 (0.7%) | 1.7 | 1.7 |
| 1975 | 22.8 | 46.8 | 64.8 | 100.9 | 152.5 | 6.2 (9.7%) | 2.4 | 2.2 |
| 1976 | 38.1 | 60.8 | 91.7 | 141.3 | 193.2 | 8.3 (9.1%) | 2.1 | 2.3 |
| 1978 | 55.8 | 77.1 | 107.5 | 159.4 | 219.0 | 3.8 (3.6%) | 2.0 | 2.1 |
| 1979 | 51.9 | 83.1 | 116.8 | 180.8 | 255.5 | 5.4 (4.6%) | 2.2 | 2.2 |

*Source*: Inland Revenue, Statistics Division

**Table 4.7** Price indices, 1846–1984

| Year | *Statist* price index[a] | Year | *Statist* price index | Year | *Statist* price index | Year | *Statist* price index | Retail price index[b] | | | Year | Retail price index | |
|---|---|---|---|---|---|---|---|---|---|---|---|---|---|
| 1846 | 89 | 1880 | 88 | 1914 | 85 | 1947 | 230 | 108 | | | 1971 | 153.4 | |
| 1847 | 95 | 1881 | 85 | 1915 | 108 | 1948 | 260 | 111 | | | 1972 | 164.3 | |
| 1848 | 78 | 1882 | 84 | 1916 | 136 | 1949 | 274 | 114 | | | 1973 | 179.4 | |
| 1849 | 74 | 1883 | 82 | 1917 | 179 | 1950 | 324 | 125 | | | 1974 | 208.2 | 108.5 |
| 1850 | 77 | 1884 | 76 | 1918 | 192 | 1951 | 401 | 132 | | | 1975 | | 134.8 |
| 1851 | 75 | 1885 | 72 | 1919 | 206 | 1952 | 380 | 136 | | | 1976 | | 157.1 |
| 1852 | 78 | 1886 | 69 | 1920 | 251 | 1953 | 366 | 140 | | | 1977 | | 182.0 |
| 1853 | 95 | 1887 | 68 | 1921 | 155 | 1954 | 361 | 143 | | | 1978 | | 197.1 |
| 1854 | 102 | 1888 | 70 | 1922 | 131 | 1955 | 370 | 149 | | | 1979 | | 223.5 |
| 1855 | 101 | 1889 | 72 | 1923 | 129 | 1956 | 384 | 153.4 | 102.0 | | 1980 | | 263.7 |
| 1856 | 101 | 1890 | 72 | 1924 | 139 | 1957 | 376 | | 105.8 | | 1981 | | 295.0 |
| 1857 | 105 | 1891 | 72 | 1925 | 136 | 1958 | 355 | | 109.0 | | 1982 | | 320.4 |
| 1858 | 91 | 1892 | 68 | 1926 | 126 | 1959 | 356 | | 110.7 | | 1983 | | 335.1 |
| 1859 | 94 | 1893 | 68 | 1927 | 122 | 1960 | 359 | | 114.5 | | 1984 | | 351.8 |
| 1860 | 99 | 1894 | 63 | 1928 | 120 | 1961 | 354 | | 117.5 | | | | |
| 1861 | 98 | 1895 | 62 | 1929 | 115 | 1962 | 360 | | | 101.6 | | | |
| 1862 | 101 | 1896 | 61 | 1930 | 97 | 1963 | 374 | | | 103.6 | | | |

| | | | | | | | | | |
|---|---|---|---|---|---|---|---|---|---|
| 1863 | 103 | 1897 | 62 | 1931 | 83 | 1964 | 401 | | 107.0 |
| 1864 | 105 | 1898 | 64 | 1932 | 80 | 1965 | 404 | | 112.5 |
| 1865 | 101 | 1899 | 68 | 1933 | 79 | 1966 | | | 116.5 |
| 1866 | 102 | 1900 | 75 | 1934 | 82 | 1967 | | | 119.4 |
| 1867 | 100 | 1901 | 70 | 1935 | 84 | 1968 | | | 125.0 |
| 1868 | 99 | 1902 | 69 | 1936 | 89 | 1969 | | | 131.8 |
| 1869 | 98 | 1903 | 69 | 1937 | 102 | 1970 | | | 140.2 |
| 1870 | 96 | 1904 | 70 | 1938 | 91 | | | | |
| 1871 | 100 | 1905 | 72 | 1939 | 94 | | | | |
| 1872 | 109 | 1906 | 77 | 1940 | 128 | | | | |
| 1873 | 111 | 1907 | 80 | 1941 | 142 | | | | |
| 1874 | 102 | 1908 | 73 | 1942 | 151 | | | | |
| 1875 | 96 | 1909 | 74 | 1943 | 155 | | | | |
| 1876 | 95 | 1910 | 78 | 1944 | 160 | | | | |
| 1877 | 94 | 1911 | 80 | 1945 | 164 | | | | |
| 1878 | 87 | 1912 | 85 | 1945 | 186 | | | | |
| 1879 | 83 | 1913 | 85 | | | | | | |

[a] For *Statist* price index, 1867–77 average = 100.
[b] For retail price index, from 1947 to 1956, 1947 = 100.
From 1956 to 1961, Jan. 1956 = 100.
From 1962 to 1974, Jan. 1962 = 100.
From 1974 to 1984, 15. Jan 1974 = 100.

*Sources*: Mitchell, 1971; Mitchell and Jones, 1971; Central Statistical Office, 1986

**Table 4.8** Geographic distribution of lawyers (judges, barristers, solicitors), per cent, 1961–81

| | 1961 | | | 1966 | | 1971 | | 1981 | |
|---|---|---|---|---|---|---|---|---|---|
| Northern region | 4.3 | | | 4.0 | | 3.9 | | 3.8 | |
| Tyneside conurbation | | 1.2 | | | 1.5 | | 1.0 | | 1.8 |
| Remainder | | 3.1 | | | 2.5 | | 2.9 | | 2.0 |
| East and West Ridings region | 6.5 | | | 6.2 | | 6.2 | | 6.7 | |
| W. Yorkshire conurb. | | 3.2 | | | 2.3 | | 2.6 | | 3.4[b] |
| Remainder | | 3.3 | | | 3.9 | | 3.6 | | 3.3 |
| North-western region | 10.7 | | | 10.8 | | 10.7 | | 10.6 | |
| SE Lancashire conurb. | | 3.8 | | | 4.1 | | 3.7 | | 4.9[d] |
| Merseyside conurb. | | 1.7 | | | 1.8 | | 1.9 | | 2.6[e] |
| Remainder | | 5.1 | | | 4.9 | | 5.2 | | 3.1 |
| N. Midland region | 5.5 | | E. Midland region | 4.1 | | 4.7 | | 4.2 | |
| Midland region | 6.8 | | W. Midland region | 6.9 | | 7.1 | | 6.9 | |
| W. Midlands conurb. | | 2.9 | W. Midlands conurb. | | 2.3 | | 2.8 | | 3.9[c] |
| Remainder | | 3.9 | Remainder | | 4.6 | | 4.4 | | 3.0 |
| Eastern region | 8.7 | | E. Anglia | 2.6 | | 2.4 | | 3.1 | |
| London and SE region | 38.8 | | South-eastern region | 53.6 | | 53.9 | | 51.9 | |
| Greater London conurb. | | 28.2 | Greater London conurb. | | 26.7 | | 28.2 | | 37.3 |
| Remainder | | 10.7 | Outer metropolis | | 17.1 | | 16.0 | | 7.5 |
| | | | Remainder | | 9.8 | | 9.6 | | 7.1 |
| Southern region[a] | 6.7 | | | | | | | | |
| South-western region | 7.1 | | | 7.4 | | 6.3 | | 8.1 | |
| Wales | 5.0 | | | 4.5 | | 4.8 | | 4.8 | |
| South-east | | 3.0 | | | 3.1 | | | | |
| Remainder | | 2.0 | | | 1.4 | | | | |
| Total no. | 29,270 | | | 31,930 | | 34,520 | | 43,580 | |

[a] Included in south-eastern region after 1961.
[b] W. Yorkshire metropolitan county.
[c] W. Midlands metropolitan county.
[d] Greater Manchester metropolitan county.
[e] Merseyside metropolitan county.

# Appendix 5

# Work

**Table 5.1** Civil proceedings commenced in England and Wales, 1910–83

| | Appellate proceedings | | | | Original proceedings | | |
|---|---|---|---|---|---|---|---|
| Years | Judicial Committee of the Privy Council | House of Lords | Court of Appeal | High Court of Justice, divisional courts | High Court of Justice | County courts[a] | Other courts |
| 1910 | 142 | 89 | 814 | 437 | 76,925 | 1,359,983 | 37,032 |
| 1911 | 128 | 90 | 862 | 483 | 74,605 | 1,309,518 | 33,006 |
| 1912 | 100 | 91 | 775 | 412 | 76,571 | 1,262,469 | 28,046 |
| 1913 | 141 | 71 | 865 | 426 | 72,414 | 1,255,542 | 25,741 |
| 1914 | 115 | 97 | 716 | 384 | 67,742 | 1,073,417 | 22,191 |
| 1915 | 162 | 69 | 621 | 302 | 63,392 | 1,060,814 | 18,905 |
| 1916 | 140 | 75 | 513 | 313 | 53,329 | 798,017 | 14,639 |
| 1917 | 165 | 83 | 521 | 259 | 46,297 | 609,526 | 10,345 |
| 1918 | 134 | 81 | 488 | 302 | 42,604 | 438,182 | 7,385 |
| 1919 | 204 | 91 | 530 | 301 | 60,290 | 444,155 | 7,962 |
| 1920 | 151 | 93 | 653 | 407 | 93,096 | 557,986 | 15,091 |
| 1921 | 127 | 101 | 647 | 475 | 124,179 | 646,043 | 40,305 |
| 1922 | 126 | 89 | 680 | 365 | 122,041 | 814,872 | 54,537 |
| 1923 | 159 | 76 | 608 | 418 | 119,948 | 912,015 | 61,431 |
| 1924 | 186 | 70 | 509 | 484 | 120,042 | 955,924 | 69,917 |
| 1925 | 125 | 80 | 480 | 395 | 112,071 | 955,774 | 73,063 |
| 1926 | 129 | 71 | 538 | 399 | 106,738 | 897,895 | 80,615 |
| 1927 | 165 | 58 | 470 | 401 | 104,246 | 1,044,300 | 94,152 |
| 1928 | 133 | 73 | 487 | 384 | 99,761 | 1,122,144 | 82,429 |
| 1929 | 141 | 60 | 456 | 320 | 103,377 | 1,134,333 | 79,193 |
| 1930 | 128 | 74 | 443 | 478 | 114,639 | 1,199,578 | 79,422 |
| 1931 | 136 | 57 | 464 | 362 | 111,829 | 1,240,517 | 80,494 |
| 1932 | 114 | 62 | 516 | 397 | 112,181 | 1,309,227 | 87,741 |

| | | | | | | | |
|---|---|---|---|---|---|---|---|
| 1933 | 110 | 63 | 522 | 365 | 101,270 | 1,303,363 | 89,092 |
| 1934 | 104 | 69 | 582 | 348 | 96,206 | 1,226,809 | 81,913 |
| 1935 | 92 | 42 | 629 | 262 | 94,001 | 1,229,401 | 85,646 |
| 1936 | 137 | 43 | 601 | 257 | 96,033 | 1,328,791 | 95,402 |
| 1938 | | | | 93,425 | 1,212,253 | | |
| 1948 | | | | | 385,171 | | |
| 1958 | | | | 99,322 | 1,300,942 | | |
| 1963 | | | | 140,003 | 1,543,324 | | |
| 1964 | | | | | 1,510,324 | | |
| 1965 | | | | | 1,516,101 | | |
| 1966 | | | | | 1,548,0212 | | |
| 1967 | | | | | 1,611,334 | | |
| 1968 | | | | 188,806 | 1,481,416 | | |
| 1969 | | | | 233,716 | 1,636,158 | | |
| 1970 | | | | 229,954 | 1,791,870 | | |
| 1971 | | | | 192,603 | 1,530,941 | | |
| 1972 | | | | 193,819 | 1,668,836 | | |
| 1973 | | | | 195,890 | 1,508,620 | | |
| 1974 | | | | 250,745 | 1,768,819 | | |
| 1975 | | | | 259,350 | 1,811,955 | | |
| 1976 | | | | 229,730 | 1,622,839 | | |
| 1977 | | | | 190,743 | 1,673,966 | | |
| 1978 | | | | 164,748 | 1,467,545 | | |
| 1980 | | | | 218,250 | 1,701,131 | | |
| 1981 | | | | 199,187 | 1,849,260 | | |
| 1982 | | | | 182,573 | 2,048,568 | | |
| 1983 | | | | 198,489 | 2,117,383 | | |

[a] Includes bankruptcy and winding up companies but excludes certain proceedings commenced in the High Court.

*Sources*: Board of Trade, Statistical Abstract for the United Kingdom, 1926: table 161; 1938: table 120; Home Office, Judicial Statistics, England and Wales; Lord Chancellor's Department, Judicial Statistics, England and Wales, 1974: tables E.2–3; 1977, tables G.3–5; 1984: tables 2.14, 3.13

**Table 5.2** Criminal proceedings, 1856–1984

| Year | Crimes tried summarily | Crimes full committal | Miscellaneous offences tried summarily |
|---|---|---|---|
| 1984 | 521,000 | | 1,664,000 |
| 1983 | 530,000 | 72,574 | 1,773,000 |
| 1982 | 539,000 | 66,186 | 1,683,000 |
| 1981 | 523,000 | 61,914 | 1,771,000 |
| 1980 | 507,000 | 57,247 | 1,872,000 |
| 1979 | 460,000 | | 1,588,000 |
| 1978 | 461,000 | 49,466 | 1,558,000 |
| 1977 | 470,000 | 53,927 | 1,623,000 |
| 1976 | 457,000 | | 1,753,000 |
| 1975 | 439,000 | | 1,672,000 |
| 1974 | 406,000 | | 1,645,000 |
| 1973 | 366,000 | | 1,674,000 |
| 1970 | 303,476 | 44,134 | 1,397,923 |
| 1969 | 288,563 | 38,127 | 1,347,316 |
| 1968 | 244,458 | 32,347 | 1,364,289 |
| 1967 | 230,664 | 30,265 | 1,381,201 |
| 1966 | 220,870 | 28,838 | 1,252,759 |
| 1965 | 207,823 | 26,864 | 1,188,741 |
| 1964 | 195,756 | 24,369 | 1,161,252 |
| 1963 | 198,427 | 25,594 | 1,142,299 |
| 1962 | 182,525 | 33,009 | 1,095,609 |
| 1961 | 158,659 | 34,324 | 1,002,648 |

| | Indictable offences | | Non-indictable tried offences |
|---|---|---|---|
| Year | Magistrates' courts | Assizes and Quarter Sessions[a] | Magistrates' courts[a] |
| 1960 | 142,877 | 30,591 | 901,956 |
| 1959 | 133,234 | 29,601 | 916,778 |
| 1958 | 128,202 | 27,801 | 875,853 |
| 1957 | 116,340 | 22,935 | 760,242 |
| 1956 | 104,111 | 19,572 | 694,690 |
| 1955 | 96,730 | 18,091 | 655,137 |
| 1954 | 95,441 | 18,736 | 646,500 |
| 1953 | 103,963 | 20,263 | 615,959 |
| 1952 | 118,387 | 22,069 | 645,465 |
| 1951 | 122,259 | 19,909 | 614,228 |
| 1950 | 105,524 | 18,779 | 593,751 |
| 1949 | 103,826 | 19,362 | 550,759 |
| 1948 | 116,642 | 22,749 | 554,439 |
| 1947 | 105,774 | 20,025 | 524,700 |
| 1946 | 99,334 | 17,497 | 436,670 |
| 1945 | 110,073 | 15,903 | 374,026 |
| 1944 | 103,451 | 12,279 | 416,509 |
| 1943 | 101,504 | 11,944 | 491,588 |
| 1942 | 104,472 | 11,565 | 609,374 |
| 1941 | 105,552 | 10,079 | 724,587 |
| 1940 | 88,392 | 7,829 | 742,603 |
| 1939 | 74,744 | 9,751 | 587,531 |
| 1938 | 75,402 | 10,003 | 744,779 |
| 1937 | 75,934 | 9,083 | 765,014 |
| 1936 | 71,948 | 8,492 | 791,577 |
| 1935 | 69,364 | 8,270 | 728,837 |

| Year | Persons proc. against for indictable offences, courts of summary jurisdiction | Number tried in Assizes and Quarter Sessions | Number tried summarily for non-indictable offences |
|---|---|---|---|
| 1934 | 75,767 | 8,675 | 610,119 |
| 1933 | 72,206 | 9,201 | 566,496 |
| 1932 | 74,413 | 10,410 | 529,176 |
| 1931 | 68,747 | 8,667 | 560,756 |
| 1930 | 66,049 | 8,384 | 597,221 |
| 1929 | 61,723 | 7,072 | 572,969 |
| 1928 | 63,194 | 7,282 | 586,053 |
| 1927 | 65,163 | 7,136 | 604,599 |
| 1926 | 79,591 | 7,924 | 590,152 |
| 1925 | 59,993 | 8,139 | 595,666 |
| 1924 | 59,746 | 7,845 | 567,710 |
| 1923 | 59,256 | 8,126 | 530,007 |
| 1922 | 60,767 | 8,435 | 505,559 |

| Year | Number of persons tried | |
|---|---|---|
| | Indictable offences | Non-indictable offences |
| 1921 | 64,276 | 531,312 |
| 1920 | 64,383 | 627,142 |
| 1918 | 57,378 | 522,248 |
| 1918 | 61,048 | 434,347 |
| 1917 | 66,016 | 511,938 |
| 1916 | 61,851 | 677,275 |
| 1915 | 59,287 | 608,421 |
| 1914 | 63,665 | 643,776 |
| 1913 | 81,776[b] | 659,095 |
| 1912 | 73,642 | 670,109 |
| 1911 | 68,575 | 641,494 |
| 1910 | 62,860 | 638,182 |
| 1909 | 74,061 | 661,543 |
| 1908 | 75,554 | 689,100 |

*continued*

**Table 5.2** (*cont'd*)

| Year | Number tried at Assizes and Quarter Sessions | Year | Number tried at Assizes and Quarter Sessions |
|---|---|---|---|
| 1907 | 13,054 | 1881 | 14,786 |
| 1906 | 13,190 | 1880 | 14,770 |
| 1905 | 12,690 | 1879 | 16,388 |
| 1904 | 12,472 | 1878 | 16,372 |
| 1903 | 12,122 | 1877 | 15,890 |
| 1902 | 11,606 | 1876 | 16,078 |
| 1901 | 11,006 | 1875 | 14,714 |
| 1900 | 10,331 | 1874 | 15,195 |
| 1899 | 11,045 | 1873 | 14,893 |
| 1898 | 11,595 | 1872 | 14,801 |
| 1897 | 11,342 | 1871 | 16,269 |
| 1896 | 11,214 | 1870 | 17,578 |
| 1895 | 11,621 | 1869 | 19,318 |
| 1894 | 12,155 | 1868 | 20,091 |
| 1893 | 12,296 | 1867 | 18,971 |
| 1892 | 12,216 | 1866 | 18,849 |
| 1891 | 11,695 | 1865 | 19,614 |
| 1890 | 11,974 | 1864 | 19,506 |
| 1889 | 12,099 | 1863 | 20,818 |
| 1888 | 13,750 | 1862 | 20,001 |
| 1887 | 13,292 | 1861 | 18,326 |
| 1886 | 13,974 | 1860 | 15,979 |
| 1885 | 13,586 | 1859 | 16,674 |
| 1884 | 14,407 | 1858 | 17,855 |
| 1883 | 14,659 | 1857 | 20,269 |
| 1882 | 15,260 | 1856 | 19,437 |

[a] 1940–5 includes offences against defence regulations.
[b] Sum of courts of summary jurisdiction and Assizes and Quarter Sessions.
*Sources*: Central Statistical Office, Annual Abstract of Statistics; Board of Trade, Statistical Abstract for the United Kingdom; Home Office, Criminal Statistics, England and Wales; Lord Chancellor's Department, Judicial Statistics, England and Wales

**Table 5.3** Divorce proceedings, England and Wales (dissolution of marriage, nullification and judicial separation), 1880–1983

| Year | Number | Year | Number | Year | Number | Years | Average |
|---|---|---|---|---|---|---|---|
| 1983 | 176,745 | 1958 | 26,397 | 1934 | 4,287 | 1900–2 | 530 |
| 1982 | 181,853 | 1957 | 28,004 | 1933 | 4,042 | 1890–2 | 336 |
| 1981 | 176,162 | 1956 | 28,579 | 1932 | 3,894 | 1880–2 | 293 |
| 1980 | 177,415 | 1955 | 28,444 | 1931 | 3,764 | | |
| 1979 | 167,511 | 1954 | 29,140 | 1930 | 3,563 | | |
| 1978 | 166,178 | 1953 | 30,645 | 1929 | 3,396 | | |
| 1977 | 170,149 | 1952 | 34,686 | 1928 | 4,018 | | |
| 1976 | 146,415 | 1951 | 38,489 | 1927 | 3,190 | | |
| 1975 | 140,064 | 1950 | 29,812 | 1926 | 2,622 | | |
| 1974 | 131,638 | 1949 | 35,325 | 1925 | 2,605 | | |
| 1973 | 116,353 | 1948 | 38,048 | 1924 | 2,286 | | |
| 1972 | 111,052 | 1947 | 48,650 | 1923 | 2,667 | | |
| 1971 | 111,106 | 1946 | 43,270 | 1922 | 2,588 | | |
| 1970 | 71,891 | 1945 | 25,789 | 1921 | 3,522 | | |
| 1969 | 61,445 | 1944 | 19,575 | 1920 | 3,090 | | |
| 1968 | 55,240 | 1943 | 15,470 | 1919 | 1,654 | | |
| 1967 | 51,235 | 1942 | 12,082 | 1918 | 1,111 | | |
| 1966 | 46,851 | 1941 | 8,357 | 1917 | 703 | | |
| 1965 | 43,223 | 1940 | 6,985 | 1916 | 990 | | |
| 1964 | 41,721 | 1939 | 8,770 | 1915 | 680 | | |
| 1963 | 37,510 | 1938 | 10,304 | 1914 | 856 | | |
| 1962 | 34,840 | 1937 | 6,016 | 1913 | 577 | | |
| 1961 | 32,105 | 1936 | 5,853 | 1912 | 587 | | |
| 1960 | 28,742 | 1935 | 5,435 | 1911 | 580 | | |
| 1959 | 26,510 | 1934 | 4,287 | | | | |

[a] Only divorces prior to 1935.

*Sources*: Central Statistical Office, Annual Abstract of Statistics (table: divorce proceedings, England and Wales); Board of Trade, Statistical Abstract for the United Kingdom (table: divorces, England and Wales)

**Table 5.4** Company formation and dissolution, bankruptcy and insolvency, 1875–1983

| Year | Companies acquired | Debtors adjudicated bankrupt[b] | Other insolvency proceedings[a] | Year | New companies registered | Companies dissolved | Debtors adjudicated bankrupt | Other insolvency proceedings | Year | New companies registered | Companies dissolved | Debtors adjudicated bankrupt | Other insolvency proceedings |
|---|---|---|---|---|---|---|---|---|---|---|---|---|---|
| 1983 | 447 | 6,555 | 72 | 1962 | 35,174 | 5,258 | 4,112 | 348 | 1941 | 7,373 | 1,360 | 575 | 220 |
| 1982 | 463 | 5,303 | 62 | 1961 | 33,997 | 5,025 | 3,482 | 338 | 1940 | 6,464 | 2,448 | 1,552 | 973 |
| 1981 | 452 | 4,730 | 90 | 1960 | 34,620 | 4,547 | 2,767 | 310 | 1939 | 11,197 | 2,980 | 2,590 | 1,465 |
| 1980 | 469 | 3,634 | 70 | 1959 | 29,467 | 4,159 | 2,277 | 279 | 1938 | 13,365 | 3,175 | 3,024 | 1,744 |
| 1979 | 534 | 3,158 | 56 | 1958 | 22,577 | 3,640 | 2,215 | 311 | 1937 | 13,438 | 2,993 | 3,034 | 1,719 |
| 1978 | 567 | 3,526 | 84 | 1957 | 20,843 | 3,279 | 2,030 | 344 | 1936 | 14,464 | 2,996 | 3,170 | 1,677 |
| 1977 | 481 | 4,078 | 99 | 1956 | 17,760 | 3,415 | 2,081 | 380 | 1935 | 13,805 | 3,064 | | |
| 1976 | 353 | 6,681 | 115 | 1955 | 17,670 | 3,353 | 2,119 | 345 | 1934 | 13,143 | 2,901 | 3,544 | 1,940 |
| 1975 | 388 | 6,676 | 145 | 1954 | 16,020 | 3,386 | 2,142 | 349 | 1933 | 12,004 | 2,947 | 4,030 | 2,182 |
| 1974 | 570 | 5,191 | 123 | 1953 | 13,454 | 3,242 | 2,179 | 345 | 1932 | 10,722 | 3,063 | 4,547 | 2,774 |
| 1973 | 1,313 | 3,363 | 112 | 1952 | 12,415 | 3,326 | 1,987 | 357 | 1931 | 8,862 | 3,194 | 4,317 | 2,501 |
| 1972 | 1,331 | 3,860 | 116 | 1951 | 13,666 | 2,965 | 1,789 | 288 | 1930 | 8,934 | 3,113 | 4,063 | 2,204 |
| 1971 | 961 | 4,353 | 159 | 1950 | 14,049 | 3,326 | 1,797 | 258 | 1929 | 9,168 | 2,954 | 3,856 | 2,044 |
| 1970 | 893 | 4,622 | 208 | 1949 | 14,597 | 3,337 | 1,463 | 230 | 1928 | 9,584 | 3,064 | 4,081 | 2,140 |
| 1969 | 944 | 4,347 | 234 | 1948 | 16,522 | 3,036 | 1,114 | 170 | 1927 | 8,929 | 2,703 | 4,234 | 1,936 |
| 1968 | | 3,896 | 168 | 1947 | 21,952 | 2,685 | 607 | 109 | 1926 | 8,366 | 2,737 | 4,149 | 1,853 |
| 1967 | | 3,995 | 194 | 1946 | 25,464 | 1,883 | 311 | 45 | 1925 | 8,606 | 2,730 | 4,627 | 1,958 |
| 1966 | | 3,672 | 228 | 1945 | 11,906 | 1,118 | 194 | 39 | 1924 | 8,542 | 2,810 | 4,706 | 1,989 |
| 1965 | | 3,375 | 227 | 1944 | 8,051 | 938 | 210 | 37 | 1923 | 8,541 | 2,859 | 4,965 | 1,891 |
| 1964 | | 3,333 | 231 | 1943 | 7,044 | 990 | 229 | 59 | 1922 | 8,562 | 2,834 | 4,733 | 1,847 |
| 1963 | | 3,929 | 274 | 1942 | 6,883 | 1,059 | 332 | 87 | 1921 | 6,834 | 2,928 | 3,472 | 1,368 |

**Table 5.4** (*cont'd*)

| Year | New Companies registered | Companies dissolved | Debtors adjudicated bankrupt | Other insolvency proceedings | Year | New companies registered | Companies dissolved | Debtors adjudicated bankrupt | Other insolvency proceedings |
|---|---|---|---|---|---|---|---|---|---|
| 1920 | 11,011 | 3,158 | 1,565 | 451 | 1897 | 5,229 | | 4,098 | 3,248 |
| 1919 | 10,725 | 1,908 | 745 | 165 | 1896 | 4,735 | | 4,170 | 3,271 |
| 1918 | 3,504 | 1,113 | 628 | 198 | 1895 | 3,892 | | 4,415 | 3,462 |
| 1917 | 3,963 | 1,233 | 1,089 | 612 | 1894 | 2,970 | | 4,794 | 3,894 |
| 1916 | 3,393 | 1,354 | 1,557 | 1,050 | 1893 | 2,617 | | 4,901 | 3,938 |
| 1915 | 4,062 | 1,648 | 2,379 | 1,652 | 1892 | 2,607 | | 4,657 | 3,333 |
| 1914 | 6,214 | 2,022 | 2,867 | 1,776 | 1891 | 2,686 | | 4,242 | 3,008 |
| 1913 | 7,425 | 1,946 | 3,358 | 2,411 | 1890 | 2,789 | | 4,044 | 3,337 |
| 1912 | 7,367 | 2,067 | 3,581 | 2,770 | 1889 | 2,788 | | 4,542 | 3,495 |
| 1911 | 6,444 | 2,061 | 3,742 | 2,950 | 1888 | 2,550 | | 4,859 | |
| 1910 | 7,184 | | 3,880 | 3,364 | 1887 | 2,500 | | 4,866 | |
| 1909 | 6,373 | | 4,070 | 3,491 | 1886 | 1,891 | | 4,857 | |
| 1908 | 5,024 | | 4,306 | 3,822 | 1885 | 1,482 | | 4,354 | |
| 1907 | 5,265 | | 4,111 | 3,488 | 1884 | 1,541 | | 4,192 | |
| 1906 | 4,840 | | 4,436 | 3,641 | 1883 | 1,766 | | 8,555 | |
| 1905 | 4,358 | | 4,764 | 3,839 | 1882 | 1,632 | | 9,041 | |
| 1904 | 3,831 | | 4,546 | 4,085 | 1881 | 1,581 | | 9,727 | |
| 1903 | 4,075 | | 4,286 | 3,622 | 1880 | 1,302 | | 10,298 | |
| 1902 | 3,929 | | 4,202 | 3,305 | 1879 | 1,034 | | 13,132 | |
| 1901 | 3,433 | | 4,244 | 3,369 | 1878 | 886 | | 11,450 | |
| 1900 | 4,966 | | 4,410 | 3,354 | 1877 | 990 | | 9,533 | |
| 1899 | 4,975 | | 4,111 | 2,974 | 1876 | 1,066 | | 9,249 | |
| 1898 | 5,182 | | 4,310 | 3,246 | 1875 | 1,172 | | 7,889 | |

[a] 1923–83: sum of compositions and schemes of arrangement, administrative orders of deceased debtors' estates, deeds of arrangement assigning property to trustees for benefit of creditors and other deeds of arrangement, 1889–1922: all deeds of arrangement.
[b] 1875–1922: sum of debtors adjudicated bankrupt, compositions and schemes of arrangement and administrative orders of deceased debtors' estates.
*Sources*: Central Statistical Office, Annual Abstract of Statistics; Board of Trade, Statistical Abstract for the United Kingdom

**Table 5.5** Industrial deaths and railway deaths and injuries, 1910–83

| Year | Industrial deaths | Railway Deaths[a] | Railway Injuries[b] | Year | Industrial deaths | Railway Deaths | Railway Injuries | Year | Industrial deaths | Railway Deaths | Railway Injuries |
|---|---|---|---|---|---|---|---|---|---|---|---|
| 1983 | 658 | 69 | 9,267 | 1958 | 1,389 | 217 | 24,031 | 1933 | 2,200 | 332 | 21,696 |
| 1982 | 675 | 57 | 8,700 | 1957 | 1,490 | 351 | 24,514 | 1932 | 2,098 | 354 | 21,033 |
| 1981 | 756 | 76 | 10,024 | 1956 | 1,364 | 265 | 24,063 | 1931 | 2,291 | 339 | 22,888 |
| 1980 | 701 | 69 | 10,850 | 1955 | 1,571 | 319 | 23,680 | 1930 | 2,714 | 380 | 24,311 |
| 1979 | 711 | 107 | 11,511 | 1954 | 1,522 | 251 | 24,548 | 1929 | 3,009 | 417 | 25,364 |
| 1978 | 751 | 114 | 11,527 | 1953 | 1,630 | 347 | 25,098 | 1928 | 2,942 | 460 | 24,324 |
| 1977 | 614 | 84 | 9,964 | 1952 | 1,618 | 415 | 26,114 | 1927 | 3,024 | 435 | 25,403 |
| 1976 | 682 | 97 | 10,321 | 1951 | 1,762 | 307 | 26,213 | 1926 | 2,404 | 374 | 23,433 |
| 1975 | 729 | 127 | 10,777 | 1950 | 1,777 | 316 | 27,016 | 1925 | 3,221 | 465 | 26,393 |
| 1974 | 753 | 78 | 11,124 | 1949 | 1,720 | 321 | 29,311 | 1924 | 3,177 | 462 | 25,641 |
| 1973 | 826 | 97 | 12,490 | 1948 | 1,921 | 367 | 30,050 | 1923 | 3,304 | 407 | 23,104 |
| 1972 | 784 | 99 | 12,005 | 1947 | 2,042 | 447 | 30,113 | 1922 | 3,106 | 402 | 19,344 |
| 1971 | 839 | 125 | 12,333 | 1946 | 1,992 | 466 | 31,712 | 1921 | 2,746 | 416 | 18,873 |
| 1970 | 911 | 143 | 13,458 | 1945 | 2,039 | 495 | 2,612 | 1920 | 3,689 | 635 | 25,143 |
| 1969 | 992 | 147 | 13,533 | 1944 | 2,303 | 559 | 2,814 | 1919 | 3,764 | 547 | 23,238 |
| 1968 | 1,067 | 131 | 12,600 | 1943 | 2,680 | 579 | 2,680 | 1918 | 4,486 | 574 | |
| 1967 | 1,010 | 201 | 13,797 | 1942 | 2,975 | 528 | 2,830 | 1917 | 4,554 | 587 | |
| 1966 | 1,207 | 125 | 13,591 | 1941 | 3,395 | 607 | 2,691 | 1916 | 4,522 | 710 | |
| 1965 | 1,089 | 161 | 14,497 | 1940 | 3,110 | 532 | 2,410 | 1915 | 4,616 | 1,066 | 30,641 |
| 1964 | 1,100 | 167 | 16,567 | 1939 | 2,694 | 411 | 17,866 | 1914 | 4,529 | 738 | 29,992 |
| 1963 | 1,101 | 192 | 17,665 | 1938 | 2,664 | 373 | 25,373 | 1913 | 4,851 | 702 | 32,521 |
| 1962 | 1,221 | 204 | 18,939 | 1937 | 2,717 | 400 | 27,169 | 1912 | 5,235 | 624 | 31,360 |
| 1961 | 1,293 | 262 | 22,241 | 1936 | 2,487 | 382 | 25,744 | 1911 | 4,297 | 659 | 30,937 |
| 1960 | 1,281 | 226 | 22,378 | 1935 | 2,502 | 391 | 23,220 | 1910 | | 648 | 28,448 |
| 1959 | 1,298 | 231 | 22,877 | 1934 | 2,651 | 371 | 22,229 | | | | |

[a] Excludes trespassers and suicides

[b] Sum of train accidents, other movement of rail vehicles and other accidents.

*Sources*: Central Statistical Office, Annual Abstract of Statistics (tables: accidents in railways; persons killed in industrial accidents); Board of Trade, Statistical Abstract for the United Kingdom (tables: same)

**Table 5.6** Road accident deaths and injuries, 1910–83

| Year | Killed | Injured | | Year | Killed | Injured | | Year | Killed | Injured |
|---|---|---|---|---|---|---|---|---|---|---|
| | | Serious | Slight | | | Serious | Slight | | | |
| 1983 | 5,445 | 303,139 | | 1958 | 5,970 | 69,166 | 224,631 | 1933 | 6,321 | 169,417 |
| 1982 | 5,934 | 328,362 | | 1957 | 5,550 | 63,706 | 204,602 | 1932 | 5,800 | 161,952 |
| 1981 | 5,846 | 78,259 | 240,735 | 1956 | 5,367 | 61,455 | 201,138 | 1931 | 5,855 | 159,257 |
| 1980 | 5,953 | 78,906 | 241,873 | 1955 | 5,526 | 62,106 | 200,290 | 1930 | 6,317 | 136,077 |
| 1979 | 6,352 | 80,544 | 247,617 | 1954 | 5,010 | 57,201 | 176,070 | 1929 | 5,817 | 132,529 |
| 1978 | 6,831 | 82,518 | 260,446 | 1953 | 5,090 | 56,522 | 165,158 | 1928 | 5,353 | 129,199 |
| 1977 | 6,614 | 81,681 | 259,766 | 1952 | 4,706 | 50,351 | 152,955 | 1927 | 4,581 | 117,239 |
| 1976 | 6,570 | 79,531 | 253,572 | 1951 | 5,250 | 52,369 | 158,874 | 1926 | 4,236 | 108,846 |
| 1975 | 6,366 | 77,122 | 241,462 | 1950 | 5,012 | 48,652 | 147,661 | 1925 | 3,535 | 102,704 |
| 1974 | 6,876 | 82,030 | 235,696 | 1949 | 4,773 | 43,410 | 128,596 | 1924 | 3,269 | 87,867 |
| 1973 | 7,406 | 89,478 | 256,896 | 1948 | 4,513 | 33,067 | 115,817 | 1923 | 2,694 | 74,290 |
| 1972 | 7,763 | 91,338 | 260,626 | 1947 | 4,881 | 35,697 | 125,651 | 1922 | 2,441 | 62,504 |
| 1971 | 7,699 | 90,868 | 253,460 | 1946 | 5,062 | 36,588 | 120,896 | 1921 | 2,328 | 55,153 |
| 1970 | 7,499 | 93,499 | 262,370 | 1945 | 5,256 | 32,537 | 100,505 | 1920 | 2,386 | 49,317 |
| 1969 | 7,365 | 90,719 | 254,810 | 1944 | 6,416 | 33,493 | 90,965 | 1919 | 2,239 | 43,305 |
| 1968 | 6,810 | 88,563 | 253,835 | 1943 | 5,796 | 30,603 | 86,137 | 1918 | 1,852 | 31,604 |
| 1967 | 7,319 | 93,757 | 268,902 | 1942 | 6,926 | | | 1917 | 2,047 | 38,326 |
| 1966 | 7,985 | 99,838 | 284,634 | 1941 | 9,169 | | | 1916 | 2,393 | 46,090 |
| 1965 | 7,952 | 97,865 | 292,120 | 1940 | 8,609 | | | 1915 | 2,564 | 54,222 |
| 1964 | 7,820 | 95,460 | 282,219 | 1939 | 8,272 | | | 1914 | 1,991 | 53,481 |
| 1963 | 6,922 | 87,776 | 261,481 | 1938 | 6,648 | 50,782 | 175,929 | 1913 | 1,743 | 38,050 |
| 1962 | 6,709 | 83,915 | 251,072 | 1937 | 6,633 | 52,224 | 174,158 | 1912 | 1,485 | 32,701 |
| 1961 | 6,908 | 84,936 | 257,923 | 1936 | 6,561 | 227,813 | | 1911 | 1,286 | 29,871 |
| 1960 | 6,970 | 84,443 | 256,138 | 1935 | 6,502 | 221,726 | | 1910 | 1,082 | 26,361 |
| 1959 | 6,520 | 80,672 | 246,261 | 1934 | | | | | | |

[a] Before 1934 the categories are fatal and non-fatal accidents.
*Sources*: Central Statistical Office, Annual Abstract of Statistics (table: road accidents); Board of Trade, Statistical Abstract for the United Kingdom (table: road accidents, England and Wales)

**Table 5.7** Gross advances on building society mortgages, Great Britain, 1910–83

| Year | Amount (£ million) | Year | Amount (£ million) | Year | Amount (£ million) |
|---|---|---|---|---|---|
| 1983 | 18,903.7 | 1958 | 374.8 | 1933 | 103.2 |
| 1982 | 15,036.4 | 1957 | 374.1 | 1932 | 82.1 |
| 1981 | 12,005.3 | 1956 | 334.9 | 1931 | 90.3 |
| 1980 | 9,503.4 | 1955 | 394.4 | 1930 | 88.8 |
| 1979 | 9,002.3 | 1954 | 373.2 | 1929 | 74.7 |
| 1978 | 8,807.8 | 1953 | 299.5 | 1928 | 58.7 |
| 1977 | 6,745.1 | 1952 | 267.6 | 1927 | 55.9 |
| 1976 | 6,183.3 | 1951 | 267.6 | 1926 | 52.2 |
| 1975 | 4,908.0 | 1950 | 269.7 | 1925 | 49.8 |
| 1974 | 2,945.1 | 1949 | 276.0 | 1924 | 40.6 |
| 1973 | 3,512.7 | 1948 | 264.0 | 1923 | 32.0 |
| 1972 | 3,630.4 | 1947 | 242.5 | 1922 | 22.7 |
| 1971 | 2,705.3 | 1946 | 188.2 | 1921 | 19.7 |
| 1970 | 1,953.7 | 1945 | 97.6 | 1920 | 25.1 |
| 1969 | 1,558.7 | 1944 | 52.9 | 1919 | 15.8 |
| 1968 | 1,589.9 | 1943 | 28.1 | 1918 | 7.0 |
| 1967 | 1,462.7 | 1942 | 16.3 | 1917 | 4.5 |
| 1966 | 1,244.7 | 1941 | 10.0 | 1916 | 4.9 |
| 1965 | 955.4 | 1940 | 21.2 | 1915 | 6.5 |
| 1964 | 1,042.5 | 1939 | 94.3 | 1914 | 8.8 |
| 1963 | 849.4 | 1938 | 137.0 | 1913 | 9.1 |
| 1962 | 613.0 | 1937 | 136.9 | 1912 | 8.3 |
| 1961 | 545.8 | 1936 | 140.3 | 1911 | 8.9 |
| 1960 | 559.8 | 1935 | 130.9 | 1910 | 9.3 |
| 1959 | 517.3 | 1934 | 124.6 | | |

*Sources*: Central Statistical Office, Annual Abstract of Statistics (table: building societies, Great Britain, number and balance sheets, current transactions); Board of Trade, Statistical Abstract for the United Kingdom (table: advances on mortgages during year)

**Table 5.8** Number and value of conveyances, 1973–81

| Month | Year | Number of transactions | Value (£ million) |
|---|---|---|---|
| Nov. | 1981 | 132,988 | 2791 |
| | 1980 | 104,213 | 2118 |
| | 1979 | 121,688 | 2393 |
| | 1978 | 127,829 | 1872 |
| | 1977 | 125,471 | 1582 |
| | 1976 | 113,052 | 1214 |
| | 1975 | 102,988 | 1035 |
| Oct. | 1974 | 96,501 | 967 |
| | 1973 | 108,946 | 1125 |

*Source*: Inland Revenue Statistics

**Table 5.9** Gross and net advances on all mortgages, 1969–84

| Year | Gross advances (£ million) | Net advances (£ million) |
|---|---|---|
| 1984 | 21,378[a] | 12,371[a] |
| 1983 | 24,948 | 14,434 |
| 1982 | 16,768 | 14,151 |
| 1981 | 13,109 | 9,276 |
| 1980 | 11,021 | 7,102 |
| 1979 | 10,366 | 6,388 |
| 1978 | 9,607 | 5,343 |
| 1977 | 7,572 | 4,275 |
| 1976 | 6,757 | 3,871 |
| 1975 | 6,057 | 3,650 |
| 1974 | 3,898 | 2,372 |
| 1973 | 4,318 | 2,831 |
| 1972 | 4,135 | 2,783 |
| 1971 | 3,129 | 1,823 |
| 1970 | 2,354 | 1,245 |
| 1969 | 1,087 | 858 |

[a] First three quarters.
*Source*: Department of Environment, Housing and Construction Statistics (table: mortgages: main institutional sources UK)

**Table 5.10** Legal aid: number of cases and budget, 1951–83

| | Civil | | | Criminal | |
|---|---|---|---|---|---|
| Year[a] | Certificates issued | Advice rendered | Bills paid (£000) | Magistrates' courts | Bills paid (£000) |
| 1951 | 37,772 | | | | |
| 1952 | 32,305 | | | | |
| 1953 | 27,636 | | | | |
| 1954 | 25,042 | | | | |
| 1955 | 23,218 | | | | |
| 1956 | 23,159 | | | | |
| 1957 | 20,663 | | | | |
| 1958 | 20,631 | | | | |
| 1959 | 23,910 | *c.*13,000 | | | |
| 1960 | 39,824 | *c.*26,000 | | | |
| 1961 | 77,530 | 46,284 | | | |
| 1962 | 92,800 | 57,731 | | | |
| 1963 | 98,407 | 61,354 | | | |
| 1964 | 100,591 | 57,941 | | | |
| 1965 | 107,641 | 58,588 | | | |
| 1966 | 113,299 | 63,196 | 10,448 | 26,192 | 549 |
| 1967 | 129,442 | 72,619 | 10,108 | 35,317 | 791 |
| 1968 | 137,098 | 76,090 | 11,795 | 51,574 | 1,205 |
| 1969 | 148,882 | 82,936 | 13,010 | 68,699 | 1,867 |
| 1970 | 159,664 | *c.*86,000 | 14,424 | 88,320 | 2,749 |
| 1971 | 202,220 | *c.*112,000 | 17,888 | 101,967 | 3,379 |
| 1972 | 187,441 | *c.*110,000 | 21,141 | 117,430 | 4,364 |
| 1973 | 179,789 | 100,298 | 23,124 | 139,272 | 6,209 |
| 1974 | 196,580 | 180,695 | 29,388 | 171,567 | 9,445 |
| 1975 | 203,908 | 254,558 | 35,654 | 213,894 | 14,371 |
| 1976 | 207,106 | 291,961 | 26,147 | 222,726 | 16,300 |
| 1977 | 179,024 | 304,343 | 30,498 | 240,323 | 20,206 |
| 1978 | 190,528 | 365,772 | 33,460 | 242,059 | 24,306 |
| 1979 | 226,695 | 438,519 | 51,071 | 243,703 | 30,307 |
| 1980 | 234,404[b] | 531,512 | 69,247 | 275,276 | 42,279 |
| 1981 | 270,451[b] | 649,496 | 93,310 | 296,134 | 48,205 |
| 1982 | | 733,410 | 119,897 | 322,813 | 56,189 |
| 1983 | | 831,561 | 144,929 | 332,352 | 62,318 |

[a] 1 April of this year to 31 March of next.
[b] Includes assistance by way of representation.
*Sources*: Lord Chancellor's Department, Legal Aid Annual Reports; Abel, 1985: 628

# References

The first section of the references applies exclusively to part I of the text; the second, third and fourth sections almost exclusively to parts II, III and IV.

## Theories of the professions

Abbott, Andrew 1981: Status and status strain in the professions, 86 *American Journal of Sociology* 819–35

—— 1983: Professional ethics, 88 *American Journal of Sociology* 855–85.

—— 1986: Jurisdictional conflicts: a new approach to the development of the legal profession, *American Bar Foundation Research Journal* 187–225.

Abercrombie, Nicholas and John Urry 1983: *Capital, Labour and the Middle Classes*. London: George Allen & Unwin.

Akerlof, G. A. 1970: The market for 'lemons': quality uncertainty and the market mechanism, 84 *Quarterly Journal of Economics* 488–500.

Arnould, R. J. 1972: Pricing professional services: a case study of the legal service industry, 38 *Southern Economic Journal* 495–507.

Arrow, Kenneth 1963: Uncertainty and the welfare economics of medical care, 53 *American Economic Review* 941–73.

Bankowski, Zenon and Geoff Mungham 1978: A political economy of legal education, 32 *New Universities Quarterly* 448–63.

Barbalet, J. M. 1982: Social closure in class analysis: a critique of Parkin, 16 *Sociology* 484–97.

Barber, Bernard 1963: Some problems in the sociology of the professions, 92 *Daedalus* 669–88.

Becker, Gary 1964: *Human Capital: a theoretical and empirical analysis*. New York: National Bureau of Economic Research.

Becker, Howard S., Blanche Geer, Everett C. Hughes and Anselm Strauss 1961:

*Boys in White: student culture in medical school*. Chicago: University of Chicago Press.

Begun, James W. 1981: *Professionalism and the Public Interest: price and quality in optometry*. Cambridge, MA: MIT Press.

—— 1986: Economic and sociological approaches to professionalism, 13 *Work and Occupations* 113–29.

Bell, Daniel 1974: *The Coming of Post-Industrial Society*. New York: Basic Books.

—— 1976: *The Cultural Contradictions of Capitalism*. New York: Basic Books.

Ben-David, J. 1958: The professional role of the physician in bureaucratised medicine: a study of role conflict, 11 *Human Relations* 255–74.

—— 1963: Professions in the class system of present-day societies, 12 *Current Sociology* 249–330.

Benham, Lee 1972: The effect of advertising on the price of eyeglasses, 15 *Journal of Law and Economics* 337–52.

Benham, Lee and Alexandra Benham 1975: Regulating through professions: a perspective on information control, 18 *Journal of Law and Economics* 421–47.

Benson, J. K. 1973: The analysis of bureaucratic/professional conflict: functionalist and dialectical approaches, 14 *Sociological Quarterly* 376.

Berg, Ivar 1970: *Education and Jobs: the great training robbery*. Harmondsworth: Penguin.

Berlant, Jeffrey L. 1975: *Profession and Monopoly: a study of medicine in the United States and Great Britain*. Berkeley: University of California Press.

Berle, Adolf A. and Gardiner C. Means 1933: *The Modern Corporation and Private Property*. New York: Macmillan.

Black, Donald 1976: *The Behavior of Law*. New York: Academic Press.

Blackburn, R. M. and M. Mann 1979: *The Working Class in the Labour Market*. London: Macmillan.

Blair, Roger D. and Stephen Rubin (eds) 1980: *Regulating the Professions: a public policy symposium*. Lexington, MA: Lexington Books.

Blau, Peter and Otis Dudley Duncan 1967: *The American Occupational Structure*. New York: John Wiley.

Blau, Peter and Richard A. Schoenherr 1971: *The Structure of Organizations*. New York: Basic Books.

Bledstein, Burton, J. 1976: *The Culture of Professionalism: the middle class and the development of higher education in America*. New York: Norton.

Bond, Ronald S., John E. Kwoka, Jr, John J. Phelan and Ira Taylor 1983: Self-regulation in optometry: the impact on price and quality, 7 *Law and Human Behavior* 219–34.

Boreham, Paul 1983: Indetermination: professional knowledge, organization and control, 31 *Sociological Review* 693–718.

Boreham, Paul, Alex Pemberton and Paul Wilson (eds) 1976: *The Professions in Australia: a critical appraisal*. St Lucia: University of Queensland Press.

Bourdieu, Pierre and Jean-Claude Passeron 1977: *Reproduction in Education, Society and Culture*. Beverly Hills, CA: Sage.

Bruce-Biggs, B. (ed.) 1979: *The New Class?* New Brunswick, NJ: Transition Books.

Bucher, Rue and Joan Stelling 1977: *Becoming Professional.* Beverly Hills, CA: Sage.

Bucher, Rue and Anselm Strauss 1961: Professions in process, 66 *American Journal of Sociology* 325–34.

Cady, J. F. 1975: *Drugs on the Market: the impact of public policy on the retail market for prescription drugs.* Lexington, MA: Lexington Books.

Cain, Maureen 1979: The general practice lawyer and the client: towards a radical conception, 7 *International Journal of the Sociology of Law* 331–54.

Campbell, Colin M. 1976: Lawyers and their public, *Juridical Review* 20–39.

Carchedi, G. 1975: On the economic identification of the new middle class, 4 *Economy and Society* 1–86.

Carlin, Jerome 1962: *Lawyers on their Own: a study of individual practitioners in Chicago.* New Brunswick, NJ: Rutgers University Press.

Carroll, Sidney L. and Robert J. Gaston 1979a: New approaches and empirical evidence on occupational licensing and the quality of service rendered, 7 *Industrial Organization Review* 1–33.

—— 1979b: State occupational licensing provisions and quality of service: the real estate business, 1 *Research in Law and Economics* 1–13.

—— 1983: Occupational licensing and the quality of service: an overview, 7 *Law and Human Behavior* 139–56.

Carr-Saunders, A. M. and P. A. Wilson 1933: *The Professions.* Oxford: Clarendon Press.

Child, John and Janet Faulk 1982: Maintenance of occupational control: the case of professions, 9 *Work and Occupations* 155–92.

Cogan, M. L. 1953: Toward a definition of profession, 23 *Harvard Education Review* 33–50.

Collins, Randall 1977: Functional and conflict theories of educational stratification. In Jerome Karabel and A. H. Halsey (eds), *Power and Ideology in Education*, New York: Oxford University Press.

—— 1979: *The Credential Society: an historical sociology of education and stratification.* New York: Academic Press.

Conrad, D. A. and G. G. Sheldon 1982: The effects of legal constraints on dental care prices, 19 *Economic Inquiry* 51–67.

Coxon, A. P. M. and C. L. Jones 1978: *The Images of Occupational Prestige.* New York: St Martin's Press.

Creedy, John 1982: Professional labour markets. In John Creedy and Barry Thomas (eds), *The Economics of Labour*, ch. 7. London: Butterworth Scientific.

Crozier, Michel 1982: *Strategies for Change: the future of French society.* Cambridge, MA: MIT Press.

Cullen, John B. 1978: *The Structure of Professionalism: a quantitative examination.* New York: Petrocelli Books.

—— 1985: Professional differentiation and occupational earnings, 12 *Work and Occupations* 351–72.

Daniels, Arlene Kaplan 1969: The captive professional: bureaucratic limitations in the practice of military psychiatry, 10 *Journal of Health and Social Behavior* 255.

Derber, Charles 1982a: Professionals as new workers. In *Professionals as Workers: mental labor in advanced capitalism*, pp. 3–10. Boston: G. K. Hall.

—— 1982b: The proletarianization of the professional: a review essay. In *Professionals as Workers*, pp. 13–34. Boston: G. K. Hall.

—— 1982c: Managing Professionals: ideological proletarianization and mental labor. In *Professionals as Workers*, pp. 167–90. Boston: G. K. Hall.

—— 1982d: Toward a new theory of professionals as workers: advanced capitalism and postindustrial labor. In *Professionals as Workers*, pp. 193–208. Boston: G. K. Hall.

Derbyshire, Robert C. 1983: How effective is medical self-regulation? 7 *Law and Human Behavior* 193–202.

DeVany, Arthur S., Wendy L. Gramm, Thomas R. Saving and Charles W. Smithson 1982: The impact of input regulation: the case of the U.S. dental industry, 25 *Journal of Law and Economics* 367.

Dingwall, Robert 1976: Accomplishing profession, 24 *Sociological Review* 331–49.

—— 1983: Introduction. In Robert Dingwall and Philip Lewis (eds), *The Sociology of the Professions: lawyers, doctors and others*, pp. 1–13. London: Macmillan.

Dingwall, Robert and Paul Fenn 1987: 'A respectable profession'? Sociological and economic perspectives on the regulation of professional services, 7 *International Review of Law and Economics* 51.

Dodge, David A. 1972: Occupational wage differentials, occupational licensing and returns to investment in education: an exploratory analysis. In Sylvia Ostry (ed.), *Canadian Higher Education in the Seventies*, pp. 135–66. Ottawa: Information Canada.

Doeringer, Peter B. and Michael J. Piore 1971: *Internal Labor Markets and Manpower Analysis*. Lexington, MA: Lexington Books.

Dolan, Andrew and Nicole D. Urban 1983: The determinants of the effectiveness of medical disciplinary boards: 1960–77, 7 *Law and Human Behavior* 203–17.

Dore, Ronald 1976: *The Diploma Disease*. London: Allen & Unwin.

Dorsey, Stuart 1980: The occupational licensing queue, 15 *Journal of Human Resources* 424.

Duman, Daniel 1979: The creation and diffusion of a professional ideology in nineteenth century England, 27 *Journal of Social History* 113–38.

Durkheim, Emile 1933: *The Division of Labor in Society*. New York: Free Press.

—— 1957: *Professional Ethics and Civic Responsibility*. London: Routledge & Kegan Paul.

Edelman, Murray 1964: *Symbolic Uses of Politics*. Urbana: University of Illinois Press.

Egelston, E. M. 1972: Licensing – effects on career mobility, 62 *American Journal of Public Health* 50–3.

Ehrenreich, Barbara and John Ehrenreich 1979: The professional-managerial class. In Pat Walker (ed.), *Between Labor and Capital*, pp. 5–45. Boston: South End Press.

Elliott, Philip 1972: *The Sociology of Professions*. New York: Herder and Herder.

Esland, G. 1980: Professions and professionalism. In G. Esland and G. Salaman (eds), *The Politics of Work and Occupations*, p. 229. Milton Keynes: Open University Press.

Etzioni, Amitai (ed.) 1969: *The Semi-Professions*. New York: Free Press.

Evans, Robert G. 1974: Supplier-induced demand: some empirical evidence and implications. In Mark Perlman (ed.), *The Economics of Health and Medical Care*. London: Macmillan.

Evans, Robert G., E. M. A. Parish and F. Sully 1973: Medical productivity and demand generation, 6 *Canadian Journal of Economics* 376–93.

Evans, Robert G. and Michael J. Trebilcock (eds) 1982: *Lawyers and the Consumer Interest: regulating the market for legal services*. Toronto: Butterworths.

Feldman, Penny H. 1980: The impact of third-party payment on professional practice: lessons from the medical profession. In Roger D. Blair and Stephen Rubin (eds), *Regulating the Professions*, pp. 245–64. Lexington, MA: Lexington Books.

Feldman, R. and James W. Begun 1978: The effects of advertising: lessons from optometry, 13 *Journal of Human Resources* (supplement) 247–62.

—— 1980: Does advertising of prices reduce the mean and variance of prices?, 18 *Economic Inquiry* 487–92.

Feldstein, M. W. 1970: The rising price of physicians' services, 52 *Review of Economics and Statistics* 121–33.

Fielding, A. G. and D. Portwood 1980: Professions and the state: towards a typology of bureaucratic professions, 28 *Sociological Review* 25–53.

Foley, Patrick, Avner Shaked and John Sutton 1982: *The Economics of the Professions: an introductory guide to the literature*. London: International Centre for Economics and Related Disciplines, London School of Economics and Political Science.

Fox, Mary Frank and Sharlene Hess-Biber 1984: *Women at Work*. Palo Alto, CA: Mayfield.

Fox, Renee C. 1957: Training for uncertainty. In Robert K. Merton, George C. Reader and Patricia Kendell (eds), *The Student Physician*. Cambridge, MA: Harvard University Press.

Frech, H. E. 1974: Occupational licensure and health care productivity: the issues and the literature. In J. Rafferty (ed.), *Health Manpower and Productivity*, ch. 6. Lexington, MA: Lexington Books.

Frech, H. E. and Paul B. Ginsberg 1972: Physician pricing: monopolistic or competitive: comment, 38 *Southern Economic Review* 573–7.

Freeman, Richard 1975: Legal cobwebs: a recursive model of the market for new lawyers, 57 *Review of Economics and Statistics* 171–9.

—— 1976: *The Overeducated American*. New York: Academic Press.

—— 1980: The effect of occupational licensure on black occupational attainment. In Simon Rottenberg (ed.), *Occupational Licensure and Regulation*, pp. 165–79.

Washington, DC: American Enterprise Institute for Public Policy Research.

Freidson, Eliot 1970: *Profession of Medicine*. New York: Dodd Mead.

—— 1983: The reorganization of the professions by regulation, 7 *Law and Human Behavior* 279–90.

—— 1984: Are professions necessary? In Thomas L. Haskell (ed.), *The Authority of Experts*, pp. 3–27. Bloomington, IN: Indiana University Press.

—— 1984: The changing nature of professional control, 10 *Annual Review of Sociology* 1–20.

—— 1985: The reorganization of the medical profession, 42 *Medical Care Review* 11–35.

—— 1986: *Professional Powers: a study of the institutionalization of formal knowledge*. Chicago: University of Chicago Press.

Friedman, Milton 1962: *Capitalism and Freedom*. Chicago: University of Chicago Press.

Friedman, Milton and Simon Kuznets 1945: *Income from Independent Professional Practice*. New York: National Bureau of Economic Research.

Fromm, Erich 1941: *Escape from Freedom*. New York: Farrar and Rinehart.

Fuchs, Victor P. 1968: *The Service Economy*. New York: National Bureau for Economic Research.

Galanter, Marc 1983: Reading the landscape of disputes: what we know and don't know (and think we know) about our allegedly contentious and litigious society, 31 *UCLA Law Review* 4–71.

Galbraith, John Kenneth 1967: *The New Industrial State*. Boston: Houghton Mifflin.

Gellhorn, Walter 1956: *Individual Freedom and Governmental Restraints*. Baton Rouge, LA: Louisiana State University Press.

—— 1976: The abuse of occupational licensing, 44 *University of Chicago Law Review* 6–27.

Glaser, Barney G. 1964: *Organizational Scientists: their professional careers*. Indianapolis, IN: Bobbs-Merrill.

Goode, William J. 1957: Community within a community: the professions, 22 *American Sociological Review* 200.

—— 1960: Encroachment, charlatanism, and the emerging professions: psychology, sociology and medicine, 25 *American Sociological Review* 902–14.

—— 1967: The protection of the inept, 32 *American Sociological Review* 5–19.

Gordon, David M. 1972: *Theories of Poverty and Unemployment: orthodox, radical and dual labor market perspectives*. Lexington, MA: D. C. Heath.

Gorz, Andre 1964: *Strategy for Labor*. Boston: Beacon Press.

—— 1976: Technology, technicians and class struggle. In *The Division of Labour: the labour process and class struggle in modern capitalism*, pp. 159–89. London: Harvester Press.

Gouldner, Alvin W. 1979: *The Future of Intellectuals and the Rise of the New Class*. New York: Seabury Press.

Greenwood, Ernest 1957: Attributes of a profession, 2(3) *Social Work* 44–55.

Griffiths, John 1986: What do Dutch lawyers actually do in divorce cases?, 20 *Law & Society Review* 135–75.

Grimm, James W. and Carol L. Kronus 1973: Occupations and publics: a framework for analysis, 14 *Sociological Quarterly* 68–87.

Hall, Oswald 1948: The stages of a medical career, 53 *American Journal of Sociology* 327–36.

Hall, Richard H. 1968: Professionalization and bureaucratization, 33 *American Sociological Review* 92–105.

—— 1983: Theoretical trends in the sociology of occupations, 24 *Sociological Quarterly* 5–24.

Halmos, Paul 1973a: Introduction. In *Professionalisation and Social Change*. Keele: University of Keele (Sociological Review Monographs no. 2).

—— (ed.) 1973b: *Professionalisation and Social Change*. Keele: University of Keele.

Harries-Jenkins, G. 1970: Professionals in organisations, in J. A. Jackson (ed.), *Professions and Professionalisation*, pp. 51–108. Cambridge: Cambridge University Press.

Haskell, Thomas L. 1984: Professionalism versus capitalism: R. H. Tawney, Emile Durkheim, and C. S. Peirce on the disinterestedness of professional communities. In Thomas L. Haskell (ed.), *The Authority of Experts*, pp. 180–225. Bloomington, IN: Indiana University Press.

Haug, Marie R. 1973: Deprofessionalization: an alternative hypothesis for the future. In Paul Halmos (ed.), *Professionalisation and Social Change*, pp. 195–211. Keele: University of Keele.

—— 1980: The sociological approach to self-regulation. In Roger D. Blair and Stephen Rubin (eds), *Regulating the Professions*, pp. 61–80. Lexington, MA: Lexington Books.

Haug, Marie and Marvin Sussman 1969: Professional autonomy and the revolt of the client, 17 *Social Problems* 53–61.

—— 1973: Professionalization and unionization: a jurisdictional dispute? In Eliot Freidson (ed.), *The Professions and their Prospects*, pp. 89–104. Beverly Hills, CA: Sage.

Heinz, John P. and Edward O. Laumann 1982: *Chicago Lawyers: the social structure of the Bar*. New York: Russell Sage; and Chicago: American Bar Foundation.

Hickson, D. and M. Thomas 1969: Professionalism in Britain: preliminary measurement, 3 *Sociology* 37–53.

Hodge, R. W., P. M. Siegel and H. Rossi 1964: Occupational prestige in the United States, 1925–1963. In Reinhard Bendix and Seymour Martin Lipset (eds), *Class, Status, and Power*, pp. 322–44. New York: Free Press.

Hogan, Daniel P. (ed.) 1983: Professional regulation, 7(2/3) *Law and Human Behavior* (Special issue).

Holen, Arlene S. 1965: Effects of professional licensing arrangements on interstate labor mobility and resource allocation, 73 *Journal of Political Economy* 492–8.

Jamous, H. and B. Peloille 1970: Professions or self-perpetuating systems? Changes in the French university-hospital system. In J. A. Jackson (ed.),

*Professions and Professionalisation*, pp. 111–52. Cambridge: Cambridge University Press.

Johnson, Terence J. 1972: *Professions and Power*. London: Macmillan.

—— 1973: Imperialism and the professions: notes on the development of professional occupations in Britain's colonies and the new states. In Paul Halmos (ed.), *Professionalisation and Social Change*, pp. 281–309. Keele: University of Keele.

—— 1977a: The professions in the class structure. In Richard Scase (ed.), *Industrial Society: class, cleavage and control*. London: George Allen & Unwin.

—— 1977b: What is to be known? The structural determination of social class, 6 *Economy and Society* 194–233.

—— 1982: The state and the professions: peculiarities of the British. In Anthony Giddens and Gavin Mackenzie (eds), *Social Class and the Division of Labour: Essays in honour of Ilya Neustadt*, pp. 186–208. Cambridge: Cambridge University Press.

Kerr, Clark 1954: The Balkanization of labor markets. In E. W. Bakke (ed.), *Labor Mobility and Economic Opportunity*, pp. 92–110. New York: John Wiley.

Kessel, R. A. 1958: Price discrimination in medicine, 1 *Journal of Law and Economics* 20–53.

—— 1970: The A.M.A. and the supply of physicians, 35 *Law and Contemporary Problems* 267–83.

Kiker, B. F. 1966: *The Concept of Human Capital*. Columbia, SC: University of South Carolina, Bureau of Business and Economic Research.

Klegon, Douglas 1978: The sociology of professions: an emerging perspective, 5 *Sociology of Work and Occupations* 259–83.

Kleingartner, Archie 1967: *Professionalism and Salaried Worker Organization*. Madison: University of Wisconsin, Industrial Relations Research Institute.

Konrád, George and Ivan Szelényi 1979: *The Intellectuals on the Road to Class Power*. New York: Harcourt Brace Jovanovich.

Kornhauser, William 1965: *Scientists in Industry*. Berkeley: University of California Press.

Krause, Elliott 1977: *Power and Illness: the political sociology of health and medical care*. New York: Elsevier.

Kreckel, Reinhard 1980: Unequal opportunity structure and labour market segmentation, 14 *Sociology* 525–50.

Kronus, Carol 1976: The evolution of occupational power: an historical study of task boundaries between physicians and pharmacists, 3 *Sociology of Work and Occupations* 3–37.

Kumar, K. 1977: Continuities and discontinuities in the development of industrial societies. In Richard Scase (ed.), *Industrial Society: class, cleavage and control*, pp. 29–42. London: George Allen & Unwin.

Larkin, Gerald 1983: *Occupational Monopoly and Modern Medicine*. London: Tavistock.

Larson, Magali Sarfatti 1977: *The Rise of Professionalism: a sociological analysis*. Berkeley: University of California Press.

—— 1980: Proletarianization and educated labor, 9 *Theory and Society* 131–77.

—— 1984: The production of expertise and the constitution of expert power. In Thomas L. Haskell (ed.), *The Authority of Experts*, pp. 28–83. Bloomington, IN: Indiana University Press.

Lazarus, W. et al. 1981: *Competition Among Health Practitioners: the impact of the medical profession on the health manpower market*. Washington, DC: Federal Trade Commission.

Lees, D. S. 1966: *The Economic Consequences of the Professions*. London: Institute of Economic Affairs.

Leffler, Keith B. 1978: Physician licensure: competition and monopoly in American medicine, 21 *Journal of Law and Economics* 165–86.

—— 1983: Economic and legal analysis of medical ethics: the case of restrictions on interprofessional association, 7 *Law and Human Behavior* 183–92.

Leland, H. E. 1979: Quacks, lemons, and licensing: a theory of minimum quality standards, 87 *Journal of Political Economy* 1328–46.

Lewis, Roy and Angus Maude 1952: *Professional People*. London: Phoenix House.

Lindsay, C. M. 1973: Real returns to medical education, 8 *Journal of Human Resources* 331–48.

Lipscomb, J. 1978: *Impact of Legal Restrictions on the Future Role of Dental Auxiliaries*. Springfield, VA: National Technical Information Service.

Luckham, Robin 1981: The political economy of legal professions: towards a framework for comparison. In C. J. Dias, R. Luckham, D. O. Lynch and J. C. N. Paul (eds), *Lawyers in the Third World: comparative and developmental perspectives*, pp. 287–336. Uppsala: Scandinavian Institute of African Studies; and New York: International Center for Law in Development.

Macdonald, Keith M. 1984: Professional formation: the case of Scottish accountants, 35 *British Journal of Sociology* 174–89.

—— 1985: Social closure and occupational registration, 19 *Sociology* 541–56.

Mallet, Serge 1975: *Essays on the New Working Class*. St Louis, MO: Telos Press.

Marcson, Simon 1966: *Scientists in Government*. New Brunswick, NJ: Rutgers University Press.

Markowitz, Gerald E. and David Karl Rosner 1973: Doctors in crisis: a study of the use of medical education reform to establish modern professional elitism in medicine, 25 *American Quarterly* 83–107.

Marshall, T. H. 1963: The recent history of professionalism in relation to social structure and social policy. In *Sociology at the Cross-Roads and other Essays*, pp. 150–70. London: Heinemann.

Masson, R. T. and S. Wu 1974: Price discrimination for physicians' services, 9 *Journal of Human Resources* 63–79.

Maurizi, Alex 1974: Occupational licensing and the public interest, 83 *Journal of Political Economy* 399–413.

Maurizi, Alex, R., Ruth L. Moore and Lawrence Shepard 1981: Competing for professional control: professional mix in the eyeglasses industry, 24 *Journal of Law and Economics* 351–64.

Mennemeyer, S. T. 1978: Really great returns to medical education, 13 *Journal of Human Resources* 75–90.

Merton, Robert K., George C. Reader and Patricia Kendell (eds) 1957: *The Student Physician: introductory studies in the sociology of medical education*. Cambridge, MA: Harvard University Press.

Millerson, G. 1964: *The Qualifying Associations*. London: Routledge and Kegan Paul.

Monheit, A. 1982: Occupational licensure and the utilization of nursing labor: an economic analysis. In R. Schoffler and L. Rossiter (eds), 3 *Advances in Health Economics and Health Services Research* 117–42. Greenwich, CT: JAI Press.

Moore, Thomas G. 1961: The purpose of licensing, 4 *Journal of Law and Economics* 93–117.

Moore, Wilbert E. 1970: *The Professions: roles and rules*. New York: Russell Sage Foundation.

Murphy, Raymond 1984: The structure of closure: a critique and development of the theories of Weber, Collins, and Parkin, 35 *British Journal of Sociology* 547–67.

Muzondo, T. R. and B. Pazerka 1979: *Professional Licensing and Competition Policy: effects of licensing on rates-of-return differentials*. Ottawa: Consumer and Corporate Affairs Canada.

—— 1980: Occupational licensing and professional incomes in Canada, 13 *Canadian Journal of Economics* 659–67.

Navarro, Victor 1976: *Medicine under Capitalism*. London: Croom Helm.

—— 1978: *Class Struggle, the State and Medicine*. London: Martin Robertson.

Nelson, Robert L. 1985: Ideology, practice, and professional autonomy: social values and client relationships in the large law firm, 37 *Stanford Law Review* 503–51.

Newhouse, Joseph P. 1970: A model of physician pricing, 37 *Southern Economic Journal* 174–83.

Newhouse, Joseph P. and F. A. Sloan 1972: Physician pricing: monopolistic or competitive: reply, 38 *Southern Economic Journal* 577–80.

Nieuwenhuysen, John and Marina Williams-Wynn 1982: *Professions in the Marketplace: an Australian study of lawyers, doctors, accountants and dentists*. Melbourne: Melbourne University Press.

Noble, David 1979: The PMC: a critique. In Pat Walker (ed.), *Between Labor and Capital*, pp. 121–42. Boston: South End Press.

Noble, Trevor and Bridget Pym 1970: Collegial authority and the receding locus of power, 21 *British Journal of Sociology* 431–45.

O'Connor, James 1973: *The Fiscal Crisis of the State*. New York: St Martin's Press.

Oppenheimer, Martin 1973: The proletarianization of the professional. In Paul

Halmos (ed.), *Professionalisation and Social Change*, pp. 213–27. Keele: University of Keele.

Parkin, Frank 1979: *Marxism and Class Theory: a bourgeois critique*. London: Tavistock.

Parry, Noel and Jose Parry 1976: *The Rise of the Medical Profession*. London: Croom Helm.

—— 1977: Social closure and collective mobility. In Richard Scase (ed.), *Industrial Society: Class, cleavage and control*, pp. 93–110. London: George Allen & Unwin.

Parsons, Talcott 1951: Social structure and dynamic process: the case of modern medical practice. In *The Social System*, pp. 428–79. Glencoe, IL: Free Press.

—— 1964a: A sociologist looks at the legal profession. In *Essays in Sociological Theory*, pp. 370–85. New York: Free Press.

—— 1964b: The professions and social structure. In *Essays in Sociological Theory*, pp. 34–39. New York: Free Press.

—— 1968: Professions, 12 *International Encyclopedia of the Social Sciences* 536–47. New York: Macmillan.

Pashigian, B. Peter 1979: Occupational licensing and the interstate mobility of professionals, 22 *Journal of Law and Economics* 1–26.

Peltzman, Sam 1976: Toward a more general theory of regulation, 19 *Journal of Law and Economics* 211–40.

Pemberton, Alex and Paul Boreham 1976: Towards a reorientation of sociological studies of the professions. In Paul Boreham, Alex Pemberton and P. Wilson (eds), *The Professions in Australia: a critical approach*, pp. 15–41. St Lucia: University of Queensland Press.

Perucci, Robert and Joel Gerstl 1969: *Profession Without Community: engineers in American society*. New York: Random House.

Pfeffer, J. 1974: Some evidence on occupational licensing and occupational incomes, 53 *Social Forces* 102–11.

Polanyi, Karl 1957: *The Great Transformation*. Boston: Beacon Press.

Portwood, Derek and Alan Fielding 1981: Privilege and professions, 29 *Sociological Review* 749–73.

Posner, Richard A. 1974: Theories of economic regulation, 5 *Bell Journal of Economics and Management Science* 335–58.

—— 1975: The social costs of monopoly and regulation, 83 *Journal of Political Economy* 807.

Poulantzas, Nicholas 1975: *Classes in Contemporary Capitalism*. London: New Left Books.

Prest, Wilfrid R. 1984: Why the history of the professions is not written. In G. R. Rubin and David Sugarman (eds), *Law, Economy and Society, 1750–1914; Essays in the history of English law*, pp. 300–20. Abingdon: Professional Books.

Psacharapoulos, G. 1975: Monopoly elements in earnings from education. In *Earnings and Education in OECD Countries*, ch. 5. Paris: OECD.

Raelin, Joseph A. 1986: *The Clash of Cultures: managers and professionals*. Boston: Harvard Business School Press.

Rawlins, V. Lane and Lloyd Ulman 1974: The utilization of college-trained manpower in the US. In Margaret S. Gordon (ed.), *Higher Education and the Labor Market*, ch. 6. New York: McGraw-Hill and Carnegie Corp.

Riera, Brian, Murray Glow, Donald Siddall and William Klein 1977: Human capital analysis: its application in the study of the consumer interest in the professions. In *Four Aspects of Professionalism*, pp. 133–94. Ottawa: Consumer Research Council.

Ritzer, George 1975: Professionalization, bureaucratization and rationalization: the views of Max Weber, 53 *Social Forces* 627–34.

Roth, Julius 1974: Professionalism: the sociologist's decoy, 1 *Sociology of Work and Occupations* 6–23.

Roth, Julius, Sheryl Ruzek and Arlene K. Daniels 1973: Current state of the sociology of occupations, 14 *Sociological Quarterly* 309–33.

Rothman, Robert A. 1984: Deprofessionalization: the case of law in America, 11 *Work and Occupations* 183–206.

Rothstein, William G. 1973: Professionalization and employer demands: the cases of homeopathy and psychoanalysis in the United States. In Paul Halmos (ed.), *Professionalisation and Social Change*, pp. 159–78. Keele: University of Keele.

Rottenberg, Simon 1962: The economics of occupational licensing. In National Bureau of Economic Research, *Aspects of Labor Economics*. New York: National Bureau of Economic Research.

—— (ed.) 1980: *Occupational Licensure and Regulation*. Washington, DC: American Enterprise Institute for Public Policy Research.

Rueschemeyer, Dietrich 1964: Doctors and lawyers: a comment on the theory of the professions, 1 *Canadian Review of Sociology andAnthropology* 17–30.

—— 1973: *Lawyers and their Society: a comparative study of the legal profession in Germany and the United States*. Cambridge, MA: Harvard University Press.

—— 1983: Professional autonomy and the social control of expertise. In Robert Dingwall and Philip Lewis (eds), *The Sociology of the Professions: lawyers, doctors and others*, pp. 38–58. London: Macmillan.

Ruffin, R. J. and D. E. Leigh 1973: Charity, competition, and the pricing of doctors' services, 8 *Journal of Human Resources* 212–22.

Saks, Mike 1983: Removing the blinkers? A critique of recent contributions to the sociology of professions, 31 *Sociological Review* 1–21.

Salaman, G. 1979: *Work Organizations: resistance and control*: London: Longman.

Sarat, Austin and William L. F. Felstiner 1986: Law and strategy in the divorce lawyer's office, 20 *Law & Society Review* 93–134.

Schudson, Michael 1974: The Flexner Report and the Reed Report: notes on the history of professional education in the United States, 55 *Social Science Quarterly* 347–61.

Schultz, Theodore 1961: Investment in human capital, 51 *American Economic Review* 1–17.

Scitovsky, Tibor 1966: An international comparison of the trend of professional earnings, 56 *American Economic Review* 25–42.

Shepard, Lawrence 1978: Licensing restrictions and the cost of dental care, 21 *Journal of Law and Economics* 187–201.

Siebert, W. 1977: Occupational licensing: the Merrison Report on the Regulation of the Medical Profession, 15 *British Journal of Industrial Relations* 29–38.

Slayton, Philip and Michael J. Trebilcock (eds) 1978: *The Professions and Public Policy*. Toronto: University of Toronto Press.

Smigel, Erwin O. 1954: Trends in occupational sociology: a survey of postwar research, 19 *American Sociological Review* 398–404.

Smigel, Erwin O., Joseph Monane, Robert B. Wood and Barbara Randall Nye 1963: Occupational sociology: a reexamination, 47 *Sociology and Social Research* 472–7.

Smith, Adam 1937: *An Inquiry into the Nature and Causes of the Wealth of Nations*. New York: Random House.

Spangler, Eve and Peter M. Lehman 1982: Lawyering as work. In Charles Derber (ed.), *Professionals as Workers*, pp. 63–99. Boston: G. K. Hall.

Spence, M. 1973: Job market signalling, 87 *Quarterly Journal of Economics* 355–74.

Starr, Paul 1982: *The Social Transformation of American Medicine*. New York: Basic Books.

Steinfels, Peter 1979: *The Neo-Conservatives*. New York: Simon and Schuster.

Stevens, Rosemary 1971: *American Medicine and the Public Interest*. New Haven, CT: Yale University Press.

Stigler, George J. 1971: The theory of economic regulation, 2 *Bell Journal of Economics and Management Science* 3–21.

Stinchcombe, A. L. 1959: Bureaucratic and craft administration of production: a comparative survey, 4 *Administrative Science Quarterly* 168–87.

Sugarman, David and G. R. Rubin 1984: Introduction – towards a new history of law and material society in England, 1750–1914. In G. R. Rubin and David Sugarman (eds), *Law, Economy and Society, 1750–1914: essays in the history of English law*, pp. 1–123. Abingdon: Professional Books.

Szelényi, Ivan 1982: Gouldner's theory of the 'flawed universal class', 11 *Theory and Society* 779–99.

Szymanski, Al 1979: A critique and extension of the PMC. In Pat Walker (ed.), *Between Labor and Capital*, pp. 49–65. Boston: South End Press.

Toren, Nina 1975: Deprofessionalization and its sources, 2 *Sociology of Work and Occupations* 323.

Tourraine, Alain 1971: *The Post-Industrial Society*. New York: Random House.

Trebilcock, Michael J., Carolyn J. Tuohy and Allan D. Wolfson 1979: *Professional Regulation: a staff study of accountancy, architecture, engineering and law in Ontario*. Toronto: Province of Ontario, Professional Organizations Committee.

Treiman, David J. 1977: *Occupational Prestige in Comparative Perspective*. New York: Academic Press.

Tullock, Gordon 1975: The transitory gains gap, 6 *Bell Journal of Economics and Management Science* 671.

Tuohy, Carolyn and Alan D. Wolfson 1977: The political economy of professionalism: a perspective. In *Four Aspects of Professionalism*, pp. 47–86. Ottawa: Consumer Research Council.

Turner, Ralph 1960: Models of social ascent through education: sponsored and contest mobility, 25 *American Sociological Review* 855–67.

Veblen, Thorstein 1915: *The Theory of the Leisure Class*. New York: Macmillan.

Vollmer, Howard M. and Donald L. Mills (eds) 1966: *Professionalization*. Englewood Cliffs, NJ: Prentice Hall.

Weber, Max 1947: *The Theory of Social and Economic Organization* (trans A. M. Henderson and Talcott Parsons; ed. Talcott Parsons). New York: Free Press.

—— 1954: *Law in Economy and Society* (trans. Edward Shils and Max Rheinstein; ed. Max Rheinstein). Cambridge, MA: Harvard University Press.

—— 1964: *From Max Weber* (ed. H. H. Gerth and C. W. Mills). London: Routledge and Kegan Paul.

—— 1978: *Economy and Society* (2 vols; ed. Guenther Roth and Claus Wittich). Berkeley: University of California Press.

Westergaard, John and Henrietta Resler 1975: *Class in a Capitalist Society*. London: Heinemann.

White, William D. 1979a: Why is regulation introduced in the health sector? A look at occupational licensure, 4 *Journal of Health Politics, Policy, and Law* 536–52.

—— 1979b: *Public Health and Private Gain: the economics of licensing clinical laboratory personnel*. New York: Methuen.

—— 1979c: Dynamic elements of regulation: the case of occupational licensure, 1 *Research in Law and Economics* 15–33.

—— 1983: Labor market organization and professional regulation: a historical analysis of nursing licensure, 7 *Law and Human Behavior* 157–70.

Wilensky, Harold L. 1964: The professionalization of everyone? 70 *American Journal of Sociology* 137–58.

Wood, Stephen (ed.) 1982: *The Degradation of Work? Skill, deskilling and the labour process*. London: Hutchinson.

Wright, Erik Olin 1979: Intellectuals and the class structure of capitalist society. In Pat Walker (ed.), *Between Labor and Capital*, pp. 191–212. Boston: South End Press.

Wright, Erik Olin, Cynthia Costello, David Hachen and Joey Sprague 1982: The American class structure, 47 *American Sociological Review* 709–26.

Wuthnow, Robert and Welsey Shrum 1983: Knowledge workers as a 'new class': structural and ideological convergence among professional-technical workers and managers, 10 *Work and Occupations* 471–87.

Young, Michael 1958: *The Rise of the Meritocracy*. London: Thames and Hudson.

## The legal profession in England and Wales

### *Books and articles*

Abbott, Andrew 1986: Jurisdictional conflicts: a new approach to the development of the legal professions, *American Bar Foundation Research Journal* 187–224.

Abel, Richard L. 1982: The politics of the market for legal services. In Philip

A. Thomas (ed.), *Law in the Balance: legal services in the eighties*, pp. 6–59. Oxford: Martin Robertson.

—— 1985: Law without politics: legal aid under advanced capitalism, 32 *UCLA Law Review* 474–642.

Abel-Smith, Brian and Robert Stevens 1967: *Lawyers and the Courts: a sociological study of the English legal system 1750–1965*. London: Heinemann.

—— 1968: *In Search of Justice: society and the legal system*. London: Allen Lane.

Alexander, Robert 1986: How real is access to legal services? 83 *Law Society's Gazette* 2301–7.

American Bar Association Special Committee on Evaluation of Disciplinary Enforcement 1970: *Problems and Recommendations in Disciplinary Enforcement*. Chicago: American Bar Association.

Anderson, J. Stuart 1984: Land law texts and the explanation of 1925, 37 *Current Legal Problems* 63–83.

Arthurs, Harry W., Richard Weisman and Frederick H. Zemans 1988: Canadian lawyers: a peculiar professionalism. In Richard L. Abel and Philip S. C. Lewis (eds), *Lawyers in Society. Vol. 1: The Common Law World*. Berkeley and Los Angeles: University of California Press.

Bailey, J. B. and S. B. Marsh 1981: Law teaching at colleges of further education, 15 *Law Teacher* 83–95.

Baker, J. M. 1977: University college and legal education 1826–1976, 30 *Current Legal Problems* 1–13.

Bankowski, Z. and G. Mungham 1978: A political economy of legal education, 21 *New Universities Quarterly* 448–63.

Beale, Diana and Barbara Stow 1986: *CABx and Access to Legal Services in South Wales*. London: NACAB.

Bennett, Paul 1985: NASPyC: an update and personal view, 82 *Law Society's Gazette* 2723–6.

Berlins, Marcel and Clare Dyer 1982: *The Law Machine*. Harmondsworth: Penguin.

Berlins, Marcel and Robert Rice 1986: Howes Percival: in the business of law, 136 *New Law Journal* 709–14.

Birks, Michael 1960: *Gentlemen of the Law*. London: Stevens.

Blacksell, Mark, Kim Economides and Charles Watkins 1986: *Solicitors and Access to Legal Services in Rural Areas: Evidence from Devon and Cornwall*. Exeter: University of Exeter (Access to Justice in Rural Britain Project working paper 6).

Bowles, Roger 1981: Unemployment amongst solicitors, 131 *New Law Journal* 252–3.

Bowles, Roger and Jennifer Phillips 1977: Solicitors' remuneration: a critique of recent developments in conveyancing, 40 *Modern Law Review* 639–50.

Bowley, Arthur L. 1900: *Wages in the United Kingdom in the Nineteenth Century*. Cambridge: Cambridge University Press.

Bridges, Lee, Brenda Suffrin, Jim Whetton and Richard White 1975: *Legal*

*Services in Birmingham*. Birmingham: University of Birmingham, Institute of Judicial Administration.

Brougham, Isobel M. 1984: Bridging the gap, 81 *Law Society's Gazette* 2289–91.

Cain, Maureen 1976: Necessarily out of touch: thoughts of the social organisation of the Bar. In Pat Carlen (ed.), *The Sociology of Law*, pp. 226–50. Keele: Sociological Review Monographs (no. 23).

Campbell-Smith, Duncan 1985a: Facing up to the global challenge, *Financial Times* 9, (15 July).

—— 1985b: The rise and rise of a new breed of lawyer, *Financial Times* 24, (16 May).

Caplan, Jonathan 1978: The criminal Bar. In Robert Hazell (ed.), *The Bar on Trial*, pp. 130–47. London: Quartet Books.

Carlin, Jerome E. 1962: *Lawyers on their Own: a study of individual practitioners in Chicago*. New Brunswick, NJ: Rutgers University Press.

Carr-Saunders, A. M. and P. A. Wilson 1933: *The Professions*. Oxford: Clarendon Press.

Chambers & Partners 1985: *Salary Survey of Lawyers in Industry, July 1985*. London: Chambers & Partners.

Christian, Edmund B. V. 1896: *A Short History of Solicitors*. London: Reeves and Turner (reprinted – Littleton, CO: Fred B. Rothman & Co., 1983).

Cocks, Raymond 1976a: The Bar at assizes: barristers on three nineteenth century circuits, 6 *Kingston Law Review* 36–52.

—— 1976b: The two counsel rule and the history of the Bar's regulation, 92 *Law Quarterly Review* 512–15.

—— 1978a: Dignity and emoluments: Thomas Blofeld's life as a Victorian barrister, 8 *Kingston Law Review* 37–48.

—— 1978b: The old two counsel rule, 94 *Law Quarterly Review* 505–11.

—— 1983: *Foundations of the Modern Bar*. London: Sweet & Maxwell.

Cohen, Harry 1984: Employed lawyers in England, 9 *Journal of the Legal Profession* 125–50.

Cohen, Phil 1982a: Born to judge, *LAG Bulletin* 8–10 (August).

—— 1982b: Racial discrimination among solicitors, *LAG Bulletin* 11–15 (May).

—— 1982c: Bar racism on trial, *LAG Bulletin* 6–10 (April).

Cooper, Jeremy 1983: *Public Legal Services: a comparative study of policy, politics and practice*. London: Sweet & Maxwell.

Cox, Steven R. 1983: *The Price Effects of Attorney Advertising Regulations*. Tempe, AZ: Arizona State University, Department of Economics (working paper EC 82/83–4).

Davies, Rachel 1985: Overseas lawyers in the UK, *Financial Times* 13 (15 July).

Davis, Gwynn and Kay Bader 1985a: Client costs: a failure to inform, *Legal Action* 9–11 (February).

—— 1985b: The legal aid clawback, *Legal Action* 7–8 (April).

Dean, Malcolm 1986a: Legal service proposed for citizens' bureaux, *The Guardian* (16 June).

—— 1986b: Publicity for duty solicitor scheme, *The Guardian* (16 June).

Dickens, Charles 1850: *David Copperfield*. London: Bradbury & Evans.

Drewry, Gavin 1981: Lawyers in the UK Civil Service, 59 *Public Administration* 15–46.

Duffy, Hazel 1986: Solicitors join barristers in action over legal aid fees, *Financial Times* (15 January).

Duman, Daniel 1973: A social and occupational analysis of the English judiciary: 1770–1790 and 1855–1875, 17 *American Journal of Legal History* 353–64.

—— 1979: The creation and diffusion of a professional ideology in nineteenth-century England, 27 *Sociological Review* 113–38.

—— 1980: Pathways to professionalism: the English Bar in the eighteenth and nineteenth centuries, 13 *Journal of Social History* 615–28.

—— 1981: The English Bar in the Georgian era. In Wilfrid Prest (ed.), *Lawyers in Early Modern Europe and America*, pp. 86–107. New York: Holmes & Meier.

—— 1982: *The Judicial Bench in England, 1727–1875: the reshaping of a professional elite*. London: Royal Historical Society.

—— 1983a: *The English and Colonial Bars in the Nineteenth Century*. London: Croom Helm.

—— 1983b: The late Victorian Bar: a prosopographical survey. In E. W. Ives and A. H. Mancheser (eds), *Law, Litigants and the Legal Profession*, p. 140–54. London: Royal Historical Society.

Duncan, Nigel and Neil Wojciechowski-Kibble 1986: Excellence and diversity: admissions policies in law schools, 20 *Law Teacher* 36–53.

Easton, John 1986: Inland Revenue, 1(2) *Counsel* 18–19 (Hilary Term).

*Economist* 1983: English justice. 2: The two legal professions, *The Economist* 46–7 (6 August).

Edwards, E. G. 1982: *Higher Education for Everyone*. Nottingham: Spokesman.

Edwards, E. G. and I. J. Roberts 1980: British higher education: long term trends in student enrolment, 12 *Higher Education Review* 7–43.

Edwards, J. L. J. 1964: *The Law Offices of the Crown: a study of the offices of Attorney-General and Solicitor-General of England with an account of the office of the Director of Public Prosecutions of England*. London: Sweet & Maxwell.

Elliott, D. W. 1963: An enquiry into the training of graduate articled clerks, 7 *Journal of the Society of Public Teachers of Law* 199–203.

Elston, Elizabeth, Jane Fuller and Mervyn Murch 1975: Judicial hearings of undefended divorce petitions, 38 *Modern Law Review* 609–40.

Fabian Society 1969: *Legal Education*. London: Fabian Society (Research Series no. 276).

Farrant, John H. 1981: Trends in admissions. In Oliver Fulton (ed.), *Access to Higher Education*, pp. 42–88. Guildford: Society for Research into Higher Education.

Fennell, Phil 1982: Advertising: professional ethics and the public interest. In Philip A. Thomas (ed.), *Law in the Balance: legal services in the eighties*, pp. 144–60. Oxford: Martin Robertson.

Flood, John 1978: Barristers' clerks and professionalism: a study in failure.

Paper presented to the 9th World Congress of Sociology, Uppsala.

—— 1981a: Middlemen of the law: an ethnographic inquiry into the English legal profession, *American Bar Foundation Research Journal* 377–405.

—— 1981b: Researching barrister's clerks. In Robin Luckham (ed.), *Law and Social Enquiry: case studies of research*, pp. 158–88. Uppsala: Scandinavian Institute of African Studies; and New York: International Center for Law in Development.

—— 1983: *Barristers' Clerks: the law's middlemen*. Manchester: Manchester University Press.

Forbes, J. R. S. 1979: *The Divided Profession in Australia: history, rationalisation and rationale*. Sydney: Law Book Co.

Foster, Joseph 1885: *Men-At-The-Bar* (2nd edn). London: Author.

—— 1889: *The Register of Admissions to Gray's Inn, 1521–1889, together with the Register of Marriage in Gray's Inn Chapel, 1695–1794*. London: privately printed.

Foster, Ken 1973: The location of solicitors, 36 *Modern Law Review* 153–66.

Friedman, Lawrence M. 1973: *A history of American law*. New York: Simon and Schuster.

Galanter, Marc 1983: Larger than life: mega-lawyers and mega-lawyering in the contemporary United States. In Robert Dingwall and Philip Lewis (eds), *The Sociology of the Professions: lawyers, doctors and others*, pp. 152–76. London: Macmillan.

Garth, Bryant 1980: *Neighborhood Law Firms for the Poor: a comparative study of recent developments in legal aid and in the legal professions*. Rockville, MD: Sijthoff & Noordhoff.

Gifford, Tony 1986: *Where's the Justice?* Harmondsworth: Penguin.

Gilbert, Michael 1977: *The Law*. Newton Abbott: David & Charles.

Glasser, Cyril 1979: The Royal Commission: the remuneration of the profession and legal aid, *LAG Bulletin* 201–5 (September).

—— 1980: After the report – remuneration. *LAG Bulletin* 29–32 (February).

—— 1986: Legal aid – decline and fall, 83 *Law Society's Gazette* 839–40.

Gower, L. C. B. 1950: English legal training: a critical survey, 13 *Modern Law Review* 137–205.

Gower, L. C. B. and Leolin Price 1957: The profession and practice of the law in England and America, 20 *Modern Law Review*, 317–46.

Green, Andrew Wilson 1976: Legal education in England, 28 *Journal of Legal Education* 137–80.

Griffith, J. A. G. 1961: Lawyers in the public service, 41 *Journal of Legal Education* 13–20.

—— 1977: *The Politics of the Judiciary*. London: Fontana.

*Haldane Bulletin* 1983: Unionisation of solicitors' firms, 17 *Haldane Bulletin* 10–12.

Hall, J. C. 1962: The training of a solicitor, 7 *Journal of the Society of Public Teachers of Law* 22–34.

Hamm, Roderick 1986: Local government, 1(2) *Counsel* 16–17 (Hilary term).

Hazell, Robert 1978a: Pupillage. In Robert Hazell (ed.), *The Bar on Trial*, pp. 82–97. London: Quartet Books.

—— 1978b: Introduction to the Bar. In Robert Hazell (ed.), *The Bar on Trial*, pp. 17–37. London: Quartet Books.

—— 1978c: Clerks and fees. In Robert Hazell (ed.), *The Bar on Trial*, pp. 99–129. London: Quartet Books.

—— n.d.: Bar Council and Senate. Unpublished draft of chapter 10 of *The Bar on Trial* (from author).

Hazeltine, Harold D. 1909: Legal education in England, 34 *Reports of the American Bar Association* 879–940.

—— 1910: The present state of legal education in England, 26 *Law Quarterly Review* 17–39.

Heinz, John P. and Edward O. Laumann 1982: *Chicago Lawyers: the social structure of the Bar*. New York: Russell Sage; and Chicago: American Bar Foundation.

Helm, Sarah 1985a: Barristers threaten 'strike' action over poor legal aid fees, *Sunday Times* (4 August).

—— 1985b: Miners' lawyer to face inquiry, *Sunday Times* (6 October).

Hermann, A. H. 1985: The legal profession at the crossroads, *Financial Times* (10 January).

Hiley, Eric 1984: Chargeable hours: Remuneration Committee survey, 82 *Law Society's Gazette* 1102.

Hilton, W. G. and Shirley W. Lerner 1965: Apprenticeship to affluence, 62 *Law Society's Gazette* 98–101.

Hobson, M. and J. D. Stewart 1969: The legal profession in local government, *Public Law* 199–218.

Holdsworth, William 1938: *A History of English Law*, vol. 12. London: Methuen.

—— 1965: *A History of English Law*, vol. 15 (A. L. Goodhart and H. G. Hanbury, eds). London: Methuen and Sweet & Maxwell.

Hughes, Everett C. 1971: *The Sociological Eye*, vol. 1. Chicago: Aldine-Atherton.

Hughes, Raymond 1985: Barristers find more work abroad, *Financial Times* 11 (5 July).

—— 1986: Akin to a large City solicitors, *Financial Times* 17 (11 June).

Jenks, Edward 1935: English legal education, 101 *Law Quarterly Review* 162–79.

Johnstone, Quintin and John A. Flood 1982: Paralegals in English and American law offices, 2 *Windsor Yearbook of Access to Justice* 152–90.

Johnstone, Quintin and Dan Hopson, Jr 1967: *Lawyers and their Work: an analysis of the legal profession in the United States and England*. Indianapolis, IN: Bobbs-Merrill Co.

Jones, P. Asterley 1956: The cost of becoming a solicitor, 100 *Solicitors' Journal* 425–6.

Joseph, Michael 1976: *The Conveyancing Fraud*. London: Michael Joseph.

—— 1984: *Lawyers can Seriously Damage your Health*. London: Michael Joseph.

*JSPTL: Journal of the Society of Public Teachers of Law* 1947: Review of legal education during the war, 1939–1945, 1 (new series) *Journal of the Society of Public Teachers of Law* 23–51.

Keeton, George W. 1939: University College, London, and the law, 51 *Juridical Review* 118–33.

Kelsall, R. K. Anne Poole and Annette Kuhn 1972: *Graduates: the sociology of an elite*. London: Methuen.

Kennedy, Helena 1978: Women at the Bar. In Robert Hazell (ed.), *The Bar on Trial*, pp. 148–62. London: Quartet Books.

Kirk, Harry 1976: *Portrait of a Profession: a history of the solicitors' profession, 1100 to the present day*. London: Oyez.

Lane, Joan 1977: The Warwickshire attorney and his apprentice, 1700–1850, 3 *Warwickshire History* 169–80.

Latta, Geoff and Roy Lewis 1974: Trade union legal services, 12 *British Journal of Industrial Relations* 56–70.

Lawson, F. H. 1968: *The Oxford Law School, 1850–1965*. Oxford: Clarendon Press.

Lawton, F. A. 1986: Costs and conveyancers, 83 *Law Society's Gazette* 3074–5, 3081–2.

Layton, Alex, Richard Tyson and William Rees 1978a: Legal education. In Robert Hazell (ed.), *The Bar on Trial*, pp. 68–81. London: Quartet Books.

—— 1978b: Legal Education. Unpublished draft of chapter 3 of *The Bar on Trial* (from Robert Hazell).

Lee, Robert G. 1984: Survey of law school admissions, 18 *Law Teacher* 165–74.

Lees, D. S. 1966: *Economic Consequences of the Professions*. London: Institute of Economic Affairs.

Lewis, J. R. 1982: *The Victorian Bar*. London: Robert Hale.

Lichtig, Jerrold M. 1986: Solicitors' offices overseas, 83 *Law Society's Gazette* 1144–7.

Lucas, Paul 1962: Blackstone and the reform of the legal profession, 77 *English Historical Review* 456–89.

McDonald, P. 1982: 'The class of '81' – a glance at the social class composition of recruits in the legal profession, 9 *Journal of Law and Society* 267–76.

McFadyen, Archibald Alan 1984: No legal aid for representation before industrial tribunals, 81 *Law Society's Gazette* 795–7.

MacFarlane, Gavin 1986: Customs and Excise, 1(2) *Counsel* 19–20 (Hilary term).

Manchester, A. H. 1980: *A Modern Legal History of England and Wales, 1750–1950*. London: Butterworths.

Marks, P. G. 1984: A statistical summary of the solicitors' profession, 81 *Law Society's Gazette* 2607–9.

—— 1985: Annual statistical report 1985, 82 *Law Society's Gazette* 2903–4, 2913–15.

—— 1986: Annual statistical report 1986, 83 *Law Society's Gazette* 3257–62.

Marsh, S. B. 1980: The last twenty years. In Michael Slade (ed.), *Law in Higher Education: into the 1980s*, pp. 6–12. Association of Law Teachers.

—— 1983: The C.N.A.A. law degree, 17 *Law Teacher* 73–123.

Mayhew, Leon and A. J. Reiss 1969: The social organization of legal contacts, 34 *American Journal of Sociology* 309.

Megarry, R. E. 1962: *Lawyer and Litigant in England*. London: Stevens & Sons.

Merricks, Walter 1982: Briefing: academic lawyers gather, 132 *New Law Journal* 891–2.

Miles, Michael 1981: The money market in the early industrial revolution: the evidence from West Riding attorneys, *c.* 1750–1800, 23 *Business History* 127–46.

—— 1984: 'Eminent practitioners': the new visage of country attorneys *c.* 1750–1800. In G. R. Rubin and David Sugarman (eds), *Law, Economy and Society, 1750–1914: essays in the history of English law*, pp. 470–503. Abingdon: Professional Books.

Millerson, Geoffrey 1964: *The Qualifying Associations: a study in professionalisation*. London: Routledge & Kegan Paul.

Mitchell, B. R. 1971: *Abstract of British Historical Statistics*. Cambridge: Cambridge University Press.

Mitchell, B. R. and H. G. Jones 1971: *Second Abstract of British Historical Statistics*. Cambridge: Cambridge University Press.

Moffatt, Michael 1986: Solicitors' profit statistics, 83 *Law Society's Gazette* 2725–6.

Molyneaux, Pauline 1986: Association of Women Solicitors – membership survey, 83 *Law Society's Gazette* 3082–4.

Mortimer, John 1982: *Clinging to the Wreckage: a part of life*. Harmondsworth: Penguin.

Morton, James 1986: Hodge, Jones and Allen – an inner city practice, 136 *New Law Journal* 1095–8.

Munby, John 1978: A look into the future. In Robert Hazell (ed.), *The Bar on Trial*, pp. 179–92. London: Quartet Books.

Murch, Mervyn 1977: The role of solicitors in divorce proceedings, 40 *Modern Law Review* 625–38.

—— 1978: The role of solicitors in divorce proceedings, 41 *Modern Law Review* 25–37.

—— 1980: *Justice and Welfare in Divorce*. London: Sweet & Maxwell.

Murray, Georgina 1988: New Zealand lawyers. In Richard L. Abel and Philip S. C. Lewis (eds), *Lawyers in Society. Vol. 1: The Common Law World*. Berkeley and Los Angeles: University of California Press.

Napier, T. Bateman and Richard M. Stephenson 1888: *A Practical Guide to the Bar*. London: Horace & Co.

Odgers, W. Blake 1901: Introductory, Changes in the common law and in the law of persons, in the legal profession and in legal education. In *A Century of Law Reform*, ch. 1. London: Macmillan.

Offer, Avner 1981: *Property and Politics 1870–1914. Landownership, law, ideology and urban development in England*. Cambridge: Cambridge University Press.

Parker, Henry Watson 1877: The extension of the Society, its functions, and powers. In *Proceedings and Resolutions of the Special General Meeting of the Law Society 1887*, pp. 51–7.

Paterson, Alan 1974: Judges: a political elite?, 1 *British Journal of Law and Society* 118–35.

—— 1988: The legal profession in Scotland. In Richard L. Abel and Philip S. C. Lewis (eds), *Lawyers in Society. Vol. 1: The Common Law World*. Berkeley and Los Angeles: University of California Press.

Pettit, Philip H. 1983: The Society of Public Teachers of Law – the first seventy-five years, 3 *Legal Studies* 231–47.

Pickman, S. P. 1981: *The Output of UK Universities by Institution and Discipline, 1980*. Manchester: Central Services Unit for University and Polytechnic Careers and Appointments Services.

Podmore, David 1977a: A survey of West Midlands solicitors. I: A review of some background data, 74 *Law Society's Gazette* 611.

—— 1977b: A survey of West Midlands solicitors. II: The work of the solicitor in private practice, 74 *Law Society's Gazette* 636.

—— 1980: *Solicitors and the Wider Community*. London: Heinemann.

Podmore, David and Anne Spencer 1982: The law as a sex-typed profession, 9 *Journal of Law and Society* 21–36.

—— 1982: Women lawyers in England: the experience of inequality, 9 *Work and Occupations* 337–61.

Read, Brian 1984: Exit from law schools: possibilities and actualities, 18 *Law Teacher* 175–80.

Reader, W. J. 1966: *Professional Men: the rise of the professional classes in nineteenth-century England*. New York: Basic Books.

Reeves, Peter 1986: *Are Two Legal Professions Necessary?* London: Waterlow Publ. Ltd.

Robson, Robert 1959: *The Attorney in Eighteenth-Century England*. London: Cambridge University Press.

Routh, Guy 1980: *Occupation and Pay in Great Britain 1907–79*. London: Macmillan.

Rule, Ella 1980: The prospects for women law graduates. In Michael Slade (ed.), *Law in Higher Education: into the 1980s*, pp. 32–40. Association of Law Teachers.

Sachs, Albie and Joan Hoff Wilson 1978: *Sexism and the Law: a study of male beliefs and judicial bias*. Oxford: Martin Robertson.

Samuel, Alec 1984: Can the silk system still be justified? 134 *New Law Journal* 503–4.

Saunders, Nicholas and Terry Faulkner 1985: Solicitors and information technology: a survey, 135 *New Law Journal* 326–8.

Sherr, Avrom 1982: Lip service under articles, or chances missed, 132 *New Law Journal* 395–8.

Slatter, Michele and Malcolm Moseley 1986: *Access to Legal Services in Rural Norfolk*. Exeter: University of Exeter (Access to Justice in Rural Britain Project working paper 7).

Slinn, Judy 1984: *A History of Freshfields*. London: Freshfields.

Smigel, Erwin O. 1969: *The Wall Street Lawyer: professional organization man?* Bloomington, IN: Indiana University Press.

*Solicitors' Journal* 1972: Lawyers in industry, 116 *Solicitors' Journal* 245.

Spring, David 1963: *The English Landed Estate in the Nineteenth Century: its administration*. Baltimore, MD: Johns Hopkins Press.

Steele, Eric H. and Raymond T. Nimmer 1976: Lawyers, clients and professional regulation, *American Bar Foundation Research Journal* 917–1019.

Sturges, H. A. C. 1949: *Register of Admissions to the Honourable Society of the Middle Temple, from the Fifteenth Century to the year 1944* (3 vols). London: Butterworth & Co.

Taylor, Adrian 1984: Ending the conveyancing monopoly, *Financial Times* (10 January).

Thomas, Phil 1986: *Access to Legal Services in Rural Dyfed, Wales*. Exeter: University of Exeter (Access to Justice in Rural Britain Project working paper 11).

Twining, W. L. 1980: Goodbye to Lewis Eliot: The academic lawyer as scholar, 15 *Journal of the Society of Public Teachers of Law* 2–19.

Van Zyl Smit, Dirk 1985: 'Professional' patent agents and the development of the English patent system, 13 *International Journal of the Sociology of Law* 79–105.

Vann, John C. 1985: Legal expense insurance blossoms, 135 *New Law Journal* 835–6.

Wallace, Keith 1977: Applying for articles – a bird's eye view, 127 *New Law Journal* 628–9.

Warren, Nicholas 1978: The Inns of Court. In Robert Hazell (ed.), *The Bar on Trial*, pp. 38–67. London: Quartet Books.

Warren, Samuel 1835: *A Popular and Practical Introduction to Law Studies*. London: A. Maxwell.

—— 1845: *A Popular and Practical Introduction to Law Studies* (2nd edn). London: Maxwell.

—— 1863: *A Popular and Practical Introduction to Law Studies* (3rd edn) (3 vols). London: Maxwell.

Watkins, Charles, Mark Blacksell and Kim Economides 1986a: *The Use of the Law List to Assess the Distribution and Characteristics of Solicitors in England and Wales*. Exeter: University of Exeter (Access to Justice in Rural Britain Project working paper 1).

—— 1986b: *The Distribution of Solicitors in England and Wales*. Exeter: University of Exeter (Access to Justice in Rural Britain Project working paper 8).

—— 1986c: *The Role of Citizens' Advice Bureaux in Rural Areas*. Exeter: University of Exeter (Access to Justice in Rural Britain Project working paper 12).

—— 1986d: *The Use of Legal Services in Three Remote, Rural Parishes*. Exeter: University of Exeter (Access to Justice in Rural Britain working paper 14).

Wedderburn, K. W. 1956: III *Actes du sixième congrès international de droit de travail et de la sécurité sociale, rapport national*, Grande-Bretagne, pp. 15–16.

Weisbrot, David 1988: The Australian legal profession. In Richard L. Abel and Philip S. C. Lewis (eds), *Lawyers in Society. Vol. 1: The Common Law World*. Berkeley and Los Angeles: University of California Press.

Wheatcroft, G. S. A. 1962: The education and training of the modern lawyer, 7 *Journal of the Society of Public Teachers of Law* 1–16.

Whishaw, James 1835: *A Synopsis of the Members of the English Bar*. London: Stevens & Sons.

Whitburn, J., M. Mealing and C. Cox 1976: *People in Polytechnics*. Guildford: Society for Research into Higher Education.

Wilby, Peter 1985a: Why you shouldn't see poly as a fall-back for failures, *Sunday Times* (18 August).

—— 1985b: Threat to students' degree hopes, *Sunday Times* (10 November).

Williams, Peter Howell 1980: *A Gentleman's Calling: the Liverpool attorney-at-law*. Liverpool: Author.

Wilson, J. F. 1966: A survey of legal education in the United Kingdom, 9 *Journal of the Society of Public Teachers of Law* 1–144.

Wilson, J. F. and S. B. Marsh 1975: A second survey of legal education in the United Kingdom, 13 *Journal of the Society of Public Teachers of Law* 239–331.

—— 1978: *A Second Survey of Legal Education in the United Kingdom, supplement no. 1*. London: Institute of Advanced Legal Studies.

—— 1981: *A Second Survey of Legal Education in the United Kingdom, supplement no. 2*. London: Institute of Advanced Legal Studies.

Winstanley, D. A. 1947: *Later Victorian Cambridge*. Cambridge: Cambridge University Press.

Winyard, Anne 1976: Legal Bar, 12 *Low Pay Bulletin* 1–3 (December).

Wojciechowski-Kibble, Neil and Nigel Duncan 1985: *Minority Entry into Legal Education: A discussion paper*. London: Polytechnic of the South Bank, Minority Access to the Legal Profession Project.

Woodhall, Maureen 1981: Overseas students. In Oliver Fulton (ed.), *Access to Higher Education*, pp. 192–202. Guildford: Society for Research into Higher Education.

Zander, Michael 1961: Cambridge University and legal education, *The Cambridge Review* 218–20 (21 January).

—— 1968: *Lawyers and the Public Interest: a study in restrictive practices*. London: Weidenfeld & Nicholson.

—— 1975: Costs of litigation – a study in the Queen's Bench Division, 72 *Law Society's Gazette* 679–84.

—— 1976: Costs in Crown Courts, 1976 *Criminal Law Review* 5–41.

—— 1980: *The State of Knowledge about the English Legal Profession*. London: Barry Rose.

## *Reports by governmental and private bodies*

AGCAS: Association of Graduate Careers Advisory Services 1980a: Becoming a solicitor: a survey of the experiences of law graduates of 1978 seeking to qualify as solicitors in England and Wales. Sheffield: AGCAS.

—— 1980b: Becoming a solicitor the hard way: a survey of the experiences of non-law graduates who took the first common professional examination in 1979. Sheffield: AGCAS.

—— 1981a: Becoming a solicitor the new way: a survey of the experiences of law graduates of 1979 seeking to qualify as solicitors in England and Wales. Sheffield: AGCAS.

—— 1981b: Becoming a barrister: a survey of law graduates who took the Bar finals course in the years 1976, 1977 and 1978. Sheffield: AGCAS.

—— 1982: Taking solicitors' finals: the experiences of law graduates of 1980. Sheffield: AGCAS.

—— 1984a: The early careers of barristers: follow-up of the 1981 survey of law graduates who began the Bar final course in 1976, 1977 and 1978. Sheffield: AGCAS.

—— 1984b: Becoming a barrister in the 1980s: a survey of law graduates who took the Bar final course in the years 1979, 1980 and 1981. Sheffield: AGCAS.

—— 1984c: Solicitors' finals 1983: a detailed report on how candidates fared at the College of Law and the polytechnics. Sheffield: AGCAS.

—— 1984d: Becoming a trainee solicitor: a report on the experiences of law graduates of 1982. Sheffield: AGCAS.

AGCAS Polytechnic Statistics Working Group 1984: First destination of polytechnic students qualifying in 1983. Sheffield: AGCAS.

Bar and Quarter Sessions 1971: Annexure to the first meeting of the Provincial Chambers Joint Committee, 5 May (Senate Archives).

Bar Association for Commerce, Finance and Industry 1977: Evidence to the Royal Commission on Legal Services (EV 244). LSE Library.

Bar Council 1984a: Report on fees collection, May 1983 to April 1984, to the annual general meeting of the Bar, July 1984.

—— 1984b: Fees collection – report to the extraordinary general meeting of the Bar, 17 December.

—— n.d.a: Survey of income at the Bar, 1981–82. London: Bar Council.

—— n.d.b: Patterns of criminal practice at the London Bar. London: Bar Council.

Bar Council Working Party on Fee Collection 1982: Report.

Bar Students' Working Party 1976: Report. Senate Archives.

Bolton Report: Bolton, Sproule (Secretary of the Education Committee of the Bar Council) 1967: Report to the chairman of the Bar Council on a survey conducted 3 January. Senate Archives.

Chambers for Young Barristers Subcommittee of the Senate Accommodation Committee 1973: Report (20 November). Senate Archives.

CHULS: Committee of Heads of University Law Schools 1984: Law as an academic discipline.

Coldstream Commitee 1973: Report on a scheme for co-ordination of the activities of the four Inns of Court in assisting pupils to find places. Senate Archives.

Coopers & Lybrand Associates 1985a: Study of remuneration of barristers carrying out criminal legal aid. London: Coopers & Lybrand Associates.

—— 1985b: Review of the Law Society's affairs. Phase 1 – The Law Society's role and functions. Report 1 – The regulatory functions. London: Coopers & Lybrand Associates.

Council of Legal Education 1976: Survey (January). Senate Archives.

—— 1982–3: Calendar.

Council of the Law Society 1944: Memorandum to the Interdepartmental Committee on Further Training. In *Annual Report, 1944*, 41–8. London: Law Society.

—— 1962: Remuneration of articled clerks and payment of premiums: a further statement by the Council, 59 *Law Society's Gazette 266–7*.

Denning Commitee 1961: Report on legal education for students from Africa. London: HMSO (Cmnd 1255).

Department of Education and Science 1984: Technical report to DES report on education (number 10). London: DES.

Doctors and Dentists 1960: Report of the Royal Commission on Doctors' and Dentists' Remuneration. London: HMSO (Cmnd 939).

Equal Opportunities Commission 1978: Women in the legal services (evidence submitted to the Royal Commission on Legal Services). Manchester: Equal Opportunities Commission.

Grand Metropolitan Ltd 1976: Evidence to the Royal Commission on Legal Services (EV 151). LSE Library.

Gray's Inn List of students desirous of being called to the Bar this term (manuscript). Gray's Inn Library.

Halifax Building Society n.d.: Evidence to the Lord Chancellor's Coveyancing Commission on its first terms of reference.

Imperial Chemical Industries Ltd 1976: Submission to the Royal Commission on Legal Services (EV 135). LSE Library.

INBUCON 1977: Survey of income at the Bar 1976–77 (evidence submitted by the Bar Council to the Royal Commission on Legal Services). London: INBUCON.

Inner Temple Treasurer's Office: Admissions and calls by Inn, 1853–1984 (manuscript).

Inner Temple Treasurer's Office: Inner Temple warrants for admission.

Knightly and Colton Report: Knightly, Betty and Mary Colton 1971: Women at the Bar: memo to Special Committee on Women's Careers at the Bar. Senate Archives.

Law Society 1977: Memorandum no. 3: Replies by the Council of the Law Society to the request for evidence from the Law Society by the Royal Commission, part I (EV 232). LSE Library.

—— 1978: Memorandum no. 5: Evidence to the Royal Commission. London: Law Society.

—— 1982: A consultative document on the future basis of premium assessment for discussion by solicitors and local law societies. London: Law Society.

—— 1985: The future of the indemnity insurance scheme: statement by the Council. London: Law Society.

Law Society Bye-Laws Revision Committee 1985: First report.

Law Society Committee on Education and Training 1985: Salaries of articled clerks. London: Law Society.

Law Society Contentious Business Committee 1986: Lawyers and the courts: time for some changes (a discussion paper).

Law Society Contingency Planning Working Party 1986: Revision of the solicitors' practice rules 1936/72 and a solicitors' advertising code (consultation paper no. 2, 30 April).

Law Society Council's Committee of Enquiry into the Law Society's treatment of the complaints of Mr L. A. Parsons against Mr G. Davies and Mr. C. Malim 1984: Report.

Law Society Standing Committee on Entry and Training 1983: A review of the system of training for entry to the solicitors' branch of the legal profession. London: Law Society.

Lincoln's Inn 1896: The records of the Honourable Society of Lincoln's Inn. Vol. II: Admissions from AD 1800 to AD 1893 and chapel registers. London: Lincoln's Inn.

Lincoln's Inn Call List. Lincoln's Inn Library.

Local Government Group of the Law Society 1977: Evidence to the Royal Commission on Legal Services (EV 250). LSE Library.

London Trainee Solicitors' Group 1977: Evidence to the Royal Commission on Legal Services (EV 227). LSE Library.

Lord Chancellor's Department 1976: Memorandum for Royal Commission on Legal Services: judicial and quasi-judicial appointments (EV 100). LSE Library.

—— 1983: The government response to the report of the Royal Commission on Legal Services. London: HMSO (Cmnd 9077).

—— 1986: The study of small claims. London: LCD.

Middle Temple 1977: Register of admissions to the Honourable Society of the Middle Temple (5 vols). London: Middle Temple.

Monopolies and Mergers Commission 1976a: Barristers' Services: a report on the supply by Her Majesty's Counsel alone of their services. London: HMSO.

—— 1976b: Services of solicitors in England and Wales: a report on the supply of services of solicitors in England and Wales in relation to restrictions on advertising. London: HMSO.

Monopolies Commission 1970: A report on the general effect on the public interest of certain restrictive practices so far as they prevail in relation to the supply of profesional services. London: HMSO (Cmnd 4463 and 4463–1).

MORI: Market Opinion and Research International Ltd 1984: Using a solicitor for conveyancing – a survey of public attitudes, 5–9 July 1984. London: MORI.

National Association of Citizens' Advice Bureaux 1981–2: Annual report and accounts. London: National Association of Citizens' Advice Bureaux.

—— 1985–6: Annual report and accounts. London: National Association of Citizens' Advice Bureaux.

National Board for Prices and Incomes 1968: Remuneration of solicitors (report no. 54). London: HMSO (Cmnd 3529).

—— 1969: Standing reference on the remuneration of solicitors, first report (no. 134). London: HMSO (Cmnd 4217).

—— 1971: Standing reference on the remuneration of solicitors, second report (no. 164). London: HMSO (Cmnd 4624).

National Consumer Council (NCC) 1984: Whose interest? Solicitors and their clients' accounts: a discussion paper. London: National Consumer Council.

—— 1985: Consumers and the professions: a review of complaints procedures: in dispute with a solicitor. London: National Consumer Council.

Office of Manpower Economics 1974: OME survey of earnings at the Bar. In Review Body on Top Salaries: Report on top salaries, appendix K (report no. 6). London: HMSO (Cmnd 5846).

—— 1981: Surveys of earnings at the Bar. In Review Body on Top Salaries: Interim report on top salaries, appendix C (report no. 16). London: HMSO (Cmnd 8243).

Ormrod Committee 1971: Report of the Committee on Legal Education. London: HMSO (Cmnd 4595).

Peat Marwick 1985: Survey of firms involved in legal aid work. London: Peat Marwick.

Polytechnic of Central London, Faculty of Law, School of Academic Studies 1985: Application for approval for part-time day or evening diploma in higher education, BA and BA (honours) course in law (1985–86).

Prosecuting Solicitors' Society of England and Wales 1977: Evidence to the Royal Commission on Legal Services (EV 161). LSE Library.

Reuter Simkin 1981–5: A survey of solicitors' salaries in London and the home counties (semiannual). London: Reuter Simkin.

—— 1986: A survey of solicitors' salaries in London and the home counties (1.10.85–31.3.86). 83 *Law Society's Gazette* 2227–8.

Review Body on Top Salaries 1978: Second report on top salaries, appendix F: Earnings at the Bar in England and Wales (report no. 10). London: HMSO (Cmnd 7253).

Robbins Committee 1963: Report on higher education. London: HMSO (Cmnd 2154).

Royal Commission on Criminal Procedure 1981a: Report. London: HMSO (Cmnd 8092).

—— 1981b: The investigation and prosecution of criminal offences in England and Wales: the law and procedure. London: HMSO (Cmnd 8092–1).

Royal Commission on Legal Services 1979: Final report (2 vols). London: HMSO (Cmnd 7648).

Select Committee on Legal Education 1846: Report. British Parliamentary Papers 1846, vol. X.

Senate of the Inns of Court and the Bar 1976a: Submission no. 1 to the Royal Commission on Legal Services on behalf of the Bar Council.

—— 1976b: Submission no. 2 to the Royal Commission on Legal Services on behalf of the Four Inns of Court.

—— 1976c: Submission no. 3 to the Royal Commission on Legal Services on behalf of the Council of Legal Education.

—— 1976d: Submission no. 5 to the Royal Commission on Legal Services on behalf of the Bar Students Working Party (EV 94). LSE Library.

—— 1977a: Submission no. 7 to the Royal Commission on Legal Services in answer to questionnaire sections I to XI.

—— 1977b: Submission no. 13 to the Royal Commission on Legal Services in answer to questionnaire sections XII To XVI.

—— 1977c: Addendum to submission 8 to the Royal Commission on Legal Services: commentary on the survey of income at the Bar 1974–75 (EV 231 add.). LSE Library.

—— 1978a: Submission no. 17 to the Royal Commission on Legal Services: speed and cost.

—— 1978b: Submission no. 18 to the Royal Commission on Legal Services in reply to questionnaire no. III on education and training.

—— 1978c: Submission no. 22 to the Royal Commission on Legal Services: Concluding submission.

—— 1978d: Supplementary evidence to the Royal Commission on Legal Services, submissions nos 1 and 2.

—— 1983: Comments on the government response to the report of the Royal Commission on Legal Services, with particular reference to those within the prerogative of the Bar to implement.

—— 1985a: Quality of entry: report of the Executive Committee Working Party (Nicholas Phillips, Adrian Whitfield, David Lloyd-Jones and Richard McCombe).

—— 1985b: Report of the Working Party on Accommodation for the London Bar (Adrian Whitfield, Jonathan Hirst and Richard McCombe).

—— 1985c: Report of the Race Relations Committee for 1984–85 (The Hon. Mr Justice Scott, Chairman).

—— 1986: Lawyers and the courts: the response of the Bar to a discussion paper issued by the Law Society's Contentious Business Committee (supplement to *Law Society's Gazette*).

Special Committee on Women's Careers at the Bar 1972: Analysis of a completed questionnaire. Senate Archives.

SPTL: Society of Public Teachers of Law 1977: Evidence to the Royal Commission on Legal Services (EV 164). LSE Library.

University of Cambridge 1976: Evidence to the Royal Commission on Legal

Services (EV 221). LSE Library.

Whitfield and Walker Report: Whitfield, Adrian and Timothy Walker 1985: The requirement for new entrants to the Bar, 1985–1989.

Williams Report: Williams, R. D. T. 1985: The work of the Bar: summary of proceedings commenced. Senate archives.

Wilmers Committee 1974: Report of the Committee on Admission, Organisation, Conditions and Needs of Pupils. Senate Archives.

## *Serials and annual reports*

All government documents are published by HMSO unless otherwise noted. General periodicals are not included in the following list. In text and references, serials are indicated by: volume no.; name or abbreviation; page nos; date.

*Bar Examination Journal* 1871–92 (vols 1–10). Edited by A. D. Tyssen and R. K. Wilson.

Bar List of the United Kingdom 1977–83. London: Stevens.

Board of Trade, Statistical Abstract for the United Kingdom 1854–1940.

Census.

Central Statistical Office 1948–present: Annual Abstract of Statistics.

Clarke's New Law List 1820–40. London: J. & W. T. Clarke.

CNAA: Council for National Academic Awards 1971–81: Annual Reports. London: CNAA.

Commissioners of Inland Revenue: Annual Reports.

*Counsel* 1985–present.

Department of Education and Science 1967–present: Education Statistics for the United Kingdom.

Department of Employment 1970–2: New Earnings Survey.

Department of Environment 1972–present: Housing and Construction Statistics.

General Council of the Bar of England and Wales 1895–1974: Annual Statement. London: General Council.

Home Office 1856–1921: Judicial Statistics, England and Wales.

Home Office 1922–present: Criminal Statistics of England and Wales.

Incorporated Law Society 1881–94: Calendar. London: Incorporated Law Society.

Inland Revenue, Statistics Division 1971–82: Inland Revenue Statistics.

John Browne's General Law List for the Year 1797 (16th edn). London: J. Butterworth.

*Journal of the Society of Public Teachers of Law (JSPTL)* 1924–38, (n.s.) 1947–present.

*LAG Bulletin* 1973–83. Legal Action Group.

*Law Notes* 1873–1986. London: Gibson & Weldon.

Law List 1841–1976. London: Stevens.

Law Society 1825–1985: Annual Reports.

Lay Observer 1975–6–present: Annual Reports. London: Lord Chancellor's Department.
*Legal Action* 1984–present.
*Legal Executive* 1963–present.
*The Legal Observer*; *The Legal Almanac, Remembrancer, and Diary* 1838–42. London: Edmund Spettigue.
Lord Chancellor's Department 1922–present: Civil Judicial Statistics.
—— 1949–50 to 1983–4: Legal Aid Annual Reports.
—— 1972–4: Statistics on Judicial Administration.
*LSG: Law Society's Gazette* 1903–present.
*NLJ: New Law Journal* 1850–present.
Senate of the Four Inns of Court 1969–73: Annual Statement. London: Senate.
Senate of the Inns of Court and the Bar 1974–present: Annual Statement. London: Senate.
—— 1983–5: Chambers pupillage arrangements and awards.
Shaw, Charles 1877–8: The Inns of Court Calendar. London: Butterworths.
Solicitors' and Barristers' Directory and Diary 1984–present. London: Waterlow.
*Solicitors' Journal* 1857–present.
UCCA: University Central Committee on Admissions 1961–2 to 1983–4. Annual Report. Cheltenham: UCCA.
UGC: University Grants Committee (UGC) 1980–present: University Statistics. Vol. 1: Students and staff. Vol. 2: First destinations of university graduates. Cheltenham: Universities Statistical Record.
Universities Statistical Record. Cheltenham.
Waterlow, W. A. 1911–20: *The Legal Pocket Book and Calendar*. London: Waterlow Bros & Layton's Ltd.
Waterlow Bros & Layton's *Legal Almanac* 1903–10. London: Waterlow Bros & Layton's Ltd.

# Index

Note: page numbers in italics refer to tables and figures

*Index compiled by Justyn Balinski*